THE ATTICA TURKEY SHOOT

THE ATTICA TURKEY SHOOT

CARNAGE, COVER-UP, AND
THE PURSUIT OF JUSTICE

MALCOLM BELL
Foreword to the Second Edition
by Heather Ann Thompson
Foreword to the First Edition
by Tom Wicker

Skyhorse Publishing

THIS BOOK IS DEDICATED
TO THE GOOD GERMAN.
EVERYONE CHOOSES
WHETHER TO
BE ONE.

And to the memory of Lenny Brown, John Edland,
Liz Fink, Don Jelinek, Robert McKay,
Frank Big Black Smith, Tom Wicker,
the Attica Supplemental Grand Jury, and
the others who strove for the truth and justice
that are too often denied.

Contents

Foreword to the Second Edition

The decades of the 1960s and 1970s were rife with both rebellion and repression. From Birmingham to Selma, from Kent State to Wounded Knee, time and again dispossessed Americans challenged injustice, and, time and again, their efforts to better the world in which they lived were met with a sometimes staggering amount of state violence. This is not to say that the many struggles citizens waged for a more just future were foolhardy. Indeed, despite the great odds they faced and the intense backlash they touched off, these grassroots battles made a real mark on history. Perhaps none better exemplifies this truth than the Attica prison uprising of 1971.

At Attica, as in cities all across the nation in the early 1970s, ordinary people—overwhelmingly poor people and people of color—suffered indignities, injustices, and inhumane treatment at the hands of state officials thanks to decades-old discriminatory policies and practices. At Attica, as at Watts and Newark the decade before, those who endured these wrongs eventually erupted in protest. And, at Attica, as at Kent State and Wounded Knee in the same decade, the state's determination to maintain power and control led to unimaginable bloodshed. At Attica, as at virtually every other uprising in which the state reasserted its power with such ugly force, officials worked hard to ensure that all fault for the violence that they wrought rested at the feet of the protesters themselves. At Attica, however, the truth of what actually happened eventually would be told. This book by Malcolm Bell, *The Attica Turkey Shoot: Carnage, Cover-Up, and the Pursuit of Justice*, is central to this truth-telling.

Bell, hired back in 1973 by the State of New York to prosecute any cases that might arise from its official investigation of crimes committed during the Attica uprising and retaking, took his job most seriously. Even though his employers seemed interested only in prosecuting inmates for laws broken during their rebellion, Bell was determined that the troopers who had killed thirty-nine hostages and inmates when they retook the prison would also be held accountable for their crimes. That, however, was not to be. State officials were deeply reticent to investigate and prosecute troopers, and the more Bell suggested the imperative of doing just that, the more his employers isolated him. Eventually Malcolm Bell had to blow the whistle on the state's unwillingness to indict its own, and his exposé of the lengths to which it went to cover up trooper crimes committed at Attica would change the course of history. With this republication of Malcolm Bell's insider account of the Attica investigation and cover-up, readers today have an invaluable historical document. Even though the history of the tumultuous 1960s and 1970s is long over, Bell's book, updated as it is with a rich and poignant new epilogue, reminds us all that the past continues to shape the present in ways both woeful and wonderful and, as the book makes clear, that we must know the past if we ever hope not to repeat it.

Dr. Heather Ann Thompson
Professor of History
University of Michigan

Foreword to the First Edition

Malcolm Bell is an American hero, a brave man who risked his livelihood, his profession, and the good opinion of his peers for the sake of truth and justice. This is his account of how he sought to prosecute New York State Police officers and other state officials for crimes ranging up to murder in the retaking of the Attica State Correctional Facility on September 13, 1971; and of how he tried to expose the blatant cover-up of those crimes by the state prosecution team—a cover-up that may well have involved two occupants of the Governor's mansion at Albany and almost certainly was furthered, if not instigated, by Louis Lefkowitz, New York's long-time Attorney General.

Bell's story has political implications beyond Attica and New York. The key episode in the official cover-up—told in detail in Chapter 17—took place on August 22, 1974, just two days after Gerald Ford, who had succeeded to the Presidency following Richard Nixon's resignation, had announced that he would nominate Nelson A. Rockefeller to be Vice President of the United States.

Rockefeller had been Governor of New York during the rebellion at Attica; it was he who had ordered the prison recaptured by force, after steadfastly refusing to go to Attica to take part in negotiations for a peaceful settlement; and it was he who said immediately after the recapture that the State Police had done a "superb job"—although they had killed twenty-nine inmates and ten hostages and wounded eighty-nine others with what repeated official investigations found to be indiscriminate and unwarranted gunfire.

After August 22, Malcolm Bell—then the chief assistant to the special state prosecutor, Anthony Simonetti—found more and more barriers in his way as he tried to prosecute State Police officers and Attica correction officers who had taken part in the recapture of the prison, and who had brutalized and tortured inmates afterward. Had Bell been able to proceed, Rockefeller might well have been shown to be so culpable for the events of September 13, 1971, that he would not have been confirmed as Vice President, or would have been discredited while serving in that office. Either development would have affected the election of 1976, in which Ford—though forced to drop Rockefeller from his ticket—was renominated by the Republicans over the challenger, Ronald Reagan, only to lose in November to Jimmy Carter.

Malcolm Bell's lonely struggle against the New York establishment also tells us much about politics and criminal justice in America. Not only did the State Police, the supposed upholders of the law, kill thirty-nine people in an orgy of wanton shooting, the State of New York then allowed the same police to play the pivotal role in investigating their own behavior—with the predictable results of missing, manufactured, and destroyed evidence, botched or superficial interrogations (or none at all, in some cases), and manifest official perjury. Then, when Bell and other honest investigators and prosecutors found that sufficient evidence existed—even after three years of bungling and malfeasance—to charge numerous officers and officials with many serious crimes, they were prevented from presenting their findings to a grand jury Bell assures us was willing to indict, and puzzled when given no chance to.

Consequently, no police officer or state official ever was found guilty of anything that happened on September 13, 1971, even with thirty-nine people dead of police gunfire, and witnesses available to tell of torture, beatings, and lack of medical care.

Only one policeman was ever indicted, and that only after Malcolm Bell had courageously made public his charges of cover-up. Even that indictment came to naught when Governor Hugh Carey—ostensibly wiping the Attica slate clean—pardoned inmates convicted of crimes during the riot and closed the investigation into other possible crimes. This apparently evenhanded action had the actual result of putting culpable police officers and officials beyond the reach of the law.

The tacit alliance of law enforcement and politics, an omnipresent reality in the American criminal justice system, has seldom been seen more clearly than in Malcolm Bell's painstaking account. The police did the politicians' dirty work, and the politicians covered up for them. Truth was outraged, justice denied, and a cynical example provided of what too many Americans already believe: of those who break the law, the powerless get prison and the powerful get protection.

But Bell tells us something else—that honesty *does* matter, that truth and justice *are* worth pursuing even if seldom attained, that one person willing to stand up can make a difference. Malcolm Bell stood up and made a difference, and of that rare experience he finds the essence: "Attica freed me in ways in which I had not known I was not free."

An unlikely hero, perhaps, but who is a likely hero? In the summer of 1973, Bell was a respected establishment lawyer, a 1958 graduate of Harvard Law School who had started at the pinnacle with Dewey, Ballantine, Bushby, Palmer and Wood. A self-described "moderate Republican" who had voted three times for Richard Nixon, and a deacon of his church, Bell had nevertheless begun to see himself as a corporate litigator "who fought over existing wealth and created nothing." He remembered the few criminal cases he had handled as far more exciting, and when the chance came to join the Attica prosecution, he took it: "Fifteen years out of law school may be late to change the direction of a career, but better late than always to wonder."

Bell left corporate law at considerable financial sacrifice, but with little idea of what his move ultimately would cost him. At first, he believed wholly in the integrity of the prosecution and still believes that it was Ford's nomination of Rockefeller that turned it sour. But when Simonetti, with whom he had once had a close, admiring relationship, suspended him, without explanation, after Bell's continuing efforts to break through what he finally recognized as a cover-up, Bell found himself out of a job during a recession and standing in the unemployment lines.

Even then, leading New York law firms were willing to interview, though none hired him. After he made his charges public—risking disbarment and the certain antagonism of the legal establishment—the interviews dried up. Bell [started] a personal practice in Connecticut . . . and, he writes, [became] a happier and freer man for his experience.

I should confess a personal interest. Before disclosing his cover-up charge, Malcolm Bell—as he recounts here—came to see me at *the New York Times*. I put him in touch with our news department, and his disclosures followed, with prominent display on page one. Later, over a period of years, I tried with no success to help him to get this book before the public. I became convinced that New York's establishment publishers either thought the public had lost interest in Attica, or that Bell's book was too hot to handle, or both. Publishers, after all, know perfectly well how to remedy whatever literary defects they may have seen in his manuscript. I had nothing to do with the present publication—other than contributing this foreword—which comes almost a decade after I first heard of the book.

Beyond that, Attica was one of those rare events that as Bell writes "has a way of holding people." I know of no one who was there who would dispute that. Having been myself on the scene during most of the riot and for what he aptly calls the "turkey shoot" on September 13, I don't expect ever to be entirely free of Attica—most particularly of the corrosive sense of a terrible failure, a failure of men and procedures, of courage and wisdom, of compassion, or the true toughness of spirit that knows no fear. Still, Attica had its few heroes, and to that short but honorable list this book will add the name of Malcolm Bell.

Tom Wicker
Rochester, Vermont
July 19, 1985

Author's Note

On the warm afternoon of November 7, 2015, roughly two hundred and fifty people gathered at Union Theological Seminary on the upper West Side of Manhattan to pay tribute to Elizabeth M. Fink, a brilliant, flamboyant, often testy, indomitable lawyer who had died that September at the age of seventy. Though Liz had started out in criminal defense—and several of that afternoon's speakers were people she had kept out of prison or freed from prison—the heart of her life's work was a civil suit to compensate hundreds of convicts for the wanton shootings and tortures that law officers had inflicted on them at Attica. Liz, aided by three other lawyers who stepped to the lectern to praise her this afternoon, fought the case for nineteen years without a payday and finally in 2000 achieved the largest money settlement in the history of prisoner litigation. Along the way, they won the largest jury award ever for a single inmate, Frank "Big Black" Smith (though this award was reversed on appeal). That afternoon Big Black's widow, Pearl, read a poem for Liz.

The huge litigation, which had been inching forward for several years before Liz joined it, was still inching when this book first went to press in 1985. While I barely mentioned Liz and her team in the book, their triumphs and defeats form a significant part of the new epilogue in this edition.

Before I spoke (the only former prosecutor to praise Liz that afternoon), it was my privilege to read a message from Michael Smith, the only former prison guard to praise her. When the shooting began, Mike, who was a hostage on a prison catwalk, survived four bullets that another guard fired through his gut. During the months of his recuperation, State officials swindled Smith and the other hostages, their widows, and their children out of fair compensation for the injuries and pain that law officers and officials had inflicted on them. It was not until 2000, though, that these former State employees and their families, stunned by the inmates' settlement, banded together as the "Forgotten Victims of Attica" (FVOA) and sought such justice as was still possible for themselves. Mike became a leader of their quest—as did dynamic Deanne Quinn Miller, who had been five years old when inmates fatally injured her father during the riot. Their quest, too, forms a significant part of the epilogue.

Attica was a volcano. First came the prisoners' eruption against the way the State was treating them. Then came the eruption when scores of law officers, who were supposed to keep the peace, rioted with their guns and clubs. In the wake of their savagery, New York's top officials fought like cornered tigers to deny to the public, and perhaps to themselves, the enormity of what their law officers had done. Their cover-up, which I detail in the book, has continued despite considerable success at revealing the truth. At Liz Fink's memorial, her legal teammates—Dennis Cunningham of San Francisco, Michael Deutsch of Chicago, and Joe Heath of Syracuse—urged everyone present to end the cover-up as completely as possible by demanding the release of still-suppressed Attica records.

Paradoxically perhaps, the prominence of the Attica tragedy has increased with the passage of time. As New York's Attorney General told a court in 2013, "[L]ike the shootings at Kent State, the violent police attacks on civil rights demonstrators in the 1960s, the My Lai Massacre, and the Watergate scandal, Attica is more than just a profoundly tragic event; it is an historic event of significance to generations of Americans."[1] At least seven elements, I believe, combine to explain Attica's prominence: the brutal beatings that inmates inflicted on prison guards and civilian employees at the outset, killing Corrections Officer William Quinn; Governor Nelson Rockefeller's premature shutdown of talks aimed at ending the rebellion without violence; the bloodbath in which State Police and guards killed twenty-nine inmates and ten hostages and wounded eighty-nine other men; the savagery that law officers unleashed upon inmates after they had surrendered; the racism that underlay much of the officers' savagery; the official cover-up of the law officers' many violent crimes; and the media attention that the tragedy still attracts.

Of these elements, probably the most significant was the law officers' unwarranted shooting that cut down inmates and hostages alike. Unfortunately, many people today believe that *all* the officers who stormed the prison were guilty of this conduct. Not so. The available evidence shows that the first dozen or so shots they fired were lawful and necessary to save the hostages whose throats inmates were poised to slash; and of the 211 troopers and a few prison guards in the assault force, more than half did not fire their guns at all.

Over the years a number of authors, reporters, filmmakers, lawyers for the hostages and inmates, and people whose lives the Attica tragedy altered forever have told me that this book showed them what really happened during and after the turkey shoot. This updated edition should serve them and others who care to know how justice really works—not simply Attica justice, but American justice.

I say *American* justice because the tortuous course of Attica justice highlights the inequality that has long blighted our nation and will continue to blight it unless enough people object. Those who committed criminal acts during the rebellion and its aftermath were both convicted felons and law officers and august state officials. When Tom Wicker wrote in his foreword, "Of those who break the law, the powerless get prison and the powerful get protection," his words fit vastly more than simply these Attica transgressors.

A point that has often been missed: what this book tells is not primarily a prison story; the prison was merely the scene of the crimes. The central story is of the ensuing prosecution that aimed to appear honest yet to fail, of my efforts to straighten its aim, and of what followed when I took the official scam public.

The beauty of the story I have tried to tell—if there can be beauty in an avoidable tragedy that put justice on trial—is that it lays bare the process by which law officers and public officials sought impunity for crimes that were sending less privileged people to prison. The back of the watch lies open. Corruption ticks inside.

The original title of the book, *The Turkey Shoot: Tracking the Attica Cover-up*, while accurate, finally struck me as being more limited than the book's scope, especially as the events of the three decades since it was published have broadened its scope. The new title better fits the new book. I have changed nothing of substance in the original text but simply clarified the writing a bit and given names to the chapters—many of them the same names that I used in a still-suppressed report on the cover-up that I sent to New York's Governor Hugh Carey forty plus years ago. The body of this book is essentially the same as the original but easier to follow.

Just as the first edition does not name the officers who became criminal suspects, I do not name them here—even though the names of many of them are now public. I consider this reticence my duty as an ex-prosecutor; and simply as a human being, I don't want to cause pointless pain by implicating men who were never indicted (albeit often for the wrong reasons) and at this late date cannot defend themselves. Some people argue that there is a duty to history to name them and that not naming them furthers the cover-up, but I am not persuaded. Indeed, I think it's a bit much if I am accused of furthering the Attica cover-up.[2]

I do not know the identities of the troopers who are seen walking outside the prison on the new cover of the book, or which of them exercised professional restraint with his shotgun or failed to during the gunfire shortly before the photo was taken.

Reverend Ray Chesbro's haunting graphic on the title page of three men being tortured to death may suggest the crucifixion of Jesus between two thieves, but more pertinently here, it stands for the brutality that state power has employed against innocent and guilty alike from Rome to Attica.

Here is a guide to the narrative: Chapter 1 gives an overview. In Chapter 2, I join the Attica special prosecutor's office two years into its work. Chapters 3-6 introduce the prison, the bloody assault that retook it from rebelling prisoners, the barbarity that followed the shooting, and the Attica Investigation. Chapters 7-16: the prosecution of the principal killers rolls forward two years tardy. Chapters 17-20: Nelson Rockefeller's nomination for Vice President changes the game. Chapters 21-30: justice was and is obstructed. Chapters 31-34: having done all I can inside the prosecution, I resign in protest. Chapters 35-43: the motley results of exposing the cover-up.

The new epilogue begins with three improbably happy endings within the Attica saga, yet even they cast shadows: The inmates' settlement with the State carried equal justice too far for many people. The resolution of the Forgotten Victims' quest omitted what some considered its most important element. And the sunshine that a federal judge let into a large, dark chamber of the cover-up revealed information that many people would rather not face. But so, it seems, does the book as a whole.

Next come four recent events: In 2013 the Attorney General joined the quest to disclose some still-suppressed documents. That year, too, saw the start of Black Lives Matter, a movement that opposes police shootings of unthreatening black men, so many of whom were shot at Attica and continue to be shot to this day. In 2014 came new insight into a likely case of murder that I had been stopped from pursuing forty years before. In 2015 the near impunity of three guards for viciously maiming a prisoner showed Attica again as representing an inequality that I hope Americans will someday find unacceptable. Finally, I note two flagrant instances of the impunity of the privileged—one well known, the other curiously ignored—that are closely akin to the unequal justice that glares from the wreckage of the Attica uprising.

While justice may have earned a mixed verdict at Attica, I close by recalling a number of people whom the quest for justice ennobled—a happy ending from which we all may take heart.

Malcolm Bell
Weston, Vermont

Chapter One

The Challenges

A reporter's camera captures a young woman, dark hair falling past her shoulders and her face averted, as she waits outside a prison. Inmates deep within hold her husband hostage. State Police retaking the prison shoot her husband through the abdomen, then try to convince the medical examiners that an inmate killed him with a spear. His death, along with the deaths of thirty-eight others at the hands of the police, shocks the nation that September. As the years pass, no one answers for those killings. The woman in the photo waits forever while her husband fades from public memory.

The Attica riot—or rebellion, as I came to understand it—burst onto the pleasant Thursday morning of September 9, 1971, inside the thirty-foot-high, cream-colored walls of the Attica Correctional Facility (maximum security prison), which rests on the rolling farmland of western New York. Slightly more than half the swollen population of inmates sacked their home, captured all the guards and civilian employees they could, and held them hostage through four tense days of negotiations. The talks accomplished much but were officially claimed to have reached an impasse. On orders from then-Governor Nelson A. Rockefeller, the State Police retook the prison in the gentle rain of Monday morning, the thirteenth. Their commander, Major John Monahan, instructed them beforehand that he did not want a "turkey shoot." But the guns of the police and a few prison guards cracked and boomed more than 450 times, speeding at least 2,200 bullets and shotgun pellets into the crowd. The gunfire killed 10 of the 38 hostages and 29 out of 1,281 inmates; it wounded 89 other men, many grievously, making Attica "the bloodiest prison riot in American history, the deadliest act of state-ordered domestic violence since the massacre at Wounded Knee in 1890."[1] And that fatal morning, a hostage was more than ten times as likely as an inmate to die.

The media that covered the riot, relying solely on the word of a State official, reported that inmates had killed all the dead hostages with knives. The next day, though, the media had to recant because Dr. John F. Edland, the Rochester medical examiner who had worked through the night autopsying the bodies of eight of those ten men, announced that bullets had killed them all. Since the police had the only guns, the conclusion was obvious. The extent of this carnage and the enormity of this official lie promptly made *Attica* a household word; yet most people have never learned what actually happened that morning, or who did what to bury these facts along with the bodies, they hoped, forever.

Within the next few days and before any investigation, Governor Rockefeller, who bore the responsibility for ordering the attack, announced that the State Police had done "a superb job." He praised their "skill and courage" and their "restraint [that] held down casualties among the prisoners as well." The officers' killing of the hostages was, Rockefeller added, "justifiable homicide."[2] Having thus predicted what a criminal investigation would find, Rockefeller and Attorney General Louis Lefkowitz appointed a special prosecutor, a former judge named Robert E. Fischer, to find out, but they gave him a staff that was far too tiny to do a proper job.

The months went swiftly by. A year after the bloody retaking of the prison, a special commission under Dean Robert McKay of the New York University Law School, which Rockefeller had appointed to investigate and report to the public about the riot, announced that the police had done "much unnecessary shooting." Unnecessary shooting inside Attica, where close to 1,300 men were crowded into a broad brick pen called D Yard, almost certainly meant criminal shooting. But the McKay Commission was a toothless tiger. It had no power to prosecute anyone, and the uproar over its findings soon faded.

Two years into the work of the Attica Investigation, which is what the special prosecutor's office was called, State officials suddenly found a way to hire more staff—not because the Investigation had finally decided to dig into the homicides by the police, but because more lawyers and investigators were needed to try the sixty or so inmates whom Fischer's meager crew had managed to indict. I was among the lawyers hired. A former New York City prosecutor named Anthony G. Simonetti soon succeeded Fischer as head of the Investigation, and I soon became his chief assistant. My job was to give a grand jury the evidence of any and all serious crimes that law officers had committed during and after the shootings. This book, then, is an insider's account of the criminal investigation into the violence by which the State got its prison back— the retaking of the buildings and rehousing of the inmates.

At Attica the veil of civilization parted and the beast sprang forth, wearing the grays and carrying the arms of the State Police. The Official Version (i.e., the line the powers that be ask the public to believe, whether it's true or not) had it that these men loosed their fire in defense against a beast in inmate green. Yet the inmates, who had killed one guard and three inmates during the riot, killed no one during the retaking. They had hundreds of knives, clubs, and other crude weapons, but apart from two tear gas pistols, they had no guns—as the police knew when they went in shooting. The only trooper to be seriously wounded was a lieutenant shot through his leg by his own men. Many of the vicious beatings and other brutalities that guards and troopers inflicted upon hundreds of inmates after they had surrendered made news at the time, but the Official Version asked us to believe that the police had unleashed their fury *only* upon men who had already surrendered, and that during their storm of bullets, they had exercised professional restraint, shooting people only as the law allows, to save someone's life from an imminent threat of grievous harm.

Most Americans who know anything about Attica think that there was only one riot, the one by the inmates. The particulars of the turkey shoot emerged so slowly, and so many facts remained suppressed, that most people never learned that the police can fairly be said to have rioted with their guns and clubs. And with lethal bigotry. The population of Attica was 54 percent black, 37 percent white, and 9 percent Puerto Rican, while the troopers and guards were 100 percent white. To the surprise and relief of many, the inmates' riot was largely free of racial animosity. Their common attitude was "We're all in this together, race doesn't matter." But to a distressing degree, the police riot was a race riot. Anger and hatred had built on both sides during a previous four-day stand-off between the inmates and the authorities. Inmates called officers "pig." Officers' favorite epithet was "nigger." Graffiti on an interior wall memorialized the hatreds: "Attica fell 9-9-71 <u>Fuck</u> you Pig!" Beside it: "Retaken on 9-13-71 32 Dead Niggers NYSP."[3] So far as I know, senior police officers made no serious effort to restrain or discipline the troopers' crescendo of racist hatred. Then came the shooting. Afterward some troopers bragged, "Got me a nigger."

The very enormity of what the police had done probably helped to assure that many people would not believe they had done it. In western New York many people still insist that the first big lie—that inmates had killed the dead hostages—was the truth and Dr. Edland was a communist. It is comfortable to trust that we live in an orderly land where, except for the proverbial "few bad apples," law officers uphold the law. At Attica, though, the State Police breached that trust as scores of them killed, maimed, and tortured with scant restraint. Their savagery triggered the destruction of evidence by their brother detectives who were supposed to preserve it. This led to a cover-up of police crimes by the prosecution, which was supposed to treat all criminals equally.

While this book includes acts of courage, restraint, and honesty by some of the State Police, it is mainly a crime story in which the police committed most of the murders. It is a detective story in which the detectives did more to bury the facts than to uncover them. It tells of law and order in collision, with order winning at law's expense. On the national level, it joins Nelson Rockefeller's ambition to become President of the United States to the fact that he ordered the armed assault on the prison—after journalist Tom Wicker, Congressman Herman Badillo, and other well-esteemed men who were at the prison, where Rockefeller refused to go, had warned him with all the passion and eloquence they could muster that the armed assault would be a bloodbath—and it links a sudden halt in the belated prosecution of his "superb job" troopers to his 1974 nomination to become Vice President.

I believe that, paradoxically, my inexperience with political realities played a significant part in exposing the Attica cover-up. Never having prosecuted anyone, I trusted that the great American principle of equal justice for all, convicts and law officers alike, would prevail. So I worked to indict the officers against whom we had substantial evidence of murder and other serious felonies. This went fine at first—a stacked deck has to appear legit—but the closer I came to indicting these officers, the more obstacles my superiors put in my path, thereby exposing more and more of their determination to obstruct justice. Indeed, they blocked my efforts so often and blatantly that I thought that any fool will see what they're doing. In the end, the equal justice that I sought was not achieved, and what a Governor called justice was not justice. But I dare say, the results turned out much better than they would have if I had not tried to do my job and then spoken out against the cover-up that blocked me.

Since I was assigned to prosecute police while most of my colleagues were busy prosecuting inmates and I refused to go along with the cover-up, some people think I must have taken the inmates' side. This is not what happened. As I show hereafter, I worked as hard to find evidence of officers' innocence as of their guilt. I simply wanted to get it right. For now, suffice it to note that Governor Rockefeller ordered the Attica Investigation to prosecute, not simply inmates' crimes, but all crimes. That is what our great principle of equal justice demands, and, naively perhaps, that is what I tried to do.

Since I tell this story as I lived it, it seems fair to note at the start that Attica changed me. This book is not written by the moderate Republican I was when the State hired me. Yet most of what I believe did not change. Because it did not, other things had to—my career, income, assumptions, perspective. Attica freed me in ways in which I had not known I was not free.

What law officers did at Attica challenged our system of justice and our proud claim that no one is above the law. It challenged Governor Nelson Aldrich Rockefeller, who had done much for the State of New York and wished to lead the nation. It challenged me, and I dare say, it challenged my superiors as they tried to restrict me to a course that they could not admit they were taking. The way that events unfolded may surprise you. It surprised me time after time.

Chapter Two

"An Honest Prosecution"

Attica has a way of holding people. The labyrinth of the riot may fascinate them as deftly as the gates and tunnels embrace the men who shed segments of their lives there. I had not thought of being captured by Attica, but I was, and I have seen it happen to others.

I knew virtually nothing about Attica when it chanced into my life in the summer of 1973. I knew they had a big riot in 1971; inmates held knives to the throats of hostages on catwalks—I imagined catwalks like the narrow iron bridges you used to see on oil tankers, instead of the long flat rooftops that they are. Throats were reportedly slashed, then they weren't. The police shot a lot of people. It was all pretty shocking, as is so much that continually happens to others. With my lack of knowledge went a lack of feeling. I enjoyed the objectivity of ignorance.

I come from a conservative background against which I sometimes rebelled. I still remember my surprise in late high school at hearing a teacher say a good word about labor unions. Through the 1960s I had supported U.S. involvement in Vietnam. In the fall of 1972 I had cast my third vote for Richard Nixon for President.

After finishing Harvard Law School in 1958, I had worked nine years for the large Wall Street firm Dewey, Ballantine, Bushby, Palmer & Wood; the Dewey was Thomas E., the former New York Governor who had lost the Presidency to Roosevelt in 1944 and to Truman in 1948. I passed six more years with two firms in mid-Manhattan in the amiable acrimony of civil litigation. More and more though, I compared litigators like myself with medieval knights who fought over other people's wealth and created nothing. Or, I saw civil suits as games of tennis—fun, but not what I came for. By the summer of 1973, I was restless and ready for a change.

I wanted to get into criminal law. The few criminal cases I had ever defended stood out among my most exciting work. Lives changed. Drama inhered. The courts were taking new steps forward and sometimes backward in the wake of the Earl Warren Supreme Court. Criminal law is a specialty, and a prosecutor's office is a good place to learn it. Though forty-one years old, I wanted to do that. Fifteen years out of law school may be late to change the direction of a career, but better late than always to wonder.

So it was that I answered a blind ad for prosecutors in the *New York Law Journal*, writing that I had never prosecuted anyone but wanted to talk about it. A reply arrived on the letterhead of the State of New York Organized Crime Task Force. It was signed, "Anthony G. Simonetti, Assistant Attorney General, in Charge." He wrote, "We are now interested in obtaining the full-time services of an attorney or attorneys with prosecutorial 'trial experience,'" for cases arising out of the Attica riot, and asked me in for an interview.

I had already cleared the personal hurdle of my distaste for prosecuting people. Someone has to do it. It is not like being an executioner, who cannot exercise discretion. Better if it is done by someone not dominated by a desire to win—since the public wins when the innocent go free. A United States Attorney for Connecticut told me once that it is important to decide whether the person before you is some poor guy who deserves another chance or a smart-ass who ought to be in. I had already applied to several prosecutor's offices, and they had not worked out. Hoping for the best, I made the appointment to try Attica.

Mr. Simonetti relaxed in his shirtsleeves behind a gray metal desk in his sunny office on the corner of a "semi-abandoned State office building" —his phrase—nine floors over Broadway.[1] The headquarters of the Attica Investigation had come to rest there, after starting at the prison, moving to Rochester forty miles away, and thence to Manhattan at the opposite end of the State. Two panels bearing an enormous diagram of the prison courtyards rested against the dirty-cream wall to his left.

Simonetti was a compact man about my age (two years younger, I learned later) and had the dark good looks of the actor Al Pacino. Simonetti had been a U.S. Marine and later an FBI agent, working for a time in the South on civil rights cases. He had prosecuted homicides under New York City's legendary District Attorney, Frank Hogan. Hogan's prosecutors had impressed me in the past as being generally fair and competent.

We discussed my lack of experience in prosecuting people. He thought my trial experience (such as it was) should transfer easily. The aspects that make prosecution unique, I would have to pick up. He impressed me by doing something that no one had ever done with me in a job interview. He told me the facts of a homicide he had once tried and asked me how I would try that case. I thought a moment, asked him a few questions, and told him. We talked about some of the problems of the case, one trial lawyer to another. He seemed pleased.

He explained that in thirty-seven indictments to date, about sixty Attica inmates had been charged with crimes, including murder, kidnapping, and assault. He said it was deemed kidnapping when inmates took hostages at the start of the riot, as it was when they took eight of the already kidnapped hostages from the Hostage Circle in D Yard up onto the catwalks on the morning of the retaking. (I would come to know those locations.) No law officer had been indicted yet, but he said, confirming a line in his letter: " . . . additional indictments may ensue."

The trials of inmates could start in Buffalo as early as that November. He was hiring additional lawyers to try these cases. Some cases were small, some big. I mentioned my past experience with complicated cases, antitrust and stock fraud, and said I was seeking wide experience. He replied that the Attica cases had already provided a great variety of legal problems, and he expected more. New law could develop; books could be written, he added, about the Attica prosecution.

To my surprise, he asked about my philosophy.

"For one thing," I replied, "if a cop and an inmate both committed a crime, I'd rather prosecute the cop."

"Why?"

"The full weight of the System will land on the inmate. The cop is more likely to hide behind the System, so that's the job that needs doing more. It's not that I have anything against cops. We need them. I feel the same way whenever a respectable person uses his position to get away with something."

He asked if I could work for $28,500. That was more than any other prosecutor's office that I knew about was likely to pay me, but it would cut my present salary by several thousand dollars. My ambition on leaving law school had been "to work on interesting cases with able and congenial men." By 1973 it was "to put together an interesting life." I thought the pay cut well worth it. I said yes. He said that if he could get my application through budget—and he thought he could—I had the job.

I was happy. The interview had gone well. I liked Mr. Simonetti—probably the most important decision one makes at a job interview. He seemed to like me. He covered the main points directly in one sitting, no one else to consult, no noncommittal promise to call me later. Here was a man who knew his mind and made it up, at ease but no nonsense, and an honorable man, as well. I had said I would rather prosecute an officer than an inmate. He offered me the job. " . . . additional indictments may ensue." The investigation had to be honest.

I took my children to the gentle island of Martha's Vineyard for a week. The radio was full of Jim Croce's song about putting "Time in a Bottle." I wished we could do that and keep those days forever. When we returned, Mr. Simonetti let me know that the necessary approvals had come through. He asked me to read the McKay Report, which Governor Rockefeller had commissioned to tell the public about the riot at the same time that he established the Attica Investigation to prosecute the crimes there. I would begin work on September 20. A letter of appointment from Attorney General Lefkowitz, Mr. Simonetti said, was on the way.

Chapter Three

The Joint

On my first visit to Attica I stood inside a cell in D Block facing the open door and tried to imagine what it would be like to live in there with the bars closed. The riot had left D Block a shambles, littered with rubble, mattresses, and the red slit corpses of Barry Schwartz, Kenneth Hess, and Michael Privitiera. Inmates had killed these inmates during the days of negotiation that occupied most of the riot. They cut and stabbed Hess forty times and Privitiera twenty. Hess and Schwartz had spoken "treasonably" to a newsman in D Yard, by telling him there were cracks in the inmates' solidarity. Privitiera kept trying to assault people. D Block was such a mess that no one found the carcass of Hess until a day after the riot ended.

The day I stood there, D Block was bare, repaired, and silent, a clean machine waiting to suck out the years. Inside the symmetry of the cell, I felt fear, some claustrophobia, and, most fearsome, snugness and safety. Attica is two ways a maximum security prison. Punishment has matured, from iron maiden to iron womb.

I had flown from New York City to Rochester early that October morning with Bill Blackford, my assigned investigator, for our first look at "the joint" as part of Tony Simonetti's orientation for all new men. Bill was tall, black-haired, Irish, and in his early fifties. The other investigators sometimes called him Blackfoot the Indian. Like most of the investigators, he had retired after twenty years in the New York City Police Department and now had a good living with his salary plus pension. Fourteen of his years as a cop, he had spent on the streets of Harlem. I guessed he had had interesting experiences and could handle himself. Tony had put both of us on Indictment No. 10, which charged ten inmates with trapping three guards in an office in C Block on the morning the riot started, clubbing them through the bars, and kidnapping them into D Yard as hostages.

From the Rochester airport we drove through the clear cold morning to the Holiday Inn at Batavia for a leisurely second breakfast with some other prosecutors—assistant attorneys general, or "assistants"—and investigators on the staff. I chafed silently, impatient that the day was slipping away in the genial company of men whose tempo beat slower than mine. This was my first taste of their "upstate fever." Perhaps we would have time to see all there was to see of the prison, I thought, and still make the return flight.

Flat Batavia lies off the New York Thruway (actually the Governor Thomas E. Dewey Thruway) a dozen miles north of the prison. Troop A of the State Police, the troop that had been in charge at the riot, centers there. Blocks of trees and lawns and houses stretch away from the taller buildings and water towers of downtown in this Anywhere, U.S.A. Among members of the Investigation, Batavia was known as the Peyton Place of western New York, basking under the benign eye of Troop A, though I never fully understood its reputation. I heard stories about correction officers' wives who drifted up to the bar at the Holiday Inn while their husbands pulled night duty. In that bar some of the troopers bragged about their exploits the evening after they retook the prison. "Got me a nigger." Someone asked the piano player to play "The Green, Green Grass of Home," not realizing that the song told of a man condemned to die in prison. That was the legend.

State Police came from all over New York and slept at the Holiday Inn, among other places, during the riot. Our staff spent a lot of time there, particularly early in the investigation. (Later, when the State Police realized we took their killings seriously, a young woman who worked at the Holiday Inn told me that one of their lawyers had questioned her about me. Fortunately, perhaps, she had nothing to tell him. I seldom stayed there after that.)

The town of Attica rests on the rolling farmland of Wyoming County east of Lake Erie, about halfway between Rochester and Buffalo though south of both cities. From the roofs of the prison you can see barns and silos among the trees and meadows. From a plane the geometry of the joint looks misshapen on the land—too squared, too big, too much like the skeleton of the minicity that it is. Bill and I drove through the little town and turned left to cross the hump of a railroad line. Over green grass off a tree-lined street lay the long light-colored wall, spaced by towers that bulged with crenellated balconies under dark conical roofs. Across the road behind us sat a restaurant in a solitary frame house, a red neon beer sign in the window. The prison opened in 1931, the year I was born. There it suddenly was, waiting for me all the time.

Disneyland North, I thought, as we pulled into the parking lot. The main gate was only a small door in the base of the center gun tower. ATTICA CORRECTIONAL FACILITY said raised letters on the wall above me. I made out the word PRISON in the concrete behind the bottom two words. They had changed the name a few years ago, as if to change the place. In the drab little sign-in room inside the iron gate, it crossed my mind to buy the warden a welcome mat.

Under the sky again but inside the walls that I felt might never let us go, we crossed a block-long sidewalk, flanked by neat, circular flower beds and a beautiful lawn, to the Administration Building. The prison buildings rose in dark red brick to gentle peaks of orange tile. The place seemed comfortably ageless, yet it had a physical awkwardness about it. It cost about $13,000 a year then to keep a person in, twice as much then as to send him to Harvard.

Another barred door, another guard slipping big flat keys in and out of a key apron as if from the pouch of an underdeveloped kangaroo. Silver castle walls surrounded the light fixtures in the square dark lobby, somebody's idea of theme no doubt. An inmate in green shirt and trousers pushed a mop in the area. As we sat waiting, two guards locked a new guest into a tiny cell I had not noticed in a corner. It surprised me to see women working near these men who cannot lie with a woman for years. Sometimes on later visits I felt the silent electric hum of the prison as I waited in the lobby, as though the mass of souls within radiated an energy that science cannot quantify and would therefore deny, but that the bars could not contain. The Administration Building had been a beehive during the riot. The State Police command post had been upstairs, with the radio on which Captain Henry Williams ordered the assault to go forward.

Electric gates stood across the hallway, or "tunnel," to A Block. A guard sat between them, facing one gate and watching the one behind him in a mirror, like a church organist or an Amsterdam whore at her window. He controlled the gates so that one was always closed, the channel from the prison like a lock in a canal. The guards used to carry batons, "nigger sticks," among the population, but guards were beaten with their own clubs during the riot. Now only one guard carried a stick inside, a burly young anachronism whose bravado seemed sad. The guards wore gray slacks and dark blue blazers with a gold Department of Correctional Services seal brilliant on the left breast, their winter uniforms, making them look like superannuated prep school boys.

The 1972 McKay Report, which I had just finished reading, ended some of my ignorance about life at Attica before the riot: wages for the inmates of twenty or twenty-five cents a day, insufficient toilet paper, rectal searches before and after an inmate saw his visitor (if any) through a wire mesh, correspondence only with people approved by the authorities. A guard might withhold a letter and not tell either the sender or the intended recipient. All in the name of security. Fourteen to sixteen hours a day alone in a cell, boredom, little productive work, less chance to learn a trade or skill, religious freedom for Christians but not Muslims. Medical aid through another wire mesh. An inmate told me once about an inmate who had just died of a heart attack after the doctor gave him aspirin for his chest pains. No one at Attica segregated violent sex offenders from frail or bonnie young men and other likely targets, so that homosexual rape remained a threat, and no one I asked could tell me how often it happened. We claim to have ended corporal punishment, but violent buggery was never authorized. Though I had visited Sing Sing in 1968 and seen the usual movies, I had never thought much about prisons. The obvious fact had never crossed my mind that as a voter and taxpayer, I bore a certain responsibility for all this.

The guards mingle with the inmates, and we mingled with the inmates, about one in five of whom was in for killing someone. We paused to discuss something in the middle of A Tunnel, where the riot had broken forth. A group of several dozen inmates with a guard fore and another one aft shuffled past my back. I vaguely waited for a kidney punch, though none seemed likely and none came.

At least three factors, I think, keep violence as low as it is in prison: the decency of most inmates most of the time, their inertia, and their fear of future punishment. The first two factors may account for most of the peace most of the time, but the third is apparently necessary to make prisons as safe as possible, so long as we solve crime with prisons. Punishing inmates' violence should make these places safer than not punishing it. This was why I wanted to do a good job of prosecuting the inmates charged in my Indictment No. 10.

Here was the C Block office, with a new door because the inmates had cut through the old one with an acetylene torch to get the guards out and take them hostage. How small the office looked. How easy to beat the guards through the bars with mop handles. However floppy the mops, the handles made brutal clubs.

White patches blotched the concrete rafters of C Tunnel where shotgun pellets had struck them during the State Police "happy hour," as we called their massive shotgunning down there. Up on the empty catwalks I pondered the number of holes in the pipe railings, a rusted residue of bullets gone by. The railings fill only a small fraction of the air space above the catwalks. To drill this many holes, the gunfire must have fallen heavy as rain.

Rust from a pipe and wire framework over upper Times Square, where the catwalks converged, had stained the pavement a dark red-brown. A correction officer who sometimes followed us around the prison asked me one day if I thought the stain was blood. At our feet as he spoke lay the corner of Times Square, where an inmate told me he saw blood running off the pavement into B Yard on the morning the patience ran out, blood and rain.

That correction officer had survived the riot only by a fluke. The inmates made him and the other blindfolded hostages in D Yard stand up when the shooting started. An inmate stood behind him, gripping his shoulder. He felt a blow like a punch, peeked beneath his blindfold, and saw that the hand on his shoulder had a hole through it. When the doctor took the bullet out of his back, the inmate's fingernail came out with it.

We saw the shop where the inmates cut sheet metal into lockers for the State and sometimes made knives for themselves. Here was the garage, from which came the gasoline for the Molotov cocktails. Out back by the power plant a guard in a tower had threatened to shoot some inmates who were beating another guard early in the riot. That stopped the beating.

HBZ is the name for solitary, the hole, the segregation cells, Housing Block Z. It and the prison's reception center form an L around a concrete exercise yard that is fenced by high wire on the other two sides. Voices inside called us "motherfucker" as we walked past. The dogs in the house bark at the dogs on the street, who do not notice.

A letter in the *New York Times* of July 9, 1974, spoke of "men in the hole at Attica who don't see the light of day for months on end." This is not true—the inmates in HBZ see the sun every day it's out, though Attica remains a temple of doomed hopes.

I was curious throughout my first visit to Attica to go up in a gun tower. There turned out to be time. Most of the towers have one entrance, at the base outside the prison wall. We looked up the smooth cream surface to see a rope wriggling down from a window. The key to the iron gate and massive wooden door danced at the end.

In the top of the tower, the guard maintained himself eight hours a shift with a hotplate, sink, toilet, rifle, and box of shells. Inmates had nearly killed this guard, sending him to the hospital for most of the riot. He had been assigned to the solitary tower ever since, so as not to have to mingle with the population. He said he was sorry he no longer had one of the Attica arsenal's AR-15s, which is a rifle that can be fired in either a semiautomatic mode, requiring a separate trigger-pull for each shot, or (unlike standard civilian models) an automatic mode, that is, like a machine gun. It was with an AR-15 in the automatic mode, I learned later, that a guard had most likely stitched the abdomen of a young guard named Michael Smith.

The smooth wall rose thirty feet up from the lawn inside the prison and the lawn outside, like a giant guillotine cleaving the green. The narrow rounded top extended to gun towers in either direction. The guard told us that an inmate once called up to him: Would he shoot if the inmate climbed a wire fence near the wall? No. Would he shoot if the inmate started to climb the wall? No. Would he shoot if the inmate jumped to the other side?

"If you jumped, I'd yell, 'Halt!' If you didn't halt before you reached the ground, I'd shoot you."

Chapter Four

Lawmen Restore Order

I began at once to learn the history of the riot[1]—to the extent it had then been pieced together—from the McKay Report and from State Police videotape, film, and other materials that Tony Simonetti used for the orientation. That history held more questions than answers. It marked the beginning rather than the end of what there was to know.

I was surprised at first by the way people in the Investigation talked about the events of 1971 as though they had happened yesterday, until I began to picture them that way myself, however many gaps riddled the picture. It was as if our suite in the semiabandoned State office building were a capsule in which time stood still. In particular, the assault by which New York restored law and order started coming together in my mind:

* * *

Spanish tile slopes above the men in gray who lie on the wet roof behind a low brick parapet in the gray morning. A video camera to their right looks down on the courtyards and the raised tunnels that cross at the center of the prison in an intersection called Times Square. Voices erupt quietly from a walkie-talkie nearby. Rifles rest with the troopers, who carry extra cartridges in their pockets. The .270 bullets, which burst from the rifles with enormous spin and disintegrate on entry, can turn a human head into a bag of shards. This horror will soon befall a hostage.

Three of the four main, red brick cellblocks, three stories high by two hundred yards long, normally warehouse the inmates behind rows of windows located across the floor so that most of them cannot look out. Security. Only in C Block does each cell have its own window; the windows on the south side face the catwalks and courtyards. Today only C Block locks inmates. Witnesses.

A Block, which adjoins C Block at the northwest corner of the great square, stands empty to rehouse the rioters; B Block and D Block are in the rioters' control. The tunnels topped by catwalks, wet now with the Monday rain, divide the great square into four courtyards, like giant windowpanes. From one of the helicopters soon to fly over, you might look down on Attica as if it were a window into hell.

Voices erupt from a walkie-talkie in the room crowded with troopers and shotguns a few steps below the doorway to the C Catwalk on the second floor of C Block. The tall, lean captain who commands the C Walk Detail briefs the troopers. "Don't use unnecessary force, but don't engage in hand-to-hand combat, and don't lose your weapon." Their job is to clear a low, jumbled barricade that the inmates have piled up midway down the catwalk, then to turn left around the wire mesh enclosure at Times Square, and to deploy along the B Catwalk in position to cover the Rescue Detail as it goes into D Yard, where twelve hundred or so inmates hold thirty-eight hostages. A trooper prays aloud. The captain figures that God has gone with them as far as He can, and now they are on their own.[2]

The troopers have taped their trouser legs tight or tucked them into their boots, and some wear towels around their necks, against the tear gas soon to fall. A few carry pike poles to rip at the barricade. Others carry fire extinguishers or stand ready to wrestle a fire hose down the catwalk, in case the inmates ignite the barricade with gasoline. Inmates have been seen making Molotov cocktails. The first troopers going out wear blue vests called body armor over their gray uniforms. All have tough plastic helmets, gas masks, and their .38 revolvers or more powerful .357 magnums. Many also carry shotguns.

Many inmates, including those who later say they did not favor the riot, have knives. Some have clubs or poles with knives lashed to the end for spears or—economically—split baseball bats or half scissors. Earlier, the inmates brought a grinding wheel into D Yard. Troopers have seen sparks flying from the inmates' weapons in the night.

Many troopers wanted to finish retaking the prison from the inmates last Thursday, the day the riot started. By early that afternoon they and the guards had recaptured half the prison, killing no one. Commissioner of the Department of Correctional Services Russell Oswald, fearful that the inmates who were cornered in D Yard would kill the hostages, stopped that retaking in order to negotiate. The inmates used the time to organize and arm as well as talk.

Oswald, new at being Commissioner of Corrections, had already promised reforms. The French Revolution started under a reform king. Trouble erupted under reforms in Russia a century later. The Attica riot broke out the week after the inmates heard a tape of Commissioner Oswald promising to give them reforms with all deliberate speed.

Attica had grown restless during the summer of 1971. Inmates in general had become less docile than before and less prone to "serve their own time." They were, in the view of many, more "militant" or "uppity," that is, they were quicker to claim that their rights were being denied when the system constrained their humanity or willfulness. They were better organized, in spite of the efforts of the administration to break up groups and transfer the organizers or trouble-makers around the State's little archipelago of prisons. Black and Puerto Rican inmates from the cities (i.e., most inmates) saw life somewhat differently from their white country keepers.

Attica was overcrowded. A critical mass of humanity becomes explosive, somewhat like a critical mass of uranium.

Events fed the unrest. The official explanation of how the police in Chicago burst into an apartment in the middle of the night and shot Fred Hampton and another Black Panther to death in December 1969 did not wash, as far as many inmates were concerned. (A federal grand jury eventually concluded that the police had slaughtered them and covered up, but no one was indicted.) At the Auburn prison a hundred miles to the east, the State Police had put down a riot without killing anyone in 1970; some of those rioters ended up at Attica. On August 21, 1971, in San Quentin, guards shot George Jackson to death. Whatever else he was, Jackson had been an articulate activist against injustice in prison. The Official Version said he had a gun smuggled in his Afro. The inmates of Attica, many of whom wore Afros themselves, had trouble visualizing that. They gave him a day of mourning on August 22. It unnerved the guards to see them wearing black armbands and silently refusing to eat. One guard admitted, "I was scared shitless."[3]

The riot at Attica began with an incident on the afternoon of Wednesday, September 8. An inmate appeared to punch a guard who was intervening in a scuffle between two inmates in one of the courtyards. After everyone was safely locked away that night, several guards came to take the alleged puncher off to solitary. Another inmate winged an unopened can of soup cleanly through the bars of his cell, hitting a guard in the head. The next morning, the guards tried to leave the soup can thrower locked in his cell while the rest of his company marched to breakfast. As the inmates passed the company lock box at the end of his gallery, one of them pulled the lever that opened his cell. He joined the others. The guards didn't dare seize him. Tension grew.

A company of inmates was halted for a moment in A Tunnel as they returned from the mess hall after breakfast. They jumped their guards. Riot spread through the prison like the smell of blood through shark-infested waters. Inmates beat guards, smashed windows, set fires. "To D Yard! To D Yard!" Inmates who did not want to go were threatened. "To D Yard or die!"

Even if the can of soup had struck the bars instead of passing through, the temper of the prison was such that the riot would likely have erupted soon anyway. A guard said later, "We had all been concerned about this trouble that was brewing in the prison. You could feel it in the air. . . . Every night we expected it."[4]

During the tense negotiations between Thursday and Monday morning, Oswald granted twenty-eight of the inmates' thirty-one demands. That was not so generous as it may sound, though yielding anything to rioting inmates angered many people. Common decency would have granted many of those demands and other reforms years earlier, would have given the inmates medical treatment, religious freedom, balanced diets, treatment for drug withdrawal, rehabilitation, fewer rectal searches, and more than one roll of toilet paper a month. The people of New York are like most Americans in refusing money for the prisons they maintain. The inmates had not seen much reform.

The demands that remain this morning are: the removal of Vincent Mancusi as warden, passage to a Third World country for the probably few inmates who wanted it (to the extent that a Third World country wanted them), and, the most important, amnesty for all crimes committed during the riot. The importance of amnesty grew with the mounting tension when Correction Officer William Quinn, whose head several inmates battered on Thursday, died on Saturday.

The underlying impasse at Attica has a tragic simplicity. The inmates say, "We are people." The authorities say, "You will obey."

The New York State Police are a spit-and-polish, paramilitary corps who seem to regard City cops as Marines regard soldiers. Their rules require them to shoot to kill if they shoot at all; their rhetoric says that this is so as not to "maim." Not incidentally to this narrative, they serve as bodyguards to the Governor.

Now, four days of calling each other "nigger," "pig" and "motherfucker" have done their work. For four days the State Police have heard a rhetoric of dying and killing boom out over the inmates' captured public address system. "If we cannot live as people, then we will at least try to die like men."[5] The State Police are not used to being defied, certainly not by a bunch of convicted felons most of whom are blacks or Puerto Ricans. The State Police are so white that years later a court has to order them to integrate. The police have not discussed their views on dying and killing over a P.A. system, but they have the guns.

Some of their shotguns carry the rifled slug, an ounce of lead that is about the size of a Civil War minié ball, useful, its makers say, in reducing a cement block wall to rubble. One of these slugs will soon let daylight through an inmate's abdomen. Another will kill Sam Melville, the radical and articulate "Mad Bomber" who is doing his time at Attica. More of the shotguns carry 00 buckshot, nine or twelve pellets, each the heft of a .32 caliber pistol bullet and each able to kill a person at several hundred yards. No distance inside the zone of contention is that great. During the days of negotiation some troopers have taken the lead pellets from shotgun shells and zipped them at inmates with elastic slingshots.

Shotguns are sometimes called scatter guns because the pellets spread out as they travel. At fifty yards the spread from these models will pattern a circle four feet in diameter; some pellets must miss any person shot at from that distance. In crowded D Yard some pellets are nearly certain to hit someone else. A single "stray" pellet through the face will soon kill Sergeant Edward Cunningham, a hostage who told the world on television on Sunday, September 12, that if Rockefeller didn't grant clemency, "I'm dead."[6]

A few inmates move about the gloomy octagon where the four tunnels meet at lower Times Square, at the center of the great Attica window. Barred gates separate the tunnels from Times Square at one end and from the first floor (which is called "the flats") of the cellblocks at the other. One of the gates at Times Square broke open unexpectedly when a mass of inmates hit it on Thursday, allowing the riot to spread through the prison. Iron rods in the floor and ceiling anchored the gates where they met in the middle. When the prison was built, one of the rods to the ceiling was too short, so the workmen added on the needed length with a light weld around the outside. It held for the next forty years, probably because everyone was too rational to test what looked solid.

The inmates in Times Square can see the figures of troopers through the bars at the other end of C Tunnel a hundred yards to the north, and down A Tunnel to the west. The gates at Times Square have sheet metal aprons across their base, which will soon save the lives of these inmates from the C Tunnel shotguns.

Restraint ran out at 7:40 this morning. Commissioner Oswald gave the inmates an ultimatum:

> I urgently request you to seriously reconsider my earlier appeal that one, all hostages be released immediately, unharmed, and two, you join with me in restoring order to the facility. I must have your reply to this urgent appeal within the hour. I hope and pray your answer will be in the affirmative.[7]

Living hostages are the inmates' power. After that there is only the good faith of the State, which prison had not necessarily conditioned the inmates to trust. Since the authorities deem surprise important, they never actually tell the inmates that an armed assault is the alternative. Many inmates expect, at worst, rubber bullets. To that extent, at least, they still trust "father."

A very large captain and a scholarly looking lieutenant wait with their men in the busy cubical cavern in A Block between the short tunnel to the Administration Building and the entrance to A Tunnel. The captain tells his men that the inmates were not organized when they were out on the street, so there is no reason to expect them to be organized now. Troopers are to shoot tear gas shells into a low barricade midway down the tunnel before the A Tunnel Detail goes in.

Above them, a narrow balcony connects the second-floor galleries of cells on either side of A Block. A door at the center of the balcony gives onto A Walk. Wooden ladders lean against the balcony. The assault plan calls for the ladders to be carried by troopers out the door onto A Walk, behind the A Walk Detail. When they pass Times Square, troopers will lower the ladders from B Walk into D Yard. Twenty-five troopers, optimistically called the Rescue Detail, will hurry down among the twelve hundred crudely armed inmates to try to rescue the hostages from the middle of D Yard, while brother officers cover them with their shotguns and pistols from B and D Catwalks, above. There is obviously no way to reach the hostages in time to save their lives if the inmates are determined to kill them.

Tents, lean-tos, picnic tables, and the garbage of four days' camping out litter D Yard. Men move about whose lives are nearly over. A man bends his arm; a bullet will soon carry the elbow away, and the wound will fester and leak years later. It's easy to forget the wounded, which, in one way or another, means nearly everyone at Attica who did not die.

A few foxholes pock the sod or burrow under the concrete sidewalk that rims D Yard. A trench runs along the pavement beside D Tunnel, rounds the right angle by Times Square, and continues a short way beside the B Tunnel pavement. This end serves as a latrine. Near the center of the yard a rectangle of mattresses piled inside an oval of benches forms the Hostage Circle, home away from home for thirty-eight men who helped to run the prison until four days ago, where Sergeant Cunningham forecast his death if his Governor did not yield. Near the Circle a kitchen deals out the food that the authorities have sent in.

During the riot, shaved-headed Black Muslims have guarded the Hostage Circle in D Yard. At times they linked arms while one of their number crashed into them, showing their ability to keep would-be attackers out. They have blindfolded and unblindfolded the hostages many times but in the main treated them well. After Oswald delivered his ultimatum, the Muslims are relieved, and other inmates tie the hostages hand and foot and blindfold them again. They take eight hostages away from the Circle.

A heavy rain has fallen through the night and tapered off to a drizzle. The inmates are wet. The hostages are wet. They share the Monday mud. Soon they will share the shots that seem to fall as indiscriminately as the slackened rain.

With Officer Quinn dead, other correction officers in the hospital, and others held hostage, a decree has gone out from the absent Governor Rockefeller forbidding all correction officers to participate in the assault, except for two who are to go in with the State Police to identify hostages. In spite of this order, guards check weapons out of the Attica arsenal or bring their own guns from home.

The Observers—a group of public figures whom the inmates summoned to the prison and who reluctantly served as negotiators between the authorities and the inmates—expect a bloodbath. On Sunday they told this to Governor Rockefeller on the telephone. The Governor, whom the Observers and inmates were urging to come to Attica, elects to stay at his estate in Pocantico Hills, far to the south. William Kirwan, Superintendent of the State Police, takes the unusual step of vacationing this Monday, staying at a motel on Lake George. It rains there, too.

"Remember the law," the troopers are cautioned before the assault. Anyone who chooses to carry a gun takes responsibility for the rules that govern its use. It takes fewer motions to shoot a person dead than to tie your shoe. The troopers have been trained in the law, which applies at Attica, that says an officer may fire his gun *only* if he reasonably believes the person he shoots is posing an imminent threat to his own life or to someone else's life.[8] No officer can lawfully be ordered to do otherwise.

The State Police know the law. State officials consider them sufficiently disciplined and detached to obey it. Major John Monahan briefs the officers who will lead the assault, telling them that he does not want them "shooting fish in a barrel." He does not want the retaking of Attica to be a "turkey shoot."[9] If the prison must be retaken now and by force, who else would do it?

Somewhere the inmates have two tear gas guns that they captured on the first day of the riot. The gas shells measure an inch and a half in diameter and can kill a person at close range. The gun must be broken open after each shot, the spent shell pulled out, and a new one put in before the gun can be fired again. It is a 37-millimeter cannon, potentially lethal, of extremely low efficiency. Other than these two gas guns, the inmates have no firearms of any kind. And the authorities know it.

A helicopter flies over. A rumor, false, ripples through D Yard that the Governor is aboard. "Stand up, stand up, so Rockefeller can see you," the inmates order the hostages. Inmates hold weapons to the hostages. One inmate wipes his knife across his hostage's blindfold, cleaning the blade to prevent infection, he says, when the knife cuts the hostage's throat.

Inmates lead the eight hostages they have taken from the Hostage Circle up a steep iron ladder inside Times Square and out of the brick blockhouse on top. (A ninth hostage is led from the Circle and made to stand on a box in D Yard.) The inmates range the hostages across Times Square and onto the A and B Catwalks. They press knives to the hostages' throats. One holds a spear to a hostage's stomach, as well. An inmate gives another hostage a Tums and combs his hair. The inmate says he wants the hostage to "die pretty."

"Hostages are on the catwalks with knives at their throats," a trooper with the video camera on A Roof says into his microphone, his emotion charging his voice.

"I don't want to die."

"Louder." The inmate executioner pulls back the head of the hostage nearest A Block on the catwalk.

"I don't want to die!"

Officials and police watch from the cellblocks. Their own are suffering and may die at the hands of convicted criminals. The police listen, their guns ready.

Hostages and inmates on the catwalks both wear prison clothes, but only the hostages are bound and blindfolded. Many inmates hold weapons in their hands and wear football helmets, turbans, and other gaily colored garb. All hostages are white, and the majority of inmates are not. It is easier to tell a hostage from an inmate before the shooting and tear gas start, but of course there is no justification for shooting either one unless he reasonably appears about to kill or grievously injure someone. But who at this point is reasonable?

"Negative, negative." At 9:30 A.M. the inmates answer Commissioner Oswald's ultimatum, his prayer that their answer will be affirmative.

Inside A Block Major Monahan surveys the interior prison through a barred window. As the commanding officer of Troop A of the New York Division of State Police, whose territory contains the prison, he has tactical command of the retaking. Although he is outranked at the prison by several officers who have come over from Division Headquarters in Albany, his primacy in the retaking, and the merely advisory role of his superiors, will emerge afterward with increasing clarity. Two years earlier Monahan had commanded the State Police at the Woodstock music festival. In two years New York added "Woodstock" and "Attica" to our vocabulary.

Voices erupt from the walkie-talkies. The assault will go forward, undeterred by the knives at the hostages' throats. The inmates' deadly gambit fails. One calculated risk begets another. The men with the .270 rifles are ordered to hold their fire until an inmate holding a weapon to a hostage makes an overt act. (I never understood what more of an overt act was required.)

Blades cut the air atop two National Guard helicopters that rest on the well-kept lawn near the neat flower beds in front of the Administration Building. They carry CS gas, also known as tear gas, which is actually a fine powder that burns the eyes, stings the skin, tightens the chest, and causes dizziness, coughing, difficulty in breathing, a runny nose, and copious tears.

Captain Henry Williams, who is Major Monahan's well-spoken chief of detectives, has taken over the radio in the State Police Command Post. Commissioner Oswald is with Williams now. Down the hall, the group of outside Observers are confined, on Oswald's order, to a room in the front of the Administration Building with a guard at the door. From there they cannot observe. The temper of the troopers who are about to retake the prison is such that some of the Observers fear for their own lives.[10]

At 9:42 A.M., the voice of Captain Williams erupts from the walkie-talkies. "All forces in position." At 9:43 he orders the power cut off, against the possibility that the inmates have electrified the barricades. At 9:44 high-powered water hoses are ordered to be connected. All available county ambulances are ordered to the truck gate at the rear of the prison. At 9:45 the troopers with the .270 rifles on the wet roof hear Captain Williams's voice: "Zero in on targets. Do not take action until the drop."

The trooper with the video camera on A Roof points his lens down at the inmates and hostages along A Walk. "The time is nine forty-five," he says into his microphone.

A helicopter skims dangerously close to the orange-tiled peak to the left of the A Roof troopers and flies along the catwalk. A white cloud falls swiftly from its belly, beaten downwards by the rotor blades. Shots crack. Men fall, as if beaten by the wind.

Inmates on the catwalks slash the throats of two hostages before the shooting sends them all down. One cut will take fifty-two stitches to close. The other will take thirty. Two other hostages on the catwalks suffer minor cuts, which could have quickly healed if law officers' bullets had not found their vitals.

Shots too clustered to count echo from the walls.[11] A figure stands on A Walk a few feet from the Times Square blockhouse. Everyone else on A Walk is down. The video camera swings crazily. We see D Walk, where little is happening, and the litter of men and tents in a blurred D Yard beyond. We glimpse the briefest flash of troopers coming at the barricade on C Walk. Back to the lone figure standing near Times Square. A white puff envelops him. When it clears, he is down and dying. The assault is only seconds old.

The assault takes the form of a cross. Troopers converge up A and C Catwalks upon Times Square, meet and mingle, then diverge down D and B Catwalks. Gunfire from the cellblocks behind them paves their path with blood on the wet concrete. Their own guns boom. The wounded and the dying cry and moan at their feet, amid the echoing shots. An inmate with a gut full of metal screams for someone to kill him. No one obliges but peace comes soon.

The video camera swings to one of the helicopters careening against the sky. Very interesting, but, again, that's not where the action is. Troopers move about Times Square. The shots grow more sporadic. Troopers spread along D Walk, their backs to the camera, their guns covering D Yard.

The troopers with the ladders follow the A Walk Detail around Times Square, descend into D Yard, and move through the rubbish and prostrate inmates to the Hostage Circle. Handfuls of troopers feed out the doors from mid-A Tunnel and mid-C Tunnel to secure the other three courtyards. Soon troopers roam through D Yard firing their shotguns into holes the inmates have dug.

The two helicopters that dropped the tear gas fly off. A smaller helicopter replaces them above the courtyards. A voice booms down like God. "Put your hands on top of your head. . . . Surrender peacefully. You will not be harmed. . . ."

Chapter Five

"You Will Not Be Harmed"

"Put your hands on top of your head. . . . Surrender peacefully. You will not be harmed," the voice repeats as the helicopter wheels above the giant windowpane of Attica.

Troopers, some with bright-orange raincoats covering their grays, line the catwalks above D Yard and point their shotguns and big pistols down at the inmates. Troopers and a few white-coated medics move among the inmates in D Yard. The inmates, obeying the troopers, converge from all over D Yard, trickle through the door in the middle of D Tunnel, and out again into A Yard on the other side of the tunnel, sand through an hourglass. Hostages climb to B Catwalk up the ladders that the troopers of the Rescue Detail climbed down a few minutes before. Troopers on the catwalks help the hostages over the rail. Young men of the National Guard, who took no part in the shooting, carry out more stretchers. The voice from the helicopter booms on.

Moving toward D Tunnel door, more inmates step across the trench, around the bodies of dead and bleeding men that lie on the mud and wet concrete between the trench and tunnel, and go up concrete steps. Troopers motion them along with guns. They keep their hands on top of their heads, surrendering peacefully. A jam develops at the door, the neck of the hourglass, so inmates sit in the mud waiting their turn to pass through while troopers cover them from the catwalks.

Inmates move rapidly down the steps into A Yard, sometimes shoved and sometimes struck by nightsticks. Troopers give them a quick pat frisk on the way. The inmates go prone on the concrete apron and onto the wet grass of A Yard, piling on top of one another before they can spread out from the door. They crawl slowly on their knees and elbows, hands still clasped on their heads. Troopers command them to strip naked and lie back down. That solves the problem of hidden weapons. Correction officers and troopers kick the heads and bodies of some of the inmates on the ground.

"The method employed to get [the inmates] to lie down was to hit them with a club across the knees," says Major John Cudmore, a National Guard doctor who was there. "If they weren't struck, it was only through their ability to avoid it. . . . Not-too-disguised attempts were made to hit them in the genitalia."[1]

An inmate speaks: "A trooper said, 'Start crawling, you white nigger lover—put your nose to the ground. If it comes up, your head comes off.' So I start crawling. I went a little ways, then they told us, 'Stop!' All this time you could hear something hitting a body. All the time you hear men groaning low and so much noise. Everything was all confused."

A correction officer: "We weren't taking any guff."

Another inmate: "I was lying here and this trooper comes up. He pushes my head down with his foot. 'Get up and get undressed,' he said. So I got undressed, and he told me to take off my watch. I took it off, and he stomped it on the ground. Smashed it."

The inmate is lucky. Others have their watches smashed on their wrists. Off with the glasses and wedding rings. Out with the false teeth. Law officers smash and trample these, too.

"Surrender peacefully," the voice booms and the walls reply. "You will not be harmed . . . harmed . . . harmed. . . ."

A guardsman carrying a stretcher with an inmate who had been shot through the groin says several troopers came over and hit the inmate with their nightsticks. The inmate screamed. A trooper replied, "Fuck you, nigger. You should have gotten it in the head."

A black prisoner—in fact, Frank "Big Black" Smith—is ordered to lie naked on a recreation table. A football is placed on his chest beneath his chin. Officers tell him he is dead if the football falls off. Hours later State legislators touring the catwalks with Deputy Corrections Commissioner Walter Dunbar see the inmate still balancing the football. Dunbar tells the legislators that this inmate is responsible for the rumored castration of a hostage. Thus, quickly they identified the perpetrator of a crime that did not happen.

Officers direct three or four other inmates, who along with the football balancer are picked out as leaders of the riot, to lie on their backs with their knees drawn up, and to balance shotgun shells on their knees or chest. "I thought they were dead at first, they were so still," a legislator says later. Officers on the catwalks spit down on them. Some flip down lighted cigarettes. The inmates must remain motionless. Since they are naked, their clothing is not damaged when the cigarettes burn out on their flesh.

"A trooper was helping the sheriffs strip the inmates," one trooper says, "and he was cuffing a few—smacking them with his hands and kicking them a little bit. So I threw him the hell out of there. . . . [Two] very emotional [correction officers were] doing a job—I mean they had nightsticks and they were smacking inmates on the head, hitting them anywhere, sheriffs' deputies were working inmates over, too."

"You don't understand what happened," a guard says to a trooper who tells him to knock it off. "Some of these men were disemboweled, and they were abused sexually." These rumors also prove false, too late to head off the brutality they inspire.

Eventually the naked inmates march in a great brown-and-white serpentine around A Yard. They enter A Tunnel and are forced to run down it, bare feet on the broken glass of Thursday. Correction officers and troopers stand along the walls, beating the walls and floor with their nightsticks for effect, beating the inmates as they run this famous gauntlet.

An inmate: "All I saw was correction officers and troopers down both sides of the hallway, and they had clubs in their hands. . . . I saw an inmate on the floor at the end of the tunnel, just before he got into A Block. They were beating him. Then the inmate furthest down the tunnel was allowed to get up and go into A Block; and the inmate midway in the tunnel started to run. As he ran down, they beat him—wacked him with clubs."

Governor Rockefeller ordered the correction officers not to take part in freeing the hostages because, he said later, "it would just be humanly impossible for them not to become involved in reprisals." The correction officers, however, remain responsible for rehousing the inmates in A Block shortly after the assault. Rumors of hostages, their own, killed and castrated by inmates incite them. In the main, their supervisors decline to supervise them—except to send some home. Over twenty guards are excused from duty that Monday. Among the reasons: "broke down" (five); "emotionally unstable," "aggressive," "incapable," "irrational," "rambling," or "incoherent" (eight); "saw bodies" (two).

A National Guardsman: "If a prisoner would take his hands off his head at any time he was running, the officers would circle him and swing from the floor. One black guy, about twenty years old, fell down because he was tripped, and they hit him for what seemed like a couple of minutes. One guard would hit him, step back and let another get a clean shot. By accident one trooper or guard hit another with his stick. The guard who got hit yelled, 'This is for him hitting me, you black motherfucker,' and he hit the prisoner. At this time they all stepped back and let the guard who got hit accidentally beat the prisoner all by himself. Then he ran the prisoner all the way through the corridor to [the] cellblock and he hit him all the way."

Deputy Commissioner Walter Dunbar leads State Senator John Dunne through the A Block flats at the mouth of the tunnel. Dunne sees naked males running toward him, officers clubbing them as they pass. Dunne turns to Dunbar and says, "Walter, I see something I shouldn't be seeing, and it had better stop right away." Dunbar gives an order. The beating stops. Later, Dunbar denies any recollection of having seen the A Tunnel gauntlet. Dunbar's boss, Commissioner Russell Oswald, remembers better. He recalls the gauntlet as being "more in the manner of an old fraternity hazing than a beating."[2]

At the end of A Tunnel more officers channel the running inmates up the stairs and into the galleries of A Block, where the actual "rehousing" in the cells occurs. The beatings follow them up the stairs and into their new homes.

An inmate: "All I could see was big troopers and correction officers at the top of the stairway, and they were calling [to the inmate ahead of me], 'Come on, nigger, your day ain't over with yet.' They called him 'cocksucker' and 'white nigger' and all this shit. Anyway, he wouldn't come. He was scared. He had tears coming down his face, and he said, 'No, I'm not going to come. You're going to kill me.' One of the troopers came over there, grabbed hold of his hair, and yanked him up by one hand—lifted him right off his feet—and threw him down on the floor and started kicking him in the stomach. Finally, they half dragged and half threw him in the second cell. The minute he got up I ran right for the [cell], because I knew if I stayed there, I was going to get hit. [A trooper stuck his shotgun through the bars and said,] 'We're going to come back and kill you.'"

The cells, built for one, now hold two or three. The inmates' belongings—clothing, books, letters from home, toilet articles, pictures, laboriously written legal papers—are emptied out onto the floor of the galleries, to be taken the next day to the prison dump and burned.[3]

A correction officer sees a trooper pick up a guitar from the pile of inmate belongings and break it over the head of an inmate who is running by. "It knocked the inmate to his knees," the guard recalls. "The troopers made a joke out of it. . . . Most of [the other officers] laughed."

National Guardsmen carry a large black man on a stretcher into the ground floor of A Block. A small, nonuniformed man, whom an inmate later identifies as a guard, comes over and asks what is wrong with the man. A guardsman: "I told him the inmate had gunshot wounds in the legs. My telling him seemingly went unnoticed. He told us to put the inmate down. [The man then] picked the head end of the stretcher up and dumped [the inmate] onto his feet. The [inmate] fell over onto his shoulder and really bounced off the floor. There was debris and slime water all over the floor. Then this nonuniformed man pulled out a Phillips screwdriver and [said to the inmate], who was lying on the floor on his back, 'If you don't get moving—if you don't get up on your feet, you are going to get this right up your ass.' Then he did stick this man right in the anal area five or six times. And the prisoner, he didn't say a word, but just sort of [got up and] pushed with his legs toward the cell block this man wanted him to go into. I know we should have stopped this man, that it was a criminal act, but it happened so quickly. We were just awed by the fact that the prison guards were standing around and seemingly not even noticing it. By the time the man was gone we couldn't do anything."

The guards take the suspected inmate leaders to HBZ, which is where solitary is, through another gauntlet outside. "You want amnesty? Well, come and get it," a guardsman hears correction officers say as they yank inmates into the doorway to HBZ and club them. Inmates say they suffer more beatings running upstairs on the way to the cells. Doctors examining these inmates eight days later find two fractured ribs, a broken arm, a broken elbow, and abrasions and contusions of body and face.

Guardsmen who do not know where they are supposed to go wander through HBZ. One opens a door to a room on the ground floor. "I didn't do it, boss." Five or six guards are beating a big black inmate with their sticks. The inmate, who is lying naked on the floor, is the one accused of castrating a hostage. "I didn't do it, boss," the inmate says over and over. One of the correction officers tells the guardsman to stay out. He retreats. The correction officers come out about half a minute later. The guardsmen find the inmate lying on a stretcher. He seems delirious and does not comprehend where they are taking him as they carry the stretcher to the hospital. He continues to moan, "I didn't do it, boss." As mentioned before, no hostages were castrated.

A correction officer explains later how this inmate received abrasions of both elbows, both buttocks, his left upper back, and lacerations of his left forehead. "I took his name and number in the same fashion I had taken everybody else's at [HBZ]. He was then directed toward the staircase. He was pushed to some extent because he wasn't responding normally. When he got into the back room of the reception building, he simply went the wrong way and fell. I think there's either three or four steps that lead into the old dormitory on the first floor, and he hit his head either on the door handle or something at the bottom of the stairs."

A National Guard stretcher-bearer who is with the wounded inmates on the grass outside HBZ: "We were just sort of getting a breather, and we heard a sort of chanting or something. I looked over and saw that one of the prisoners was sitting up on his stretcher and was singing. Somebody yelled to him to be quiet and to lie down. He was just sort of singing to the sky, and he started yelling, 'You're going to kill me, brother.' Then about three or four uniformed prison guards appeared. He stopped singing as soon as they started walking over toward his stretcher. They dumped him up and led him onto the steps of the recreation building, took him into the vestibule, and they just beat the hell out of him with nightsticks. He was on the floor in a fetal position. 'Enough! Enough!' They just kept beating on him."

Another guardsman hears correction officers telling injured inmates, "You fucking nigger, see what black power has gotten you," and things to that effect.

Some of the injured are taken to E Block, a small cellblock behind the main quadrangle on the same side as the prison hospital. Inmates locked in E Block hold mirrors out of their windows, a common inmate practice, and watch correction officers dump injured inmates from stretchers and beat them with nightsticks, the inmates say later. The officers finally hang blankets at the end of the gallery to block the inmates' view.

Major Cudmore, the National Guard doctor, tells his wife that night what it was like at the prison: "For the first time, I could understand what happened at My Lai."

Was it likely, I asked myself, that the police and prison guards fired their weapons with lawful restraint during the retaking and lapsed into criminal savagery only afterward? A State Police officer who had watched the retaking from the roof of a cellblock told me later how he had walked out on the catwalks the same night. They were empty and silent, and he could not believe what he had seen there only a few hours before.

In the traditional police brutality case, it was the word of several officers against that of the lone prisoner, and the prisoner had some injuries for which the officers gave an innocent explanation. "He fell." Back then, who would believe the convicted felon against the officers who are too much like the rest of us to commit such cruelty and then lie about it afterward?

In many of the potential Attica "rehousing cases," National Guardsmen saw the police commit the crimes. The guardsmen served mainly as litter-bearers.

They have never been accused, except in ignorance, of hurting anyone.[4] They articulate well. Unlike the inmate witnesses, they are of us and we believe them. With the help of the guardsmen, it looked, from my beginner's standpoint, as though it would have been comparatively easy to have indicted and convicted many perpetrators of the assaults they witnessed, which were as serious as the crimes that had put many inmates inside Attica in the first place.

Inmates, then police, had scrawled across a wall in the prison: "Attica Fell 9-9-71 Fuck you Pig! Retaken on 9-13-71 31 Dead Niggers."[5] I have often thought that graffiti epitomized the spirits at war during the riot.

The police brutality after the shooting, killing no one and causing relatively few serious injuries, was widely reported. The cruel and gory details seem to have aroused more than their share of the decorous outcry over Attica, in proportion to the wanton taking of human lives by law officers earlier that morning. I suspect this happened largely because the public remained ignorant and confused about the shootings until it forgot them. The facts, which could have ended that ignorance and confusion, spent the years that followed aging in the dark vaults of the State, like rare whiskey in a country that has gone on the wagon.

Since World War II impressed me at a wide-eyed age, I have thought it unrealistic for Americans to assure themselves that the excesses of Nazi Germany could never happen here. If we share our humanity with everyone else, then we share our capacity for evil—as we share with the Good German the capacity to look the other way. My orientation to what happened during the retaking and rehousing did nothing to alter my view that Americans can be as brutal as anyone else, notwithstanding the fact that after the shooting stopped, no one apparently died from the "old fraternity hazing."

Chapter Six

Programmed to Fail?

I came to know three central characters apart from my new colleagues: Attica the prison, Attica the event, and the Attica Investigation. I have introduced the prison and the event as they were introduced to me that fall. I grew acquainted with the Investigation by doing some of its tasks and while looking at it as intently as I could.

Warnings that the Investigation had been programmed to fail—at least in prosecuting crimes by law officers—were plain to see in hindsight; but I was immersed in the moment and focused on learning my way around and doing my new job. I did notice several of the warnings as I worked along, but I was not alert for trouble and did not connect the dots. I was less aware then than I became later, that this long after the shootings, it would require a major effort to make sound cases against criminal police; but I did not doubt that Tony Simonetti, head of the Investigation, had the will and was about to be given the power to pursue those cases. That this would happen late was too bad, but better late than never.

My ignorance about criminal practice made me uneasy, and my anxiety helped me to learn. I looked up to the assistants who surrounded me, most of whom were younger than I. Nearly all had previously prosecuted in other offices. Several besides Tony had worked in District Attorney Frank Hogan's homicide bureau in Manhattan. Gerry Ryan, one door down the hall from me, had helped to convict three people for killing Malcolm X. With Tony's permission and my hundred dollars, I spent the Friday and Saturday of my first week on the job attending a symposium on criminal practice. I would be ready to try my cases against inmates whenever I had to, I told myself, but it would be fine with me if the trials were delayed until I learned more about the best ways to try them.

While we were not yet ready for the inmate trials, it was obvious that the

Investigation was rolling in hot pursuit of their crimes. It had succeeded so far in indicting dozens of them and usually in winning the defense motions that their lawyers kept making in court. As the Investigation was busy, I became busy at first, prosecuting inmates. I found this an interesting and important job, though I wondered why it was not a smaller job than investigating law officers who had killed ten times as many people as the inmates had. Yet I saw everybody treating it as just about the only job.

Tony had me read the big office Administration ("Admin") File. In it I saw inconclusive memos about the fatal shooting of two hostages on the catwalks, I read fragmentary memos about the deaths in the Hostages Circles, but there was no coherent story. An assistant named Ed Hammock had tried to prosecute a few officers, though none had finally been indicted. The reasons why, and why Hammock no longer worked there, I did not know. The Investigation, I was beginning to see, had shown little more than perfunctory interest in pursuing officers' crimes during its first two full years. But it did not enter my mind that the people in control may not have wanted it to, that they may have preferred all those homicides to look as "justifiable" as Rockefeller had claimed they were. As I understood it then, the full investigation and possible prosecution of law officers had simply not been reached yet. Exhilaration from the fascinating new job and new world I was entering buoyed my optimism.

Prosecuting only inmates during the months and years that mattered most must have been seductively pleasant. Their crimes were disturbing in ways that our ex-prosecutor assistants and ex-cop investigators found comfortable. Most cops don't like to go after brother officers. The game is cops and robbers, not cops and cops. Though I understood such loyalty, I did not like it. I was a pretty conservative person then, but fair is fair. I admired the New York City cop Frank Serpico for blowing the whistle on corruption among his brother officers. Above the entrance to the Supreme Court of the United States are the words "Equal Justice Under Law." As long as I can remember, I have believed in those words and been proud that my country does, too. All stand equal before the law. All deserve equal justice: cops and robbers, good guys and bad guys, us and them. Right?

The inmates' crimes deserved punishment if any crimes did. They had savagely beaten a number of guards. Most beatings had not even been necessary to help the riot succeed. One or more inmates had broken the skull and battered the brain of the young guard, Bill Quinn. Color autopsy photos of his brain shocked me. Kenneth Hess, one of the three inmates whom inmates had killed, had met a particularly ghastly end. In much of the prison, one set of bars that are three floors long covers each vertical row of windows. Hess squirmed out of a third floor window, wedging himself between the bars and the red brick wall between the top two floors. Though his throat was partly cut, he was able to scream for help, but the officers on the grass below could do nothing for him. Arms thrust from the window below. Hands clutched his legs. He vanished into the interior. The day after the police retook the prison, his decomposing body was found in a closet. Tales of the riot were small talk among our staff. This was one of them.

The Organized Crime Task Force (OCTF), which came into being in 1970 and of which I was now pleased to be a part, was tasked with attacking crime that occurred in more than one county. The name impressed me, though I never heard that the OCTF had accomplished very much. Until a criminal indictment becomes public, that sort of work is supposed to remain secret. One could always suppose that the OCTF was working on something important, like organized crime.

The OCTF existed under the New York State Department of Law, which was headed during the Rockefeller and Malcolm Wilson governorships by Attorney General Louis Lefkowitz. Voters knew him as "Looey"; we called him "General." Deputy Attorney General Robert E. Fischer, who was sometimes called "Judge" because he had once been one, presided over the task force mainly from its office in Binghamton in New York's "Southern Tier." Rockefeller had appointed Fischer to two other posts before the OCTF and was apparently pleased with his work. As the riot ended, it was decided that prosecuting the crimes that had occurred there would be too much for the local District Attorney, Louis James. (Later I wondered whether James was also too honest to be trusted.) The next day Rockefeller appointed Fischer and the OCTF to do the job. The Attica Investigation was thus a part of the OCTF; we were all employed ultimately by Louis Lefkowitz. Somewhere in my mind I knew that Lefkowitz was totally loyal to Rockefeller, but the thought did not surface then. It had no reason to.

The Attica Investigation faced a mammoth task—forty-three homicides and many times that number of serious assaults and other crimes to investigate, perhaps three thousand witnesses to interview, a growing mountain of documents to digest, and more thousands of items of physical evidence and photographs to fit into the giant jigsaw puzzle of who did what to whom. The Investigation should have moved quickly, before witnesses forgot the faces of the perpetrators and before inmate witnesses started returning to the streets;

but to do this mammoth task, Fischer extracted from the Rockefeller-Lefkowitz Administration just one full-time assistant, Tony Simonetti, who was already working for Fischer in the OCTF Rochester office, plus one part-time assistant, nine investigators, and a dozen detectives of the State Police (SP). A second part-time assistant soon came on board. And that, during the crucial, irretrievable beginning, was all.

Maxwell B. Spoont, an able and genial lawyer who had worked with Fischer in private practice, was his lieutenant for the OCTF proper. Tony Simonetti acted as Fischer's chief executive officer for the Attica Investigation, the tail of the OCTF that outgrew the dog. Except for the New York City ex-cops whom Tony hired for the Attica Investigation, the OCTF had no investigators of its own; it depended for its investigative work, and thus for its success, upon the detectives of the New York State Police.

While these State Police detectives may not have been investigating the shootings, beatings, and other assaults by their brother officers (at least not that I saw), they were nonetheless on the same team with our investigators who were. They were in the same offices, and sharing access to the same files. This goodbuddy proximity had to damage, if not destroy, the vigor and objectivity of these inquiries into State Police crimes; and it gave the State Police access to information that they should not have had about how these (few) investigations of their brother officers were proceeding.

At the outset Fischer made a portentous decision: he decided to investigate the riot "chronologically," that is, to devote the main effort of his woefully inadequate staff to the four homicides committed by inmates before the thirty-nine homicides by law officers. During the next two-and-a-half years, the special Wyoming County grand jury, which received only such evidence as the Investigation chose to give it, charged sixty-two inmates with 1,289 crimes, and no law officer with anything.[1]

It is obviously vital to question witnesses and show them photos while their memories are still fresh, to marshal evidence before it deteriorates or is lost, and to hunt down additional evidence while it still exists. To an extent that appalled me later, our investigators had not done this, at least not for the turkey shoot and subsequent police brutality. They questioned the inmates about the events of the Thursday, Friday, Saturday, and Sunday of the riot, and Monday up to 9:45 a.m., in enough detail to support those 1,289 criminal charges against inmates. But for the most part, they did not ask the inmates what they witnessed during the next ten or so minutes while all around them policemen were shooting 128 people. It would have taken our few investigators only a short time to have asked ask those inmates what they saw, heard, felt, and did during those crucial minutes.

Since our investigators were, most inappropriately, working with State Police detectives and sharing fellowship with them, it may have been hard for the investigators to ask inmates whether they saw a trooper shoot an inmate. But hard or not, those crucial questions had to be asked. But it was not the investigators' decision, it was their superiors' decision, that these key questions were not to be asked.

Possibly Fischer and whomever he may have consulted about halting the questioning at 9:45 had feared that inmates would lie, though not against specific officers since, wearing gas masks but not their name tags during the shooting, they could not be identified. This fear could have been remedied by cross-checking the inmates' stories, the stories of troopers and other witnesses, and the ballistics, autopsy, and photographic evidence. But if the fear was that the inmates would tell the truth and make a record that could not be ignored, that would have been harder to remedy. Best for Rockefeller and any and all criminal officers, I saw later, if such a record did not exist.

The decision not to question these thousand or so eyewitnesses about all these shootings—about the most significant slaughter in the modern history of New York—may have flowed from the decisions to have a tiny staff and to investigate the riot chronologically. From the standpoint of effective prosecution, the decision to have no questioning instead of intense questioning at this crucial point constituted a terrible blunder. But to protect the police from being prosecuted for murder and other serious felonies, all three decisions were perfect—as I saw much later.

State Police detectives and our own investigators did question troopers and prison guards (though not inmates) about what they themselves were doing during the shooting. When an officer admitted firing his weapon, as 111 of them did, they asked him what he shot at and why. Those officers' answers, including the many answers that were provably false, turned out to be among the Investigation's most valuable evidence. But the questioners curiously failed to ask officers about the shootings by other officers that many of them must have seen. Here, too, apparently on the instructions (no competent investigator would do so on his own), the investigators failed to collect crucial evidence it was their duty to collect.

Tony and I would talk often about the failures of the SP detectives to gather evidence, but seldom about the similar failures of our own investigators. The failure to question inmates about whatever shootings they may have witnessed frustrated me, but once again I did not grasp what the failure implied. I have asked myself since why I did not catch on sooner. And what would I have done if I had. Through dumb luck, my remaining a team player for as long as I did enabled me to expose as much of the truth as I eventually did, and as much of my seniors' efforts to bury the truth. Had I caught on sooner, I'd have left the Investigation sooner and exposed fewer of the decisions and deeds that furthered the cover-up.

In the fall of 1971 Governor Rockefeller had proved reluctant to provide another Attica inquiry with an adequate staff, but this time he didn't get away with it. Right after the riot, the public demanded to be told what really happened, by someone more credible than an Administration that had maintained as long as it could that inmates had killed the dead hostages. Rockefeller responded by launching the McKay Commission to report to the public in one year. To assure its independence, Rockefeller asked a panel of the State's chief appellate judges to select its nine members. Conflict quickly rose between the Administration and the Commission; by November the members were threatening to quit en masse unless Rockefeller granted them the people, tools, and powers they felt they needed "to make a full and impartial investigation."[2] To avoid this embarrassment, Rockefeller yielded. One must ask, though, why he resisted in the first place—and why he failed to give the prosecution similarly adequate tools to do its job.

The Attica Investigation had a far bigger job than McKay. It had to determine what had happened—which was McKay's only job—and *also* to marshal the specific evidence sufficient to identify and convict individual perpetrators of the inmates' and officers' crimes arising out of all those shootings, kidnappings (i.e., hostage takings), and assaults. But, because the McKay people insisted on having the tools to do their job, the Rockefeller Administration permitted McKay to hire a staff of thirty-six full-time workers, half of them lawyers, and sixty part-time workers. It seems that, unlike McKay, Fischer never fought for the staff he needed, though the Rockefeller people should have given it to him without a fight. In fact, they should have insisted that he have it.

The Meyer Commission, which would later investigate the Investigation, would conclude that responsibility for the Investigation's tiny staff "rests largely with Fischer, and not with [Rockefeller's] Executive Chamber or Simonetti." (The Executive Chamber were the bright, savvy men who worked directly for

Rockefeller.) Long afterward when I became aware of this history, I would agree with Meyer's exculpation of Simonetti but certainly not of Rockefeller and Lefkowitz. Those two pros administered the law in the State. They could have had as adequate a staff as McKay if they had wanted one. That they didn't have one meant that they didn't want one.

By the summer of 1973, it finally looked as though the first inmate trials would begin that fall. Up till then the Rockefeller-Lefkowitz Administration had permitted the Investigation's staff to grow only slowly and still very inadequately, despite repeated pleas from Simonetti that he needed more people. These pleas, which I saw in the Admin File, reassured me that Tony wanted a fair investigation. As the prospect of trying inmates loomed, however, Lefkowitz suddenly let the Investigation double the number of assistants and add ten more investigators. That is how Simonetti was able to hire me and several other lawyers two years after the events in question.

I had first seen the A Roof videotape of the retaking on a small hookup in the back office of the Investigation. Someone had put up a sign there that said, "Support your Attica Brothers." That is what the inmate defendants called themselves. Most of them pooled their efforts under the standard of the Attica Brothers Legal Defense (ABLD), represented by lawyers from around the country and across the political spectrum. Former U.S. Attorney General Ramsey Clark represented one of the two inmates charged with murdering Billy Quinn. William Kunstler represented the other.

I knew Kunstler only by reputation as the outspoken radical lawyer who had represented Bobby Seale at the Chicago Eight trial and served controversially as an Observer during the Attica riot. Some assistants at the Investigation combed the tapes of what Kunstler had said in D Yard to see if they could indict him for "inciting a riot." They seemed disappointed that he always saved himself by qualifying his "inflammatory" remarks. Tom Wicker, on the other hand, credits Kunstler's cool talk with saving some Observers' lives when some inmates' emotions in D Yard threatened to get out of hand. I used to think it a tribute to our open society that it would tolerate a Kunstler. I came to consider him a necessity.

Defending the Attica Brothers had automatically become a cause. From the perspective of the cause lawyers, the riot had been a rebellion for human rights and dignity. "If we cannot live as people, then we will at least try to die like men." The prosecution, they said, merely continued the oppression. It was a political prosecution; the coming trials would be political trials. Indicting scores of inmates but zero police, they said, highlighted the unfairness and proved their point. Law students, college students, and other volunteers helped the lawyers. A motley group of them sometimes filled the spectators' benches in the Buffalo courtroom—in jeans, the men bearded, the women braless, occasionally an interracial couple of whom our investigators tended to disapprove, all looking like fugitives from a rock concert. I think politics permeate life, and I had enjoyed many rock concerts, but this was not what I expected in court. Our investigators joked pointedly that the ABLD supporters were dirty and smelly. In court and in meeting them up close, I never noticed that.

Donald Jelinek, a lawyer out of Berkeley, California, acted as coordinator for the ABLD and their main spokesman in court. He stood before the judge with a loosened tie and ragged hole in the elbow of his jacket and spoke against oppression. Yet beneath the rhetoric he was very effective. He reminded me of some lawyers I had opposed in commercial lawsuits in New York City, the practical salami slicer working away beneath the soapbox, shaving off morsel after morsel for his clients. The Brothers could do worse than have Jelinek speak for them. Later I learned that he had indeed once worked on commercial cases in the City.

In my experience in civil cases, the opposing lawyers generally try to cooperate with one another except when it matters. Incidental cooperation usually saves time and helps their clients and their blood pressure. But, with the notable exception of Tony, most of the assistants and investigators showed animosity if not hatred for the ABLD, the price perhaps of wearing a white hat. We have a job to do, I thought, why hate?

The notion of the riot as a rebellion may have unified the inmates and, in the minds of some of them, justified their bloodletting. What are four lives in a rebellion—right? Paradoxically, this may also have offered the State Police a more appealing defense for their shootings than the Penal Law permits. To put down a rebellion, to fight a war, one need not satisfy himself that each shot he fires is necessary to save someone's life. War is hell. Shooting is tactics. It's them or us. Such an argument legally has no place in a courtroom. Whether it entered the jury room would be another question—if a case against a trooper ever reached a jury. As it stood, though, the State Police insisted that all their shootings were legally justified, so that the war-is-hell defense had not come up.

A problem inherent in causes is that the cause lawyer may sacrifice the client for the cause. A man who is nearly sure to be convicted of murder, for example, may be wise to plead guilty to manslaughter, but his lawyer may bring

on a trial that convicts him of the murder in order to create a platform to publicize the cause. Tony, Max, and I wondered whether the ABLD would do this.
Tony's concern that the defense lawyers not sacrifice any inmates for the cause
impressed me again with his fairness.

One of my first jobs in the fall of 1973 was to read the testimony that supported my Indictment No. 10, which charged inmates with beating and kidnapping three guards, to be sure that the grand jury had heard enough evidence
to indict each of those inmates. Sure enough, the evidence seemed to be there.
The judge agreed with me and with the Investigation's work in the grand jury,
for he denied each defendant's motion to dismiss.[3]

All the same, the scantiness of evidence against some defendants bothered
me. I wondered whether our people had uncovered all the possible witnesses,
so Bill Blackford and I searched the files for new ones. If the case against a
defendant was sound, I wanted it stronger. If there wasn't enough evidence to
make it sound, I wanted to throw it out. Tony, too, wanted to dismiss any case
that was weak; he said that to me and at staff meetings. My record of winning
convictions did not matter much—I was here simply to learn—but Tony had
to be concerned about his record. Yet I saw him risking it in order to be fair.

Blackford and I went to the prison to interview a few witnesses on
Indictment No. 10. One inmate, whom we had never met before, burst into
the stark room where we sat behind an empty table. Trembling, he shouted at
us to stop bothering him and burst out again before either of us could say hello.
We looked at each other and shrugged. More often than not, though, I had
no trouble in talking with inmates I wanted to talk with. So far as I heard, the
others at the Investigation had the same success. The FBI claimed later that its
own investigation of the riot had been stymied by inmates' refusal to talk to its
investigators. A number of people told me the FBI didn't try very hard. I found
that interesting though not ominous.

Another inmate talked freely, or almost freely. He was a bluff, hearty man
with a reputation for being a "faggot"—the investigators always used that epithet, no matter what other attributes they left out. This man usually tried to
trade an interview for some favor, a transfer to another prison or, better, a work
camp or a good word with the parole board or some help in his endless quest
to persuade the courts to let him out. The game was to keep him cooperating
without promising him anything. Some inmates always asked for these things.
More did not. I saw letters in the Admin File in which an assistant told the parole
people of an inmate's cooperation, for whatever consideration they wanted to

give it. Nothing wrong with that, I supposed. Was a prosecutor's "good word," which might get an inmate released years early, enough to make him bear false witness or shade the truth? Even having to ask myself that question showed my inexperience, yet experienced prosecutors were writing these letters.

One evening Blackford and I took a room in a Holiday Inn not far from the prison to talk to a witness I'll call Daltry,[4] who had gotten four years at Attica for stealing some tools. Another assistant and investigator were there to talk to Daltry about another case. We expected them all to arrive at about the same time. A knock sounded. Blackford's snub-nosed .38 lay loaded on the dresser, Blackford having retired to the can. Was it Daltry or one of us? I slipped the revolver, heavy for its size, into a pocket of my jacket and opened the door. Our investigator stood there.

Those few moments were the only time I carried a loaded gun at the Investigation. It took me a while to get used to working with men who had .38s sticking out of their belts. Not that I was a stranger to firearms; I had owned a .22 as a boy and enjoyed being on a company rifle team in the army. Sometimes you would open a desk drawer to look for a paper and find someone's "biscuit" instead. I pictured the war that would break out if any defendants tried to raid our files. The longer I studied the riot, particularly the full color blowups of the naked dead, the more I grew to dislike violence. My children had an easier time watching television than I did.

The evening at the Holiday Inn, the other investigator questioned Daltry in a way that upset the other assistant, who told me later that investigators often messed up his interviews. The investigator was telling Daltry what Daltry saw, heard, and did at the riot. The object, I knew, should be not to force the witness to memorize your script, but to preserve and refresh his own recollection; but discouragingly often, investigators (never Blackford) took some version of an event based on someone else's recollection, their own shrewd or hasty guesswork, or whatever, and loudly talked a mumbling, pliant, and sometimes frightened witness into making it his own. I expect they sometimes did this simply out of impatience at the witness's sometimes semiarticulate meanderings, sure they were telling him what really happened. They seemed to want a simple, probable, and therefore marketable story—if it fit the truth, so much the better, but don't confuse us with the facts. Sometimes, I expect, the inmate figured his main chance lay in telling the story the cop wanted him to. I wondered how often these investigators had done this during their collective years in the New York City Police Department, this tiny handful of alumni; how many of their colleagues did it still; and how many likely but innocent suspects spend years in our Atticas as a result. Inducing a witness to testify to something that is not true is called suborning perjury and is a felony. When it was part of law enforcement, I did not see anyone prosecuted for it.

After that evening at the Holiday Inn, I stopped this activity a few times when I encountered it, though with an almost guilty sense that I was showing my inexperience and not playing the game. Once or twice I was told to let an investigator talk to a witness alone "because they can do things you can't." My education in criminal practice was not going quite as I had expected. As a boy I used to wonder why the Ten Commandments bothered to forbid people to bear false witness; now I wondered no more.

And so the Investigation worked, earnestly and sometimes ineptly or worse, two years and more after the bodies went under the sod. In its rushed yet leisurely routine, it prosecuted the people who had done one-tenth of the killing, but who were often sullen and inarticulate and lacked any power except to destroy. It mostly ignored the evidence against the people who had done most of the killing, but who were friendly, well-spoken, politically powerful, and *of us*. Unless this changed radically, the main killers were going to remain at large. But the Investigation had just doubled its manpower. Tony Simonetti was soon to be its new head. Where Fischer had failed, he would do it right. He, I was convinced, was an honorable man.

Honorable, though not without flaws. Finding more witnesses for Indictment No. 10 was one of the jobs that Blackford and I never finished before Tony assigned us to do other work. Tony constantly reassigned people before they finished the jobs he had given them. I saw this then as sometimes necessary but often inefficient, a personal quirk. Tony's impatience left him a better lawyer than administrator. That is a lawyer's occupational hazard, and I had seen it hurt several law firms. The new assignment that was to preempt me from Indictment No. 10 was to prosecute police.

Working on the inmate cases gained me Tony's confidence and moved me into this position. I did not plan it that way. I simply did the jobs Tony gave me as well as I could and was at that point, I believe, the only assistant who had much interest in prosecuting such crimes by law officers as nestled like nuggets in the mass of inconclusively investigated information about the shootings. This job obviously needed doing and just as obviously wasn't being done. I did not stop to wonder why I was now the only assistant who had this interest, or why Bob Fischer and Tony had not required this job to be done back in 1971.

The welter of jobs by which I was picking up the new practice, I realized later, were also the jobs by which the Investigation defined itself. What it chose to do highlighted, silently but starkly for anyone who cared to look (not me yet), what it chose not to do. People tend to see the patterns they want to see and to miss those that might unsettle them. This can make it hard to prove a case that goes against the bias of the jurors. A cover-up can be such a case. I did not see any ominous patterns during my early months at the Investigation. My suspicions were not engaged. Maybe I did not want them to be.

I found myself immersed and perhaps submerged in on-the-job training, learning by doing, over my head but keeping up, more or less. In the main, getting on top of Indictment No. 10, the facts that comprised the big picture of Attica, and my other assignments filled my days. Though I had generally enjoyed my work at the law, I was happier with it now than I had ever been. I continued to see the same commuter crowd on the trains from and to Connecticut, but now I was working on an important and fascinating prosecution, while they were mostly making money in the same old ways. I did not wonder if many of them considered the Attica prosecution important, or were any more aware of it than I had been before I answered Tony's ad in the *Law Journal*, or cared whether justice prevailed for a prison riot that was long out of the headlines.

One morning that fall, Bill Blackford and I drove out to the Troop A barracks, a low-keyed, efficient-looking office on a rural road near Batavia. We wanted to visit their garage, which held the inmates' weapons and some other evidence from the riot, and to see the heavy iron crank handle. Normally such handles were used to crank all the door locks open or shut in a gallery of cells. One of the defendants in Indictment No. 10 was said to have used this one to smash the inch-thick bulletproof glass window in the door of the C Block office. Then he dropped it on a guard inside. I once tried breaking a piece of this glass with a similar handle. It would be embarrassing if the defense proved to the jury that it could not be done after my witness testified that he saw it happen. I knelt on the floor of a shop at the back of the prison, wearing safety goggles and surrounded by a little group of onlookers. My first blow smashed the glass easily.

This morning a friendly State Police investigator unlocked the garage and the wire cage inside that held the weapons. Our eyes watered as we stirred up some powdered tear gas from two years before. We found three crank handles, all about the same weight, all once painted orange. There was no way to tell which, if any, was the one the inmate had dropped on the guard, though under the rules of evidence that did not really matter. An inmate witness had described the crank handle as weighing about twenty-five pounds. I asked the State Police investigator if I could weigh it.

"What do you want to do that for?" he shot back, suddenly tense and defensive.

It startled me to see him turn from friendly to uptight over this routine question. In that instant, he made me feel that the State Police feared us and that guilt underlay their fear. I did not suppose that this investigator was afraid we would invent nonexistent crimes. He wasn't even a shooter. Why did he jump so? The crank handle weighed eight pounds.

Chapter Seven

"Much Unnecessary Shooting"

During most days at the Investigation, its flaws of organization and technique did not touch me. I enjoyed working with the people. The investigators joked a lot and were generally jovial. I knew I had a lot to learn from everyone. I was happy to be aboard, eager to pick up the fine points of criminal practice from the seasoned prosecutors, pleased that my work seemed to please Tony, anxious to climb on top of my cases, and fascinated to spelunk further into the labyrinthine facts of Attica. This was a far cry from my days of wearing a homburg in the subway, a vest in the library, and looking up the law for The Chase Manhattan Bank. The vitality of this job mattered here and now, was somebody else's but also mine.

One assistant was wont to say that the Investigation had been mishandled from the start. "It's a salvage operation," he would repeat, like a lonely Greek chorus. I did not find that sinister. When Tony and I talked business, we often had trouble sticking to a subject, the side avenues of Attica held such interest. I never had that problem on a job before. I could not remember ever looking forward so much to going to work each day.

There was the outer life, what I said and did to push Indictment No. 10 and the general effort of the office to prosecute inmates. Tony came to involve me more and more in the latter. Then there was the inner life, the reconstruction of the riot that grew in my mind. This raised far more questions about law officers since the inmates' situation seemed under control. The A Roof videotape, the McKay Report, the Admin File, Tony's orientation to the riot, and all the stories that went around the office made me wonder: What happened? How much was true that passed for fact? (Tony warned me against accepting what I was told.) What had really happened?

Tony had his own copy of the McKay Report, as did a number of other lawyers and investigators. Secretaries read it. It gave a concise and very accurate overview of the riot, in 500 pages. It was, however, too short to include the specifics of most of what we were looking for; the McKay Commission had not wanted to prejudice any prosecution with premature publicity.[1] Thus it had a large, intentional gap; for the most part it left out the worst that happened at Attica, individual criminal acts. All the same we found it a handy place to check some of our work.

Reading the McKay Report recalled some doubts that the Official Version had raised in my mind back in 1971. I had not really believed Governor Rockefeller when he praised the State Police right after the retaking for doing "a superb job" and for showing "skill . . . courage . . . and . . . restraint" in saving hostages and holding down casualties. I like to quote Otto von Bismarck's dictum, never believe anything until it is officially denied. Too many had died at Attica for the Governor's words to ring true. He hadn't been there. Being responsible for the retaking, he had every reason to say it went well, whether it did or not. Even so, it chastened me to read in the McKay Report how "in the cellblocks, on the catwalks, and in D Yard there was much unnecessary shooting."[2] That suggested much criminal shooting, if McKay rather than the Governor was right.

As the McKay Report described the assault, the shooting of the inmate executioners who held knives to the hostages on the catwalks struck me as good shooting, regrettable but necessary (if you accept the need for an assault then) and good police work. Then came the "unnecessary shooting." The shooters described the inmates as a band of fearless fanatics who, without leaders, training, or discipline and immune to the tear gas that zonked the hostages, rushed with knives and spears into the blazing shotguns, undaunted by the awful cannonading or the bullets spattering, and the bodies riven around them. This version reminded me of Heinz Guderian's laconic footnote to the German blitzkrieg into Poland in 1939: "The Polish *Pomorska* Cavalry Brigade, in ignorance of the nature of our tanks, had charged them with swords and lances and had suffered tremendous losses."[3] Had the inmates shown the fatal courage of the Polish patriots?

It looked from the McKay Report and from the accounts I saw at the Investigation as if the State Police retook Attica in two separate assaults at the same time, in the same place, and with the same people. Supporting the Polish cavalry version were the troopers who admitted doing the shooting and a few other State Police and officials. Supporting the other version were most of the troopers who held their fire, the inmates, and the strangely sparse photographic record. It would be fair to say that this version added up to a massacre.

Through most of my years as a lawyer I had consigned facts to three categories: the ones I believed, the ones I didn't, and the "suspense file" in which I neither believed nor disbelieved but simply waited to see what else would turn up. By the time I finished the McKay Report, Tony's orientation, and my first look at the evidence in the office, the facts about the criminality or justification of all the shootings remained in the suspense file. It looked bad for the troopers, but appearances often change and maybe change back again. I cared deeply that any version of the facts that I ended up believing, and trying to convince a jury to believe, would be the true version. It is bad enough that innocent people go to prison; it would be terrible to send one there.

Beyond preferring to find that people have not misbehaved, I did not care which way the facts about the shootings came out. Through the years that followed, I have questioned my feelings and conduct many times on this point, as others have seen fit to question them; and I realize that merely acknowledging the power and subtlety of self-deception does not make one proof against it. That said, I do not believe I cared one way or the other whether a person whom the evidence showed to have committed a crime was an inmate or a law officer. I could be wrong. My emotions were engaged. Who among us thinks he speaks—or listens—with an accent?

In any event, the summary accounts and incomplete evidence that I saw during my first months at the Investigation gave me a lot to ponder. For example:

The riflemen of A Block and C Block said they fired at inmates who were running to attack hostages—even where there were no hostages or anyone else in the direction in which the inmates were running. The inmate witnesses said they saw them as fleeing from the troopers. Riflemen also said they fired at inmates who were running toward the assault force or attacking crawling hostages. The photos do not support these accounts, nor do the inmates who watched from C Block, nor do the trooper witnesses who did not fire, nor, it seemed to me, did common sense.

Some troopers said they fired when inmates mounted the C Walk barricade brandishing swords and a spear. Color slides of the assault simply show the empty barricade. Could inmates bent on suicide have mounted it in the seconds between the photos? If so, where were their riddled bodies? Again the inmates and the troopers who did not shoot said they did not see this.

A Molotov cocktail is a bottle of gasoline, or other inflammable, with a rag stuffed in the neck for a wick. You light it and throw it. If it works right, it shatters and flares up. Many troopers sought to justify many shots by saying that the inmates were throwing Molotov cocktails. Some inmates did indeed have these devices, made with gasoline from the prison garage, I was told; but no one at Attica was burned by a Molotov cocktail. I saw no report by anyone that any Molotov cocktail even flared up.

Shooters on A Walk said tear gas canisters came at them over that barricade. Does a tear gas canister lobbed outdoors pose an imminent threat to the life of men in gas masks? To anyone's life? The assault forces were deluging the inmates and hostages with tear gas in order to save lives.

Yet after all the death threats the inmates had just made, after inmates were seen holding knives to the throats of hostages, after the sparks that troopers had seen flying off the inmates' grinding wheel in the night, was a trooper obligated upon pain of being charged with a felony to analyze what was being thrown at him before he shot back? The troopers had a duty to move forward quickly to try to save the hostages. They had a duty, not to mention the instinct, to save themselves and their brother officers. Would they not have violated both duties had they paused to examine the inmates' missiles or to engage in moral calculus? What would I have done if I had been a trooper with a shotgun?

Several troopers on C Walk said they fired at inmates holding weapons in their hands and running toward Times Square over on A Walk. The photos and spectators support the claim of inmates running, as does one inmate who was shot seven times while running yet survived. Through gas masks and tear gas, the shooters saw figures running seventy yards away. Could they really see weapons in their hands? That morning did they have to? How fair is it to the cop to put him in a situation where he has to act quickly, then to second-guess him at leisure and charge him with a crime if you differ?

One trooper, not atypical, said he fired at inmates who were "shouting obscenities, throwing Molotov cocktails at our group, [and] running at our group with pipes, bats, knives, and various other weapons."[4] Running into the booming shotguns on the catwalks, heedless of the massed firepower in the cellblocks? The photographs and other evidence not only fail to corroborate these justifications; they tend to show them false. I am not aware of any report that any member of the assault force (except for Lieutenant Christian, discussed below) was hurt by a knife, spear, club, or sword.

About a dozen correction officers fired from A Block, some using rifles or shotguns they had brought from home, at least one a submachine gun, one a snub-nosed pistol. The ones who fired said they never heard Governor Rockefeller's order that correction officers were not to participate in the assault. Few of the people they admitted shooting at could have posed an imminent threat to anyone's life. Major Monahan, the State Police troop commander, testified that he would not have been out on the catwalks if he had thought correction officers would be firing, because he was contemplating retirement. His remark typified the troopers' attitude toward the guards.

When the inmates in D Yard realized that real bullets were striking among them, they hit the dirt, dived into holes and into the trench, or took ineffective cover, behind benches and tents. Inmate executioners who had replaced the Black Muslim guards at the Hostage Circle repeatedly made the hostages stand up—setting them up for what became known as "the Christian Incident" or whatever it was that caused several of them to be struck by shotgun pellets. The incident is hazily recorded about four minutes into the A Roof videotape of the action. On the soundtrack we hear the shooting burst suddenly intense again after it had died down. Seeing the tape a number of times under the tutelage of Investigator Lenny Brown, I made out a clump of figures in D Yard who topple from left to right when the shooting reintensifies.

According to the Official Version: Lieutenant Joseph Christian, armed with a shotgun and two pistols, leads the Rescue Detail across D Yard to the Hostage Circle, as they come one by one down the rickety ladders from B Walk. He leaps the trench near Times Square and moves out front alone. As he nears the Hostage Circle, an inmate suddenly rises up and fells him with a blow of a club on the back of his plastic helmet. To keep the inmate who is poised over him from finishing him off and grabbing his guns, troopers back on B Catwalk fifty yards away let go with their shotguns. They shoot the lieutenant through the leg and in the arm. He is the only member of the assault force to be seriously hurt. Tragically, he lies between the shooters and the hostages, the clump of figures who topple from left to right, when the shotguns spread their lethal loads to save him. The State Police rely on the Christian Incident, which doubtless happened in at least some part, to explain their killing of hostages in the Hostage Circle.

At the start of the assault, inmates in D Yard struck one hostage over the head, breaking a hole in his skull, stabbed another, and killed no one. Officers' gunfire, besides killing eight out of thirty hostages in D Yard, killed about thirteen out of the more than twelve hundred inmates.[5] In D Yard an inmate had a twenty-five times better chance of surviving the rescuers' gunfire than a hostage did. On the catwalks the ratio of mortality went the other way.

In D Yard, too, troopers told of inmates shot while attacking, while inmates told of inmates shot while surrendering. Curiously few photos exist. One trooper testified that the police understood that "anyone who doesn't obey orders gets waxed."[6] The police gave their orders through their gas masks during a confused uproar. An inmate who disobeyed or hesitated or missed an order in the din automatically posed an imminent threat to someone's life, no doubt. Other troopers in D Yard fired into tents and holes in order, they said later, to warn inmates to come out and surrender. The logic of the troopers' warnings escaped me then and since. Tony Simonetti didn't see it, either. How do you come out into a blasting shotgun except dead? This was supposed to be the police restoring law and order, I thought, not the Marines mopping up on Iwo Jima.

On the videotape we see troopers move on the catwalks. A jaunty little officer marches down A Walk toward Times Square with big quick steps, a bobbing scissors. When I asked the cameraman why he lingered on him so long, he turned out to be the cameraman's boss. Odd, I thought, that the cameraman could find his boss on the catwalk, but his tape fails to show troopers during all their shootings down there.

We see figures begin to emerge into A Yard from the center of D Tunnel. Officers on each side of the door shove at them as they come out. The inmates struggle to lie prone at the bottom of the steps. The camera leaves and returns. The fan of wriggling bodies on the ground broadens from the tunnel door. Four troopers hurry a stretcher across the top left corner of the picture, across A Yard from mid-D Tunnel to mid-A Tunnel, which is the way to the ambulances out front. I wonder if they are carrying Lieutenant Christian. The shooting peters out. The cameraman says on the soundtrack that some of the shots must be coming from inside the cellblocks. People mill. The action grows less interesting. Gunshots have penetrated nearly 130 people. Most of the dead have died by now, their bodies ripped and emptied by the bullets' random butchery. We reach the part of the videotape I won't bother to see so often later.

Tony had cautioned me to keep an open mind. He was right. He had his own suspense file. Our job as lawyers, if not as people, requires us to see for ourselves the evidence that matters, to the extent that we can. Cases that look "open and shut" often turn completely around upon a further look. The McKay Report was hearsay. It was on its face not perfect. The nub of its argument on why Governor Rockefeller should have gone to Attica—because the State's long neglect of its prison system, which now needed major reform, "was a major contributing factor to the uprising"—looked illogical to me, though it was clear enough that the Governor should have gone.[7] Any bias may distort, and the report struck me as having a left-of-center bias. Though no one mentioned it to me in 1973, keeping an open mind also meant realizing that the McKay Report may have been unduly soft on the troopers, guards, and officials it criticized, as well as unduly harsh.

And suppose McKay had not been too harsh. Suppose there had been "much unnecessary shooting" or worse. We as prosecutors had problems, which McKay as a reporter to the public did not have, of sorting out the facts and the law, meshing the fragments, assembling the individual scenes, identifying the perpetrators, and resolving the conflicting reports as best we could, so as to prove where possible that specified individuals had committed specific crimes beyond a reasonable doubt. A column by Tom Wicker in the November 18, 1973, *New York Times* that criticized us for not having indicted any troopers bothered me. It wasn't that simple.

Why, I wondered only later, had the Rockefeller government authorized a staff for Dean McKay that was several times larger than our staff, particularly during the crucial first year of the Investigation, when McKay's job was significantly simpler than ours?

Upon the evidence available, the long and tortuous portion of the Attica saga that followed the shootings neither helped nor hurt the dead.

Chapter Eight

What Evidence?

One question that buzzed in the back of my mind as I worked on the inmate cases was: when the investigation reaches the troopers, will we have anything to work with? Bureau of Criminal Investigation (BCI) detectives had collected the evidence of what troopers did during the retaking. How they collected it—or didn't collect it—was not specifically part of our orientation. That came together for me from the McKay Report, the Admin File, and stuff I heard in the office. Here, roughly, is how it looked:

* * *

Spanish tile slopes above the men in gray who lie on the wet roof behind the low brick parapet in the gray morning. Rifles rest with the troopers, on the roof of A Block and the nearly identical roof of C Block, ready to pour their crossfire into men on the catwalks below. More troopers wait inside the windows of A Block and C Block with rifles ready.

Each rifle bears a serial number, its unique identification. Standard police procedure requires each trooper's name to be recorded along with the serial number of his rifle when he checks it out. Unless a bullet is badly mangled, it can be traced from the body to the rifle to the shooter. If there is much shooting, how else do you keep track of who shoots whom?

With a few exceptions, no one keeps track of what trooper has what rifle at Attica. Not before the shooting. Not after the shooting. After the bodies litter the prison, the detail commanders release their little squads of riflemen. The troopers turn in their rifles to the quartermaster trucks outside. The troopers at the trucks receive them. The rifles rest in the trucks, indistinguishable except for their unique serial numbers, the unique markings on the bullets that leave their muzzles, and the other unique markings their firing pins make on the cartridges as they fire. The troopers who fired them go on about their lives.

State Police rifles at Attica kill ten inmates and four hostages. They injure many more, taking off this one's elbow, smashing that one's leg. The bullets that kill three people are later traced to a single rifle. Another rifle kills two more people and injures a third. Who fired these rifles? We did not know and were never able to learn.

The State Police use a form called a Discharge of Firearms form. It is standard procedure for a trooper to fill out one of these forms after he fires a weapon. The form has a little box for the trooper to fill in the serial number of the weapon he fired, another little box for him to say at whom or at what he shot, and a big white space for him to describe the circumstances of the shooting. There are more occasions to use these standard forms on September 13 than ever before, but they are not used at Attica on this most bloody day.

The rifles at Attica carry cartridges in a clip. After each shot, the shooter turns and slides a bolt that ejects the spent cartridge and strips a new one off the top of the clip and into the chamber for the next shot. The Ithaca model shotguns are pump action, the trooper ejecting the spent round and chambering a new round from the tubular magazine by sliding a comfortable wooden grip along the underside of the barrel. A revolver, of course, carries cartridges in a cylinder. The troopers carry extra cartridges.

When the assault begins, the shots explode too fast to count. Afterward the law officers admit firing about 450 shots. Since most shotgun shells contain nine or twelve pellets, at least 2,200 deadly pieces of metal flew toward the crowd in Attica.[1] In fact, the officers fire even more, since shots are proved to have been fired in places where no one admits firing. No one ever knows how many shots are fired because there is no ammunition accountability today. No one keeps track of how many bullets a trooper has before the assault or how many he has afterward.

Ammunition accountability is almost as basic to police procedure as weapons accountability. The law and the New York State Police *Manual* require each trooper to account for each shot he fires. They require him to account before a grand jury if necessary. If you do not know how many bullets a trooper starts with and finishes with, you have nothing but his word for how many times he shoots. He need not justify any shots he does not admit firing.

Standard procedure requires the expended cartridges at shootings to be picked up, tagged as to their location, and preserved as evidence. This record tends to show where the shooter was when he ejected each expended round, since the unique mark of the firing pin on the cartridge can be traced to the weapon that fired it. This procedure is particularly important at Attica because there is so much shooting. It would not be futile (notwithstanding the general failure of the police to keep track of who had what rifle or shotgun) since records did exist for tracing most or all pistols, a few rifles, and at least one shotgun to the troopers who fired them. Even placing a particular rifle at a particular location could help. But the police failed to follow their standard procedure for collecting and tagging expended cartridges at Attica. One State Police detective told me of seeing expended rifle cartridges still lying about on a cellblock roof several days after the shootings.

"Don't move the body until the police get here," goes a familiar line in detective fiction. Just as we all know about tracing bullets to guns by ballistics, we all know about preserving the scene of the homicide until the police take their pictures, make their measurements, pick up any weapons, and do the other things they do in a routine investigation. This evidence is basic and essential.

At Attica there is no need wait for the police. They are there already. Detectives of the New York State Police Bureau of Criminal Investigation follow the assault troopers down the catwalks and into D Yard. They follow so closely that one is in position to fire a shotgun slug into the chest of Sam Melville, the "Mad Bomber," killing him when Melville allegedly sallies forth from a bunker brandishing a Molotov cocktail. The BCI detectives fail to make the measurements around this or any other body. To a large extent, they fail to give the Investigation pictures of the death scenes. They fail to keep track of any weapons lying near the dead men, which might help to justify the killings if they were really there. Tony theorized that one reason the State Police destroyed the death scenes was that the weapons they claimed in their justifications simply weren't there.

An exception comes to mind. A photo of a dead inmate near Times Square shows a sword lying beside his body. The sword, which is curved like a scimitar, is one of the more ingenious inmate artifacts. The problem is that an earlier photo of the same scene shows no sword. It shows nothing in reach of the dead man but an Afro comb. Who planted the sword?

These two photos successfully run a gauntlet of curious coincidences between the assault and our investigation. Many other police photos have different luck. The State Police photograph the retaking, but, we are told, they do not make adequate preparations beforehand. The photographic record they produce is far from complete. Sometimes, we are told, troopers fail to operate simple cameras properly. Sometimes it's a failure to develop the film with minimal competence. Sometimes there is simply a failure to take the pictures the trooper was sent to take. The police give us hundreds of pictures, but few of death scenes and none of shootings. The reasons vary but the result is the same, no photos where photos matter most.

One of the two video cameras assigned to cover the retaking does not receive adequate power from the car battery that is on hand to operate it after the electricity is shut off before the assault begins. (I always thought this might have been a legitimate snafu.) The other video camera, which the State Police have set up to the right of the snipers on A Block roof, jumps and cuts crazily during the action and somehow fails to show any of the shooting in spite of the volume of fire on the catwalks below and on the soundtrack of the videotape.

All this comes out about the cameras and the videotapes afterward. Such photos, film, and tapes as we ever see remain a strangely long time in the exclusive custody of the State Police before they are turned over to the Investigation and to McKay. The big and well-placed gaps in the photographic record are the more regrettable since State officials barred the outside Observers and the press from witnessing the retaking.

BCI detectives take written statements from most of the State Police riflemen on the afternoon of September 13. By and large, we are told, they do not take statements from the rest of the troopers who took part in the assault until September 15. (What the State Police do on the fourteenth remains, for the most part, one of the mysteries of the Investigation; Tony Simonetti often mused aloud about that.) The statements that the State Police detectives take from the troopers are remarkably uninformative, particularly when one considers that they have thirty-nine homicides to account for. The major thrust of the statements that these professionals take from the shooters and eyewitnesses seems directed toward what the inmates were doing—their hostile acts and words—before the firing commenced.

One of the bigger myths of Attica lasts barely a day. On the afternoon of September 13, Correction Department officials announce, and the press duly (some say, obediently) reports, that inmates killed all the dead hostages, most by slashing their throats, some by stabbing and beating with clubs and lengths of pipe. One emasculation is also officially reported.[2]

The autopsies of the dead hostages actually begin in Rochester about midnight on the thirteenth, with troopers watching the pathologists as they pull bullet after bullet from the carcasses of the supposedly slashed hostages who were wondering that morning what was going to happen and, maybe, when they could come in from the rain. As people are reading the throat-slashing version in their morning papers on the fourteenth, the true story begins to filter out. That afternoon, Dr. John Edland, the chief medical examiner, formally announces that all dead hostages died of gunshot wounds, and that none was emasculated. Since the officers had all the guns, that points the finger at the officers. They killed their own.

The same afternoon the Correction Department tells the press, in the first official reaction to the truth:

> We have eyewitnesses who say the hostages' throats were cut—and we believe their reports. . . . We have unconfirmed reports that the prisoners had zip guns. We have not yet seen the coroner's report and have not been able to study it . . . but from our point of view we note two things: (1) we have eyewitnesses that saw throats cut and (2) there were various types of arms in the possession of the inmates that could have inflicted bullet-type wounds.[3]

These official statements, repeated even after the truth is known, suggest the intensity of the officials' will to disbelieve for themselves and to hide from others the enormity of Attica. In the years that follow, Dr. Edland, the medical examiner, will pay the price for his simple honesty.

The sensible procedures for collecting evidence prescribed by the State Police *Manual* are, of course, designed to learn what really happened and, where a crime has been committed, to convict the criminal. One would suppose that police with nothing to hide would follow the procedures that they were trained, accustomed, and supposed to follow. I have often thought that the State Police at Attica practiced evidence collection as if they had consulted their manual in order to do exactly the opposite of what it required.

Tony called me into his office one day during the fall of 1973 and told me, with the door closed, that he had been keeping a file since the inception of the Investigation on how the State Police had refused to cooperate with us, had been uncandid, withheld evidence, then fed it to us piecemeal, and generally obstructed our efforts to learn and prove what happened from the moment the cloud of tear gas fell on the catwalks. A number of times, for example, they would say in effect, "This is all the evidence we have," and Tony would press them, and they would produce more. It is the policeman's job to help the prosecutor. They refused to do that, and they eviscerated the evidence. (Any distinction between failing to collect what is your duty to collect and actively destroying it has always escaped me; the State Police did both.) Then, as Tony told it, they stonewalled us.

By memo dated November 15, 1973, Tony asked me to "evaluate our evidence and write a legal opinion re . . . CONSPIRACY BY STATE POLICE TO OBSTRUCT JUSTICE AND/OR TAMPER WITH EVIDENCE."

I began to consider the fact that Tony, his two part-time assistants, and his nine investigators—most of them ex-City cops he had worked with when he had been prosecuting homicides in Hogan's New York district attorney's office—had the help, as it were, of about a dozen State Police detectives until June 1972. How do you prosecute the State Police, I wondered, with these personable BCI detectives in the office every day sharing your efforts and quietly goodbuddying you to death?

Tony told me he threw them out. That is, he had the BCI detectives physically reassigned away from the Investigation's offices and their routine access to its files. He relied on them, however, for prosecuting of inmates throughout my time at the Investigation. Not that that was necessarily Tony's fault. He was not in Albany controlling the budget. I had seen in the Admin File that he had complained to Albany periodically about the Investigation's minisize. Bob Fischer, not Tony, was the person "In Charge," under Lefkowitz and Rockefeller.

Anyway, in the fall 1973, Fischer was on the way out. Tony would now be calling the shots. It encouraged me vastly that the State Police's obstructions of the prosecution had concerned Tony early and constantly, that he had been keeping book on them, and that he was taking me into his confidence to try to do something about them. Their obstructions might add up to a crime. Under New York law[4] it is called "hindering prosecution" and is substantially the same as the federal crime of obstruction of justice, which was often being mentioned about the Nixon Administration's handling of the Watergate scandal.

We had no reason to think that the police had bothered to hinder a prosecution that could not hurt them. We did have evidence against the perpetrators of several specific shootings that looked criminal. In light of the evidence they had destroyed, what could we do about the bulk of their killings and maimings? Tony had one answer, and I developed another. Tony went into his during a trip we took to the grand jury and to Binghamton to meet with Bob Fischer.

Chapter Nine

Report But Not Prosecute?

One day in early November 1973, I entered a grand jury room for the first time in my life, in Warsaw, the Wyoming County seat, a short drive south of Batavia and Attica. I wanted to watch Frank Cryan present what I understood (incorrectly, it turned out) was the Investigation's first murder case against a State trooper.

Like Tony, Frank had worked in District Attorney Hogan's homicide bureau. That meant trying murders in New York City. Frank had a very conservative outlook, the dry, pixie humor of a mature Irishman, and a habit of nearly missing airplanes. It was Frank who convinced me, soon after I came to work, that the police did indeed need shotguns loaded with 00 buckshot, at least for backup during the retaking. What if all those crudely armed inmates had charged the first troopers into D Yard? Tragically, the police did not save the shotguns for backup.

Frank had put a lot of the Investigation's evidence into the grand jury since it was convened two years earlier. He was now Tony's chief trial man. (Tony did not plan to try any cases himself.) In this case the trooper had finally admitted to our investigators that he shot the inmate, after first insisting that he had gone through the retaking without unholstering his pistol. Now he sought to justify himself for shooting the inmate by saying that the inmate, who had already been shot several times and was lying on the pavement, had given a "fish kick" with one of his legs. The trooper said that the fish kick showed him that the inmate was about to leap up and attack. To us it indicated that the inmate was still alive when the trooper shot him. Frank went over the evidence that the jury had previously heard in bits and pieces over the preceding months and told them the law they were bound to apply. Standing bespectacled behind the lectern, he looked and sounded objective, dispassionate, and convincing, a grim professor expounding a fatal subject.

Frank, the court stenographer, and I left the room while the jury deliberated. I expected them to indict. A few minutes later they opened the door, thus telling us they had voted. We reentered the room. Frank glanced at the slip of paper that showed their vote, placed it on the shelf inside the lectern, and continued in his scholarly way with the next piece of business. I sat against the back wall watching him in vain for some sign of how the vote had gone. Not for nothing was Frank called the Desert Fox. Finally, the session ended. Frank told Tony and me outside that the jury had voted not to indict. Our dismay was plain to see. How, I wondered, could the jury consider the evidence and not indict this trooper?

That cold fall afternoon after the jury's vote, an investigator drove Tony, Frank, and me 160 miles southeast from Warsaw to Binghamton in one of the Investigation's dilapidated state cars. We were on our way to dinner with Max Spoont and Bob Fischer at the Binghamton Treadway Inn. Fischer had been awarded the Silver Star and several Purple Hearts during World War II. From 1951 to 1955 he had served as District Attorney for Broome County. Governor Rockefeller selected him to perform an investigation in Buffalo in 1965, to sit as a county judge in 1967, and in 1970 to head the Organized Crime Task Force, where he was dubbed "supercop." Now he had just won election to the New York State Supreme Court (though called "Supreme," this court sits beneath two appellate courts). He was very popular around Binghamton. Everyone had expected him to win.

Judge Fischer, like General Lefkowitz, kept himself more formal with his staff than with his constituents. A tall, graying, handsome man, he spoke of his enthusiasm for skiing and of having us back to his house that evening, though this did not come to pass. He had to leave us after dinner.

Tony, Frank, Max, and I returned to a table in the bar and drank possibly two dozen bottles of beer. Max spoke glowingly of how we might form a public interest law firm after the Investigation ended. It had to end sometime. For some people "public interest law firm" means liberals charging into court with impractical pet projects. That was not our subject that night. Max talked of bringing realistic suits that would really help people, and make up to us in satisfaction and fascination what they would not pay. Max and I warmed to the idea. Tony showed interest. These were good men to be working with, not narrow-minded, selfish, or cynical. Frank puffed on his pipe, drank his beer, and smiled his bemused smile.

Tony, Max, and I also discussed a grand jury report during the Binghamton trip. Besides deciding whether or not to indict people for crimes, a grand jury has the power to issue a presentment. That is a recommendation for administrative discipline of an official who has done something wrong but whose activity does not amount to a crime. Or a grand jury may issue a report that describes a situation that needs describing. The grand jury hears evidence in secrecy and issues a report of public concern—light from darkness. For example, a federal grand jury had issued a thoughtful and damning report on the so-called "shoot-out" in which the Chicago police killed Fred Hampton and another Black Panther in the middle of a night in 1969.[1] It charged those police with "misfeasance and nonfeasance" (Tony's summary) for their massive and apparently unwarranted shooting and their bizarre failure to follow the most basic rules of evidence collection afterward. Tony and I found the description in that report remarkably similar to the State Police conduct at Attica. He soon had the report photocopied and distributed to the other assistants.

In Binghamton, Tony was alive with the idea of our publishing a report on the entire riot, based on the evidence we had given the grand jury. He, Frank, and I would divide up the initial drafting, he said. One person would then rewrite the whole thing, to integrate it and improve the style. Tony spoke of hiring a professional writer. I said I really liked to write and offered to do the final rewriting as well as my segment. I was eager to do it, though afraid it would take me away from trying cases. Tony and Max seemed willing to let me go ahead.

Tony said we would offer our draft of the report to the grand jury. If it was going to come out as their report, they would obviously have the final say on what it said. They would doubtless want to make some changes in what we wrote. That would be fine. We had no commitment to any particular interpretation of the riot except a fair one. If the jury rejected our approach (whatever it turned out to be), Tony wanted the Investigation to submit the paper as a "Report to the Attorney General." As such it could still be published, perhaps more readily than if the grand jury adopted it. The court has the power to seal a grand jury report and would likely do so, at least until all the trials had ended.[2] Not that the Attorney General would release a report prematurely, but at least it would be up to Louis Lefkowitz, Tony's boss, rather than the court to control the release. We agreed that this would improve the chances for early release. Early public release of the facts about Attica was the objective all three of us said we were aiming at as we talked.[3]

This report would finally tell the public key aspects of the riot that the McKay Report had not been able to cover or had not even known about, particularly about the shootings. Tony said he had heard that the McKay Commission had had to slant their report to satisfy some "constituency" of blacks or liberals or both. None of us knew what that meant, or even if it was true, but in any event we were beholden to no one. (I did not yet know that the McKay Commission had questioned far more witnesses in far greater detail about the shootings than the Investigation had.)

Tony also wanted the report to discuss the problems of conducting the Investigation. I sensed that two years of frustrations had put this aspect particularly close to his heart. "Perhaps those problems can be avoided," he said, "if, God forbid, there's a next time." Our report would give the world the full and final word on the enormity of Attica. None of us questioned the importance of doing that.

Nor did I feel the slightest cause for doubt that Tony wanted this story told. In the next few days he committed the forces of the Investigation to telling it. He dictated outlines of what to cover. Tight as we were for staff help, he even let me hire a paralegal, Elyse Colton, to work exclusively on the report. Tony knew how to get a project started.

Many years later I would wonder whether, during the trip to Binghamton, Fisher had pushed on Tony the idea of reporting but not prosecuting the crimes by the police. My own preference was always to prosecute. That's what prosecutors usually do, and simply writing a report in response to the killing of thirty-nine men would be an industrial-strength travesty.

The entire Investigation, as well as some other OCTF people and Ed Hammock, who had earlier tried to prosecute a number of troopers, gathered at Hizzoner's Restaurant across from City Hall in Manhattan the next afternoon for a farewell party for Judge Fischer and a young assistant who was also leaving. The unblinking report on the State Police and prison guards at Attica that Tony was initiating, not to mention any systematic prosecution of officers who had transgressed, had yet to go forward. I have often thought since then that Judge Fischer, from his standpoint, got out at the right time.

* * *

As autumn passed, Tony and I grew closer on the job. He came to use me increasingly to answer the questions of law that arose in the Investigation. I had probably done more law look-ups in the past than any of the other assistants had; they had been prosecuting criminals.

Tony, who freely admitted that he was not a law man in the bookish sense, often phoned Max Spoont for legal advice or to consult on strategy. My background was more like Max's. Once or twice I noticed Tony watching like a spectator at a tennis match while Max and I discussed a legal question. The OCTF was going to split upon Fischer's departure. Tony was to head the Attica Investigation, and Max, the OCTF proper—both, of course, under the benign hand of General Lefkowitz. As the time for the split approached, Tony came to consult Max less and me more.

Tony continued to impress me. He used to say that telling the truth was the only way he could get along because he wasn't smart enough to follow a lie through. Though he repeated that he loved cops, he complained that some police lie when they don't even have to. While he headed the Investigation, he spoke of letting the chips fall where they may, on inmates, on law officers, on anyone else. I believed he would let them fall on Nelson Rockefeller himself if that was where they belonged. He told me once that the trouble with law enforcement in this country is that the people who do it don't know the difference between right and wrong. I have never doubted that Tony knew the difference.

He called me to his office more and more, on problems of law, strategy, and running the office. He liked to confer, discuss, and bounce ideas off others. Ideas and energy burst from him, subsided, and burst out again. Like many volcanoes of creativity, he needed an editor. He and I got along well. I liked him and believed he liked me. Each of us understood easily what the other was saying. We usually agreed with each other's conclusions. We came to have lunch together a good deal. Away from work, we did not socialize—quite naturally, since he lived on Long Island and I, in Connecticut—and seldom spoke on the phone.

By the end of 1973, Tony had me acting as his chief assistant. In January after he had succeeded Fischer as head of the Attica Investigation, he circulated a memo that formally named me "Chief Assistant." Tony's choice, which I guess he came to regret, put me in position for what was to come. In name my new position made me to Tony what he had been to Fischer. This did not diminish my respect for Tony's far greater experience and for his judgment.

Chapter Ten

Behold a Handle of Justice

The turkey shoot has been an American sport for generations at county fairs. Traditionally, a live turkey was tied out at a stake. The first shooter to draw blood from the head or the neck got the bird. As we entered a more gentle time, paper targets came to be substituted for living targets at county fairs.[1]

Major Monahan had briefed the troopers that he did not want the retaking of Attica to be a turkey shoot. Afterward, much turned on whether it had been one, in the traditional sense. If so, the proud, professional New York State Police came off as a savage mob inside of stuffed gray shirts, and a proud Governor who wanted to be President may well have blown it.

With the savvy brass that usually served him well, Governor Rockefeller had promptly announced that the troopers had done "a superb job." That then was the Official Version. Every State employee who served Rockefeller, who served what usually passes for self-interest, or who served Official Versions for the employee's own peace of mind, became obliged to honor Rockefeller's description and, if necessary, make it true after the fact.

Besides honor, image, and perhaps the Presidency, a lot of money turned on what really happened within the walls of Attica. Waiting in the wings, in case the troopers proved to have used excessive force,[2] stood the widows and the wounded with their damage claims for millions of dollars against the State and Rockefeller and some other officials. If Rockefeller's hopes for the Presidency suddenly brightened, the chances for a truth to emerge that rebutted the Official Version would dim further.

Of course, the Official Version had already taken a considerable beating. A year to the day after the retaking came the McKay Report's measured conclusion that the troopers had done much unnecessary shooting. McKay had reported as an official of the State, but he had been an academic before and could go back to that life. Reports, too, come and go. Even though McKay confirmed what many had felt from the start—and what the inmates and their radical supporters were saying to anyone who listened—it lacked the clout to displace the Official Version in a popular way. The Official Version, if wrong, created a danger. If a turkey shoot had not happened, then changes were not needed to avoid another one.

Now Tony Simonetti was going to issue another report, not to repudiate McKay but to add to the McKay Report, in detail and in impact. Our report, as Tony described it to Max Spoont and me, had to add to McKay because our evidence increasingly showed that what McKay had concluded was true. Our report had to be more of the same, the true facts, but this time in all their particular horror. Like McKay, Tony had apparently not gotten the word about State employees honoring the Official Version and making it come true. Coming from a grand jury or the Attorney General, I thought, our report was likely to pack more clout than McKay's. We were more official than he.

So long as the Attica Investigation failed to indict any troopers, it endorsed the Official Version for anyone who noticed. Indictments, on the other hand, would rebut the Official Version very noticeably indeed. Picture a group of State Police officers answering those criminal charges in court. Their inevitable outcry over being indicted would capture more public attention. Perhaps those indictments—and convictions—would elevate the truth itself to the eminence of Official Version. Perhaps they would not only bring justice but move a bewildered and complacent public.

All this I saw in hindsight, when I considered why things happened as they did. The Attica Investigation, I understood, was an apolitical office of State employees. I did not consider this an oxymoron. My main thoughts when Tony announced our report were: Great, but why stop with a report? Why not get indictments, and whatever convictions would follow? Charge the police with their crimes. Convict all whom propolice passion or some unforeseen hole in the evidence would not rescue from a guilty verdict. I felt strongly that the truth about Attica should come out and the guilty should be prosecuted, but the reasons—beyond the theory that we live in an informed and just democracy— grew clearer to me later.

My mind was still open to the extent that I remained perfectly willing to accept evidence that made sense and still supported the Official Version as to any number of shooters whom this version might fit. Keeping an open mind, however, did not mean rejecting without reason the evidence I saw more and more of on the job. Tony knew, and I saw as I worked, that Rockefeller was wrong, McKay was right, and Major Monahan had been disobeyed. Attica was a turkey shoot.

But was there a handle—to lift the lid of secrecy, bring the police to justice, let the light in and the truth out? Upon what specific evidence chosen to prove what specific crime do you indict individual State Police and guards for shooting people, after they had destroyed so much of the evidence? How could we identify specific perpetrators of individual acts, beyond a reasonable doubt, with little ballistics, fewer photos than there should have been, few death scenes measured, etc., etc.? Had the police really engineered their own escape from justice? The unfairness and the challenge nagged me through the fall of 1973 as I worked on prosecuting inmates. I wanted to look into it. The first place to look was in the books, a task that would take time from my assignments. I asked Tony's permission. He said, "Go ahead."

The law seemed straightforward. If you intentionally shoot and kill someone without justification, that is murder. Having a sufficient disregard for whether you kill someone or not is the same as intending to kill him. If you shoot and wound him, that is assault in the first degree. If the shot misses, that may be reckless endangerment. Reckless endangerment in the first degree is a Class D felony in New York, carrying a maximum penalty of seven years in prison. The statute says:

> A person is guilty of reckless endangerment in the first degree when, under circumstances evincing a depraved indifference to human life, he recklessly engages in conduct which creates a grave risk of death to another person.[3]

Shooting at people who weren't doing anything to be shot for sounded depraved to me.[4] Surely, it created a grave risk of their deaths. Could the answer be so easy, the handle so obvious? Many of the unnecessary shots fired at Attica had missed; I often marveled at how many had missed. With very little ballistics evidence to prove who fired into whom, we would have to treat other shots that actually hit people as though they had missed. One hundred and eleven troopers, by Tony's count, had given written statements to the State Police BCI detectives in which they admitted shooting at people who, they usually claimed, were doing something that justified shooting them. "I fired at an inmate in A Yard who was throwing a spear up at the catwalk." If the evidence showed that the justifying act had not happened, that the inmate had not been throwing a spear at that time and place, then the shooter may have admitted committing a felony—not to mention a wanton and brutal act—even though there was no way to prove he hit anybody.[5] Reckless endangerment in the first degree.

The Investigation's files already held two short memoranda about reckless endangerment. Tony had written one of them. Both memos concluded that we could not apply reckless endangerment to what the police had done at Attica. How, I wondered, could anyone have reached *that* conclusion? Neither memo explained how. They simply and summarily said no to reckless endangerment. Thus they threw away the handle. My approach was not to confront Tony, but to convert him if I could.

I spent a good part of December looking up the law. I thought it a good plan to explore all the side alleys, what-if's, and ramifications I could think of, but the heart of the work was rather simple. Reckless endangerment (R.E.) was a comparatively new crime in New York. Few reported cases interpreted it. One case found R.E. when the defendant pulled the trigger of an unloaded pistol that he was pointing at the victim's chest, then fired a bullet past her head, notwithstanding his claim that he was an expert marksman and had merely wanted to show her that he "meant business" during an argument they were having in the restaurant where she worked.[6] The court in another case held it was reckless endangerment when the defendant pointed a loaded shotgun at the victim's stomach and had his hand near the trigger; the victim was a policeman.[7] I did not think "a depraved indifference to human life" meant wild eyes and slavering over the rifle. Surely, if anyone had fired without justification toward the crowd at Attica, he had shown a more depraved indifference than the defendants in either of those two cases.

In *People v. Jernatowski* I met an old friend I had studied in law school. It was the leading "reckless murder" case, and it had been decided by the New York Court of Appeals, the State's highest court, half a century earlier under the statute upon which the R.E. statute was based. In *Jernatowski*, the defendant, who was supporting a railroad strike in Buffalo, saw lights on and heard voices in the house where the victim lived with her husband, who had refused to join the strike, and three other people. Mr. Jernatowski fired shots into the house, killing her with one of them. The court sustained his murder conviction, saying:

> So in this case when the defendant fired two or more shots into the house
> where he knew there were human beings he committed an act which the

jury certainly could say was imminently dangerous and which evinced a wicked and depraved mind regardless of human life . . . .[8]

The Practice Commentary in the Penal Law, which explains what the New York legislature had in mind when it passed the reckless murder statute, gives as examples: shooting into a crowd; placing a time bomb in a public place; or opening the lions' cage at the zoo.[9] If such acts are reckless murder when they kill someone, they must be reckless endangerment when they do not. Certainly many officers fired into a crowd at Attica. Leaving a time bomb in a public place showed the same indifference to human life, it seemed to me, as firing a shotgun blindly into the D yard foxholes, into which one would expect inmates to have dived to escape the gunfire.

Looking at the evidence unsystematically (which was the only way we could look at it then), I saw case after case in which we could take a shooter's BCI statement admitting that he shot at someone and establish by other evidence that shots had indeed been fired in that person's direction when he was not doing anything that justified shooting him. The seven years maximum sentence for reckless endangerment in the first degree is a long time to go away—maybe longer than a trooper would be sentenced to, even if we had additional evidence to prove that his unjustified shots struck someone. It was not perfect, but justice could be approximated. We had 111 people who admitted shooting, and we had 39 corpses and 89 wounded. If the rest of the evidence held up on close analysis, we had our handle. A number of felony indictments should make the police more careful whom they shoot hereafter, I thought. Apparently, we would still be powerless against the shooters who had not admitted firing their weapons.

On January 7, 1974, I finished a thirty-eight-page memorandum concluding that reckless endangerment could be very useful indeed to the Investigation. Tony, with whom I had been talking about the memo as I worked along, agreed with it. Max Spoont phoned me to say he had read my memo and he, too, agreed.

At that point I did not give much thought to how Tony or the other assistant who had looked up reckless endangerment could have gone so wrong in their own memos. I was merely pleased to have turned Tony around. My conclusions on reckless endangerment, and Tony's and Max's agreement with them, played a major part in Tony's decision to ask the court a few months later to convene a second Attica grand jury to consider crime by the police. My memo, of course, would not have had the impact on the Investigation that it did if Tony and the other lawyer had reached its simple conclusions in the first place.

Tony's editing of my R.E. memo had significance I did not realize at the time. I had given it to him to edit before it was typed in final form. He made very few changes, most coming at the end. Here is my Conclusion, the words in italics being what he added, the words in brackets showing what he asked me to delete:

Any belief by a shooter that he was firing in order to prevent an escape from the "custody" of the Attica Correctional Facility or to effect an arrest was not *in most cases, if not all cases,* in the opinion of the writer, a reasonable belief within the justification statute.[10] Each shot, therefore, that was not fired in order to defend the shooter or a third person against "the use or imminent use of deadly physical force" constitutes a prohibited use of weapon, a class A misdemeanor. If the shot also created a grave risk of death and the shooter was indifferent to whether he killed anyone or not, the crime of reckless endangerment, a class D felony, was also committed.

The only realistic defense against charges arising from random or reckless shots appears to be the extra-legal defense that the retaking was essentially an emotionally charged war or combat situation, to which the Penal Law does not apply and was not intended to apply. The law, however, creates no such exception. [The shooters had all the firepower, so that if it was a war, it was a one-sided war.] The assault troopers were directed to use their weapons responsibly. The troopers had a duty to use their weapon responsibly, not to fire warning shots, and to consider themselves answerable for each shot in court. Most of the shooters adhered responsibly to their duty. [A number of deaths are doubtless attributable to those who did not.]

[Attica is in large measure a tragedy of people who put the law aside in order to reach goals they considered justified. The rioters took the law into their own hands, in part, as a response to oppressive prison conditions, yet indictments have been returned without regard to this extra legal defense.] If some of the assault force ignored the law and their duty in firing their weapons, they should be equally subject, *as the inmates,* to prosecution for any crimes they thereby committed, with similar disregard for any extra-legal defense. [Otherwise, it may appear that the prosecution itself is not following the law.]

What Tony had me take out of the memo foreshadowed our later differences. At the time the foreshadowing got lost in the sunshine. Tony and I were agreeing on nearly everything. He said he was deleting subjective conclusions that had no place in my memo. They struck me as little enough editing and did not concern me. I thought he could be right. I still can't say he wasn't. It also occurred to me afterward that he was protecting the Investigation's file.

The statement in the Conclusion for which I probably had then seen the least evidence is "Most of the shooters adhered responsibly to their duty." I was uncritically accepting the office view and Mc Kay's view about that.

Tony and Max's acceptance of my rather elementary conclusion that R.E. fit many of the shots at Attica did not settle the issue in the office. In fact, the R.E. debate showed as little inclination as a snake to stop wriggling after it was dead. Tony even staged a debate between me and my most vocal critic the following June, well after the second grand jury had gone to work, though nothing came of it. It opened my eyes to see the myopia that Attica pulled down like a window shade across the intelligence of many, and I have always wondered how I may be deluding myself when I feel comparatively objective.

Tony circulated my memo among the other assistants. One of them wrote a memo in opposition, unburdened by citation to any cases. It touched on a number of points that Tony and I discussed both before and after I finished my own memo, and it still fascinates me as an example of another prosecutor's thinking about R.E. Here is part of it:

> I did not . . . in many cases, read the case law cited by Mr. Bell. I . . . have not done extensive research . . . .
>
> Did the firing clearly create the grave risk of death? . . . Does firing into the ground[11] create a grave risk of death? . . . I find no authority which states that said conduct created a grave risk of death instead of merely serious physical injury. I did not think that this assumption can be made. In making an argument to the jury as a prosecutor, I would much rather argue that the trooper's conduct created the possibility of serious physical injury but I feel that it would be difficult, if not impossible, to convince the jury that a trooper fired [his shotgun at Attica] knowing that there was a grave risk of death to a non-target.
>
> Is there evidence of a depraved indifference to human life? . . . The factors which must be considered here are:
>
> a. Is [the shooter's] deviation more than gross? . . .

The [Bell] memo baldly states that the troopers fired with reckless indifference as to whether an inmate could be killed . . . . This begs the question and is an assumption which should certainly not be considered as a conclusion. Reasonable people using hindsight will agree that the troopers should have used other methods to clear the holes (e.g., tear gas), but was the decision not to do so depraved, reckless, negligent or just stupid? No parameters are set out in the memo and yet they must be determined and explored before any conclusion can be drawn . . . .

It appears from the language of the memorandum up to page 30 that the writer of the memo is convinced that a great deal of the shooting was unjustified. I would dispute that point in many cases . . . .

. . . I submit that no inmate in "D" yard is an innocent person within the meaning of the [justification] statute and that a police officer was certainly intending to arrest or at least detain each of these persons.

State police regulations and the Penal code are cited in the memorandum. Both the law and the regulations were not specifically drawn to cover a riot situation such as occurred in Attica. In reviewing the State Police regulations they, of course, can be used as a guide. However, deviation from them would not be too strongly considered in this instance . . . .

So the police would have been justified in shooting all of the inmates in D Yard dead. The writer of the memo, a very likable guy, epitomized to me the problem of the honest cover-up (which was one of the cover-ups at Attica) and suggested how prosecutors who are usually fair often fail to prosecute police whose actions are no less criminal than those of the felons who happen not to belong to the brotherhood of law enforcement.

Between outright acceptance and outright rejection, several issues arose over R.E., some of which deserved consideration and some of which did not but got it anyway. A prosecutor may be a doer, but he is also a lawyer.

Several times that winter and later, Tony and I agreed that when a trooper had actually done wrong but a debatable point of law might get him off, it was not our duty as prosecutors to decide the point in his favor. We talked, for example, about a trooper who fired his shotgun into a foxhole without looking first to see if anyone was down there. Plainly reckless endangerment in the first degree, as far as Tony and I were concerned. But some assistants said we would have to prove someone was in the hole—impossible, except for the hole that held the shotgunned corpse of Ramon Rivera—before we had a case. No decision that I could find had decided this issue. In such cases Tony and I agreed to seek the indictment and let the court decide if proof of occupancy was required. That could be done before a trial. The prosecutor might decide the clear questions in favor of a wrongdoer but not the questions that were, at best, wide open. If we did, we recognized, we would be arrogating to ourselves the duty and responsibility of the judge. I never heard Tony depart from that conclusion.

Tony told me a number of times that the State Police might be justified in their shots because they were simply carrying out orders and performing an official duty when they retook the prison. He asked me to cover that argument in my R.E. memo. The opposition made a similar argument, and I have heard it many times since. It resembles Adolph Eichmann's defense for murdering Jews. There cannot be a lawful order to commit an unlawful act. A felony is no less a felony if someone orders it. The order simply makes the person giving the order guilty, too. An order to retake the prison is not an order to shoot people who are not threatening anyone. Major Monahan did not tell the troopers he wanted a turkey shoot, and if he had, it would not have exculpated the perpetrators. Tony's failures to see through the "following orders" defense surprised me.

The Practice Commentaries after the justification statute explains that if an officer "both intentionally shoots the robber and recklessly kills a bystander, the fact that he was authorized to do the former does not justify the latter. On the other hand, his justification for shooting the robber is not negated by his reckless shooting of the bystander."[12] The fairness of symmetry! Under logic and the law, a trooper at Attica could be a hero with his first shot and a criminal with his second. I thought some were. Should it be this way? I thought so. A piece of good work should not give an officer a license to kill. The judge could always consider the trooper's good work in passing sentence.

Getting back to the law of justification as it applies to reckless endangerment, it is not the *fact* that the person shot at was actually posing an imminent threat to someone's life that justifies the shot. Rather, it is the reasonableness of the shooter's *belief* that this was happening. This rule protects, for example, the cop who shoots someone who is sufficiently suicidal to pull a toy gun on him. On this point my memo said:

> Factors bearing on the reasonableness of the shooter's belief that he was protecting himself or someone else from the use, or imminent use, of deadly physical force, include: the shooter's knowledge of the inmates'

arsenal of weapons, of inmates' sharpening delineators[13] in D yard, of the inmates' statements to fight to the death, and so forth, in addition to the inmates' hostile acts that he actually saw when he fired.

Another point: A person cannot be convicted of a crime solely on the strength of his own admission. The law requires independent evidence, or corroboration, that establishes the existence of a crime. Once the crime is shown, a person's uncorroborated admission that he was the one who committed it is generally sufficient to convict him. This doctrine protects crackpots who confess to non-existent crimes, though it does not always protect crackpots who claim credit for real crimes. Though Tony and I never finally resolved the issue of corroboration as to most of the R.E. cases, it did not pose a serious problem to me, nor, so far as I ever heard, to Tony.

Besides the saving of someone's life, the law, in theory, provides two other justifications for an officer to shoot: to arrest certain felons, or to prevent their escape from custody. I have considered both of those justifications as being too remote from the context of the turkey shoot to treat seriously—the retaking was not an arrest situation, and no one at the riot was about to escape the custody of Attica. But this did not stop some of the assistants from arguing them. They said over and over, for example, that it was okay to shoot any inmate who was trying to flee the storm of bullets up on the catwalks by going under the rail into D Yard, because the inmate might then mingle with the population down there and avoid identification (if he had not already been adequately identified). The inmate might then escape prosecution for any crimes he may have committed against the hostages up on the catwalks. Their arguments struck me as vexing nonsense—iffy mights to kill someone over! The statute speaks of escaping custody, not prosecution. Nowhere does the law allow an officer to take another human's life simply to forestall a possible problem of identification later on. I do not recall that Tony ever sounded impressed by the escape argument, or that it ever impeded the prosecution. As best I recall, the State Police always sought to justify firing at inmates by claiming there was some imminent threat to life, never to prevent an escape.

Yet, as far as Tony and I could figure out, this was how an unknown trooper on C Roof came to kill hostage John D'Archangelo: he was wearing prison clothes, had slipped off the identifying blindfold, and was probably trying to get off B Walk and away from the splattering bullets. The trooper apparently shot the "inmate" before he escaped.

When I was still working on the R.E. memo, I found a section toward the end of the New York Penal Law that appeared to make any unjustified firing whatsoever a misdemeanor.[14] I thought it would make a good back-up charge to include in what I expected to be our indictments for reckless endangerment in the first degree. Among other things, it would leave a milder alternative if some jurors concluded that a trooper had done wrong but they did not want to convict him of reckless endangerment, or if a court found a hole in our R.E. theory. I brought the statute into Tony's office.

"That's the handle I've been looking for!"

By handle, he said, he meant a way to charge the police with their wrongful shots. He sounded quite enthusiastic. This puzzled me. I wondered where he had been looking for his handle during the past two years. I also wondered why the hell he did not consider reckless endangerment the handle, since he seemed to be agreeing with me about it, notwithstanding his earlier memo in which he had thrown it away.

The bottom line was that a few months after I submitted my memo, Tony called for a Supplemental Grand Jury to be convened. Tony planned to have many cases presented to it, upon the basis of my conclusion—which superseded his own opposite conclusion—that many reckless endangerment cases could be proved against the State Police and correction officers who had perpetrated a turkey shoot.

A lockbox is a panel of levers or handles that controls all the locks on a gallery of cells. Each cell may be locked or unlocked by its individual lever, or all the locks may be operated at once by a master handle—a big crank such as the one that smashed the glass and crashed down on a correction officer in the C Block office in Indictment No. 10, and the one that upset the State Police detective when I wanted to weigh it.

Like a person struggling in vain to pull the levers on a few cells, Eddie Hammock had worked on his individual shooter cases one by one without success. Now Hammock was gone. Tony had told me that he himself had been looking for the big handle. Now, reckless endangerment gave it to us, the legal instrument to open a significant number of cases that deserved to be opened against shooters. With one great pull on that handle—it would be a hammer of justice—we could indict them. Official action would finally follow the conclusions of the McKay Report, instead of repudiating them. Verbal conclusions were one thing. The criminal indictment of a number of the State Police would be another. The secrets would come out, the public would know, Pandora's box would lie open (and therein lay the problem). And behind the big handle of reckless endangerment stood the back-up handle of the full, honest grand jury report that Tony had committed the office to write.

It has been said that those who know don't talk and those who talk don't know. Well, the Investigation knew, and the Investigation was going to talk. So much for those who said government could not be candid or deal justly with its own.

Superb job or turkey shoot? Conflicting reports had made it easy for people to think what they wanted and do nothing. The question had hung so long that most people no longer cared. Not caring, they did not demand what was needed to avoid another Attica, or to force greater restraints upon the guns of the law. But the truth had served a two-and-a-half-year sentence at Attica, and the truth would soon be out. The Investigation might be slow, but it was honest.

Chapter Eleven

The Shooter Conferences

"Shooter conferences" is what we called the meetings that Tony Simonetti held through February and March 1974 in our big room with the sign that said "Support your Attica Brothers." They were his first major project on taking command of the Investigation from Judge Fischer. We tried to analyze all the evidence we could find about each shot by each of the 111 troopers and guards who admitted firing their weapons. As Tony put it in a memo dated January 21, our "focus and purpose is:

1. to write a report;
2. to present 'true bills' [i.e., cases in which we expected them to indict] to Grand Jury;
3. to present 'no true bills' to Grand Jury [i.e., cases that we wanted them to consider though we expected them not to indict]; and
4. prepare [our evidence] for referral by the Grand Jury to the State Police or other departments those cases in which administrative action is recommended."

On November 11, 1973, a *New York Times* article had quoted Tony as saying that the grand jury was "approaching an end." Why did Tony say that then? I recall feeling a flicker of apprehension when I read it, knowing that the real work on the police crimes had yet to be done. Then, of course, Tony had not yet grasped the "handle" of reckless endangerment. By the time the shooter conferences began in February, I had forgotten he had said it.

Late in 1973, Tony assigned each of us new assistants—whom Albany had let him hire last summer to try inmates—to study each shot fired by each trooper who had admitted firing his weapon as part of one of the assault teams. I drew the team that had gone out on A Catwalk. Several investigators joined the conferences, most notably Mike McCarron, the big, white-haired retaking expert, and Lenny Brown, who half-jokingly called himself the Investigation's token black and who kept our photographic file.

Tony recognized that not everyone would be comfortable prosecuting police. He announced that anyone, lawyer or investigator, who did not want to work on any phase of the Investigation should tell him. He would assign him to other work and not hold the request against him.

Getting ready for the conferences was a big job. Jim Grable, a young assistant in our Buffalo office who was conscientious, industrious, and the only one of us ready on time, got to discuss his C Block riflemen first. Everyone contributed whatever he could as each of us in turn presented each of his shooters' shots. We considered where the shooter said he aimed, when he said he fired, and why. The information from our separate studies converged on the inmate targets, as had the gunfire two-and-a-half years earlier. We keyed in the information from the autopsy photos and reports and considered whom each shot may have struck. We reviewed the statements of others at the scene, whatever photos we had, the A Roof videotape, and everything else we could think of, in considering the truth or falsity of what each shooter said about why he fired. The evidence before us pointed to few heroes and many criminals and liars. At the end of the discussion of each shooter, Tony or I redictated each assistant's memo (including my own), cranking in the added evidence and our thinking on whether or not to seek an indictment. We found a few murders, more attempted murders, some assaults, and some "no bills." The most common conclusions were: indict for reckless endangerment, investigate further, or both.

Day by day the evidence brought the turkey shoot forward in time, making it more and more vivid. Some color blowups of the dead still come back to me:

- A black man lies naked on his back. A deer slug has drilled his abdomen, in the side, out the front. Shiny gray guts rest in a little heap on his belly.
- The loins of a brown man show a black hole at the base of his penis where a shotgun pellet entered and another hole, the exit wound, halfway along the shaft.
- A hostage (all the hostages were white) lies in repose with a small round hole from 00 buckshot in his cheek.
- The face of another hostage changes shape with each photo that shows him in a new location, because a .270 bullet has shattered his skull and the bones shifted when he was moved.

- A red-lipped surgical incision cleaves the torso of a white inmate lengthwise. A cluster of pellets fired from a few yards away caught him in the side.
- A black man lies on pavement by the wire mesh of Times Square. An oval an inch-and-a-half across gapes from the side of his neck where a full load of buckshot went in.
- Fourteen entrance wounds perforate another body.
- A small hole marks the upper right of a buttock, the only wound the man took.
- A dark brand, ruled across a man's head, slices diagonally through his left ear. Neater holes mark the entrance of other pellets into his back and brain.
- A black man lying face up on the Times Square pavement has empty slits where his eyes used to be. Pistol bullets shattered his skull; bone splinters punctured the eyeballs.

Dr. Michael Baden, then Deputy Chief Medical Examiner of New York City, had taken many of these photos when he performed second autopsies on the Attica dead. He was one of the pathologists whom Tony, Fischer, and Commissioner Oswald had called immediately to check the work of the Rochester medical examiner, Dr. John Edland, after Edland had announced to the world that it was bullets (police) rather than knives (inmates) that had killed the hostages. Tony told me, and I agreed, that it had been prudent to call in outside experts to confirm Edland's findings, as they did. Afterward the Investigation used Baden as its main pathologist. Lively, scholarly, and about my age, Mike Baden supervised autopsies and did them himself daily at the City's Institute of Forensic Medicine, sometimes called "the morgue," up on First Avenue. The fact that he had taken most of the color autopsy photos in our dead men's files had no significance for me then, though it must have for Tony.

Dr. Baden fascinated us for two full days with his explanation of how life had departed the thirty-nine dead. X-rays, which he used in pale counterpoint with the color blowups, tracked the fate of the inner man in black and grays and empty film. Dr. Baden told us:

- The shotgun pellets spread about an inch each yard they go from the gun, so the pattern you see here means the man was shot at about five yards.

- Notice on the X-ray the characteristic fishtail spray of .270 fragments as the bullet disintegrated while it traveled through the subject.
- We found over a quart of blood in this man's lungs, meaning he bled to death from the bullet in his chest.
- The bullet in this man's back has an upward track, but that does not necessarily mean he was shot from below. He may have been running bent over when he was shot, or he may have been down already from one of these other bullets.
- The irregular entrance wound in this man's back means that the bullet had probably already struck something else and was yawing. People were shot in the back more often than not at Attica, but, of course, the man could have been spinning when shot.
- This little entrance wound does not look serious, but the bullet severed the main artery in the man's abdomen. Probably little could have been done to save him under the best of conditions.
- The white circle you see on the X-ray inside the pelvis is probably a shotgun pellet, though it could be a pistol bullet directly facing the camera.
- This man's smashed wrist, together with the jagged entrance wound in his chest, is consistent with a single rifle shot as he held a knife to the throat of a hostage. Could this man have attacked any one after receiving this wound? You never know. Some people would lie down and die, but now and then someone will run a block after he's been shot through the heart.
- This .38 bullet traveled through the musculature of the man's back and probably would not have killed him. Any bullet wound can eventually prove fatal, but we'll call it a nonfatal bullet. What killed him was this other .38, which traveled upward through his chest and came to rest against his spine.
- The size of the hole in this man's neck (viz., the one-and-a-half inch oval) and the absence of powder burns mean that he was shot at from between three and ten feet. I'd say about five feet. Several of the pellets fractured the vertebrae in his neck, killing him instantly. Otherwise, he might have lived another ten minutes, no longer, on account of the bullet in his chest.

Baden often said that something was "consistent with" something when he could not say for certain how it happened. Saying for certain was what the other evidence was for, when we had it. I wondered what so many inmates were doing to get shot in the back, certainly not all spinning around. X-rays of people killed by .270s characteristically showed a cone of disintegrating silvertip. I used to wonder how you got all those fragments out of someone who lived. The answer is that, short of amputation, you didn't. Living with the fragments would have been preferred, I suppose, by a surviving inmate who had his penis shot off. The bullet that entered an inmate's right buttock was the one that severed the main artery in his abdomen. It troubled me, among other things, that someone who was shot in the ass could die so easily. Don't we consider that almost funny? Troopers who swore they remembered little else of the retaking recalled the black inmate with the empty slits gazing upward, as if from hell, at the sky over Attica.

Analyzing each shot by each shooter had to be done, reckless endangerment or no reckless endangerment, public report or no public report, destruction of evidence or no destruction of evidence. With 128 people shot, it was as important for us as prosecutors to search for what had gone right as for what had gone wrong. Not to mention that everyone knew that the Investigation had indicted sixty-two inmates and zero police. Shortly after Attica, Governor Rockefeller formally issued an Executive Order directing Attorney General Lefkowitz to investigate any and all crimes connected with the riot and the retaking before one or more grand juries. The Governor's order was fair. His public statements usually were. It plainly applied to any and all crimes by law officers as well as by inmates. It had to. It served as the charter for the Investigation, our marching orders, our reason for being.

Equal justice under law is a basic principle of America. Equal justice, impartially applied, differentiates us from the pharaohs' Egypt, Hitler's Germany, Stalin's Soviet Union. Any nation can prosecute the people it "knows" are guilty, or that it otherwise does not like. It takes an advanced nation, a just, a great nation to apply the law equally, without fear or favor, to rich and poor, powerful and weak, favored and disfavored, officer and inmate. I learned that in high school civics, and earlier from a radio adventure called *Mr. District Attorney*. If all this were as obvious as it should be, people would stop asking me how I could ever defend a person I know (how?) is guilty (of what?). And they would stop seeking ways out when I wanted to prosecute an officer against whom there was probable cause to prosecute. The same law, the same vigor of enforcement, and the same unwillingness (or willingness) to accept excuses apply to officers and inmates who may have committed crimes. In theory. In fact, equality exists only when the people who enforce the laws, and their constituents, want it to.

Earlier in 1973, Tony and three of the more senior assistants had done an analysis of the shots fired. Each had written a memo on the shooters he had studied. So why was Tony repeating the job? Those earlier memos rested almost exclusively on what each shooter had reported about himself, without reference to the photos, witness statements, and other extrinsic evidence in our files. First the BCI detectives, and later our own OCTF investigators, had simply written down what each shooter had to say on his own behalf, with few if any clarifying or follow-up questions by the interviewer. Had each shooter told the truth and not tried to protect himself? The assistants accepted the statements as uncritically as the interviewers had. Even where a trooper admitted an unjustified shot, as a number did, the lawyers usually failed to raise the possibility that the officer had committed a crime. Reading those memos by those special assistant attorneys general, I did not wonder that Tony ordered the work redone. Their inadequacy slapped you in the face. If those memos were the only prosecutorial analysis of 128 shootings, that fact alone would cry, Cover-up!

With one exception. Of the four lawyers, only Tony appeared to have done a conscientious and intelligent job. He analyzed many shots in terms of their clear impropriety and raised serious questions about others where serious questions struck me as existing. Not that the other three assistants were necessarily *trying* to cover up. Not that they were stupid. But they struck me as not wanting to take a hard look at whether the cops had committed crimes. I expect they did biased, superficial, unprofessional, and slipshod work in relative innocence. Why dig when you can see what you're looking for on the surface?

Frank Cryan made what struck me as an outstandingly strained but otherwise typically propolice argument one sunny afternoon in Tony's office. Was a trooper up on the A Catwalk justified in shooting an inmate who was just standing down in A Yard? There were few inmates, no officers, and no hostages in A Yard. Tony, Ned Perry, and I said no. Frank disagreed. He explained that the inmate probably had a knife and may have intended to run into the door in the middle of D Tunnel, run the fifty yards down the tunnel to D Block, run up the stairs, run the hundred yards of open catwalk back to Times Square in the face of the dozens of guns in A Block and on A Walk, and try to knife one of the hostages on the far side of Times Square. Thus, this seasoned prosecutor concluded, the inmate standing in A Yard posed an imminent threat to the lives of those hostages, and it was okay to kill him in order to save them. I called this "Cryan's Run." Its logic would have justified slaughtering all 1,200 inmates in D Yard.

Not that Frank's argument should have come as all that big a surprise. Police and prosecutors are natural and working allies. Comradeship grows during their common battle against crime. Each depends on the other to make his efforts matter. When the cop becomes the criminal, it may be only natural for the prosecutor to remain his ally and to excuse him, heart ruling head, loyalty to person ruling out loyalty to principle, and duty and fairness be damned. If the retaking of Attica shows how brutal we can be, the prosecution shows how tribal we can be. And shows the need for truly independent prosecutors and investigators when police conduct is at issue.

A problem in analyzing the Attica Investigation is sorting out conscious cover-up from innocent cover-up. The former arose from an intent to deceive, the latter from a desire to be deceived. Each, I suppose, supported the other on occasion in the same person at the same time. As of early 1974, I saw a majority of our prosecutors as wanting to be deceived about the crimes by cops, to cast themselves unasked into the role of the cops' defense counsel—eager to accept, to rationalize, to overlook, to condone, to go blank on what our job was.

Law and order apparently mean different things to people of different temperaments. Among those inclined to become prosecutors, the more common emphasis may be on order. It confuses order to prosecute a law officer, even though the law may require it. Prosecuting a large number of law officers is probably more unsettling than prosecuting a single renegade cop. We depend on the police to protect our property, loved ones, and selves from people like three-quarters of those slain at Attica. Plus, the officer is an authority figure.

In any event, most of our prosecutors who declined to prosecute criminal cops struck me as starting in the innocent category—not unlike much of the public who wanted to forget Attica quickly. As time and the Investigation wore on, it must have been increasingly hard for an assistant to know what was happening and call it innocent. But it was easier and safer to mind one's own business (of prosecuting inmates) and protect one's self from knowing too much. That is what I saw most of them do. Like the Good German.

Once, when Tony and I had been discussing the intentional cover-up by the State Police, he paused and asked me if I thought it really existed. I knew enough facts by then to be convinced that it did. I told him about the scene in the movie *Deliverance* in which Burt Reynolds is leading his intrepid band of city slickers in search of the river they intend to canoe on. "We'll find it," Reynolds says heroically. One local yokel remarks to another, "It's only the biggest fuckin' river in the state." I told Tony the State Police cover-up was only the biggest fuckin' river in the state. He repeated musingly, "Only the biggest fuckin' river in the state."

The destruction of evidence by the State Police definitely hurt us at the shooter conferences. That was why reckless endangerment was the most common crime for which we recommended indicting troopers.

The shooters had commonly given two statements, one to BCI investigators within two days of the assault, and one, the OCTF statement, to Mike McCarron and Tom Dolan, our investigators assigned to the 128 shootings. The State Police refused to let their shooters talk with Mike and Tom unless they were being chaperoned by a BCI detective. The BCI had kept nearly all the statements in longhand, which made them a chore to read. Sometimes an officer gave additional statements, some giving as many as five. Without exception, as I recall, the later the statement, the more it justified the shots it described. Improved stories meant inconsistent stories. One or another was not true.

It was the assistants' job to figure out which statements were true or false or garbled. We could usually draw a reasonable inference about this from what we already knew, but finding sufficient evidence to prove a case was not so easy. The question recurred whether we could prove guilt, not to a mathematical certainty, but beyond a reasonable doubt. You cannot ask a jury to decide an individual's case from the "feel" that you as a prosecutor get from studying the evidence in all the cases combined. I would sit in my office, my feet on the desk and my lap full of statements, and wonder at the officers' lies.

The troopers' statements were of enormous help in that they identified so many shooters. Many people have asked me how you can possibly identify who fired specific shots years ago in all that confusion where they all wore gas masks and the same gray uniforms. The answer in scores of cases came from these signed statements, admissions, demiconfessions. Inadequate as they were in many ways, they told which assault detail the shooter belonged to, how he was armed, where he said he was when he fired, and his version of why. How do you know who shot whom? Scores of shooters' statements gave the key, at least, to who shot *at* whom.

Time and again, the assistant reporting his cases at the shooter conferences said that all of a trooper's BCI and OCTF statements were consistent with one another. This surprised me. The statements of my own A Walk troopers often varied from one another significantly, sometimes so much that it sounded as if different men had given them. Why should my troopers lie or embellish so much more than the troopers assigned to other assistants? I checked a few of the statements they reported as being "all consistent" and found significant discrepancies there, too. I discussed all this with Tony, who assigned Don Schechter to check it out but reassigned him before he had finished.

Tony sometimes expressed concern that some of the troopers may have claimed shots they did not fire, lying, as it were, in order to share in the glory. We had heard about officers bragging on September 13 around the prison or at the Batavia Holiday Inn about how they "got me a nigger." The danger of indicting an innocent braggart did not concern me. It would be one thing to brag in a bar that night, another to do it soberly two days later while giving an official statement to a BCI detective. If the trooper had merely been bragging, I felt he could explain that to a jury

Tony was particularly appalled at several officers who admitted in their statements that they fired at inmates who were running down B Catwalk toward B Block. There weren't any hostages in that direction, Tony expostulated, and no troopers; these inmates had to be seeking safety, to be *removing* themselves from where they could threaten anyone. The officers who fired at them were almost certainly committing crimes, as Tony and I saw it. Some assistants disagreed— the logic of Cryan's Run.

If a majority ruled, we all understood that any vote on what cases to present to the grand jury would turn largely on who voted. A panel of Tony, Ned Perry, Charlie Bradley, and me, for example, would almost certainly vote for more cases than a panel of Tony, Frank Cryan, Bill Nitterauer, and Jim Grable. These office votes would not determine the number of actual indictments, but only the number of cases that we would present to the grand jury for *their* vote on whether or not to indict. Given the biases in the office, a vote of the entire staff would probably mean very few cases for the jury to consider.

Prosecutors generally have enormous discretion to follow their biases—to "not see" obvious facts, to take silly conclusions seriously, and otherwise to pervert justice to their emotional bent—when it comes to *not* prosecuting, *not* presenting available evidence, *not* asking pertinent questions, *not* going forward. The law has various safeguards to help prevent prosecutors from acting improperly, but (unless a case hits the newspapers) there is little to stop them from improperly failing to act.

I told Tony the story of the time President Lincoln's whole cabinet voted one way and he voted the other, and he won. Tony seemed not to have been thinking in those terms. He acted somewhat startled that I was telling him that he could alone make the decisions or overrule any vote that went against his judgment. I thought he would have known he had that power.

I also urged Tony that whenever there was a close question of whether or not to let the jury decide on an indictment, let them decide. Let it be their judgment, not ours. Tony said he agreed.

In the more usual "street" situation, the evidence of a crime and against a suspect is often so simple that indictment is the sound and obvious choice. However easily a prosecutor may be able to persuade a grand jury to vote for indictments in other contexts, to act as a "rubber stamp" even in questionable cases, none of us had reason to feel we could get indictments automatically against the police at Attica. Tony and I often discussed our expectation that any Attica grand jury would take a close independent look at the evidence before it would indict a law officer—the same close independent look a grand jury *should* take in any case.

We hear a lot about the theory that everyone is presumed innocent until proven guilty. Perhaps stronger in many people's minds is a touching faith that prosecutors don't prosecute people unless they're guilty. The stellar defense lawyer Clarence Darrow used to rail against this faith. We hear less against it today.

A grand jury ordinarily has no more evidence to work with than the prosecutor chooses to bring it. The Attica jury was no exception. For all the evidence on the shootings that had thus far been presented, far more in our files had not. Very little had been brought to the jury that contradicted the self-serving justifications of the shooters. Though Edward Hammock had labored hard to indict a few shooters, no one had presented the bulk of the evidence on possible shooting felonies to a jury systematically or at all. Apparently, no one had been given an assignment to do that. The "handle" had not been found to make it matter. By allowing some shooters to tell the jury their versions unchallenged, and by reading the statements of other shooters to the jury with no effort to add the evidence that showed that the justifications could not have happened, the Investigation had (knowingly or not) set up the jury to endorse the ultimate fiction that the troopers, faced with attacking fanatics, had done a superb job.

Now, however, it was different. Tony's February 21, 1974, memo to the shooter cases team spoke of interviewing marginal shooters (i.e., those against whom a case looked doubtful) to see if they would cooperate with us. Tony wanted to make a deal with them, if possible, to give evidence against other troopers.

In a memo of February 22, Tony listed thirty-two cases against troopers and guards that "are tentatively recommended for true bill," meaning indictments. They include a few attempted murders, a few perjuries, and mostly reckless endangerments. Tony tentatively listed two more officers who had already been no-billed by the jury on murder charges for reconsideration and indictment. Another of Tony's memos, also of February 22, suggested five more indictments and twelve no bills.

My notes of February 25 show that of the shots we had studied by then, fifty-five could be considered criminal, sixteen looked like no bills, thirteen merited report and reference for possible administrative action, and for forty-two we had only enough evidence to write them up in the forthcoming grand jury report. That covered only 126 of the 450 or more shots that we knew about. My notes showed that Tony concluded: "Evidence of actual resistance by inmates, outside shooters' statements, is almost nonexistent. . . . Patterns of embellishment on question of justification. . . . Patterns of false official statements."

As far as I could tell, all of the assistants who attended the shooter conferences expected that a lot of troopers and maybe a dozen guards would be indicted. The assistants varied mainly in their satisfaction, apprehension, or indifference. By late April we had approximately seventy State Police and prison guards lined up for possible indictments by a grand jury. We had still not considered a large number of the admitted shots and alleged justifications.

During the days that Tony and I redictated the shooter memos recommending indictments, I thought of the movie *Z*. Jean-Louis Trintignant, as the quiet bespectacled prosecutor, questioned Greek officials about a political assassination. The keys of the typewriter beside him pounded like tiny trip-hammers of justice. One after another uniformed official found himself indicted. In the winter of 1974, the Attica Investigation had finally gained momentum, our typewriters reaching the tempo of the typewriter in *Z*—only words, but words that promised to give substance to the ideal of equal justice. I did not concern myself with who besides the guilty officers stood to lose by a fair and even-handed prosecution of the crimes at Attica, or what they might do to avoid the loss. In *Z* the prosecution was aborted, the prosecutors and witnesses finding themselves demoted or dead, but that had happened in a totalitarian Greece. Tony and I were doing our job in the land of the brave and free.

Chapter Twelve

Trouble Ahead?

An odd meeting gave rise to my only real fear that winter that the prosecution of police crimes would go awry. Tony called me into his office for one of our frequent closed-door conferences. He said he had a message that the Attica Brothers Legal Defense wanted to discuss an overall settlement of the inmate cases. He named a prominent New York Republican (whose name I am no longer sure of) who, he said, had been contacted by a lawyer named Victor Rabinowitz on behalf of the ABLD. The ABLD, on the other hand, always claimed it was the State (i.e., Rockefeller people) that initiated the talks. Both, of course, wanted the Attica prosecution to go away.

On February 28, Tony told me we should make it clear that if the ABLD could show us we had indicted any inmate who was innocent, that defendant would have "no problem"; we would ask the court to dismiss him. I agreed. Tony said he was afraid that they would use the meeting to make a "record" for some wild assertion. We decided to ask them to keep the meeting secret and, beyond that, to take the risk. (They never used the meeting as a basis for wild assertions.) I suggested that we explore whether some of the inmate defendants or their defense witnesses could help our cases against the shooters. The ABLD obviously had better communications than we did with inmates who saw and survived the shootings. Tony agreed.

The meeting came on a rainy Saturday, March 2, in the plush, dark, empty offices of Botein, Hays, Sklar & Herzberg, a prestigious Park Avenue law firm that constituted "neutral ground." Tony, Max Spoont, and I represented the prosecution. Don Jelinek and Haywood Burns, a criminal law professor at New York University who was taking over Jelinek's job as coordinator of the ABLD, represented the defendants. Victor Rabinowitz was there more or less neutrally on the inmates' side. *New York Times* columnist Tom Wicker was there at the start, but he excused himself after both sides agreed on secrecy, since this might conflict with his duty to report news.

After Tony and Jelinek talked a while, Victor Rabinowitz proposed that we all take the stance of statesmen and agree on a general amnesty for Attica. "Let's put Attica behind us." That was the first time I heard the amnesty proposal. Beneath the mask that one strives to keep at such meetings, I was shocked. Inmates had committed murder, rape, kidnap, and assault at the riot. Either you prosecute crimes or you don't. Where was the evenhanded administration of justice if you washed the Attica inmates? Why prosecute street crime, white-collar crime, or Watergate? Tony and Max weren't buying amnesty that day, either. Max spoke eloquently about administering justice.

As the meeting wore on, Tony seemed to be covering all we had planned to cover except the possibility of finding witnesses to the officers' crimes through the ABLD. That puzzled me a little. I had been silent up to now. I whispered to Tony about raising it. He said go ahead. I did. Jelinek and Burns said they would consider it, though they did not hold out hope of results. (Long afterward, they and Rabinowitz told me they had not considered my proposal sincere.)

Back in Max's hotel room, he broke out a new bottle of scotch. We rehashed the meeting as the rain poured down outside. The conversation took what struck me as a dangerous turn. Max began to argue that we'd never get a jury to convict troopers where no one was hurt! Two months earlier Max had phoned specially to tell me that he agreed that reckless endangerment applied to the shootings at Attica. Incredibly but clearly, he was now reversing himself and attacking the effort to apply it. If he convinced Tony, I saw the prosecution of the main criminals disappearing down the drain. Max, how could you?!, I thought but did not say.

Tony had built the shooter conferences around reckless endangerment. It was not that no one was hurt. One hundred and twenty-eight were hurt, thirty-nine of them fatally. Could Max be right about the juries? If so, let the juries prove it, in full view of the evidence and the world. I was appalled at the specter of prosecutors deciding in a hotel room over a bottle of scotch what the juries would do with the butchery of Attica, and depriving them of any chance to decide for themselves.

In the past Tony had generally deferred to Max on questions of law and sometimes judgment. More recently he had deferred to me, but this was the first time that Max and I had opposed each other. Had I possibly gone ahead of Max in Tony's eye? And did it matter? Tony had ample ability to think for himself. During the shooter conferences he had repeatedly shown his commitment to prosecuting for reckless endangerment the scores of officers who deserved no less and, in many cases, more.

That afternoon or later Max also stated that "it would be politically impossible" to convene a second Attica grand jury. The conversation turned to other subjects and grew less cogent as the scotch sat lower in the bottle. Fearful for the Investigation, I took the train home.

Monday dawned a better day. Tony held fast. The prosecution of officers for reckless endangerment would proceed. The secret settlement talks with the ABLD sputtered on through sporadic phone calls for the next five weeks and came to nothing.

* * *

As I look back on the stimulating routine that winter of preparing to administer justice to the law officers, a number of other events stand out against the background of what happened later.

At one point Tony began to talk about "putting the troopers into the other end of the pipe." By that he meant arresting them first and asking the grand jury to indict them afterward. As prosecutor he could do that. Making the arrests first would put great pressure on us to secure the indictments rapidly if at all. It would create a hue and cry. I imagined the headlines, the statements and posturings in the press, if we placed several dozen New York State Police under arrest. But it would show the grand jury and everyone else our conviction that many officers had committed serious crimes. It would also show them (as I recall, Tony thought they might need to be shown) that they had no hidden assignment not to indict law officers.

I liked the boldness and commitment of this proposal, which Tony was discussing with me and turning over in his own mind, but I feared it would backfire on account of the technical difficulties of presenting a large number of cases to the jury quickly. The idea was eventually dropped, before we reached such nuances as which troopers merited arrest and who would be asked to arrest them. To me the fervor and force with which Tony approached the idea, even though it was well to drop it, showed him at his best, determined to go forward without fear or favor and let the chips fall where they may.

I felt, incidentally, that any trooper against whom we presented a case should be given a chance to tell his story and be questioned about it in the grand jury before they voted whether or not to indict him. Tony told me that law and custom give this risky chance to reputable citizens who may be facing prosecution, and he thought the troopers should have it, too. At the time I accepted this as how things are, wondering only later how it squared with the notion of equal justice for all.

On February 24, the papers reported that a federal grand jury was finally taking up the 1970 fatal shootings at Kent State, long after a local grand jury had indicted some students who may or may not have done the "provoking," and exonerated the National Guardsmen who did the killing. Then and at some other times I discussed with Tony my concern that if we did not do our job right, federal prosecutors would come in and do it for us. I did this as a quiet goad that I hoped he did not need.

Tony called me into his office one day, door closed, and asked if I thought Frank Cryan was "a Rockefeller plant." He did not say why he suspected this or how Frank could be serving Rockefeller except perhaps as a spy. I knew of no basis for Tony's suspicion, though it did not strike me as particularly bizarre for Tony to wonder. He was often suspicious. How much of it came from his nature and how much from his experience I cannot say. He went through a suspicious phase about others at the Investigation, and eventually, I suppose, about me.

An assistant named Louis Aidala, a dapper dresser with an elegantly waxed moustache, worked on the homicide of William Quinn. Some State Police were helping him to make that case while I was working to indict other State Police. Eventually, he won the only victory a trial jury ever gave the Investigation against inmates, convicting inmate John Hill (known on the defense side as Dacajeweiah, his Native American name) of murdering Quinn.

I respected Louis's abilities and thought it surprising that winter when he started to talk in favor of one of Tony's strangest theories, what I came to call "the Divisible Lie." As noted before, the heart of most of our reckless endangerment cases was the shooters' signed admissions that they shot at somebody, coupled with the fact that the photos and other evidence showed that their claims of shooting to save their own or somebody else's life were false. That left the troopers intentionally shooting at people without justification: reckless endangerment.

First Tony and then Louis Aidala started saying that if the shooters lied about their justification, then their admission of shooting at someone had to be thrown out, too—as a "divisible lie" rather than lie coupled with truth. So no case. This argument left me very quietly flabbergasted. Another seasoned prosecutor I talked with confirmed that Tony and Louis's theory was nonsense. The law I looked up said that not only was it nonsense but that the troopers' "false exculpatory statements" constituted further evidence against them since these lies showed their "consciousness of guilt." The theory is that people don't generally make up an excuse unless they feel they need one.

I told Tony I was going to do a memo on this, though I did not finish it until the next fall. There seemed to be no hurry since its bottom line was not in doubt. Though Tony never told me he was giving up his strange theory, he let me go forward with shooter cases as though he never doubted the evidentiary value of officers' admissions that they had shot at people.

Tony's analysis of "the Divisible Lie" was one of many little puzzles or disharmonies that developed along the busy way. They buzzed quietly, mostly inaudibly, in the back of my mind without changing my trust in Tony or in the ultimate soundness of the Investigation during the bustle and progress on prosecuting the police. That's how life is, at least for me. Some things that don't add up now, do later. Some things never add up. Most things don't matter.

Tony and I continued to be good office friends. We often ate lunch together, sometimes with Ned Perry or Louis Aidala or others. When we talked about Attica or about life, we usually shared similar points of view and appreciated what the other was saying. Tony spoke of having been a loner in Hogan's office. I had been somewhat of a loner. Mindful of each other's faults, we respected each other's abilities. We shared a common purpose.

"The bottom line" was a phrase I used a lot then, as so many people did. For some reason Tony began attributing the phrase to me. "The bottom line, as Malcolm would say. . . ." One reason I used it was to try to shorten my daily or several-times-a-day conferences with Tony. The subjects were always fascinating and "important"—Attica had this way, too, of holding people, a morass of fascinations, one subject leading half-finished to the next, and none resolved if you didn't take care. Also, I enjoyed the importance that Tony gave me in the Investigation. But the conferences cut into the work I was always behind in. The bottom line was that the phrase shortened the talk, but I remained behind.

In March 1974, Tony decided to ask several State Police commissioned officers down for some Q and As about the retaking of the prison and the State Police cover-up. A "Q and A" simply means taking a person's statement in question and answer form—a deposition. It is a way to practice the venerable investigative technique called asking the witness what happened. During the two-and-a-half years since the retaking, no one had asked these officers the questions Tony had for them now.

For all my studies of Attica, my direct contact with the New York State

Police had been limited to weighing the crank handle with the tense detective at Batavia and receiving a speeding ticket on the way home from skiing several years earlier. On the day of the first Q and As I saw the two officers stride into the end of our dim and dingy hallway, large men in their pressed grays, physically impressive even without their quaint and imposing Smokey Bear hats. The impact of their bearing put me one down. The New York State Police tend to be physically big. Bearing and appearance, not to mention pride, go with their job. Not until I started questioning one of them with a court reporter tapping out a transcript—I doing my thing and the officer not doing his—did my awe disappear.

Tony demonstrated his abilities as an examiner on another pair of commissioned officers. I was questioning one of them in my office when Tony, who often vented his impatience, came in and took over. He continued (with me intermittently resuming the questioning) alternating one officer and then the other, sometimes shouting but more often calm, until well into the evening with no hint of slackening or (more importantly to me) eating. He shook the officers and virtually undid the woman at the stenotype machine. Before he let her go, he had me read her the statute that made it a crime to disclose anything she had transcribed. She left in tears.

Tony's questioning that day showed less system than mine, but more drive, incisiveness, and economy. Questioning a witness fascinated Tony. I always enjoy watching a good examiner and did then. He had the art of fencing off the information he wanted with simple sharp questions that gave the witness little or no room to squirm and made him say more than he may have wanted to.

Tony told me that something big had happened among some State Police officers in a diner in the early morning hours a few days after the riot. That meeting, according to what a high-ranking State Police detective had told Tony in September 1971, held the key to a big part of the State Police cover-up, to the murder of inmate Kenneth Malloy (the one with his eyes shot out), and to a report that one of Malloy's killers had given about taking a shotgun from an inmate, a report that the killer soon admitted was false. The high-ranking detective had told Tony that he got "the answer" at that meeting in the diner, the answer to what, he had not said. One of the men whom Tony questioned so long in March 1974 told us he had been sitting in the diner at that meeting. To my surprise, Tony stopped the questioning short of asking him what happened. Why Tony stopped then, I never knew. He told me he was going to pick that up next time we questioned the man. Next time never came.

In his search for evidence since the riot, Tony had laid a series of requests and subpoenas on the State Police to turn over all their evidence. Each time they produced a little more, which showed that they had not come clean before. In June 1972 when Tony threw the rest of the BCI detectives out of the Investigation, the State Police also gave us a file cabinet of evidence they should have given us at the start. In the winter of 1974, Tony shared the game with me, telling me to go to the top and phone State Police Superintendent William Kirwan directly. I did. A day or so later Captain Henry Williams got back to me, my first contact with that man. Then and thereafter, he called me Malcolm and I called him Captain. I guess he and I both figured it's harder to contemplate indicting someone you're friendly with. Tony and all of our other people called him Hank.

Williams was fat, serious, tough, and, when he wanted to be, one of the most personable members of the entire Attica cast. One story had it that when a toothache seized him during a party, he asked for a pair of pliers, reached into his mouth, and yanked the tooth out. I hoped it was true.

Williams was the BCI captain at Troop A at the time of the riot. A film showed him before the assault stressing to a group of troopers that none of "our boys" get hurt. His was the voice on the Command Post radio during the assault, leading some reports to conclude that he rather than Major Monahan was in command. He was the third-highest officer in charge of collecting and preserving evidence after the assault. During the first four months after the riot, Williams worked with Tony at Attica as the State Police "liaison" with the Investigation. The State Police claimed that we got Williams into that job, and Tony claimed the State Police did.

The Investigation obviously committed a blunder or worse by letting Williams stay inside it. Tony seemed willing to face up to that blunder in our current quest to learn and tell what happened. That Tony and Fischer had allowed Williams and some other State Police detectives to remain at our office and files as long as they did bothered me as early as the winter of 1974. Tony told me he suspected that Williams had been spying on the Investigation for the State Police. No shit.

Tony badly wanted to win the inmate trials that were coming up in 1974 and 1975. Having to rely on State Police detectives to do this put pressure on him not to prosecute State Police. He told me once, in defense of the decision to go after inmates ahead of officers, that he did not expect to get from the State Police the cooperation he needed against inmates once he started indicting them for their own crimes. His admission only stated the obvious. It was not Tony's doing that the Rockefeller Administration kept the Investigation so understaffed that it had to remain dependent on the help of the State Police.

The State Police often struck me as cozying up to our people, particularly with our investigators, the ex-City cops who belonged to a different chapter of the same fraternity. I suspect that apart from their assumption of being superior, the State Police felt as close to our investigators as the investigators felt to them. The State Police being *us*, it was not so serious that they had killed some of *them*, the law-breaking tribe.

Besides my phone calls to Kirwan and from Williams, Tony had me lay another half-dozen subpoenas on the State Police. I drafted catch-all clauses for the catch-all clauses, as it were, so as once and for all to get *all* the evidence they should have given the Investigation in 1971. On the return date of the sub-poenas, Captain Henry Williams and two other officers appeared in my office to make the State Police response. They brought affidavits swearing to their compliance and some more documents, though fewer than we had hoped for. I had a court reporter there to make a transcript as I questioned Williams about their compliance, as in a Q and A. I had read some of his previous testimony and knew to expect a filibuster. He did it well. To help me to "understand," as he put it, he buried me with words. I kept him more or less to the point. After a page or so of verbiage he would say, as he had not said on previous occasions, "But to answer your question . . ." and finally give a responsive answer. After a very long time, but before we had covered everything, I decided to adjourn this questioning to another day. I did not know that here, too, another day would never come, though I did not stop at a point that mattered. On reading the transcript a few days later, Tony said grimly that Henry Williams "has a problem."

Another State Policeman whom the Investigation had relied on unduly was Bob Horn, their chief ballistics man. I have no evidence on which to doubt Horn's integrity, but it was stupid or worse for the Investigation to rely as it did on a State Police ballistics expert to trace as many bullets as possible from bodies to guns to troopers. The State Police had taken until around February of 1972 to do that job, they told us, due to the press of other ballistics work. (I do not believe they were preoccupied by a war at the time.)

Bullets suffer nearly as much in a shooting as people do. Some remain nearly intact, some are torn and twisted. Nearly all bullets lose weight as they pass through flesh, losing more when they strike bone. Some can easily be traced to the gun that launched them, some cannot be traced, and some can be traced only if the expert really tries. Neither Tony nor I had confidence that the State Police had done their best work to incriminate their own. As of 1974, Fischer and Tony had not had the job redone by an independent expert.

Not that an independent expert was so easy to find. Tony told me he had tried several times to get one and had run into difficulties, such as other assignments that made the best men unavailable, a reciprocal relationship with the State Police that the expert did not want to jeopardize, etc. We sensed that if the brotherhood of the police was strong, that of ballistics experts was even stronger. An able man I finally spoke with was as knowledgeable and fascinating in his field as Dr. Mike Baden was in his. Like Baden, he enjoyed his work and made it exciting to understand.

Before obtaining this expert, we had to endure Entwistle, as I shall call him, the ballistics man Tony brought to the shooter conferences. With white sideburns and puffed-out sports jacket, he reminded me of a dapper rabbit. He was always at ease, always assured, and often spoke nonsense. He insisted, for example, that I could stand in A Block, he could stand at Times Square, I could shoot at him all day with a .38, and the bullets would have lost so much force in the hundred yards that they would just bounce off him. He said the same for 00 buckshot. This crap angered me to the point of wanting to try it on him. Later, the real expert mentioned how a low-powered N.Y.P.D. .38 had gone off by accident in Manhattan and killed somebody across the East River in Queens.

Entwistle caused one of the zingier office scandals. "Preserving the chain of custody" of a bullet is a holy ritual that law officers observe routinely. The officer who recovers it may carve his initials in it so he can identify it in court. It may be photographed. It is sealed in a plastic bag, and the bag is labeled. Records are kept of each person who has custody of it, however briefly, so that the defendant cannot raise a reasonable doubt that the bullet in court is the one that was recovered from the body and traced to his gun. It is a human chain of careful custody. The State Police and the Investigation followed this ritual. Up to Entwistle.

Two of our investigators, rummaging in the State Police garage behind their Batavia barracks on August 28, 1973, had found two spent bullets when they pulled apart the gray sweatshirt and the raincoat, stiff with dried blood, of eyeless Kenny Malloy. One of the bullets was in nearly perfect condition. Lieutenant Raymond "Sam" Slade of the State Police inspected it and said, "I guess that's the answer to your question and what you are looking for." He asked them if they had planted the bullets in Malloy's clothing, and had both of them sign a receipt for them.[1] Later, they photographed the bullets and turned them over to Bob Horn in Albany, getting a receipt from him.

We had identified two of the officers who shot Malloy, and I suspected that there might have been a third. The nearly perfect bullet should have been easy to trace to the pistol of whoever put it through Malloy. In the winter of 1974, Tony had it sent to Entwistle for analysis. Entwistle lost it. At first he tried to pass off another, damaged bullet as the nearly perfect one. Our photos proved him wrong. Then he told me on the phone that losing the bullet did not matter. That infuriated me. As it turned out, I guess he was right.

* * *

My notes of a private conference with Tony on February 14 show "GJ → Liab—60 days AGS → LL." This meant that Tony told me he had talked with Attorney General Louis Lefkowitz about presenting the evidence of shooters' liability to the grand jury. Liability meant criminal liability. My notes show that at a conference with me and seven other assistants on February 15, Tony said, "Our staff is committed to the Attorney General to produce significant grand jury action within 60 days regarding the retaking." This turned out to be a pretty fair estimate.

As the shooter conferences, the Q and As, and our other pushes to accumulate evidence continued, it grew increasingly clear that we would need to convene a second grand jury. Max Spoont had said that "it would be politically impossible" to do that. But fairness to the jurors who had served so long, and to the prospects for indicting the many shooters who deserved indictment, required us to try. This was a big enough step to require approval or rejection by that master politician, the General himself.

Chapter Thirteen

A Proper Grand Jury

Tony and I sat in Attorney General Lefkowitz's ample office on the forty-seventh floor of Two World Trade Center, near the foot of Manhattan and overlooking New York Harbor, the Statue of Liberty, and the cities of eastern New Jersey. Tony told the General of our plans to convene a second grand jury in order to present the evidence against the State Police and prison guards.

Smallish, bald, and plain, the General was gruff but pleasant, relaxed but to the point, solicitous but brief. Though he looked somewhat sleepy in pictures, alertness and casually controlled animation sparked his manner. His appearance was disarming, considering the competence within. I have heard people call him mean and have reason, recited elsewhere, to believe it; but I never experienced it in my own dealings with him.

An impression gradually grew on me that in presiding over the New York Department of Law, the General made an art out of running a loose ship. Beyond question, he had made an art out of survivorship in the three-dimensional chess game of New York State politics. He billed himself as the consumers' advocate in subway ads, yet he did not seem to disturb the Establishment. A Ralph Nader he was not. He took pride in his long service to Nelson Rockefeller, for whom he was as quick, perhaps, as Eisenhower's Nixon or Jack Kennedy's Bobby, while looking more benign than either. The avalanche always seemed to land beside him—a nursing home scandal, the Attica cover-ups, the indictments of one of his assistants and of his personal secretary—leaving him erect and smiling and, after perhaps a word of regret, going on as before. Eternal Louis. Already Attorney General when Rockefeller first ran for Governor in 1958, he had taught Rocky to campaign by eating blintzes, the man from the Lower East Side tutoring the hearty, immaculate patrician. He treasured his friendship with the Governor.

When Tony and I met with him, there was some question whether he would seek reelection because of his age. He would be seventy on July 3. He did and he won. Tony told me from time to time how much the General loved his work. After that meeting Tony also told me from time to time that the General would ask him how "the trooper cases" were coming along. It mattered that the General asked.

The reasons for seeking a second grand jury, which Tony outlined for the General, had grown increasingly sharp as we marshaled more and more evidence. A New York grand jury usually sits for one month, hearing evidence and voting on whom to indict. As of March 1974, the Attica Grand Jury had been sitting, though not every day, for two years and three months. I saw an item in *Time* magazine (January 28, 1974) on the extraordinary length that the Watergate Grand Jury had been sitting. The Attica Grand Jury had been sitting six months longer. A pair of the jurors had married. Lesser alliances had formed. The jurors had every right to be tired of serving. They had long since earned relief.

A grand jury starts with twenty-three members. It can function with sixteen, a quorum. It takes an affirmative vote of twelve in order to indict someone (i.e., a bare majority when the jury is at full strength but three-fourths when it is down to sixteen). In 1974, weeks would pass with no assistant asking John Gowrie, the investigator who served as the jury's good shepherd, to call them together in the Warsaw courthouse. It had grown increasingly hard for John to gather a quorum even in the winter. Some jurors were farmers, and we proposed to sit them during much of the spring planting. This would not be fair to try or likely to succeed. Tony and I were concerned by the fact that if the jury were down to sixteen or seventeen, even a small faction that opposed indicting a law officer could block the indictments of those who deserved it.

I was bothered then and later by the "City-liberal" prejudice that assumed propolice prejudice in these upstate jurors. Nonetheless, though Judge Carman Ball had screened them to some extent during selection, he could have done better. Tony couldn't get over the fact that Judge Ball selected as foreman of the jury the man who ran the Attica Village school buses. Prison guards drove those buses. How could he avoid favoring his people? Each time the evidence showed an officer shooting an inmate, Tony told me, another juror used to mutter, "Nice shooting." They removed him for bias.

A number of those jurors had stood strong for equal justice; and I did not doubt that, like most people I have seen on juries, the majority of them took their responsibilities seriously. As was reported after the fact, this jury did vote to indict a trooper—until Tony and Judge Fischer hastened to Warsaw to undo the vote.[1] Tony persuaded me (and I have never been unpersuaded) that the vote has rested upon insufficient evidence. It did show the willingness that the jury once had to indict a trooper. Tony used to say that this episode had "lost" that jury from indicting any more troopers. Possibly this was why the jury no-billed the trooper I had watched in the murder case Frank Cryan presented the previous fall. Wholly apart from whether the jury was "lost," we had good and sufficient reason to convene a new one.

Now Tony was telling the General we needed one. Max Spoont had called that prospect "politically impossible." Louis Lefkowitz, the consummate politician and, I have always supposed, one of the last people to let a scandal over Attica hurt Rockefeller's remaining chances for the Presidency, said no such thing. He listened to what Tony had to say with interest. He permitted us to go ahead.

* * *

Tony and I sat in the chambers of Justice Carman Ball in the old Erie County courthouse in Buffalo, upstairs from the courtrooms and the Investigation's quarters in the suite the District Attorney once occupied. Tony told the judge of our need for a fresh grand jury. He asked if we thought the present jury would never indict a trooper. While the reasons Tony had just given him for a new jury were sufficient, the judge had not too surprisingly hit upon the best part of our thinking. Tony said as much.

We agreed with Judge Ball that we would apply formally to him for the second jury, and he would repeat that application to the appellate court that sat above him.[2] None of us doubted the appropriateness of a second grand jury, but even the judge was a bit uncertain about the right procedure for getting one in the novel circumstances of the Attica prosecution, and none of us wanted to see indictments thrown out because the jury had not been duly constituted. The Executive Order that created the Investigation had authorized it to proceed through "one or more grand juries." Out of caution, Judge Ball decided to name it the "Supplemental Grand Jury." I guess that made it sound more like part of the first one than something new, and I didn't see that it did any harm. A few days later the judge had me research some more procedure for him, a new experience for me.[3] Leave for the Supplemental Grand Jury came down from the courts in due course.

Tony put me in temporary charge of the Investigation while he vacationed from April 8 through 19, 1974. Sitting at Tony's desk gave me a new perspective on the Investigation. Being Numero Uno is radically different from Number

Two. The two weeks went well, and I started some projects to organize the files, etc., that needed attention. I noticed that the office was quieter and more relaxed while I sat at Tony's desk. This was because I had less authority than he, regardless of my new physical location, and because of our personalities. Tony could be relaxed, too, but lately he had not been.

Before Tony left, I was afraid I did not know enough to handle his job for even two weeks, partly from my general ignorance of prosecution and partly from being out of touch with large areas of activity, like the prosecutions of inmates. The two weeks passed more easily than I had expected. This had to be largely because nothing unusual came up, except on one subject I knew a lot about.

On Good Friday, April 12, the news of the new grand jury broke, well before Tony or I had expected it. I had my first experience in answering reporters' questions and in providing the General with some information about the new jury so he could answer them, too. I tried to cooperate with the reporters, but between the rules of grand jury secrecy and Tony, whose general policy was to tell the press as little as possible, I could say almost nothing beyond repeating the contents of an affidavit that Tony had sworn to in support of our application for the new jury. That affidavit, which was now a public record, said that the first jury had served an extraordinary length of time and was depleted, and we wished to present evidence on "substantial additional matters." I did not admit or deny to the reporters that our purpose was to conduct a systematic prosecution of criminal officers. Neither I, nor anyone else who knew, mentioned our fear that the first jury was beyond indicting them, but this, of course, was the speculation.

The president of the State Police Benevolent Association, Patrick J. Carroll, was quoted as calling the second jury a "continuing inquisition." He said Tony was conducting a "last-ditch effort . . . to get a trooper conviction. . . . There can be no other reason for seating the new jury, because in well over a year the prosecutor has failed to come up with any evidence to link a trooper to an indictable offense. . . . [Simonetti is] obviously under pressure from various groups" to produce an indictment of State Troopers.[4]

* * *

Tony and I sat at a dark glossy wood counsel table in the Wyoming County courthouse in Warsaw on April 24 with Judge Ball presiding, and prospective jurors and the press filling the spectators' seats at our backs. At the start of his questioning, Judge Ball asked us how long he should tell the prospective jurors they would have to sit. Tony virtually assured him we expected the work to take three months. "Don't promise," I whispered to Tony. No way on earth could we give the jury the evidence we had of the crimes by the police in three months. The first jury, concerned mainly with inmates' crimes, had now been going nearly two-and-a-half years. "Don't promise."

Judge Ball called the prospective jurors to the witness box one by one and asked them whether they could take the time from their lives to serve on the jury, or had friends or relatives who worked at the prison, or had any other reason why they could not be fair and impartial. It did not surprise us that many of them knew some guards; Attica was one of the main industries in Wyoming County. Laughter sounded as the crowd recognized Franklin "Pappy" Wald, a genial white-haired retired captain of the guards who was one of the D Yard hostages, when he walked forward to be asked if he had a bias. He was also one of the guards the inmates had beaten up in the C Block office case that I now no longer worked on. Judge Ball excused Pappy Wald with a smile and no questions. The judge weighed the answers of each of the other 119 people he questioned, selected 23, and told 96 of them that they need not serve.

When the jurors were finally chosen, on a second trip to Warsaw on May 2, Judge Ball called us to the bench and asked Tony whom he wanted as foreman. They discussed three people who they thought stood out, two men and June Bardeen, a slender, attractive, quiet woman who supervised several people on her job and whom I had already picked in my own mind. Tony passed the choice to me.

"You're the one who's going to be working with them, Malcolm."

"Mrs. Bardeen." I never regretted the choice.

Tony and I were both happy with the jury Judge Ball had chosen. "They don't want to serve," Tony said. "That means they'll do a good job." If someone wanted to serve on this jury, he reasoned, that probably meant wanting to vent a bias for or against the police and guards. While predicting what a jury will do is an elusive art, Tony and I agreed that these twenty-three stood as good a chance as anyone to indict the officers who deserved it and to no-bill the ones who did not. We both believed the jurors wanted to do a good job, and perhaps to show the world that Wyoming County could do justice among its own. I never wavered in that belief, and I don't think that Tony or his superiors in the State did, either.

Chapter Fourteen

Cases against Shooters

And what were these "trooper cases" that came together in the shooter conferences, divided the office, required a Supplemental Grand Jury, provoked the
State Police Benevolent Association, interested the General, and put the question of whether we mean it about equal justice in this fair land? I cannot describe
them all and can give only a few specifics of these that I do describe. The sample
that follows is essentially what I swore to do in an affidavit in 1978.[1] I am
barred by law, soundly I believe, from using the suspects' names. According to
the evidence that we discussed in the shooter conference and were preparing to
present to the new jury:

* * *

Trooper A fired his pistol many times into inmate Kenneth Malloy in the C
Yard corner of Upper Times Square when, as appears from pictures taken a
few seconds before and after the shooting, Malloy was surrounded by troopers and apparently not posing a threat to anyone. Four .357 magnum bullets taken from Malloy's body were ballistically traced to Trooper A's pistol.
Malloy was the inmate mentioned in chapters 11 and 12 whose eyes were
shot out. Trooper A soon complained that he was having nightmares about
seeing brains.

* * *

Trooper B also shot Malloy up to six times. Cases against him for murder and
lesser crimes were presented to the first Attica Grand Jury, which voted no bills
on each. Tony concluded that the evidence against Trooper B and the fact that the
first jury had been "lost" by the time it voted on these cases warranted our making

an application to the court for leave to resubmit Trooper B to the Supplemental Grand Jury for votes on murder, attempted murder, and/or other crimes.[2]

* * *

An inmate we identify as James Robinson is lying against the wire fence on the B Walk side of Times Square. His backside faces C Block, so we come to call this "the James Robinson Tushy case." His position does not change from well before the C Walk Detail reaches him until well after. We see this from color slides that State Police Sergeant Jerry O'Grady took from C Roof during the assault. While O'Grady's slides show Robinson before and after the C Walk Detail reach him, there is a gap of one or two slides *when* the C Walk Detail does reach him. We know about this gap because Investigator Lenny Brown had the curiosity to peel back the cardboard mountings on O'Grady's slides, after the State Police belatedly turned them over to us, to see the consecutive numbers that Kodak puts on its film and that are normally hidden by the cardboard slide mountings. There is a break in the numbering that shows either one or two slides missing, depending on how the film was cut and mounted.

(Four of O'Grady's slides are missing for the time in which Troopers A and B were blowing Kenny Malloy away a few yards from Robinson and a few moments later. It is O'Grady's slides that show Malloy surrounded by troopers before and after Troopers A and B kill him.)

James Robinson is already dying before the C Walk Detail reaches Times Square. A .270 bullet has smashed his wrist and torn a jagged hole in his chest. He is bleeding to death inside. Dr. Michael Baden, who studied Robinson's wound, gave him ten minutes to live, tops, after the bullet spun apart in his lung. We know he is already shot and dying as he lies on the catwalk because his chest with the hole in it faces D Block at all pertinent times. There are no .270 rifles in or on inmate-controlled D Block.

In fact, the .270 bullet in Robinson's chest does not kill him. This is because Trooper C, who is in the forefront of the C Walk Detail, blasts Robinson in the neck with his shotgun at a range of about five feet as Robinson lies on the catwalk. This kills Robinson instantly. A hole over an inch in diameter gapes in the right side of Robinson's neck. There are several holes on the left side where some of the pellets came out. Others smashed vertebrae and did not exit.

Trooper C admitted firing his shotgun at an inmate at Times Square. He told one of our assistants that the inmate was Robinson but said Robinson was running at him with a knife. To have done this, the mortally wounded Robinson would have had to jump up from where he lay, run toward Trooper C, present the right side of his neck to Trooper C's shotgun, have his head nearly blown off, and fall back into precisely the same position as he lay before, all within the seconds between the O'Grady photographs that are not missing. The eyewitnesses to that part of the retaking saw no such activity. Tony and I concluded that it did not happen.

Some of the assistants said that what Trooper C did really wasn't murder because the helpless Robinson was dying anyway. So are we all. Lenny Brown called it "an execution." I agreed with Lenny and wanted to hear what the Supplemental Grand Jury would call it.

Trooper C admitted firing a total of nine rounds from his shotgun. We seemed to have a clear and simple case of reckless endangerment on his last one. When he reached the end of B Catwalk by B Block, a group of inmates came out the door from the block. Trooper C does not claim that they attacked or that he was threatened. He says, though, that he fired his shotgun into the brick wall beside the door a foot or so to the right of these men at a range of eighteen feet. Highly dangerous and no justification. Three years later in front of B Block, I spread my right hand and pretty well covered the pattern that his pellets had left in the brick.

* * *

Trooper D admitted firing at inmates who were running down B Catwalk toward B Block, *away* from the hostages and troopers.

* * *

Inmates had dug a number of holes in D Yard. Several holes burrowed under the sidewalks that rimmed the yard along B Tunnel and B and D Blocks. The most natural places to flee the bullets, I supposed. Among the Rescue Detail that descended the rickety ladders into D Yard came troopers who fired their shotguns into these holes. They admitted not looking inside before they shot. None of them claimed that any inmate was attacking from these holes or that they feared such an attack. Behind these troopers came two correction officers who fired Thompson submachine guns into the holes and, more dangerously for the crowd in D Yard, into tents that stood around the yard.

The statements of the "holes shooters" inspired more sarcasm and ridicule in the office than any other group of statements. I found it wonderful and odd that only one inmate, Ramon Rivera, was found shot to death in a hole. Tony said he was fascinated by the fact that none of these troopers' statements placed their target holes anywhere near Rivera's corpse. The discovery of that body had been a conversation piece among the police well before their statements were taken.

The State Police officials who read these troopers' statements at Division Headquarters in Albany apparently recognized the criminality of these blind shots into the holes. Ranking officers asked for and got "Supplemental Statements" in which the troopers suddenly chorused that they had not fired into the holes at all, but merely into the ground in front of the holes. It impressed Tony that the State Police thus violated the first rule of police procedure: Don't change your story. Besides showing inconsistency, the changes may constitute an admission that the first version betrayed guilt. Someone writing a whitewash of the police, however, could quote the later statements and ignore the first. Tony said that obtaining the Supplemental Statements showed the willingness of the top brass to sacrifice the individual troopers for the sake of the State Police image. Here are some of what we called the Holes Cases:

Trooper E jumped into a tunnel, according to his September 15 BCI statement—we thought he must mean into the entrance—and fired two rounds of 00 buckshot into it. He told our OCTF investigators on November 30 that he fired in order to force any inmates in there to evacuate the tunnel. By August 1972, his reason evolved to claim that Captain John McCarthy, the leader of the Rescue Detail, had said that D Yard might be booby-trapped, so he fired to set off any booby traps that might have been left in the tunnel—thus risking his own death if one of them exploded? He admitted to Investigator Gowrie that he had not known if anyone was in the tunnel before he fired, but he looked inside afterward and did not see anyone.

Trooper F told the BCI on September 15 that he jumped down into a tunnel that was apparently near D block and said, "Anyone in there surrender, come out with your hands up," waited a few seconds . . . repeated the order, waited again, and then fired five rounds of 00 buck from his shotgun into the tunnel. "I didn't hit anyone in the tunnel." By November 29, Trooper F had managed to recall that he had really fired the five rounds into the dirt in front of the hole, in order to flush out any inmates secreted inside. He later admitted that he had called to anyone inside to come out while he had his gas mask on, which lessened the chance that anyone in there could understand him.

Trooper G fired one round of 00 buckshot at a "dugout," according to his BCI statement two days later, and the dugout had a mattress on the ground in front of it. This constituted a warning shot for anyone inside to come out with his hands up (if he still could). Trooper G also gave a verbal warning. The "bunker" was empty. By the end of November, Trooper G had changed his target from the bunker to the mattress. In August 1972, he said he looked into the hole after he fired.

Trooper H jumped into a tunnel under the concrete sidewalk that runs along the D Block side of D Yard. He fired five rounds of 00 buckshot, reloaded, and fired five more rounds into it, in order, he said, to flush out inmates. He later changed his story to say he fired all ten rounds into the ground in front of the tunnel. He and Trooper F both say they were down in their tunnels at the time they finally remember firing into the ground in front of them. A neat trick as I visualized it, and maybe not so safe for themselves.

Trooper H was among the last third of the Rescue Detail to descend into D Yard. He said that before he reached his tunnel he fired one round at a young, "colored" male in blue dungarees and a shirt who was running at the detail with an ax handle that had a metal spike on top. No one else claims to have seen any such attacker. By August 1972, Trooper H was saying that other troopers had told him there were "armed inmates" in the tunnel he fired into. How those unidentified troopers knew this and why they were not removing these inmates themselves (perhaps by a less final solution) are not mentioned. I thought that instead of justifying Trooper H's conduct, his afterthought about the armed inmates in the tunnel made it more wanton. The issue was not whether the inmates were armed, or else why not gun down all the inmates in D Yard? The issue was whether they were imminently threatening anyone's life. All that the afterthought really did was to admit that Trooper H believed he was firing at human beings.

* * *

Correction Officer Z says he fired his personal .44 Ruger magnum carbine from a window on the third floor of A Block at the inmates' barricade down on A Walk. The bullet entered the chest of hostage John Monteleone on A Walk about seventy feet beyond the barricade, perforating his aorta, and ending his life. An accident? Criminally negligent homicide? Worse? Correction Officer Z's attorney agreed with me to let him testify to the Supplemental Grand Jury under a waiver of immunity—meaning they could still indict him for any crime he told them about—though in the end Tony did not let me call him to the jury. Other shots that Z admitted firing may have warranted reckless endangerment charges, as well.

* * *

Several troopers admitted firing their shotguns from A Catwalk down into nearly empty A Yard at an inmate who may or may not have thrown an object up onto the catwalk approximately fifteen feet above him. The object is not claimed to have struck anyone. Throwing it disarmed the inmate of it. William "Taxicab" Allen was the indicated deceased—"Taxicab's last ride," we called it. Would the Supplemental Grand Jury consider that Allen had been posing an imminent threat to the lives of the troopers so as to warrant their taking his? While I was preparing for the shooter conferences with Mike McCarron, he said sarcastically, "I don't know what they were shooting at down there." I would have voted these shots criminal, but decisions like that are what grand juries are for, and I am glad of it.

A similar event happened in D Yard below D Catwalk, though one trooper said he was struck in the leg by the stick that the inmate threw. Inmate Willie West died for throwing the stick; he took several bullets in the body, and his right elbow was shot away. The .38 bullet that ended his life traveled upward through his chest. Since it was fired from above, West was almost certainly already down. State Police ballistics failed to trace it to the pistol of the trooper who finished him off, though it traced a second, nonfatal .38 to a commissioned officer. We kept getting more eyewitnesses to this event. Tony and I used to call it the "D-2" case, meaning the second D Yard case we considered.[3] Between William Allen's death and the D-2 case alone, the jury would have to decide whether to indict about six troopers and the commissioned officer.

* * *

The correction officers were under orders, which came down from Governor Rockefeller, not to take part in the assault. (Tony used to consider it anomalous that the correction officers were considered too upset to take part in the assault but not in the rehousing of inmates right afterward, during which they committed so much brutality.) Only two exceptions were deemed necessary, two guards who were to go into D Yard with Captain McCarthy's Rescue Detail to identify the hostages. Everyone seemed to know about Rockefeller's orders on the thirteenth except the people who violated them. Most notably among the latter were a group of guards, some of whom had come over from the Auburn prison, who stood at the third-floor windows of A Block, a floor below Lieutenant William Shurter's snipers on the roof and a floor above A Walk. One of these guards was Correction Officer Z, who killed hostage John Monteleone. These guards had no legitimate targets except the inmates acting as executioners on A Walk, all of whom fell in the first seconds of the assault, and possibly William "Taxicab" Allen down in A Yard. The inmates on D Catwalk and the few across A Yard by D Tunnel could not have imminently threatened any hostage or trooper because there were no hostages or troopers there to threaten. D Tunnel's red brick mass blocked much of D Yard from these guards' view, and none of them claimed to have been trying to shoot anyone in D Yard. But any shot they fired at a person on D Catwalk or any overfire at people standing in front of D Tunnel stood an excellent chance of hitting an innocent person in D Yard. Such shots amounted to shooting into a crowd. An unjustified shot is an unjustified shot, whether or not these guards heard the order that they were not to participate in the assault. If they heard and disobeyed, that would evidence more wantonness. Here are some of their cases of reckless endangerment:

Correction Officer Y fired six rounds from another officer's personal .22 automatic rifle at the door leading from D Catwalk into D Block. He said he did this to prevent anyone from entering or leaving D Block, so as to protect the troopers in D Yard. One witness confirmed that Correction Officer Y fired. At least two witnesses, as well as photos, confirm that there were inmates near that door. Those inmates were one flight of stairs and half a tunnel's length from any of those troopers; they posed a far less "imminent" threat to those troopers than did all 1,200 inmates in D Yard.

Correction Officer X fired two rounds from a .351 prison-issue rifle at D Tunnel wall, he said, to force armed inmates back into D Block.

Correction Officer W fired three rounds of .30-.30 Savage from the Auburn prison arsenal at the wall at the edge of D Block door, allegedly to keep inmates in if they were hiding there.

Correction Officer V fired two deer slugs from a 16-gauge shotgun at a shack in A Yard next to the D Tunnel door, to provide cover fire, he said, for troopers and prevent inmates from entering or leaving. Witnesses and photos corroborate the location of the inmates and the shack near the D Tunnel door.

"Cover fire" may sound fine, but there were no troopers anywhere nearby to cover for.

Correction Officer U fired three rounds from a .30-.06 rifle, which had been given him by another officer, into the ground in A Yard near Times Square, for "coverage." Witnesses place inmates in that vicinity. Again, there was no one to cover for, much less anyone being imminently threatened.

Correction Officer T fired three rounds from a .351 rifle at the door from B Catwalk into B Block, 200 yards away, to stop inmates from entering B Block. Any inmate entering B Block would have been going away from the troopers and hostages. Another guard corroborated this shooting. Witnesses and photos place inmates at the target area, to be endangered by those shots. Tony and I considered T as murderous as Trooper D—both of them had admitted shooting at inmates who were moving *away from* the hostages and troopers. I used to wonder if maybe no one had briefed these shooters about who was where around the prison. I had trouble believing that some of them could be that wanton if they had known what they were doing.

Correction Officer S stated that he fired twice from a .38 pistol, which he had gotten from the Attica arsenal, at the door from A Yard into D Tunnel, because inmates "were standing there." I found his confession refreshingly candid.

Correction Officer R, down on the second floor of A Block, fired twice with a .38 revolver at the shed in A Yard near D Tunnel door, "to keep inmates from returning."

Correction Officer Q, also on the second floor, fired one round from a .38 revolver. His first statement says he fired at D Tunnel door to give cover fire to advancing troopers—as unjustified as Correction Officer V's shots at the same place. His OCTF statement says he fired at an inmate in A Yard who was about to throw a Molotov cocktail at advancing troopers. The evidence indicates that Q made this version up. We proposed to reinterview Q and confront him with what an OCTF file memo of February 24, 1974, calls "the glaring inconsistencies between the two statements he has given." We were also going to have ballistics expert Entwistle check a .38 slug found in William Allen against a test bullet from Q's pistol, as well as test bullets from the pistols of Correction Officers S and R.

Correction Officer P claimed to have been armed with a .351 semiautomatic rifle and admitted firing three clips, meaning 18 shots. His BCI statement of September 16 says he fired at inmates behind a barricade in the middle of D Catwalk. He gives no reason for firing. The evidence shows that inmates were there, they posed no threat to anyone, and beyond them lay the crowd in D Yard. P gave additional statements in March, May, and October 1972 in which he claimed his target was actually a "male Negro" carrying a gas gun in the same place. The photographs and eyewitnesses disclose no such person or gun.

P's many shots at D Catwalk were incredibly dangerous. The odds that he killed or wounded someone in D Yard were excellent. One of my projects was to see whether P was actually the officer who was reported to have fired into bodies on A Catwalk[4] and/or the officer who may actually have been armed with an AR-15 and who machine-gunned a hostage named Michael Smith.[5] In either event the charges against Correction Officer P would rise from a flagrant case of reckless endangerment to assault in the first degree and attempted murder.

* * *

Inmate Ramon Rivera huddles in a hole a few feet under the sidewalk beside B Tunnel not far from where the inmates' long curved trench ends in a common latrine and where the Rescue Detail just put their ladders into D Yard. The gunfire booms and echoes above him. He threatens no one. A dark pipe wavers for a moment in the entrance to his hole. Flame, smoke, and pressure explode from the pipe with an intolerable bang. A swarm of lead rips through Rivera's left thigh and into his right. His life bleeds quickly out. Another inmate who is in the hole catches a pellet in the heel. He climbs out and limps away in silent obedience to the troopers who are herding the inmates toward the D Tunnel door. Eventually, he tells us about it.

Our leading suspect in this case was Trooper A, the only trooper to admit shooting an inmate at this location. He told State Police investigators that he came upon an inmate here who was holding a shotgun, shot him with his pistol, took away the shotgun, and later turned in the shotgun at the Command Post. In fact, it had been carried into D Yard by one of the correction officers who had accompanied the Rescue Detail to identify hostages. We wanted to establish precisely how the shotgun got from the correction officer to the trooper, the most likely hypothesis being that he simply handed it to Trooper A at the Hostage Circle. Trooper A soon admitted that he had made up the story about an inmate having a shotgun because he thought it would help the State Police to explain all those shootings.

The State Police were equally creative but less ready to admit it. They tried immediately after the retaking to establish that Rivera had died long beforehand,

and that his rigor mortis was well advanced by the time he was found on the thirteenth. If he had been shot before the retaking, that would mean the inmates had a shotgun even if none was found, and the State Police could claim a mystery and assert their own innocence of more deaths than Rivera's. The medical examiners, however, thwarted this subterfuge by the police even before the surviving inmate told us about being in the hole when Rivera died.

A very high-ranking State Police detective told the Investigation a cock-amamie story about failing to retrieve an expended shotgun shell that he saw on the lip of Rivera's hole, because, he said, someone kicked up tear gas and they had to retreat, and when they returned a day or so later, the hole was filled in (although our photos showed that it wasn't). Tony saw no excuse for the shell not being picked up, tagged, and preserved immediately after the allegedly kicked-up tear gas settled, since this detective already knew that an inmate had been shotgunned to death in the hole. Of course, they also knew that an expended shotgun shell can be traced to the weapon that fired it. Would the shell, if retrieved, have shown that Trooper A had ejected it at the lip of Rivera's hole from the shotgun he turned in? If so, would that evidence have completed a murder case against him? Or would the shell have helped to clear him of suspicion? The very high-ranking detective had fixed it so we'd never know. Tony talked from time to time about indicting the detective for perjury.

The same very high-ranking detective allowed or persuaded Trooper A to resign from the State Police, ostensibly because he had lied in his statements, and had another trooper drive him home to another part of the state. Tony said he did not then have the staff to follow him. The ploy made Tony angry even when he talked about it two and three years later—but even when he had a bigger staff, he did not press the case.

* * *

Trooper I resolutely maintained that after he passed through the A Walk barricades as part of Captain William Dillon's assault detail, he fired a shotgun slug at a Puerto Rican who was wearing a blue football helmet with a yellow stripe across the top, a yellow "M" on the side, and a red cloth band tied around it and who had thrown one Molotov cocktail and was turning to pick up another from the catwalk behind him. I saw no way on earth or in hell that an inmate could have stood on A Walk then under the massed guns in A Block, much less be throwing Molotov cocktails. Nor do the photos or eyewitnesses corroborate this trooper's tale. They fail to show any Molotov cocktails (i.e., anything resembling a bottle) at that time and place, or anyone trying to throw one, or any inmate standing. On the other hand, the C Walk Detail had already reached Times Square by the time the A Walk Detail got through its barricades, so that any shot that Trooper I fired toward Times Square would have jeopardized other troopers as well as hostages and surviving inmates. A shotgun slug passed through inmate Melvin Ware on A Walk, though there is no way to prove whether it came from Trooper I's gun, and Ware was beyond talking about it. Even the State Police lawyer with whom I discussed this case in Buffalo on May 10, 1974, seemed surprised that Trooper I stuck to this story.

Trooper I said that he next fired a slug from A Walk at a big black man who was standing with a curved sword by Times Square. A tall black man with a curved sword, who eventually became an inmate defendant and was acquitted of murder, was seen around Times Square before the assault, but neither the eyewitnesses nor the photos place him there after it began. In fact, the only people standing by Times Square then were C Walk troopers. Trooper I thus admitted firing an unjustified, and probably criminal, shot.

Inside the Times Square blockhouse, Trooper I said he saw a black male going down the steep stairs holding a sword; he fired one shot at this inmate, who was probably not threatening anyone then even if he had the sword. Trooper I saw the shot strike the wall inches from the inmate's head. We did not expect to be able to do much about this shot, except that Trooper I's account of it may have placed him as a likely witness to a homicide by Trooper J outlined below.

Trooper I next went around Times Square onto D Walk, where he admitted shotgunning an inmate indicated as Lorenzo McNeil in the back of the head as McNeil was allegedly getting off the ground down in D Yard to throw a hatchet at Trooper M. To the best of my information, it was never established that Trooper M was down there then. We found no support for the claim that any inmate tried to throw a hatchet at anyone. No hatchet was recovered, and none is shown in the photos of McNeil's body lying on the mud. The pattern of the pellets that entered McNeil's head and back and sliced through his left ear is consistent with the blast that Trooper I admitted firing. Among my litany of questions for witnesses in the Supplemental Grand Jury were several designed to see how much of a case might or might not exist against Trooper I for the murder of McNeil.

* * *

Trooper J admitted firing his shotgun at an inmate who was coming up the nearly perpendicular Jacob's ladder from Lower to Upper Times Square inside the blockhouse and allegedly attacking Trooper J with a knife. Tony used to ask, "Where's the knife?" Trooper J admitted that the attacker's head had not even reached the level of the floor on which he was standing at the time he says the inmate attacked him. I pictured the inmate coming up the ladder, seeing the boots and shotgun, twisting to flee, and taking the hit. When Trooper J told this to Mike McCarron and an assistant, according to Mike, they just looked at each other.

How J said he fired was consistent with the pattern of pellets in the side of inmate Edward Menefee. A big, wet compress covered a surgeon's incision down the center of Menefee's torso, and according to the hospital records, he called for his mother and his teddy bear during the nearly two weeks it took him to die. Two State Police commissioned officers told me that a body they saw lying at the foot of the Times Square ladder looked like pictures I showed them of Menefee, though they stopped short of making a positive identification. Later, a correction officer gave me a list of people who were likely to have seen the body. (He made the list on the thirteenth, but the Investigation had never gotten it from him.) I was never to question the people on the list or show them Menefee's pictures. His murder was another case I looked to midwife in the jury, if indeed the case existed.

* * *

A lull comes immediately after the shooting from B Catwalk into D Yard to "save" Lt. Joseph Christian from an attacking inmate has subsided and the clump of hostages has fallen from left to right.[6] A group of eight or more black men armed with clubs and other weapons suddenly rushes from the corner where D Block meets D Tunnel, heading for the fallen Christian, who is lying in front of the Hostage Circle. Trooper K is standing in the middle of B Catwalk. He has just heard someone to his right fire to save Christian. Now he lets go four rounds of 00 buckshot across D Yard at this black platoon, and they fall.

The problem with this story, which sprang into being in Trooper K's BCI statement and no one else's, is that no such platoon existed. This case of K's black platoon bothered me enormously. Here was a trooper who admitted firing thirty-six to forty-eight deadly pellets into crowded D Yard at people who did not exist. He said he fired low. That's where the people were. The pellets from each round would have spread into a pattern four feet in diameter by the time they reached the Hostage Circle. I was morally certain that Trooper K's unjustified gunfire killed and/or wounded innocent inmates and/or hostages, though we could never prove which ones. I considered this reckless endangerment at its worst and wanted to see if it would bother the jury, too.

* * *

State Police Noncommissioned Officer M fired his shotgun from D Catwalk at one or more inmates down in D yard. His statements gave five versions of what he fired at, ranging from an inmate diving into a trench (clearly not justified) to an inmate running at troopers (sounds justified but did not happen). We considered cases against him for false official statement as well as reckless endangerment.

* * *

Such were the cases that Tony Simonetti assigned to me, and to some extent to Ned Perry, to present to the Supplemental Grand Jury. If the jury voted indictments in all of them, it would mean five officers charged with murder, about twenty-five charged with reckless endangerment in the first degree, plus some other charges. These do *not* include a host of other officers who probably committed felonies when they joined the turkey shoot—A Roof and C Roof and C Block .270 snipers (after their initial justified shots at the inmate executioners), A Walk and C Walk cannoneers, revelers who fired their shotguns massively at nothing but bricks and iron at the C Tunnel "happy hour," some State Police and correction officers whose main fault seemed to be that they wanted to get into the act, except that they may have killed someone—and more.

Beyond the law officers' barbarity and falsehoods, their statements disturbed me for the mentality, approach, outlook they reflect. "Cover fire," "dugout," "foxhole," "bunker," "armed attacker," "prevent inmates from entering (or leaving)," "force armed inmates back," "flush out inmates. . . ." Their fatal and often militaristic jargon bore little relation to the questions that mattered: Is the person I shoot about to kill someone? Whom else may my bullets hit? Is there a less lethal way?

It may also reflect on the all-white troopers' states of mind that although only 54 percent of the inmate population of Attica were blacks, they described all (or virtually all) of the fictitious attackers whom they invented to justify their shots as being black or brown.

Tony and I recognized that we did not yet have all of the evidence we needed for all of the cases, and that new evidence might exculpate some officers who now looked guilty. We hoped and expected to receive more evidence as we questioned witnesses in the jury and outside it, followed leads, and otherwise finally pressed the investigation of the shootings. The bottom line remained thirty-nine killed and eighty-nine injured by police bullets, comparatively few legitimate reasons to fire, and no one yet held accountable.

Chapter Fifteen

The Grand Jury Hits Its Stride

On May 8, 1974, I got up at 4:45 A.M., excited by what the day promised and fearing it a little because I had never before worked with a grand jury. That day I would start putting in the evidence on the Shooter Cases. I took a seven o'clock flight from LaGuardia through the clear morning to Buffalo, then walked across the terminal parking lot and checked in at the Airways motel, soon to be a second home. An investigator drove Assistant Charlie Bradley and me through the rolling farmland of Wyoming County to the weathered brick courthouse that stood among the freshly green trees in the village of Warsaw, the county seat.

At 10:00 A.M. Charlie and I would meet with the twenty-three men and women who had survived Judge Ball's questioning and undertaken to vote their consciences about indicting law officers for shootings and other crimes—and maybe indict some other State employees. I gave little thought to the possibility that it could go as high as Rockefeller, since we did not have proof that he had committed an indictable crime. We were busily seeking more evidence about Attica, on innocence as well as guilt, through our own investigations and now, we hoped, through the jury. A grand jury is a traditional instrument of investigation. This jury was to be largely mine. New facts had to come out as the Shooter Cases went in because the Investigation had not yet done its job on these cases. Where the facts led I did not really care, so long as they led to charging those who deserved it and no one else. I was damn curious to see where they led.

As ten o'clock approached, familiar faces from the two days of jury selection began to fill the hallway outside the grand jury room. Being terrible at new names, I went over the jurors' seating chart several times, mindful that I still wouldn't know who was who for some time. Mrs. Elaine Deazley, the juror who had been appointed secretary, took the roll. All were present. I explained the law of murder, assault, and reckless endangerment that we would be asking them to apply, put a big chart of the prison into evidence, and called a correction officer to describe what he had seen, heard, and done from Thursday to Sunday, September 9 through 12, the days before the turkey shoot. That witness was part of the background that Tony and I had planned for the jury, along with the A Roof videotape and Jerry O'Grady's color slides of the assault.

Our picture show immediately raised an encouraging curiosity in the jury. Why, they asked, don't all those pictures show anyone shooting anyone?

Charlie Bradley sat out the day in silence. He was an experienced prosecutor who had worked with grand juries before. Tony had sent him to Warsaw to help me in case I needed it. I didn't. Charlie would not return to the jury until the next October.

Simple was the word for most of the cases we had planned for the jury, but presenting them had to take time. Our investigators would read the shooters' statements to the jury,[1] a short process; but establishing that the shots lacked justification meant questioning the many eyewitnesses. Tony and I decided that I would start with the nonshooters, the State Police who went out in the assault but stated that they had held their fire. These nonshooters were refusing to discuss their recollections with us except as they had to when we put them into the jury. That made it unduly hard to learn the facts. You nearly always learn more and learn it more quickly when you talk with the witness informally first. Their refusal to cooperate made it tedious for the jury, too, since I had to explore what each witness did not know, as well as what he did, on the jury's time. Police are supposed to work with the prosecution, not against it, even when their own are involved—Attica through the looking glass.

Ned Perry occasionally took the jury for a day of evidence that was not likely to contain surprises or new information, for example, reading in the shooters' written statements or putting in ballistics evidence. Mostly, though, it was just me with the jury; Tony and I planned it that way because we wanted the bulk of the evidence going in through one person who would know what the jury had heard and still needed to hear to make each case. After asking each witness his name, rank, and present assignment, I took him through his day at Attica, including such postshooting brutality as he would talk about, and whatever happened after the thirteenth that seemed to matter. The testimony of the live witnesses largely supported the cases we had previously put together on paper, but I kept turning up nuggets of evidence that the Investigation had not previously found— because it had never asked these witnesses these questions.

The word was out that the Investigation finally meant business about the police. Up to now our investigators had driven the roads of western New York as if there were no speed limit, the State Police had winked, and, in effect, there wasn't. Now Tony warned the investigators to slow down, and they did. Over at the prison, we had pretty much had the run of the place, coming and going nearly as freely as the guards who escorted us around. Now the guards at the front gate tuned up their airport-style metal detector and made us go through it several times if necessary, emptying the keys and pens out of our pockets until we "passed." Then they made us report our business (which was basically none of theirs) to the warden, a genial man who seemed embarrassed by the new procedure, before we could get on with it. Plainly, the word had been out up to now that the Investigation had not meant business. Both times the word seems to have been well informed.

Petty harassment by our nominal allies could not dim the excitement of putting the evidence into the jury and turning up new information as I went along. Another clear May morning I asked a young, retired correction officer named Michael Smith to meet me at the courthouse before the jury began. Tony said that Smith had a philosophy that the jury ought to hear. Smith felt that inmates are human beings and treating them as such helps all concerned. More to our point, Smith had been one of the hostages whom the inmates had placed on the prison catwalks on the morning of the thirteenth, with inmate "executioners" holding knives at their throats. They sat Smith blindfolded in a school chair that had a writing arm on it, with another inmate poising a crude spear over his belly for good measure. When the assault began, the inmate with the knife at Smith's throat went down without using it. A sharpshooter killed the inmate with the spear. Another bullet, I was told, struck either a pipe railing or the concrete floor of A Walk and disintegrated, the fragments entering Smith. Tony said that Smith was a very sick boy when he saw him afterward. Those wounds were why Smith retired early.

As Smith told me about his wounds in the judge's small robing room that doubled as our workroom at the jury, I began to think that I had been misinformed by our people. Fragments? I asked Smith to let down his pants. Instead of the scars one would expect from the fragments of a single bullet, I saw four full round holes in a vertical line down Smith's white abdomen, misplaced navels of death. The bullets came out in horrible exit wounds, he told me, one or two taking chunks out of his flesh "as big as grapefruits." No wonder he looked sick to Tony. Add him to the miracle that more did not die at Attica.

The placement of the holes indicated that Smith had been shot four separate times with an automatic weapon. Anything hitting him less rapidly could almost certainly not have stitched him so neatly. They were fired from A Block, probably by an AR-15, not a Thompson, judging from what the ammunition of each does to flesh. They must have been fired by a correction officer since the State Police in and on A Block had no automatic weapons. Several AR-15s were checked out of the Attica arsenal on the thirteenth. A State Police officer had told me of seeing one in A Block, though none of the correction officers there had admitted to having one. When I reported my discovery back to the office later, an investigator still tried to convince me that Smith had been hit with only the fragments of a single bullet. How, I wondered, could the Investigation not have discovered the true nature of Smith's wounds two-and-a-half years ago? (And how could the McKay Report have missed it?)[2]

Those wounds also made it clear that Smith could not have been hit by a stray shot accidentally, as everyone had been assuming. Rather, someone had most probably aimed and fired a burst at this human being who was not attacking anyone. (A radical friend once asked me whether another correction officer may have shot Smith for his radical beliefs about inmates being human.) Whether someone had shot Smith for a reason or just on principle, it looked like assault in the first degree and attempted murder. From the shooters' written statements and other evidence, I had a fair idea which correction officer had done it, as noted in the previous chapter. I added a guard's machine-gunning of Smith to my list of fact situations to ask the witnesses about in the jury.

Working with the Supplemental Grand Jury was one of the best times I ever had as a lawyer. I gave them evidence building the cases against the shooters, usually three days a week, from May 8 through August 1. I came to regard these three months as the simple, straight, sunny phase of the jury. On Tuesdays I would get up at 4:45 A.M. for the early flight, often working on the plane and in the car all the way to Warsaw on my questions for the day, which ran from 10:00 A.M. to around 3:30 or 4:00 P.M. Then my investigator and I might stop at the prison or in Buffalo or somewhere else to interview witnesses. Then a necessary nap. Dinner with the investigators and assistants who were preparing for the inmate trials was fun, but it burned up too much of the evening, maybe six beers' worth, so I took to eating alone. Then back to the room to work until midnight or later. Wednesdays and Thursdays began with a pleasant breakfast with the investigators. We looked for the latest news on Attica in the Buffalo paper; every few days brought news even then. After the jury on Thursdays, I flew home tired.

Mondays and Fridays in the City, I planned which witnesses to call next and prepared the questions and exhibits to go over with them in the jury, always afraid I would leave something behind. I still had administrative chores as Chief Assistant, though Tony let me pass off more and more of these to others, usually to Ned Perry. I conferred with Tony whenever he summoned me, more than I wanted in light of all else I had to do. Besides the long evenings in Buffalo, I worked at home, though not so much as Tony seemed to. My agenda of legal look-ups and other projects for Tony stayed well behind. I could have asked for more help than I did, though Tony could have told me if he wanted my agenda cleaned up faster, or reassigned more of my other jobs to less busy assistants. He and I agreed that my main job now was to put the witnesses to the shootings through the jury and make the cases against the guilty shooters.

Tony kept me under a vaguely explained pressure to pump the witnesses through the jury as rapidly as possible. Maybe he was thinking that he had almost promised the jurors we'd keep them only three months, I thought, or maybe it was his constitutional impatience. Many supervisors find virtue in speed. Afterward, but not at the time, I pondered why Tony had been pressing. Haste made waste when it came to learning everything useful that these reluc-tant troopers could tell us. I stayed slightly torn between Tony's pressure to hurry and my desire to learn all I could.

Tony read the transcripts of all my witness examinations and wrote little memos of comments and further questions for me to ask and leads for me and others to follow. His supervision made particular sense to me, since I was so new at the grand jury business. This is how it should be going, I thought, this is helpful. Generally, Tony approved of my work. He complimented me for my patience with the many State Police witnesses who were obviously lying or claiming falsely to forget.

"1 don't know how you do it, Malcolm. I'd never have the patience." That was how things were with Tony then. Patience was to grow more useful.

Tony did give me some staff support for a time, in the form of Mike McCarron, the investigator who knew the most about the retaking and its thirty-nine homicides. Tony had nearly thirty investigators then, most of them working on the endless preparations to try inmates. On the other hand, I did not ask for more help. Mike would examine my lists of proposed witnesses and write out more questions for me to ask them. I told Tony how helpful I found this. Soon he assigned Mike away from me.

With white hair and a benign pink face, burly Mike lacked only the back-wards collar to pass for a priest. Inmate leader Frank Smith had taken the name Big Black; I thought of Mike as Big White. I gained particular confidence in Mike, not only for his knowledge and intelligence but also for a story he told me about his days in the N.Y.P.D. He had been called on to investigate the deaths of two people who had been watching out of upstairs windows during a riot in Harlem. The police had drawn their pistols and fired into the air, and, according to Mike, "for a while it sounded like a fucking war." Then, none of the City cops reported firing. Nobody seemed to want to do anything about an investigation. Mike had test bullets taken from the revolvers of all the cops in the area and finally traced the fatal bullets to two rookies who, he said, had been scared stiff at the riot. Mike was perfectly willing to help me now, whenever he was free.

Other investigators reacted variously to my work. The ones who exercised the option that Tony had given them not to work on prosecuting police had little to say to me but never seemed hostile. They did their job, I did mine. The rest were friendly, though we did not talk much about my work. One investigator driving me to Warsaw said he had been reading the transcript of my questioning of a BCI detective. "You really had him on the ropes," he said. "Where?" I asked him then and later. He never told me, and I had to go find it in the transcript. Another investigator, with a candor I admired, tried to talk me out of my work. "Anyone can make a mistake with a gun," he said. "You or I could. Then what are you going to do?" Similarly, a State Police lawyer used to tell me how an officer's little girl was asking at breakfast, "Daddy, are you going to be indicted?" I was always supposed to sympathize with the transgressing cop. Quite a few people, I thought, spend large chunks of their lives in Attica for making mistakes with guns.

I enjoyed the feel of being a prosecutor, as I'd put on my sunglasses and be driven away from the courthouse on a warm afternoon. Lenny Brown and I decided that the brooding tower of a telephone relay near Warsaw was really how Captain Henry "Hank" Williams and Lieutenant Raymond "Sam" Slade of the Troop A BCI team kept watch on the Investigation. That September after Nixon had resigned and been pardoned by President Ford, Lenny and I invented the Watergate Shuffle: you step right out and say, "Pardon me." Though the investigators seemed to feel that their jobs depended on following Tony's game plan, to the extent that they could discern it, Lenny was the one who I sensed was rooting for me to bring equal justice to the brethren of the law.

The investigators often had little to do but sit around the courthouse between driving me to the jury, lunch, and driving me back. Once or twice I drove myself, but I had no eagerness to drive through State Police country alone.

Other investigators shared some of their adventures, recent and back in the N.Y.P.D., during these drives to and from the jury:

- Investigators stole some ducklings from a farm and hid them in an office they were using at the prison. A guard came in. "What's that? It sounds like ducklings." "What sound? We don't hear nothin'." They smuggled the ducklings back out of Attica and set them free in the aisle of the jet flying to New York.
- An investigator, a religious man, told me how it had bothered him as a cop to be on the take. It plainly bothered him still. I was surprised to be his confessor.
- An investigator had kept a roll of coins inside his glove. A suspect at the stationhouse gave him some lip. The investigator punched him to the floor. The suspect smiled and said, "Man, you sure can hit." Two more of our investigators said they had wrung a confession from a suspect by flushing his head in a stationhouse toilet.
- A suspect told the judge an incredible story about how badly one of our investigators and some other cops had beaten him up. Afterward the suspect's lawyer apologized to them in the courthouse elevator. He said his client's story was so incredible that even he didn't believe it. The thing was, the investigator told me, the story was true.
- Some investigators expressed nostalgia for the bygone days of stationhouse beatings. With the courts, as they believed, so soft on criminals, those beatings were often the only real punishment the criminal received.

I listened. I'm only hearing this, I thought, because I'm on the inside, one of them. (To the extent that I won't say who did what, perhaps I still am.) What might I have heard from the State Police if they had reminisced in the car instead of forgetting in the jury? One trooper testified so vaguely about what he did and saw during the assault that I finally asked him if he was sure he had been at Attica at all that day. On reading his transcript, Tony talked about indicting him for perjury.

Every day that I had even one trooper witness in the jury, meaning nearly every day, a State Police lawyer based in Albany came to Warsaw to talk with the troopers before I put them in and to debrief them afterward. This had to be giving their lawyers a good idea of where we were going and how far we were getting. Tony did not like that, but he did not seriously challenge it.

Usually the State Police lawyer was a young and able ex-prosecutor named Bernard "Bud" Malone. He started out by telling me I was being unfair to the troopers because I was putting in only evidence that cast them in a bad light. I was not doing that but did not feel I could tell him. Later he told me he saw I was trying to be fair.

I had each trooper check his gun—usually by leaving it with the next trooper witness or the last one—before he went into the jury. Sometimes when I forgot to ask a BCI detective, I would see the butt of his revolver protruding from under his sports jacket as he took the witness chair. I felt freer when the questioning grew acrimonious if the other man was not armed. One day I walked a witness back to the room, behind an unlocked door on a public corridor, where we had left the other trooper witnesses. The room stood empty. His loaded pistol, looking enormous, lay in the middle of the desk. Anyone could have walked in, taken it, and used it. I asked the State Police lawyer to try to see that this didn't happen again.

Another day I was questioning a generally congenial captain who towered over me about the circumstances under which a trooper is authorized to use his weapon. The captain explained that if he had to get through the door behind me and I tried to block him, he might have to shoot me. His voice had an edge to it that I did not like. Tension rippled through the jury, as I think his tone surprised them, too. I wanted to discourage his presumption without losing him as the partly helpful witness he was.

"But you're a much bigger man," I said. The jury laughed, and he admitted that that was something to consider.

Acrimonious questioning was the exception. My approach is somewhat scholarly until the witness makes that hard. When it comes to learning from even a hostile witness, I favor my mother's adage that you catch more flies with honey than with vinegar. The State Police are a big deal in rural New York, to an extent that a Brooklyn boy like me found hard to believe, and of course the Attica area is Guardsville. Controlled anger has its uses, but I stayed mindful that as between me and the witness, I was usually the outsider. I tried to be the last person in the room to grow angry with him.

A particularly bitter examination developed with a tall trooper who seemed to be seeking the Best Supporting Actor award in the drama of the missing State Police assault photos. I felt the jury's anger rising with my own at the tall tale he swore to. The tension grew. I thought as I listened to his words that we would have to check them for a perjury indictment. Afterward, the trooper told the State Police lawyer that I was "a master of innuendo." I wondered what he meant by that. I only asked him if he destroyed the photos.

Not that the jury was proinmate. I felt them freeze against a man who had been shot during the assault, when he announced with fierce pride that he was in prison for murder. A juror had asked why he was in, and though that information was not relevant, I had not wanted to close off the juror. I could have thawed the jury, I think, if I had asked the inmate what had happened to his teenage daughter while he was in, but I didn't see any point in doing that then. She had been raped and murdered in the Bronx that January.

My controlled anger arose during a tooth-pulling exercise with a particularly difficult officer. Among other things, he admitted that he had watched the whole retaking from C Roof overlooking the catwalks and courtyards, but he swore he had not seen any shooting whatsoever. This was the dumbest lie I had heard to date. After I dismissed him as a witness, he hung around outside the jury and asked several times if there was anything else he could do for me. His demeanor now was not snotty but servile. Strange.

Making an evidence film at Attica one afternoon after finishing at the jury, I took a corrections sergeant over to where that State Police officer had stood. What would the sergeant say, I asked, if I told him an officer had watched the retaking from here and swore he saw no shooting? The sergeant looked at me for a moment. C Walk and A Walk stretched below us to Times Square, silent and empty in the afternoon sun.

"I'd say he was buying himself a perjury indictment."

A good moment came the day I questioned an officer whose penchant for splitting hairs, misapprehending the question, and giving evasive answers made him the most exasperating witness I have ever encountered. Ned Perry had found him the same way. We commiserated with each other for having to deal with him. He was also one of the few nonshooters who supported the shooter version (which was also the Official Version) of the State Police shootings as being a necessary defense against frenzied inmates. Now he swore how inmates with spears and a sword had mounted the C Walk barricade and stood there impervious to all the guns against them, brandishing their weapons to repel Captain Malovich's advancing men. I handed him our 8 x 10 blowups, which depicted that barricade during the assault.

"Why," he said in astonishment, "there's nobody there."

Those blowups, incidentally, did not even exist for the first jury. That jury apparently saw O'Grady's assault slides flashed on a screen once in two years, and that was that. I had the blowups made from the slides and found them invaluable. Time and again I saw new things as I pored over them. Hardly a day passed in the jury without using them. "Isn't that trooper holding two shotguns?" a juror asked me one day, pointing to a detail I had never noticed in a crowd by the Hostage Circle.

I used another photo as a code with the jury. Anthony Yazback, a Monroe County deputy sheriff, had taken pictures inside Attica soon after the shooting stopped. He gave a set to the State Police, who gave sets to the Investigation and the McKay Commission. We had reports that the State Police had forced inmate Frank "Big Black" Smith to lie naked on a table with a football balanced between his chest and chin, promising that if the football fell off, they would blow his fucking head off. Two other inmates were made to lie with shotgun shells balanced on their raised knees, under the same threat. Very interesting, but we had no photographic proof that it ever happened.

Now, the Investigation needed another set of Yazback's photos. Instead of asking the State Police or having new ones made from ours, Lenny Brown asked Yazback himself. Lo and behold, the set Yazback sent us included several we had never seen before. One showed Big Black lying with his football and the other inmates with their shotgun shells. Those men on those tables would have been hard to miss if you spent any time in A Yard that morning. Sometimes in the jury a trooper who had been there then would admit to having seen them. More often he would not. Then I simply handed the jurors the photo. I never told them why, and I never doubted that they knew.

"I have one trouble with my clients," a State Police lawyer told me outside the jury after we had been going for a while. "They think they're above the law."

The best that could be said of most State Police witnesses is that they helped the prosecution as little as they civilly could. I could say worse of many. The memorable events of the turkey shoot had happened nearly three years earlier, as they were fond of reminding us. On average, the witnesses who were not troopers remembered at least twice as much that mattered as the troopers did. Tony assigned Don Schechter to analyze the troopers' testimony for possible perjury indictments or criminal contempts.

Three troopers who left A Yard together through A Tunnel during the time of the famous gauntlet in that tunnel gave us a neat capsule of State Police veracity. Each of them admitted being in the tunnel with the other two. I asked each if he had seen officers clubbing inmates, who were running past naked. "No," said two of the troopers with open innocence. "Yes, I saw that," the third one said sadly.

The truthful trooper had been jumped by an inmate in A Yard a little earlier. Instead of trying to shoot him, he handed his shotgun to another trooper and wrestled the inmate to the ground.

Another insight came from a BCI detective who had worked with the Investigation during its early days at the prison and whom Tony called "very honest." He happened to mention in the jury that he had never expected the State Police to be prosecuted for Attica. I did a double take. "Why not?" I asked him.

"The brotherhood of the police."

* * *

Working in the Airways motel in the evenings, I used to tell myself over and over, "I hope they'll just leave me alone until I finish." Who *they* were I did not think about, but I believed some *they* must be lurking someplace. The image of the New York State Police faced a great stain. Dozens of troopers faced criminal prosecution. Nelson Rockefeller faced large political injury while he still sought to be President. The Investigation remained under Louis Lefkowitz, who was not only Rockefeller's long-time Attorney General, fellow campaigner, and friend, but who was also defending the State as well as Rockefeller and other officials personally against claims that the widows of the Attica dead had brought for millions of dollars. Would *they* really leave us alone to indict seventy or more State Police and prison guards? Week after week *they* did leave us alone, as I put in more and more evidence against the perpetrators of the turkey shoot. I continued to hope and to wonder if it would last.

Bringing the turkey shoot to Warsaw in May 1974 marked a triumph for the Investigation and for what justice is supposed to mean. Say that for Tony. The road to Warsaw had been hard. Though Attica lay to the northwest only twenty minutes away by car, it took over two-and-a-half years to travel that distance. For most of that time the Investigation had looked as though it would not go that way at all.

Now we were finally reconstructing September 13, 1971, in the jury. The evidence unfolded the retaking like a series of in-depth but fractured photos of the echoing courtyards. In the clean, quiet jury room as the weather grew warm, we pieced the turkey shoot together like a four-dimensional jigsaw puzzle, the fourth dimension being time. As we did, we lived it and grew angry, and suffered with the terrified and the dying.

Chapter Sixteen

The Cases Build

It was a privilege and a pleasure to work with the Supplemental Grand Jury. Except for a woman who broke her leg, they were rarely absent. Their questions, which they whispered to me and I asked the witnesses when I had finished with my own questions,[1] showed their intelligence and alertness, and that they were seeing what I was trying to show them. They often picked up points with a witness that I had missed. As the weather grew hot, some of the jurors found it hard not to doze off. A juror told me once that she fought to keep awake because she did not want to miss anything that might affect a trooper's future. A few of them told us they were being hassled by people at work for sitting on this jury; and I have always believed that they saw it as their job to right some wrongs even at cost to themselves. Many people said then and later, with such certainty that I am not sure they realized they were speculating, that no Wyoming County grand jury would indict guards or troopers. I who knew this jury never agreed with that.

While I was sharply aware of the cases my questions to the witnesses were probing, I could not tell the jury or outline a map to show them where I was heading. If I did, Tony said and I believed, I would create a risk that anyone who was indicted would claim I had prejudiced the jury into indicting him. They had to see the patterns for themselves or else remain confused as we went along. Not to worry. Their questions showed they were following. Also, when it came to vote the cases, I was to read them the shooter's statements, the testimony that bore on each case, and review the other evidence and the law that pertained. They would then see and vote on each case as a unified package.

Tony and I planned to have them vote on most of the Shooter Cases in a bunch at the end of all that evidence. In most cases we would not know if we had the best evidence that either supported or undercut the case until we had questioned all the people who might have seen the pertinent events. We always planned, however, to let the jury vote a few simple cases quite early, in June then in July 1974, in order to motivate them, hold their interest, and give them a sense of accomplishment (whichever way they voted). We also foresaw a salutary impact on the police if we got some indictments early in the process. With Tony's approval, I told the jury from time to time that they would have a few cases to vote on soon. They responded warmly to the prospect.

* * *

The patterns of the assault that emerged from the witnesses who came through the jury pretty well fit the patterns I have already described, except that the trooper witnesses were curiously oblivious to the shootings. To summarize the assault: Details of troopers advanced down two tunnels—which were really hallways somewhat higher than the ground in the courtyards they divided. At the same time, more troopers went down the catwalks that formed the roofs of the tunnels about fifteen feet above the courtyards. The troopers were launched from A Block and C Block, the two cellblocks at right angles to each other that the authorities controlled. They met at Times Square, at the center of the four interior courtyards, then ranged themselves along the B and D Catwalks on the far side of Times Square, covering D Yard, which contained most of the inmates and hostages, while troopers of the Rescue Detail climbed down ladders from B Walk and struck out across D Yard for the Hostage Circle.

Not much happened with the troopers who advanced down A Tunnel. They walked through a white fog of tear gas. They said some objects were thrown at them. They held their fire, except that one trooper, in his BCI statement and to me on the phone, maintained he had used his pistol inside A Tunnel. Everyone else in that detail whom I talked with swore he hadn't seen or heard this firing. No one was shot in there.

Some of the A Tunnel troopers fanned out into A and C Yards as they reached the doors leading down a few steps to these courtyards, midway down the tunnel. Only one trooper admitted seeing inmate Kenny Malloy being executed in the C Yard corner of upper Times Square a few moments later. The rest of the A Tunnel Detail proceeded down that hallway to where the gate to Lower Times Square stood locked, barring their passage and possibly saving their lives. The first officer I questioned about reaching Times Square admitted that he saw sparks flying on the other side of the gate, where pellets from the C Tunnel "happy hour" were striking the walls. Apparently realizing he'd said something helpful, he immediately grew uncertain about this recollection. The troopers who had been with him, whom I questioned later, denied seeing this evidence of the C Tunnel shooting at all.

"Were you aware of gunfire as you proceeded down the catwalk?" I asked the witnesses who had advanced down A Walk overhead. "Where was it coming from?" The most they usually admitted was hearing gunfire from A Block behind them. (Everyone knew that guards as well as troopers had been shooting from there.) The BCI statements, on the other hand, showed that a number of troopers had admitted firing shotguns from right beside or just in front of these witnesses.

Inmates had strung two wire barricades across A Walk before the solid one of junk. Troopers ripped down the first wire. The second one proved too tough until a big trooper threw his body across it and the others ran over him Marine-style, knocking off his gas mask as they passed. He was badly tear-gassed and had to be led out to an ambulance. This added to the evidence that the police used discriminating gas at Attica; it zapped every law officer and hostage it touched but had no effect on the inmates, allowing them to make their banzai charges into the blazing shotguns.

The big question down in C Tunnel was, why all the shooting? Some of the troopers who had been there saw no reason for it. Since they were usually standing too far back in the crowd to see what was happening up front, I doubted that their testimony helped the prosecution as much as it might seem. The Official Version had it that a tear gas projectile had come down the tunnel from lower Times Square. Troopers in front emptied their shotguns in that direction and fell back to reload while other troopers stepped forward to fire. Tony and I thought it sounded like something out of Rudyard Kipling's stories of British imperial warfare. The inmates at Times Square saved their lives by lying behind the metal apron at the bottom of that gate. We considered it quite possible that the C Tunnel troopers had simply fired on general principles, which almost certainly made their shooting criminal, and that they, reaching the same conclusion, had invented the projectile. Some new evidence led me to explore the possibility that a puff of wind outside had suddenly blown a cloud of tear gas in through the broken windows, provoking the troopers in their gas masks and high emotion to open fire. That, if true, could have helped them.

The big Kiplingesque shooting happened before the troopers passed the midpoint in C Tunnel. Once there, some of them deployed into B and C Yards. We traced Troopers A and B, the two we knew to have shot Kenny Malloy, out into C Yard and up a ladder onto C Catwalk, a few feet from where Malloy was in Times Square. One of O'Grady's C Roof photographs shows a trooper reaching the top of that ladder—before the gap in those photos while Malloy was being shot. The rest continued down C Tunnel. As they approached lower Times Square, they opened fire again. They said they saw a "flash of light" and thought they were being fired on again. The "flash of light" could serve not only to justify the later volley but also maybe the earlier barrage, on the theory that the first shooting could not have been excessive if an inmate was still able to shoot a tear gas projectile at them afterward. Tony said, with a degree of certainty that surprised me, "The flash of light never happened." How, I wondered, do you disprove a flash of light that several troopers swear to when there are no other witnesses?

Questioning for the C Walk Detail went much the same as for the A Walk Detail. It grew more interesting for both as they reached Times Square, with the executions of Malloy and James Robinson and shotgun blasts into several other inmates.

"What were they doing to be shot so many times?" the jurors asked about these inmates. I can't tell you, I thought, but time and the evidence will: nothing.

A correction officer told me that it was terrible for the police to go into D Yard firing shotguns where the hostages were held. Of course, firing the shotguns would have been all right, he thought, if there were only inmates in D Yard.

Some of the C Walk Detail, which spread out to the left along B Walk after they reached Times Square, saw parts of the Christian Incident, in which an inmate clubbed Lt. Joe Christian to the ground in D Yard, and troopers back on B Walk say they fired their shotguns to save him. A number of these witnesses also saw the D-2 case, the shooting of Willie West over by D Tunnel. Puzzlingly, none of the A Walk Detail, who spread themselves along D Walk in time and place to have seen the Christian Incident, said they saw any of it. Nor did any trooper admit to seeing or hearing a trooper put four pellets (i.e., a load that partly missed) through an inmate's thighs. Then as that inmate lay on the ground below B Catwalk, another trooper standing a few yards from him and apparently irritated by his screaming from the pain of the pellets, fired a shotgun slug through his ankle.

The testimony in the jury built another Attica anomaly. While shooters had admitted firing about 450 shots, the nonshooters who surrounded them were swearing that they had not seen or heard these shots. Since the nonshooters were all mixed in among the shooters during the assault, they were swearing in effect that those shots had not been fired. All we needed to complete this miracle was for the dead to resurrect, with their butchered carcasses sucking back the blood and closing up the holes, as in a film run backwards.

The troopers in the Rescue Detail testified more openly than most other troopers, I thought, mainly because, after Captain George Russell Tordy's A Tunnel Detail, most of them had shown more courage and restraint than most of the others. They were candid enough to recall seeing one or two correction officers firing into tents and holes in D Yard, but not the half-dozen troopers who admitted doing the same thing at the same time and place.

Sometimes I called hostages to the jury to describe the other end of the rescue mission. They were survivors, had hurt no one, and were always willing to talk with me outside the jury, altogether a pleasure after the State Police.[2] Their loyalty to the State Police amazed me. One man, who had survived a State Policeman's pellet that passed through both his lungs and narrowly missed his heart, told me fervently that he would never say anything to hurt the troopers. The shot that hit him may have been part of the effort to save Lieutenant Christian.

The Christian Incident posed several mysteries. Sometimes it seemed that there were two Christians in D Yard—a remark that brought laughter at the Investigation. Most of the witnesses place him in front of the Hostage Circle, as does a photo.[3] Some of the troopers who said they fired to protect him, however, place him fifteen or twenty yards to the right, which means that the overfire from their shotguns would have missed the Circle, which would mean fewer dead hostages and more dead inmates, which is not what happened. The second Christian may have arisen from the shooters' reluctance to admit to others or themselves that they had probably shot hostages.

According to the Official Version, Christian had raced across D Yard for the Hostage Circle far ahead of the other Rescue Detail troopers. An inmate rose up behind Christian and struck him down as he passed, forcing several officers on B Catwalk, fifty yards behind, to let go with their shotguns in order to save his life from that inmate's attack and keep inmates from seizing his shotgun and two pistols. (He was carrying an extra pistol in his belt to arm the hostages and form a defense perimeter—such were the pictures in his mind.) The police, Rockefeller Administration, and other proponents of the Official Version claimed that the Christian Incident accounted for the tragic but unavoidable deaths of eight hostages in the Circle behind the fallen Christian—unavoidable if one accepts the unavoidability of using scatter guns in such a crowd.

The further I went, the more suspect this Official Version became. We had known from the start that three of those eight dead hostages were killed by rifle bullets, though none of the troopers on B Walk had rifles, and none of the riflemen admitted firing at the Circle. Tommy Hicks was the only dead inmate supposedly found near Christian, and the only one who could have been shot while attacking him. But the few and seemingly random holes in Hicks's body did not look consistent with the Official Version. I also wondered why the State Police failed to keep track of where Hicks had been found and what his death scene looked like if he really supported the Official Version.

The troopers who crossed D Yard with Christian, however, and the hostages who saw them coming do not put Christian out front alone. They said he came with the other troopers roughly in a line, being at most only a little ahead of the others. That, too, contradicts the Official Version, but not so much as this: there seems no doubt that an inmate did strike Christian on the back of his plastic helmet. He and those near him describe this in convincingly consistent detail. Also convincing was the trooper who told me how he crossed D Yard with Christian and felled Christian's assailant with a butt stroke from his shotgun. So was the trooper next to him who told how he saw that trooper knock the inmate down. Neither of them was hit by the scatter shot from B Walk—could they have been so lucky? Lt. Christian, on the other hand, caught a pellet in the arm and a one-ounce slug that tunneled the long way through his calf. He was still limping when I met him. The deeper I went into this mystery, the more fascinated I grew.[4]

While the 111 officers who admitted firing their weapons constituted less than half the total assault force, it bears considering that a large number of the troopers who went down the comparatively narrow catwalks were not in a position to fire without hitting or endangering the officers immediately ahead of them. The catwalk details found no targets in B Yard and C Yard and only one target in A Yard on the flanks of their advance (i.e., where those not at the head of the details could get off a clean shot). With one possible exception, the A Tunnel Detail did not fire at all. The Rescue Detail, following the A Walk Detail, had no one to shoot at until they reached crowded D Yard; once there they did relatively little shooting, except for the notorious holes shooters. As to the rest of the assault force—meaning the officers in and on the cellblocks, in the front rank of the A Walk and C Walk Details, and the rotating front rank of the C Tunnel Detail—all the independent evidence we had was confirming that most of them did shoot, mostly with a criminal lack of justification. Except for the blow to Joseph Christian and whatever it was that Willie West and Taxicab Allen died for throwing, attacks by inmates that the shooters claimed to justify their carnage had not happened.

* * *

Time and again I came up with little nuggets of evidence that the Investigation had not learned before, like the machine-gunning of Michael Smith described in the last chapter. Tony's lack of pleasure at these nuggets puzzled me. His most surprising reaction came when I told him how a trooper who had been standing on B Walk wearing a tear gas pack (i.e., an army flamethrower converted to squirt tear gas instead of napalm) had shouted down to a trooper in D Yard below him to stop firing his shotgun into a foxhole so that the first trooper could gas it. Here was important evidence, probably about the killing of Ramon Rivera, and a potential eyewitness to that killing. I thought Tony would be elated. Instead, he replied testily that we already knew about this. I checked. So far as the people I asked knew and the files showed, we had never known it.

Discouragingly often the nuggets led to "nevers." Here are a few examples:

- A trooper had told us and McKay that he and troopers with him had received instructions after the assault to falsify their BCI statements and, in his words, "Cover your ass."[5] Fine, but how to corroborate this? No other trooper we questioned admitted being told it. One day I gently led an officer, whom the Investigation had somehow never questioned, to admit that he had actually given his men these instructions. The jurors were furious. Tony was furious. The officer now had immunity from prosecution, but we could use his confession in the big Hindering Prosecution Case that lay down the road and in our Report.[6] We never did.
- Our hearts wrenched one day to hear a hostage who had been slightly wounded tell how he held another hostage's head in his hand during the ride in the ambulance. He found his fingers going inside the man's skull. Inmates had taken this man from the Hostage Circle before the assault, along with the hostages they took to the catwalks, but they stood him on a box in another part of D Yard. When the assault began, someone banged a hole in his head with a hammer. Cut throats and all, that was the most serious injury by any inmate to any hostage during the retaking; but it was somehow the one least mentioned afterward. When I talked

with the victim more than two years later, he spoke very slowly. The Investigation had looked lightly into this crime, and Tony put an investigator on it at my urging, but evidence on which to identify and prosecute the inmate perpetrator was never found. (It occurred to me later that asking the potential witnesses, viz., all the inmates in D Yard, about it would have meant asking them what they saw during the assault; thus the Investigation, unlike McKay, had chosen to ask very few inmates.)

- Someone reported seeing Kenny Malloy, who was black, with white stuff on his face. The white may be visible in one of O'Grady's photos. A trooper told me how he had squirted an inmate at Times Square from his tear gas pack. It occurred to me that maybe the reason Malloy kept trying to get up (if he had) when he was surrounded by troopers was that he had caught the tear gas in the face. All the less reason for shooting him. Tony, however, was never to give me the chance to test this theory by calling the rest of the people who were there.

- Trooper L seemed more frightened of testifying than any other trooper I ever talked to. He said he had exited through a tunnel door early in the assault into C Yard. He stood facing the corner of Times Square, about twenty-five yards away, while troopers were killing Malloy there. He insisted, quavering, that on somebody's orders, he spent that whole time in C Yard with his eyes glued to the latrine door in that corner of the yard (i.e., in the outside of lower Times Square). Because his eyes were glued so intently on that door, he swore, he failed to notice that troopers shot Malloy twelve times, not six feet above it. When I made the evidence film at Attica, I had the cameraman stand where Trooper L had stood in C Yard and pan a full view of what Trooper L must have been looking at as he faced Times Square and the latrine door. I proposed to Tony that we call Trooper L into the office with counsel of his choice, show him the film, and give him to understand that he could either tell us the truth or let the jury judge his present story on a perjury vote. Tony agreed but never let me do it.

- A number of inmates claimed that after the main shooting stopped, correction officers on the catwalks pointed out certain inmates for execution, whereupon troopers shot them. The one case in which I thought the evidence indicated that this could possibly have happened was the shooting of Sam Melville, an articulate radical of the 1960s known as the "Mad Bomber." A BCI detective who followed the C Walk Detail out during the assault testified that as he was standing on upper Times Square, an inmate emerged from a bunker down in D Yard with what appeared to be a Molotov cocktail in his right hand. The investigator, fearing the inmate would throw it, fired his shotgun, putting a deer slug through Melville's chest. Another BCI detective standing beside the shooter corroborated this version.[7] First reports were equivocal as to whether any Molotov cocktail was found close enough to Melville's body to have been in his hand, though no one claims that any lighted Molotov cocktail flared up in that area. One inmate reported that he had seen a guy trying to surrender. He had his hands folded on top of his head as the loudspeaker in the helicopter said to. He was walking toward the wall. A trooper was standing on the wall. The guy kept walking toward him and the trooper shot him in the chest.[8]

Inmates often described the catwalks and upper Times Square as being the top of the wall; very few inmates in D Yard could be said to have been shotgunned in the chest. Another inmate testified that he and Melville had been in an entrenchment in D Yard until the helicopter started its surrender message:

> then I saw troopers coming down ladders from the tunnels and Times Square and start to move towards the hostages. "They're here already," I said to Sam. Sam turned to me. "Well," he said, "we did the best we could." We shook hands and I understood that we would go out and surrender. Then I heard a shot. I turned to Sam and saw that he had been hit by a bullet in the chest . . . .[9]

Significantly, this second inmate's testimony was not given until October 1975. The Investigation should have heard it years earlier, and I expect I would have obtained it if I had been permitted to do a thorough job on the Melville homicide, but that was never to be.

* * *

Tony, the jurors, and I all decided it would be for the best if the jury recessed during the first three weeks of August 1974. That ended the three months that Tony had originally told them was all they would have to sit. We had obviously come nowhere near finishing the Shooter Cases, not to mention the Rehousing

Brutality and Hindering Prosecution Cases that lay ahead. The jurors had earned a rest and needed a chance to attend to their lives. I welcomed the chance to fly with my children to visit my brother and his family in San Jose, Costa Rica.

As the August recess approached, I reminded Tony again that we had planned to give the jury some votes along the way. I said I had three cases ready now. One was a reckless endangerment against a correction officer who admitted firing a Thompson submachine gun out of A Block at several inmates who were not posing an imminent threat to anyone. Any overfire—the muzzle of a Thompson tends to rise as you fire it—would threaten the additional lives in D Yard. The second was a reckless endangerment against Trooper Gregory Wildridge, about whom more later. The third was the perjury case against the officer who swore he had looked down upon the retaking from C Roof and failed to notice any shooting.

With Tony's approval I prepared two packages of evidence for each of the three cases. Each package contained the target officer's statements in evidence, the testimony that concerned him, and a summary of the law that the jury should apply. I left one set of packages on Tony's desk on the warm Monday evening of July 29 when I finally finished putting them together and took the other set with me on the flight to Buffalo the next morning, to present to the jury along with that week's witnesses.

I phoned Tony and asked him to release me to present these cases to the jury. He refused. He never faulted the cases I had put together. He just said no, and on August 1, 1974, the jury recessed.

Chapter Seventeen

The August Switch

The day after the jury recessed, my children and I flew to Costa Rica. Total change. After a few days among the green volcanoes, purple bougainvillea, and wild city traffic around San Jose, my brother and I drove west with our families out of the mountains to their house, roofed with Spanish tile, at a beach called Flamingo on the Nicoya Peninsula. The surf is so warm you can stay in it five or six hours a day if you like, as the children did. Evenings we sat in high-backed rockers on the tiled veranda and watched the sun set behind rocks that rose like an echo of Stonehenge far out in the Pacific. One night we found a turtle maybe four feet long plodding up the beach to lay her eggs in the cool sand for the hot sun to hatch later.

Watergate finally toppled President Nixon. On August 8, 1974, the day before we left for the beach, we watched him mouth his resignation on San Jose television and heard his voice out of sync on English-language radio. On August 20, two days after we returned with our sunburns and no-see-um bites, the newly inaugurated President Ford ended the suspense by announcing that he was nominating Nelson Rockefeller for Vice President. I listened to the English-language radio give background on Rockefeller and told my sister-in-law and brother that I thought Rockefeller was the best person the Republicans could nominate under the circumstances.

I considered Rockefeller strong and effective as Governor and big enough to deal with the nation and world. He had served Presidents Roosevelt and Eisenhower and dominated New York State politics after he was elected Governor in 1958, winning an unprecedented fourth term ten months before Attica. His hearty, honking "Hi ya, fella!" signaled his energy and activism. He was a doer, spender, architect of the State University of New York (SUNY), the great university system that sprawls across the state, builder of the monumental mall at the Albany capitol, unflinching advocate of the right of every man to make a million and every woman to choose an abortion, given to facile super-latives (the troopers' "superb job"), passionate collector of art and sometimes women. I found him, by turns, liberal and reactionary, patriot and opportunist, idealist and indifferent to distinctions between right and wrong. He unleashed enthusiasm, skill, a well-honed team, and often money in his quests to get his way. He usually got it, except what to him mattered most.

"I always took it for granted I'd be President," he once said, "It was always there, in the back of my mind."[1] "After all," he said another time, "when you think of what I had, what else was there to aspire to?"[2] He had challenged Nixon for the Republican nomination in 1960 and 1968, and Barry Goldwater in 1964, the year Rockefeller stood waiting to address the convention in San Francisco through sixteen minutes of boos, catcalls, and heckling by con-servatives, gaining more respect through that stalwart silence, perhaps, than by anything he ever said. Those conservatives were plainly the ones he had to convert if he was ever to win the nomination. He rammed harsh drug laws through the New York legislature, laws that, without noticeable benefit, cost those at the opposite end of the material spectrum thousands of years in prison. (Tony and I had agreed when he hired me that neither of us would want to enforce those laws.) The drug laws were widely considered a device to win those conservatives. So was his intransigence on Attica. (I cannot believe they were wholly that.) Though he and Nixon were antagonists in 1960 and 1968, he had courted Nixon in recent years and fallen into line as a loyal party regular. Nixon had disappointed him by nominating Gerald Ford for Vice President when Spiro Agnew was forced to resign in October 1973, making it Ford instead of Rockefeller who became President when Nixon resigned.

This chronology seems important: The Watergate crisis came to its head during the first days of August 1974. On August 5, President Nixon admitted that he had ordered a halt to that investigation.[3] A story in *the New York Times* datelined August 7 was headed, "Gov. Rockefeller Viewed as the Front-Runner to Succeed Ford if Nixon Resigns." The story went on to note that "In what many have viewed as an exploratory campaign for the 1976 Presidential nomi-nation, Mr. Rockefeller has issued increasingly conservative statements on such issues as welfare that have softened his old opposition in the South and West."[4] Nixon resigned on August 8. Ford took longer to make his selection than many expected. Stories in the *Times* on August 11 and again on August 13 placed Rockefeller at the center of the speculation about Ford's choice. On Tuesday, August 20, Ford announced the nomination of Rockefeller, news that was widely greeted with relief and approval. A profile of Rockefeller in the *Times* noted that:

> Since 1971 a major topic of complaint has been his handling of the Attica prison uprising, in which he declined to go to the scene and finally ordered a trooper raid, after a period of negotiation, that left 39 inmates and hostages dead from state gunfire.
>
> "There was more at stake even than saving lives," Mr. Rockefeller has said. "There was the whole rule of law to consider. The whole fabric of society in fact."
>
> For some liberals, this affair was the nadir of Mr. Rockefeller's public service, and some observers have predicted a pressing Congressional inquiry into the Rockefeller nomination, given his critics on both ends of the political spectrum.[5]

Tony Simonetti phoned me in Costa Rica to call me back to the office early for some sort of conference that had already begun when I arrived. I had planned to return on Monday, the 26th; instead, I found myself on Thursday, the 22nd, sitting with Tony and half-a-dozen investigators in the big room with the sign that said, "Support your Attica Brothers." I tried to follow what they were talking about, fretting because Tony's whole concept seemed wrong, and wanting to see him alone so I could try to talk him out of it.

On Friday, the sixteenth, while I was at the beach in Costa Rica, Tony had written a surprising memo directing Ned Perry, Don Schechter, and me to speed up the presentation of the Shooter Case evidence to the jury and put in a new Hindering Prosecution Case against the State Police, all by the end of September; we were then to analyze the evidence in October and present cases for the jury to vote on in November. This timetable was not realistic. I do not recall seeing the memo when I returned to the office and do not recall that it was referred to during the months that followed. On Monday, August 19—the day before Ford formally nominated Rockefeller, but well after Rocky had been publicly discussed as the number one contender—the first of the Hindering Case conferences, which is what I joined on Thursday, had begun.

More than the strange names, events, and fragmented allusions that went past me during that Thursday, the strangeness and size of the mistake I saw Tony making bewildered me. *Tony was stopping the presentation to the jury of the Shooter Cases, though they were far from finished. He was starting the presentation of the Hindering Case, though it was far from ready.*

Tony had always spoken of presenting the Hindering Prosecution—or, State Police Cover-up—Case after we had finished the Shooter Cases. I learned later that he had even considered convening a third grand jury for that case. From the standpoint of effective prosecution, however, this was about the worst time he could have chosen to switch cases on the jury. We were far from finished with the State Police nonshooter witnesses and the hostages in the Shooter Cases. I planned soon to give the jury the nonshooter correction officers who had watched the assault from the third floor of A Block. I had not yet begun with the National Guard stretcher-bearers who saw things that mattered, such as which body lay where. Then there were those three cases Tony had not let me present to the jury before the recess. I had sent to Buffalo for the files of the inmates who had had the grandstand view from the south side of C Block during the assault, to see which of them I might put into the jury. I hadn't even finished identifying the inmates in D Yard who saw people shoot or get shot, or everyone else who saw the assault. The jury had not heard all the shooter statements read, or the rest of Dr. Michael Baden's testimony on how the dead had died, or the men who survived their gunshot injuries telling what happened. I had not yet tried to refresh the memory of frightened Trooper L about watching the execution of Kenny Malloy; and I had not yet questioned the people who might be able to identify the body at the foot of the Times Square stairs—two or three possible murder indictments right there. Not to mention the perjuries or criminal contempts by State Police witnesses in the jury so far. Not to mention. . . . I learned that Tony had canceled the fifteen or so Shooter Case witnesses I had asked to be called to the jury next week.

I knew parts of the Hindering Case pretty well, but large gaps still perforated my knowledge. Now Tony wanted me ready by the following Tuesday to examine witnesses I had never heard of, about facts I had never heard of, as part of a picture I saw only in part, for reasons that escaped me entirely.

Late Thursday afternoon I finally got Tony alone in his office and told him my concerns. We had at least a month more of witnesses on the Shooter Cases, I said. (In retrospect, at least three months was more like it.) We were plainly not ready with the Hindering Case. Even now it needed more field investigation, as Tony himself was soon to say. Switching presentations now would confuse the jury. I did not think it was worth it.

If we "broke" the Hindering Case, Tony replied, that should end the perjuries and evasions the troopers were giving us on the Shooter Cases. "We can break the Hindering Case and then break the Shooter Cases," he said.

I disagreed. Our targets in the Hindering Case were a few ranking officers.

Indicting them, I said, was not likely to persuade the average trooper suddenly to remember seeing his buddy shoot someone. "Our best chance to improve those recollections," I said, "is to indict some troopers for perjury!" I mentioned the officer I had wanted to indict for that crime before the recess. "A lot of troopers have lied under oath," I said. "We haven't given them any reason to think we intend to do anything about it. If we indict a few for perjury, maybe they won't lie so much." I told Tony this was a better way to reduce their perjuries than indicting a few remote officers for something else, and besides, it could be done without interrupting the flow of the Shooter Cases for the jury.

Tony disagreed. He was the boss. We did it his way.

This is only a postponement of the shooter witnesses, Tony said and I believed, not a cancellation. My disagreement with Tony was professional, not personal. I was perplexed but not suspicious. I did not see the significance of the August Switch, as I came to call it, that I saw later when I coupled it with events in the Investigation and nation. I simply thought that Tony was making a bad mistake. I did not see it then as a reversal of plans that threatened the completion of the Shooter Cases and indictment of those criminal police, or that permitted the making of a national decision that public knowledge of the facts might have barred.

Nelson Rockefeller's handling of the Attica riot may well have been the biggest single count against him going into his nomination for the Vice Presidency. "Probably the most egregious single error of judgment Mr. Rockefeller made during [his] time [as Governor] involved his handling—or mishandling—of the Attica prison riot." So said the *New York Times* in an editorial on December 10, 1974, which concluded that he ought finally to be confirmed as Vice President, on the basis, I suppose, of what was then publicly known. Whether it would have hurt Rockefeller's chances for confirmation by the Senate, and probably his last chance to become President, if we suddenly indicted sixty or seventy or more of the "superb job" troopers whom he had ordered into Attica is a question that hardly needs asking. All it would have taken to precipitate the August Switch was the fear of such a hurt by, say, Rockefeller's long-time friend and aid—and Tony's boss—Attorney General Louis Lefkowitz.

The Attica Investigation had inadvertently plodded into position to threaten Rockefeller's highest ambition, at the same time that the often-delayed uncovering of the Watergate crimes had put him closer to realizing that ambition than he had ever been before. Four of the previous seven Vice Presidents had become President.[6] If the Senate confirmed him, he would stand the proverbial heartbeat away. But like a time bomb, the Investigation ticked beneath the ambition.

I have no direct proof that either Rockefeller or Lefkowitz ordered the August Switch. Nor do I think that really matters in the scheme of their acts and omissions that frustrated the Attica prosecution. Perhaps it was entirely Tony's idea—though I have never believed this—and they and their other minions simply sat back and reaped the benefit: the August Switch assured that an unprecedented number of State Police would not be indicted for the killings at Attica during the months that the Senate considered whether or not to make the man who had ordered the assault the Vice President of the United States.

Chapter Eighteen

"Who's Going to Tell Gerry Ford?"

"Who's going to tell Gerry Ford?" Tony asked somewhat frantically the next Monday, as I returned from a weekend of wondering about the August Switch and the unfamiliar witnesses I would question in the jury the next day. "Who's going to tell Gerry Ford?" he repeated. Tell him what, I wondered. About Governor Rockefeller's involvement in Attica? What was there about it that had not long since been public knowledge?

It seemed to me that Rockefeller had taken a partially bum rap because "he did not go to Attica." Hindsight might show more clearly than could be seen at the time that by relying on the second team instead of coming himself, he made a tragic mistake. Tom Wicker, Congressman Herman Badillo, and two other Observers at the prison had urged Rockefeller on the phone the day before the assault to come to Attica in order to avert a "bloodbath."[1] Even Russell Oswald, Rockefeller's man in charge, on whose judgment he said he was relying, asked him to come. According to Oswald, however, Rockefeller replied, "Do you feel it will be productive? Will it save lives?" Oswald answered, "I don't believe so."[2]

So why should Rockefeller have come after his man in charge told him it would do no good? The McKay Report said that "the Governor should not have committed the state's armed forces against the rebels without first appearing on the scene and satisfying himself that there was no other alternative and that all precautions against excessive force had been taken." I agreed. McKay added that this was true because "state neglect [of the prison system] was a major contributing factor to the uprising" and that "Commissioner Oswald had requested him to come."[3] However much State neglect contributed to the riot, McKay's second reason struck me as a non sequitur. It faulted the Governor for not making a pilgrimage of contrition.

Regardless of McKay's reasoning, the realities had stood stark for even the absent Governor to see: a major riot ran taut with peril. Negotiations between the State and inmates faltered. The lives of thirty-eight hostages and thirteen hundred inmates hung at issue. So did the lives of the troopers, though they had the guns. The Observers told Rockefeller that an impasse meant a blood-bath, less than twenty hours before he ordered the assault. We had elected Rockefeller, not Oswald, to run the State. If Attica did not call for the top man to take charge, what did?

I do not know the extent to which Rockefeller's decision not to come rested upon his belief in Oswald and in not "surrendering" to criminals, those being the reasons he gave, and how much may have rested on political posturing or flaws in his common sense or character.[4]

But two conclusions I can reach. First, the assault came at the worst time possible. Tempers, hatreds, passions, and frustrations had built to their peak on both sides. The inmates' spirits had not yet begun to flag. During the hours before the assault they had been soaked with rain. Minutes before the assault, inmates in D Yard had cried out, in ignorance informed by hope, that Rockefeller was in the helicopter overhead. Only by coming could he have recognized the temper of the troopers and taken steps to bolster their self-control. If he had come, that plainly would have bought time. The worst time to attack would have passed.

Second, the negotiations had not reached the dead end that the Official Version has claimed. The key to the impasse was the inmates' demand for amnesty for their acts at the riot, most notably for killing Correction Officer Billy Quinn. Rockefeller held that he had neither the disposition nor the power to forgive that murder. That, however, did not end the possibilities for negotiation.

Quinn was killed during the riot. The riot was a felony. The venerable and often harsh felony-murder doctrine makes all participants in the felony guilty of murder if someone dies from it. All 1,300 rioters could be charged with murder for Quinn's death. The inmates knew it and feared it.[5] That fear unified them and made them stubborn. Before Quinn died, Louis James, the Wyoming County District Attorney, had written that he was "unalterably opposed to . . . indiscriminate mass prosecutions" and that he deemed it his obligation to prosecute only where he considered that "there is substantial evidence to link a specific individual with . . . a specific crime."[6] Inmates in D Yard, who apparently had a deep distrust of the authorities, laughed at the letter. News of Quinn's death, however, sobered them sharply, as they realized that it implicated all of them.

Rockefeller was Big Daddy in the sky. I have long believed that if he had come to Attica and personally assured the inmates that no one but the actual killer or killers of Quinn would be prosecuted for that murder, the riot might well have been resolved in peace.[7] It would have been ridiculous, monstrous, to prosecute all 1,300 inmates for Quinn's death. In fact, two alleged actual perpetrators were the only men the State ever sought to prosecute for it. Would the riot have ended peacefully if Rockefeller had offered the inmates this painless compromise? It was worth trying. Other avenues for compromise may also have lain open.[8]

Rockefeller said at the time that the decision to launch the assault was the toughest in his thirteen years as Governor, but, "There was no alternative but to go in."[9] An obvious and less fierce alternative, though, was expressed by Dr. Vernon Fox, deputy warden and chief psychiatrist at South State Michigan Prison: "My method is to keep talking and outwait them."[10] In any event, Rockefeller's mistake in not coming to Attica, whether cynical or shortsighted or both, is separate from his responsibility for the cover-ups that followed.

* * *

"This man Rockefeller has devoted his life to public service. We have a great responsibility not to do anything that might unnecessarily hurt his chances to realize his life's ambition." Tony told us this several times, in words or substance, during the same days he was asking us who would tell Gerry Ford.

I took Tony to mean simply that the Investigation should take more care than ever to act responsibly and to say nothing to anyone about Rockefeller that was not fully supported by the facts. I agreed with that. I did not connect Tony's remarks about telling Ford and protecting Rockefeller's ambition with the jolt he was now giving the jury. The August Switch was irrational from the standpoint of a straight prosecution, though not, as I saw later, from that of protecting Rockefeller. I had seen Tony seem irrational before, though never as grandly as he seemed now.

I have imagined Tony telling himself that the Shooter Cases have waited this long since the riot, the Hindering Case has to go to the jury sometime anyway, the indictment of a large number of troopers is not the same as convicting them, but it might create a wave of feeling against Rockefeller; therefore, the responsible course is to hold off on the Shooter Cases until after Rockefeller is confirmed. These thoughts, of course, may have been too kind; it may have been Tony's job never to indict a trooper all along. My speculation is not evidence. If Tony did go through the scenario I imagined, it is not as bad as what he did later, as the waters deepened around him.

Tony told me that General Lefkowitz asked him from time to time how the trooper cases were going. I imagined a scenario in which the General told him, "It's your Investigation, Tony, and you must follow it through, but it would be a shame to hurt the Governor unnecessarily while he's up for Vice President." If Lefkowitz, whose Investigation it really was, said something like that to Tony, that's all it would have taken. In any event, that was pretty much what Tony was telling us.

The Senate and public obviously deserved to know the facts about Rockefeller when he was up for Vice President. They deserved to know (and to have known long before) whether the troopers he ordered into the prison had rioted with their guns. The chips were not falling where they may when it mattered.

* * *

On Tuesday, August 27, I entered the grand jury room to start the unfamiliar witnesses on the unfamiliar case. Tony sent a couple of other assistants and several investigators with me, as he was often to do while the Hindering Case progressed. I realized for the first time how helpful it would have been to have had that much support on the Shooter Cases.

I didn't even know how to pronounce the name of the first witness for Wednesday, the 28th. This elderly man was not prepared to testify, and Tony's crash schedule did not allow time to prepare him now. You nearly always have to talk for a while with a person before he can sort out his recollections of several years before. This witness was not a trooper; he was willing to talk freely with us outside the jury. (Like correction officers, civilians and even inmate witnesses generally cooperated with us much more readily than the State Police.)

I barely had a chance to talk with this man before the time came to swear him in. He seemed plainly honest, but he stumbled. Who wouldn't? Yet a defense lawyer at trial could hammer at this grand jury testimony as showing contradictions and uncertainty. I considered it unprofessional to make him testify cold, to embarrass him as it plainly did, confuse the jury as it must have, and provide ammunition for a defense lawyer later. It was not necessary except to fit Tony's new plan.

In the middle of my questioning, the door opened behind me, and I was called out of the jury. Tony was on the phone. He wanted me on the next plane to New York. One investigator would drive me to the airport in Rochester. Another would pick me up at LaGuardia. Tony could really move it.

Before I left, I turned the witness over to another assistant with a few hasty words about what to ask. The assistant had not heard me start the questioning and knew even less than I about what was going on. He told me afterward that he had had to "destroy" the witness through an incisive cross-examination. "I hated to do it," he said, "but I had to destroy him." Why? Here we had a friendly witness who was doing his best to help us, for a change. The assistant had not been given even that much understanding about the new case. I read the transcript later. The assistant had wrought less destruction than he thought.

I sat in Tony's office in New York, the door closed, with Tony and Mike McCarron that afternoon, wondering what was happening and why I was not still questioning witnesses in Warsaw. Tony told us that the FBI wanted to talk with the Investigation as part of a background check it was running on Rockefeller for his nomination. Tony wanted us to Q and A half-a-dozen people immediately, in preparation for talking with the F.B.I. He had drawn up a list: Howard Shapiro, Bobby Douglass, and Michael Whiteman, all members of Rockefeller's Executive Chamber who had been at Attica; Louis James, the Wyoming County District Attorney whom Rockefeller and Lefkowitz replaced with Bob Fischer as the Attica prosecutor; Superintendent William Kirwan and First Deputy Superintendent Robert E. Denman of the State Police. Each of these men might be questioned in the Supplemental Grand Jury later—I hoped all would be— but Tony wanted, now and on the record, whatever they could tell us about Rockefeller. Evidently the Investigation had not sought that information before.

Tony asked me to phone each of them and try to schedule their Q and As. For this he rushes me back to New York? It was not to discuss the decisions he had already made. Calling me back to phone these men, whom he knew and I did not, hardly seemed worth it. I was a little steamed but got myself into it as best I could. I asked him if I should tell them that we would ask them to sign waivers of immunity and that they could bring lawyers to the Q and As. He said yes.

Howard Shapiro was First Assistant Counsel to the Governor at the time of the riot. Now he worked in our building as Chairman of the State Investigation Commission. He sounded very surprised when I told him on the phone what Tony had in mind. He asked to speak with him.

They talked for some time, with the door closed, while Mike and I waited outside. Afterward Tony told me I had been too abrupt with Shapiro. Apparently Shapiro had given Tony second thoughts about having the head of the State Investigation Commission advised that he had a right to counsel and would be asked to waive immunity from prosecution. Tony had even agreed to write out our questions and send them to Shapiro in advance. After that Tony notified the other witnesses himself, except for Louis James, who was to be my particular witness and who took me several days to reach because he was in Canada, fishing.

Tony, Mike, and I met at the Tarrytown Hilton Inn on the rainy morning of Friday, August 30. We drove to Albany to question Michael Whiteman— intelligent, smooth as mercury, Rockefeller's counsel, and Shapiro's boss at the riot. Tony planned to question him first. I was to ask any questions Tony over-looked. Mike was to remind us of anything we both missed.

A string of offices led to Whiteman's inner sanctum, where he now served Governor Malcolm Wilson, Rockefeller's longtime understudy who had finally succeeded him. Pleasantries about the bad weather bounced off the tension in the room like a child on a trampoline. Tony treated Whiteman more gently and covered significantly less ground than our talk in the car had led me to expect. Without actually saying so, Tony gave me a strong impression that he did not want me to ask Whiteman much else. At first, feeling somewhat intimidated, I did not. Near the end, though, with everyone acting awkward except Whiteman, I finally questioned him about why the Attica Investigation had been underfunded—underfunding had assured it was too small to do its job properly—though my questioning was not as full as I later wished. I was surprised that Tony had dropped our sensible plan to go into that himself. Whiteman, when I finally asked, revealed little.

Bobby Douglass had been secretary to Governor Rockefeller and one of his closest aides in September 1971. We questioned him in his office at the law firm of Milbank, Tweed, Hadley & McCloy, where Douglass had become a notably high-priced partner, high up in The Chase Manhattan Bank Building. Milbank, Tweed did much of the bank's legal work, with Dewey, Ballantine (the firm I once worked for) doing much of the rest.

I was up for this questioning, and damned if I was going to feel intimidated again. I asked Douglass some questions that we had planned and Tony again had not asked. Douglass gave us little, for all his apparent frankness. Sitting with Mike in front of Tony's desk later, I was surprised to hear Tony say I had sounded too much like a prosecutor. He assigned Mike to talk with me about how to tone myself down. Mike seemed embarrassed. I was curious to hear what he would tell me later, but we never had the conversation.

The questioning of Kirwan and Denman in Tony's office went unremarkably. Tony left out less than he had with Whiteman and Douglass. Superintendent Kirwan repeated the State Police Official Version that the troopers had failed to fill out their standard and informative Discharge of Firearms forms at Attica because the police used that form solely for shots fired at animals, not at people, even though the form itself asks "at *whom* or what" was the shot fired. A few weeks later Kirwan was to depart from his testimony in the jury to lecture those good citizens on why they should vote for Malcolm Wilson for Governor in the coming election.[11] Some people said that Kirwan was just a figurehead (which seemed untrue) and that the white-haired Denman, who had retired and looked unwell, was the person who had actually run the State Police (which I could believe, nevertheless). Kirwan impressed me as the promoter, Denman as the professional. On the afternoon Denman came in, several of our investigators more or less bowed and scraped before him as if he were a visitor from Olympus. They called him "Chief" with a reverence I had never heard them use.

The formal Q and A suggested that Denman honestly did not know much that concerned us. Afterward he told Tony and me with a confidential air that he would deny what he was about to tell us if we ever repeated it. It was to save Lieutenant Christian, he then confided, that the police shot hostages in D yard. The Official Version as a private secret! I wondered whether the poor man actually believed it. He had been in charge at Division Headquarters in Albany on Bloody Monday, while Kirwan vacationed at Lake George. Denman struck me as a strong and honorable man though intensely loyal.

Loyalty caused more problems for the Investigation than any other virtue I can think of. This includes my own loyalty to Tony and the Investigation that made me slow to see the cover-up. The question must always be: loyalty to whom or what? Please consider, if you disagree, the fact that the despicable Adolph Eichmann was *loyal* to a profoundly evil regime.

Two more witnesses remained. Tony was to question Howard Shapiro in New York, and I was to take Louis James in Buffalo, both on September 5, the day I came to call "Thursday in the Sky."

My Chevy Nova failed me that morning. I missed the 7:05 A.M. flight to Buffalo and had to catch a 9:00. I phoned ahead to let James know I'd be late. While I sat waiting at LaGuardia, an investigator came by and told me to be sure to phone Tony from Buffalo before I questioned James.

I went over my questions on the plane. What about the communications James had with Rockefeller? What about Rockefeller's replacing him with Fischer as the Attica prosecutor? The underlying question, which I would probably not ask outright, was what information, if any, did James have on whether Rockefeller put his own man, Fischer, in charge of the prosecution in order to keep it under control. The Official Version had it that the initiative to replace James had come from James. Really? I also planned to see what James could tell us about the State Police efforts to hinder prosecution. He had gone to the prison on the morning of the assault and was present with the State Police brass and some of Rockefeller's Executive Chamber people in the Administration Building at the time and place I believed the conspiracy to cover up was hatched.

James was waiting along with Charlie Bradley in the Buffalo office. Some surprises awaited, too. Tony had assigned Charlie instead of me to question James, though he had flown me to Buffalo solely to do that. Charlie's questioning was not to be a Q and A transcribed by a court reporter, as the others had been, but merely an informal off-the-record interview, with Charlie making his own memorandum of what James said. And Tony did not want me to assist Charlie or even attend the interview. Instead, I was to fly straight back to New York.

I suppose I would have been more astonished than I was if Tony had not accustomed us to his occasional "off-the-wall" decisions. Charlie had not been privy to the long discussions among Tony, Mike McCarron, and me about what questions to ask. Charlie had no idea of what we had asked Whiteman, Douglass, Kirwan, or Denman. Apparently Tony had not given him much idea what to ask James. Steamed again, I again tried to get into it. I quickly told Charlie my points on what to ask and left for the plane. Not until long afterward did it occur to me to wonder why Tony had not had the investigator who found me at LaGuardia that morning simply ask me not to go to Buffalo in the first place. By the time I wondered that, I was sure Tony wanted me out of the way during Shapiro's questioning too.

So I gazed from a window of an American Airlines 727 at the blue sky over New York for the second time that Thursday morning, wondering what the hell was going on. Back in Buffalo Charlie made an inevitably feeble pass at questioning James. Tony questioned Howard Shapiro beyond the horizon in New York City. For what special crisis was Tony rushing me back this time? Surely it had to be more important than making the few phone calls he brought me back for last week, I thought. But no task at all awaited me in New York.

The memo that Charlie produced from his interview of James ran slightly more than one page. It was virtually worthless, for which I did not blame

Charlie. The transcript of Tony's Q and A of Shapiro was probably even worse, in that it looked a respectable length but read like old friends lobbing marsh-mallows at each other. When anything that mattered came up, Tony might as well have asked, "Mr. Shapiro, can you recall anything useful?" and Shapiro have answered, "No, Mr. Simonetti, as a matter of fact I can't." (I learned long afterward that Shapiro remarked to Tony on the way out to the elevator that it would be a shame if this Attica business impeded Rockefeller's nomination. Others, of course, may have suggested that to Tony, too, and he himself had said as much.) At least that Thursday was a perfect day for gazing at the sapphire sky above green New York.

* * *

Up to now Tony had consulted me on nearly every important matter he dealt with in 1974. Except on the inmate trials, I was his chief consultant. He kept me with him during his trips and his meetings with people outside the office—at the inmate settlement conferences last winter, one day with Trooper A's law-yer, at meetings with the General and others. Just the previous week he had rushed me out of the jury and back to New York to ring me in at the start of our investigation for the FBI. Until Thursday in the Sky, he had kept me with him at every step of that effort. He rehearsed with me what he was going to tell the FBI agent who was due in the office the next day, Friday, September 6. I remained Tony's Chief Assistant. As I listened to him, I even suggested that he was planning to tell the agent more than necessary.

I worked at my desk that Friday morning waiting for the call to Tony's office for the meeting with the FBI agent. It never came. I finally asked Tony's secretary when the agent was due. She told me he had come and gone. That surprised and disappointed me. It even hurt a little. It was a sharp break with Tony's usual way of operating. Why, I wondered, had he not wanted me present?

Thursday in the Sky culminated Tony's effort to look without finding. Friday in the Cold struck me as his way to protect the FBI from any helpfulness on my part. I wondered later if it also freed him to lie.

The FBI agent had surprised him, Tony said, by asking less than Tony had expected. Recalling his own experience as an FBI agent, he said that when agents receive an assignment to ask only certain questions, those questions are all they ask. I was soon to reflect on this when Tony narrowed the questions I could ask in the jury.

Thus Tony investigated Rockefeller so as to have little to give the FBI The FBI apparently investigated so as to have even less to take from Tony.[12] Rockefeller's nomination appears to have been in good hands.

The assault that Rockefeller ordered led to the bloodbath he had been told it would. The August Switch put the lid on the indictment of a host of troopers for that, at least for the crucial time being. Yet the fact that the assault resulted in thirty-nine deaths was old hat. What else lay hidden? If nothing, why the calculated superficiality at both ends of the FBI investigation? Routine caution? If so, whose? I assume, without knowing, that Tony discussed the FBI check with Lefkowitz. Does the FBI generally don blinders and act as if the official it is investigating has something to hide? Did someone merely assume the American public could not take further problems after Watergate? (It infuriates me whenever people claim the American public cannot take something. The American public has taken everything it has ever been asked to take.)

Nixon's White House had struggled during the Watergate cover-up to keep that F.B.I. investigation narrow. I asked myself in passing whether the FBI check on Rockefeller was merely a ritual to satisfy appearances. The Constitution requires the Senate to consent to the nomination of people the President chooses for high office. That is one of our treasured checks and balances. But what if the FBI (which is under the President) keeps the Senators in the dark about the nominee, at the same time that it deludes them into thinking they are being enlightened? "The FBI has conducted a thorough investigation and finds the conduct of the nominee to have been above reproach." Thoughts to sleep by.

A week or so after our investigation of Rockefeller had fizzled into oblivion, Tony told me he had made a mistake in having me do all that flying on Thursday in the Sky. It interested me that he should apologize. It puzzles me a little now to recall that I did not really believe Tony's apology, yet I was not really disturbed by the events that brought it on. For the most part, I still liked and trusted Tony, was still loyal to him, and considered the work for the FBI check as only a diversion from our main job.

"Who's going to tell Gerry Ford?" Tony and the FBI and Rocky's loyal staff supplied the answer on Attica: no one.

Chapter Nineteen

The Rockefeller Runaround

The Rockefeller Runaround completed Tony's trilogy of what I thought then were atypical acts following Rocky's nomination for Vice President—the August Switch and the bogus check for the FBI being the others. Members of the Supplemental Grand Jury wanted Rockefeller. They wanted Russell Oswald. They wanted Major John Monahan, the State Police troop commander at Attica. They asked for every witness necessary to do their job and did not seem to care who he was, or how low or high his so-called station in life.

Rockefeller had been questioned by the McKay Commission in 1972, though not very probingly. So long as I worked at the Attica Investigation, he never became a target of the prosecution. I know of no evidence linking him to any of the shooting crimes or postshooting assaults; and barring the monstrous, I do not see how he could have been part of those crimes. He had ordered the assault without much evidence of immediate need, without seeing the situation for himself, and after being told it would result in a bloodbath. Whatever that says of him as a Governor and person, it does not make him a criminal under any extant law that I knew about.

I did not know of any specific evidence that linked Rockefeller with the State Police cover-up after the assault, though Tony had just shown his intention to go no further than through the motions of looking for it. I could, however, conceive that such evidence might exist. Rockefeller's aides were in the building and perhaps the room where I believe the cover-up was hatched, they participated in many high-level decisions at the prison, they clearly had a motive to protect Rockefeller, and they showed a lack of scruples on other occasions. Rockefeller faced a tremendous image problem, to say the least, if that cover-up failed. These facts obviously don't prove anyone's guilt, but they indicate a prosecutor's need to consider the possibility of guilt. I have little difficulty picturing a tough and loyal Rockefeller vowing to protect the troopers who did a tough and thankless task for the people of New York at Attica.

Though not a target, Rockefeller was indeed a logical witness. On the basis of what information did he authorize the September 13 assault? Received from whom? When? Upon what information did he announce after the assault that the police had done "a superb job"? Who told him what and when about how the assault progressed? He told McKay at length about his concern before the assault to protect human life. What steps did he take to learn what need there had been for killing thirty-nine people? From whom? With what result? What assignments, if any, did he give to his personal team, Gen. A. C. O'Hara, Bobby Douglass, Dr. T. Norman Hurd, Michael Whiteman, and Howard Shapiro, before or after he sent each of them from Albany to Attica? What reports did each of them make to him? When did he learn that State Police Superintendent Kirwan had taken the day off on the bloody thirteenth? What, if anything, did he do about Kirwan's apparent dereliction of duty? Why, or why not?[1]

Before the assault, Rockefeller had ordered that the correction officers not take part because he expected they would engage in reprisals if they did. On the basis of what information did he expect this? From whom? What did he know about the temper of the State Police before the assault? Upon what information, received from whom? What steps, if any, did he take to prevent the bloodbath he had been told the assault would be? To whom did he say what about the failure of any such steps to work? Did he participate in the decision to bar the press and the Observers from witnessing the assault? Why? On whose information or advice?[2] Oswald reports that Douglass was on an open telephone line with the Governor during the assault.[3] What did they say to each other? Did anyone else join the conversation? Did Rockefeller know about or approve any aspect of the State Police cover-up? Did he have any knowledge, before or after the fact, that the State Police had snatched Trooper A from Simonetti and the Investigation, allowing him to resign from the State Police and whisking him away from Attica before he could be questioned? Did Rockefeller ever make or approve a decision that no trooper would be prosecuted for crimes at Attica? If so, when, why, on the basis of what information, and in conjunction with whom?

Rockefeller stated among his reasons for refusing amnesty to inmates during the riot that "the very essence of our free society [is] the fair and impartial application of the law.[4] Upon substituting "our good friend Bob Fischer"[5] for Louis James as the Attica prosecutor, what discussion did Rockefeller have with Fischer about that job? What were the full circumstances of the substitution? What steps, if any, did Rockefeller take to assure that the prosecution was indeed full, fair, and impartial? What status reports did he seek or receive on its progress, when, and from whom? How did he respond? Did he ever ask why dozens of inmates and zero troopers were being indicted? There was no shortage of questions to ask Rockefeller within the ambit of his order to investigate all crimes at or after Attica. How would he answer or not recall?

Even before the August recess, grand jurors had asked to have Rockefeller called and questioned. His nomination intensified their requests. Tony finally had to respond. He asked the jurors to wait. He stressed that an orderly presentation of the evidence was essential. He said that as yet the record contained "no foundation" for calling Rockefeller, and we had not yet reached the point of deciding whether it would be proper to call him. He asked them to bear with us and wait until the end of September.

I marveled at Tony's chutzpa. He had just pulled the August Switch on the jury. Now *he* stressed to *them* the need for an orderly presentation! It would have fit easily in the new order to call Rocky then. Tony's claim that the record lacked a foundation was untrue and unnecessary. The record had plenty of facts linking Rockefeller with Attica, raising questions like those just noted. And there is no requirement of "foundation" as Tony used the term; otherwise, you could never call the first witness.

When Tony asked the jurors to wait, what could they say? Actually there were several things, but Tony made sure they did not know about them when it mattered. One day when they were asking for Rockefeller, he lectured them on how they lacked the power to subpoena the executive. Now, whether or not that is legally sound, Rockefeller was not then the executive. No longer Governor and not yet Vice President, he was merely a private citizen. Tony's reference to subpoena power was doubly beside the point because all the jury probably had to do was *ask* Rockefeller to come. If they simply wrote him a letter, what could he say? In the spotlight of the Senate deliberations, how could he gracefully refuse a grand jury of the Investigation he had established? We were supposed to advise the jury, not mislead it. A request had been all it took to bring him before McKay.

Repeatedly, I told Tony that his advice about the jury's lack of subpoena power had misled them into thinking they could not simply ask the man to come. Repeatedly, I asked Tony to correct this to the jury. He did not refuse. He delayed. He asked to see the transcript of what he had told them. That took time. When it came, it confirmed how misleading he had been. He delayed some more. Finally one day, when the jury was involved in something entirely different, he mentioned very casually in passing that they could always ask

Rockefeller to come. None of the jurors gave the slightest sign of seeing the import of that remark. None of them responded to it. Yet Tony had gotten it into the transcript where he could always point to it later. Nicely done, I thought, you protected your record and still duped the jury.

* * *

In mid-September—as best I recall, at Tony's request—I drafted a statement about Rockefeller for Tony to read to the jury. I made it as close as I could to what he was discussing with us in his office, including his views and omitting mine where they conflicted. Of all the jobs I ever wrote for Tony, he reacted most strongly against this one, cutting half of it out and noting some sharp comments. His critique has always fascinated me for the insight it gives into his desire to shield Rockefeller and his nervousness about doing so.

My draft said that the jurors' concern to hear Rockefeller was understandable and serious, and we were passing it along to Attorney General Lefkowitz. Tony took all that out. It said that the FBI had the primary job of checking out Rockefeller, and they could assume the FBI was doing its job. He took that out, even though the FBI check was public knowledge. He left in the fact that a grand jury can only subpoena people within New York State, but he struck out my view that Rockefeller would not stay away from New York in order to avoid such a subpoena. He strengthened the point that for a grand jury subpoena to be valid, the testimony sought must be material and relevant to any crimes, malfeasance, or misfeasance committed *during* the retaking, but he struck from the areas of relevance "any destruction of evidence or hindering of prosecution of those crimes," even though these were the very areas he had just switched the jury into. He left in our intention "to call every witness we consider necessary and proper . . . regardless of where the chips may fall."

Concerning materiality and relevancy, my draft said that Rockefeller spoke with Oswald on the phone on the morning of September 13 "concerning the decision to retake the facility that morning. In addition, members of the Executive Chamber were present at the facility before, during, and after the retaking." Those facts were either in the record or about to be. Tony struck all that. He struck the sentence "In our judgment, there is not enough evidence before you at this moment to justify calling the Governor at this time." The reference to "our judgment" meant in Tony's judgment and therefore the Investigation's judgment, because Tony was saying it though I was disagreeing with it. Tony underlined the words *at this time* twice, even though he took them out, giving me the impression he did not like them at all. He left in "you can ask me any questions and make any further statements." He struck out that the jury could ask us to leave the room and take "any vote you deem appropriate," even though it was equally sound advice.

The comments Tony wrote on my draft disturbed me even more than his deletions of the points he had been discussing with us:

Mal
1. This statement would confuse & prejudice this jury beyond Hope.
2. More importantly, it confuses me as to your thinking.
3. This in no way represents the logical and exhaustive outline of the law and situation as I gave it to you.
4. Query: Would it help if you and Charlie changed places for a while?

What had I said that was so wrong? I did not believe Tony's first three points. His claim that the draft did not represent his "logical and exhaustive outline" was self-serving hogwash. His last point distressed me most immediately. To have me take over Charlie Bradley's inmate trial assignment and Charlie take over the presentation of the Hindering Case to the jury signaled disaster. Charlie lacked the long factual background and the motivation for my job. At that point I lacked the same for his. I puzzled over what I could have said in the draft that made Tony react so. How thoroughly wrong was it?

I took my distress to Tony. Soothingly, he said he was not suggesting that Charlie and I trade places except very briefly (i.e., a brief but total waste of time), and he withdrew even that idea. I do not recall what Tony actually told the jury in place of my decimated draft, but I do remember being surprised at how close he came to repeating most of my original version. Possibly I should not have been so surprised; most of my draft was what Tony had been saying all along.

* * *

The news had recently been filled with Nixon's Watergate tapes. Around this time, an astute juror said to me that since everybody seemed to have tapes these days, why didn't we see if Rockefeller had any tapes about Attica. Good thinking. If he did not bug his own office as Nixon had, at least he might have taped his phone calls. I passed the juror's idea to Tony. He responded with the lecture he sometimes gave about not talking with jurors off the record.[6] I asked him in all innocence if he wanted me to put her remarks on the record (i.e., telling them to the jury with the court reporter taking them down).

"Come on, Malcolm, you know better than that."

In that moment, never repeated, Tony dropped the mask, the pretense, the deception and opened the window into the Rockefeller Runaround. The juror's idea belonged on the record, and we should have gone after any tapes or notes of phone calls concerning Attica that Rockefeller had. We never did.

* * *

Thus was Nelson Rockefeller spared any questioning in the Attica grand jury while it mattered to his nomination for Vice President.

So why didn't the Rockefeller trilogy alert me at the time that the Investigation was covering up? I am not sure but have pondered the following possibilities, uncomfortable at seeing myself look that stupid (and stupider as more happened): I am sometimes blind and insensitive. Nelson Rockefeller was not a target, only a potential witness. I am not positive to this day that there are hidden facts about him. He was not then our main concern. I expected that if we were ever to find anything implicating him, it would not be by a quick pass at his inner circle, but by a methodical working through of all the witnesses below him, something we could not really do except as we finished the Hindering Case, the Shooter Cases, and, hopefully, the postshooting brutality cases. I saw our job then as prosecuting the police lawbreakers, not protecting the nation from a possible suspect who had insulated himself from Attica with a layer of loyal aides.

The trilogy took over a month to play itself out, from late August through September. Organizing and giving the jury the evidence of the State Police cover-up was taking most of my attention and time. The first lesson of the trilogy was not that Rockefeller was guilty of anything but that Tony was being very protective of Rockefeller, and of his own future. The little guy's protectiveness does not prove the big guy's guilt. Tony obviously wanted to save Rocky the inconvenience and possible embarrassment of testifying, and maybe more, but I did not ponder the trilogy, the pattern, or even put them together. Books are mined from the ore of life, and I was not even prospecting.

More introspection and/or rationalization: I am not sharp as often as I would like and am not particularly suspicious when my job does not seem to require it. Ideas traverse my consciousness at times from back to front, from vague feeling through awareness to an articulated conclusion. I assume that such a process is common with others. The idea that the Investigation was intentionally covering up, or that Tony was not basically honest, had not yet penetrated forward. His unwillingness to rock Rocky's boat was a far cry, in my mind, from blocking evidence of police homicides, etc. As I saw it that September, Tony was not cutting out any part of the Investigation. He was simply imposing his own erratic sequence on it. The overriding factor in my September complacency, I think, was that, consciously and emotionally, I still trusted Tony.

I was, however, admiring him less. I saw us more and more often getting into tugs of war, in which I pulled toward finding and presenting evidence to the jury, and he resisted. I often don't judge until I'm angry. Except for a few specifics like Thursday in the Sky, that had not happened yet. I continued to pull. That was my job. I still believed that basically and in the long run it was Tony's.

Chapter Twenty

Evidence of Obstruction

"They're fucking it up," a ranking BCI detective told Bob Fischer in confidence (according to what Tony told several of us) at Attica shortly after the retaking. The detective was referring to the way his brother officers were conducting the collection of evidence.[1] He quickly had a change of heart, according to our own evidence, and became one of our targets.

The Mosaic is what Tony called the case of hindering prosecution (obstructing justice) against the State Police. That was how he pictured it and I came to picture it. Its pieces were the morgues, the statements, the photos (or their absence), the subpoenas, and so forth. They were what Tony had been talking about the previous November when he took me into his confidence about the book he had been keeping on the State Police. In late August he wrote fifty-three pages of notes, questions, outlines, and diagrams that filled out the Mosaic.

The Hindering Case was not against the troopers who may have falsified their statements or lied when asked if they saw anybody shoot anybody. Those troopers, however plentiful, were small fish, a school of miscreant minnows, most of whom we probably could not catch. Rather, the case was against the four ranking officers who had had authority over the collection of evidence of all the shootings, and who, as far as we could tell, had consciously done it wrong or overseen others doing it wrong, failing to collect what it was their duty to collect and sometimes affirmatively destroying it.

The Hindering Case depended upon circumstantial evidence. No one had come forward and said, "I covered up." We did not expect that anyone would. Circumstantial evidence—evidence that depends on inferences derived from proved facts—is as valid as direct evidence—evidence sufficient unto itself. In fact, circumstantial evidence can be better, for example, than the direct evidence of an eyewitness to a crime who identifies the wrong perpetrator. Judges have to impress this circumstance on juries, because the popular assumption is that direct evidence is always best. Consider that a "smoking gun" is no more than circumstantial evidence. Maybe the person found holding it shot the deceased, or maybe he just didn't know better than to pick it up. The other circumstances matter. For a case to exist, the circumstantial evidence can and should exclude every reasonable explanation for what happened except the guilt of the accused.

If we were going to prove a Hindering Case, it would be by piecing together sufficient circumstances to make the four officers' guilt clear beyond a doubt that was reasonable. The more pieces we had of the Mosaic, the better. People can look at a whole mosaic and not see a picture they do not want to see.

Notwithstanding possible difficulties, the Hindering Case, as I saw it, was a serious, provable case. That was part of its beauty, if and when Tony would ever have to justify the August decision to switch the jury away from the Shooter Cases that could wreck Nelson Rockefeller's nomination, and onto this long, complex, circumstantial case that almost certainly could not. Even if the jury voted true bills in the Hindering Case, they would be against the few remote police brass who may have misbehaved solely out of loyalty to their men, not against scores of the troopers whom Rockefeller had ordered to retake the prison.

The August Switch, then, could be called a matter of judgment. It is inherently hard for outsiders to second-guess a prosecutor's judgment. People realize that he or she is better positioned than they to balance the circumstances. Even if Tony's judgment was later judged "bad," what then? Bad judgment alone is not a crime.

The Hindering Case had enough to it so that presenting it to the jury might be stretched out until after the Senate voted on Rockefeller's confirmation. That is, if Tony saw enough of a case to let it go to the jury for a vote. A prosecutor has broad discretion to chuck a case at the preindictment, grand-jury level—as a matter of judgment. Even if the jury voted before the Senate did, indictments here would, as noted, probably not reflect on Rockefeller. The August Switch permitted Rockefeller to reach the Vice Presidency as deftly as a key block may permit a fullback to score.

* * *

As I worked into the Hindering Case, I had more and more disagreements with Tony, who showed two minds about really intending to press it. I focused not on the disagreements or on the two minds that Tony was showing, however, but on piecing the Mosaic together for the jury. Lawyers who work together always disagree; it's part of the job.

Several elements of the Mosaic stood out from the start, but we had to show how they came into being. How did it happen that no one kept track of which trooper had which rifle or how many cartridges? Who decided not to use the standard Discharge of Firearms form, and not to collect expended shells and write down their locations on tags? Through whom or what did key photos not reach us? Whose idea was it that the team of BCI detectives who interviewed the assault troopers were not to ask obviously key questions such as: Did you see any trooper shoot anyone? Who authorized the premature destruction of the death scenes, the carting off of bodies before they could be photographed, and the locations measured where they fell? Who in the State Police decided to withhold evidence from the Investigation as long as they did, in the face of our repeated requests and subpoenas and their plain duty to cooperate with the prosecutors? We knew from the start who sent Trooper A away from the prison before his part in the killing of Kenny Malloy and maybe of Ramon Rivera could be investigated. That high-ranking detective came to head our list of four targets of the Hindering Case.

Tony assigned Ed Burbage, a quiet and conscientious investigator, to assemble lists of potential witnesses for each piece of the Mosaic—the BCI detectives who took statements, the State Policemen who took and processed the photos, the morgues people, etc. Ed and I reviewed what they might be able to tell the jury. Other investigators and assistants prepared additional questions. Ed prepared kits of questions and evidence for each witness. I put witnesses into the jury.

The BCI statements formed a central piece of the Mosaic. Taking statements from witnesses who were at the scene of a homicide is of course a basic police procedure. It seems too elementary to mention that the detectives should ask the witnesses all they saw at the time. Here the State Police had thirty-nine homicides to explain, homicides committed by and in full view of themselves. So you'd expect . . .

On the afternoon of September 13, several BCI detectives interviewed a number of the .270 snipers and dictated the results onto plastic belts. Statements typed from the belts duly reached the Investigation. Those BCI interviewers, however, were mysteriously sent away from the prison, and a new team was brought in. On the fifteenth the new BCI interviewers took, and the troopers signed, handwritten and grossly inadequate statements that formed the bulk of trooper statements we received. The State Police told us that they reflected "administrative, non-evidentiary" interviews. If so, what happened to the real interviews? Did they ever exist? And what happened on the fourteenth?

We had some evidence that the State Police withheld a full first generation of trooper statements about the assault. One early statement, which a trooper of the C Tunnel Detail wrote on yellow paper in his own hand, did reach our files. Could he have been the only trooper in any assault detail to make such a statement? Importantly, it contained more of the trooper's observations, including shooting by other troopers, than the statement that the BCI took from the same trooper on the fifteenth.

I questioned witnesses about a first generation of statements. Some officers had some recollection of giving, taking, or seeing other statements that we never saw. A high-ranking officer stated that a certain captain knew about the full first generation of statements. Tony never let me question the captain.

I tried to get Tony to pursue, and let me pursue, the reason why the State Police changed interviewers between the thirteenth and the fifteenth. Maybe there was nothing to it, or maybe the State Police made the change so they could instruct the new arrivals to ask only a narrow set of questions for the "administrative, nonevidentiary" interviews.

Tony repeatedly speculated, without mentioning his foundation, that the reason the State Police switched the interview team must have been that the first team was tired from being such a long time at the riot—during which most of them had little to do. I repeatedly reminded Tony that the only BCI man I had asked about this said he had not been called to come to Attica until early on the thirteenth, the riot's last day. After he had interviewed only two .270 shooters at the prison, he was sent away. So our only information contradicted Tony's speculation.

Speaking of speculation, I have imagined the following: The State Police command know immediately that there has been a bloodbath. They decide to protect the troopers who may have overreacted to the inmates' provocations while doing the dirty and thankless task of retaking the prison. The Executive Chamber people, who are with the State Police at the Command Post, join the cover-up. The State Police command see to it that the troopers' rifles and shotguns are turned in without recording their serial numbers. They decide that the standard Discharge of Firearms forms, which call for these numbers, are not used. They commence the statements that obviously have to be taken. But at least three of the first statements come back with the rifle serial numbers on them anyway. What to do? The statement taking is halted. The statement takers are sent away. All statements that have not been dictated for typing are suppressed, except the one on yellow paper that got through. A new group of detectives is called in, given the carefully curtailed questions for "administrative, nonevidentiary" purposes, etc.

This imagined scenario includes many facts we learned and is consistent with the rest. It is not original with me; most of it started as Tony's. A drawback of covering up is that it deprived the State Police of a chance to show, if they could, that this is not what happened. Mystery after mystery at Attica was like a detective story with the last chapter torn away.

In any event, the statements that the BCI did take on the fifteenth are inadequate beyond belief. They dwell at length upon inmate hostility that the troopers saw out the windows and down the tunnels before the assault. They say what kind of gun or guns the trooper carried but do not note the serial numbers of the rifles and shotguns.[2] They do report what shots each trooper says he fired at what targets—thus supporting the reckless endangerment cases that none of the police may have contemplated when the statements were taken. They could not have related any fewer facts without becoming totally laughable. The telegraphic brevity of the troopers' admissions of shootings told us that the experienced BCI interviewers simply accepted at face value whatever story the troopers told, without asking follow-up questions, without seeking details, without probing, without questioning the absurdities that many stories contained.

With thirty-nine homicides and eighty-nine gunshot wounded to account for, and with scores of trooper witnesses to shootings done by scores of troopers, these BCI detectives failed to ask troopers if they saw any other trooper shoot anybody—or shoot at anybody, or shoot period.

Good detectives that they were, they did ask the troopers if they saw any "members of other departments" shoot. That meant correction officers, who did almost no shooting except from the third floor of A Block, where almost no trooper could have observed them. The BCI interviews of the correction officers were also significantly more complete than they were of brother troopers, loyalty to tribe versus justice taking another turn. As many troopers had shown indifference about shooting correction officers who were hostages, so now the State Police showed relative indifference about implicating correction officers who were shooters.

The BCI statements of the troopers who admitted firing followed the same half-assed format as those of the troopers who did not. What McKay says about the former equally fits the latter:

> The BCI statements of those troopers who fired contained detailed accounts of the alleged actions of inmates just prior to and during the assault. These accounts were much more detailed than parts of the statements concerned with the activities of the troopers themselves. In fact, the

structure of the statements points to a preoccupation with establishing hostile activities on the part of inmates. *When those statements are compared with all of the other available evidence, the conclusion is inescapable that many of them were exaggerated, if not fabricated . . . .*[3] [Emphasis added.]

The troopers did not choose the format of these statements. It was the BCI interviewers who failed to ask what they should have. These failures resulted from, and led us to, the officers who told the interviewers what to ask. Those officers designed the format to omit what was vital to include. They hindered prosecution, almost certainly preventing it in many instances. The evidence against them mounted. Tony shifted us to other pieces of the Mosaic before I could question all the witnesses whom Ed Burbage and I had selected for their knowledge about this piece.

I have already noted how a chorus of troopers whose statements admitted that they fired blindly into D Yard holes all changed their tune to claim in Supplemental Statements that they had fired into the ground in front of the holes. The uniformity of these changes raised the inference that the State Police brass realized that the troopers' initial honesty admitted criminal shooting and told them uniformly what to change it to.

Supplemental Statements were also taken to "clarify" a number of other situations, mainly to place a weapon in the hands of inmates who were not said to be armed the first time the troopers admitted shooting at them, or simply to omit the unjustified shots. How had the decision to take the new statements been reached? By whom? I questioned the officers who had done the re-interviewing. Two captains admitted that at times the Supplemental Statements created justification for shooting where no justification existed in the troopers' original statements. One .270 sharpshooter had admitted in his first statement firing five shots, the last two at inmates who were not threatening anyone. The captain who described the Supplemental Statement that omitted these two shots did so in a tone of disbelief that never reached the record, but that I doubt many of us listening ever forgot.

Generally, the BCI interviews of inmates covered the period from the start of the riot on September 9 through the events just prior to the State Police assault on the thirteenth. Then it was as if time fell off a cliff. The BCI failed to ask the hundreds of inmate eyewitnesses, and even people who were shot, about the gunfire they saw, heard, and felt burn through their flesh.

Why, the jury had asked when we first introduced them to Attica, don't all those photos of the assault show anyone shooting anyone? The answer, as the

State Police told it, was the damnedest series of snafus you ever heard. Trooper after trooper claimed to have been unable to operate the camera he was assigned to cover the assault with. Part of the Mosaic was to cross-examine them on the precise mechanics of what they said they failed to do or their cameras failed to do. The more specific the questions forced them to be, the more incredible their answers became. Would that the State Police had had as much trouble operating their guns.

One State Police investigator stated at first that comparatively few of his photos had come out. I pressed him with cross-examination. He admitted that many more of his photos had come out than he said at first. He struck me as a candidate for perjury. One of his photos shows an inmate lying apparently unconscious in D Yard. A later one shows the inmate still unconscious with a weapon beside him. Did the inmate wake up, put it there, and go back to sleep? The investigator admitted that he had placed the weapon beside the inmate before taking the second photo, claiming that he had found it inside the inmate's clothing. This State Police officer was fabricating evidence, for its poetic truth no doubt. What made him think, right after the assault, that it would matter to show a weapon beside an inmate?

Sometimes the State Police seemed to vie with one another for the honor of having screwed up the pictures the most. A trooper I have already mentioned claimed credit for wrecking many color slides by developing them improperly with the standard, small-operation equipment that it was his usual job to operate correctly. Another trooper said, rather, that it was he who had taken it upon himself to throw out the evidence slides that he claimed had wholly or in major part not come out. Then a third trooper said a fourth trooper had done this. How was it, I wondered, that the innocuous slides taken at nearly the same time and place and by the same person and camera survived so much better than the ones that mattered?

Yet another trooper began taking pictures from inside A Block as he waited for the assault to begin, continued as he went down A Walk to Times Square, and thence down into D Yard. There weren't very many of them. He said he thought there should have been more. They came to us consecutively numbered on one roll of film. The trooper thought he had taken about seventy photos (i.e., at least two rolls). He had a distinct recollection of finishing one roll, stopping to reload his camera at Times Square or on B Walk, and continuing on with the new roll. He was also sure he had taken pictures down in D Yard that were never given to us. Did the State Police weed out incriminating slides and reproduce the innocuous ones on one new roll? We heard one opinion that this trooper's slides that the State Police gave us were copies rather than originals. A juror who knew something about photography thought so, too. I was never to have the chance to pursue this question.

The State Police at the Command Post had a picture show on the thirteenth as soon as the assault photos could be developed and rushed back by police car to the prison. Who saw what at that show? Could the Executive Chamber people have somehow not been present? How much of that show ever reached McKay or us? These, too, are questions I sought to pursue with the Hindering witnesses.

From time to time Tony said that the State Police failed to tag inmate weapons by location as they picked them up because there were not enough weapons at or near the dead and injured to justify the police for shooting them. That was his theory. A lieutenant who oversaw the weapons collection in one of the nearly empty courtyards, B Yard or C Yard, where it didn't matter, tagged them properly by location. The lieutenant who had this job in D Yard and the two who had it on the bloody catwalks failed to do this. The State Police did not claim that the job was too big for them to do right. When they said anything, it was that they had to rush so that inmates—gassed, cowed, surrendered, covered by scores of guns, 10 percent of whom had been shot—would not pick up the weapons and attack.

One of these lieutenants, we heard, went around kicking inmate weapons off the catwalks. Ned Perry questioned him under oath about it. He denied it. But when I questioned him, also under oath, he admitted it. I asked him why he had lied to Perry. Perry, he said, had angered him by referring to the retaking as "the assault." (I heard State Police call it the assault all the time.) So, perjury out of pique.[4] What piqued me was his scorn for duty and truth, and his (correct) assumption that he enjoyed impunity.

Two pieces of the Mosaic struck me as particularly bizarre and nervy: the State Police morgues and the Night Riders. I found it hard to comprehend the mentality that could have tried to get away with either one, yet the evidence shows that they did.

Typically curious circumstances surround the initial State claim that inmates had killed the dead hostages by slashing their throats. The police removed their bodies from the death scenes before they were even pronounced dead. Tony pointed out that that action violated State law.[5] The State Police lieutenant in charge of the temporary morgue for hostages at the prison—segregated from the morgue for inmates—swore that he did not see bullet holes in the bodies he handled, only cut throats. He squirmed when I displayed the photos of the dead, which a State Police photographer had successfully taken in the morgue. They showed that the lieutenant was swearing to nonsense. He tried, too, to claim that, well, bloody rags around their necks had made it look as though their throats were slashed. That might have sounded fine, until you looked at the photos. They showed few if any bloody blindfolds or shirts or anything else that could have led anyone to such a mistake. Corrections Sergeant Edward Cunningham, for example, lies as if asleep, unmarked save for one round hole in his cheek. While it may have been theoretically possible that some inmates had knives or picks that could make an entrance wound that looked exactly like a bullet hole, the obvious inference from looking at these bodies was that they had been shot, not slashed. The two hostages who had their throats seriously cut were then under repair in a hospital.

That afternoon the State Police had the bodies of the hostages trucked from the prison to local funeral homes. That sent one undertaker scurrying around town for lumber to lay across sawhorses, since he didn't have enough on hand to hold his allotment of bodies. The game ended when a State Police investigator, who wasn't in on it, phoned the Command Post at the prison to say that the funeral homes were completely inadequate for the necessary autopsies, since they had no X-ray equipment—vital in these multiple gunshot cases—inadequate sewage, etc. The State Police dutifully brought the bodies back to the prison, trucking them out again that night along with the dead inmates, mainly to the Monroe County medical examiner in Rochester, Dr. John Edland, who shocked the world and shattered the Official Version the next day by announcing that all of them had been shot to death. So ended the State Police effort to whisk the dead hostages into the ground under the official lie that inmates had killed them.

How do we know that the local undertakers would have cooperated with or been bamboozled by the State Police? Enter the Night Riders. When I first joined the Investigation, an assistant named Brian Malone told me how the State Police rode around in the middle of the night getting local undertakers to say that the dead hostages had been stabbed, not shot. When I mentioned this to Tony, he told me not to take Malone too seriously. That made sense. Malone's story of the Night Riders, as he called them, was hard to believe.

As I put the Hindering Case together for the jury, I found that the story was true. The State Police had made these trips and persuaded at least two under-takers[6] to make written statements to the effect that there was no evidence of gunshot wounds on several of the dead hostages—after a number of State Police officers had watched Dr. Edland and his associate, Dr. Richard Abbott, take bullet after bullet out of these same bodies.

Now it is true that the entrance wound made by the .44 Ruger magnum bullet that Correction Officer Z had fired into the chest of one hostage, John Monteleone, had in fact been destroyed during the autopsy, but the State Police knew that this bullet had killed him—and that it was not State Police ammunition—before they got the undertaker to deny seeing any bullet wound in Monteleone. Specifically, Dr. Edland showed Bob Horn, the State Police ballistics expert, a tray full of bullets taken from the hostages' bodies. Horn said, "It looks like our stuff," though when Horn examined the .44 magnum slug, he said, "That's not ours."[7]

Nevertheless, an undertaker, "being duly sworn," made the following handwritten statement, dated September 14, 1971, 11:15 P.M., on the letterhead of a local funeral home:

> I am an officer of _____ Funeral Home Inc. and have been employed in the funeral home business in excess of twenty years.
>
> At approximately 8-30 PM, 9-14-71 in company with Inv. _____ _____ & Inv. _____ of the New York State Police, I examined the body of John Monteleone in the preparation room of the funeral home, an autopsy had already been performed and the body embalmed. In my opinion there was no evidence of a gunshot wound to the body of John Monteleone. There was a laceration on rear area of the neck, approximately three inches in length and running horizontally.
>
> I can read and write English and I have read this statement and it is the truth to the best of my knowledge.
>
> [signed]
>
> Witnesses
>
> [signed]
> [signed]

Another undertaker who had been in the business for many years stated that he could find no bullet hole in another hostage, and he concluded that the hostage had been stabbed to death. The State Police announced these "findings" to the media.[8] Dr. Michael Baden, the medical examiner who had arrived from New York City on September 15 to check Dr. Edland's work, drove to that funeral parlor at close to midnight, rolled the body over, and pointed to the bullet hole in the middle of the man's back. The undertaker and the trooper who was there looked in silence. Then the undertaker reportedly phoned his wife and told her she'd better stop talking to the press.[9]

One of the four targets of the Hindering Case had directed the Night Riders' effort. While Tony did not bar me from giving the evidence of the Night Riders to the Supplemental Grand Jury, he claimed several times to be baffled by what I was trying to prove. He said, in substance, "Go ahead, Malcolm, if you really want to, but I don't see the point." I replied that it looked to me like part of a State Police effort to hide the truth that was desperate to the point of irrationality. (Technically, it evidenced motive and intent. It added weight to the conclusion that the pieces of the Mosaic were not simply goofs but constituted a deliberate effort to hinder the prosecution of the guilty shooters.)

The dig was a State Police stunt that Tony did complain about. Police bullets had riddled the tents, tables, mattresses, and trash in D Yard. So long as these objects lay in place, they constituted valuable evidence of trajectories, volume of fire, etc. Some bullets had probably lodged in them. They should have been promptly photographed and/or tagged for location and collected. What part of the bullets fired during the Christian Incident, for example, ended up within the large rectangle of mattresses piled in the Hostage Circle? How much other evidence lay scattered about D Yard—clothing, notes, spent shells, maybe spent bullets—we never knew.

The police, Tony used to complain, simply scooped up everything in D Yard and buried it behind the prison. They said something about preventing disease, though I do not recall any medical warnings about that. If threat of disease was really a problem, the obvious solution was to collect the evidence quickly. They had dozens of detectives and perhaps could have found one competent photographer. I am fairly certain that the Investigation tried digging it all up later to see if any evidence remained usable but came up with a mucky mess that was beyond salvaging. At least the State Police found time to pick up all the inmate weapons in D Yard. They and Bob Fischer called a press conference to display these weapons on the sixteenth—after Fischer had imposed an official silence about the riot and retaking.

A radio log is a written journal of what messages come in and go out over a radio, with the time noted beside each message. The State Police kept such a log at their Command Post at Attica. First, they told the Investigation they hadn't.

Then, the log they gave us looked strangely sparse for the period during the assault. We knew a lot more of what went over the State Patrol radios then from a "log" that a *Los Angeles Times* reporter had made when he jumped into an empty police car outside the prison and took notes while looking at his watch. The State Police admitted when we questioned them that they did not write their log at the time they sent and heard the messages surrounding the assault, at least not the log they turned over to us. Rather, they reconstructed that part several days later in their Batavia barracks, from "notes" they had made at the time. They had apparently destroyed those "notes."

Did their original log or notes contain more than they wanted us to know? The main State Police radio operator admitted to me that the times recorded on the log for the transmission of messages during the assault were not accurate. He admitted that much substance of the messages was omitted, though he claimed that all the notes they had at Batavia were transcribed onto the log before being destroyed. The radio operator on the night shift early on the thirteenth stated that he had made notes on a yellow pad of messages for which he did not see entries on the reconstructed log. Taken alone, the destruction of the original record of State Police radio transmissions might prove nothing beyond an incredibly sloppy departure from State Police standard practice. In context, it fit the pattern. Another piece fell into place in the Mosaic.

A blotter is a traditional and standard police accoutrement. It is a journal kept at a stationhouse, command post, etc., in which the police note by date and time the significant events that happen and the noteworthy people who come and go. Tony used to say that the first thing the police do when they establish themselves someplace is to set up a blotter. The State Police had a blotter at the Auburn prison riot in 1970. They had a blotter at the Woodstock rock music festival of 1969 (which I read in 1974 with great interest). But they said they did not have a blotter at Attica until some days after the retaking, starting around September 16, as best I recall. Why had they not set one up before the assault—if they hadn't—during the days of negotiations when they had relatively little to do? Since they could not realistically have given us a blotter with the pages for the assault and its desperate aftermath torn out, the realistic question was, was their original blotter so incriminating that they chucked the whole book and started over?

The blotter that should have existed should have proved invaluable—told in many instances who was where when, noted the turning in of the shotgun that had probably killed Rivera, maybe included useful notes about the Rockefeller people who were there, etc. Questions about a blotter were on my list for the Hindering Case witnesses. Most of the troopers who should have seen one said they did not recall seeing it. A few had some recollection. Were they confused, constructing in their memory what should have been there but was not? I never learned for sure about the blotter.

The Department of Correctional Services people made tapes of their phone conversations between Attica and their Albany headquarters during and after the riot. So did the State Police. The Department of Corrections turned their tapes over to the Investigation early on. Naturally. In late summer 1974, Tony assigned Investigator Jimmy LoCurto to listen to this pile of cassettes and cull anything useful. The State Police tapes had to contain spontaneous, excited, and otherwise revealing conversations. But the State Police told us, under oath, that they had destroyed their tapes by routinely reusing those cassettes and thus taping over all that had been recorded during the critical time. Would a jury swallow such a claim?

Tony used to call September 14 the "missing day." We pretty much knew what the State Police were doing, and failing to do, on the thirteenth after the retaking, and on the fifteenth, but not on the fourteenth. The taking of troopers' statements was supposedly suspended. The panoply of assault photos that had to depict people shooting had been shown late on the thirteenth. The news broke on the fourteenth that the hostages had been shot—telling the public what the State Police had known all along and literally tried to bury. Then what? We knew at least what pieces of the Mosaic to pursue for the thirteenth and fifteenth. In that vivid yet misty aftermath of Attica, in the Mosaic that shimmered somewhere between Franz Kafka and Alice through the Looking Glass yet had really happened, the fourteenth of September gaped as a nonpiece, a void, a black hole. What had we missed? With inconsequential exceptions, the State Police I asked said they did not recall.

Yet we need not answer everything. The Hindering Case grew stronger. While I did not expect the existence of the State Police cover-up to be admissible against any trooper in a Shooter Case, I found it overall a monumental admission by the State Police that they had much criminal shooting to hide.

* * *

That September, which marked the third anniversary of the turkey shoot, was a halcyon month, peace on borrowed time, notwithstanding Thursday in the Sky following Labor Day, an afternoon I call Mad Friday later in the month, and a number of other hassles. Expecting to return to the Shooter Cases, I warmed to the Hindering Case as I dug deeper into it. The jury warmed to it, too. The case looked stronger and stronger, the deeper we went. Much remained good, in the jury and out. Several interviews at the prison went well. For some reason that Tony never mentioned, he had his secretary go around and collect everybody's notes of the first August conferences on the Hindering Case. He had never done that before. I was distrustful enough to keep a set of mine. His secretary finally came to Buffalo. One gentle evening some investigators and I took her to dinner on the Canadian side of Niagara Falls, the first time I'd been there. I still believed that the new troubles with the Investigation would be gotten through, that things would improve even as they worsened.

Mad Friday came the long afternoon of September 20. Tony assembled eight or so of us, mainly investigators, in the big front room overlooking City Hall. Starting at about two o'clock he harangued us loudly in a strange voice I was hearing more and more then, pacing the room, and with repetition that seemed endless at the time. In part, his words were a pep talk for the investigators to dig into investigating as he had never before asked them to. He also sounded as though he wanted to stop using the grand jury for uncovering new evidence. I thought that this had been progressing rather well. Perhaps his problem was that he did, too.

To those of us sitting on the gray metal desks around the room, Tony sounded as if he had gone crazy. "Field investigate!" he thundered. "Field investigate!" Cases like the Hindering Case, his tremolo continued, are solved by investigators questioning witnesses in motel rooms. Several times he challenged anyone who was not with him to get up and leave the room. Several times an investigator named Frank Keenan did get up, only to sit back down. Frank told me later that he was getting up not to accept Tony's challenge but to lead him away.

Finally, at close to 6:30 P.M. Tony subsided. The rest of us went quietly to our weekends. On Monday Tony was back to his new version of normal. "I hated to have to do that," he told me a little later, quietly but still in the strange voice, "but I had to." Which day, I wondered, was he putting it on?

Crazy like a fox is the expression that came to mind afterward. No matter how off the wall Tony acted following the August switch, his bottom line was always the same: keep the evidence of official crime away from the jury. His "aberrations" never cut the other way. Mad Friday fit the mosaic of Tony's behavior.

Chapter Twenty-one

Obstruction of Evidence

Voices from the past startled Lenny Brown as he worked in his cubicle next to the one in which Jimmy LoCurto had chosen to listen to tapes. Tony had assigned LoCurto to review all the tapes that the Corrections Department had given us of their riot-time conversations between Attica and Albany—their counterpart to the tapes the State Police claimed to have routinely erased. The subtle, white-haired LoCurto had great ability to find facts, to reason, and to cope with people, though I never felt he put his heart into investigating other cops. Now he was listening to the tapes sometimes with an earplug, sometimes over a speaker. Lenny heard the voices on the speaker and reported to Tony and me what they said.

The first voice belonged to Warren Cairo, an official of the guards' union, who watched the retaking from A Block and was reporting back to the Corrections Department Command Post in Albany that same afternoon. Here is the core of what Lenny and Jimmy heard:

Cairo: I took one of the hostages out and he said, "Boy, I love you."
CP: Did he—
Cairo: He didn't give any information. He was in shock. You know, he just couldn't give any information.
CP: What did you see? Point out any things that you seen.
Cairo: Relative things. I was standing next to a correction officer with a rifle as—
CP: Where was that?
Cairo: In cell block A on the top tier on the right.
CP: During the attack?
Cairo: At the beginning—before, beginning and after. When the hostages with threats, they had three of them facing the cell block A and

the helicopter came down with the gas, then the inmates started to attempt to cut and then there was a complete fire from all sides. The officer next— they were all laying down now on the crosswalk and the officer next to me was firing into the bodies on the walk and I pushed the rifle away.

And I said, "Gee, get those targets over there, the leaders with all those, you know, weapons. You got hostages there, you know."

You know, I think all the display here by the State Police was the coordination and training that they had. If they had to go through two wire barricades to get to a third barricade and what they did, they sent men out with firepower and then right back of them come in the men with the snips and cut the wire and the more firepower, over the wire and so forth. It was really—it was such a short duration I don't think they ever anticipated that kind of firepower. I think it took them completely—

CP: By surprise?

Cairo: Yes.

CP: They must have been expecting this all along.

Cairo: They were expecting it, but they never expected the firepower that came out. You know, they had barricades and they thought, you know, that was going to do the trick, but it didn't.

When they saw all—when they were mowed down like wheat on that—on top of that crosswalk and there was nothing moving on that walk once the fire, that initial burst.

And that helicopter hovered over and told them, "Put your hands on your head, give up to the nearest officer," and mister, they were giving up.

Tony found the greatest significance in the words, " . . . they were all laying down now on the crosswalk and the officer next to me was firing into the bodies on the walk. . . ." I agreed. Tony sounded as horrified as any of us by this shooter, whose prostrate targets had not been posing an imminent threat to anyone. This correction officer came, I thought, to be one of the targets of the Shooter Cases, a perpetrator probably of attempted murder and certainly of reckless endangerment. It was vital to try to identify him, if possible by Cairo. That should have been done three years ago; McKay had quoted Cairo, and his transcript became publicly available in 1972.[1] It could still be done now.

Cairo's tape belonged in the Supplemental Grand Jury. It might well be the key to indicting and ultimately convicting a criminal correction officer. It gave a firsthand feel for the volume of fire. It suggested the conclusion that few if any inmates moved on A Walk after the initial barrage. It also deserved its place in the jury's Report.

With Tony's approval I called Warren Cairo to Warsaw in early October to put him and his tape into the jury. Our investigators had talked to him and reported back that he could no longer recall what he had said to the correction officer next to him. My first reaction was to disbelieve Cairo, but I talked with him myself outside the jury and found him convincing. Cairo maintained that he had no recollection of the conversation with the shooter, but he knew he spoke on the phone as the tape shows he did, and he had no reason to doubt the truthfulness of what he had reported.

I told Tony, who was at the jury that day, that under these circumstances I considered the tape admissible in evidence, and thus proper for the jury to hear. Before leaving New York that week I had looked up the law on this.[2] I asked Tony to let me put the tape into the jury through Cairo and play it for them on a machine we had brought for that purpose.

Tony wasn't so sure. I asked him to let me recheck the law with Mike Sawicki, an assistant who was one of the best book lawyers the Investigation ever had. If Sawicki agreed with me, we could put Cairo into the jury and play them his tape. Tony agreed. I phoned the question to Sawicki in Buffalo. About forty minutes later he called back to confirm that the tape was indeed admissible. I told Tony. It was too late. To my surprise and chagrin, Tony had sent Cairo home.

Tony never disagreed that the tape was admissible, never disputed his initial view of its importance, but he never allowed me to bring Cairo back to the jury, or to play the tape for them.

Cairo had other evidence the jury should have heard. He had told our investigators on September 30 that:

he observed the troopers coming from A block down the catwalk
diagonally and . . . firing into the barricades as they were advancing. Mr.
[Cairo] did not see any resistance from inmates and stated that everyone
was down. He stated that he did not see anyone get shot . . . .[3]

His corroboration of this shooting mattered, since the nonshooters who came down that catwalk among the shooters were swearing that they were not aware of it.

Cairo recalled seeing fifteen or twenty correction officers on the third floor of A Block with him. Our investigators had showed him pictures of only eight. Presumably, some of those—like so many of the Investigation's pictures of correction officers—were years out of date, depicting middle-aged men in their vanished youth. Cairo was not able to identify the man who had been firing into other men's bodies. The obvious move was to show him current photos.

One drawback of Tony's rush into the Hindering Case was that it looked as if we would run out of witnesses to fill the three-day weeks with the jury. If that happened, Tony wanted to tell the jury not to come in. That made no sense to me. Why not put in the Shooter Case witnesses who would have to go in eventually anyway? That would help Tony's objective of speed. Apart from letting me bring Cairo to the door to the jury room, however, Tony did not want any more Shooter witnesses called. We argued. He was not immune to logic if it was repeated often enough. I finally persuaded him. Then we did not run out of Hindering witnesses, and the argument became moot except as another piece in the new mosaic of Tony's efforts to obstruct the prosecution of the Shooter Cases—efforts that I had been experiencing since he refused to let me present, and let the jury vote on, the two shooter cases and one perjury case at the end of July.

The pressure Tony had put me under during the Shooter Cases to hurry witnesses through the jury increased during the Hindering Case. Now, though, Tony had an explanation. He said he'd promised his wife he would finish with the jury in six weeks. Wishful promise or no, I did not see how he could cut off the cases forever if they were not complete.

Tony was insisting with increasing stridency that he alone understood the Hindering Case, what comprised it, how to solve it. When you disagreed with him, the subject was not debatable, you simply didn't understand. This was a new Tony. He said what he said to us singly or in groups and refused to permit comment. I made a note, "Pro[cedure]: *You* ask a q—then go on when I try to ans. *I* start to ask & get cut off before I finish."

The failure of the State Police to use their standard Discharge of Firearms form at Attica was a piece of Tony's Mosaic. Don Schechter wrote in a memo dated October 25, 1974, regarding State Police Superintendent Kirwan:

> *Recommendation*: I suggest that we obtain *all* of the forms relative to the discharge of firearms maintained by the N.Y. State Police from two years before 9/9/71 until the present. Let us examine their procedure rather than be told about it.

I agreed. Kirwan was not the only officer who told us that the form, which asked at whom or what was the shot fired, was solely for shots fired at animals. This fiction was the State Police Official Version. A captain who went out with the assault, on the other hand, stated that if he had fired on the thirteenth, he would certainly have filled out the form. Sometimes such an obvious truth came like a breath of fresh air. How had the decision not to use the form been reached? Whose decision was it? I pursued these questions in the jury. The answers were beginning to come. One captain had already told us which of our four main suspects had told a second captain not to use the form. But Tony would not permit me to question the second captain. He refused to ask Superintendent Kirwan the number of forms the State Police had used for shots fired at people in recent years. He refused to request or subpoena all forms filled out by the State Police in recent years. He refused to understand why Schechter or I thought any of this mattered.

Nelson Rockefeller had announced in September 1971 that unfortunately the hostages had gotten caught in a "crossfire."[4] That was, of course, not what happened. I did not see that tracking down the origin of his use of the term was either possible or a very useful way to expend our investigators. Rockefeller had either misunderstood the fact or thought it sounded like a good phrase to explain away those killings—so what? Tony disagreed. He and I barely discussed it. The same thing happened with an inaccurate diagram of D Yard that some officer had drawn. For a time Tony expended our forces on them as though they were the keys to the Hindering Case. Was he simply being foolish, I wondered later, or trying to divert our forces away from what mattered?

The BCI failure to ask witnesses if they saw troopers shoot anyone was a key element in Tony's Mosaic. Now Tony himself suddenly directed me to stop asking the same question. That appalled me. Many of the BCI detectives I was putting through the jury had followed the assault troopers down the catwalks. They had excellent opportunities to see people shoot people. Some of them must have seen that. Not to ask? It was a simple question, basic to our purpose. Who was hindering what? Tony and I discussed this a number of times. One clear morning as our flight from LaGuardia settled toward the Buffalo airport, I finally persuaded him to let me continue asking it.

Leading questions are a good and common way to get reluctant witnesses like the State Police to tell as much as they will, and maybe more. A "leading question" suggests the answer it calls for—not that the witness has to accept the suggestion. "What did you see when you went down the catwalk?" is a non-leading question. "Did you see an inmate throw something up at the catwalk?" or "Did you see a body lying face up with no eyes?" are leading questions. I generally asked the troopers both kinds of questions, to learn as much as possible and to pin down what they saw so they couldn't "suddenly remember" seeing something new in defense of a brother officer later. Those questions were proper, routine, and helped the jury and us to learn as much as possible about police crime. During May to August of 1974, all this had been fine with Tony. In all his memos on my examinations of witnesses and in all our conversations, not once had he criticized me for asking the troopers leading questions. Suddenly in September, he told me to stop. I protested. We finally had a big debate in his office with Ned Perry and Charlie Bradley and possibly Frank Cryan. The vote went my way. Tony yielded.

Later, however, Tony took to asking to see the questions I intended to ask the witnesses and directing me not to ask many of them. He had never done this before, either. Sometimes I held my peace. There are only so many times you can argue with the boss and still hope to remain effective. Sometimes he and I argued over what was "proper" to explore, what was "cumulative" and therefore unnecessary, and what there was "no foundation" for asking.

"Show me the foundation," Tony would say. That became one of his favorite ploys. It, too, was new since the August Switch. Laying a foundation means asking a witness if he has direct knowledge of what you are about to ask him about. "Were you able to hear what A said to B?" "Yes." lays a foundation for asking, "What did A say to B?" Laying a foundation protects the jury from hearing hearsay and rumor, is easy to do, and is not really what Tony was talking about. Laying a foundation, I quickly learned, meant demonstrating to Tony's satisfaction that what I wanted to ask about related to other evidence in our inquiry. That foreclosed the new. Tony had never had trouble in seeing why I wanted what I wanted to ask about before. Now he acted obtuse beyond belief. Where he used to see how A led to Z, he was now refusing to see how A led to B.

I did what I could about Tony's new blindness to his own Mosaic. Explaining over and over the connections that he would have seen in an instant two months ago took a lot of time from my proper work, hurting the Investigation doubly when I lost those little debates. He even had me explain over and over why it mattered that the State Police slides taken while troopers were killing Kenneth Malloy and James Robinson were missing, and how we concluded that missing slide numbers meant missing slides. Tony had seen all this during the first eight months of the year.

So it continued. The evidence that the State Police had obstructed the prosecution of State Police was mounting. Tony's obstruction of his own case against them mounted with it. So far as I could see, Tony's dealings with the cases against inmates and with the people working on those cases during this time remained as reasonable as they had ever been. Off-the-wall as some of his decisions about cases against State employees may have seemed on the surface, they remained exquisitely rational and consistent in terms of keeping the evidence of crimes and possible crimes by State employees from reaching the jury—whom the law, their oath, and our system required to consider such evidence.

Lenny Brown told me that the way Tony was leaning on me and keeping evidence from the jury was similar to the way he had leaned on Ed Hammock when Hammock approached the indictment of a few troopers. Hammock had then left the Investigation before I was hired. Lenny's news raised questions I could never answer. Had Tony been committed, once or always *before* the August Switch, to protecting Rockefeller and the State Police by keeping the prosecution of officers from reaching indictment? Note that, no matter what his commitment, it was his job to make the Investigation look as though it had tried. Note that without explanation, he had stopped me from letting the jury vote on indictments of two troopers and a correction officer on August 1, before the August Switch. Fischer had been In Charge (i.e., the head person) when Tony leaned on Hammock. To what extent, if any, was Fischer responsible for that? The Investigation had always been under Attorney General Lefkowitz. Did he order no indictments of officers? Tony had convinced me on the evidence (lack of evidence) that he and Fischer had been right to persuade the first jury to unindict a trooper whom Hammock had had them indict. Did Tony's treatment of Hammock reflect a legitimate loss of confidence in him after that? I had done nothing like that, yet Lenny said Tony's conduct was similar. What mix of motives may Tony have had? With all that was happening, I had yet to conclude that Tony was intentionally covering up. I plainly did not want to. Possibly if I had sat in silence and thought things over for an hour or so, I would have.

One day Tony and I pulled briefly on the same end of the rope. He was working in the anteroom outside the jury. I was questioning a State Police investigator who knew a fair amount about the perambulations of the shotgun that Trooper A had turned in. That shotgun had always fascinated Tony. I came out of the jury and told him what I'd learned from the investigator. Tony sent me back with additional questions I hadn't known to ask. Again I came out and told him what I'd learned. Again he sent me back with more questions. This is great, I thought, this is how Tony can be; he's caught the fever. But Tony's temperature quickly returned to its new normal. Although a second State Police investigator was supposed to know even more about that shotgun, Tony repeatedly refused my requests to call him.

Before turning it in, Trooper A had discussed the shotgun in C Tunnel with a correction officer who, we were told, wrote Trooper A's name on a slip of paper at the time. The Investigation had never sought the slip! That was the slip I have described getting from the correction officer in Warsaw. It had Trooper A's name on one side and on the other the list of people who may have been able to identify the body at the foot of the Times Square stairs.

Under questioning by Ned Perry, Lieutenant X had admitted that Sergeant Y had deleted State Police slides, probably on Lieutenant Z's order, by removing them from the slide trays before the police turned them over to the Investigation. Tony grew angry with me two or three times for asking such an unfair question of Lieutenant X "without foundation." He claimed he did not know what Lieutenant X meant by "deleting slides." Each time, Ned or I explained that it was Ned who elicited this testimony, that its foundation was painfully apparent, and that the lieutenant had said what he meant by deleting slides—he meant taking them out of the trays. Lieutenant Z was another witness Tony refused to let me call to the jury.

Lieutenant X had gone out with or close behind the C Walk Detail during the assault. That would probably have placed him at or near Malloy and Robinson at the time Troopers A, B, and C were killing them. Perry had called Lieutenant X to the jury to ask about State Police photographs; he failed to ask him if he saw these shootings. That lapse was correctable, as I told Tony. Lieutenant X should have been brought back and questioned about these killings and the deleted slides. This, too, Tony refused to allow.

Ned Perry made an ideal examiner for Tony's present priorities. More by personality than plan, I believe, Ned often failed to ask witnesses about anything that mattered beyond some narrow and specific questions. That fit what Tony had told me, during the FBI check on Rockefeller, about this practice. As it happened, Tony and Ned had known each other in the FBI. Ned lived on Long Island and often talked about sailing his boat. Like me, he was single. One peaceful afternoon in Tony's office, Tony and I were speculating on the extent to which Ned might use his boat for romance. Tony inquired casually how I made out in Connecticut. I had a quick instinct that he was trying to "get something" on me in case he ever needed it. I replied that I didn't fool around with married women. That ended the conversation.

Tony began to use Ned more and me less for the Hindering witnesses. Tony also turned to others among the more docile assistants and questioned some witnesses at the jury himself. Before September he had not been to the jury since they were empaneled on May 2. Now he gave me a distinct impression that I was being chaperoned at the jury, lest I bring out more facts than he wanted them to hear.

We sometimes worked with Emerson Moran, who had been employed by the OCTF proper since before the riot. Howard Shapiro was Assistant Counsel to Governor Rockefeller and one of his Executive Chamber who went to Attica at the time of the riot and was questioned by Tony at the end of the FBI check. When Moran and I were both in Warsaw on October 8 or 9, he told me how Shapiro first reacted on hearing Dr. John Edland's findings that all the dead hostages had been shot. "Who is this guy, Edland?" Shapiro said, according to Moran. "We've got to get something on him."

I phoned Tony in New York for permission to have Moran tell this to the jury. Tony refused to see any significance in Shapiro's words. To Ned and me, they obviously evidenced a willingness by Shapiro to use improper means to suppress or discredit Edland's findings. They suggest a willingness of the Executive Chamber people at Attica to help and maybe to encourage the State Police cover-up. I could not make Tony see any part of this. He said there was "no foundation" for giving the jury this evidence. I finally agreed with him on the phone that Moran should not tell the jury what Shapiro had said without some further investigation by us. I have since been told I was wrong to agree with Tony.[5] But since I was not going to put Moran's testimony on the record in defiance of Tony's orders, I saw no practical choice. Thereafter, Tony refused to investigate the circumstances surrounding Shapiro's words.[6]

An account by Rockefeller's speechwriter, Joseph E. Persico, appears to dovetail with Moran's report on Shapiro:

> Bob Douglass (of the Executive Chamber) had an open telephone line to Nelson at his Fifth Avenue apartment and reported as each hostage was freed . . . . State officials initially reported that the ten dead hostages had been murdered by prisoners. The Governor judged the attack a success, and said that he was "amazed" that so many hostages had been saved.
>
> The next day the bottom dropped out. The Monroe County medical examiner [Dr. Edland] studied the bodies of the hostages and concluded that they had not died by their captors' hands. The atrocity reports were

untrue—they had been killed by State Police gunfire during the assault. State officials on the scene disputed the medical examiner's findings.

Back in Albany by now, I had been instructed to call Attica, get the facts and prepare a statement that would, if possible, put the state in a defensible light. These conversations soon turned grisly. As the corrections officials described the hostages' bodies, I found myself uncomfortably pressing for more detail. Wasn't there anything else? Just a scratch on the neck? A contusion on the arm? Don't you see anything besides the gunshot wounds? There was little evidence of the atrocities that I was supposed to recount. One hostage had required fifty-two stitches, but he was one of the survivors.

Soon after, the Governor called. One of his counsels wanted to discuss the medical examiner's report with him, and I was told to listen in on an extension for whatever information might prove useful. In describing the medical examiner, the counsel said, "Of course, he's a known leftist." Rockefeller muttered, "Sure. It all fits." . . . I was surprised at how eagerly the Governor seized upon the rationale of extremist conspiracy, including the medical examiner's presumed politics, to explain the tragedy.[7]

When I first read the Admin file, I had noted the foolishness, but not the politics, implied by an early Investigation assignment sheet. It showed, as best I recall, seven investigators put on inmate crimes, two on the 128 shootings by police, and seven on the alleged inmate conspiracy to riot.[8] Nothing came of the last, and it was a dead letter by the time I reached the Investigation. Rockefeller's first public statement following the retaking had begun, "The tragedy was brought on by the highly organized revolutionary tactics of the militants. . . ."[9] I did not ponder until afterward the priorities of Fischer's understaffed Investigation in solving the thirty-nine homicides, etc., versus trying to prove Rockefeller's pet conspiracy theory.

We had a huge diagram of the prison with two transparent overlays attached at the top so they could be pulled on or off. The State Police had "reconstructed" these overlays a week after the fact, rather like their radio log. One overlay showed where the dead hostages supposedly fell; the second showed the dead inmates. The problem was that these body locations were only approximate. They could be wrong by dozens of feet, or even show a body in the wrong courtyard. All this mattered when it came to trying to show who shot or could have shot whom. Where inmate Tommy Hicks died may have been a key to the Christian Incident.

As noted before, the State Police had rushed the bodies away before the death scenes were measured or (they claimed) competently photographed. Some State Police said they hadn't been sure the dead were dead and were trying to save them. Really? All the dead? A body with a hole in its head stares freeze-frame at the sky, and you try to save it? Was there doubt about more than a small fraction? Did death come so differently at Attica, so that only here were the State Police unable to take the pictures and make the measurements they customarily take and make before they moved the dead?

Emerson Moran and a BCI detective both said that they saw body markers in the ground in D Yard. Markers are a far cry from photographs and not as accurate as measurements, but they would have compensated in some part for the troopers' walking off with the bodies. Moran added that one of our four Hindering Case suspects had pointed out these stakes to him and to Bob Fischer as being "body markers" when the three of them had toured the yard together. Later (i.e., too soon), these stakes had somehow disappeared, so that the State Police had to prepare the overlays for the diagrams without even their imprecise help.

I wanted to ask Fischer whether he could corroborate Moran about the markers and the suspect. Tony replied that he would be the one to ask Fischer. Later I asked Tony if he had done so. Each time I asked, he said he had forgotten. A phone call would have done it.

Tony directed me several times *not* to ask witnesses who had been in D Yard when Moran said the body markers were there whether they had seen them. He claimed he did not see any significance that the body markers had for the Shooter Cases or that their premature removal had for the Hindering Case.

In considering the Hindering Case, Tony and I and others at the Investigation had originally asked one another, "Fuck-up or cover-up?" The BCI's reputed competence counted against them. Now a correction sergeant told me how efficiently he saw the BCI collecting evidence in D Yard after the assault. I wanted to put this into the jury. Tony told me not to. I also suggested that we compare the efficiency of the State Police in preserving death scenes, collecting evidence, etc., for the three inmates killed by inmates with their efficiency for their own homicides. Tony said they did the same quality job and declined to pursue it. I had heard otherwise and asked Lenny Brown. He confirmed that the State Police did a far superior job with the homicides by inmates. New Yorkers could remain confident in their State Police, at least where they weren't the killers.

My view of Tony grew more ambivalent. Others at the Investigation were beginning to say he had been reached.[10] To them, I defended him. Yet I kept picturing him as a little man running around the floor of a big paper bag. He charged off toward one paper wall and then another, changing his direction each time before he could punch through—meaning indict troopers. Crazy? Incompetent? How did he manage to indict sixty-two inmates, to punch through their side of the bag sixty-two times in the first two years?

The Report I was to write in January 1975 for Governor Hugh Carey, the newly elected Democrat who ended sixteen years of Republican rule, concluded on the Hindering Case and on what the Investigation was doing about it:

> The evidence shows that the SP [State Police] systematically hid, destroyed, delayed and fabricated the evidence material to crimes and possible crimes committed by SP members during and after the assault. Their effort was not to enforce the law but to protect their own. [Simonetti] at first pursued this aspect of the Investigation, at least in some respects, with more energy than he pursued the shooter cases. As we came closer and closer to getting something indictable, however, he himself threw repeated obstacles in the path of the full, logical, honest effort. Once again it appeared to be his object to do enough to look like a game try but not enough to indict the perpetrators.

Chapter Twenty-two

Bathing a Big Fish

A standard way to prove a conspiracy such as the Hindering Case is to give up the little fish in order to catch the big fish. The prosecutor may agree to a plea bargain or not to prosecute a witness at all if he or she agrees to "talk." Or under New York law, he may force witnesses to accept immunity from prosecution by subpoenaing them into a grand jury. Once he questions them about a transaction in the jury, the statute automatically gives them immunity for whatever their own role was in that transaction,[1] so that they can no longer claim their Fifth Amendment right to remain silent on the grounds that what they say may tend to incriminate them. The immunity they have just received makes self-incrimination impossible. That is why we questioned only nonshooters in the jury about the Shooter Cases.[2] To have questioned the shooters would have been to have "bathed" them, making it impossible to prosecute them if their shots were criminal. The same would be true, of course, for perpetrators of the Hindering Case.

Tony and I agreed early in the Hindering Case that there was no point in going after all the low-ranking BCI investigators who failed maddeningly to pursue the right questions when they took statements or who added to the other parts of the Mosaic. We needed those BCI men to tell the jury who created those parts of the Mosaic and how it was done. This need to immunize the little fish in order to catch the big fish contributed to our having, as of October, only four prime targets in the Hindering Case. We had not finally limited ourselves to those four. In our thinking, at least two or three other ranking officers contended for inclusion. Nor had we reached the question of who among the Executive Chamber and other Albany officials may have participated in the State Police cover-up. We were not about to call any of the potential new targets of the Hindering Case into the jury, since it would be ridiculous to give them immunity before we had decided whether to add them to the four definite targets.

By signing a paper called a "waiver of immunity," a grand jury witness may agree to preserve the possibility that he can still be prosecuted for what he testifies about. Why do it, I used to wonder. Perhaps it did not look good for a police officer to refuse to give evidence without a guarantee that he would not be prosecuted. Perhaps machismo and honor were motives. A number of State Police shooters, sergeants and above, had signed waivers of immunity and testified about their shots in the first grand jury. Then, almost as if by tacit agreement, the assistants who questioned them showed virtually the same blind trust, lack of inquisitiveness, and willingness to take nonsense seriously as the BCI had shown when they first took statements from these shooters. How had Tony allowed his staff to do this, I wondered in passing, when the same BCI conduct was part of his Mosaic of the Hindering Case?

The word being out that the Supplemental Grand Jury meant business about officers' crimes, the State Police had now united in refusing to sign these waivers of immunity. State Police Superintendent William Kirwan and Captain Anthony Malovich were exceptions. Kirwan's position at the top of the State Police, and his being on vacation the day of the turkey shoot, made it practically obligatory for him to sign.

Captain Malovich, on the other hand, I saw as something of a hero; alone among all State Police who participated in the assault, shooters and nonshooters, he seemed to me to have waived his immunity out of honor and courage. The jury liked him, as did I and everybody I knew about at the Investigation. He was quiet to the point of shyness (when he wasn't being tough), yet in the first few minutes of talking with him, you suddenly found him on the wavelength next to yours. One day when Ned Perry and I were chatting with Bud Malone, the State Police lawyer, by the stairs outside the jury, we mentioned that Malovich had been a captain for a long time and asked when he was due for promotion. "Promotion!" Bud snorted. "He's in Siberia." Why? Because he had broken ranks and signed the waiver.

I spent three full days in the jury with Captain Malovich, longer than with any other witness. He had led the C Walk Detail, been part of the State Police command, and knew a lot that I could use. Talking with him was like picking up a rich pile of cards at gin rummy—something for here, something for there, and a much stronger hand. At the same time he managed, as he answered my questions, to present the State Police side to the jury better than any other witness. I wondered if the State Police would have sent him to Siberia if they knew how well he was doing for them.

I badly needed a fourth day with him in the jury. He had told me some facts that the jury needed to hear, not necessarily against any of our four targets but for filling in the picture of what happened on the thirteenth. Also, I had yet to question him about events in the State Police Command Post when he was there at the time and place I believed the State Police cover-up was born. With Tony's approval, I scheduled his fourth day in the jury in early October. Then Tony took the transcript of his first three days of testimony home to read over the weekend. Afterward, Tony had the fourth day canceled and never let me call Captain Malovich back to the jury.

* * *

Major V was the only one of the four targets of the Hindering Case who had refused to sign a waiver of immunity and testify before the first grand jury, though he did testify before the McKay Commission. Faced with the choice of granting him immunity or not calling him to the first jury, Tony and Judge Fischer refused to call him. Instead, they simply had his McKay testimony read to the first jury.

That jury never focused on the State Police cover-up. That was not their choice, but Judge Fischer and Tony's. Now the Supplemental Grand Jury had focused on that cover-up nearly exclusively for about seven weeks. We had developed considerable evidence, in addition to what we had had in the files, which tended to prove that a conscious, concerted State Police cover-up occurred and that Major V deserved his place as a target. Substantially more evidence against Major V, or possibly in his favor, seemed within easy reach if we but called the right witnesses and asked them the right questions.

How did Tony respond to all this progress, and imminent progress, in the case against Major V? Despite the fact that Major V still refused to sign a waiver of immunity, Tony told us that he had decided to put Major V into the jury— meaning that Tony had decided to immunize Major V from prosecution! If Tony actually did it, automatically and by operation of law, Major V could never be prosecuted for his role in any transaction he told the grand jury about. I was at a loss. I thought our job was to prosecute the major criminals, not to make it impossible for anyone ever to prosecute them.

Why was Tony doing this? He said it was to drag Major V out from behind his Fifth Amendment right not to incriminate himself, to get the information he could give us about the State Police cover-up case. What information? All Tony knew, so far as the rest of us could tell, was what Major V had told McKay: not much. Tony could not know what information he had decided to immunize the Major for. He was immunizing this big fish on a fishing expedition.

The traditional and prudent way for a prosecutor to immunize a suspect is to assure himself that the suspect has essential information about the other suspects, that the information is not available from other sources, and that the suspect will actually give the information in exchange for the immunity. It was a pretty good bet that Major V did have information incriminating the other targets, though there was no way to be sure without talking with him—off the record and, if he wanted to be careful, through a lawyer. But he was refusing to talk with us.

We had no agreement from Major V that he would tell us anything whatsoever once Tony did immunize him. Loyalty to the State Police, to the men and the image, had to be a prime reason for his participation in the cover-up in the first place. He struck me as a loyal man, courageous in his own way, and subject to some unwarranted abuse by more senior officers. I considered it absurd to suppose that, especially with no new incentive, he would depart from his own code, contradict his sworn testimony to McKay, stain the State Police image, and implicate his brother perpetrators. I saw nothing to expect from him beyond the same innocuous stuff he had given McKay. Tony was bestowing prosecutor's prize on a man who looked to us like a criminal, for nothing in exchange.

Again and again I argued to Tony against immunizing Major V. I tried to make him see that we had yet to question many witnesses who were likely to complete our cases against all four targets including Major V. We had no way of knowing how much these other witnesses would give us until we questioned them. Repeatedly I told Tony, and he refused to see, that we already had much evidence against the targets and had yet to analyze several thousand pages of testimony to see how much we really had. If we should ever immunize him, I repeated, we should certainly do all these things, exhaust all these alternatives, first.

This was my most serious difference with Tony, the first time his conduct was an order of magnitude more flagrant than his previous post-August Switch obstructions of evidence, the first time I thought he might fire me. After the jury went home on Wednesday, October 16, Tony and I argued all this again in the boardroom adjoining the jury room, while the two investigators who were with us bided their time outside and until we were told that the courthouse was closing. Then Tony and I walked the streets of Warsaw in the raw, red late afternoon still discussing it, more calmly, with more reason. I thought as we drove back to Buffalo that perhaps reason had prevailed. Major V was scheduled to be at the jury the next day.

Morning saw Tony restored in his determination to immunize the major. Back in the boardroom, I tried again. "All right," Tony challenged, "What witnesses would you call first?" I sat down at the long, polished conference table and wrote on a sheet of legal paper in five or ten minutes the names of seventy-four witnesses and groups of witnesses who should be thoroughly questioned, and had not been, before we could responsibly even think of immunizing the major.[3] I handed the list to Tony. He glanced at it quickly, set it on the table, and did not refer to it again. He talked briefly, too quietly for me to hear, with the major, an ordinary-looking man, well into middle age, who had met many challenges during his career but was about to evade another.

As Tony had announced to all of us back at the beginning of the Shooter Conferences, anyone could be excused from working on any aspect of the Investigation that went against his conscience without having it held against him. I had never thought I would have occasion to invoke that policy. Now I did. Any participation in immunizing Major V, even being in the jury room when Tony immunized him, went painfully against my conscience. Though I still looked to Tony for guidance on how to be a prosecutor, I was about 98 percent certain he was wrong now. I reminded him of his policy.

"As a matter of conscience, Tony, I don't want to participate in immunizing him. Not even be in the room."

"I'd like you to," he said with forced casualness.

Tension entered the boardroom.

"Are you directing me to?"

"Yes."

I affirmed briefly in my mind a decision I had already made that if Tony ordered me to sit in the room, I would, and that if Tony actually immunized the major, I would then do my best to see that he was questioned as fully as possible, so at least we would get as much return as possible for this horrible mistake.

Tony called Major V before the jury and had him sworn by the stenographer. He began to question him about the events at Attica. I sat to one side of the room with Charlie Bradley, who was making one of his brief appearances at the jury. Now Major V could never be prosecuted for the State Police cover-up.

The main purpose of a grand jury is to decide whether to indict a suspect or to clear him. These dutiful men and women did not seem to comprehend that

Tony had just taken this decision away from them forever on this target of a case that was ostensibly so urgent that it had preempted them from considering thirty-nine homicides. There was no reason for the jury to comprehend this. Tony did not consult with them about his decision to immunize the major. He did not tell them he was making it. They hardly ever knew who our witnesses would be until they saw them sworn or maybe recognized the local witnesses out in the hallway first. They had heard the law of immunity, along with a lot of other laws, some time ago. They did not know our overall plan (such as it was). It took only a minute or two from the time Major V entered the room until Tony placed him, by operation of law, beyond the law's reach and the jury's reach. There was no way the jury could pull it all together and clap their hand to their forehead and say, "My God, you're taking away a quarter of our big case!"

Tony sounded businesslike in his questions to Major V, but he was not doing a very good job. He failed to probe. He failed to ask questions that should have been asked, in terms of his own Mosaic. He failed to follow up. He failed to take Major V much beyond his McKay testimony. Shades of the faux BCI interviewers! Major V's activities at Attica had made him potentially a vulnerable witness, yet Tony proceeded as if by a private agreement not to press him, embarrass him, put him on the spot, or learn from him. For this Tony immunized him?

The major's tone bothered me, too. He called Tony "Tony" in front of the jury and on the record. To me this came across as arrogant familiarity and condescension from a chief suspect, though possibly it was nervous gratitude for the bath Tony was giving him. My objectivity was not at a high point then. He finally asked Tony, still on the record in front of the jury, if Tony minded being called "Tony." Our Assistant Attorney General In Charge of the Attica Investigation ventured that he did.

Well into Tony's questioning, he had to leave the room to take a phone call. His logical choices were to declare a short recess or maybe ask me to continue the questioning, though he would not then know what I had covered. To my surprise and disappointment, he asked Charlie Bradley to continue. Knowing virtually nothing about the Hindering Case and totally unprepared for Major V, Charlie had no idea what to ask. He tried gamely and foundered. After a few minutes of groping questions, he called a recess.

In the boardroom Charlie told Tony, who was not yet able to return, that it was ridiculous for him to try to question Major V.

"Why don't you let Malcolm do it?"

Tony acquiesced. I sailed into Major V like a happy warrior and was just warming up when Tony returned a few minutes later and took over. The questioning went back to eliciting what did not matter or we already knew.

Later that Thursday afternoon, I began to draft a memo to Tony about our differences on immunizing Major V. It was my first serious effort to commit to writing any of our disagreements. I typed it at home, so that no one on the staff would see the scope of the rift between us. I wrote it partly in the hope that by seeing it, Tony would apprehend what he had done better than he had from our hours of conversation, and partly to try to persuade him not to immunize any of the other three targets. To me the memo was like arguing with the umpire in a baseball game, not to get him to reverse his last call—too late for that—but to try to win the next one. I included as much affirmative as I could, to offset the glaring negatives. Here, without the identities, is the memo:

STATE OF NEW YORK
ATTICA INVESTIGATION
MEMORANDUM

TO: A.G. Simonetti   OFFICE: New York City
FROM: M.H. Bell   DATE: October 17, 1974
SUBJECT: Supplemental Grand Jury

This is to record my respectful but deep dissent from your decision to grant immunity from prosecution to Major V at this time, as expressed in our conversations of yesterday and today prior to the time you questioned him in the Grand Jury, thus immunizing him; my request made to you as a matter of my conscience that I at least not be required to participate in immunizing Major V at this time; and your direction to me to participate nevertheless. A summary of my stated reasons for not immunizing Major V now were:

1. The record contains substantial evidence that members of the Division of State Police withheld evidence, destroyed evidence, fabricated evidence, and failed to collect evidence in violation of their duty.
2. Major V was _____ at Attica, located physically and by authority at or near the center of events there.
3. Evidence exists which tends to establish that it was Major V's decision not to obtain rifle and shotgun serial numbers from individuals who shot circa 100 people,[4] and that at one point he shared with [a second target] the questioning of Trooper A.

4. At your request I gave you, prior to your immunizing Major V, a list of 74 witnesses and categories of witnesses all or many of whom, I suggested, should be questioned before Major V, both as to the facts he might supply and the facts they might supply about him. (The list was prepared in haste and is not complete.)

5. Since late August several thousand pages of testimony have been taken in the jury on the current SP investigation but not digested or appraised by our office. Some of this evidence concerns Major V. Besides not knowing the future evidence, we do not yet understand the past evidence concerning him.

6. The appraisal of evidence which you contemplate shortly should be time enough to decide whom to immunize at or near the center of the case.

My respect for your judgment and my own view of the Major V situation were such that I complied with your direction. Once Major V was immunized, I questioned him myself as aptly as I could at one point, and I hope to complete his questioning as thoroughly as possible when he is recalled. Nevertheless, occasions are conceivable in which you or I or anyone else would be required not to follow the direction of a superior, no matter how sincere the superior's motive. Only last week, for example, it was your decision not to immunize Capt. _____ on account of his prior testimony (given under waiver of immunity) to the effect that he had followed directions of his superiors which may have contravened his duty as an officer.

My basic fear, as you know, is that our investigation of a possible cover-up by the State Police may itself become a *de facto* cover-up. That may occur through not calling sufficient witnesses, crowding the schedule so that the witnesses' knowledge cannot be thoroughly explored, and failing to follow leads. I recognize the problems of time, manpower and SP-created difficulties which have confronted this investigation throughout, but I question whether these factors compel a premature or unnecessary grant of immunity to individuals who may be central to a case of hindering prosecution, destruction of evidence and official misconduct. A perpetrator usually possesses important knowledge, but it would usually seem prudent to exhaust other sources first.

I also recognize that we are dealing in matters of judgment, that your general knowledge and experience exceed mine, and that the burdens of judgment which confront you in the present situation are inherently monumental. As you know, I have great respect for your judgments. I generally agree with them and accept them when I disagree. I have later realized you were right and I was wrong on some occasions when I did disagree. In addition, I hope that my occasional dissents are of use to you.

I note that we had conversations similar to the foregoing, relative to the possibility of immunizing [the third and fourth targets], as to both of whom the evidence of involvement in culpability appears to be substantially stronger than as to Major V. I request an opportunity to compile such evidence during the period of analysis which you propose once the currently contemplated presentation to the jury has been concluded.

I left the memo with Tony in his office the next day, which was Friday. I kept a carbon and did not make a copy for the file. A few minutes later Tony called me to his office and asked me to close the door. I sat down.

"I don't need this!" he screamed, his voice shrill, the only time I ever heard him scream. He flung the memo at me across the desk. The two pages, stapled at the corner, fluttered down.

He called the memo unfair because it did not list his reasons for putting Major V into the jury. All I could have said about his reasons was that he immunized the Major in the unfounded hope of learning unspecified facts that we did not then need, that we had an excellent and yet unexplored chance of getting elsewhere, and that Tony did not then seek from him.

It interested me that Tony called the memo unfair. I wrote it to make a point to him, not as a report for the file. Tony talked as if he were concerned mainly for what posterity might think of the memo. His reaction made me think that some posterity might find it of interest.

"I typed this myself," I said. "No one else has seen it. I wrote it for you to consider what it says, not to throw it back at me."

He calmed down. He kept it.

By unilaterally deciding to immunize Major V, Tony usurped the grand jury's function by abusing his own. Under his direction I had established the major with the jury as a prime target. They were the ones charged with the duty of deciding whether or not to indict him. Given the evidence against the major, Tony had more than discretion, he had a duty to give the jury that decision. Prosecutors enjoy enormous discretion, meaning power, not only to immunize suspects but to violate their own duty. Tony showed the potential for abuse.

Those who write the laws, draft the standards, and guard the bar might consider what can be done about this.

Major V was due back at the jury to finish on October 29. The main damage was done, but I wanted to salvage what was possible. I offered to finish the questioning. Tony agreed and asked me to prepare to do that. Then he decided to do it himself, saying I could ask the major whatever he left out. That sounded familiar. Sitting in the jury on the 29th while Tony questioned the major, I filled nearly two yellow sheets with additional subjects. Tony ended his own examination by telling the jury that he did not think Mr. Bell would have much else to ask!

With the jury in brief recess and thus prepared to go home a few minutes later, Tony went quickly over all the questions that I thought still needed asking. He told me, don't ask this, we don't need that, we already have the other. I disagreed, sometimes saying so, sometimes resting on the obvious fact that I had just put the question on the list. He watched as I wrote in silent anger "NO AGS" [his initials] in red across the subjects he vetoed. We returned to the jury with most of my examination axed, and I was surprised to find myself questioning Major V as briefly as Tony had predicted.

The subjects that Tony forbade me to probe, on which I wrote "NO AGS," included:

- The authority for the briefing of the State Police on the thirteenth before the assault.
- The authority for the assault itself.
- The failure to record which trooper returned which rifle to the SP quartermaster trucks after the assault.
- Whether Major V saw any police, particularly the two lieutenants assigned to collect inmate weapons, on the catwalks kicking weapons off into the yard after the shooting stopped.
- Whether there was any legitimate purpose in having inmate leader Frank "Big Black" Smith lie naked in A Yard with the football balanced between his chest and his chin after the surrender.
- Which procedure (if any) was followed for keeping track of which trooper had which rifle during the alert, or dry run, of the assault that had occurred on Sunday the twelfth?
- The procedures for collecting and identifying expended shells, and for the ammunition accountability that should have occurred but did not.

- Orders to the State Police not to use prison guards in the retaking.
- Handgun records in the troopers' personnel jackets.
- The State Police "shoot to kill" policy.
- Any hostile acts by inmates on the catwalks after the initial volley.

Major V was eminently fit to discuss all of these subjects, and Tony knew they mattered. The first question is not, why did Tony veto my probing them? It is, why did Tony not probe them himself?

One of Tony's arguments for immunizing Major V was that if he lied in the jury we could always get him for perjury. That argument was fatuous, as Tony had to know. You can be pretty sure someone is lying, but to establish perjury requires that the lie be both intentional and material, beyond a reasonable doubt. The overwhelming number of perjuries that occur are simply not pursued. Tony himself had refused to let me give the jury the case of the lieutenant who looked down upon the retaking and swore he saw no shooting.

Now, in comparing Major V's testimony to McKay with his testimony on October 17, I found a flat contradiction. One time he testified that certain troopers were authorized to fire into a certain location. The other time he testified they were not. Sometime before October 29, I told Tony I thought the major should be confronted with the discrepancy in the jury. He may have perjured himself, the jury deserved if possible to hear the true version if he could and would now give it, and I thought a confrontation might make the major more candid with his other testimony.

Tony refused to allow me to do that. I pressed. Finally, he said I could confront the major outside the jury. I put it to him in the hallway where he was waiting to testify. He replied that he did not see a discrepancy.

I passed this on to Tony. He still refused to let the major be confronted in the jury. He also refused to let me read to the jury the portion of the major's McKay testimony that would complete the discrepancy on the record.

A week later I wrote Tony a memo asking to pursue Major V's discrepancy. (Unlike the major, Tony saw that it existed.) Instead of disagreeing unpleasantly as he had at the jury, Tony quietly agreed. I decided to write Tony more memos. He assigned Ned Perry the job of pursuing Major V's conflicting testimony—whatever pursuing it meant now that all that remained was to give it to the jury. As a practical matter, it meant tabling it. So long as I was at the Investigation, it did not reach the jury.

Major V's two versions of where those troopers were authorized to fire came two years apart. Memory plays tricks. Anybody can make a mistake. Though the discrepancy related to homicides, maybe in full context it did not matter that much, was not material. I was not convinced that the major had perjured himself. I did not know—though his refusal to see the discrepancy escalated my concern—since people usually like to clear up their honest mistakes. The point was that the System gave these issues to the grand jury, but Tony refused to. Tony had immunized Major V from the substantive crime, using the remote possibility of perjury as part of his reason. But when that possibility actually arose, he quashed it. Once again, no State Police officer was to be indicted. No State Police officer was even to be placed at risk of indictment.

About the same time that Tony told the jury that I would have very few questions for Major V, he told them I would have very few questions for another witness I was about to question. On a gray morning a day or two after October 29, he and I were standing alone in the lobby of the Airways motel, and I told him I wished he would not make these predictions to the jury because they were not necessary and pressured me to rush.

"That's the idea," he said.

Twenty-three

Immunizing the "Chief Perpetrator"

Tony had no doubt that Captain T, second of the four targets of the Hindering Case, would sign a waiver of immunity. He assured us of that several times as we built that case in the jury. I never knew any basis for Tony's confidence other than the facts that he knew the captain well, liked him, and considered him a helluva fellow.

Sometime between Tony's assurances that Captain T would sign and the time he was to testify, our investigators learned that he was consulting a lawyer. Why was he doing that, Tony wanted to know, even though Tony had made him a target. After reading through a Q and A that I had taken from the captain earlier that year, Tony told me one day in his office that he saw why the captain was consulting a lawyer. The reason was not apparent to me from the Q-and-A, but Tony knew better than I the likely criminal implications of what the captain had said. I knew, though, that the Q-and-A aside, he had many reasons to consult a lawyer. Time after time as we studied pieces of the Mosaic, he turned up at or near the center of the piece. He created it or helped create it or was present at the creation. Tony knew all that. That was why he had made and kept him a target.

Until he decided to immunize him, too! The captain told us, after conferring with his lawyer, that he would not sign the waiver. So Tony decided to put him into the jury anyway—after some more arguments with me.

All the reasons for not immunizing Major V applied to Captain T in spades. We had much more evidence against him. We had no agreement with him to give any particular evidence in exchange for immunity, or knowledge of what evidence he could give, and we had the same host of likely alternative sources. If I was 98 percent sure the major should not have been immunized, I was 100 percent sure about the captain. Don Schechter told Tony that, in his opinion, the evidence was already sufficient to indict the captain. Tony asked me whether that was my opinion, too. I said it was.

Before Tony finally told us he had made up his mind, he asked me again and again to go over the evidence we had against the captain, evidence that Tony knew perfectly well already. I reviewed it for Tony in the car driving to the jury. I reviewed it for him in New York. We went over it with other people on the staff. I put down on a legal pad the areas in which the evidence implicated the captain. I grew intensely bored repeating the evidence. It became harder, almost physically, each time I spewed it out.

My handwritten notes of October 21, which I went over with Tony that day, include the following areas of evidence that we had developed in varying degrees about the captain:

- His key position in the State Police investigation of the assault.
- The failure to order rifle serial numbers to be recorded on the 13th.
- His authority over inmate weapons collection.
- Collection of the assault film; first viewing; missing pictures.
- Expended shotgun, pistol, and .270 cartridges, which should have been but were not collected and tagged by location and checked ballistically.
- Tents, mattresses, and tables that police bullets had riddled in D Yard and that they scooped up and buried behind the prison.
- The defective State Police radio log.
- The Night Riders, whom our evidence indicated he had directed, though apparently he, in turn, was directed from above.
- Instructions to the BCI on how to interview inmates about the riot, up to but stopping short of the assault and the brutality that followed it.
- The BCI's woefully deficient interviews of the troopers on the 15th.
- The more "thorough" BCI questioning of the correction officers.
- The original trooper statements and [their] Supplemental Statements that were missing from the Troop A file on the assault that the State Police turned over to the Investigation.
- The deficient returns by the State Police on our subpoenas to them.
- His probable knowledge that the dead hostages had been shot to death as early as the afternoon of the 13th arising from his visit to the hostage morgue then.
- Initial BCI investigation of Trooper A.

These notes also bear patterns of harsh, jagged doodles, suggesting perhaps my mood as I went over and over this litany with Tony.

Apparently, he took partly to heart my point that we had not known what the record in the jury already contained against Major V before he immunized him. Now Tony assigned several investigators to review the several thousand pages of testimony since the August Switch and make a note of each reference to Captain T. As time grew short on Tony's mysterious calendar, he assigned Schechter, Perry, and me to help them finish the job. We found the captain's name a lot. I knew we would—I was still putting most of the testimony into the jury in spite of Tony's recent dilution of that effort—and so did Tony.

We showed him each place Captain T was mentioned. That was it. We just showed him the pages with the captain's name. No discussion. No analysis. No seeing how it hung together. Point out the name, and on to the next. When I tried to show Tony the context, he brushed it aside. He was too busy for that. For what? Half-a-dozen people could testify later, if anyone asked, that Tony had reviewed each mention of the captain's name in the record before he decided to immunize him. Who could prove that the review was the sham it was? As usual, Tony did not explain the rush. He followed the first rule for cover-ups: appear to do the job without actually doing it. Once again.

Tony brought Captain T out to the jury two or three times before officially deciding to put him in. Tony's wavering, I thought, he can't go through with it. Captain T would meet us at the Airways motel before driving out to Warsaw. I stood alone with him on the curb outside the lobby one cold gray morning. Stuck for something to say to this usually personable man who was now silent, I told him that I liked criminal practice better than civil, because criminal practice was more honorable. I meant it.

I watched Tony and Mike McCarron climb into the captain's car across the Airways parking lot. Ed Burbage drove me to the jury as usual in one of the Investigation's cars. They're allowing a chief suspect to chauffeur them, I reflected.

"I tricked you into riding in a different car," Tony told me in the boardroom. Captain T was afraid of me, he explained, and would talk more freely to Mike and him if I was not there. I pondered that one. Afraid of me? Why? Not afraid of Tony? Why not? Suddenly I am such a tiger? The image was not wholly displeasing. The captain felt freer to talk with Tony about what?

At the same time, I was puzzled and disappointed that Tony felt he had to trick me. In spite of everything, we were still on the same side, weren't we? He could simply have told me he wanted to talk to the captain alone. Tony had complained that some police lie when they don't have to. He was tricking me when he didn't have to. I said in my report to Governor Carey the next January, "Though my experience in law enforcement is not so great as AGS's, I do not believe it is customary for the chief prosecutor to accept rides from a chief suspect."

While I was standing at the head of the stairs in the Warsaw courthouse, one of the State Police lawyers told me that Captain T found his present dealings with Tony, and being a target of an investigation, personally awkward since he and Tony had been so close in the past. That made sense to me, from what I knew about Tony and the captain. I passed the lawyer's remark along to Tony in the boardroom. He answered coldly that he and the captain were never close. I didn't believe him.

I told Tony, as I had with Major V, that as a matter of conscience I did not want to participate if he immunized Captain T. I had resolved that if Tony ordered me into the jury this time, I would refuse to go, and I began to think about looking for another job. Possibly Tony had been thinking, too. He told me, without my bringing it up again, that he would not require me to be in the jury when he did it. That was considerate. And it also assured him that I could not ask additional questions.

Tony kept Captain T on the stand several hours during two days, pursuing the case he had now given half of away for no benefit. His actual examination of the captain was worse than it was of Major V. My report to Governor Carey called it "a long somber joke." Again Tony failed to probe, to press, or even to ask many vital questions. Again, the unwritten agreement not to embarrass. He did not even begin to exhaust the areas of the captain's participation in the cover-up that I had gone over and over with him. He accepted bullshit answers without a whimper and, more important, without the few simple follow-up questions that he had shown me last March he could ask so incisively—questions that he condemned the BCI for not asking the troopers on the fifteenth and that would now have exposed the captain's solemn words for what they were. Tony accepted testimony that we had reason to believe was perjury with no effort either to dispel the falsehoods or to nail them down. At one point the captain recalled turning certain evidence over to Tony at Attica after the retaking, a recollection that supported Tony's own position. Tony responded before the jury and on the record, "God bless you . . . . Withdrawn." At the end Tony said, "Thanks, _____," using the captain's first name.

Thus, and for little or nothing, Tony bathed Captain T. He and Major V, two of the four main suspects, half the Hindering Case, were now free forever from prosecution for the broad and flagrant obstruction of justice by the State Police regarding their own deadly riot at Attica.

An early problem with the Watergate investigation apparently arose when the regular prosecutors, who were later replaced, improvidently immunized a likely target whose memory promptly went bad.[1]

One evening shortly after Tony immunized Captain T, a group of us went out to dinner at a restaurant on the outskirts of Buffalo. Tony and three assistants sat at one table. Brian Malone, half-a-dozen investigators, and I sat at another. We had the narrow dining room virtually to ourselves. The conversation at my table turned to Captain T, what a great guy he was, and how often he had helped out with chores for the Investigation. Someone recalled that he had once set up a relay of State Police to drive some papers 400 miles up the New York Thruway from one end of the state to the other, when one of our investigators inadvertently left them back in the City. Someone else brought up the fact that Tony had just granted immunity to Captain T.

"The curtain of charity covers many things," Mike McCarron said solemnly.

Back in New York I walked into Lenny Brown's cubicle on his return from a short vacation and told him that Tony had gone ahead and done it.

"He's immunized the chief perpetrator!" Lenny exclaimed with a mixture of mock horror and, I sensed, disgust.

Twenty-four

Playing Catch-22 with the Commissioner

Besides wanting Nelson Rockefeller, the Supplemental Grand Jury wanted Russell Oswald, the Commissioner of Corrections whom Rockefeller had placed in charge at Attica. Oswald had ordered the retaking of the prison to cease the day the riot began, and he commenced negotiations with the inmates, since he feared they would kill the hostages if he forced the showdown then. Rockefeller among others would criticize that decision in hindsight. Oswald risked his life by going into D Yard among the rebels to negotiate. He accepted twenty-eight of the thirty-one inmate demands. "I felt most of the twenty-eight points were reasonable—and the rest were part of the price we would have to pay to save thirty-eight precious lives," he wrote later, raising the question of why the State had not adopted these reasonable reforms years earlier.[1] Then it was Oswald who transmitted Rockefeller's order for the assault on Monday, the thirteenth.[2] Another victim of Attica, he had since left the Department of Correctional Services and was serving in Albany as a member of the Crime Victims Compensation Board. And he shared with Rockefeller and a number of other officials the distinction of being sued for millions by the wounded and the widows of the dead.

By wanting Oswald, the jury again showed their seriousness. This time Tony was willing to let them have their way, though he opined several times that he did not see what Oswald could add to the testimony of the other witnesses. Often now, Tony was claiming his ignorance of what a witness could say as the reason for not finding out.

I did not share Tony's doubts about what Oswald might contribute. Besides transmitting Rockefeller's authorization for the armed assault, he was present in the Administration Building while it went forward. He was there and probably elsewhere in the prison later on the thirteenth. He was in an excellent position to know what State Police, members of the Executive Chamber, and other officials really knew about the turkey shoot and how quickly they knew it. The same for the birth of the State Police cover-up—he may even have been present in the delivery room, which I took to be the State Police Command Post. Perhaps he could tell us how it was decided that, after all that gunfire, troopers would turn in their rifles without recording who had what weapon.

Tony vacillated among Donald Schechter, himself, and me, or some combination of us, as to who would question Oswald in the jury. His initial choice was Schechter, who knew the least of the three of us about what to ask. He assigned me to prepare the questions. Then he asked me to join Don in the questioning. On October 21, he wrote that he himself would examine, assisted by me. Then, by Don and me.

I reached Oswald by phone and found him friendly, open, and quick to cooperate. He impressed me as being among the more candid officials I would examine. We arranged for him to testify on the morning of November 6. I warmed to the task of questioning him. Perhaps we would really get something from this witness who had participated in many of the high-level discussions at the prison.

* * *

Riding back from the jury to the Airways motel on a gray afternoon the week before Oswald was to testify, Tony told me that Frank Cryan would be the one to question Oswald in the jury. He asked me if I knew why. Surprised and disappointed again, but in another sense not surprised by now, I drew a blank. I said the only mentionable thing I could think of was that it was so Cryan could keep Oswald from talking about events before the assault that bore on the inmate indictments that Cryan was responsible for. Oswald was not likely to get into those events no matter who questioned him, since nearly all the Hindering Case questions for Oswald concerned events after the assault when the hindering happened. If, however, Oswald should mention anything that helped the inmate defendants, their lawyers would be entitled to know it under the *Brady* doctrine, and the prosecution would be weakened accordingly.[3] If that was Tony's objective, it was not noble (recall that prosecutors are to seek justice, not convictions), but it was the only one other than a cover-up that made any sense at all.

Tony told me I was right and asked me to prepare an outline of questions for Cryan to ask (i.e., to continue the job I'd started). It was obvious that Schechter and, even more so, Cryan did not know what to ask. Tony, in effect, admitted this by asking me to write out the questions for them. In every other instance I knew about, each assistant prepared his own questions.

I worried as we rolled toward Buffalo that even with my outline, Frank Cryan would not know enough of what to ask or how to spot and follow the leads that Oswald's answers were likely to give. He had no contact with the thousands of pages of testimony we had developed in the Hindering Case. He was probably the least willing of any assistant to catch misconduct by any trooper or other State employee. Remember Cryan's Run—his absurd argument, described in chapter 11, that would have justified shooting all inmates who posed even the remotest threats to anyone. I asked Tony if I could ask Oswald supplementary questions to fill in what Frank missed. He answered yes in the harsh voice; then he added that I could ask only such questions as I cleared with him first, and he would be in New York City on the day Oswald testified in Warsaw. It would plainly be cumbersome to the point of unworkability for me to phone Tony, fill him in on what Frank had covered, and debate the additional questions while Oswald and the jury waited.

Tony's requirement that I clear those questions with him had the beauty of stopping me from questioning Oswald without actually forbidding it. I did not ask Tony to explain his purpose, and he did not offer an explanation. He had thought impressively fast. Tension filled the car for the rest of the ride to the Airways motel, the investigator at the wheel keeping discreetly silent.

I did a growing burn over the weekend. The more I thought about it, the more troubled I grew over what a mistake it would be for Cryan to examine Oswald. All of us were to be in the New York office on Monday, November 4. Tuesday was Election Day. Frank and I were to fly up for the jury on Wednesday. I resolved to talk with Tony Monday morning and ask him to reconsider.

In the office on November 4, I learned that Tony was at home. I phoned. His wife told me he was out. I asked her to ask him to call me. Next I phoned Frank Cryan, who was also at home. Frank said he thought it would be a mistake for him to be the one to question Oswald. He said he did not know the Hindering Case. While he had often appeared before the first grand jury, he had never appeared before this one and did not want to go before them one time for one witness this late in their life. He said he saw no problem in my keeping Oswald from testifying on the areas of his indictments. Fine, I thought, this will help when I talk with Tony. Tony often listens to reason when it comes from more than one quarter.

Comes now the one-two punch.

One: Frank tells me on the phone later in the day that he has spoken with Tony, who has not returned my call, and Frank is all set to question Oswald. I tell Frank I have an examination outline for him and will get it to him by Ned Perry, who will be with him and Oswald at the jury, because . . .

Two: Tony has suddenly assigned me to spend Wednesday and Thursday in Buffalo helping Charlie Bradley and Brian Malone get ready for the inmate trial of Indictment No. 10 that I have not touched since the beginning of the year. I won't even be at the jury to go through the charade of questioning Oswald in Warsaw through Tony in New York.

After Frank hung up, I completed the outline of questions for Oswald. Here is how it aimed to help the Hindering Case:

STATE OF NEW YORK
ATTICA INVESTIGATION
MEMORANDUM

TO: Anthony G. Simonetti   DATE: November 4, 1974
      Frank Cryan
FROM: Malcolm H. Bell   OFFICE: New York City
SUBJECT: Supplemental Grand Jury

Suggested Questions for Russell Oswald
1. What knowledge of the authorization to retake on 9/13/71?
   (a) Authorization from whom?
   (b) Authorization to whom?
   (c) Any discussion with N.Y.S.P. members (Miller, Quick, Infante, Monahan, Albany, Kirwan)?
   (d) Any discussion with members of government other than N.Y.S.P. (Exec. Chamber, O'Hara, Rockefeller)?
2. What knowledge of/participation in retake plan?
   (a) Present at Monahan's briefing?
   (b) Knowledge of any change in retake plan when hostages brought to catwalks?
3. Knowledge of order that C.O.'s not participate in/shoot during retake?
4. Location and observations during and after retake?
5. What information re retake received 9/13? From whom? What information re retake given 9/13? To whom?

6. Present at 10:30 C.P. [SP Command Post] meeting? Hear what? Say what?

7. First knowledge of gunshot wounded hostages?

8. First knowledge of gunshot dead hostages?

9. Visit D yard 9/13?—Observations— [Death] Scenes—Evidence collection—Monahan—Infante—Quick—Williams.

10. Visit catwalk 9/13—Observations—scenes—evidence collection—Monahan—Infante—Quick—Williams.

11. Knowledge/observations of A Yard and rehousing? See anyone struck?

12. Any knowledge of S.P. investigation?

13. Any knowledge of evidence collection?

14. Any knowledge of Weapons Accountability—S.P.—C.O.?

15. Any knowledge of [Death] Scenes?

16. Any knowledge of Deceased location diagrams? S.P.—C.O.?

17. Any knowledge of decision on what coroner to use?

18. Any knowledge of decision to send hostages' bodies to Marley's [local funeral home]?

19. Any knowledge of decision to return hostages' bodies [to prison morgue] from Marley's?

20. When did you first see prints, slides, movies, video [of the retaking and aftermath]?

21. Do you know when S.P. first saw prints, slides, movies, video?

22. Present when (knowledge of) film given to Capt. Williams on [at] C.P. on 9/13 (by Wilcox)?

23. Any knowledge re shotgun reportedly taken [by Trooper A] from inmate?

24. Any knowledge re Trooper A?

25. Any knowledge re dead inmate [Ramon Rivera] pulled from hole?

26. How long did you remain at A.C.F.? Any further knowledge of after-investigation?

27. Any communication with Executive Chamber, Nelson Rockefeller during retake, after retake, re retake/re investigation?

(a) [Rockefeller's Executive] Mansion conference?

(b) Any other conference?

28. Any knowledge of S.P. investigation of Correction Department retake?

29. Any knowledge of Correction Department's investigation of self re retake?

30. Any communication w/[SP] Kirwan, Infante, Monahan, Williams, Slade re retake/ re investigation?
31. What were the assignments and duties on 9/13, 9/14, 9/15 of [C.O.]:
    Dunbar?
    Mancusi?
    Vincent?
    Pfeil?

MHB:BB

Distribution:

Retake Admin

Supp'l Grand Jury

R. Oswald

Messrs. Bell, Perry,

Schechter, Brown, McCarron,

Savino, LoCurto

I really wanted to see what Oswald would say about these questions and the follow-up questions that many of his answers would inevitably lead to. I still do. I sent the original of this outline to Tony's desk, and I handed copies to Ned Perry for himself and for Cryan. Later that same Monday afternoon, I was somewhat startled to meet Tony marching down the hallway. He had come in after all, and his attitude seemed to say, "Surprise! Surprise!" as if he expected to catch us in a palace coup or something.

On Wednesday, November 6, while Frank was, I assumed, exploring the outline with Oswald, I sat on a gray metal desk in one of the Investigation's Buffalo offices fifty miles away, occasionally drumming my heels against the metal side, while Charlie Bradley and Brian Malone prepared an inmate witness for the trial of Indictment No. 10. Since I was there, I tried to contribute. Since I was so far out of the case, I added nearly nothing. The trial did not occur until the following spring.

The next day, when Oswald had finished and I might far better have been questioning other witnesses in the jury, Charlie Bradley quite sensibly told me he would not need me at all for Indictment No. 10, and I spent most of the day sitting in another office fuming through the transcript we had just received of Tony's examination of Captain T.

I also had an interesting conversation with Charlie. Although Tony's plan the previous spring had called for him to join Ned Perry in putting routine evidence into the jury, Charlie had been absent from the jury from the first day they sat until mid-October, the day he tried to question Major V. This morning, November 7, in Buffalo, Charlie told me he had stayed as far away from the jury as he could.

"Why?" I asked.

"Because nothing's going to happen there," he said.

* * *

Back in New York, Tony returned the outline of questions for Oswald that I had sent to his desk before he reached the office on November 4. Across the upper right-hand corner he had written: READ & RECEIVED ON 11/6 @ 3:20 P.M. WHAT VALUE WHEN CRYAN PUT OSWALD IN EARLIER TODAY? WAS CRYAN FURNISHED A COPY? Of all the memos I had ever sent Tony, this was the only one I ever got back with a note of a date or time received. I thought the date and time were probably false, that Tony had received the outline when he should have on November 4. In any event, they created a record that I had finished the outline too late for Cryan to have used it. That record, of course, was false. After seeing Tony's note, I checked with Ned Perry. He assured me that he had given Cryan the outline before Cryan questioned Oswald.

Tony had also written on my outline, "If necessary have Bell & an Inv. Interview Oswald on unans'd questions." So Tony, who claimed not to know whether Cryan had it, assumed Oswald may not have answered some of the questions on it. Could he possibly have supposed that without such an outline Cryan would have known to ask Oswald more than a smidgen of what needed asking on the Hindering Case? After the trouble Charlie Bradley had had on that score with Major V? I thought not.

As soon as the transcript of Oswald's testimony arrived in New York, I looked at a copy, eager to see what had happened. It was short. It was far worse than anything I expected. Frank Cryan had ignored the Hindering Case, Tony's Mosaic, my outline, the reason Oswald had been called. Instead, he reviewed with Oswald precisely the events that happened before the assault, the very areas Tony had told me he wanted Oswald not to be asked about, his stated reason for having Frank, not me, question Oswald in the first place.

Not that Frank took much risk. Whereas Tony had become increasingly critical of me for asking leading questions to uncooperative witnesses, who needed them, Frank led Oswald, a cooperative witness who didn't, far more intensely than I had ever led a trooper, leading him on about as short a leash as a lawyer can ever lead a witness. It looked like this:

Q. And then you did A, B and C, is that correct?
A. Yes.
Q. And then you did D, E and F, is that correct?
A. Yes.

Since the phrasing was almost all the prosecutor's, there was not much help an inmate defendant was likely to get from Oswald.

I went to Tony with the problems of substance and style I found in Cryan's examination. What a pain in the ass Tony must have considered me for mentioning that Frank asked Oswald nothing that mattered, and for my other efforts to pursue the stated purpose of the Investigation. Yet he must have taken some pleasure from the quick skill with which he parried so many of my efforts. His only response this time was to assign Lenny Brown and me to interview Oswald in Albany and explore with him the questions Frank had not asked, just as he had written on my outline.

Thus did Tony Simonetti play Catch-22 with the Supplemental Grand Jury over Russell Oswald. Thus did Tony win. They wanted Oswald. He gave them Oswald—in a meaningless display that gave them nothing but an illusion of substance.

Twenty-five

The Witness Shutout

In early October Tony had surprised us with a list of thirty-nine witnesses and groups of witnesses to be put through the jury during the nine days the jury would sit between October 8 and 24. I found the list striking in several ways. It specified very limited and inadequate questions for each witness. It was too crowded to permit adequate questioning. It omitted many important witnesses, with no indication that they would ever be called, though it did provide for field interviews of a few. Ominously, it included a number of shooters, some of whom should certainly be indicted, and others, possibly indicted, but who would be immunized forever if Tony put them into the jury.

I had responded with the following memo, dated October 8, 1974, which I considered mild (and still do) though it was my first written protest:

> I suggest that it may be in the interest of the investigation if I am con-
> sulted before plans are made concerning the Supplemental Grand Jury. (1)
> Though my knowledge of the evidence, and its interrelationship before this
> jury is imperfect, it is probably more complete at this time than anyone
> else's; (2) my knowledge of matters for presentation or possible presenta-
> tion to the jury is sufficient so that I may be helpful to your planning in
> other respects; (3) I may be of use in forming estimates of the time that
> certain projects will require.

As I was to write in my report to Governor Carey:

> I recognize[d] that AGS was In Charge and had the right and duty to be
> responsible for the jury presentation, but as the man most often before the
> jury I believe I had a duty to try to keep him from blundering (as I then
> thought it was) . . . . Item 3 on the 10/8 memo reflects the fact that the

investigators assigned to the [jury] and I were being driven to distraction by AGS's constant and apparently unnecessary deadlines. I then considered AGS's artificial deadlines and refusals to listen to others as merely idiosyncratic to him, though they did have the effect of making the jury presentation less adequate than it would otherwise have been.

Tony paid no heed to my October 8 memo, except that so long as I remained at the Investigation he did not immunize those shooters, and he declined to put five State Police commissioned officers into the jury when they refused to sign waivers of immunity. Those five included the other two targets of the Hindering Case! Tony let me range more broadly with some of the witnesses than his narrow list of questions allowed, though he kept up the time pressure. We argued at times when I wanted to cover more ground than he wanted me to—but he never wanted me to cover more than I wanted to.

After Tony immunized Major V, the question arose about what to do with the list of seventy-four witnesses and groups of witnesses I had given Tony in the effort to forestall that immunization. I found Tony reviewing the list in his office in New York on Friday, October 18, when I returned from lunch. Four investigators were there, along with Ned Perry and Don Schechter. Tony was going down the list, asking in the harsh voice what each witness could contribute, though he already had to know that about most or all of them.

As I was to report to Governor Carey:

> . . . he rushed quickly through such answers as those present ventured to give, in an atmosphere definitely not conducive to thoughtful consideration. He was [close to halfway through] the list when I entered, and never gave me a chance to . . . answer on the ones I had missed, though I asked him if he wanted my answers.

The bottom line was that fifty-six witnesses and groups of witnesses on my incomplete list who should have been called were not. Of those who were called, at least four, including Russell Oswald, were not questioned adequately; and Frank Cryan and I talked outside the jury with one inmate on my list, and we concluded that he was out of touch with reality and hence should not be questioned in the jury.

The same day that I read Cryan's nonexamination of Oswald, I read the transcript of Ned Perry's effort to examine another Corrections Department official, on the day after Oswald, the second day of my exile from the jury. It was nearly as bad as Cryan's, covered nearly as little ground, and showed nearly as little interest in Tony's Mosaic, which Perry knew far better than Cryan. As a prosecution, the Attica Investigation was becoming a joke, at least for crimes by State employees. As a cover-up of those crimes, it was doing fine.

Before Tony began replacing me with Ned Perry as an examiner of non-routine witnesses, he was replacing me with Perry as his chief assistant for administration. That made sense, since I had been so busy so long with the jury. Perry was also replacing me as Tony's sounding board, confidant, and chief discusser-with. That went with the administration. Also, Ned did not hassle Tony about his decisions against prosecuting law officers. More and more Tony was using Ned to tell me things, rather than telling me directly. That had to be pleasanter for Tony, since these messages were often about truncating the prosecution, which predictably provoked my disagreement. It also shrank the slim chance that I might talk Tony out of (or into) doing something.

One evening in late October, Tony, Ned, and I had dinner in a restaurant outside Buffalo that I'd not been to before. They reminisced about their times in the FBI. We relaxed. It was the first pleasant time I had with these men in weeks, and the last time ever.

The transcript of the Supplemental Grand Jury had reached 9,000 pages. As things deteriorated during fall 1974, I came to think of that transcript as my monument, an unshakable pillar of what the cases against State employees were or could have been, that would "speak for itself" (if anyone who knew what he was doing took the trouble to read it). It would stand regardless of how Tony or anyone else might cloud or misrepresent what had happened or seek to justify the refusals to prosecute by making the plausible yet specious arguments that all lawyers can make and the best refuse to.

November 7, the day I burned in Buffalo over the transcript of Tony's nonexamination of Captain T and Charlie Bradley said nothing was going to happen at the jury, was the last day the jury was to sit before Tony's "period of evaluation" of the evidence they had received as well as what they still needed to receive.

Twenty-six

"Only Two More Weeks"

Tony had been saying for some time that he wanted to finish the Investigation and "get back to the real world," meaning his regular OCTF job or maybe some other prosecutor's job. The quantity of new memos, plans, and outlines he often brought in on Monday mornings showed what the Investigation was doing to his weekends. That may have provoked his promise to his wife after the August Switch to finish in six weeks, but I saw no way he could keep the promise. Wholly apart from the cases against State employees, there was no way—short of dropping all prosecutions—that the inmate cases could end in six weeks or six months or short of a year or two. Theoretically, the Investigation could continue without Tony—I believed that under Tony it had continued better without Fischer—but that alternative did not come up. Though Tony said he wanted to leave the Investigation, he wanted to leave it by finishing it. The six weeks came and went.

It was a good idea to evaluate the record, to index what was in the jury and see what we had, but I saw no need to halt the jury presentation while we did that. Putting in most of the evidence myself and reading the transcripts of the rest, I had a pretty good idea of where we were and still had to go with the jury. I could easily have kept giving them the witnesses they needed while somebody else evaluated the evidence. That was the quickest way to finish with the jury, or so it seemed to me. Speed, however, was Tony's priority, not mine. I did not make an issue over his desire to suspend the jury for the period of evaluation.

At first Tony did not say very clearly what he meant by that period, beyond the obvious. I found his talk about it hard to grasp, amorphous, somewhat mysterious, far less precise than Tony, the great planner and schedule maker, usually was. As October passed, he clarified his plan: We would stop the jury in early November, appraise the evidence so far, and see what cases we had completed by then. We would then reconvene the jury, give them any little bits of evidence they needed to fill in such small gaps as we found in the existing cases. The jury would vote to indict or not indict the troopers and guards involved in whatever cases we had so far.

And that would be that!

No month or three months or whatever it would take to give the jury the evidence they needed on all the other Shooter Cases, the evidence that Tony had said was merely being deferred when he made and I opposed the August Switch. No more of the many additional witnesses we needed to complete his Mosaic of the Hindering Case. No rehousing brutality cases. No chance for the jury to write the Report on the shootings, brutality, and State Police cover-up, to which Tony, common sense, and I had all given high priority—notwithstanding that the first grand jury had been working for months on their part of the Report, on what the inmates did during the riot, specifically leaving the later events for this jury. Of course, Tony was not going to let the jury look beyond Attica to Albany. Rockefeller's nomination for Vice President continued to pend before the Senate.

Tony's intention penetrated slowly. On October 31, I heard him tell the jury that what remained for them to do was basically to vote the cases we came up with during the period of evaluation. He mentioned that there were no plans to recall Captain Malovich, the helpful witness whose fourth appearance at the jury he had already canceled unbeknownst to them. Tony told the jury that the presentation of evidence they had already had was "thorough." That was false. Tony knew it was false.

The day that Tony told the jury the lie that the presentation was thorough was the last day he allowed me near the jury. I was not to speak with any of these dedicated and unwitting pawns in the State's game again—except long afterward, on the phone.

The next week, while Tony kept me in frustrated futility in Buffalo, the period of evaluation began. On November 7, Ned Perry told the jury that after they recessed that day, they would reconvene *"for only two more weeks, tops."*

The jury had sat for five busy months, for the not-thorough parts of the many cases we had given them so far. "Only two more weeks" in the jury meant six days of about five hours each, thirty hours of witnesses, instructions, deliberations, and any votes on indictments. "Tops." Finis. The end. Sorry. The troopers may have gotten a little carried away, but no indictable crimes, or maybe a token trooper or two. Equal justice for all.

Could Ned Perry have misspoken to the jury? He was virtually Tony's alter ego by then, certainly his messenger. He and Tony were conferring hours a day.

Tony had taken one step after another to prevent a thorough presentation. He had as much as told the jury the same thing as Ned, the week before when he told them that the presentation had been thorough and all that remained for them to do was to vote.

I did not learn of Ned's statement until the week after he made it. I was reading what happened in the jury in my absence as quickly as the mail brought those red-bound transcripts to New York. Shocked at Ned's prediction, I immediately wrote the following memo:

STATE OF NEW YORK
ATTICA INVESTIGATION
MEMORANDUM

TO: Anthony G. Simonetti   November 13, 1974
      Edward J. Perry
FROM: Malcolm H. Bell   New York City
SUBJECT: <u>Supplemental Grand Jury</u>

This is to express my concern that the jury was told, in the colloquy following the 11/7/74 testimony of _____ . . . that the jury can expect to be reconvened for no more than two weeks. This estimate appears inaccurate and unfair to the jury, if we are to provide them with an opportunity to give proper consideration to the evidence available, for the following reasons:

1. At least a month of presentation appears needed to complete the shooter cases. That was my conclusion in late August, and nothing since has occurred to shorten it, as virtually all the subsequent jury presentation has concerned the hindering prosecution case.
2. Substantial additional evidence is needed for a fair presentation of the hindering case. How much may be determined by the evaluation which has not yet occurred. It is already apparent, however, that additional witnesses should be called and that those who were called have not yet been asked many material questions.
3. The evidence in and not in the jury on brutality indicates the need for further presentation in this area.
4. Additional interstitial evidence will almost certainly be needed for the report contemplated for this jury. The time and method for their participation in writing the report should also be considered.

5. The jury has indicated on the record its interest in reading and reviewing the evidence, another time-consuming process.

6. It appears that a substantial number of shooter cases will warrant presentation to, and vote by, the jury. In addition, there is a substantial likelihood that the hindering case should be presented and voted. All of this will take additional time before the jury.

Apparently, the jury's concern is similar to mine. "A JUROR: . . . I feel as if there is a lot of questions unanswered. A JUROR: I feel as if I am being hung in the air. All of a sudden, we just quit now . . . . A JUROR: Mr. Perry, after your appraisal of the evidence and the testimony that has been given . . . can you introduce any more witnesses to us?" Obviously, not all questions in the Attica situation can be answered, but the fact is that substantial additional evidence that we have available has not been given to the jury, numerous indicated questions have not been asked, and the indicated remaining field investigations may produce still more evidence. The Attica cases remain too big to squeeze into two weeks of additional presentation, or even perhaps into two months.

This morning I received, and declined to comment upon, telephonic information from Mark Benenson that the rumor among his correction officer clients at Attica is that the Supplemental Grand Jury is about to close up.

There is no need to give the jury such predictions of little additional work. It artificially creates the undesirable alternatives of either doing a rushed and inadequate job of presenting the available material evidence, or else disappointing the jury's expectations once again.

I recommend that such predictions not be made to the jury and that steps be considered to correct the impression presently left with them.

MHB:kbc
Retake Admin
Messrs. Schechter, Bradley,
Bell

Tony's thoughts on receiving this neatly typed memo, which would routinely appear in the Investigation's files, did not cross my mind. I simply but urgently wanted him to change his plan. He called me in that afternoon and demanded angrily why I had addressed the memo to him as well as to Ned. I reminded him of his own rule that all memos should be addressed to him and noted that the memo did not attribute Ned's statement to him. That calmed him down.

He said, in a strange voice, that he agreed with the memo and Ned had been in error. Two weeks, he agreed, would be far too short a time for what remained for the jury to do. Feeling guarded elation, I took that as Tony's way of saying that he himself was also in error and that my memo was leading him to correct it. (I am touched now at my tireless optimism, dismayed at how slowly I learned.) Since Tony said he agreed that the jury should sit a lot longer than two weeks, I repeated to him the suggestion in the memo that we tell the jurors that, so they could revise their plans accordingly. No reaction.

That voice, in which Tony agreed with my memo, often issued forth at the times he was blocking the Investigation. It sounded harsh and not natural. It had a loudness to it even when he was speaking quietly and reminded me of the "onstage" voice he used before the jury. If his voice was a tray on which he served his thoughts, it sounded at those times as though he were leaning down on the edge of the tray. Later I recalled the remark he made during the time of openness, that the trouble with law enforcement in this country is that the people who do it don't know the difference between right and wrong. Tony knew. His voice betrayed his knowledge.

I asked Ned Perry about his "only two more weeks, tops" statement, in the secretaries' area outside Tony's and Frank Cryan's offices, one day after I had read it. He replied that he believed he had given the jury Tony's true thinking. By that point I had no reason to doubt him. I had asked Tony again, some days after he and I discussed my memo, to tell the jury that they would have to sit a lot longer than two weeks. So long as I was with the Investigation, he never did, and he never took any other step that showed he planned to continue the jury longer than two weeks. As time passed, he acted increasingly as though my memo were wrong, Ned and the October 31 Tony were right, and the jury were virtually finished. "I feel as if there is a lot of questions unanswered . . . I feel as if I am being hung in the air. All of a sudden, we just quit now . . . can you introduce any more witnesses to us?" Those plaintive, stifled cries from the jurors were to follow me through the years.

One sunny warm morning in Warsaw well before Tony began his talk of a period of evaluation, a juror named Mrs. French had taken me aside and told me about a nightmare. She dreamed that we were all in the jury as usual. At the end of the day I did not say, as I usually did, "That's all for today. I'll see you at ten o'clock next Tuesday," or whenever. Instead, I said in my usual voice, "That's all. Good-bye." I sent them away with no more witnesses, no votes, nothing. That was her nightmare, and I had reassured her that nothing like that was going to happen. Her nightmare haunted me as the fall of 1974 deepened. It was coming true.

Twenty-seven

The "Old Fraternity Hazing"

A stone monument stands in front of Attica for the dead hostages, but nothing for any dead inmates. It seemed obvious even from the newspaper accounts of September 1971 that the police shot some innocent inmates. Bullets sent sufficiently awry to kill ten hostages cannot have threaded through the crowd solely into inmates who were attacking people. But while much of the public who read the news seemed upset about the dead hostages, I do not recall more than passing concern in myself or others in 1971 over the deaths of innocent inmates. In this, we, the public, showed as little inclination to distinguish the inmate targets as the bullets had.

After Attica some criminals, their loved ones, and radicals of the ilk that joined the ABLD cried, "Massacre"—a faint cry lost quickly in the winds of time. My friends and family on the right, who were usually quick to say "remember the victim," seemed comfortable ignoring or forgetting about the victims of Attica who were inmates, while some friends on the left looked askance when I mentioned that the event included brave, restrained, and compassionate troopers. When the police shoot someone, it is comfortable to presume that the person asked for it or that it was an accident. Thinking otherwise can lead to a nightmare from which there is no awakening. Such a nightmare is Attica.

To the extent that the public did show concern for what befell the inmates, it was mainly reserved for the postshooting brutality. The beauty of that brutality, as recounted earlier, was the abundance of eyewitnesses to whom people would listen, the National Guard stretcher-bearers. Unlike the police, they were not gagged by loyalty or guilt. Unlike inmates, they could say what they saw and be believed. They rent the veil of ignorance and rebutted the presumption that the officers had obeyed the law. The picture that emerged from the National Guard witnesses was of police and prison guards smashing watches, glasses, bodies, and heads; running the inmates barefoot over broken glass through a gauntlet of club-swinging officers; letting cigarettes burn out on the flesh of inmates who were told they'd be shot if they moved; and beating people sense-less on the basis of rumor, whim, or general principles. Anyone who doubts that the retaking was a turkey shoot might consider the likelihood that the police and guards exercised reason and restraint during the shooting and went on their rampage only at the cease-fire.

Whereas the shooting ended in the space of a few minutes, the brutality lasted several hours and, out of sight, for several days. Whereas the shooters wore gas masks, fired mostly untraceable weapons, and would have escaped identification almost entirely were it not for their BCI statements, the perpetra-tors of the brutality had taken off their masks and were easy to recognize. Many photographs showed who stood where during the brutality. That happened without the smoke, noise, anonymity, and confusion of the assault, in slow motion by comparison, and with disinterested witnesses all about. Some of the perpetrators worked inmates over for minutes or even longer, not the second or so it took a shooter to dispatch an inmate. Prosecuting the assaults by officers upon surrendered inmates ("You will not be harmed . . .") should have been comparatively easy. You simply arm investigators with current photos of all the officers who went inside the prison that day, interview all witnesses promptly before they forget the faces, and ask the simple questions. That, however, did not happen.

For the most part, the State Police and Attica Investigation investigators who interviewed the troopers, inmates, and correction officers present at the assault did not ask anything about these crimes of brutality, which were widely reported at the time. Fischer and Simonetti, not to mention the men in charge of the BCI, had to know about these failures to ask. The failures have to have accorded at least with their wishes and probably their instructions at the time.

Shortly before I went to work for the Investigation, Tony had assigned Brian Malone and Lenny Brown to look into such evidence of brutality as was collected anyway. They put together a red-covered binder containing portions of some inmates' statements about brutality that had slipped through the bar-rier of the interviewers' nonperformance. Before Brian and Lenny could finish their work, Tony apparently reassigned them to do something else. That ended any systematic effort to investigate or prosecute those crimes.

In all our talks, Tony—who had initiated the Shooter Cases and Hindering Case and who was, after all, In Charge—never discussed the brutality crimes

Outside the front gate of the prison during the rebellion. Note the flag at half-staff.
[Source: AP Images]

Troopers of the A Walk Detail approach an inmate barricade right after two helicopters dropped the tear gas that began the assault. The photo was taken from a barred A Block window above C Yard. Smokestack of the powerhouse rises in the distance behind B Block. [Source: Liz Fink Collection]

The A Walk Detail has rounded Times Square and spread out along D Walk over D Yard. The nearest body on the ground may be that of Willie West, whom troopers shot after he threw a stick up at them, thereby hurting no one and disarming himself. [Source: AP Images]

Troopers guard surrendered inmates in D Yard. Rescue Detail troopers had descended into D Yard on the ladders seen leaning against B Tunnel. [Source: Liz Fink Collection]

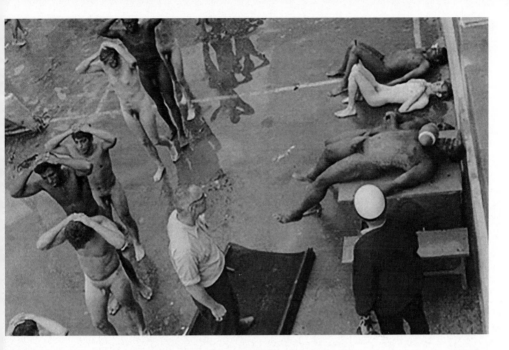

Frank Big Black Smith balances a football on his chest while two other inmates balance shotgun shells on their knees, on pain of instant death, as inmates pass them in A Yard. Most of the troopers who spent hours in A Yard denied seeing this spectacle. When they did, I would hand the jury this photo.
[Source: Liz Fink Collection]

Kenny Malloy, into whom, our evidence showed, Troopers A and B had emptied their revolvers. The absence of his eyes was so gruesome that the troopers who asked me to believe that they remembered little else admitted they had seen this. [Source: Liz Fink Collection]

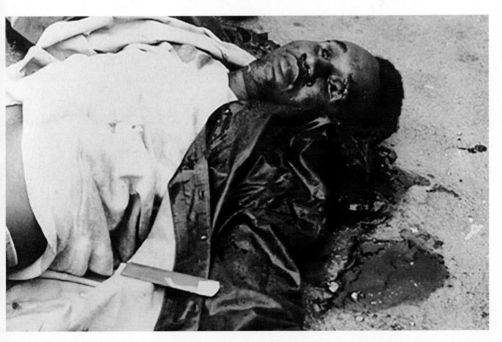

James Robinson lies not far from Malloy on upper Times Square after, our evidence showed, Trooper had fired a load of buckshot through his neck killing him instantly. [Source: Liz Fink Collection]

A State Police detective admitted to me that he had planted the sword at Robinson's dead hand. [Source: Liz Fink Collection]

Monroe County Medical Examiner Dr. John F. Edland, who exposed New York officials' first great lie about the Attica tragedy: that inmates killed the dead hostages. (The second great lie: that there was no cover-up.) [Source: AP Images]

Nelson Rockefeller, Vice President. His path to that job, and toward the goal he never reached of becoming President, was paved with the bodies of the Attica dead. [Source: AP Images]

Attica inmates' champion, Liz Fink. [Source: Rochester *Democrat & Chronicle*]

Liz's champion, Frank Big Black Smith. [Source: Rochester *Democrat & Chronicle*]

Mike Smith was a hostage who survived four bullets that another correction officer fired through is belly. He became the chief advocate for the Forgotten Victims of Attica (the FVOA), that is, the hostages and their families whom the State swindled out of fair compensation for their injuries.
[Source: Rochester *Democrat & Chronicle*]

United States District Judge Michael A. Telesca, who presided over the inmates' settlement in 2000 and the FVOA settlement in 2004. He compiled the most complete and accurate record there is of what the inmates suffered as a result of police savagery during the retaking and the hours, days, and decades that followed.
[Source: Rochester *Democrat & Chronicle*]

Dee Quinn Miller beside the monument that Attica guards and civilian employees erected for their slain comrades. Dee was five years old when inmates fatally bludgeoned her father, Correction Officer William Quinn. She became the leader of the FVOA. [Source: AP Images]

with me seriously or at length or on his own initiative. When I raised them with him from time to time, he generally pooh-poohed the subject. He would say that blows to inmates that did not cause serious injury were not worth our effort. There was some fairness to that, since the Investigation had made it a policy not to prosecute inmates whose blows to officers had not caused serious injury. Officers, however, had hurt quite a few inmates seriously, at least as seriously as several inmates whom the Investigation chose to prosecute had hurt officers. Tony knew this when he pooh-poohed prosecuting officers' brutality.

Virtually the only evidence I was able to give the Supplemental Grand Jury on brutality went in in fragments, at the end of a witness's testimony on the other cases. After going through what the witness saw and did during the shooting, I would routinely ask him what he saw and did afterward. The investigators could routinely have put the same question to all the witnesses three years earlier, but usually they did not.

One inmate had told us how a correction officer, whom he named, came in and beat his head with a baton the night of the thirteenth as he lay, shot through both legs, in the prison hospital. But to my surprise, he refused to tell it that way in the jury. Al Gonzales, the investigator who was in the jury that day as "warden" to guard the inmate witnesses and translate some Spanish, pointed toward the door. I turned and saw the correction officer who had brought this inmate over from Attica standing just inside. No unauthorized person is ever supposed to enter a grand jury. I went over and asked him to leave. He said he had to stay to guard the inmate. I had never had anything like this happen and was not sure what to do. I walked back to the lectern and continued my questioning. I was wrong, and it did not work. The inmate plainly feared to tell his full story with the guard in there listening. Two or three minutes after I first asked the officer to leave, I went back and told him he had to go. He went. Since Al, who was tall and burly, was there to guard the inmate, I should have insisted the first time.

Back in New York, I described the episode to Tony. He did not seem particularly disturbed by it. We decided that I should call the guard back to the jury, swear him in as a warden, and swear him to observe the rules of grand jury secrecy. A week after the episode, I did so; and that, I thought, was that. The next year, though, some people would use the episode, which had happened in June 1974, to try to discredit me. While I clearly should have put the guard out immediately, I did not see that this had any bearing on my main effort.

We sometimes got nuggets on brutality. I heard more than I had heard before about guards dumping inmates off stretchers and onto their wounds, and jamming night sticks into their wounds. Twice I heard eyewitnesses tell about how an officer ripped a bottle of plasma from the arm of a fallen inmate. I wondered how to classify that deed—assault, reckless endangerment in the first degree, attempted murder, all three?

The best witnesses to the brutality, the National Guard stretcher-bearers, had simply not been questioned at all by anyone. I recall seeing in the office Admin File the job of interviewing them listed on one of Tony's agendas from 1971. It still waited doing. I prepared a questionnaire. Tony let me send two investigators up to Camp Drum in northern New York to interview some of these men on a catch-as-catch-can basis during their summer camp. Even at that late date about eight or ten of the interviews looked as though those guardsmen could help make cases against law officers.

I was too busy with the jury to pursue those leads myself until the period of evaluation, and the job had remained undone. In a memo to Tony dated November 4, 1974, I said, "Litterbearers whose investigative interviews show promise should be interviewed by an assistant for possible presentation to the jury." Tony asked me what I meant by that and how many of them I had in mind. I told him. By memo dated November 13, he wrote, "indicate basis for conclusion that 'about 8-10 further interviews are needed'. Thereafter, after discussion and as indicated, assignment to [Investigator Jim] LoCurto will be made." I had no doubt that it was obvious to Tony why these interviews were needed, particularly after I just discussed it with him.

In my November 4 memo, I also said:

> Brutality to inmates during the rehousing should be pursued, particularly the evidence we have of hard blows with gun butts (teeth out, torso damaged) and bottles of plasma being ripped from the arms of injured inmates (a black in A tunnel, a white in the prison hospital). Were any cigarettes thrown on inmates and allowed to burn there? The [jurors] keep asking about inmates being driven barefoot across broken glass, a matter which at this date can probably rise at best only to the report level.

I had more in mind with the National Guard than brutality cases, as I believed Tony also knew. If one of them could identify the body at the foot of the Times Square stairs, that might well complete a murder case against Trooper J.

Tony's November 13 memo was full of little obtusenesses similar to his

request to show the need to interview litter-bearers, aimed at killing my pro-
posals to follow leads. It also typified his penchant for creating a record that
bore little relation to the reality in the office, but which he could always point
to later if he ever had to defend his refusals to gather evidence and present it to
the jury. Smart bureaucrat, I thought. Demanding to be shown what he already
knew, then refusing to see it when I showed it to him, came to serve increasingly
as a *modus operandi* for Tony. The feeling of frustration that his tactics gave me
was almost physically of being in a straitjacket.

As our conflicts about giving the jury the evidence intensified, Tony did
not quite know how to handle me, the person, however deftly he might use his
authority to block my efforts. I'm sure that many people would have fired me by
then, and I suspect that Tony would have handled me more surely if he had not
been in conflict with himself. Nothing more came of the belated effort to gather
the remnant recollections of the fraction of the National Guard witnesses. The
following April, a Buffalo newspaper reporter named Joe Ritz turned up more
brutality evidence in two weeks of talking with National Guard witnesses than
the Investigation had gathered from them in three years.

An inmate named Richard Moore received a buckshot pellet in the
abdomen during the retaking. The authorities did not "discover" this until the
next day. Moore died in Meyer Memorial Hospital in Buffalo on September 22
as a result of the wound and infection. I never knew how he came to be shot but
considered the incident an answer to the Official Version that nobody died as a
result of the abysmal lack of medical attention after the assault, and as a hint of
what the rehousing was really like.

An investigator told me that one of the prison chaplains had witnessed a
guard beating an inmate in the prison hospital and had probably seen some
other brutality. The Investigation had never formally questioned the chaplain or
asked him to give his evidence under oath to either grand jury. The chaplain, I
was told, liked his job and his life among the guards, and testifying would jeopardize his snug position. Our people seemed reluctant to put him on the spot,
or force him to make the awkward choice between God and Mammon. Feeling
a qualm or two myself, I fully intended to call him before the jury, swear him
to tell the truth, and ask him every question I could think of about his seeing
brutality. I was never permitted to do that.

I planned to make a systematic presentation to the jury on brutality as soon
as the Shooter Cases and the Hindering Case came in. That presentation *had*
to be made, and the underlying investigation *had* to be completed, if we were

to do our job. Knowing, and to some extent only suspecting, all the work on brutality that lay down the road heightened my chagrin when Tony and Ned erected their sign for the jury that said Dead End.

The small size of the Investigation's staff may explain the failure to interview the National Guard witnesses during the first weeks after the riot in 1971. It cannot explain that failure during the years that followed. Nor can it explain the decision not to ask the few additional questions it would have taken to cover the brutality with the hundreds of troopers, inmates, and correction officers who were interviewed right after the riot. Nor does it explain Tony's demands in November 1974 to be told why the National Guard witnesses should be questioned. And it raises once again the questions of who decided to keep the staff so small, and why.

Of all the gaps in the Investigation, the failure to pursue these primitive and easily prosecuted crimes probably gapes the widest. It illuminates the true intent of the people who were running the Investigation, meaning Louis Lefkowitz's Department of Law and the State itself. Rockefeller and Lefkowitz knew about the brutality, and they had to know that no one was being indicted for it; they had a duty to find out why—if, indeed, they were not the reason why. Here everyone in charge of the Investigation violated the first rule for cover-ups: they failed even to look as though they tried.

Twenty-eight

Rocky's Men Speak No Evil

"It's fascinating . . ." or "I'm fascinated . . ." were among Tony's favorite expressions. Fascinating to me was Tony's turnaround commencing with the August Switch—his decision to postpone the Shooter Cases first for the Hindering Case and then forever, his charade of investigating Rockefeller for the FBI, his closeout of the Hindering Case, too, when indictments look likely, his refusal to pursue the postshooting brutality, and beyond all this, his refusal to investigate the extent, if any, to which the Attica cover-ups led to or emanated from the Executive Chamber, from his own boss, Louis Lefkowitz, or from Rockefeller himself. Tony's conduct stood in sharp contrast to his pursuit of official crimes before indictments loomed and Rockefeller's ambition rose as expectant and exposed as a bridegroom approaching the altar.

Fascinating, too, were Tony's own words, as he set them down by hand in the fifty-three-page memorandum that he gave me and I dated August 24, 1974.[1] It was his sketch of the Hindering Case, and it shows his speculations, facts, questions, frustrations, and concerns pointing in the direction of Nelson Rockefeller, all of which he had now determined not to investigate. It suggests what a good job he was capable of.

I particularly valued the memo for its account of the birth of the Attica Investigation in mid-September 1971 and for its demonstration that Tony understood as late as August 1974 what we needed to investigate in order to finish proving the Hindering Case, an understanding that he would almost immediately "lose." In the memo Tony went far toward describing the cover-up that he and other State officials would later deny existed. (These official deniers would include a once and future judge named Bernard Meyer who would take on the job the next April of investigating the Investigation.)

Among Tony's greatest concerns in his long memo were not only the State Police decision not to keep track of, or "account for," which trooper had which rifle during the shootings, but also whether Rockefeller or his Executive Chamber took part in the decision to forego this basic and key routine of weapons accountability. Here, like jagged little fragments of an exploded shell, are the rough notes that Tony wrote about this and the other early efforts by the Executive Chamber and the State Police, as it were, to starve and strangle the Investigation in its crib:

> Essential Question. After there was knowledge re the cause of death what . . . was happening at the C.P. . . . re telephonic or radio traffic, or conversation relative to the [decision] to forego accountability especially any conversation on the phone by anyone particularly Monahan re [argument] foregoing {word illegible}[2] weapons or any other type of accountability—
>
> Consider whether perhaps Kerwin is not at Bolton Landing . . . at the time of the retake, but instead he is either at Division or Pocanto Hills {i.e., Rockefeller's home} (distance all ways) in a, in effect, three-way conversation with Monahan, the executive or his representative, relative to accountability (weapons).[3]
>
> * * *
>
> [Remember in connection with our accomplishments & the remaining work: we are lot better than "they" permitted us to be.
> 1. Handle . . .
> 2. Double Cover-up or triple Cover-up?
>   (a) Phone call—No weapons acct. = cover 270 shooters.
> 3. Trooper A attempt to cover-up = cover the 38, 357 & shotgun shooters ({Hostage} circle).[4]
>
> * * *
>
> On about September 15th there is a meeting in our (OCTF) office at the facility attended by {SP} Infante, Monahan, Williams (Sullivan & Connally,) {OCTF} Fischer, Spoont, (Bisher, Case, Moran) and myself for the purpose of discussing, as I recollect, the fact that we (OCTF) were not being given access to S.P. files, statements (their investigation). I, at the outset of the meeting ask Fischer if I may say something, whereupon I state in fairly forceful terms that Infante et al must think we're school boys in not furnishing info & files or words to that effect. I seem to recollect Fischer stating that he was placing me in charge of the technical aspects of the investigation. The meeting concluded on the note of better

cooperation. On Sept. 17 . . . we receive what (Infante) purports to be the files of the S.P. for the first time (From whom? How?).

Theory: By the 15th rather than the 17th, the cover-up was complete. Notice that [coincidentally] Fischer is appointed as in charge . . . of the investigation on the 15th. Infante has always leaned back on the fact that Fischer was in charge from 15th, but we can prove that all aspects of the investigation were [covered] complete by the 15th, i.e. scenes, morgues, evidence, Photos, Statements, weapons accountability, ballistics, Trooper A, the circle, & records. This is the mode of cross-examination for this point.

In reference to the above meeting the following should be determined:
1. What exactly did I say?
2. What was the purpose of the meeting?
3. What was decided at the meeting?

Notice that Bischer's (steno at meeting) steno book was (was it?) destroyed when she left OCTF.

Note that at the time of this meeting {SP} Sullivan and Connally . . . were assigned to me. Following the meeting I unassigned them because they saw the beginning of the meeting (left at outset—ran out because of what was transpiring) my judgment could have endangered their careers had they remained assigned to me following this confrontation with their boss (Infante). Notice (responsibility) that Infante is doing the talking & ordering from the outset.

It is noted that on the 14th {SP} Stillwell drives me to Edland's office. Stillwell is now assigned to me until 6/72 (By whom? For what purpose?).

Check tolls from ACF to Governor's office coincident with the time the decision to forego acct. would have been made.

Questions for Executive Chamber: When did you learn that there was no weapons acct? How etc? What did you do as a result of [learning] this information? {n.b.: During the September F.B.I. check, Tony did not go into these questions of possible key involvement of the Rockefeller team in the SP cover-up.}

Theory & Questions:
1. By foregoing weapons acct. the image of the Governor & S.P. is saved from further embarrassment by preventing it from being shown how the shootings happened.

Query: Is it the motive for the cover-up to protect image from further embarrassment.

Query: Time cause of death(s) known (2:45 PM on 9/13/71—where are weapons?)[5]

* * *

An essential question: would the S.P., an executive department creature, under the Governor, forego accountability (no photos, no proper {death} scenes, no evidence, denial of morgue knowledge on question of time of knowledge of the time of the cause of death(s) & withholding of the death certificates & certifying doctor's filling out same until after possible cover-up many months later, statements lacking weapons acct. question, ballistics being neglected, essential records missing which leads to an inability to show the how and the who of who shot whom) without (permission) ascertaining "the will" of the executive department—

Query: Why, for 2 years, was there a complete lack of manpower {at the Investigation} to do the job? . . .

Notice that in 7/73 I write a blistering memo which prompts a meeting at the Governor's office among the Governor, the AG, the director of the budget, the Gov's press-secretary, Fischer and I. The gist of the meeting is we need 10 additional lawyers and 10 additional investigators to address the trials {of inmates} & complete the remaining work. Why? Indictments create need for more work. We are granted our request.[6]

* * *

Essential question [For Every Appropriate witness]: By whom are you told to forego weapons accountability.

Ask everyone near enough to . . . ask it up the chain of command . . .

{There follows a list including witnesses Tony refused to let me call.}[7]

Here is the Tony who refused to follow up with State Police Superintendent Kirwan, or anyone else, about the State Police failure to use the Discharge of Firearms form:

who testified that {SP} Monahan (Malovich & Elbel . . .) consulted with Kirwan . . . to make the decision to forego weapons [acct.] discharge forms which require serial numbers of weapons fired.[8]

At another point in the memo, Tony wrote, "For two years [this is our proof] we conducted the most meticulous investigation imaginable on the question of liability for the shootings . . . ." That was simply not true. Could the Tony who wrote it actually have believed it? What, I wondered, did it say of his capacity for self-delusion if he did? He wrote it in the context of considering whether the obstacles the Investigation met "suggest a cover-up by a legal mind," specifically, one of Rockefeller's counsel.[9]

Recall that when the Supplemental Grand Jury asked for Rockefeller after the August Switch, Tony put them off by telling them that there was "no foundation" for calling him, and by denying that they had the power to subpoena the executive, even though Rockefeller was no longer the executive, and he would probably come if they simply invited him.[10] Here is what Tony had written on that subject in his memo, before he turned (was turned?) around:

> Recall, the first Grand Jury requested that Rockefeller be called (Fischer's view adopted by the office was that you could not call the Executive with respect to the proper exercise of his discretion, i.e. the decision not to go to Attica).
>
> The question arises, however, did the first grand jury wish to ask the Governor about the decision to forego accountability because that is a question relative to the "improper" exercise of discretion (ask the first Grand Jury what it was they wished to ask the Governor?).
>
> This possibility relates back to {Rockefeller counsel Michael} Whiteman's statement that "if I am called before the Grand Jury I will refuse to testify on the grounds that there exists 'executive privilege' and lawyer-client relationship" (which is patently absurd in so far as his own acts, i.e. he went to Attica & dealt with the S.P. & Fischer).[11]

On the motivation of the State Police and the Governor's counsel, Tony wrote:

> The S.P., and apparently Whiteman, were interested in explanation rather than responsibility from the outset.
>
> Remember that on about 9/14 Whiteman wished to release evidence . . . photos depicting "inmate executioners with hostages." I objected. Fischer [then] objected on the ground of free press-fair trial. Whiteman relented and finally those photos . . . which appear in the press are released [How? By whom? With what knowledge?], but Whiteman during the [controversy] discussion states his sole interest is the "image of his client" (Motive).[12]

Recall that Tony now refused to see the point to the evidence about the State Police Night Riders who sought statements from the undertakers that the dead hostages had not been shot.[13] Here is what Tony had written, apparently implicating Rockefeller's Secretary, Robert Douglass, to whom he did not ask about it during his questioning for the F.B.I. check:

An Aspect [Evidence]
Consider Calling the two BCI men who took the BCI statements from
funeral directors . . . re their instructions . . .
    Douglas
    ↓ direction
    Infante (he says)
    |
    BCI men
    |
    Funeral Directors
Queries:
When? was the direction given . . . ? With that knowledge? For what
purpose?[14]

Here, on Tony's information and in Tony's hand, are two of Rockefeller's closest aids, Whiteman and Douglass, who were both at the State Police Command Post at Attica, the one saying his sole interest is Rockefeller's image, and the other working with the State Police in a bizarre efforts to shield that image. And now Tony refuses to explore whether Rockefeller's minions are implicated in the State Police cover-up!

Tony's refusal to explore, of course, also cut off the chances to establish that the Executive Chamber was *not* implicated. For example, Tony said that Douglass's request to Lieutenant Colonel George Infante was to see if the hostages bore "additional trauma." Was it a fact that Douglass had no intention of repudiating Edland's findings and simply wanted to see what injuries might support the throat-slashing reports and/or murderous intent by inmates? Was it the State Police alone who decided to take the additional step of trying to repudiate Edland? Tony's current cut-off assured that any answers to such questions would remain speculative.

A vital question, which Tony referred to repeatedly in the memo, was when did the State Police and Executive Chamber first learn that some or all the dead hostages had been shot? As noted, our evidence showed that they had to have known soon after the retaking on September 13, notwithstanding the Official

Version to the media that the hostages had been slashed. As Tony put it in his long memo:

> The info furnished on the death certificates must have been <u>superfluous</u> by 2:45{?} P.M. (check) because it should have been known & must have been known to the people at ACF by virtue of what was seen happening (the retake) and what was seen thereafter in the way of scenes, evidence & morgues that the hostages & inmates were dead of gunshot . . . .[15]

Tony also added in the memo:

> <u>Important</u>:
> If Rockefeller's office does not know (Shapiro) the cause of death on the 13<u>th</u>, the S.P. lied to them (at least by silence) because on the evening of 9/13/71 Shapiro stated to me that there was no need for autopsy by medical examiners (Baden—Siegal) from New York City because the cause of death (impliedly no GSW {gunshot wounded}) could be verified by later consultation if necessary. (Did Shapiro know causes of death at that time?)[16]

That, too, was a question Tony did not see fit to press with Rockefeller's assistant counsel, Howard Shapiro, during the FBI check and was now foreclosing forever. I, and I am sure the old Tony, would have great difficulty in concluding that Shapiro did not know. If he did know, his suggestion to call off the back-up medical examiners from New York may be taken as direct aid to the State Police effort to whisk the hostages' bodies into the ground, hopefully forever, while the world believed the Official Version that they had been slashed to death; and his remark the next morning, "Who is this guy, Edland? We've got to get something on him," reflected his consternation and the remedy that apparently sprang to mind when Edland did not endorse the Official Version.

On the other hand, the investigation that was now being cut off might have shown, I suppose, that, notwithstanding the motive and power to cover up, Rockefeller's men at Attica did not do so and did not notice that the police were doing so. The cut-off denied the chance for certainty, though the cut-off itself suggested that there were things to hide.

Don Schechter wrote several memos to Tony during fall 1974 about investigating Nelson Rockefeller's possible active participation in the Attica cover-ups.

Tony directed him to stop. Don complied by addressing his next Rockefeller memos to me. I understood that Tony kept his copies of Don's memos in a discrete little pile in his desk, so he could produce them if he had to, but they would not burden the Investigation's files.

Tony went over much or all of his fifty-three-page memo with Jim LoCurto, Mike McCarron, and me on August 26, 1974, the Monday after the conferences that called me back from Costa Rica and introduced me to the August Switch, and the day before we jerked the jury into the Hindering Case. My handwritten notes of that Monday conference, which run fifteen pages, contain a great many of the actual phrases that Tony had used in his memo. I was surprised that he did not ask Gloria to collect his big memo when he had her collect the memos of those Hindering conferences in September 1974. Those conference memos betrayed his knowledge of and interest in that case but did not show the need to probe the Executive Chamber as this one did. Perhaps he simply forgot.

In November 1974, Tony committed the Investigation to not seeking answers to the questions that Tony had known to ask, been eager and angry to ask, in his big August memo. That handwritten memo shows the Tony who wanted to know, the investigative tiger before his claws were plucked and his teeth pulled. Had Tony alone chosen to render himself impotent (on the official side, not the inmate side)? By whom or what was he turned around? What mattered to him? Security, ambition, respect for authority, a good life for the wife and kids, the same things that matter to most good people?

Twenty-nine

Leads Going Nowhere

Tracking the gaps, if any, in the State Police videotape, which depicts the retaking without showing any of the shooting that bangs like blazes on the tape's audio, makes a detective story without an ending. The month between November 7, 1974, when Tony recessed the jury, and December 6 gave me some time to follow the track.

"Where is all the shooting?"

"Why don't we see anyone being shot?"

The grand jurors had asked such questions during their initial orientation in May, when we showed them the State Police videotape and slides of the assault. I believed that the slides were snapped enough seconds apart so that they could theoretically have missed the instants of shooting by coincidence—though the slides missing at the murders of Kenny Malloy and James Robinson make it pretty clear they did not—but for a nearly continuous videotape to miss all the shooting by accident was not to be believed. The question, then, became: Did the State Police cut the shootings out of their videotape?

An inmate I'll call Townshend watched the assault from his window in the C Block flats and made notes in the front of his Bible of the times things happened. He noted "continuous" gunfire from 9:45 A.M. to 9:55 A.M. That was several more minutes than you can hear on the videotape. The "9:45" checked sufficiently with our evidence that the assault started at 9:45 or 9:46, but the elapse time, not the starting time, was what mattered here. The shootings that Townshend saw on the catwalks and the blood he saw running off Times Square upset him, but I thought that this was hardly likely to have distorted his reading of his watch. What did he mean by "continuous" gunfire? His evidence alone did not prove an amputated videotape, but it probably helped to.

A very high-ranking State Police officer, who had not been at Attica on the thirteenth, told us that according to what he saw on the videotape, people seemed to be getting off the catwalks as fast as they could after the shooting started. The A Roof tape that the State Police gave us after he had watched it does not show anyone doing that. Had he seen parts of the tape that we had not?[1] The State Police had kept this tape an unaccountably long time before turning it over to the Investigation.

Enter now two Smiths, Frank and Donald, and two *Times*es, the *Los Angeles* and the *New York*.

Frank Smith (not to be confused with inmate Frank "Big Black" Smith) was the trooper who took the videotape up on A Roof during and after the assault. Tony had told me soon after I joined the Investigation what a lousy job Frank Smith had done, directing the camera up at a helicopter when he should have been taking the troopers coming down the catwalks, and generally not showing the action that he should have. The entire tape barely shows any of the troopers' advance down A and C Catwalks. It does not show them struggling to clear the barricades, or rounding Times Square, or continuing onto B and D Catwalks, or any shotguns going off, or any people jerking or crumpling when hit, all of which you would expect someone photographing the action to have shown. Frank Smith was not a regular video photographer, but how much experience does it take to point the camera at the action? Smith, when I met him, seemed able. Had he really taken so little of what he should have?

A Sergeant Chamot of the State Police had stood beside Frank Smith on A Roof watching the assault and helping him decide where to aim the video camera. Chamot had to be an important witness to what happened during the assault and to whether Frank Smith had shot it. I asked Tony several times, orally and in writing, to let me call Chamot to the jury. He never did.

The important thing that Frank Smith told us was that he had run the video camera almost continuously throughout the assault, with only very minor gaps when he shifted to a new scene. That is what one would expect. Not until after the shooting died down did he turn the camera off very much, taking additional footage only as he saw new scenes of interest, like the inmates passing from D Yard to A Yard through D Tunnel as through the neck of an hourglass, or his boss marching down A Walk with big quick steps like a bobbing scissors. Frank Smith, too, seemed to consider the gunfire important. How, then, could he not have shot it?

"The time is nine forty-five," Frank Smith says on the soundtrack, ten seconds before the helicopter drops the first tear gas. The A Walk Detail and the C Walk Detail advance the hundred yards to Times Square. The Rescue Detail lower their ladders into D Yard. Lt. Joseph Christian is felled by a blow from an inmate and shot by other troopers. The overfire from the barrage to save Christian (probably) reaps the hostages like wheat. That shooting bursts suddenly intense on the video soundtrack. Lenny Brown and I spent an evening in the Airways with the videotape, putting the interesting scenes into slow motion or freeze-frame, trying to count shots on the audio, and learning as much else as we could from it. After several replays under Lenny's tutelage, I was able to see the hostages fall, from left to right in the blurry distance across D Catwalk about a hundred and fifty yards from the camera. Once I was able to see this, there was no doubt about it. We see and hear it *four minutes* into the assault, as we timed it on the videotape.

If that shooting actually came four minutes into the assault, the tape probably had little if any cut from it. If it was more than four minutes, that strongly suggests cutting. At the very least an intensive further investigation would be warranted.

"Surrender peacefully. You will not be harmed," the voice booms down like God from the State Police helicopter over the prison. You first hear that on the A Roof videotape *four minutes and forty seconds* into the assault. You hear it begin in the middle of the message. I doubted that State Police Senior Investigator Donald Smith, the man on the loudspeaker in the helicopter, had started reading his message in the middle. Then Donald Smith told me he had *not* started in the middle. A couple of years earlier while watching a public broadcast of the McKay Report on his home television, he said, he first formed the impression that the videotape had missed the first part of his message and also had recorded him delivering it substantially earlier in the assault than he remembered starting. Cutting a tape, of course, makes everything on the far side of the cuts seem earlier than it happened.

A pleasant, mild man, Donald Smith struck me as being less guarded than most of the State Police. Talking with him after I had grown used to his voice booming on the videotape was like seeing the Wizard of Oz step out, small as life, from behind his paraphernalia. I guessed that Donald Smith was not in on the State Police game, in any sense. He easily agreed to sit down with us and see if he still thought his message started sooner on the videotape than he remembered starting it.

I recommended to Tony, orally and eventually by memos dated November 4 and 14, that we show Donald Smith the tape. Tony declined. Instead, he assigned Lenny Brown to write a short memo, dated November 29, which concluded:

> If absolutely necessary arrangements will be made to show subject [i.e., Smith] N.Y.S.P. videotape that we have . . . . However, it is common knowledge that television news programs and television documentaries

edit material to fit a telecast time schedule, therefore the material referred to by Smith [i.e., the McKay broadcast] cannot be compared to our evidence videotape.

Somebody's "common knowledge" that television documentaries shorten their material was, of course, no substitute for the simple step of showing Smith "our evidence videotape" and seeing his response. Our tape would be compared to Smith's recollection, not to McKay's tape, whether edited or unedited. I do not know who composed that memo, except that Lenny was too intelligent to have written it by himself, and Tony was too intelligent to have accepted it if he cared to know the facts.

So how do we establish the actual time from the start of the assault until the shooting of Christian and the hostages? How do we establish the elapse until the beginning of Donald Smith's surrender message?

A message on the State Police radio ordered the tear gas to drop and the assault to start. A radio message ordered the National Guard helicopters that dropped the gas to leave the air space over the prison so that the State Police helicopter carrying Donald Smith could fly over and he could deliver his surrender message. A trooper called for help for the fallen Christian on his walkie-talkie; and we knew that call came only a few seconds after Christian was shot. Our best chance to establish the crucial time elapses seemed to lie in the radio logs.

Standard State Police procedure requires their radio operators to keep a contemporaneous log of when and what is said over the radio, but as described above,[2] the State Police first told the Investigation that they did not keep a log during the assault and later produced a grossly inaccurate and incomplete log that they fabricated a few days later from "notes" that they then "destroyed." We had, however, two other logs that were far more complete and consistent with such other evidence as we had. One was some notes that we understood a reporter from the *Los Angeles Times* had made by listening to a radio in a State Police car that was parked outside the prison. The other showed up in the *New York Times* of September 14, 1971, as a detailed account of what the State Police radio was saying at what minute. The Investigation had never learned how the latter log came into being.

The *Los Angeles Times* log shows an order for a National Guard gas helicopter to remove itself from the area of the prison at 9:52, six or seven minutes after the assault began. That helicopter had to fly away, and Donald Smith's had to fly over, before his message could begin. That meant significantly more time elapsed than the four minutes and forty seconds into the assault when the videotape first recorded his message in its middle.

"A rescue unit to the center of the yard. Expedite. Expedite. I've got an officer down." The *New York Times* log apparently shows 9:54 as the time of that call to help Christian.[3] The *Los Angeles Times* log has that message at 9:53. At the time Christian is shot and we see the hostages topple from left to right, the surrender message has not yet begun on the videotape. Instead of coming four minutes into the assault, the Christian Incident must have come seven to nine minutes into it. Instead of four minutes and forty seconds for the surrender message to begin, it was even longer than those seven to nine minutes.

It looked increasingly certain that the State Police had cut the evidence against their shooters out of their videotape, but two points still required covering: Did the tape itself show signs of having been cut? And how did the *New York Times* log originate? I pressed Tony on the first question, writing on November 14:

> I phoned [an expert who had seen the tape some time ago] yesterday afternoon and learned that apparently it is possible to omit portions of an original tape so as not to show on a copy, but the fact that a copy is a copy should be evident on the copy . . . . Consideration should . . . be given to putting him into the [jury], whichever he concludes.

Tony assigned Lenny Brown to take the tape to the expert uptown. Without asking Tony, I went, too, to the expert's cluttered studios over Times Square. He showed us that the tape could not have been physically cut and spliced, and that any editing would have had to be done by making a copy that omitted such scenes as the State Police wanted out. One way to detect whether a tape is a duplicate, he said, is to use an oscilloscope. He then used an oscilloscope on our tape and said it did not show up as a duplicate. That did not satisfy me. I asked him to use the oscilloscope on a tape he had handy that he knew was a duplicate. He did. That tape did not show up as a duplicate, either. So much for the oscilloscope test.

The expert also said it is very hard to make a duplicate tape without having a horizontal "headline" show separately across the bottom of the tape, generally out of sight below the picture that you see on your screen. The original tape has its own headline, he explained, and a separate headline will show on a copy unless the copy is made with the skill and patience needed to keep the second headline exactly on top of the first. He looked at our headline and concluded that the tape was either an original or a duplicate skillfully made. He added that if we wanted a more knowledgeable technical opinion than his, we should take the tape to Minnesota Mining and Manufacturing Company, which made it.

When Lenny and I returned to the office, Tony assigned him to write a memo about our trip. Lenny showed me his memo before giving it to Tony. It concluded that in the expert's opinion of the tape "he believes it is an original and not tampered with." The memo left out the inconclusiveness of the oscilloscope test and the possibility of matching headlines to make a duplicate look like an original. I asked Lenny to add those points. He did, in his genial way, without changing anything he had already written. His memo ended, "If further analysis is needed it was recommended that Minnesota Mining Co. be contacted." Further analysis was obviously needed. So far as I know, the Investigation never sought it; Tony never let the tapes be sent to the manufacturer for a definitive opinion on whether it was a duplicate.

I was somewhat disappointed in Lenny for writing that memo and the one about television documentaries editing their material. But what could he reasonably have done? I never saw Tony have Lenny write two memos in a week before or after. I suspect that besides wanting the memos themselves, Tony was not displeased to force my ally—as Lenny plainly was—into providing him with support.

A potentially conclusive lead to whether the State Police had cut the videotape was the *New York Times* radio log. Tony believed that they had had a radio in a rented house near the prison during the riot.[4] I discussed with him how marvelous it would be if they had actually made a tape recording of the State Police radio transmissions during the retaking. That tape, if it existed, would show us the exact timing of the State Police radio messages as well as all the audible words of all the messages from both the Command Post radio and the walkie-talkies that went in with the assault troopers. Even the notes of a second reporter listening to a State Police radio and looking at his watch would be important to corroborate and supplement the *Los Angeles Times* log, if that turned out to be how the *New York Times* log was made. Obviously, we ought to find out and get it, whatever it was.

I asked Tony in September about going after the *New York Times* log. By memo of October 1, I asked him again, "Is it possible to try to obtain the New York Times radio log?" My November 4 memo to him put it, "The Los Angeles Times radio log should be obtained . . . ; and the New York Times radio log, if it exists, should be obtained, both cautiously so as not to cause publicity." Tony had told me that he feared publicity if we asked those newspapers about their logs. In a memo of November 18, I reviewed the sure benefits and possible benefits of seeking the *New York Times* log, in detail that would not have been necessary for the Tony of before the August Switch. He still demurred, saying that the *Times* might print something about the Investigation. He had survived their previous articles about the Investigation without noticeable trauma, even the one that included a "choirboy" photo of him a year earlier and an interview he gave Fred Ferretti that was published June 10, 1974. The intensity of his presently stated fear of publicity was more than I could account for, except as an excuse not to go after the log. He said that if we approached them through their counsel, that would reduce the danger that a news item would appear in the paper.

Without really agreeing, I decided to try it. I checked around and found that the firm of Cahill, Gordon & Reindel represented the *New York Times*. I phoned their managing clerk's office and found out which partner handled the account. I asked Tony to let me approach that lawyer about the log. He refused permission. As best I recall, which is not very well on this point, his only reason this time was an unexplained "not now." In any event, Tony never let me or anyone else to my knowledge go after the *New York Times* radio log, or the underlying tape recording of State Police radio traffic that Tony and I both believed might well exist, or any original notes the *Times* might well have had.

Besides having interviewed Tony in 1974, Fred Ferretti was the reporter who wrote the September 14, 1971, story that contained the only version we ever saw of the *New York Times* log. Long afterward and without provoking a news story, I asked Ferretti about his log. He told me there was no tape recording. He had been outside the prison on the morning of the assault. He and the other reporters knew it was coming, as they could see the armed troopers going inside. When they tried to go in, too, in order to watch the assault, Gerry Houlihan, the Department of Corrections public relations man who had come to Attica for the riot, refused them permission. It was Houlihan who later that day told the press the official lie that inmates had killed the dead hostages. Having talked with Houlihan, I believed that he himself had believed the Official Version when he announced it; but had the reporters been allowed in, they would have seen the truth for themselves and for everybody else.

In any event, a UPI or AP reporter who was with Ferretti that morning had a shortwave radio and happened to tune in the State Police frequency. The two of them jumped into Ferretti's car, rolled up the windows, and listened. Ferretti transcribed all he could, noting the times from his watch. He considered the times he reported to be accurate. He later destroyed his original notes, as was his practice, but believed that virtually all of what he noted appeared in the September 14 article, since the *Times* was giving him "unlimited" space for that story. The Attica Investigation, he said, never sought to obtain any information from him about the *New York Times* radio log. Neither did the Meyer Commission when it investigated the Investigation the next year.

So much for that radio log. You don't know where a lead goes until you follow it. Ferretti's testimony about the actual log would not have been as conclusive as a tape recording—almost nothing else would have been—but far better than an unexplained newspaper story that Tony, by refusing to follow the lead, left floating.[5]

And so much for all the other leads that Tony refused to follow, as he refused to prove as conclusively as we easily could have whether, as already amply appeared, the State Police had cut the best evidence from their televised overview of the turkey shoot. Tony had refused before the August Switch to let the jury vote on a perjury indictment of the officer who looked down on the retaking and swore he saw no shooting. Now Tony refused to pursue the State Police's apparent crime in rendering their videotape as blind as that officer. So nobody fired; nobody died.

* * *

Spending five days a week in the City for Tony's period of evaluation, I undertook to dictate digests of the 8,500 pages of actual testimony that the jury had heard since May, the main job I worked on but did not nearly finish that month.[6] Tedium gave way to the excitement of sifting the useful evidence from page after page that led nowhere. It was like picking dozens of simple jigsaw pictures from thousands of pieces that did not fit anything. My digests included new or overlooked questions for the witnesses who should be brought back to the jury and new projects that the testimony suggested. That month I dictated thirty or so red plastic Dictaphone belts that summarized about half of the testimony the jury heard before the August Switch. Working faster than the women who were available to type them gave me time for projects like tracking the gaps in the State Police videotape.

Tony had asked me, as part of the evaluation, to list projects that still needed doing. I described nineteen in my memo of November 4, such as interviewing some nonshooter correction officers from the Auburn prison, inmates who had had the grandstand view of the retaking from their cells in C Block, gunshot-wounded inmates, and many others in D Yard, none of whom had been adequately questioned about what they saw of the shootings; further efforts to identify the inmate who banged a hole through the skull of Correction Officer Fred Smith and the correction officer who put four rounds of silvertip through the guts of Correction Officer Michael Smith; and so on. Tony responded by an evasive memo of November 13, mainly by assigning those projects back to me—though he had a staff of about forty people who had less to do—or by asking me to provide him with further particulars of why these obviously needed projects were needed. I would conclude on page 83 in my Report to Governor Carey that the fact that those projects still needed doing "reflect[s] a harsh commentary on the failures for over three years to investigate."

I continued as I could to respond to these needless new requests and to write other memos pursuant to Tony's assignments. I even finished the memo of law on the "Divisible Lie"—Tony and Louis Aidala's erroneous notion that if a trooper's justification was false, his admission of firing at someone (and hence the possibility of convicting him) had to be thrown out—that I had put off since the previous winter.[7] Tony, who seldom spoke to me now, took me aside one day. Almost whispering in the strange voice, he said, "Let's stop the paper war."

I could not do my job without writing memos. Tony had asked me to list projects and particularize the need for projects and given me other assignments that required me to generate paper. He may have seen everything I wrote to push the Investigation forward as being part of a paper war, and I saw that Tony would be happier without a paper record of what he was doing and refusing to do, but I was not about to give up on that account. I also saw that his failure to force a showdown and fire me over the immunizing of Captain T was having the great benefit that each time he squashed one of my efforts to do our job, he made the prosecutorial cover-up more blatant. I did not think that anyone could read his November 13 memo without seeing what he was up to. He, too, must have seen that he was increasingly exposing his hand. Hence the gag.

On the afternoon of November 21, I received a copy of a memo from Edward J. Perry Jr. to Anthony G. Simonetti re: "Mal Bell's Presentation." It said:

> Mal is to devote himself to marshalling facts in the shooter cases, then proceed to marshal facts in whatever other cases he believes to exist.

He is not to generate any further memos on any topic until he has completed presentation on all cases he believes to exist.

A memo from Ned to Tony struck me as an odd way for Tony finally to direct me to stop the paper war. Tony was making virtually all his communications to me those days through Ned. I understood, though no one really told me, that Tony had replaced me with Ned as Chief Assistant. One day Mike McCarron's voice carried from the investigators' front room down the hall to my office, "Mal Bell's wondering what happened to him."

I was furious at the direction to stop writing memos, delighted that it should make the cover-up even more obvious, and intrigued to see what moves it opened on our little chessboard. Finally, I wrote this memo dated a fateful day:

STATE OF NEW YORK
ATTICA INVESTIGATION
MEMORANDUM

TO: Anthony G. Simonetti   December 6, 1974
FROM: Malcolm H. Bell   New York City
SUBJECT: My Recent Memoranda

This is written pursuant to permission from Mr. Perry to write a response (at my request) on my own time to his memoranda dated 11/21/74 and 11/22/74 directing me not to generate any further memoranda on any topic until I have completed presentation of all cases I believed to exist.[8]

1. I welcome the opportunity to marshal the facts of the cases which now exist and indicate the areas where further facts are needed for cases which may exist.

2. I had previously advised Mr. Perry that I estimated four weeks to prepare the shooter cases and another four weeks to prepare the hindering case, insofar as evidence of them is now before the Supplemental Grand Jury, and he acquiesced. His memoranda thus seek to "gag" me for at least eight weeks. This is amazing. I submit that it is counterproductive to the common purpose of the office.

3. I tried in all ten memos complained of to further this common purpose. [Memos discussed.][9]

4. Mr. Perry's list omits at least four other memos I wrote in the period he designates and a fifth written a few days before. How is one to

know which memos will be judged sufficiently valuable before they are written?

5. Mr. Simonetti's memo of 11/13/74 appears to call for further written response. Does or does not this take precedence?

6. If the concern was that my memos were diverting my time from case preparation, I should have been told. I have given hundreds of hours of my own time to the jury presentation to date, and would gladly do more memos on my own time if speed in finishing the jury is an important concern.

7. If speed in finishing the jury is an important concern, I suggest that more of the projects in my various memos be pursued now, during the present record analysis, rather than waiting until after.

8. I would like to submit a further list of projects designed to aid the cases in question, if am no longer forbidden.

9. The Attica investigation is not complete. The question is whether this office will complete it.

I sent this memo to Tony on December 11 by certified mail, return receipt requested (and received), with a note that I had drafted it on December 5 and that "It belongs in the files of the Attica Investigation." Later I would give a copy to the Meyer Commission in case it had never reached them.

Chapter Thirty

"The Dead Do Speak!"

Dr. Michael Baden had to go back to the Supplemental Grand Jury if anyone did. I hoped Tony would agree to that. Mike had yet to finish his basic testimony on how the bullets had killed the thirty-nine dead men. In particular, he had not yet given the jury his complicated explanation on the sequence in which the dozen bullets had entered Kenneth Malloy. That evidence might complete murder indictments against Troopers A and B. Even the first jury had heard him give it, through the work, never to bear fruit, of Eddie Hammock.

The jurors liked Baden. Several of them told me he was their favorite witness. The vitality of his descriptions modulated the grotesqueness. I believe the jury saw the importance of his testimony. They wanted him back. They were supposed to get the witnesses they wanted.

I had been working for nearly a year with Mike's autopsy reports, and those of Dr. John Edland and the other pathologists, single-spaced protocols of the dead, brought figuratively to life by Mike's bright descriptions and color stills. Seeing what actually happened at an autopsy, I thought, will have to help me do my job. I had mentioned that idea to Mike several times, and he was cordial. On the brisk, sunny morning of November 22, I went uptown to the Institute of Forensic Medicine at First Avenue and 31st Street, the day after Tony imposed the gag order, briefly mindful that eleven years earlier, President Kennedy's autopsy had been partly mangled, and the results of it partly suppressed.

Feeling more curiosity than apprehension—after all, the photos of death had hardened me, I supposed—I accompanied Mike downstairs. It was just a random morning in that long basement shop, a wall of refrigerators outside the autopsy room resembling a row of big lockers in a railroad station. Beyond the brotherhood of death, the corpses that comprised the morning's work had nothing to do with the men killed at Attica. I shall not forget the morning. Watching Mike preside over or participate in nine autopsies moved me to try writing a poem, which I nearly never do, because death, the sacraments of death, and a civilized casualness about killing overshadow this narrative.

When I showed the poem to them later, Mike Baden and another pathologist asked me for copies of it so that their wives could see what their work was like. The autopsies I saw struck me at first as being more fluid and chancy than the single-spaced pages of the protocols suggested. Behind the dry typed certainties lurked facts slippery with blood. Here, for instance, is what the poem said about finding two bullets in one of the morning's corpses—the buzzes are from the electric hand saw that Mike used for cutting bone:

> the scalpel halos the scalp
> pull down the face
> buzz
> skullcap the skull
> draw out the great gray wrinkled oyster
> slice it into bread
> track the bullet
> worm burned black through an apple
> a silver pearl rests inside the forehead
> squashed
> his life's revenge on the lead
>
>   * * *
>
> the one through the cheek's harder
> probe to the mouth
> maybe he swallowed it
> pour out the handy sack
> no luck
> squirm the tongue aside from below
> up the throat into the mouth
> where's the goddamn bullet?
> buzz buzz the skull's floor
> break it back creaking
> to the probe in the hard palate
> we'll have to x-ray
> no here mostly in the jaw
> only some fragments carried through
> cratered brown covering
> white fibrous as a coconut thick to bursting

years of skinpopping
he was sitting in a restaurant
next time he should pay for his heroin
later above the bloated arms
his handsome mustached face sleeps in the distance
a mask over nothing

Tracing the bullet through this man's brain and the other one in his jaw struck me as probably being similar to the autopsy work that Drs. John Edland and George Richard Abbott performed the night after the turkey shoot. Having watched these autopsies, I appreciated better the problems of the reautopsies Mike had done after Dr. Edland and the other pathologists. Watching the doctor probe the many stab wounds in a huge-breasted woman, I saw how it must have been to probe for some of the State Police bullets. The doctors' ladling blood out of a chest cavity showed vividly how a person can bleed to death from a bullet in his lungs.

The cause of death that an autopsy reveals is only the immediate cause. Baden never pretended otherwise. Yet the sureness of what a corpse can tell the living grew on me as I reflected on the morning's work. The dead do talk, as Mike triumphantly exclaimed during the morning's work.

One of the morning's bodies was that of a man who had been nearly decapitated when he stepped into traffic. Accident or suicide? "The dead do speak!" Mike exclaimed triumphantly, pointing to old cuts on the man's wrists. The dead may speak, that is, unless officials suppress their last silent cry.

I expected what I witnessed that morning to help me as I continued to fit the autopsy reports into our other evidence and question Mike Baden in the jury about the rest of the dead. At least Tony would let me do that! It should also help when I summarized the evidence to the jury for such votes as we would give them, for their Report, and for such trials of troopers as might come later.

The morning impressed me once again with the enormity of needless killing, one human smashing the temple of another's life. Too many temples had tumbled at Attica, leading the State to its litany: they deserved it, we cannot know who did it, we'd best forget it.

When I reached the office, Ned Perry demanded to know why I had visited Baden. His question, which I took to be Tony's question, told me again that Tony was exaggerating my ability to open up the Investigation. Ned's nervous question reminded me, when I reflected on it, of the State Police investigator at Troop A who had asked so tensely a year earlier why I wanted to weigh the orange crank handle. I told Ned why I went.

"Am I being criticized for going?" I added.

"Oh, no," he said and dropped the subject.

That same day or a day close to it, we were standing in the hallway between the elevators and the Investigation's front door at about lunchtime. I started to tell Ned what was going wrong with the Investigation's work.

"I don't want to know," he said.

"That's a dangerous position," I said.

"I know," he said and disappeared inside the Investigation, while I headed for the street.

Thirty-one

Suspended!

I told Tony several times starting in September that I had the feeling that a person with high State Police connections, whom I had questioned at some length and whom I shall call Morrison, had more to tell us if we asked him. We ought to do that fairly soon, if ever, because Morrison said he planned to leave the country. Tony never warmed to the idea and never assigned anyone to do it. I might fault Tony's spirit for that but not his judgment. The Investigation could not check every hunch.

On Wednesday, December 4, Morrison phoned the office. He asked one of the secretaries, then me, about some travel expenses that were due him. Then he told me he had some important information for the Investigation. He would give it to me, he said, if I would meet him without telling anyone.

I had to make a quick decision. The man was in a position to know a lot. I did not think he would approach me if he did not have something important. Did I have authority to get it in confidence? Until recently I had been the Chief Assistant. It was still our stated mission to investigate. Yet I felt that if Tony knew what was up, he would either bar the meeting, assign it to someone to flub, or otherwise avoid the risk of learning anything important. That, after all, was now his *modus operandi*. Need I obey Tony's desire, unspoken but abundantly expressed in other ways, to learn nothing new about official crimes at Attica?

I agreed to meet Morrison in confidence on Friday, December 6, at the Tarrytown Hilton. Having some qualms about meeting him without telling Tony, I made it for 8:30 in the morning so it would happen on my own time.

On the morning of December 5, Ned Perry came into my office for a long talk. His (Tony's?) bottom line was that if I was not happy at the Investigation, why didn't I resign?

The first thing Morrison asked me the next morning, after we found an empty booth in a corner of the Hilton's coffee shop, was whether I was wired.

"No, I've never been wired in my life."

He said he would deny ever saying what he was about to tell me if I ever disclosed who he was. Before he would give me his information, I must agree to keep his identity confidential. "Even from Simonetti?"

"Even from Simonetti."

Another decision. I had crossed the bridge of not telling Tony beforehand about this meeting, but it might be legitimately important for Tony to know the man's identity. That was a bigger decision, fatefully bigger. Could I do that? But what had I come here for? I gave my word.

Morrison told me, amid the quiet bustle of the other breakfasters, that he had learned during the past month that the tapes the State Police had made of their telephone conversations between Attica and Albany during and after the riot, tapes the State Police had sworn were routinely destroyed by reusing the cassettes, still existed. He gave me the names of the State Police custodian of those tapes and of four high officers and one very high officer who knew of their existence. I questioned Morrison about this and some other aspects of the Hindering Case.

Those tapes had to contain all kinds of spontaneous and otherwise truthful insider-to-insider statements about things the State Police had spent the next three years covering up. If Morrison's information proved correct, those tapes, and the identities of the State Police who were presently hiding them from the Investigation, could, as they say, break the Hindering Case wide open. Had the deleted film that showed shootings been discussed on that State Police hotline, or the strange way the State Police shielded Trooper A? The tapes might complete some murder convictions. If we had found nuggets before, the tapes could provide a solid vein. If they exist, I thought, they can give a quantum jump to the evidence of what happened.

One would expect that those tapes of the day the State Police shot 128 people would have been routinely preserved. The State Police, however, asked us to believe they had inadvertently stood routine on its head once again. One lieutenant had already given us his conclusion that the tapes still existed, based on his general knowledge of State Police procedures. Tony had repeatedly refused my requests to follow up on that lead. When questioning the very high State Police official now named by Morrison, Tony had refused my requests (including one in writing) that he ask him if those tapes existed. It is so simple to ask a question. If Morrison were right, the man would have had to say yes or risk perjury.

My mind raced ahead to pursue Morrison's lead. I shook hands with him in the Hilton parking lot and phoned the office to say I'd be in late—so much for meeting Morrison on my own time—and wanted to see Tony when I got there. (I could no longer simply walk into his office.) Back at the Investigation, Perry intercepted me in the hallway. He told me to tell him whatever it was I wanted to see Tony about. I repeated the informant's information and described my agreement not to identify him. Ned disappeared, returning soon to say that Tony wanted me to dictate a full report. I did that at once, adding ideas about how to pursue the lead.

It was my practice to proofread my typed memos before they went out. After more time passed than I thought was needed to type this one and return it to me, I went to the desk outside Tony's closed door and asked Kathy how it was coming. She said she'd finished it and Tony had taken it from her, even though she told him I wanted to proofread it first. I never wanted my work to go out uncorrected and found this unsettling for that reason and, I think, that reason only.

I passed the afternoon in one of the cubicles dictating more summary of the jury testimony. I was conscious that Perry was closeted with Tony, but less concerned than I might have been. Tony, too, must have seen that if the State Police tapes still existed, they threatened a quantum jump in our evidence. The fire suddenly threatened to flame out of control just when Tony thought he had the lid nearly clamped shut on the jury and on me.

At around four o'clock I was summoned to Tony's office. The door was closed. I faced Tony, Ned Perry, and Investigator Bill Mulligan. It had grown dark and wet outside those large windows that had been filled with sunshine the morning I first met Tony a year and a half earlier. The atmosphere now felt like thunderclouds before the lightning.

Tony asked in quiet tension whether I had anything to add to my memo, which I still had not seen. I gave him a few minor afterthoughts on how to go after the tapes.

"Is there anything else you're willing to tell us?"

"Nothing else I'm able to tell you, under my commitment to the informant. It's all pretty much in the memo."

"You're suspended, pending investigation."

A moment of silence followed. I did not know what "pending investigation" meant, except that it did not sound like an investigation of whether the tapes existed and who had them. I saw no point in asking. Most likely, I guessed in the silence, he meant an investigation to identify the informant. I noticed that Tony did not ask me to name him.

"May I have a copy of my memo?"

"No."

Silence.

"Ned, you and Bill go with Mal and take his keys to the office and his identification cards. Mal, you tell Ned where you want your paycheck sent on Tuesday."

Back in the cubicle in which I had been dictating, I said to Ned, "Did I break any rule?"

"You should never not tell the boss," he said. Bill echoed agreement.

"I'd think at worst, he'd say, thanks for the information, don't do it again," I said. "I might try telling my informant I was suspended for keeping his confidence and see if he releases me."

"I'm not sure if that would do any good," Ned said, with a hesitation that made me suspect that he and Tony had not considered that possibility before Tony decided to suspend me. Tony, I thought, was too happy for the chance to get rid of me to think much about alternatives.

I told Ned I would not try it unless Tony asked me to. I was soon to wonder how I could put it to Morrison without making Tony sound like an asshole. At best, I thought, that was how he would look. For all that had happened, I still did not want to expose his failings to an outsider, such was the momentum of my loyalty.

Bill Mulligan suggested that I not do anything until the weekend passed.

"Don't do anything rash like go to the newspapers," Ned added.

"Don't worry, I won't," I agreed with both of them.

We moved to my office. I turned over my keys and identification and pointed out generally what papers piled on the desk and table should go to what files. I thought of an old movie in which a British army officer is being cashiered: another officer reaches out and rips some fabric down from the shoulder of his uniform. I had seen in the past when Tony had put "the suicide watch," as I thought of it, on an investigator he was firing. A couple of other investigators would sit and commiserate with the man for a while, agreeing if he said life was hard or Tony was a bastard or whatever else was on his mind. It was a compassionate touch. Besides, the investigators tended to be older men who drank and carried .38s. Defusing the feelings of the man being fired protected Tony, too, from anything rash. Now I seemed to be having a suicide watch of my own. As Tony knew, I did not carry a gun or drink much, but I liked to write.

"How do you feel? I'd feel mad," Ned said.

"I don't know. I feel relieved if anything. I don't want to analyze what I feel now." I did not know what I felt, except maybe that a great lid was coming off inside my head.

"If you have any stuff at home, return it at office expense," Ned said.

"I have a lot of stuff I was working on at home." I knew that Tony and Ned knew that. I guessed they had talked about retrieving it.

"Should I put in a travel voucher for using my car to meet the informant?"

"Yes."

Soon afterward I decided not to. Putting in for my travel to Tarrytown might help them to identify Morrison.

My agreement with Morrison was the only reason I did not tell Tony who he was. Had he not obtained my word as the price of the information, I would have identified him to Tony and Ned automatically, without being asked. It impressed me that, throughout, they showed no consideration or respect whatsoever for the fact that I had given my word.

"I don't know what's going to happen," Ned said.

"I don't expect to be called back and told, thanks for the information, you did a great job."

"You've done a great job," Ned said.

"You don't have to say that."

I felt great warmth for Ned and Bill at that moment, in spite of their complicity in my suspension and the games we were playing about the informant's identity and the papers at home that Tony and Ned had to fear. I shook hands with Ned and Bill and told them they were both gentlemen, no hard feelings. They replied in kind. I never did have hard feelings against Ned, notwithstanding his agreement to act as Tony's tool in the cover-up or his role in the events of the next few weeks. I never knew Bill Mulligan as anything but a nice guy. No one ever explained my suspension further.

I took my dictionary, records of travel money due me, and the few personal items. As I was leaving, Denise, a stenographer who was working in the next office, said, "Are you leaving for the day?"

"I'm leaving for the day."

"Have a nice weekend," she said.

Outside, I walked on raw, wet Broadway a few blocks south to the New

York County Lawyers Association on Vesey Street. In their warm, dry library where I had researched the reckless endangerment memo a year ago, I wrote on a legal pad all I could recall of the memo I had dictated for Tony earlier that day, my suspension by Tony, and the few conversations with Perry and Mulligan, as described above.

A few Fridays before, when Perry was away, Tony had called me into his office to discuss whether he should fire an assistant for taking time off, a rare and final time he sought my advice. I prevailed on him to think about it over the weekend. He did, and neither fired nor suspended the assistant. He did not fire or suspend another assistant who, according to Tony, had violated Tony's express instructions not to have the first grand jury vote on a trooper indictment. Nor did Tony act so decisively when he learned that one of our investigators had vacationed in Italy with an important Mafioso.

Afterward I wondered now and then whether I could possibly have been set up for dismissal through the informant. It was possible, but I thought not. The informant always seemed what he seemed. He was not a likely person to do the Investigation such a favor. They could not have known I would keep his confidence throughout. Tony, I thought, had simply seen his chance and grabbed it. I also thought that occasional touches of paranoia are an occupational hazard when you oppose a large organization. I was to get a kick out of the joke "Just because you're paranoid doesn't mean they're not out to get you."

The one thing that hurt now was Tony's refusal to trust my judgment that the informant looked sufficiently reliable so that we ought to follow his lead swiftly to its end. To that extent I was still accepting Tony at face value emotionally. I was not able to feel that his ostensible lack of trust in my judgment was beside the point, however circumspectly I thought it. Morrison's lead might have brought the Investigation a bonanza. To the extent that Tony feared that, I suppose he did trust my judgment.

I had planned to see Genesis, then a rather spacey rock group, at the grungy old Academy of Music on Fourteenth Street that Friday night. I did not see that being suspended should interfere. I climbed to my seat high in the balcony and pulled out the pocket notebook I used that year for jotting down ideas for the Investigation. As one impelled, I began to write down everything I could think of that Tony had been doing to subvert it. Throughout the loud and colorful concert—the members of Genesis donned costumes and acted out skits as they played—I pulled out the notebook repeatedly and wrote more and more, oblivious to the music, my mind crossing and recrossing the state of New York and the months of 1974. Nothing like this outpouring ever happened to me before, or since. It was as if a dam had burst inside my brain. Freedom, anger, and a joy of combat drove the events past my inner eyes like freight cars loose on a downgrade. Those jottings in the dark were the first rough outline of the Report I was to send Governor Carey eight weeks later, and my first effort to marshal the events I have described in this book.

At one point a young couple sitting in the row in front of me turned around and asked if I was a reporter. I said no. They were talking about the concert. In a sense, though, I guess I was.

Thirty-two

The General Tips His Hand

The decision to resign in protest came simply. I can do no more inside the Investigation to make it honest, I concluded, so this is what I do now. I did not weigh alternatives or consequences or give the decision systematic thought. It took from Friday until around Monday to form. Part of the time, I think, I was collecting momentum for the way I was to go.

In sixteen years and three job changes since law school, I had never missed a paycheck and had always been fearful of doing so. That fear was absent now. Maybe I'll find work by next March, I thought, though you never know.

Outwardly the decision changed my life. Not to have made it—to have returned to Tony's charade, told him the informant's name, and followed his orders to abort the Investigation—would likely have continued my career in whatever direction it was going, but it would have changed the inner me. I did not consider doing that.

I saw a lot of my children during the days that followed my suspension. I told them that we were not going to have much money for a while. Apart from not going to work the next week, I did pretty much what I always do, though I stayed away from home except to sleep. I did not want to be there if Tony sent some armed investigators for the papers I was holding. Of all the places I might hang out, I chose Judy Nathanson's. She was a warmhearted friend whom I saw so seldom that even someone who knew my habits would be most unlikely to look for me there. Also, she had an electric typewriter for the letter I was shaping for Attorney General Lefkowitz.

About then I started squirreling away Attica papers with people I trusted around Fairfield County, where I lived, with instructions to pass them to Tom Wicker or Jack Anderson[1] if I should end up in, say, a perfectly plausible accident with a truck. I did not mean to be dramatic but saw no harm beyond some inconvenience in taking that precaution. I also started going out to make the phone calls I did not wish to share if someone had arranged a tap on my line. I phoned Morrison a couple of times at Perry's request. I did not tell him that keeping his confidence was the peg on which Tony was suspending me. Partly I did not want to put that pressure on him. Partly it was none of his business. I still did not want to tell him that Tony was acting badly, and I felt that keeping his confidence really had little to do with why Tony suspended me.

Though I was pretty sure Tony had simply seized the excuse to be rid of me, I wanted to be certain I had not unknowingly transgressed some canon of the prosecutor's code. I phoned my friend Bill Looney in Boston. Bill had been a roommate in law school, a federal prosecutor, and a person whose judgment I always respected. He said that if I had come to him as I had to Tony last Friday, he might have said, "Don't tell me about it if you do that again," but that would have been that. (A former prosecutor who was a member of the Meyer Commission was to tell me later that suspending me for not disclosing the informant's name was "bullshit . . . not even a good excuse . . . a reflection on Simonetti's limitations.")

I told Looney my concern about keeping my office papers. Giving them up would obviously help assure the cover-up, but how could I claim a right to keep them? He suggested that I take the position that I was keeping them in my capacity as an officer of the court. Excellent! Every lawyer is an officer of the court, though I doubt if many of us think of that from year to year. Looney also gave me the best nugget of advice I ever received on resigning in protest: "When this thing breaks, Malcolm, a lot of people are going to make assholes out of themselves. Try not to be one of them."

I felt quite concerned that Tony would persuade Judge Carman Ball to dissolve the Supplemental Grand Jury. Except for Tony's momentary agreement with me that Perry was wrong to tell them "only two more weeks, tops," he had shown no wavering in his intention to finish them off as quickly as possible. A grand jury exists separately from the people who comprise it. Once it is dissolved, you cannot call the same people back and resurrect it. Even if a new jury were convened, the evidence would all have to be presented afresh. If Tony had his way, I saw another precious year going down the tube.

I finished drafting my letter of resignation on Tuesday, December 10. That evening I telephoned Judge Ball at his home in Buffalo, so he would know my concerns if Tony told him it was time to end the jury. The judge sounded distressed, particularly when I told him how Tony had immunized Major V and Captain T. I told him I was keeping copies of Investigation papers "as an officer of the court." I did not request, and he did not offer, an opinion on whether that was proper. My notes on the judge's reaction to my call say: "He and I agree it's first for Lefkowitz to settle—I tell him of letter to Lefkowitz—he says he'd think I'd want to see Lefkowitz in person. I shouldn't talk to foreman of jury so long as suspended. Nothing Ball can do except Beware."

When I had raised the possibility of taking my concerns directly to the jury, Judge Ball specifically warned me that I might be considered to be "tampering," a crime, if I did. Going to Lefkowitz first was the only step I saw open, even though I recognized the possibility that he was directing the cover-up. There was still a chance he wasn't, and I felt bound to go through channels before going outside. Since I had warned Judge Ball about the threat to the jury's existence, I felt reasonably assured that all that could be lost by going through channels was a limited amount of time.

Here is the letter that I typed out on Judy's electric typewriter and sent, certified mail, return receipt requested, to Attorney General Lefkowitz on December 11, 1974. Only the names of the bathed have been changed:

Dear General Lefkowitz:

I hereby tender my resignation as Special Assistant Attorney General assigned to the Attica Investigation. My basic reasons are that the investigation lacks integrity, and I am no longer able to hope that integrity will be restored so long as Anthony G. Simonetti remains in charge.

I

The investigation has developed substantial evidence before the Supplemental Grand Jury and in its files that numerous members of the State Police and Department of Correctional Services committed crimes involving homicide, assault and reckless endangerment by shooting people and shooting at people without justification during the retaking of the prison on September 13, 1971. Mr. Simonetti has repeatedly refused to allow witnesses to be called, questions to be asked, leads to be followed, and legal and logical conclusions to be utilized which will allow a fair presentation of these shooter cases to the jury.

The investigation has developed substantial additional evidence that the State Police have withheld, destroyed, fabricated, and failed to collect material evidence of these homicides, assaults and reckless endangerments, thereby indicating the further crimes of hindering prosecution, obstruction, and perjury. Mr. Simonetti has similarly blocked the full development of this evidence.

Moreover, Mr. Simonetti has needlessly, prematurely, and without justification or particular benefit, granted immunity from prosecution to two of the four leading suspects in the obstruction case. See Exhibit A hereto.[2] After immunizing former Major V over my strong protest as there described, Mr. Simonetti took the even more amazing step of immunizing Captain T.

II

I joined Mr. Simonetti's staff on September 20, 1973. Prior to that time my experience in criminal law was not great, the longest portion of my fifteen years since law school having been spent in the litigation department of Dewey, Ballantine. Earlier this year Mr. Simonetti made me his chief assistant, and I had the privilege of meeting you at that time. Mr. Simonetti left me in charge of the office during his two weeks' vacation last April. Since the Supplemental Grand Jury was empaneled in May, I have presented most of the evidence before it, insofar as I was permitted to. I think that close to 8,000 pages of the about 9,000 pages of testimony reflect my work. I have spent large amounts of my own time on this job.

Commencing at the end of last August Mr. Simonetti suddenly switched the jury presentation from the shooter cases, on which I then estimated to him that at least a month more evidence was required, to the obstruction case, which was not yet ready for presentation. Besides creating confusion, Mr. Simonetti increasingly restricted the scope of the questions I was allowed to ask witnesses in the jury. It was a fight, for example, even to be allowed to ask witnesses to the retaking whether they saw anyone shoot anyone. Later he increasingly refused to let me question witnesses much or at all, leaving them to be examined superficially by assistants who lacked the knowledge or the will to inquire fully. He himself failed or refused (when I asked him) to ask many pertinent questions of the witnesses he examined, most notably, Major V and Captain T, whom he said he was immunizing for the information they could provide. He refused to call many witnesses who should have been called. He and Sp.A.A.G. Edward Perry, his current chief assistant, have indicated to the jury small need for additional presentation, to the apparent consternation of the jurors.

In October Mr. Simonetti asked me to list projects for further investigation during the period of evaluation of the Grand Jury record. As I continued to do so, however, I received the, to me, unprecedented direction to cease writing all further memoranda for at least eight weeks.

Mr. Simonetti may now claim that he has intended to investigate fully all along, and then go ahead and do so. If he does, that would be a most welcome and surprising benefit from my resignation.

Last Friday, December 6, I received information from a man I consider reliable that tapes which were made of telephone conversations between State Police at Attica and Albany during the riot are presently in existence and in the custody of the State Police. The information, if true, is substantively valuable and makes liars out of certain ranking members of the State Police who have told one or both Grand Juries that the tapes were routinely destroyed. As a condition of giving this information, the informant required me to agree to protect his identity even from Mr. Simonetti. I provided Mr. Simonetti with the information and dictated a memorandum of it at his direction. He refused to let me proofread the memo or retain a copy and I have not seen it. That afternoon he suspended me from the office.

Mr. Perry informed me by phone on Saturday that my agreement to receive the information in full confidence violates no law that he is aware of but does violate certain customs. As an apparent afterthought, and possible admission of the weakness of Mr. Simonetti's position, Mr. Perry phoned me on Monday afternoon to relay Mr. Simonetti's "direct" order to me to break my agreement and identify the informant. All my requests to have my position respected have been for naught.

Meanwhile, at Mr. Perry's request, I had asked the informant if he would release me from my agreement of confidentiality. On Monday he was willing to consider doing so if Mr. Simonetti would be the only additional person to know. Mr. Perry, however, was only willing to say that the "office" would know and protect the informant's identity. When I asked the informant Tuesday morning if that was sufficient, he refused to allow even Mr. Simonetti to know, and signed off. I am afraid the office has thus lost a valuable informant.[3] The main point about the acts leading to my suspension is that they are not the main point. My acts presented Mr. Simonetti with a choice. He could thank me for the information, follow it up incisively, and encourage me to develop the source. Or he could say that the information provides a fine lead, but don't make an agreement like that again even if it blocks your access to the information. Or he could do as he has done. I am forced to conclude that I have violated some commitment of Mr. Simonetti's to eschew important investigation at this time.

III

The inmates killed four people and about 60 have been indicted. Law officers killed 39 and none have been indicted. Was all the shooting justified? The evidence makes it plain that it was not.

The investigation to date has done prodigious work, particularly as to inmate crimes. As to crimes by law officers, however, it is as though Mr. Simonetti has managed to load the bases in every inning, and it is now the bottom of the ninth and he has yet to score a run.

After the Black Panther shoot-out in Chicago, in which only Fred Hampton and one other were killed, a Federal Grand Jury charged the Chicago Police with misfeasance and nonfeasance, after the local authorities had failed to fault them. It was essentially the same story at Kent State, where only four were killed. The retaking of Attica dwarfs these shootings. "Attica" remains a household word, in spite of the desire of many that it go away. I think that expedience as well as justice and honor compel the Attica Investigation to do its job. One Watergate in this decade is enough.

I am sorry, General, to have to burden you with all this. Far more is at stake, however, than my personal future. At stake is whether the knowable facts of a terrible tragedy will be presented or buried, whether equal justice will apply to inmates and law officers, whether more law officers will hereafter be more careful why they shoot people, and whether they keep the circumstances of their shooting from coming before juries of citizens afterwards.

My objectives have been to see that all the facts which are necessary for the Grand Jury's votes and report are placed before it, and that equal justice applies to inmates and officers. Mr. Simonetti speaks of letting the chips fall where they may, but since August Mr. Simonetti and I have had dozens of arguments, the nub of which was that I wanted to put evidence before the jury and he wanted not to. His actions convince me that, in his eyes, my objectives are my transgressions.

IV

The jury investigation is described in greater detail in a status memorandum which I am now preparing, subject to the fallibilities of my memory and the absence of records to refer to while I write all this away from the office. I would be happy to discuss anything that would be helpful to you, with

Mr. Simonetti present, without him, or both. I am available by phone at [phone numbers deleted].

In conclusion, Sir, I would like nothing better than to complete the full investigation before the Supplemental Grand Jury, and participate in any trials thereafter. It is now clear to me, however, that the investigation is being aborted, beyond my power to help. So long as Mr. Simonetti remains in charge of the Supplemental Grand Jury investigation, I do not believe I can be of any further use to it.

> Respectfully yours,
> Malcolm H. Bell

I hoped, as the letter allowed, that the General would be honest, would remove Tony and/or his obstructionism, and permit me to continue with the jury. That job mattered; and I was most curious to see, if it was done thoroughly, how it would come out. Yet I realized there was scant hope that my wish would be realized. What if the General were not only honest but should ask me to take Tony's job on the law officer side? Though that heady possibility crossed my mind, I gave it even less thought than I did the desire somehow to get back to work with the jury. In real terms, the fact that I was writing the General required me to take the stance that he was honest and Simonetti was the problem. I couldn't very well write, Dear General, You're probably in it even deeper than Simonetti, but in case you're not, I think you should know . . . .

I knew in theory, but was not mindful during this period, that what I said in my letter about police shootings would, if proved, undermine or destroy the defense that the General was providing for Rockefeller and other State employees against the civil damage claims on behalf of the men who had been shot. Nor did I consider at that time the General's flagrant conflict of interest in conducting that defense and overseeing the Attica prosecution at the same time. Had I considered these factors, I doubt that I would have done differently or been less surprised at the outcome.

On Thursday morning, December 12, I returned to the office early—I preferred to come and go before Tony arrived—to turn in the few papers I had decided to give up: a red-covered folder on the postshooting brutality that was the only original office file I had, a folder of my interview notes, a copy of Captain Malovich's "confidential report" on the riot, and a few other papers

I did not feel I needed in order to make the best possible case I could against the cover-up. As I walked in, Denise, who had wished me a good weekend the previous Friday, warned me tearfully to be ready for a shock because they had dismantled my office. As I was leaving I asked Nick Savino, Tony's chief investigator, to tell him that if he wanted any more of my papers, he should send me a written request. Tony never did.

* * *

Ned Perry soon identified Morrison as my informant. He told me when I asked him about it that he had just guessed. Morrison told me on the phone in March 1975 that they had called him up to Warsaw on January 8, but they wouldn't put him into the jury when he wouldn't sign a waiver of immunity. (Considering whom Tony had already immunized, I couldn't comprehend that.) Ned Perry, Mike McCarron, and another investigator questioned him. "I felt they were jerking me off, and I told them, 'You're jerking me off.'" He said he suspected they were trying to get something on me for withholding information from them. He swore to them that he had sworn me "to absolute secrecy" about his identity and had told me he would deny anything I repeated if I broke his confidence. (I assured him I had not broken it.) Then he did deny part of what he had told me on December 6, saying that when he had claimed to have received information about the State Police tapes "from a higher source from headquarters," he did not in fact have a higher source but had lied about it "to give more credibility" to what he was telling me. Which time, I wondered, was he lying? He went on to tell me, however, of a conversation he had had with some unnamed State Police officers shortly after September 13, in which he said, "It's too bad all this isn't preserved for [State Police] training," and they said, "It's all on tape anyway." Like the State Police lieutenant whom Tony had not let me recall to the jury, Morrison said that from all he knew of State Police procedures (he, too, had been an officer), the tapes still existed. "They don't destroy them," he said.

* * *

On Friday, December 13, General Lefkowitz's secretary phoned to say that the General could see me at noon the next Tuesday.[4] I arrived then at his corner office on the forty-seventh floor of Two World Trade Center above the

New York harbor. Also in the room were Samuel A. Hirshowitz, an elderly man who had been the General's first assistant since 1959, and Tony and Ned Perry. Tony said at the start that he did not feel required to answer me since he was there "as a matter of courtesy." I found that remark as opaque as his saying I was suspended "pending investigation." He then sat silent. Perry sat stiffly in his double-breasted navy blazer and said nothing. I wondered as I talked whether I was on tape. For some reason I suspected a slim briefcase that stood on the floor beside Hirshowitz, who was sitting between the General and me. A prosecutor friend had advised me to wear taping equipment myself. I declined to do that.

The General and Hirshowitz showed great interest, to say the least, in what I was saying. Tony's presence made it a little hard to get started—if looks could kill, I would not be here today—but I soon warmed to the task and told the General as much of the cover-up as I could, adding specifics to the charges in my letter, during the hour of my audience.

I told the General about the Shooter Cases, giving him some examples, and mentioned Tony's refusal to let me vote the three indictments before the August recess. I went into the August Switch and my efforts to talk Tony out of it. I described the Hindering Case, and many of the specifics of how Tony kept evidence from the jury, refused to permit key questions to be asked or leads to be followed. Bringing the General up to date, I said, according to my notes:

> Now comes the appraisal of the SGJ record, after which it is possible to put in the needed additional evidence, BUT . . . I'm told to look for the cases existing now, with a very great burden on me to justify calling any additional witness. Perry told me that AGS told him there are no shooter cases.[5] Perry told the jury they would be back for 2 weeks tops, I wrote a memo strongly opposing this, whereupon AGS told me he agreed with my memo and that Perry was wrong, but Perry was trying to reflect AGS when he said 2 weeks—quote AGS to the jury on 10/31 where he as much as said they'd have very little new work . . . .

The only point I deliberately left out was Rockefeller's possible involvement in the cover-up. Implicating Rocky would be largely on inference (as it is now), whereas I had plenty of hard evidence against the police and in support of my charge that Tony was aborting the investigation of them. Mainly, I felt it would be silly to attack Rockefeller to Lefkowitz then. I felt as I spoke that Lefkowitz knew I suspected him of directing the cover-up I was revealing to him.

He and Hirshowitz asked a few questions as I went along. Like Judge Ball, the General seemed particularly concerned about how Tony immunized Major V and Captain T. Several times the General said, "These are serious charges, Malcolm." Once he said, "These are very serious charges."

The General said that he and Hirshowitz would look into my charges; they would get back to me with any questions they had about all I had said, as well as some papers I had handed them as I went along. As I was leaving, Tony wished me well.

Of this meeting, I wrote in my Report to Governor Carey:

> The Attorney General asked me at the December 17 hearing if the matters I was describing to him, that spell cover-up, were not matters of judgment, and didn't I respect AGS's experience and judgment. I tried to avoid taking a hard position on whether I thought they were simply matters of judgment. I obviously would not be there saying that the Investigation lacked integrity if I did, but I wanted the facts I was reciting to speak for themselves. As to AGS's experience, I said I had great respect for AGS's experience . . . .
>
> The story of my last three months at the Investigation is that AGS would take a position that sounded wrong, and I would accord it prima facie validity, until I was satisfied of its unsoundness by checking the facts, the law and the opinion of others. AGS may have had more experience, but experience does not assure integrity. In spite of my comparative newness to criminal prosecution, I am sixteen years out of law school and felt reasonably confident to see what any fool could see.

* * *

AGS and Perry were present before I arrived and after I left. They heard everything I said and had their opportunity to make their answers. I heard nothing they said and of course could not answer them. In that respect the hearing had the simplicity of playing to a stacked deck.

I heard nothing during the days that followed. How could the General and Hirshowitz have listened to all I told them about these "very serious charges" and not have questions? Why weren't they getting back to me with the questions

I must have left unanswered, as the General said they would? On December 27 the following letter, dated December 23, arrived:

Dear Malcolm:

I accept your resignation as Special Assistant Attorney General with the Attica Investigation effective December 11, 1974.

I want to take this opportunity to wish you success in all your future ventures.

Best wishes.

Sincerely,

LOUIS J. LEFKOWTIZ
Attorney General

A personal invitation to forget it. Suitable for framing on my office wall, to remind private clients of my period of loyal public service. If Louie wasn't part of it before, I thought, he is now.

On December 19, 1974, Nelson Rockefeller had been confirmed as Vice President of the United States.

Thirty-three

My Report to the Governor

The nation's economy was slumping then. I read that being out of work and seeing what your town looks like at 10:00 A.M. on a weekday is depressing. I did not find it so. The town looked beautiful, sun, rain, or snow.

I served my time on the lines at Unemployment. When I applied for compensation, I had a heart-to-heart talk with a veteran worker about why I was there and how much to explain in writing about my resignation. I phoned a nervous Ned Perry to tell him my application was on its way and that Unemployment was not the forum in which to air our differences. Standing on the lines for the biweekly stipend, I noticed several faces from the Darien commuter platform and felt, as I had when I was drafted into the army, that I was participating in an experience of my generation. Eventually some of the people who worked there behind the counters came to know why I was there. They liked what I had done. One had me speak about Attica to the kids in a neighborhood youth program. Another, who was moving to Boston, said I could stay with her and her husband anytime I went there. It heartened me that most people I talked with were for me. One who wasn't for me, though, was a man I was introduced to in the middle of a restaurant who started immediately to rant about inmates: "Oughta cut their balls off. Oughta cut all their balls off."

Status, I'm told, has three traditional sites: job, community, and family. Being without the job took some psychic getting used to. I had not realized that belonging to an organization was a part of me until I did without it. It disappointed me not to be quite as independent as I had thought and to miss belonging. Yet I adjusted quickly and concluded that my dependence on a job for feeling whole had been artificial, an easier habit to kick than coffee. Thus began a freedom I had not realized I lacked.

"You save it so slowly, it goes out so fast," I told a bank teller. She nodded. My savings helped. I stopped buying bacon and started getting oil for the car at the department store. I stopped filling up the gas tank, though I still drove as much as before. I supported my children as before. I paid all my second wife's alimony, though not so regularly, and she was patient. At noon I ate cheaper, faster, and better at home than I had at Manhattan lunch counters. I found it important to keep getting up at 7:00 A.M., even though I had no train to catch. I welcomed an excuse not to waste money in some of the ways we are expected to waste it. Spending far less changed my life surprisingly little, and I wondered how I had spent so much before without, I thought, being extravagant. I discovered the truth that there are two ways to have money, to earn more and to spend less, and that the latter can be the more satisfying, unifying. I contemplated, relaxed, and saw more of the beauty of the world.

On the darker side, I would be driving along at night, during the weeks after I resigned, and the headlights in the car behind me actually knew me—an eerie anthropomorphism I never experienced before or since. I suppose that some "paranoia" may serve a sound purpose, as one becomes unreasonably alert in times of a danger that is palpable yet too elusive to confront. My papers and live testimony could embarrass and maybe convict some powerful people and many who carried guns. It would be foolish for them to hurt me, but the story of Attica had not been free from foolishness. I reminded myself that John Dean had survived. (I was not aware that Karen Silkwood had been killed in November 1974 in an ambiguous auto wreck while she was on her way to tell a *New York Times* reporter about falsified safety records, etc., at a Kerr-McGee nuclear plant.) My gentle landlady asked me if someone was likely to take a shot at me. I wondered if she was worried about the hole that might make in the wall. "If they do," I assured her, "I'll call the police if I can."

One of the stranger evenings came in January when my children, first wife, and I went to see *Godfather II* starring Al Pacino. We hoped to see a friend who had been an extra in several of the street scenes on the Lower East Side, and I had forgotten about my impression that Tony looked like Pacino. The resemblance came back powerfully as I sat in the dark and watched Al/Tony somberly designating people for death.

While I waited for Lefkowitz to get back to me with the questions he never asked, I saw no point in going to Governor Malcolm Wilson. His term ran out at the end of the month, and he had been Rockefeller's loyal Lieutenant Governor for years, before Rocky stepped aside and allowed him a short term at the top.

In Hugh Carey, the Democrat who had beaten Wilson in November, I had hope. I felt some disappointment but no surprise when Lefkowitz sided openly with the cover-up that he may have arranged all along, but with new Governor Carey of the other party, I thought, it should be another matter. What was the two-party system all about? What indeed. I was not then aware that Rockefeller had helped Carey's career. Nor did I concern myself with how unpopular it would be for any politician to take on the New York State Police, the Governor's bodyguards. Right was right. While I had some real hope that Carey would do it, I did not expect miracles. I began to organize a report to him on the Attica cover-up, the "status memorandum" referred to in my letter to Lefkowitz.

* * *

About this time I sought out another friend whose judgment I respected and who had also been a prosecutor. Late one evening in his comfortable living room I told him what had happened. "I admire your instincts," he replied. His words mattered, particularly now that I was soloing. He urged me to send Carey a written report. "Then they'll have to deal with it," he said. "An oral report would be too easy to brush aside." After Lefkowitz, I had already known the report to Carey would have to be in writing, yet I had hesitated to face the task. My friend's advice gave me the needed push.

I reviewed my notes, made a few false starts, organized the topics, and began to write them out in short chapters. It was tough, though I was feeling pretty tough then myself. On Saturday, January 11, 1975, the writing finally began to flow as I tended a bad cold in the base lodge at Magic Mountain in Vermont and my children appeared from time to time to tell me how great the skiing was outside. As long as the money holds out, I thought, why should I miss skiing with the kids just because I worked for a dishonest investigation? Starting the report felt good.

Back in the barn where I lived in Connecticut, I drummed away at my old manual typewriter. I felt the handicap of no access to the files, grand jury transcripts, and recollections of others, but I couldn't very well ask Tony to make them available. My head seethed with a turmoil of facts, the problem being less to recall them than to sort them out. The quality of my hasty writing embarrassed me somewhat, but I considered it more important to get the product to the Governor and Judge Ball as quickly as possible, before Simonetti tried to discharge the jury. What emerged were eighty-nine typed pages plus seventy-one pages of supporting documents, the best of the office papers I'd kept copies of. It was a short, choppy, impersonal ancestor of what I have written here. The report had twenty-seven chapters, from one to eleven pages long. Any documents that went with a chapter were sandwiched after it.[1] I made copies for the Governor, the judge, myself, and for safekeeping. I bound it in orange covers and titled it *Preliminary Report on the Attica Investigation* because the final report could obviously not yet be written. It concluded:

> The Attica Investigation pursued the serious crimes by inmates with all the vigor that its inadequate staff allowed, but it has lacked integrity in its investigation of crimes and possible crimes by law officers and other public servants. It has not properly investigated or presented to the Supplemental Grand Jury the shooter cases, the hindering prosecution case or the potential rehousing cases. As to these cases, it has sought with varying degrees of art to give the appearance of a full and honest investigation, without the substance of such an investigation.
>
> * * *
>
> Anthony G. Simonetti is the apparent architect of the Investigation's failure to investigate, though I note the Attorney General's apparent prompt failure to find substance in the facts I reported to him on 12/17/74. I do not believe I have any particular qualification to speculate on where the present cover-up goes beyond AGS, or whether he invented it by himself. Likewise, possible motives for the cover-up should occur to others as readily as to me.
>
> I assume that following my 12/17/74 report to the Attorney General, in the presence of AGS, the Investigation will at least appear to plug some of its more glaring gaps, though it cannot unimmunize Major V and Captain T. Any such steps by the Investigation need close scrutiny.
>
> * * *
>
> My object in this matter has been, and remains . . . to see that the law is applied to officers and inmates equally. Prisons should be safer if inmate crimes against their keepers and fellows are punished. Law officers may be more careful whom they shoot if they are held accountable for their shots, as the law and SP Manual require.
>
> How can it rehabilitate an inmate to see an officer get away with murder? Must it not leave him cynical and hostile? How can it improve the humanity and performance of the New York Division of State Police if

they are allowed to see themselves as being above the law? It should have a salutary effect on everyone if the law is fairly applied to all, without fear or favor. To the best of my knowledge and belief, that is not happening.

That did it. Rectifying the Attica cover-up should now be out of my hands, except as I might be called on to explain or testify. A few bad apples misdirecting the Investigation did not make the whole barrel of New York politics rotten, nor mean that the vast majority of public servants were not honest and hardworking, shocked by the shocking, and quick to do their duty to the public that employed them, to clean up the mess and let the chips fall where they may.

I sent the report, certified mail, return receipt requested, to Governor Carey on January 30, 1975, with a letter saying who I was and why I was sending it. I phoned his secretary first to assure that my "very serious charges" and all the accompanying grand jury secrets would go to the Governor and not into the bureaucracy. I sent another copy to Judge Ball, also certified mail, return receipt requested, and stowed other copies with trusted people and prudent instructions. The covering letter enclosed with the judge's copy said:

Dear Judge Ball:

With great difficulty I have managed to commit to writing the events I outlined briefly to you on the phone on December 10, and am enclosing herewith the resulting report. I am sending the original to Governor Carey, having apparently failed to convince the Attorney General that anything was amiss.

I consider it important for you to have this, since you are the judge assigned to the Supplemental Grand Jury and it is plainly important for you to be apprised of what I take to be misconduct in the presentation to it . . . .

My objectives have been to give the Supplemental Grand Jury the material facts as fairly as possible, and to seek to apply the law equally to inmates and law officers. That may be naive, but I think it important. Why else are we here? . . .

Unbeknownst to me, Lefkowitz and Simonetti had met with Ball on December 23, and Lefkowitz sent my resignation letter to Carey on December 27, before the new Governor took office. Ball told me long afterward that my December 10 phone call had come as "a bolt from the blue." He got in touch with Lefkowitz and told him two of his staff were fighting, he had better investigate. That key and obvious advice Lefkowitz refused to follow. At the December 23 meeting, Ball said he could not come between Simonetti and me, it was a matter for Lefkowitz not the court to settle. That, too, seemed obvious to me if Lefkowitz were not part of the cover-up. I heard afterward that Simonetti wrote a memo in late January saying that both Attica grand juries would be discharged on February 28.

* * *

When I had heard nothing from the Governor by February 11, my apprehensiveness about the demise of the jury grew great enough that, reluctantly, I phoned his secretary. The report, she said, lay on his desk unread. I said I was sure his new administration gave him a lot to do, but time mattered to the life of the jury. Still hearing nothing by February 18, I overcame my reluctance to nudzh a new Governor and wrote:

Dear Governor Carey:

Not having received a response to my letter of January 30 (copy enclosed), I most respectfully urge your prompt attention to the report on the Attica Investigation which I sent you therewith.

Fairness in the administration of justice requires the salvaging of the Attica Investigation, if that is still possible. I have no reason to question the fairness of the principal indictments against Attica inmates. As described in the report, however, there appears to be a whitewash of certain State Police and other public servants who committed serious crimes at and after the riot. The whitewash itself may well be criminal.

Saving the investigation requires speed. The Supplemental Grand Jury investigating the shooting and cover-up crimes by public servants, was convened in early May 1974. My superiors were trying to end the jury's work when I left the job in early December. If the jury is ended on the basis of the deficient presentation described in my report, nearly a year's work will be lost, at a time that is already woefully distant from the events of September 1971.

Some people have asked me, who cares about Attica any more. They might as perceptively ask, who cares about justice.

Please accept my apology for writing again, in the event this matter is already being attended to. As I indicated before, I would be happy to give any assistance I can to you or your designee in this matter.

Respectfully yours,
Malcolm H. Bell

In the days that followed, nothing. Again the disappointment outweighed the surprise. Principle and the facts were with me, I knew then and later, but the realities were against me and, I believed, against the public.

Thirty-four

Waltzing with the Perps

A symposium called "The New York Correctional System: Three Years after Attica" drew me to the stately hall of the Association of the Bar of the City of New York on Wednesday, February 26, 1975. The panel was Robert McKay of the McKay Report, an ex-inmate, a man from the guards' union, and the Commissioner of Correctional Services who had replaced Russell Oswald. An ample crowd gathered. None of the panel thought that prisons had changed much; "cosmetic changes" summed it up. Attica had a new gym. Whereas guards were hired with no psychological screening before, they now had to pass "rudimentary screening." The panel all agreed that correctional facilities do not correct.

A lawyer named Robert Patterson asked the last question from the floor: "Since no State Police or correction officers have been charged with crimes in the three-and-a-half years since Attica, have we any assurance at all that a large cover-up is not being engaged in; and what can we as a bar association do about it?"

The question drew applause. Dean McKay responded that Patterson had asked "a blockbuster of a final question" and added, "I do not know whether there is a cover-up or not." He, too, was surprised that some cases against officers had not been easily proved. He called on Stephen Rosenfeld, a lawyer in the audience who had been on the staff of his Commission. Rosenfeld invoked the conventional City wisdom that "it is probably very difficult to get indictments from citizens in Western New York against correctional officers and State Troopers from Western New York." He said he knew the Attica Investigation had made efforts to prosecute officers because he had received phone calls from them about that. I sat there thinking, "Yeah, those were my phone calls."

Robert P. Patterson, Jr., was the senior partner of Patterson, Belknap & Webb, a well-respected firm of about fifty lawyers filling a well-appointed floor high in Rockefeller Center. Among other good things, he had served for four years as president of the Legal Aid Society, the organization that had given me my first exposure to criminal law. He had gone to Attica after the riot as a member of the Goldman Panel to assure that inmates were receiving their Constitutional rights, whereupon more of them did. I had met him in 1968 when we both represented defendants in a stock fraud prosecution.[1] He had impressed me at the time for being the only defense lawyer conscientious enough to sit through several days of an evidentiary hearing that constituted my first effort to present evidence in court for longer than an hour. I understood that Patterson had good standing in the New York legal establishment, even though he gave more time to the public welfare than most of its well-heeled members said they could afford. He was a very careful lawyer, possibly suffered from too much tact, and was enormously likable. As the crowd left the hall at the Bar Association, I caught up with him at the top of the wide marble stairs.

"I can answer your question," I said. We agreed to meet on Friday.

In Patterson's corner office, he and I quickly agreed that he would act as my "lawyer." He was not to represent me in the usual full sense, and I was not to pay him, but we could invoke the attorney-client privilege if anyone tried to force us to disclose what we were about to say to each other.[2] Having seen what he saw at Attica in 1971, he needed little persuasion that a cover-up existed. As he was soon to put it in a letter to Judge Harry Goldman of the Goldman Panel:

> I and the other members of the panel quickly became aware of the fact that the Deputy Attorney General of New York, Robert E. Fischer, was not investigating the crimes committed against inmates after the riot, although such investigation was a part of his assigned duties and obvious crimes had been committed. The crimes consisted of assaulting inmates after the prison was under control and, in some cases, while those assaulted lay wounded on stretchers or were receiving medical treatment.

After our meeting that sunny Friday, Bob told our concerns about the cover-up to Governor Carey's counsel, Judah Gribetz, to U.S. Assistant Attorney General Harold R. Tyler, Jr., in the Justice Department, and to Cyrus Vance, who was then in practice in Manhattan and advising Governor Carey on criminal law matters. It felt good to have someone with a little clout on my side finally, though I soon realized that Bob and I were traveling on somewhat different wavelengths. As events unfolded, he struck me as somewhat too cautious for what we were trying to do, though I knew that this is a common complaint clients make about their lawyers. My antennae went out when he told me there was no profit in pursuing Rockefeller, since I understood that his firm did some work on Rockefeller foundations. His advice, though, made perfect sense, like saying don't fight City Hall, and I was to hear it soon enough from others. I wanted to pursue Rockefeller no farther than the facts and fair inferences warranted, but certainly that far. Rockefeller was Number One at Attica, even when he refused to be there.

After my first meeting with Bob, I crossed Manhattan for lunch with Mike Baden. Mike told me that he had been called back to the Supplemental Grand Jury since I left, only to be asked routine questions covering familiar ground, boring him, and apparently adding nothing to what he had already testified. I shared my concern about the cover-up. He turned serious and sad. "We better stop talking," he said. "We may have to testify about this conversation later."

Phase One of my involvement with Bob Patterson lasted until March 27, a month that passed slowly. It contained my last futile effort to balance the Attica prosecution, short of going public. I met with Bob in his office several times, with phone calls in between. Any time we phoned about something that mattered, I left my snug barn for a pay phone outside. The colder the day, the more I doubted that anyone would actually bother to tap my phone.

The first reaction I received from Bob's efforts came on March 7 when Paul Gioia, assistant counsel to the Governor and Judah Gribetz's assistant, phoned. I had spoken with Gioia a few times while I was with the Investigation. Now he told me that he had been with Tony back in Frank Hogan's office, but he added that he had not known Tony well because Tony had been a few years ahead of him. He said he considered Tony to be able.

More to the moment, Gioia said that he and Gribetz had read my Report and were concerned by it; he called it "a big accomplishment." I told him of my concern that the Supplemental Grand Jury would be disbanded in the middle of its work, meaning another year lost. He understood. I assured him the jurors were good, serious people who should be given the evidence and allowed to vote on it. He asked if it would be all right to talk with Attorney General Lefkowitz about my Report. I replied that I could not direct him what to do, but Lefkowitz had already heard the same things I said in the Report, and "I struck out with Lefkowitz." Gioia asked about giving Tony a chance to answer the Report. "That should happen at some point," I said, "but not now." I made a formal request for permission to let Bob Patterson see the Report, saying I did not feel free under the Executive Law to show it to him without clearance by the Governor or his counsel, but I thought my attorney should not have to remain in the dark about what he and I were talking about. Gioia said he would let me know. He never did.

Apart from the certified mail receipt I got back and my February 11 phone call to the Governor's secretary, this March 7 call from Gioia, after Patterson had intervened, was the only acknowledgement I ever received from Governor Carey's office that I had sent him a Report on the Attica cover-up. When I applied later to be reimbursed for the expense of duplicating copies of the Report for Judge Ball and myself (I never asked compensation for writing the original), my application was refused on the grounds that I had been acting voluntarily and not at the request of the State.

* * *

I was informed afterward that on March 6 Simonetti advised Lefkowitz that, except for some incidental witnesses plus Rockefeller himself, the presentation of evidence to the Supplemental Grand Jury would be completed by March 14. That beat dismissing the jury on February 28, as Simonetti had scheduled in late January, but not by much. On March 7, I understand, Gribetz and Gioia met with Lefkowitz, Simonetti, and Perry to discuss my Report. When Gribetz mentioned my concern that the jury was about to be closed out, Lefkowitz and Simonetti assured him that it would be hearing evidence for at least three more months. Apparently my rocking the boat was having some effect. At the meeting, Lefkowitz expressed "complete faith" in Simonetti; Gribetz said he "relied implicitly" on the General's judgment. He let Lefkowitz and Simonetti know that he would give them my Report for their comments.

I learned later also that Lefkowitz and Simonetti were more prepared than I was for me to go public: a few days after their meeting with Gribetz, Simonetti sent the General a draft press release that called my anticipated charges false, said all that was involved was a disagreement over professional judgments, and that the courts and bar association were being asked to consider the ethics and legality of my conduct. So, Simonetti, at least, wanted to discipline, disbar, and maybe prosecute me. I had been wondering at the time whether they planned such steps. With some fear, I was relishing the chance that such moves would likely give me to question both of them under oath and bust everything I could wide open. My guess is that Lefkowitz realized that that is how I would probably respond and told Simonetti to cool it. In any event, that draft was not the press release Simonetti finally used.

* * *

Bob Patterson phoned me on March 11 to say that Gribetz wanted him and me to sit down with Lefkowitz and Simonetti and let them clear themselves. To us! Upon what basis had Gribetz himself concluded they were clear? Lefkowitz had to have concurred in this proposal for Gribetz to have made it. Bob said he had replied that that was highly unwise—what if we were not satisfied? He told Gribetz he had checked around and found some independent corroboration for my cover-up charges. Gribetz seemed to ignore that and to act as if what was at issue were merely a personal dispute between Tony and me. How painless, even plausible, if you ignored the substance of the disputes.

After I had finished a job interview about noon on Monday, March 17, Bob and I reached Gribetz on the phone to try to get official approval at last for Bob to see my Report. We were concerned about Section 63(8) of the Executive Law, which made it a misdemeanor to disclose results of an official investigation without the Governor's approval. It was Bob's opinion that as my counsel he could see the Report anyway. I would likely have agreed and given it to him if we could not get approval, but I wanted the approval if possible. Gribetz said it was his opinion that my counsel could see the Report, but that he was not speaking in his capacity as the Governor's counsel when he gave that opinion. Mumbo jumbo. Bob and I decided that this constituted approval.

Gribetz also said that following my conversation with Gioia on the 7th, Gribetz had told Lefkowitz and Simonetti that I was concerned I'd be indicted if I showed Bob the Report, and they said they had no such intention. I replied that I had not told Gioia I feared I'd be indicted but just that I might violate Section 63(8). That was a small distinction, perhaps, but important to me. I was sure that people who talked about their work violated Section 63(8) in little ways all the time, and I had never heard of anyone being indicted for that. Interesting, I thought, the twist they gave my words.

Gribetz repeated the proposal that Bob and I hear Lefkowitz and Simonetti answer my charges. Bob said he would react to the proposal after he had read the Report. I asked Gribetz if he had shown them the Report. He said no. He assured us that, according to Simonetti, the jury had another three months to sit. That news fascinated me in light of the Perry-Simonetti statements to the jury the previous fall that they had already received a thorough presentation and were to finish in only two more weeks. I supposed my cover-up charges were at least making the State go through the motions of giving the jury more evidence. My experience with Simonetti and Lefkowitz and my conversation with Baden gave me scant hope that they were giving the jury anything that mattered.

Off the phone, Bob and I agreed that so little was likely to come of meeting with Lefkowitz and Simonetti that it would not be worth the inevitable price of letting them read my Report, and that the proper way to proceed would be for them to be asked about the subjects it covered (which they had already learned from me at the December audience) and their answers transcribed *before* they saw it. Once they saw the Report, they could and doubtless would start tailoring their answers to meet its specifics. The truth would suffer accordingly. On the other hand, I had already gotten nowhere by talking to Simonetti and Lefkowitz alone; all Bob would know of the situation, he would know from me and my Report.

* * *

Judge Ball was to give me his own conclusion to the same effect long afterward. When he had been a District Attorney, he told me, someone had made accusations against one of his assistants. He called in the assistant and a court reporter and said, "Here's the accusation. What do you have to say?" Giving Simonetti the Report, in Ball's view, was like giving him a detailed trial brief to tailor a tale to.

* * *

Back in my good old days (1968–1970) at the firm of Mermelstein, Burns & Lesser, we often used the term "pfumpf." A pfumpf is a statement or proposal that sounds good, means nothing, and serves to delay or avoid. "He called and I gave him a pfumpf," said with relish. "I called and he gave me a pfumpf," said in exasperation. A pfumpf is a deft little runaround.[3] The proposal that Bob and I sit down with Lefkowitz and Simonetti was a quintessential pfumpf.

Leaving Bob's office on this afternoon of the St. Patrick's Day parade, I watched an impressive formation of the New York State Police march smartly up Fifth Avenue. Any grand jury witnesses in that bunch, I wondered, any Attica killers? I can't go through life reacting like that to troopers, I thought; the time will come when I have to let go. There was a fair chance that the factual answer to both my questions was yes.

I met with Bob before another job interview the next morning. He had read the Report. Would it, I was wondering, fall flat for this outsider? To my mild relief, he reviewed with me the wrong decisions and wrong acts of the Investigation that it catalogued and made a few suggestions that could make it more complete. For example, I could add what the witnesses Tony would not let me call would likely have told the jury, and give more detail on what questions he would not let me ask the witnesses who were called.

Bob told me he had checked on how Simonetti had been regarded back in Hogan's office. He heard he was a loner and not considered particularly able. I could see the loner part; Tony had told me as much himself. The part about not being particularly able did not ring true. Paul Gioia had just confirmed my own observation of Tony's considerable abilities. In other conversations, Bob put increasing emphasis on what he heard of Tony's weakness and incompetence and even alleged emotional problems.

By Friday, March 21, Bob said he was leaning toward taking a position that the Investigation's long failure to indict law officers should be our main point of attack. That long failure existed beyond question, but Bob's proposal struck me as a retreat. It would put him back where he stood when he asked his question at the Bar Association, before he read my Report. It would avoid a contest of credibility between Simonetti and me, in which I would point out all he had done to keep the evidence from the jury and he, presumably, would say it didn't happen that way. I saw Bob's proposal as letting the Investigation off the hook. Sitting in Bob's quiet office, I visualized Tony pointing to the file memos in which he had periodically asked for a bigger staff and falling back on the defense that, given the small staff, the decision to prosecute inmates before officers had been merely a question of judgment. Suppressing the evidence, on the other hand, clearly was not. I was ready to go to the mat with Simonetti on which of us was telling the truth (if he didn't tell it). I believed I had enough supporting evidence to resolve any fair doubt in my favor.

Bob added that questions were being raised about the propriety of my conduct when the prison guard had listened to the inmate witness for a few minutes in the jury,[4] but that Simonetti had denied it ever happened! If that's what they have against me, I thought, they're pretty desperate. I shouldn't have let it happen, but what did it have to do with three-and-a-half years of covering up? Bob's bottom line was to seek through Gribetz to have the Governor replace

Simonetti as head of the Investigation and/or seek a federal investigation of the Investigation.

Why, I wondered, did Governor Carey and his counsel need a letter from Bob Patterson to tell them to investigate the Investigation? It may or may not be part of the answer—though I think it is at least a symptom of the problem— that at about this time the State Police were making expensive and desirable improvements in Governor Carey's vacation home on Shelter Island, in the name of making it more secure.[5]

From time to time during our talks, Bob had been telling me that he had "the ear" of someone at the *New York Times* who was "very interested" in a possible Attica cover-up. For some time I had had a modest plan of my own to go to the *Times* in the hope they would run a short inside-page squib to the effect that I had resigned from the Investigation over policy differences. I wanted that protection if and when the Investigation's failure to do a competent job came out, and especially if the Investigation's corruptness came out. When I had dropped in on a friend at Dewey, Ballantine in December, he had said he was surprised not to have seen a note about my resignation in the papers.

Tom Wicker would be the person for me to see at the *Times,* especially if I were to go beyond the mere fact of my resignation. I was reading his book, *A Time to Die,* about his own experiences as an Observer at the Attica riot. I had met briefly with his assistant, David White, at the *Times* on January 31, the day after I mailed my Report to Governor Carey and Judge Ball, and again on February 19, a week before Bob Patterson's fateful question at the Bar Association. Both times, as well as on the phone with White, I had been quite guarded in what I was willing to say, though I went a little further each time. I had not gotten past White to Wicker.

Sometimes I felt discouraged at the lack of official reaction to my Report. (I even toyed with the idea of moving to Canada, though not seriously.) The State's new Democratic administration was showing the same aggressive lack of interest in delving beneath the Attica cover-up as had the Republicans, who owned it. The option of going public with more than a simple notice of resignation began to attract me more and more. It started to appeal to me as the only way to bust out of the straitjacket that seemed to bind my hands, arms, and mouth so long as I tried to right the wrongs through proper channels. The Gribetz-Lefkowitz pfumpf landed like the bale that broke the camel's back.

I now began to court the idea of going public with more than a squib, though I did not know quite how to do it. I did not want to commit the crime of disclosing grand jury secrets. I did not want to lose control, whatever control I had. But I was damned if I wanted to continue the way I was going, down the State highway to nowhere.

The spark of interest at the *Times* finally kindled. I met Tom Wicker on March 25 in his book-lined office, an enclave of calm on the hectic third floor of the *Times*'s big building. I had told Patterson about the meeting before-hand, and he had cautioned me to be careful what I told Wicker about naming individuals and so forth, so as not to violate the secrecy laws. Wicker was a large man about five years older than I, and he spoke surprisingly rapidly for a Southerner. David White said as we walked to Wicker's office that I would have twenty minutes before Wicker had to leave for a luncheon appointment. Moments after we met, we were back inside Attica reliving the day of the turkey shoot. Forty minutes slipped quickly away.

I described how I had been stopped from calling witnesses and following leads. I told how two prime suspects had been granted immunity, though I declined to say they were State Police. I said the Investigation had been under-staffed and had gone after inmates almost exclusively from the start. Wicker stressed that he did not want me "to destroy" myself with what I told him, though he assured me that we spoke in confidence. I said I did not want to be unfair to any future indictees or to destroy my usefulness as a future witness to the cover-up. We agreed it would not be a crime for me to say I had resigned and sent a report to Governor Carey, and that I would not be in trouble if the *Times* were able to obtain my Report from someone else. Wicker promised to protect my identity and position. He said he would speak to the metropolitan editor about sending an investigative reporter to talk with me.[6]

The next morning I heard through the grapevine that (some of?) the Investigation's lawyers in Buffalo were seeing now what I had seen about the cover-up last November and December. They feared, my source said, "the Investigation will end up with a bad name and Simonetti will save himself and blame them for screwing it up." Morale in the office was said to be "very low" with people "afraid of getting involved." The talk around the office was report-edly that Morrison was my informant, that "nothing" he had told me was true, and that he had a grudge against the State Police. Investigators (which ones?) thought that I was "not familiar with procedures" but that Simonetti should not have landed on me so hard for the way I got Morrison's information. The effort, I noted, was still on discrediting Morrison, instead of on following his lead to the crucial tapes. The version that Morrison had fabricated his information about the State Police tapes in order to settle a grudge must have appealed only to someone who wanted to believe it. How, I wondered, was it going to discredit the State Police if he told an assistant (me) about tapes that an investigation quickly showed did not exist? If he did have a grudge, it would be served far more effectively if the tapes did exist. Even though Morrison was now reported to say (truthfully?) that he had lied to me about his information—or, as he had told me on the phone, about the source of his information—his overall story about the tapes still sounded more credible than the State Police version that the tapes had been routinely erased. But speculation is endless. The Investigation should have gone after the tapes, if any, thoroughly and hard years before Morrison made his move. The grapevine seemed to bear sour grapes this morning.

Myron Farber of the *Times* phoned that afternoon. He reached the landing outside my apartment at 8:40 that evening, carrying a folder of clippings of my 1957 engagement and wedding and half-a-dozen letters to the editor that the *Times* had published (including letters of 1965 and 1967 in which I supported the United States involvement in Vietnam). Thorough, I thought. I noted the comparative speed of the State and the *Times* in responding to my cover-up charges.

Farber was the investigative reporter who unearthed the story of "Dr. X," Mario Enrique Jascalevich, the New Jersey surgeon accused of killing patients with curare. Dr. X was brought to trial twelve years after the deaths, "too late to prosecute" being a flexible concept. Farber looked to be in his thirties; he had a deep laugh and mildly diabolical sense of humor though he was all business this evening. He took my history, the history of the Investigation, and the history of the cover-up, not neglecting a few questions apparently aimed at testing whether I was disreputable or crazy. It mattered to him to see the memo in which Tony had named me Chief Assistant. He grasped what I was saying about the cover-up more readily than anyone else but Wicker.

The next morning in New York, Patterson showed me a letter he had drafted to Gribetz, in which he said that, based on reading my Report and obtaining some information "of a general nature" elsewhere, he saw "no purpose to be served in your suggested meeting with Attorney General Lefkowitz and Mr. Simonetti to hear their explanations of the various points and criticisms raised by the report." Instead, Bob called for "the appointment of one or more persons to investigate the management and affairs of the Attica Investigation while the Grand Juries are still sitting." This draft sounded short of asking for a federal investigation or seeking to replace Simonetti. Still, it did not sound bad to me if the investigation of the Investigation would be out from under Louis Lefkowitz.

Bob's draft also said, "As you pointed out, matters of judgment and personality seem to be involved . . ." with my charges. "That plays right into their hands," I told him, adding how important it seemed to Simonetti, Lefkowitz, and Gribetz to reduce my cover-up charges to a personal dispute with the boss. I told him it was not accurate and gave our position away. He took it out.

His draft also referred to the fact that "not a single non-inmate has been charged with a crime against an inmate" but went on to say, "Since three and one-half years have now passed, the necessary identifications will be far more difficult and the likelihood of charges being brought is slim. . . ."

"You can't say that, Bob. You don't know the evidence."

I went on to remind him that the shooters had identified themselves in their BCI statements. He seemed to be focusing mainly on the officers' attacks on inmates after the shooting had stopped, with which he had been concerned when he went to Attica on the Goldman Panel. He changed the letter to say that "the likelihood of charges being brought for such crimes has been reduced."

Why, I wondered, had it been necessary to make these points to Bob Patterson? He said the object should be to get our "head in the tent" with Gribetz, then pursue a full investigation. (He explained long afterward that he believed that once an investigation of the Investigation began, then all aspects would be opened up, and the most effective way to initiate this was by a simple, uncluttered approach—nice words that did not answer my question.)

I filled him in on my conversations with Tom Wicker and Myron Farber. Where he had calmly advised me beforehand to be careful in talking with the *Times*, and had talked about talking with his own person there, he now sounded quite upset. He didn't want to look to Gribetz, he said, as if he were "playing press." (He told me long afterward that he thought he had made it clear beforehand that his advice was not to talk to Wicker at all and that his own talks with a *Times* reporter had all antedated his February 26 question at the Bar Association. Actually, he had made neither of those points clear.)

He phoned me that afternoon to read me a paragraph he was adding to the letter to Gribetz, with copies to Cyrus Vance and Robert McKay, saying that he was resigning as my attorney. Here is how it finally came out in the letter, toned down from what he read me on the phone, tactful to the point of being cryptic: "I believe my services are now complete. I hope you [Gribbetz] will follow my recommendation."

I was sorry to have caused Bob distress over the *Times*, especially after not being the most agreeable client in other respects. My disappointment at his unexpected resignation was leavened by the knowledge that even with him, I still stood partly on my own, still had to think critically for myself, still tested all his advice against the question, Is his way my way? Often, it seemed to me, it was not. I was angry and may have been unfair. He went out on a limb for me, or with me, for justice.

Besides seeming to steer me away from Rockefeller, Patterson told me at one point that it was not politically popular to pursue the State Police, as they were a big political power outside New York City. Again I recognized his appraisal as realistic, yet worried at hearing him say it. When the question was reality versus right, why did so many people take the answer for granted? A quixotic question, no doubt. If I had been realistic . . .

Where, I wondered, was Bob Patterson coming from? From the Establishment, of course, but from the part that had a social conscience. What had he thought was going to happen when I told him I was going to speak with the *Times*? How much of everything he said to me reflected his political orientation and personal attitudes toward life, the police, and the law? Doesn't all advice, my own included, reflect such things? Bob was talking to Gribetz who was talking to Lefkowitz. Who, if anyone, was conning whom? It would be unduly suspicious, I supposed, to wonder if anyone had asked Bob to keep a leash on me. (He assured me afterward that no one had.) What was I coming to, I wondered, if I distrusted Bob Patterson?

I phoned an old family friend. "Bob Patterson," he told me, "is close to being a thoroughly good man. He is an idealist, a person of integrity. . . . People love him."

From Bob's perspective I may have seemed like something of a wild man. I realized during the time we talked that, were I in his place advising me, I would have advised more caution than I, in my place, felt like practicing. Plus I knew far better than he how valid my charges were. I reminded myself several times that March that he had the welfare of a big firm to consider, whereas I enjoyed the freedom that comes from being out of work and out of the Establishment. To a large extent Kris Kristofferson's mournful lyric from "Me and Bobby McGee," "Freedom's just another word for nothing left to lose," had become my happy song.[7] Bob may have risked more even when he stepped on the brake than I risked by stepping on the gas, as we each sought action on the Attica cover-up.

It later fascinated me that various official positions, all false, that Bob passed along to me in March 1975 turned up as the Official Version as concluded by, among others, the Meyer Commission or Governor Carey or both: too little evidence remained on which to prosecute the officers for their crimes; Simonetti was weak and incompetent so that the failure to indict officers (though not inmates) happened by accident not design; and my cover-up charges stemmed largely from personal differences with Simonetti.

Who says Kafka wrote fiction?

Thirty-five

The Cover-Up Hits the Fan

My letter of resignation to Lefkowitz in December formed the heart of my going public in April. I photocopied the letter, cut narrow strips from the copy with a small knife to excise the parts I thought would violate the grand jury secrecy laws, rephotocopied the slightly tattered product, and gave the resulting copy to Myron Farber. I told him all I believed I could about the cover-up in long conversations in my barn apartment and held back when he pressed for more.

He wanted my Report to Governor Carey. I would not give it to him. I held up my orange-covered copy to confirm that it existed, read him some parts that seemed safe, and told him that giving it to him would defy the secrecy laws and risk wronging the people whose names appeared. He assured me that the *Times* would not print any names to harm anyone. I believed he meant it but still would not give it to him.

He said he would go to prison before he would ever violate my confidence. I felt certain that Myron meant it—which meant that I could give him the Report, swear I had not, and he would never give me away. I had resolved, though, that if I ever volunteered the details about how I went public or a court ordered me to give them, I would do so truthfully. That hampered me and, I am sure, frustrated Myron.

I was interested to watch and to feel, almost as if in a field of magnetic forces, the opposing pulls as free access to information on which democracy depends tugged against grand jury secrecy on which criminal justice importantly depends.

All through going public I sought to steer between saying so little that the cover-up could continue and saying so much that I would hurt someone unnecessarily or commit a crime. I considered then and later the irony if I should be the only law enforcement person to be convicted over Attica.[1] I had no wish to enter the custody of men I had been trying to indict, and I did not want to break the law. Inmates broke the law at Attica. Law officers broke it. The prosecution was still breaking it. I considered it a duty and challenge not to.

The *Times* ran a fast but detailed background check on me. By taking me public they were in a sense backing me. I guess they did not want to back a kook or a crook.

"Is it possible that no one connected with the Investigation will support your charges?" Myron asked.

"It's possible," I said. He who does not hope will not be disappointed. Myron checked around and found partial support from three former assistants. When asked about their views for publication, two of the three were to back off.

The long trial in Buffalo of John Hill (Dacajeweiah) and Charles Pernasilice for the murder of Correction Officer William Quinn was drawing to a close during my conversations with Myron. That was the biggest Attica trial so far and the biggest that was to be. William Kunstler represented Hill; Ramsey Clark represented Pernasilice; and Louis Aidala represented the People of New York. It began to look as though the *Times* would break my story before the jury went out or while they were deliberating, and I feared that the news of my charges would influence their decision. I had no idea whether Hill was innocent or guilty—the charge against Pernasilice fell during the trial from murder to attempted assault because the Investigation turned out not to have any evidence that he had struck Quinn—but it would have been wrong, I felt, for the jury to reach a verdict on an emotional reaction to charges that had no bearing on the evidence before them. But Myron did not want to interfere with the *Times*'s timetable.

"The jury will be sequestered," he said. "They'll be locked up in a hotel until they reach their verdict."

"I can see Bill Kunstler lowering a newspaper on a rope outside their window. You can't be sure they won't hear," I said, adding that in my opinion, "It would be responsible journalism to hold my story until after the verdict."

He took my concern back to the *Times*. They agreed and held up the story. The jury convicted Hill of murder.

On Monday, April 7, as my story was about to break in the *Times*, Bob Patterson phoned, cheerful and full of advice. Apparently he had decided to be my lawyer again. Well, okay, I accepted his return without comment on his departure.

Myron phoned about 6:30 that evening to say the story had gone to the printers. It would be on the front page, hitting the street about 10:20 P.M. The television stations generally looked at the *Times* as soon as it came out, he said; I could expect the story on the eleven o'clock news.

"You're part of the story of Attica now."

"That really puts the steaming turd out on the ballroom floor," I replied. Myron savored the metaphor. I understand he spread it around the *Times*.

Driving alone on the Connecticut Turnpike an hour later to pick up a date, I said, "God help me. God help Tony Simonetti. God help everybody." No matter what I do, I thought, I'll be a temporary hero to some and villain to others. I wondered what it was going to be like to be a has-been after the story had passed. It seemed like a good time for a quiet evening at the barn. A friend phoned at 11:10 P.M. to say she'd heard the story on NBC television.

CHIEF PROSECUTOR ON ATTICA ACCUSED
OF JURY COVER-UP
Ex-Aide Says Inquiry of Way State Police
Acted During Revolt Lacked Integrity
BY M.A. FARBER

A key member of the Attica special prosecutor's office has resigned and charged the chief prosecutor, Anthony G. Simonetti, with covering up possible crimes by law-enforcement officers who put down the rebellion at Attica prison in September 1971.

The accusation was made by Malcolm H. Bell, who was once Mr. Simonetti's chief assistant. Mr. Bell charged that the inquiry into whether crimes were committed by state troopers and correction officers "lacked integrity" and was being "aborted" by Mr. Simonetti.

Mr. Bell made the statement in his letter of resignation to Attorney General Louis J. Lefkowitz last December 11. A copy of the letter, from which information about certain cases before the grand jury was deleted, has been obtained by The New York Times.

After Mr. Bell concluded that Mr. Lefkowitz did not intend to pursue his charges, he sent a 160-page report on Jan. 30 to Governor Carey.

LEFKOWITZ TO REPORT

Mr. Carey asked the Attorney General yesterday to submit a written report responding to Mr. Bell's charge. At the same time, Mr. Lefkowitz said he had been exploring the allegation since it was made. He declined to comment on the merit of the charge.

Mr. Simonetti said that the allegation was "both false and shocking" and that "we have held a very open investigation of Attica and we will continue to look at all aspects in a logical and thorough manner." A spokesman for the Governor said that Mr. Lefkowitz had expressed "complete confidence" in Mr. Simonetti following the charge by Mr. Bell . . . .

That was how it began, on page one of the April 8, 1975, *New York Times*. The story continued for another 65 inches with liberal quotes, full background, and a stern picture of me on an inside page. I was happy to read that the Attica grand juries "will remain in session at least until these charges are again reviewed by the Attorney General."

So Governor Carey finally asked Lefkowitz to respond to my charges when he knew the *Times* story was about to break, after sitting serenely on my Report as long as no one was telling the public. Myron laughed, I laughed, and others laughed at Lefkowitz's expression of "complete confidence" in Simonetti. Lefkowitz's statement that "he had been exploring the allegation since it was made," with zero questions to me who made it, struck me as self-serving crap. He knew to say it; why didn't he know to do it? The sad part was that however sure I was by now of Lefkowitz's guilt, I had the mass of evidence only against Simonetti. Lefkowitz seemed content to leave Simonetti alone out front. *Time* magazine soon quoted Lefkowitz as saying, "I have complete confidence in what's-his-name—Simonetti."[2]

Besides the headline, Tuesday morning brought many calls from friends and reporters. Local CBS-TV was sending someone up for an interview, then national replaced local, sending Bob Schakne, a first-class person who had been at Attica during the riot. Gabe Pressman came up from the City and seemed a bit put off when I had to ask him what time and channel to watch us on. The psychiatrist who had the apartment downstairs from mine asked the camera people to show it, so his mother could see where he lived. A couple of staff people from the Investigation phoned to express support for me, as did one of the prosecutors.

In Berkeley, California, Don Jelinek, the former coordinator of the ABLD, read the *Times* story and literally danced on his bed.[3] He and the ABLD had been charging the cover-up for years, and virtually nobody to the right of the far left had been paying heed.

The front page of the April 9 *Times* ran a picture of Bob Patterson, a two-column headline, and a hundred-plus inches (I did enjoy measuring) of article beginning:

CAREY DEFERS A DECISION
ON ATTICA TRIALS INQUIRY
**Says Lefkowitz Should Meet
With Lawyer for Ex-Prosecutor**
BY M.A. FARBER

Governor Carey deferred a decision yesterday on a request that he appoint an independent individual or group to investigate the "management and affairs" of the state's prosecution of crimes connected with the Attica prison rebellion of September, 1971.

Instead, the Governor urged a meeting "without delay" between Attorney General Louis J. Lefkowitz and Robert P. Patterson Jr., an attorney for a former key member of the Attica prosecution team. The prosecutor, Malcolm H. Bell, resigned, charging that his chief, Anthony G. Simonetti, had covered up possible crimes by law enforcement officers at Attica . . . .

So, out rides the pfumpf.

The article included my resignation letter as fully as I had given it to Myron including, to his embarrassment, my phone numbers. He offered to change them at the *Times*'s expense if crank calls grew heavy, but none came. The article went on to say:

Mr. Patterson's proposal for an independent inquiry drew support yesterday from Cyrus Vance, president of the Association of the Bar of the City of New York, and Representative Edward I. Koch, Democrat of Manhattan.

* * *

Mr. Lefkowitz said that his report to Mr. Carey would be based on an analysis by Mr. Simonetti of Mr. Bell's report to the Governor, plus other materials in Mr. Simonetti's possession. "In effect Simonetti will do the reply to the Governor," the Attorney General said. "I will pass it along."

* * *

Two other prosecutors resigned from the Attica investigation because, they said yesterday, they were unhappy with the way the investigation was proceeding. Neither of the two prosecutors was critical of Mr. Simonetti.

But one, Herman Graber, said he had "the feeling that 'someone didn't want the investigation to succeed.'"

So, the accused would get to see and answer the Report, and the Attorney General would pass the answer along, a sort of postman or valet, barely soiling his hands. Poor Simonetti remained alone out front. Here is his full statement as printed in the April 9 *Times*:

The allegations made by Mr. Bell are entirely false and wholly irresponsible. I will not engage in debate or rhetoric concerning Mr. Bell in any form. He has brought wholly false accusations against me and my office, and I will not dignify his bearing false witness against me.

The Attica investigation has been conducting investigation painstakingly and fairly under my direction. Law, ethics and common fairness prevent me from speaking specifically about the case, but I assure the public that the two grand juries which have sat for approximately three years have considered and continue to consider every relevant and material aspect of the case as presented by me and my staff including law enforcement participation at Attica.

Contrary to the impression given by Mr. Bell that his criticism has been ignored, at the direction of Attorney General Lefkowitz and in his company, we conferred with Justice Carman F. Ball on Dec. 23, 1974, the Justice presiding over the Attica Investigation, and gave him a copy of Mr. Bell's criticisms. On Dec. 27, 1974, Attorney General Lefkowitz turned over a copy of the criticism to Governor Carey.

"Wholly irresponsible"? It would have been irresponsible to remain silent. The "false witness" part stung, even though I knew it was not true. I guess Tony and I learned it from the same book.

The following editorial in the April 9 *Times* made excellent sense to me:

ATTICA BOMBSHELL

Former Attica prosecutor Malcolm H. Bell has dropped a bombshell into the state's law enforcement machinery that requires a good deal more than the usual "we'll look into it" response which it has elicited from Governor Carey's office.

Mr. Bell, once the chief assistant Attica prosecutor, has charged that his former boss, Anthony G. Simonetti, still the top Attica prosecutor, interfered with attempts to investigate crimes which law enforcement officers may have committed in the course of retaking the prison after the rebellion in September 1971. Mr. Simonetti says the charge is "both false and shocking." Attorney General Lefkowitz has agreed to look into the problem, while at the same time expressing "complete confidence" in Mr. Simonetti. Governor Carey says his staff has talked with Attorney General Lefkowitz on the subject and will do so again.

Those ritualistic expressions of good faith and promises of action might suffice if the case involved an everyday allegation of corruption; but the timing and manner of retaking Attica may have been the most controversial set of decisions of the Rockefeller administration—and the lives of 42 human beings were lost in carrying them out. Mr. Bell charges that there has been a cover-up of official wrong-doing and the suggestion is inescapable that the Attorney General has been sleeping on those charges since December.

* * *

Even without the Bell allegation, an investigation which resulted in indictments of 62 individuals—all of them inmates—was bound to leave large questions when the McKay Commission took eyewitness testimony that law enforcement officers did commit crimes. Beyond those circumstances and Mr. Bell's key role in the investigation, the handling of his charges since his resignation last December throws the Attica prosecution into even deeper shadows. Attorney General Lefkowitz has had Mr. Bell's charges in hand for almost four months and Governor Carey has had Mr. Bell's 160-page letter in his hands for two months of silence and apparent inaction.

It is entirely possible, as Mr. Simonetti says, that everything simply flows from a disagreement of prosecutorial judgment and that the investigation has in fact been "very open." The trouble is that the facts now known don't automatically support that view. The circumstances which are known raise large questions about the priorities and the vigor given to various aspects of the investigation. Mr. Bell's charges go beyond that to suggest that the state's law enforcement system has been twisted into a mockery of justice.

Only an independent inquiry, as suggested by Mr. Bell's counsel, can put this particular humpty-dumpty together again.

That afternoon James Wechsler in the *New York Post* made a point that pleased some friends of mine and me:

[Bell] can hardly be dismissed as a disgruntled headline hunter; he with-held the news of his resignation for four months while he sought to obtain a comprehensive private review of his charges by the state's Attorney General and then by the office of the newly elected governor.

The front page story in the April 10 *Times* began:

> Governor Carey said yesterday that his counsel, Judah Gribetz, would meet shortly with senior judicial officials of the state to discuss the alleged cover-up of possible crimes by law enforcement officers during and after the Attica prison revolt in September, 1971.
>
> Asserting that "justice will be served in my administration," Mr. Carey said the purpose of the meeting was to "determine what action, if any, is warranted by the judicial branch of the government" to resolve the allegation of a cover-up. He did not speculate on the outcome of the meeting . . . .

Myron and I asked each other what the judges could possibly do. Apparently the judges did not know, either. Nothing came of the meeting, as the State scuttled down another blind alley in its haste to escape its own derelictions. The April 10 article quoted National Guardsmen who had witnessed the post-retaking brutality and never been questioned, or questioned only after several years, by the Investigation. It also reported:

> [F]ormer Attica prosecutor, Donald Schechter, said he quit the prosecu-tion team because he was not satisfied with the way the prosecution was being handled. Like the other two former prosecutors, Mr. Schechter was not critical of Mr. Simonetti. But he said he "would have handled the investigation differently." "Whether there was a cover-up remains to be seen," Mr. Schechter said.

Don's caution disappointed me, though he had not been exposed to the cover-up as directly and often as I.

The April 10 *Times* included a personal profile. It began, "Throughout his career in the law Malcolm H. Bell has spoken his mind, argued with his supe-riors, stood his ground and, sometimes, suffered the consequences." It ended by quoting a friend at Dewey, Ballantine that I am somewhere in between "a bit of a maverick" and "an independent thinker." "It's marvelous," my first wife said of the profile. "It makes it perfectly clear why no one could ever live with you." We laughed.

Diane Dumanoski, a reporter with the *Boston Phoenix*, interviewed Donald Schechter, Herman Graber, and Ed Hammock and wrote the following in the May 13 issue, starting with Don's view of the August Switch:

> Atty. Donald Schechter, who was working on the Attica Investigation at the same time as Bell, also observed the shift that August. But this wasn't the first puzzling Simonetti decision that Schechter had noticed. To Schechter, who had spent time as a prosecutor in the Queen's County D.A.'s office, Bell's very presence at the head of the Grand Jury inquiry seemed inexplicable. Of all the attorneys hired in the fall of 1973, Bell, Schechter says, had the least criminal prosecution experience. That's not to suggest, Schechter continues, that Bell didn't do a respectable job. "What Malcolm lacked in criminal experience, he made up in time . . . he's a hard worker." Sitting in his modest Manhattan office, where he recently opened a private criminal law practice, Schechter recalled nights in the motel room in upstate New York when at 1:00 and 2:00 a.m. Bell would still be reviewing evidence he'd spread all over the bed. But despite Bell's conscientious efforts, the question still remains. Why, Schechter asks, were the really experienced prosecutors assigned to inmate indictments but not to law enforcement officer cases?[4]

I, too, wondered from time to time if giving the Supplemental Grand Jury to someone of my criminal inexperience had not struck Simonetti, Lefkowitz, or both as a safe move, a handy way to appear to pursue police crimes with comparatively little danger of succeeding. Not too surprisingly, I was not as inclined as Donald to think that this was their game. When asked about Simonetti's decision to immunize Major V and Captain T, Don said, "I agree legally with Malcolm's position. The immunization wasn't necessary." Of Simonetti's suspension of the jury for a "period of appraisal" in November, Don said, "[A]ll of a sudden the Grand Jury was put in cold storage." He agreed with me that there was no reason to do that.

Dumanoski quoted Herman Graber on his decision to join the Investigation shortly after it began:

> "I went up there because I felt the truth had to be known. I wasn't interested in indicting anyone. My purpose was to find out what happened and to prevent it from happening again."

It took Graber four months to decide this wasn't going to happen through the Special Prosecutor's office. "We had all kinds of problems. At times it seemed like pettiness, but now I'm not so sure it was pettiness."

According to Graber, among the not so petty problems were the investigators assigned to the Attica inquiry by the state. Half of them, it turned out, were state troopers. State troopers were to investigate possible crimes committed by their own? As if this wasn't enough, the officer in charge, Graber says, had also been present at Attica on September 13. "The whole thing was incredible."

Because of the presence of state troopers, Graber says, the decision was made to concentrate on the inmate crimes and delay the major work on the retaking until after the troopers had left the staff. That finally occurred the following June, 1972.

Graber himself departed after concluding the effort "was not serious." In his view, the investigation was headed for trouble even without a deliberate cover-up. "Nobody wanted the truth to come out . . . . All the parties in my opinion were covering up for all their reasons . . . fear, politics, position." And even without explicit instructions from the higher-ups, he says, it's not hard for a young ambitious man to get the message about what the boss wants.[5]

Ed Hammock's experience foreshadowed my own. Not surprisingly, he had reached the same conclusion that I had from the relative sizes of McKay's staff and the Investigation's. Dumanoski wrote:

For Ed Hammock, a black lawyer who is now a commissioner in the City Bureau of Investigation, what started as six weeks on the Attica investigation turned out to be a year and a half. As Hammock sees it, the criminal investigation of Attica started out in the "back seat." Bowing to political pressure, Rockefeller had also set up the McKay Commission with duties and powers paralleling those of the Special Prosecutor's office. Both groups were working at the Attica prison and both were investigating the events. But there was one major difference. The Special Prosecutor's office had a harder job: it had to build cases that would stand up in court, while McKay had only to write a report. Yet the McKay Commission had a staff many times the size of that assigned the Special Prosecutor. "That indicated to me the attitude of the powers that be," reflected Hammock.

Like Bell's, Hammock's departure, as he recounts it, followed a deteriorating relationship with Simonetti and disagreements about how the investigation should be conducted. Hammock had been hard at work on the investigation of state police conduct when the disagreements started worsening.

"We got to the point where we disagreed on many things. I was in no way able to prove Louis Lefkowitz or Governor Rockefeller had told Simonetti not to do something. I didn't know what was going on, but I felt something was happening, and making it more difficult to do the job."

Like Bell, Hammock says grand jury secrecy prevents him from explaining the details of why he left. "It's tied in with why there are no indictments."

Hammock stresses that he doesn't have a shred of evidence to prove there has actually been a cover-up, but he says he and Graber used to talk about what was happening. "We couldn't figure out where the pressure was coming from. Maybe Simonetti was making his own decisions."

" . . . I think Malcolm Bell believes what he is saying. I don't think it's simply that he and Simonetti had a spat. My impression is he was taken up by Attica. His background is not that of a bleeding heart or a public interest lawyer."[6]

The April 10 *New York Times* confirmed some bad news:

Mr. Simonetti received Mr. Bell's 160-page report from the Governor's office and began preparing a response for Mr. Carey. Mr. Patterson said he was "saddened" that Mr. Simonetti had been given the report in advance of any independent inquiry.

* * *

Mr. Patterson said that this was "not an appropriate time" for Mr. Carey's office to have given Mr. Bell's report to Mr. Simonetti. "It looks to be that it means no step will be taken toward an independent inquiry," he said.

Mr. Bell himself said "it is not my place to tell the Governor how to conduct his investigation." He went on:

"But giving Simonetti my report, which contains the foundation for serious charges against him, was a highly questionable move now. Of course he should have a full opportunity to answer the report down the road."

That quote was me in full restraint. I was furious that Simonetti should be given the Report now. That was the contemptuous opposite of an independent inquiry. Carey's office was making it as easy as possible for Tony to get himself and the Investigation off the hook. That, of course, was what Lefkowitz contemplated when he said that Simonetti would answer the Report. To what Attica inmate defendant, I wondered, would Simonetti or any other prosecutor worth his salt have given the guide to the charges? Lefkowitz had acknowledged my charges as "very serious." So had Carey's office. So they hand Simonetti the key to escape and perpetuate the cover-up. He, I had slowly learned, was not a truthful person. With his back to the wall, I was sure he would say nearly anything he felt he could get away with. And if he escaped, who could point a finger at Lefkowitz?

The story continued on the front page of the *Times* on Friday, April 11, under the headline "EX-ATTICA PROSECUTOR SAYS EVIDENCE WAS DENIED HIM." Tom Wicker's column that day concluded:

> . . . Gov. Hugh Carey of New York has no decent option but to force Attorney General Louis Lefkowitz, or some special panel, into a thorough investigation of charges by Malcolm Bell, once the Assistant Special Prosecutor in the Attica matter, that there was a systematic prosecution cover-up of criminal offenses committed by the Attica attackers and their supervisors. (The word "force" is not too strong since Mr. Lefkowitz has failed since last Dec. 11, when Mr. Bell made his charges to the Attorney General, to act on his own.)
>
> * * *
>
> It is not just a matter of elementary justice, although it is that above all. To ignore law officers' crimes, if any, at Attica, as well as a state cover-up of those crimes, if there is one, can only increase the disrespect and contempt for the law and those supposed to enforce it that already are major causes of crime and corruption and much bitter alienation from American society.

How beautiful that last, I thought, and how ignored!

Saturday's story finally began on an inside page: "REPORT ON ALLEGED ATTICA COVER-UP CITES POSSIBLE MURDER CHARGES." I was surprised to read about the homicides of two named inmates, Kenneth B. Malloy and Ramon Rivera. Where Myron had dug that out I did not know, but could guess. The story said, "At the direction of the Governor, Mr. Simonetti is preparing a 'line by line' response to Mr. Bell's allegations. It is expected to be ready in two weeks."

That night I saw a friend who reminded me that when I had told her a few things about the Investigation back in October, she said it sounded like a cover-up, and I responded by defending Simonetti.

The Sunday *Times* carried the Governor's announcement that a special deputy attorney general would soon be appointed to evaluate the Attica prosecution:

> A spokesman for the Governor said the appointee would be a lawyer of "outstanding integrity, ability and reputation" and would have "complete independence" and broad powers to inspect secret documents and take sworn testimony.

My marvel at the power of the press grew. The politicians stonewall as long as they can, I thought, then at long last they announce for truth and justice as if they'd been for them all the time, once the people finally learn what they're up to. How fine their words are now!

> The spokesman said that Mr. Carey and Mr. Lefkowitz had agreed on the appointment of a special deputy attorney general "to assure public confidence" in the Attica investigation being directed by Mr. Simonetti.

Again, the prejudgment that the Investigation deserved public confidence, after my shocking assertions maligned it.

> The Governor's spokesman said the special deputy attorney general would report within 30 days of his appointment to both Mr. Lefkowitz and Mr. Carey.

That "report within 30 days" sounded ominous. The only report that could happen within 30 days would be a whitewash. The facts were too complex for any responsible person to reach in so short a time the conclusions that the facts warranted. I recalled the many times that Tony had burdened our work by artificially short deadlines. The common denominator between Simonetti's short deadlines and the Governor's was Louis Lefkowitz.

I watched with interest how the *Times* orchestrated the cover-up story for maximum impact. If they had run my resignation letter, some interviews with other people, and everything else they had on the first day and the final denials on an inside page the next day, that would have been that. Instead, they let it out more slowly, fanning public interest, and goading an increasingly apt response from the unwilling State. They did not manufacture news; they elicited news. Myron had said, "When this thing breaks, people will come out of the woodwork." They did. And the pressure mounted.

The week after the cover-up story broke, Vice President Rockefeller flew to Taiwan to attend the funeral of Chiang Kai-shek. The morning news showed a reporter asking him, as he boarded the plane, to comment on the charges of an Attica cover-up. He tensed. He refused to comment, he said, because this was a sad occasion. Again the reporter asked, and again he refused to comment because this was a sad occasion. Crocodile tears, I thought as I watched in the barn. When the plane landed in Taiwan, no one asked Rockefeller about Attica, and he commented jovially on everything he was asked about. Apparently he had worked out his grief during the long flight.

As I watched Rockefeller refuse to comment on the cover-up charges, his tenseness, his tone, his manner, I suddenly felt for the first time that he had played an active part in covering up. It reminded me of when I asked to weigh the crank handle at the Troop A barracks and suddenly felt the guilt of the State Police in the officer's reaction. Being right the first time did not necessarily make me right the second. An accuser's gut reaction is not usually evidence, but a jury may judge a witness's demeanor. Accuser I might be to the public, but I was juror to the event. In that instant, Rockefeller looked guilty to me.

For the most part my family and friends were great about what I was doing. That had to be a particular challenge for my mother and father, who were very conservative people. Yet I believed I was expressing their deepest values. Their support mattered much.

An old friend told me that her father had said, "Malcolm is doing the wrong thing."

I was sorry to hear that. I had great respect for her father, considering him as a good person who had had a successful career with a major corporation. "What would he be doing in my position?" I asked.

"He would never let himself get in your position," she replied. I realized sadly that that was true and was part of the problem.

The telephone was never better than after my story broke. A friend: "You have courage. It's the only thing you could have done." A Buffalo politician: "We're with you." A person from the Investigation: "I'll support you. You're marvelous." Another person from the Investigation: " . . . tremendous." A friend in Maryland: "That's vintage Malcolm." An employment agent: "I admire you. I feel you're telling the truth. Why would you lie?" A friend: "I'm glad you did it. It takes guts." A former employer: "I'm bug-eyed in admiration at what you've been able to accomplish." One of my older Sunday school students: "I really appreciate what you're doing. That's really beautiful." I did not keep notes of what people said in person but remember their remarks warmly. If some friend of yours sticks his or her neck out, say something nice. It will mean a lot. I was surprised at the number of people who mentioned courage. I had not been thinking of it that way.

Not everyone, though, appreciated what I was doing; an unsigned postcard from Queens said that the writer looked forward to reading my obituary.

Unfortunately, my family and friends did not run the law firms in which I was seeking a job. An employment agent told me: "You know, a lot of people won't touch you. They won't say it, but they won't do it." Another agent said: "Nobody who wants to do business with Rockefeller is going to offer you a job." That covered a lot of business, starting with The Chase Manhattan Bank, whose chairman and chief executive was Nelson Rockefeller's brother David. Why should a firm risk losing a client for the sake of hiring me? Rockefeller's power was such that it radiated impact without the need for him to lift a finger. Plenty of able lawyers wanted jobs, and if I saw something I considered crooked, I might report it. Even more basic, where stability matters, who wants a boat rocker?

For whatever reason, going public confirmed my worst fears about human nature in the job market, even as it confirmed my best hopes on the personal side. I was answering ads and sending out résumés at a pretty constant rate. I had fifteen job interviews in the three months before going public, and three in the three months after.

My father cautioned me repeatedly to be careful about talking to reporters, far more than Bob Patterson had. It is hard, though, to go public without talking to reporters. Almost without exception, the ones who questioned me were as fair and accurate as anyone could ask.[7] More than once they protected me when I may have said a little more than I later thought discreet. One reporter bought me a steak lunch and spent it trying to get me to implicate Rockefeller. The steak was nice, but no dice. All in all, I found it a bit of a trip to read what I said in the papers or see myself saying it on television. I reminded myself it would soon end and tried not to let it take me too far.

After I went public I seemed to be about the only person I knew of who did not think I had "changed sides." I was still trying to do my job as I conceived it, see justice done, and support the System as it was supposed to work—same old me. I went to Buffalo on an inmate defense subpoena, making myself easy to serve by driving over to Bridgeport to pick it up. Several of my former colleagues on the same early flight did not "see" me. Tom Goldstein of the *Times* asked me to share a cab from the airport with him and Bill Kunstler. I declined.

Investigation people steered clear in the courthouse hallway, except for Frank Cryan, who gave me a cheery "Hi, Malcolm!" On the stand, I found myself being a fairly hostile witness to the defense lawyers who questioned me, not giving them what they wanted unless they asked the precise question. Two investigators watching from the jury box looked grim when I started and were smiling by the time I finished. I was not trying to please or displease anyone, but to answer accurately and volunteer no more than I felt like—at that point not much.

One of the nicest results of going public was an invitation to speak at Hampshire College in Massachusetts. The students gave me a standing ovation, the first my professor-host said he had seen them give anyone. In a seminar beforehand I had expected to be attacked from the right. Instead I caught it from the left.

"Just by practicing law in the System, weren't you perpetuating the status quo?"

The question sounded like an accusation. I reflected. "I guess that's partially true," I said. Attica may have radicalized me, but not all at once.

The story of the cover-up continued in the *New York Times* through a second week. "We don't want this thing dragging on," Lefkowitz was quoted as saying,[8] though he was to drag it on unconscionably. A group of twenty-three New York legislators were reported as saying: "Whether one agrees with all of Mr. Bell's charges or not, we must agree with his statement that 'One Watergate in this decade is enough.'"[9] A news analysis pointed out that before I spoke out from the inside, Simonetti had been able to fend off cover-up charges by saying that two grand juries were still sitting to consider the evidence of the riot— the trite but ever-effective official dodge, "We know what you can't, so bug off."[10] An editorial concluded that "an ad hoc parallel law enforcement system is beginning to develop because the formal system of enforcing the laws in this state has broken down so regularly."[11]

Referring to the proposed investigation of the Investigation, Arthur Liman, who had been general counsel to the McKay Commission, stated in a published letter:

> It would be a mistake . . . if the new investigation was devoted only to resolving the dispute between Mr.. Simonetti and Mr. Bell. Mr. Simonetti, who did not succeed to the role of chief prosecutor until more than a year after the events, did not set the priorities of the investigation. Rather, I submit that the decision to focus entirely upon inmates' offenses until the evidence against correction and police officers had become stale and unreliable accurately reflected the attitude of [the] state government . . . .[12]

Bravo again, though it bothered me to see Liman accepting the Official Version that my involvement was merely a dispute. On the same subject, for example, my Report said, as Liman could not know:

> The meager forces of the Investigation were deployed in inverse proportion to the magnitude of the problems they faced. The inmates had killed four people; the law officers had killed 39 . . . . The decision to investigate the riot before the retaking, and inmate crimes before law officer crimes, was crucial to the failures of the Investigation to date.

I was also concerned that Liman was repeating the Official Version (as Patterson had) that the evidence had grown too "stale and unreliable" to prosecute officers. I assumed he believed it, but I was noticing that conservatives who wanted to let the cops off, as well as liberals who sought amnesty for the inmates that could be gotten only if the cops got off, were both saying it then.

At last the April 18 *Times* reported, front page:

> Bernard S. Meyer, a former State Supreme Court justice in Nassau County, was named yesterday to head the independent inquiry into the charge that the chief Attica prosecutor covered up possible crimes by law enforcement officers.

Cyrus Vance and Bob Patterson were quoted as praising the selection of Judge Meyer, Patterson calling him "an honorable fellow, a fine man, a person of integrity and a first-rate lawyer, by all accounts." Patterson had asked me on the phone to tell the press something nice about Meyer. I refused. I knew nothing about the man. I expected to testify before him and did not want to flatter him in advance. I would form an opinion of him as I saw what he did. The *Times* continued:

> Some lawyers . . . suggested that Mr. Meyer was "not tough enough" and expressed concern about his lack of experience in criminal matters. Mr. Meyer has never tried, defended or presided over a criminal case.

Some of Simonetti's people had been claiming that my charges could not be sound because of my own relative lack of prior criminal experience, a non sequitur that they abandoned with the appointment of Meyer. The April 18 *Times* repeated the ominous timetable:

> The special investigator, who will not present evidence to a grand jury, is scheduled to report to both Mr. Lefkowitz and Mr. Carey within "30 working days." Although some lawyers doubt that Mr. Meyer can complete his assignment by that deadline, a spokesman for Mr. Carey said the Governor's office expected any extension to be "only a matter of a few days."
>
> * * *
>
> The former judge, who was divorced and is remarrying today, plans a "working honeymoon" in the next few days while he examines documents relating to the alleged Attica cover-up.

Getting action by going public, after failing to get it through channels, decreased my faith in the two-party system and increased it in the press enormously. I felt the vitality and directness of the press, as opposed to the pretense, fear, and fumbling of the officials. But the press, I suppose, has the simpler task. A free press does much to make America great; but freedom to publish is only the second link in a three-link chain. Foremost comes free access to the news. To the extent that anyone suppresses information that matters, a free press means nothing more than freedom to print gossip, government propaganda, and crossword puzzles. And ultimately the public must act on news that concerns it. To the extent that good people mind their own business, freedom withers, and we subside into a large piece of land where America used to live. Official cover-ups and public indifference are equally un-American.

The power of the press, I realized for the first time, derives from the decency of the people. Newspapers and public servants proceed on the premise that the people will not tolerate raw conduct, as and when they hear about it. Some public servants seek to deceive the people—appointing an "independent investigator" only when their deceptions fail for the moment, thanks to good journalism.

An investigation of the Investigation at last! A powerful newspaper and an insider did in ten days what needed doing, what no one else had been able to do in years, and what the insider could never have done alone. A working honeymoon for Judge Meyer? I pictured my orange-covered Report lying beside the bed.

Thirty-six

A Judge Misjudges

I met Judge Bernard S. Meyer for the first time at 8:30 on the sunny morning of May 15, 1974, exactly four weeks after Governor Carey and Attorney General Lefkowitz had appointed him to report within "30 working days." Clearly he was not going to meet their artificial deadline. He was tall, thin, and pleasant-looking, with glasses and gray hair, two weeks short of his fifty-ninth birthday, suggestive of a lawyerly Jimmy Stewart. I always found him courteous, almost courtly, in person.

The State was paying him $150 an hour, to a limit of $35,000, for investigating the Attica Investigation. That was a cut in his hourly rate.[1] He remained the senior partner of the Mineola, Long Island, law firm of Meyer, English & Cianciulli. He had sat on a State court for Nassau County from 1959 to 1972, presiding over exclusively civil cases, and had been Democratic chairman for Nassau County in 1957 and 1958. He had a reputation for working 16-hour days.

In accepting the Attica appointment, Meyer said he realized that there was no way he could please everyone. Finding a cover-up could lead to Lefkowitz and Rockefeller. Failing to find it would likely bring charges of a whitewash. An interview in the *New York Post* that May quoted him as saying:

> I'm not so thin-skinned that it would sway me, the fact that someone won't like what I've decided. I took the job because I considered it important. We're dealing with the restoration of public confidence in the criminal justice system.[2]

In 1969 and 1972 Meyer had run for election to the New York Court of Appeals, the State's highest court, which he called "one of the great courts in the country." He was candid this May about his desire to sit on that court. "I will go to the grave with that ambition if I don't realize it," he said, adding that the only reason he had entered politics was to become a judge. Referring to his Attica job, though, he said: "It would be a shame if people thought the results were tainted by that because they won't be. My ambition is nowhere near as important to me as my integrity."[3]

A shame or not, I was apprehensive. Merit alone does not determine who becomes judge. A person ambitious for that job has to feel the pressure to play the game, not to rock the boat. The people who covered up were not likely to admit it; Meyer would have to examine the circumstances and either infer the cover-up or not infer it. People often stare at two and two and won't see four. The Attica cover-up was more complex than two and two. Seeing it could rock the ship of state.

Sitting beside Meyer the day I met him were the first two lawyers he had hired for what came to be called the Meyer Commission. Malachy T. Mahon was a professor of criminal law and the founding Dean of the Hofstra Law School. Eric A. Seiff was Chief Assistant of the Criminal Division of the New York Legal Aid Society; he had served five years in Frank Hogan's office. They asked me about leads they might follow, who else at the Investigation might help them, what, if anything, I had concerning Rockefeller and Lefkowitz, whether the Attica Investigation was too big a job for Simonetti, and what about his sanity and mental balance. I asked Judge Meyer if he was completely independent. He assured me he was. I asked whether he was free to follow if a trail should lead to Mr. Lefkowitz or Mr. Rockefeller. He indicated that he was, with what struck me as an instant's hesitation. According to a memo I wrote at the time:

> I asked if I will have a chance to see or reply to Simonetti's answer to my Report. Meyer said he is not sure. I may simply be asked to reply to specific questions they will ask me without being shown the answer (i.e., the way Simonetti should have been questioned without being shown my Report) . . . .
>
> * * *
>
> I mentioned that I was among the last to believe ill of Simonetti, trying to find legitimate reasons for his acts during the time last fall when others in the office were saying that Simonetti had been reached. I asked, somewhat rhetorically, where are those voices today.

When Meyer was first appointed, Simonetti and I had immediately offered him our full cooperation. That was the obvious move; I obviously wanted to make it. Meyer and his people asked me for some papers and suggestions on how to proceed, I volunteered others, and they received them all. Simonetti and his office provided voluminous papers, though I don't know which ones. He and I both went to Meyer's Mineola office a number of times to testify, under oath with a transcript being taken.

Meyer eventually added a total of eight lawyers to his Commission, but only one investigator. The ability and motivation I saw in the lawyers encouraged me, but how much could Meyer investigate, I wondered, with only one investigator? The lawyers would read and analyze papers. They would depose witnesses, a slower and more cumbersome process and one that gives you less feel for what happened than Tony's vaunted "field investigation." At least he had four times as many lawyers as Fischer and Simonetti had had at first. On May 27 Meyer asked through the press for anyone with pertinent information to get in touch with him.

I gave the Meyer Commission my first testimony on May 28 and 29. He advised me of my rights, said everyone would now be questioned on the record—the reporter was tapping away as he said it—and turned the examination over to Edward "Mike" Shaw, a former federal prosecutor who had been three years behind me at the Harvard Law School. I kept trying to answer fully, and Shaw kept impatiently cutting me off by putting a new question, while Eric Seiff, the member of Meyer's staff with whom I felt some kinship, sat in silence. On one of those warm afternoons, Shaw said, with what I took as rudeness, "Your answers are making me sleepy."

"Your questions are making me sleepy," Seiff said amiably.

Seiff asked me to meet with him about the investigation on Sunday, June 8. "I hope someday Shaw wants to hear what I have to say," I told him then. Shaw did not question me again (perhaps he had exhausted his area of interest), and the Meyer people who did question me never again cut off my answers.

That same Sunday, Seiff told me that either Simonetti or I would "be badly hurt" by Meyer's work. I had not doubted it. He also referred to the fact that in my Report to Carey I had noted that Simonetti said, "God bless you . . . withdrawn," to Captain T when he bathed him in the jury. My implied criticism did not follow, Seiff said, because the captain could have sneezed. "This will give us a chance to ridicule you," Seiff added, "if our findings go against you." I wondered why they would add gratuitous ridicule to whatever hurt they might find necessary to inflict.

The lawyers who took the most testimony from me were Irwin Rochman, Arthur Vivianni, and Bobby Lawyer. Rochman had been a prosecutor in Hogan's office and now specialized in criminal defense. Vivianni had been an FBI agent for five years before becoming a federal prosecutor. Lawyer had been a federal prosecutor with extensive service looking into official corruption. They questioned me at considerable length about the particulars of the Shooter Cases, but not as much as I had expected or would have liked about how the cover-up worked. That made me wonder a little about their direction, particularly when Vivianni remarked one day something to the effect that he could understand a trooper firing his gun in the excitement of the retaking.

I testified about how Tony and I used to discuss the D-2 case. They told me Tony denied knowing what the D-2 case was. Several times during the summer of 1975 the Meyer people told me that Rockefeller had been nominated in September of 1974. Each time I assured them it was in August. Why do they keep getting it wrong, I wondered. Why don't they look it up? Don't they care that it happened right before the August Switch, not after it?

On July 25, a couple of the Meyer people mentioned that the jury had no-billed Trooper A since I'd left. That was a Grand Jury secret and technically a crime for them to tell me, but I found it reassuring that they did, as if to say, however momentarily, "You are one of us." I wondered a lot in those days what the Meyer people were up to, but I did not really worry: I was doing what I could, mindful that events were now largely in the hands of others.

They scheduled Simonetti and me so that we would not run into each other in the Meyer firm's pleasant offices. I had asked to see his response to my charges again when Shaw questioned me. "Not yet, but soon," I was told then. I kept asking and getting put off. Besides being curious, I was sure I could help them test what Simonetti was telling them, confident I could spot crap more readily than they and show them how to wade through it. They did not need my help with what Simonetti said, Mahon told me on the phone on July 29.

In a memo of May 21 to Meyer I had said:

> Further on Mr. Simonetti's mental balance: I am sure he felt the pressures
> of his job, and I believe he felt the pressures of doing the cover-up since he
> is far from being all bad and his dishonest acts must have created conflicts
> within him; but there was too much method to call it madness.

I found it very disturbing both during Meyer's investigation and talking with his people afterward that, undeterred by their lack of qualifications, they kept questioning Simonetti's mental balance and even asserting negative conclusions about it. They did not originate the idea. Rather, they were echoing an insiders' Official Version that Bob Patterson had been told and passed along to me before I went public. Discrediting people by calling them crazy is for the Soviet Union, I kept thinking, not the United States. One Meyer person cited the fact that Simonetti had filed some notes on paper napkins. So he thinks at lunch; the best people do. At least he didn't have a fetish about getting everything typed. After I resigned, I had been called "flaky" myself, and probably worse. And my jury had been called too biased to indict a law officer.

The Meyer people said repeatedly that Tony did things "off the wall"— meaning without reason that they could see. I agreed, while wondering if they would agree with me that those seemingly impetuous acts—reassigning people before they'd finished a job, launching crash new areas of investigation, the August Switch—actually had the logical, consistent, and inevitable effect of keeping evidence of officers' crimes from reaching the jury. I had worked closely with Simonetti. He was not a great administrator, was sometimes emotional and impetuous, a human being. I never doubted his balance except for Mad Friday—the day the previous September when he had harangued the staff for hours to "field investigate" and so on—and then only until he had told me a few days later how he'd hated to have to do that. Beginning to wonder if my opinion was unique, I finally asked Donald Schechter. "Tony's very competent indeed," Don said. Mike Baden told me, when I asked, that he thought so, too.

It was possible, of course, that something had happened to Simonetti's mental balance since I'd seen him last, and that the appearance that won the Meyer people to the Official Version accorded with some new reality. Personally, I doubted that Simonetti had undergone any fundamental change, though I'm sure that the need to cover up the cover-up drove him to extreme caution.

When Karen Silkwood blew the whistle on the mishandling of plutonium by the Kerr-McGee Corporation, its lawyer argued that she was emotionally unstable and suggested that she was kinky. When Sam Adams of the CIA charged that enemy troop strength in Vietnam was being officially understated, he, too, was said to be emotionally unstable. Frank Serpico, the cop who blew the whistle on corruption in the N.Y.P.D., was repeatedly called "psycho." Calling someone crazy may be just another way of calling him inconvenient and of distracting people from the merits of what he is saying. It fit the pattern to call me flaky. What was unusual was for the State to be doing this to Simonetti, who sought to remain the insider; but this, too, served the State's purpose as it sought to distance itself from him even as it supported him. Witness Lefkowitz's masterful and perhaps instinctive "I have complete confidence in what's-his-name—Simonetti." The Attica hostages who served the State were sacrificed in the retaking. Now it might be Tony Simonetti's turn. On August 8, Bob Patterson told me as scuttlebutt, for whatever it might be worth, that Simonetti "may have a serious emotional problem."

I did not see that Simonetti's alleged craziness or mine made much difference, except emotionally, to the cover-up issue. What happened happened, whether or not I was crazy to say so, and it could be seen beyond my testimony. Or if craziness *motivated* Simonetti, so what? His motive could just as well have been ambition, procop bias, or orders from Lefkowitz. If sixty-two State Police and zero inmates had been indicted, someone above Simonetti would surely have stepped in and made certain he was doing a proper job. In my experience, he checked his big moves with Lefkowitz before he made them. Fischer was In Charge of the Investigation for over two years, and it was always under Lefkowitz; I never heard anyone question *their* balance. And even an unbalanced or incompetent mate cannot excuse the captain for driving the ship in the wrong direction for four years.

I continued through that spring to look for work, sending out as many résumés as ever but with sparse responses now, and to make the biweekly trips to the unemployment line. Finally, on July 2, Peter C. Dorsey, the United States Attorney for Connecticut, interviewed me for a job.[4] I told him about the Meyer investigation.

"He could come out against me," I said.

"If he does, I'd doubt him," Dorsey answered, to my everlasting admiration.

He offered me the job, at a salary of $25,000; but the longer I weighed the offer, the more I came to realize that, somewhat to my surprise, I did not want to be on the prosecution side then. That $25,000 turned out to be more than five times my adjusted gross income for the following year. Shortly after I turned down Dorsey's offer, my landlady's son-in-law was indicted for stock fraud and asked me to defend him. Seven codefendants were convicted, but after a six-week trial the next winter in the Manhattan federal court, the jury acquitted him—largely, I believe, because he was innocent. So my private practice of law began.

During my testimony at Meyer's office, Bobby Lawyer asked me one day to argue my case against Simonetti.

"I don't want to do that," I said. "I want to tell you the facts and let the facts speak for themselves."

"That's right," Irwin Rochman said. Possibly, as it turned out, my making an argument might have helped Judge Meyer, and more likely I think, whatever I might have argued would not have made the slightest difference.

I kept offering the Meyer people my help in explaining what I could, analyzing notes, suggesting questions for witnesses, and so on. They accepted every paper I handed them and surprisingly little else of what I offered. The questions they asked me sought significantly less information than I was offering to tell them. I noted later that the Watergate prosecutors utilized John Dean, who was an admitted lawbreaker, to investigate that cover-up far more than the Meyer Commission ever utilized me.

May through September, I drove from my home in Connecticut to Meyer's offices on Long Island fourteen times, testifying six whole days and parts of two others to the extent of 1,400 pages. In a way, giving that testimony was therapeutic; getting it out, I felt relieved. I hoped they were hearing what I was saying. At the end Rochman showed me three places where I had been inconsistent. I hadn't expected any inconsistencies, yet there they were. I cannot recall what they were—they should be in my still-suppressed testimony to Meyer— but I do remember that I did not consider them major and wondered whether he did or not. I reflected on each one and gave him my best recollection of which of my statements was correct. I was glad to see that at least they'd spent the time with my transcript. For years I had known about innocent inconsistent statements and had told clients not to be thrown when opposing counsel brought them up; but ever after, I have been less prone to pounce when I caught a witness in an inconsistency. I never again heard any comments on my inconsistencies, though such may lurk in the portion of Meyer's report that are also still suppressed.

On August 20, my testimony behind me (except for some clean-up questions on September 26), I was finally allowed to see Simonetti's written response (or some of it) to my charges. I do not remember the specifics of Simonetti's response except that it bore little relation to the facts I knew. I spent two days at Meyer's dictating a reply, which I hoped his people would find useful.

I would later learn that Simonetti had repeatedly told the Meyer people that he never sought to limit my questioning of witnesses, though even Perry contradicted him on this. Simonetti insisted that he had not planned to close out the jury with little more presentation the fall of 1974; his own words that fall contradicted him on that. He argued at length that he had not immunized Major V and Captain T, because it was conceptually impossible to immunize people who, in his judgment, had not committed crimes. He complained that he had originated the bulk of the leads that I had been urging him to follow in fall 1974. Absolutely true. I never claimed otherwise. That fact made his failure to follow those leads, or permit me to follow them, all the more incomprehensible except as part of the intentional cover-up. He told Meyer's people that he had nothing against me except that I had libeled him and lied about him.

Vice President Rockefeller, accompanied by two lawyers, was questioned by the Meyer Commission on August 7 for five hours. "I answered fully and frankly," the Vice President assured the press afterward, adding that his answers had been "frank and straightforward, simple and open . . . [T]here was no mention of a cover-up." Echoing Rocky's evaluation of his own testimony, Meyer said: "He answered every question that he was asked and his answers were satisfactory."[5] On reading this in the *Times* the next day, I wondered how Meyer could have known, immediately and without talking those answers over with his staff, that all of them were satisfactory. Then on August 29, Rockefeller testified "voluntarily" before the Supplemental Grand Jury. Referring afterward to the retaking of Attica, he said, "We should have gone right through in the beginning."[6] That struck me as reasonable hindsight from his perspective.

On September 5, 1975, Lynette Alice "Squeaky" Fromm leveled a loaded .45 at President Gerald Ford at a range of about two feet, but a bodyguard grabbed her, and she did not shoot. On September 22, Sara Jane Moore fired a .38 at the President from across a street in San Francisco, but she missed. If either woman had been as competent with her gun as Lee Harvey Oswald,[7] Sirhan Sirhan, James Earl Ray, or Troopers A, B, and C had been, then Nelson Rockefeller would have become President of the United States.

* * *

Everyone who was following Meyer's investigation knew that October that he was taking longer than expected to finish his Report. Everyone was asking what it would find. The October 7 *Boston Phoenix* quoted me as saying of the Meyer people:

> [T]hey were slow to understand what I was saying and quick to grasp at explanations offered by the other side." [Bell] says he suspects the report

will be critical but will stop short of accusing Simonetti of a conscious cover-up, which Bell believes was indeed the case.

On October 10 the Supplemental Grand Jury indicted Trooper Gregory Wildridge on charges of reckless endangerment in the first degree for a shot-gun blast he fired during the retaking.[8] Wildridge was one of the three officers I had wanted to present to the jury for indictment on August 1, 1974, but Simonetti had not let me. The State Police announced that they would not suspend Wildridge while the charges were pending. Patrick J. Carroll of the State Police Benevolent Association said it was "a travesty of justice to indict a trooper who was risking his life to quell a prison riot." (Any risk to Wildridge, I happened to know, had been negligible.) Carroll branded the indictment as well as the still secret Meyer Report "a political move to silence Bell." I don't know how it would silence me, unless a token indictment was supposed to satisfy me. A "knowledgeable source" (viz., me) was quoted as saying, "They can't have just one token indictment, they have to have at least several token indictments." The president of the Buffalo Police Benevolent Association stated that in indicting Wildridge the jury "went along with the aims and goals of the Communist party in Russia."[9] I was delighted that after all this time and mismanagement, the jury had the opportunity and moxie to indict a man I felt deserved it on my reckless endangerment theory. It was their first and last hurrah.

"Reverend Bell?" said a deep voice on the phone at 6:30 P.M. on October 27. Myron Farber, who had always been struck by the fact that I was a deacon of my church, was calling to say that the Meyer Report, consisting of 570 pages in 3 volumes, had gone to Governor Carey and Attorney General Lefkowitz at 3:30 that afternoon. Bob Patterson phoned on October 30 to say that Judah Gribetz, Carey's counsel, was taking the position that "the so-called cover-up" was merely a personal dispute between Simonetti and me, and "a pox on both their houses." Eric Seiff had told him earlier, Patterson said, that "it took guts for Bell to do what he did"; he had asked Seiff to tell that to Meyer. Suspense quickly grew over the question of when the State would release the Meyer Report. One Sunday Farber asked me if I'd gotten the answer in church.

That November, a couple living in Scarsdale, New York, who knew about my situation over Attica, sent me a check for $3,000 "to help you through a rough patch." It did, but the fact that strangers would do that for me helped even more.[10]

Tom Wicker's column in the November 18 *Times* called for a general amnesty on Attica. I phoned to say I was glad he wrote that. Yet only a few months earlier I had favored full prosecution of all Attica criminals. It was largely by watching myself say and do things that I saw how Attica was changing me, as when I turned down Dorsey's job offer. I did tell Wicker that I was concerned that an amnesty not be "the last step in the cover-up."

The phone rang on the evening of Saturday, December 19. A reporter was calling for my reaction to the news, which I had not heard, that Simonetti's office had released the names of four troopers and three correction officers whom the Attica juries had no-billed. I forget what I said, but know what I felt. I had been investigating all seven of these men; except for the one presentation I had attended, I wondered how their cases were presented to the jury. With that one exception, these no bills left me with no confidence at all that they had been done right.[11] Why, I wondered angrily, was this information suddenly released now? It wasn't necessary, and it did the named officers no good at all. I supposed it was a ploy to delude the public into believing that the Attica Investigation had done its job, and that it was the juries, not the prosecutors, who refused to indict.[12] At that moment I knew, and I knew that Simonetti as well as Lefkowitz knew, how Meyer came out on the question of a cover-up. Some of us who were discussed in Volume 1 of the Meyer Report had received it in confidence—130 pages of findings, recommendations, and background. It was not handed to the press until December 21.

Here are Judge Meyer's full "findings" as printed in the front portion of Volume 1 of his Report:

1. There was no intentional coverup in the conduct of the Attica Investigation. There were, however, serious errors of judgment in its conduct. Moreover, there were, immediately after the retaking assault was over and before the investigation commenced, important omissions on the part of the State Police in the gathering of evidence. The combination of those errors and omissions has resulted in an imbalance in the prosecution.

2. Governor Rockefeller's selection of then Deputy Attorney General Robert Fischer who was head of the Organized Crime Task Force and well qualified by his background to head the criminal investigation, was prompt and appropriate. However, the dual role of the State Police (i) in the retaking of the prison, during which 39 men were killed and 89 wounded by law enforcement personnel, and (ii) as the investigative

arm of OCTF created for it a possible conflict of interest and for the Attica Investigation other problems which Fischer should have dealt with more firmly. Moreover, Rockefeller's remarks immediately after the retaking in praise of the State Police as a group were inappropriate in view of the possibility that the degree of force used by enforcement personnel may have been excessive and of the possible effect of those remarks upon the course of the investigation.

3. The Attica Investigation was from the outset woefully under staffed. The responsibility for the inadequacy of the staff rests largely with Fischer, and not with the Executive Chamber or Simonetti.

4. The decision to conduct the investigation sequentially or chronologically rather than topically was a serious error of judgment. Investigation in depth of the later occurring events was thus deferred, which skewed the investigation's inadequate manpower away from possible retaking, rehousing and hindering of prosecution crimes by law enforcement personnel. The Attica Investigation should be continued long enough to assure presentation to a Grand Jury of all such possible crimes.

5. The charge that prosecution of law enforcement personnel for murder or other shooter crimes and for perjury was obstructed by the Attica prosecutor is not sustained by the record. The deficiencies in evidence gathering immediately following the retaking left so little available to the investigation that determination of possible criminal liability in shooter cases became inordinately difficult in all but a few extraordinary cases.

6. The First Grand Jury returned 42 indictments containing 1,289 counts against 62 inmates, but in the four cases presented to it with respect to law enforcement personnel refused to indict. This one-sidedness was partly the result of the decision to investigate chronologically which caused cases against inmates to be presented first and over a period of a year, thereby saturating the jury with evidence of inmates' guilt before any law enforcement case was presented, partly the result of partiality and emotion on the part of jurors in considering charges against enforcement personnel who were their friends or neighbors, partly the result of the fact that indictment for "technical" offenses was asked for against inmates but not against law enforcement personnel, and partly the result of legal errors by the prosecution and the presiding judge that may have created tension between the prosecution and the Grand

Jury and confusion of the Grand Jury members, particularly as to the standard guiding their decision whether to indict.

7. Investigation of crimes of brutality against inmates which occurred during their rehousing and for several days thereafter was neglected, despite the fact that the area was one requiring a broad-scale investigation, quickly mounted, in order to obtain information and identification while memories were fresh. In consequence, available sources of information were not tapped nor has the investigation to date been well organized in the rehousing area. This resulted from the decision to investigate chronologically, from the inadequate staffing of the investigation and from a mistaken and misguided sense of values amounting substantially to indifference.

8. Simonetti conducted a detailed and logical investigation of the possibility that his investigation of possible law enforcement crimes may have been deliberately hindered by the State Police, but many steps should have been taken sooner.

9. Simonetti's decisions with respect to the granting of immunity demonstrate in the case of two high ranking State Police officers a lack of good judgment in failing adequately to interview them before putting them before the Grand Jury, and in a third case involving a State Trooper, both the lack of good judgment and an unreasonably lenient view of what should be regarded as a technical crime.

10. The charge that the investigation was switched in August 1974 from shooter cases to possible hindering of the investigation crimes and that the Grand Jury was recessed in November 1974 in order to frustrate presentation of possible cases against enforcement personnel is not sustained by the evidence. Those decisions were made in good faith, and except as to the brutality area, in the proper exercise of prosecutorial discretion.

11. The evidence does not sustain the charge that certain of Simonetti's actions demonstrate his desire to prevent Bell from effectively investigating the shooter and hindering cases. Some of the actions were entirely proper; others appear to have been motivated more by the strained relationship between Bell and Simonetti than by concern for the orderly progress of the investigation, or were simply the result of poor administration, but, fortunately, it appears that none of the actions resulted in any harm to the investigation.

12. Though Bell's charge of a coverup has proved not well founded and
in some parts was based more on emotion than on fact, a substantial
portion of the public shared his misgivings. In bringing the matter to
public attention and investigation, he has performed an important
public service.

So Meyer refused to bite the bullet. I was disappointed, but not surprised, and
bemused that Meyer had bought and was now peddling chunks of the Official
Version—too little evidence left to prosecute all but a few officers; "partiality and
emotion on the part of juries" (whom, I understand, the Meyer people did not
interview). He confronted only the most glaring unpleasantness and wished away
the merely obvious. He did not seriously rock a boat that deserved to be capsized.

I was angered that while Meyer openly disagreed with my conclusion that
the cover-up was intentional, he was not too modest to take sole credit for my
conclusions that the Attica Investigation had been terribly one-sided, "grossly
understaffed from the start,"[13] wrong to investigate the riot before the retaking,
and so on. Right up front in Finding No. 2, Meyer slapped Rockefeller's wrist
for his "inappropriate" prompt praise of the State Police. Finding No. 12 struck
me as more of a snide slam than a compliment. So, emotional and misguided
Bell sparked a good result for the wrong reasons. Anger, not gratitude, was my
emotion as I figured Meyer was trying to add stature to his finding that the
cover-up was inadvertent by a deft little putdown of the person who said otherwise. Meyer reached his conclusions after he and his staff reportedly reviewed
33,000 pages of grand jury testimony, more than a thousand documents
totaling "tens of thousands of pages," and interviewing 37 witnesses.[14] All those
trees examined, and the good judge declined to see the forest.

During the fall of 1974, my opposition to Simonetti's efforts to drop the
investigation of police crime forced him time and again into the increasingly
open acts of suppressing evidence that I have here recounted. I came to believe
that no one who examined those acts could fail to see the intentionality of the
cover-up. I had not foreseen Meyer. So much for another naive belief.

Meyer also found it "indelibly clear that more force was used than was
necessary to accomplish the retaking"[15] and that "criminal acts of brutality to
inmates occurred during the rehousing." "Clearly the State has dealt unfairly
with the inmates and affirmative action is necessary to correct the situation."[16]
He rejected the idea of a general amnesty that would drop the charge against
Wildridge and foreclose any more charges against law officers because that

"would foreclose the possibility of trial and thus dilute, if not prevent, the catharsis that the public airing of such charges would bring."[17]

He recommended that Simonetti be replaced as head of the Attica Investigation, adding, "Not that I have found any venality on his part; quite to the contrary, he has sought properly to carry out his task."[18] When Governor Carey and Attorney General Lefkowitz released the Meyer Report, Volume 1, they also announced the appointment of Alfred J. Scotti, seventy-one years old and Frank Hogan's chief assistant for almost twenty years, to replace Simonetti, "to determine whether indictments should be sought against law enforcement personnel and others and to conclude all aspects of the Attica probe 'justly.'"[19] Scotti was first appointed to the Manhattan District Attorney's office in 1938 by my old boss, Thomas E. Dewey, who had been District Attorney before Hogan; Scotti had served there for thirty-six years. Irwin Rochman and an assistant named Lewis R. Friedman, who had already served as Simonetti's personal adviser in defending himself against my cover-up charges, were to assist Scotti.

I found Meyer more impressive as a literary critic than as an analyst of reality when he wrote about the charges in my letter of resignation to Lefkowitz and Report to Carey:

> Evaluation of those charges has not been as easy a task as it might have been, however, had Bell, who has a flair for writing, cast his report in the more pedestrian but more clearly analytical form of a legal brief.
>
> Bell's literary bent, the obvious personality conflict between him and Simonetti prior to Bell's resignation and Bell's emotional involvement at the time he prepared the 160-page report in sustaining the position earlier taken in his letter of resignation, have in some instances resulted in subjective characterizations which manifest nothing more than the disagreement between Simonetti and Bell. Perhaps the best illustration is that whereas Bell states that Simonetti "repeatedly refused to allow witnesses to be called" (MBR 4), his testimony was that Simonetti failed to respond to his suggestion that certain witnesses be called and then recessed the Grand Jury . . . .[20]

So Simonetti refused to let me call witnesses by not saying yes when I asked permission to call them. (That was one of his ways of refusing; and as Meyer does not mention, another of his ways was simply to say no.) If that was Meyer's best illustration, I didn't see his problem or mine. If Meyer wanted a legal brief, why didn't he ask me for one? "[E]motional involvement . . . in sustaining [my] position" is what made me tell Carey what I'd told Lefkowitz? And not simply that Lefkowitz showed no interest in saving the prosecution of police crimes after I'd warned him it was being aborted? Maybe Meyer needed to involve his emotions before he could relate the same facts twice, but I've never felt that need. Bob Patterson had phoned on December 18 to read to me from my copy of Meyer Volume 1, which the State had delivered to him instead of to me.

"I think we should claim vindication," he said.

"It's a little hard to claim vindication," I replied, "when it keeps saying my charges are not sustained."

Unfettered by such restraints, Simonetti gave what I have since thought was the perfect response to Meyer from a person in his position. "I welcome it," he said, and thanked Meyer "for his objectivity leading to his findings clearing my good name and reputation."[21] Judge Fischer disputed many of Meyer's factual findings in a seven-page, single-spaced letter and said Meyer was "simply supplying his judgment in place of mine in retrospection."[22] If Simonetti could say that about me, I guess Fischer could say it about Meyer. Bob Patterson stated with judicious detachment that "whether by intention or by poor administration and serious errors in judgment, as found in the report," it was now "futile [to] attempt to prosecute" any officers.[23] My own statement "strongly dissented" from Meyer's conclusion that the cover-up had not been intentional and added:

In this respect, the Meyer report is like a pyramid without a point . . . . I appreciate that it may be harder for him to see what happened after the fact than it was for me who lived it. Nonetheless, it is like being at a holdup and then being told by the investigator, "the money's gone and the bodies are here, but there wasn't any holdup."[24]

A *New York Times* editorial on December 29 called for a general Attica amnesty, commenting, "The harm already done to the notion of equal justice is breathtaking." But a letter in *Time* magazine about a riot on Riker's Island was less abstract:

I could scream every time I read about a prison riot [Dec. 8].

When people go to prison because they walked into a store with a gun and held it up, they have given up their right to have any rights. I don't give a **'$*! about their gripes. Just shoot them when they riot. That will put a stop to it.[25]

As usual in those days I had the family Christmas Eve party in my barn. It was a happy time. A column by James Wechsler in that afternoon's *New York Post* made the rounds of my parents, children, brother, and his family, adding to the warmth:

> . . . Beyond the anticlimactic inconclusiveness of the result [of the Meyer Report], there is reason for special dismay over the treatment Meyer accorded Malcolm Bell, the 44-year-old Darien Republican whose cry of conscience impelled Gov. Carey and Attorney General Lefkowitz to initiate the inquiry . . . .
>
> The Meyer report almost grudgingly acknowledges that "in bringing the matter to public attention and investigation, he [Bell] has performed an important public service." But this minimal tribute is accompanied by nitpicking derogation of Bell's charges of cover-up, including a remarkable exercise in literary criticism . . . .
>
> This is an unjust rap, rendered even more gratuitous by the extent to which Meyer's findings confirm the key contentions Bell advanced when he resigned . . . .
>
> . . . Meyer's downgrading of Bell's critique is peculiarly incongruous. The line between "deliberate cover-up" and chronic negligence and ineptitude becomes almost a semantic irrelevance.
>
> For the moment, however, these comments are primarily dedicated to Malcolm Bell. He deserves better from the Meyer report. In a time when we reproach so many in public life for playing it safe and going along, he spoke out forthrightly. If his statements were tinged with "emotion," the Attica horror-story surely merited more spirited tones than the "pedestrian" language of a turgid legal brief.
>
> There are worthy passages in Meyer's report. But that document would not exist if Malcolm Bell had observed the vows of bureaucratic silence and submissiveness.

I sat alone in the barn a week later as dusk settled through the branches outside. My long stock fraud trial was in full swing and heavy with documents, and I called it a good night when I got five hours' sleep. The judge, however, had let us out early for New Year's Eve, and I was finally taking the time to read the

Meyer Report Volume 1 beyond its findings, recommendations, and the passage about my charges.

I could not believe the simpering, weasel-worded, illogical analysis in Meyer's "Factual Basis for Findings" that made the findings themselves look blunt by comparison.[26] This is just the background, I thought, what do Volumes 2 and 3 look like? I didn't write a brief; Meyer wrote a brief, an incredibly weak brief, as the prologue for pulling his punches on the cover-up. Why this garbage bothered me more than the findings I did not know, but it did. Talk about emotion—seldom if ever has dudgeon moved me toward action as it did then. But what to do as dusk settled on the end of 1975? I phoned Tom Goldstein, a colleague of Farber's who also wrote about Attica at the *Times*. He was still there.

"It's bullshit!" I said. "I can't believe it! Do you know what he says?"

"I know," Tom said soothingly.

I put Meyer Volume 1 aside for a New Year's Eve party, but I wasn't done with it. When people would ask what I thought of it, I generally said, "It sucks." I went to work on a more analytical critique as soon as the stock fraud trial ended in mid-January and sent it to the *Times* Op-Ed editors. They accepted it, mentioning that while they did not usually let people respond to their pieces, they'd let Meyer respond if he wanted to, in view of what I was saying. He didn't. My piece, which the *Times* printed on February 14, 1976, shows how far emotion can drive me. Here it is:

Bernard S. Meyer, the special state investigator of the Attica prosecution, asked me if I wanted to make a statement when I was testifying in his offices last spring. I said I thought he had a unique opportunity to restore the faith of a lot of people that non-partisan honor is still possible in government. For me the Meyer Report does not do that.

The report . . . made substantial progress. It found that the prosecution of crimes at the 1971 riot discriminated in favor of the New York state police and prison guards. It found the prosecution woefully understaffed from the start, too close to the state police, and guilty of bad judgment in focusing on crimes by inmates before crimes by law officers. I charged all this a year ago. Why then am I dissatisfied?

The one-sided prosecution of crimes by inmates had the effect of covering up crimes by officers. It gave Mr. Meyer the choice of calling the head prosecutors, Robert E. Fischer and then Anthony G. Simonetti, knaves or fools.

Either they intended a cover-up or they perpetrated it without knowing what they were doing. He chose, in effect, to call each of them a fool.

He attributed the cover-up to serious errors in judgment, mistakes of law, mismanagement, personality factors and indifference—to anything, in short, except conscious decision. Concluding that the cover-up happened unintentionally, he did not have to decide who directed it.

Actions prove intent. If X consciously shoots Y dead, that is enough to convict X of murder for intentionally killing Y.

The officers of Attica fired over 450 times, hitting 128 people, and killing 10 hostages and 29 inmates. Insofar as those shots were not fired to save someone from an imminent threat of death, they were not justified and were probably criminal.

Then the officers assaulted scores more inmates. The Attica prosecutors had a duty to prosecute these crimes. By constant decisions over a four-year period, they determined not to do that. Intentionally? Mr. Meyer says no.

He rests his charity on three pillars of salt, each of which should dissolve on inspection:

1. Mr. Meyer says that deficiencies in evidence-gathering by the state police at the riot left too little evidence to prosecute any but a few extraordinary shooting crimes. The state police did the opposite of what sound evidence-gathering required.

In addition, the prosecution never questioned hundreds of eye-witnesses about many shootings, and committed many other sins of omission in the pursuit of evidence.

In blaming the state police for the missing evidence, Mr. Meyer may create the false impression that the prosecution does not also bear heavy responsibility. It does not follow, however, that many cases against shooters did not survive.

As the McKay . . . Report of 1972 made clear, much film and many photographs remain. Ballistics remains, though it is of limited value since the state police did not record which trooper had which rifle.

Eyewitnesses should be able to say even now whether *anyone* was attacking *anyone* so as to justify the various shootings. Each trooper also gave a written statement within days after the riot, thus identifying many shooters. Insofar as the statements admit shootings that can be shown to be unjustified, at least the felony of reckless endangerment may be provable. A single trooper was finally charged with this crime last fall.

2. Mr. Meyer says that "a mistaken and misguided sense of values amounting substantially to indifference" motivated the prosecution's four-year neglect of the notorious brutality that followed the shootings.

A panel appointed by then Gov. Nelson A. Rockefeller reported only two months after the riot that the prosecution was not concerning itself with these crimes.[27] How Mr. Meyer can attribute such a glaring dereliction to indifference rather than intention escapes me.

3. Mr. Meyer suggests that the grand juries were too biased to indict officers. A grand jury however, can only act on the evidence the prosecutor gives it. When Mr. Simonetti put me in charge of giving evidence to the second Attica grand jury in May 1974, he and I agreed to present at least several dozen possible shooting cases before going on to brutality and a possible obstruction of justice by the state police.

Starting the next September, however, he and I had increasing disagreements, the nub of which was that I wanted to give adequate evidence to the grand jury and he did not. The grand jury attended well, asked probing questions after we finished questioning a witness, and sought important witnesses. It is not fair to blame a grand jury for the faults of the prosecution. I have no reason to doubt that that grand jury would have done its job according to its oath if given the chance.

I said in my resignation in December 1974 that my object was to see that all the facts necessary for the grand jury to vote on indictments were placed before it, and that equal justice applied to inmates and officers. That is how the system is supposed to work. I wanted it to work. Apparently my superiors feared the result if it did.

Some people tell me not to waste sympathy on inmates. Sympathy has nothing to do with it. The inmates of Attica were sentenced to a prison, not a game preserve. It is never open season on humans. The law protects inmates as well as the rest of us from being wantonly shot or bludgeoned. Moreover, almost all inmates get out. How we treat them in prison affects how they treat the rest of us afterwards. Humanity, the Constitution and common sense all require equal justice.

Some people want to forget Attica. It is old hat. Who likes to contemplate the police gunning people out of anger, hate or fear? Yet as the riot recedes into history, the full story remains hidden.

Brotherhood failed at Attica. The failure reached bottom when officers shot and beat without justification. It continued while the prosecution pursued inmates yet sheltered officers from answering for their crimes. It continues with Mr. Meyer's conclusion that the prosecutors made the prosecution one-sided unintentionally. The split between the ins and the outs, the good guys and the bad guys, us and them, is alive and well in New York State. Denying the facts will not avoid their repetition.

Thirty-seven

Dr. John F. Edland

Dr. John F. Edland, the medical examiner of Monroe County, had shocked everyone (or nearly everyone) by announcing on September 14, 1971, that all the dead hostages had died of gunshot, after the State had announced and the media had duly reported the Official Version that inmates had slashed their throats. Though the Investigation had known that troopers watched Edland pulling bullets out of the dead through the early hours of the fourteenth, it had never questioned him about the State Police cover-up. I had put his name on my list of seventy-four witnesses to call to the jury, but Tony had not let me call him. I had written to Meyer in May 1975: "Someone told me that John Edland . . . thought there was a cover-up. Perhaps he should be asked what he thinks and the basis for his thoughts." But the Meyer people did not talk with him.[1] As Rockefeller's assistant counsel had asked on the fourteenth, who was this guy, Edland?

I decided to find out in 1976 while my son Brian, who was eleven, and I were visiting relatives in Edland's part of the state. Edland sounded cordial on the phone and welcomed us into his large corner office in the medical examiner's building in Rochester. He was about my age and size; he, too, had black hair and glasses. A microscope stood on a table near his desk, and near it a milky screen for reading X rays. A small human skeleton suspended in the next room fascinated Brian. I had hoped to talk with Dr. Edland for an hour or two. We talked for eight hours, ending up at his home after dinner with his family and after our kids had ridden "Evel Knievel" bikes through the neighborhood into the darkness.

Dr. Edland gave me a copy of a memorandum, dated September 22, 1971, in which he reported in detail his activities, with whom and when, starting "shortly before 6:00 P.M." on the thirteenth. He referred to it repeatedly as we talked. It was the skeleton on which he fleshed out his recollection. I had never seen it before. The jury should have seen it and heard him.[2]

With a feeling of impending doom, he said, he had followed the events of

September 13 as best he could on the radio and TV. He feared there could be "considerable loss of life" at Attica, by which he meant maybe six to ten dead. At 6:10 P.M. his phone rang at home. State Police Captain Nicholas Giangualano asked him to take as many bodies as he could for autopsy and storage.[3] Edland said he would take twenty-five, but only on the condition that they included all the dead hostages. He had already heard enough about mutilations, and so forth, that he wanted to see for himself what really happened. The captain told him to expect the bodies by 7:30 P.M.

He summoned his staff. State Police and men from the Monroe County Sheriff's Office placed his building under heavy guard, as busloads of armed blacks were rumored, falsely, to have taken to the highway from New York City. During the long evening, some police talked with pride about shooting "niggers" that morning. "Did you get one?" "Oh, I got one." They talked like that, heedless of Edland's black assistant, who became so furious he had to leave. At 12:10 A.M. the bodies finally arrived in two trucks with a State Police escort, nineteen inmates, and eight hostages, which were all but one of the hostages who had died by then. Edland showed me a large color photo of the stretchers covering the floor of the garage outside his office. I would not let Brian see it.

Edland and his associate, Dr. George Richard Abbott, did a complete external examination of each man in the clothes he died in, a complete description of the naked body and its wounds, and a complete internal examination. They had to do anal swabs for semen because they had been told to treat the hostages as rape victims. Those results proved negative.

Photographing the wounds forms an essential and elementary part of the autopsy. Mike Baden's grisly prints had been invaluable at the Shooter Conferences and in the jury. I had watched Mike routinely take photos the morning I saw the nine autopsies in New York City. Edland told me he always took the autopsy photos himself or had his staff do it. That night, though, he and his staff faced a unique mass of work. The State Police offered to take the photos. They had two experienced photographers there for that purpose. They would need the photos for their investigation of all those homicides. Letting them do it would save Monroe County a little money. Edland let them.

The State Police photographers took hundreds of pictures as Edland and Abbott worked. They told him afterward that they had somehow neglected to keep track of what photos went with what body. What good is a close-up of a bullet hole in an unidentified back? They had the grace to call their failure to take usable photos "very embarrassing."

Keeping track of what pictures went with what body was as elementary as keeping track of what rifle went with what trooper. If anyone on Edland's staff had been guilty of so gross a failure, he said, he would have fired him. Edland repeatedly asked the State Police to see those hundreds of pictures anyway—maybe some of them could be matched up, some must show faces, unique wounds, etc.—but all the police would ever show him were a handful of pictures without identifications. Why didn't the Attica Investigation go after all those hundreds of State Police pictures?

I recognized both of those State Police photographers as participants in the picture-taking failures back at Attica earlier that day. The State Police had not fired them, or anything like it. Talking to Edland this summer afternoon in 1976 was the first I ever heard about the State Police photo "failure" at the autopsies. The jury should have been given this evidence, too, of the State Police cover-up.

Simonetti, who had reached Attica on the thirteenth and investigated ever since, had to have known about this failure. He had to have known that the photos belonged with Edland's autopsy reports but were not received with them, and he had to have known why this huge hole existed in the normal and expected evidence. Yet Tony had not included it in his Mosaic of the State Police cover-up. He had not insisted that Edland be questioned about it, nor included it as events to question the two State Police photographers about in the jury. Instead, he prevented me from calling Edland.

Edland's first autopsy was of a hostage whose skull looked at first as if it had been shattered by a club, in other words by an inmate. This was the corpse whose face changed its expression in the various photos that the State Police had seen fit to give the Investigation. The culprit turned out to be a .270 bullet. Dr. Abbott, who knew a lot about firearms, examined a slug from the chest of John Monteleone, a father of five who was not supposed to be working at the prison the day he was taken hostage. "Jesus Christ!" Edland remembered Abbott saying, "That's from a .44 magnum." They asked the troopers in the room if the State Police carried .44 magnums. The troopers said no, telling Edland that the killer was a guard. (In fact, it was Correction Officer Z.)

Some troopers did what people usually do at an autopsy: they left. Others milled around. It was terribly obvious to Edland and Abbott as they worked that all the dead had been shot, but the police seemed oblivious. Repeatedly an officer would say, "Was he stabbed, Doc?" and they would say "No." The doctors would say things like, "That's a beautiful .270," or, "Gee, there are fourteen double-O's in this guy." Edland said he and Abbott assumed that the police beside them were taking all this information in, but he thought afterward, maybe they weren't. His memorandum says, "By 4:30 A.M. it became apparent that the hostages had all been shot, and that there were no slashed throats or genital mutilations."

At about 6:30, Edland decided it was time for a break. All the hostages had been posted, along with four inmates, and no one seemed in a hurry to finish the rest. The police have been here, he felt, they have seen what we found, the information will filter back up. He did not foresee the impact his findings would have on the police, the public, and his own future. He went home, lay down, and looked at the ceiling. Then he showered, ate breakfast, and returned by eight o'clock.

The State Police had been pressing him to release the bodies of the hostages as quickly as possible, he said, so they could be treated as fallen heroes. Before going home he had made what he later considered the mistake of agreeing. While he was gone, the eight bodies were taken away. This made it hard for the pathologists who were called in later to check his work to do that. (Not knowing his findings, officials had not yet decided to call them in.) It also permitted the State Police Night Riders to try to have the local undertakers repudiate his findings.

At 11:00 A.M. State Police Lieutenant Fred Penfold, the officer in charge of their morgue detail, arrived. With him came Bob Horn, the State Police ballistics expert from Albany. Seeing them there made Edland realize the concern of the State Police. He saw in them "considerable apprehension . . . a palpable anxiety . . . concern as only you can feel when things haven't gone right." They kept asking him if he was really sure various bullets came from the various hostages. Edland said he was. It was then that Horn said generally of the bullets on the tray, "It looks like our stuff." Penfold and Horn asked to take the bullets with them. Edland refused. They were the property of the Medical Examiner's Office. He could not release them yet. (Good save, I thought.)

Reporters mingled everywhere on the morning of the fourteenth and were pressing to know his findings. The police did their best to keep them away from the rooms that held the bodies. A TV reporter started grinding way with his camera, until the police stopped him. At 3:00 P.M. when all the autopsies were finished, Edland held a press conference. He had expected to meet with "a few local reporters." Instead he found "wall-to-wall" representatives of the national media. That surprised and shocked him. He had come without a written statement. He told me that that press conference was "the most outstanding job" he had done in his life, "flawless, detailed, concise, cutting out all the previous misinformation." He told his wife afterward that he expected no contradictions of what he had reported. He was right, in spite of heroic efforts by State representatives to prove him wrong and otherwise discredit him.

Edland's press conference was not the first news that the hostages had been shot. That morning, according to Edland, a reporter named Dick Cooper from a Rochester paper had been chatting with one of Edland's staff named Lupo. Lupo asked Cooper where he got the idea that all the dead hostages had had their throats cut. Cooper replied, the *New York Times* and U.P.I. Cooper left. Outside he realized what Lupo had said. He rushed back inside, got the first story of the hostages being shot, and won a Pulitzer Prize.

Simonetti wondered aloud from time to time at the Investigation how Lupo came to "leak" that story. He considered that significant on the issue of when the State Police knew for sure that the hostages had been shot. Consider, too, that the State Police got their ballistics expert from Albany to Edland's by 11:00 A.M. on the fourteenth. All that Edland was telling me bore significantly on this issue. It should have gone to the jury.

At 4:00 P.M. on the fourteenth Simonetti walked into Edland's office. He asked Edland to go over what had happened again and again. Edland found himself being almost apologetic, sorry it turned out this way. Edland, who was accustomed to being questioned by prosecutors, found Simonetti to be a skilled interrogator, "an intense and extremely competent questioner." Judge Meyer notwithstanding, I knew the Tony that Edland was describing.

During the hour they talked, Simonetti did not mention that he had already summoned Dr. Henry Siegel, the senior pathologist from Westchester County, to review Edland's findings. Edland felt amazement, dismay, and anger when Siegel arrived at about 6:30 P.M. He was even more amazed when Dr. Michael Baden phoned around eleven o'clock to say he would be up from New York City the next morning on the eleven o'clock flight. Edland's "inner voice finally awoke" to ask, "What's going on? Don't they believe Abbott and me?" He felt suddenly left out. Baden told him, "Don't worry." That worried him. He hadn't known there was anything not to worry about.

Baden told me afterward that he was called in to see if Edland could tell the difference between a bullet hole and a knife hole, and Edland could. Corrections Commissioner Russell Oswald had contributed to the original fiction. "Not only were the guards murdered by the prisoners," he had announced on the thirteenth, "but atrocities were committed on the hostages. A twenty-two-year-old guard was killed, castrated, and buried in a foxhole." Though Oswald summoned Baden as an independent medical examiner, Baden has stressed that Oswald was hoping Baden would find that the hostages had indeed been cut and not shot.[4]

Dr. Henry Siegel was older than Dr. Baden, had a greater reputation, and a higher position. Lieutenant Fred Penfold escorted Siegel, while Baden was escorted by a trooper. Siegel looked at the bodies and took some pictures. Baden actually reautopsied them and took hundreds of color photos that largely replaced the original photos that the State Police ruined. That was how we ended up having them for the Shooter Cases.

Siegel initially bought two State Police versions, according to Edland. One was that Ramon Rivera had been shotgunned in his foxhole in D Yard well before the State Police assault. If that were true, it would "prove" that the inmates had a shotgun, and the State Police could claim that inmates had used the same shotgun to kill hostages. Baden and Edland showed Siegel that it wasn't true, and that Rivera was shot during the assault.

The State Police also persuaded Siegel that hostage John D'Archangelo was killed by a thrust in the abdomen from an inmate spear, until Edland and Baden showed him that a State Police .270 had put the hole in D'Archangelo. A photo that stays with me is the one a newspaper photographer snapped of D'Archangelo's wife three days before a trooper sent the bullet through to his spine. She was the young woman with dark hair falling past her shoulders and her face averted, who waited outside the prison at the mercy of others.

I had not heard how the State Police had snowed Siegel until I talked with Edland, and also asked Baden about it, in 1976. The jury should have heard this, too.

Wednesday, September fifteenth, brought Edland a barrage of phone calls from midnight on, from all over the country, from the media, from pathologists, some purporting to come from the White House and the Governor's office. That evening Simonetti, Drs. Baden and Siegel, and Penfold and Horn of the State Police came to Edland's office, as well as Michael Whiteman, Counsel to Governor Rockefeller, for a detailed, scientific, five-hour meeting on the deaths of the hostages. Simonetti, the former homicide prosecutor, "wore the mask of ignorance" about pathology, Edland said, making him feel "grilled" as he had to repeat simple explanations. Whiteman said little. During the meeting the news announced that a Batavia mortician had been unable to find a gunshot wound in one of the hostages, so Baden left to see for himself. It was then that Baden rolled the body over and pointed out the bullet hole in its back.

The next morning Lt. Penfold, "smoking furiously," drove Edland and Abbott on "the white knuckle flight" to a meeting at the prison. They "hit speeds approaching 100 miles an hour" on the country roads, until the terrified Edland told Penfold there was not that much need to rush. Edland noted that in violation of normal procedure, they did not sign into the prison—another uncollected piece for Tony's puzzlement over the missing sign-in records at Attica.

At the Administration Building Edland felt that the guards were looking at him and Abbott "with absolute hatred." He chatted in the corridor with two troopers who apparently did not share the guards' animosity. When he told the troopers it seemed strange that (as he apparently already knew) there was no way to trace the bullets from the corpses to the guns to the shooters, "they just gave me a big wink." That wink, too, belonged in the jury.

On entering the conference room, Edland was startled to see Dr. Milton Helpern, Chief Medical Examiner of New York City, Baden's boss, and a legend in his time. The State had flown Helpern in from London, though not much came of his presence. Siegel, Simonetti, and Robert E. Fischer were already there, too. Fischer "was very much in control . . . . Simonetti deferred to him on all occasions." Edland was called on again to do most of the talking. "I was practically defensive," he said, "about facts I considered very obvious."

He met Captain Henry Williams for the first time at the meeting, finding him open, friendly, and personable. Of all the officials there, Williams was the nicest to him and did not seem to begrudge his findings. Williams brought out a movie of the retaking for the doctors to see, to the apparent consternation of Fischer and Simonetti. Edland said that the film showed a trooper on his knee firing a shotgun well after the prison had obviously been retaken. (If so, Tony had known that film existed, yet to the best of my recollection, the jury and I did not see it. Am I mistaken, or did the State Police withhold it from the Investigation, or cut it before turning it over?) Edland said that on seeing that shooting, Baden wept.

Edland asked Fischer to whom he, Edland, was responsible. Fischer answered him with silence. No one else would tell him, either. He also asked Fischer if Fischer would have his findings confirmed, because his phones had been ringing constantly and he wanted to get people off his neck. Again Fischer and the others sat silent. Fischer, Simonetti, and the Investigation never did answer; Edland's findings were not officially confirmed. A day or so after the meeting, Baden publicly confirmed Edland's findings on his own. Edland kept trying to have his status defined. Eventually his boss, the Monroe County Manager, wrote to Fischer on the need to define Edland's role. Simonetti wrote back that it was "the traditional role between prosecutor and medical examiner which you understand fully."

At that meeting at the prison on September 16, Fischer directed that no more information was to be released, imposing this official silence, he said, "to protect the rights of the accused." His blackout, however, did not extend to himself or to the Official Version. That same day, he and Major Monahan held a news conference at which they described the assault and released pictures of hundreds of the inmates' weapons—thus jeopardizing the rights of any accused inmates and boosting the defense of any accused officers. Also that day, Governor Rockefeller told the press that the hostages may have been caught in a "cross-fire," and that from what he knew, the killing of the hostages was "justifiable homicide."[5]

The Investigation asked for and got from Edland all the bullets, the clothing from the dead hostages, and his autopsy reports, though he also kept copies of the reports. He kept the original X-rays, since he considered that they established more clearly than any other evidence the authenticity of his findings. When the Investigation called for them, he took them himself or had an assistant take them. He would only turn over copies.

My former colleagues called Edland to Warsaw often on short notice, he said, to answer brief or trivial questions before the first jury. "You're needed in Warsaw this afternoon." One day they asked him to bring the files on ten or eleven of the dead. He hoped he would have a chance at last to give some full testimony, as prosecutors usually asked him to in grand juries, but all they asked him in case after case was "name and cause of death." It ended in a few minutes. The only time they questioned him fully in the first jury was about the death of William Quinn, killed by inmates.

Efforts "to get something on Edland" or otherwise to discredit him continued. Friends told him that investigators had questioned them about his personal life. When he moved a few blocks to a new house in 1975, a report circulated that he had "skipped town." The police, TV, and floodlights converged on his old house, making a memorable evening, no doubt, for the folks who had just moved in. Edland thought that many people felt even in 1975 that if he disappeared, so would his findings. Spooky.

Edland saw himself as a messenger whom the king beheaded for the tidings he bore. For years he received abusive mail, late night phone calls, accusations about his integrity, and an official cold shoulder. The police stopped consulting him about homicides. He had been, he said, the Western New York expert in his field, whom the State Police called on in special cases before Attica but not afterward. A prosecutor from a rural county had recently come to ask him about a local homicide. The interview over, he thanked Edland but said that if he called him before the jury, he would probably lose the case. Some people still believed, Edland said, that he had been covering up for the inmates when he told how the hostages died. He didn't just confuse people with the facts, I thought, he won their hatred.

In evaluating what anyone says about Attica, it seems necessary to weigh possible bias. Attica is a Rorschach, and its events often take strange shapes through the prism of the beholder. A Goldwater Republican in 1964, Edland had let his hair grow long following the riot and took to referring to the NYSP as *Staatspolezei* who do two things, write traffic tickets and shoot unarmed men. How much of Edland's feelings grew from the actual horror of what the police had done, and how much from their leaving him out? It is not sufficient to conclude, as I do, that Edland is an honest man. Bias often colors any witness's testimony in ways he does not recognize. For the most part, Edland's sympathies seem to have lain with law enforcement at the time he witnessed the happenings of mid-September 1971. He changed as time passed, the horror sank in, and events passed him by—another person "radicalized" by Attica, at least for a time. His hair was fairly short when I saw him in 1976 (if hair length means anything), and he seemed to be speaking of a prior Edland when he told me of his remarks about the *Staatspolezei*.

But bias could not have invented the State Police photographic failure at the autopsies; that failure should have made a significant contribution to the Hindering Case. His September 22, 1971, memorandum antedated any shift of bias. Nor is it likely that bias imagined the troopers' wink. He seemed straightforward to me in August 1976 (which could possibly mean we shared similar biases then), and he said many things that meshed with details that I knew about and he almost certainly did not. As often happened when I questioned a new witness about the State Police, he related a few facts that helped them—they were human and not totally bad about Attica—and far more facts that strengthened the Hindering Case against them. In fact, very few, if any, witnesses helped that case as much as Edland would have, if he had been called to the jury.

He told me that no one had ever suggested to him that he lie about his findings, though events probably moved too quickly before his press conference bombshell for anyone to have had an opening to do that discreetly. Then Baden and Siegel were too honest to disagree with him. Yet he was made to feel, he said, that he had transgressed by "violating the chain of command [and] not releasing the information through channels."

He considered those channels deep enough that his information might well have sunk into them forever. According to the scenario he believed likely, it would have been announced that the autopsy findings were "under investigation" or "awaiting the grand jury" or "would prejudice the rights of the accused." Belief in the Official Version would then have hardened until nobody cared. I am repeatedly amazed at how many people still think that inmates killed the hostages. (Consider the suppression of the findings and photos of John F. Kennedy's autopsy, and of the X-rays that showed the bullet tracks through him.) From Edland's familiarity with prosecutors and with what else happened after Attica, he feels that it would have been relatively easy to have buried the truth, leaving the bullet-ripped bodies to rest in their graves while the world went on believing that inmate knives had put them there. His scenario is certainly consistent with the way the State Police whisked the bodies to sympathetic but unequipped undertakers on the afternoon of the thirteenth and, after Edland and Abbott's autopsies, sent out their Night Riders in the vain effort to kill the truth.

Honesty may be the enemy of a cover-up, but at Attica as elsewhere, this proved more true in theory than in practice. It was the unpredicted or uncontrolled, random incidence of honesty that ripped such holes as appeared in the Official Version. Like so much else, Edland's account shows that Attica was too big to keep the lid on, yet the cover-up largely succeeded anyway. What a tribute to official power, public conformity and indifference, and the complexities that drive us to seek order at the expense of law. The power of the people to deceive themselves writhes through the story of Attica like a great serpent. It proved a sinuous ally for the intentional cover-ups, sometimes even making them redundant.

Sometimes when disgusted at the persistence of the deceivers and the deceived, I reached moments of asking myself whether the truth, after all, was not better buried along with the other Attica dead. The serpent of Eden tempted with knowledge. Today's serpent tempts with ignorance.

Edland said he felt there was a cover-up from the first day he met Simonetti. He "couldn't believe it" when he heard the Supplemental Grand Jury was being formed. He was "flabbergasted and delighted" by my cover-up charges. The Meyer Investigation puzzled him. He thought "it was superficial [and] failed to live up to its great promise."

Honesty was Edland's burden and his glory. He shattered the first magnificent State lie about State crime at Attica. His instinct for telling the truth rather than playing the game was anomalous, anathema, and costly. Yet if everyone plays the game, we shall all end as losers. If he had it all to do over again, John Edland said that, save for releasing the hostages' bodies to the State Police, he would.

Thirty-eight

The Prosecution Peters Out

The winter of 1976 saw the end of the entity called the Attica Investigation. The equal justice that finally arrived was different from what I had sought, but radically better than what had existed before I went public. I do not believe it would have arrived at all, or that the State would have admitted the need for it, if I had not gone public.

The prosecution of inmates had peaked two years earlier with 62 of them charged in 42 indictments with 1,289 crimes. The Investigation's only triumph was the March 1975 conviction of John Hill (Dacajeweiah) for the murder of William Quinn and a codefendant for attempted assault. By the time Al Scotti succeeded Simonetti as In Charge of the Investigation, four other trials (before and after Hill's) had ended in acquittals, a number of indictments had been dismissed, nine inmates had pleaded guilty to reduced charges, and only eight indictments of inmates remained to be tried. Only one of them, against eleven inmates charged with kidnapping hostages, was scheduled for trial soon. The dismissal rate for most prosecutors' offices ranges between 10 percent and 20 percent. For the Attica Investigation it had already gone well over 50 percent.[1]

On January 26, 1976, Scotti asked the court to dismiss four more indictments. The court complied.[2] On February 26 he asked the court to dismiss the remaining indictments against inmates, except for a charge that Mariano Gonzales, who had been released and become a fugitive, had murdered another inmate. Again the court complied,[3] as courts nearly always do when the prosecutor moves to dismiss.

Though Carey and Lefkowitz had appointed Scotti "to review evidence to determine whether indictments should be sought against law enforcement personnel,"[4] Scotti made it clear, in an eight-page February 26 statement to the court, that he had not found and would not find enough evidence to do that. His overture to inaction sounded even better than Meyer's had, but he, too, was not about to bite any live bullets. He told the court that there was "indisputably excessive use of force by law enforcement personnel during the retaking," but he went on to say:

> We have concluded that, with the possible exception of two matters involving serious criminal conduct of law enforcement officers, there is no available evidence which would justify an additional indictment against anyone for a "serious offense." One matter involves a possible intentional killing by a state trooper and the other matter involves a possible serious obstruction of the Attica investigation by a member of the State Police. These matters are being reviewed to determine whether indictments should be sought.[5]

Lest there be any suspense, nothing was to come of these reviews.[6] Citing the State Police failures to record serial numbers, take adequate statements, label and preserve evidence, and account for vanished photos, Scotti's statement continued:

> My two associates and I have found that the unavailability of evidence required for successful prosecution of those serious offenses resulting from the unlawful excessive use of force by law enforcement personnel was caused by flagrant deficiencies in the State Police investigation of the retaking. The State Police inexplicably failed to collect and preserve evidence.

I don't see how Scotti found those failures inexplicable; the explanation was clear to me. He continued:

> These serious failures to comply with basic investigatory practices make it impossible, now, to conduct an effective investigation of the circumstances concerning the thirty-nine deaths and eighty-nine woundings caused by weapons fired by law enforcement officers during the retaking of Attica. It should also be acknowledged that the failure of the Attica Prosecution to perceive these deficiencies at the very outset of the investigation and to take whatever action could have been taken to develop evidence pertaining to those offenses has, in large measure, contributed to making an effective investigation impossible. There is evidence which strongly suggests that

unjustifiable homicides were committed by individual law enforcement officers. The tragic fact is that prosecution has been rendered impossible.

Impossible my eye! Simonetti, incidentally, did perceive those deficiencies at the very outset; he also told us that no less an authority than a ranking BCI detective had told Fischer, referring to State Police evidence collection after the retaking, "They're fucking it up." Scotti also asked for and got dismissal of the reckless endangerment charge against Trooper Wildridge, reasoning:

> Our investigation has confirmed that there is ample evidence to support the conclusion that many other law enforcement officers used excessive force during the events of September 13, 1971. Also, *the evidence strongly suggests that the crime of reckless endangerment was committed by many law enforcement officers during the Attica retaking.*
>
> However, the appalling deficient investigation by the State has made virtually impossible the development of a legally valid case against any of these other law enforcement officers. It would not be just, therefore, to single out one state trooper for prosecution for the crime of reckless endangerment. [My emphasis.]

So Scotti agreed with me and sometime Simonetti that many officers were probably guilty of reckless endangerment (though Scotti thought not provably so)—in contrast to Meyer's curious failure to make any mention at all of all those crimes in his findings.

Scotti told the court that he had reviewed the eight no bills of officers that the juries had already voted and found sufficient evidence to resubmit one of them except that, "[S]ince that state trooper has already received immunity from prosecution, prior to my appointment, he cannot, now, legally be prosecuted." This must have happened after my departure; I would have been fascinated to know more about it.

Scotti went on to note that he was not condoning the "barbaric" acts of some inmates or the "brutal" acts of some officers. That allocation of adjectives may have been politic and expected, but it did not accord with the reality of the turkey shoot and tortures that followed. As to the allocation of justice, 62 percent of Attica's inmates were in for violent crimes, including homicide, robbery, assault, and rape, whereas 100 percent of the officers who committed homicide and assault at Attica remained at large.

Scotti ended his statement by saying:

This is a unique situation made possible solely by the unfairness of the State investigation. In the absence of such unfairness there would be no reason not to prosecute anyone who committed a crime at Attica.

There is one standard of justice for all. The name "Attica" should be a symbol, not only of riot and death, but also of the capacity of our system of criminal justice to redress its own wrongs. I, therefore, believe that the amply demonstrated lack of fairness and evenhandedness by the State in the conduct of the Attica investigation compels, in the interests of justice, the dismissal of these pending indictments.

Much of what Scotti said was honest and accurate, and I suppose in this day and age that is an accomplishment. Certainly his statement was a far cry from Lefkowitz's answer when I first broadcast my charges, that he had complete confidence in what's-his-name.

Ever the attentive pupil of Simonetti, I knew what to say this time when the *New York Times* asked me to comment on Scotti's actions: "It's nice to be vindicated. I hope this doesn't lead to sweeping what really happened under some carpet someplace."[7] The *Times* could not reach Simonetti for comment.

Judge Ball dismissed both Attica grand juries at Scotti's request on March 30, telling them that they were bound for life by their oath of secrecy as to what they learned and did during the investigations.[8] The first jury submitted a 118-page report to the judge; it was sealed and I have heard nothing of it since. Asked about the end of the juries, I said, "The problem is the de facto amnesty now satisfies many of the critics and that removes a lot of the impetus for having the story told."[9] Tom Wicker wrote in the April 2 *Times* that the dismissal of the juries "puts an end to one set of injustices but perpetuates another." He called the one-sidedness of the prosecution "an American atrocity. The state's dismissal of the grand juries merely puts on it the final seal of official indifference."

In April, Scotti recommended executive clemency for "some" of the eight convicted Attica inmates; suggested departmental discipline against twelve troopers, seven guards, and one civilian employee at Attica; and recommended that Volumes 2 and 3 of the Meyer Report be released. Thus he signed off.[10]

Patrick Carroll of the troopers' Benevolent Association was quoted as saying, "Scotti's rude, prejudicial to-hell-with the canon of ethics statements against the troopers should be investigated by the bar association. The true fact is that Scotti has set himself above the law . . . ."[11] A headline in the April 23 *New York Daily News* was more dispassionate: "Attica Prober Asks Clemency for Cons, Spanking for Cops."

But lest anyone think that Attica had gone away: within three weeks after Scotti closed out the Attica Investigation, 150 guards picketed to protest under-staffing and overcrowding. Three stabbings of inmates and an unarmed attack on a correction officer in May led to a cell-by-cell search that turned up a large but not surprising collection of knives, clubs, and garrotes. In July, eight guards and an inmate were hurt in a flare-up over a routine cell search; and Governor Carey prepared to go to the prison himself if the situation demanded it. Attica then housed 2,000 inmates, 240 fewer than in 1971, when overcrowding was a major cause of the rebellion, though officials said that the prison was designed to hold only 1,600. After investigating the situation, Scott Christianson, Director of the Correction Commission's State Prison Unit, announced that conditions at Attica were "just as bad, perhaps worse" than in September 1971. "What we have," he said, "is a combat situation . . . [that] can go off any time. Both sides have the power of death in their hands." Attica Superintendent Harold J. Smith concurred, adding, "I'd be a damn fool to say otherwise."[12]

Instead of rioting—a lesson learned perhaps—the inmates commenced a general strike on August 23, with most refusing to leave their cells. Both inmates and officials succeeded in keeping the tense strike nonviolent through six days of negotiations that resulted in reforms that included a promise to reduce the population by 300; expansion of work-release and furlough programs; allowing inmates to touch, kiss, and hug their wives, children, and other visitors; showers daily instead of twice a week; fewer rectal searches; a greater effort to hire black and Hispanic guards, at least some of whom spoke Spanish; and greater efforts to house inmates closer to their homes. About 60 percent of Attica's inmates were from metropolitan New York, a trip of about 400 miles each way that was particularly hard for a family that did not have a car. Otherwise, life at Attica remained much the same.

Within two weeks after the strike ended, the State fired Scott Christianson for his "independence" in disclosing the conditions and predicting the trouble. He responded by saying of Governor Carey and other officials, "They don't want to improve conditions in prison. They don't want anything done except to keep things quiet."[13] If Christianson were not correct, I expect conditions at Attica would have changed more before the strike or, for that matter, after it.

Thirty-nine

The Book Won't Close

On December 31, 1976, Governor Hugh Carey sought to "close the book" on Attica. His statement said in part:

> No government can command the confidence and respect of its people without a firm commitment to the principle and practice of even-handed justice.
>
> [T]he state, through its highest officials, failed abysmally in upholding this principle in the handling of [the] Attica investigation and prosecution in the first half of this decade. Due to insensitivity to their constitutional responsibilities, equal justice by way of further prosecutions is no longer possible.
>
> * * *
>
> I have come to the most distressing, indeed the most disappointing moment in my tenure as Governor of this State. For I now must conclude, that the conduct of this investigation and prosecution has been such that we now confront the real possibility that the law itself may well fall into disrespect. Hence, I have concluded that, as Governor, I have the final responsibility to bring this tragic affair to a conclusion which, however unsatisfactory, will foster respect for our system of justice as one capable of recognizing and correcting its wrongs.
>
> * * *
>
> Attica lurks as a dark shadow over our system of justice. The time has come to firmly and finally close the book on this unhappy chapter of our history as a just and humane state . . . .[1]

The Governor accordingly pardoned seven Attica inmates, as Alfred Scotti had recommended. He commuted the sentence of John Hill, the man convicted of killing William Quinn, making him eligible for parole, but the parole board then decided to keep Hill in. The Governor ruled that no action would be taken against the nineteen officers and one civilian against whom Scotti had suggested departmental discipline. Governor Carey did nothing at all to end the suits on behalf of the gunshot wounded, the widows of the dead, or the inmates whom officers tortured.

The New York Court of Appeals ruled back in 1973 that people shot during the retaking could win money damages if they could prove "excessive force."[2] The McKay Commission, the Meyer Commission, and Scotti's Attica Investigation all concluded that the police had indeed used excessive force. Rockefeller (whose personal exposure to liability in the inmates' suit theoretically exceeded $4 billion) then swore that in his opinion the State Police had "absolutely not" used excessive force.[3] The State refused to admit any liability or enter settlement talks. The State's stonewalling actually caused the Court of Claims to hold the State (Attorney General Lefkowitz) in contempt.[4]

I was involved in the civil suits only by accident. The same day in December that Governor Carey "closed the book" on Attica, he requested the Attorney General to take whatever legal action is necessary to effect the prompt release of Volumes 2 and 3 of the [Meyer] report. . . .[5]

This "request" was a "direction," as the General's office admitted, and I waited for the General to obey. Months passed. Nothing happened. In late March, I dialed the General's office and was referred to Charlie Bradley, who still worked in the Department of Law. Never available to take my calls until I caught him with a person-to-person on May 9, Charlie told me he knew nothing about any effort to free up Volumes 2 and 3.

The next day I wrote to the General, noted that it was "now over two years since you said you did not want this thing dragging on," and respectfully urged him to secure the prompt release of Volumes 2 and 3. Within a week Attorney General Lefkowitz sent me a reply that left me mystified and somewhat suspicious:

I am in receipt of your letter of May 10th concerning the status of the Meyer Report. The issue of disclosure of the entire Report is presently before the Appellate Division, Fourth Department, on appeal from a decision of the Court of Claims in *Hardie v. State* and *Jones v. State*. The claimants' request for disclosure of the Report for purposes of pre-trial discovery was implicitly denied by Judge Quigley.

The *Hardie* and *Jones* appeal was argued April 13, 1977 and I am constrained to hold in abeyance any application for release of the entire Report until the Fourth Department renders a decision in the matter.

What, I wondered, was that all about? *Jones* and *Hardie* were suits claiming twenty million dollars on behalf of the wounded hostages and hostages' widows. Their lawyers were seeking to discover evidence from the State, which the General was defending. I could find nothing in the decision by Judge Robert M. Quigley that "implicitly denied" the widows Volumes 2 and 3. On appeal from the *Jones* and *Hardie* decision, the General was asking the Fourth Department to render an advisory opinion (i.e., an opinion on a question not at issue) that Volumes 2 and 3 could not be released.

The Fourth Department was the appellate court above both Judge Quigley in the Court of Claims and Judge Ball in the Supreme Court, Wyoming County. Since the overtly sensitive parts of Volumes 2 and 3 involved Judge Ball's grand juries, the application to release these volumes would be made to Judge Ball. But if the Fourth Department issued the advisory opinion the General was seeking, then Judge Ball would almost certainly deny any application to release them. The General had not given notice of his maneuver to the many of us who had an interest in release or suppression. How ingeniously sneaky, I thought, Lefkowitz is trying to suppress the volumes that the Governor directed him to try to release.

I wanted those volumes released and was concerned lest the Fourth Department issue the advisory opinion without realizing the ramifications. Even if Meyer's reasoning was as flawed in Volumes 2 and 3 as it was in Volume 1, the later volumes had to disclose a host of significant facts that I did not feel free to disclose and presumably other facts that I did not know about. Meyer's findings still grinned at the world like the head of the Cheshire Cat, without visible means of support. Until the body of his Report appeared, they could not be understood, appraised, or attacked with precision.

I phoned the clerk of the Fourth Department, who told me it was too late to appear *amicus curiae* (as a friend of the court). Would I be out of line, I wondered, to phone or write one of the judges anyway, or at least explain the problem to his law secretary? I learned that Judge Harry Goldman (of the Goldman Panel) had disqualified himself from considering this appeal. He and I had had a good chat after a talk I gave in Rochester back in November 1975, and calling him now would not be an improper communication with a judge considering a case. With some apprehension nonetheless, I phoned him on Monday, June 6. He seemed pleased I'd called, listened to my concern, and found that the court's decision had come down the previous Friday. He read it to me—no mention of Volumes 2 and 3. So the good ship Liberty glided past another iceberg in the night.

My interest in *Jones* and *Hardie* quickened when I phoned the hostages' lawyers to discuss the General's gambit to suppress Volumes 2 and 3. They told me that they had started simply as lawyers trying to win for their clients. They had no ax to grind, no cause to fight, no cover-up to expose. They had the conventional sense that having a cause could hurt their claims before the presumptively Establishment-oriented judge who would decide the claims without a jury. Yet the further they pressed the suits, the more maddening they found the State's obstructions of civil justice and the more intensely they wanted to bring out the facts about Attica simply for the sake of bringing them out. One of Lefkowitz's assistants had even admitted to them that he was under instructions to drag his feet and be as uncooperative as possible.[6] Realizing that the General could jerk them around on pretrial discovery until their cases grew too stale to try, they decided to forego discovery and mark the cases "Ready." The trial was set to start on October 3.

Admiring their spirit, I found that the amount they did not know about the turkey shoot was awesome; I wanted to do what I could to fill them in. Four months was a frighteningly short time to prepare for such a trial. I suggested that they subpoena me to Buffalo so I could officially tell them as much as I could. They did.[7]

On the morning of June 29, 1977, I flew to Buffalo and met Gene Tenney, Nelson Cosgrove, and Bill Cunningham, the main lawyers for the hostages. My old colleague, Dave Flierl, was there as the assistant attorney general for the State. He recited, portentously and maybe a bit self-consciously, the crimes I would be committing under the grand jury and executive secrecy statutes if I went ahead and complied with the subpoena to testify for the hostages the State had sacrificed. The transcript continues:

MR. FLIERL: Do you . . . concur on matters that I've gone over this morning, that it would appear that you'd be prescribed from revealing anything learned in the Grand Jury?

MR. BELL: No. I definitely would not agree with that . . . . I believe that generally the facts I learned in the Grand Jury have been disclosed, and in one way or another, and therefore, the statute that prohibits disclosure is not applicable.

MR. FLIERL: Therefore, one crime justifies another?

MR. BELL: . . . I absolutely disagree with that statement. It is not a crime if you state things from the Grand Jury that are already disclosed.

MR. TENNEY: . . . Apparently, you're advising Mr. Bell as to the statutes of the State of New York, and almost under terms of a threat, if I may characterize it as such, that if he does testify pursuant to a lawful subpoena of this Court, that you are telling him that there are certain laws under the criminal Procedure Law and the Penal Law of the State of New York for which he maybe arrested or indicted. Is that the way I understand it, Mr. Flierl?

MR. FLIERL: No. I think that's incorrect . . . . I'm not trying to intimidate the witness, but I want the witness to be aware of them, so there will be no charges later on, which he says, gee, I didn't know that.

As I sat at the conference table with these usually pleasant men, I had the most immediate sense of risk I had yet had over Attica. It was a solemn thing to hear a prosecutor threaten to indict me if I said what I was planning to say, knowing that once I said something there was no way I could unsay it. I was also pondering the possibility of being disbarred even if I were not charged with a crime. The adventurer in me hoped to be indicted, to run my own show, to question Simonetti, Lefkowitz, Rockefeller, and everyone else publicly under oath, to let it all hang out as far as the courts would let me. On balance, though, the total Malcolm wanted very much not to be indicted. I did not need that in my life. But I said to myself, Fuck it, I'm going ahead.

MR. BELL: As to your review of the statutes at this time, Mr. Flierl, and in no way meaning to question your subjective intent, I took your review of the statutes . . . as having a dual function. One was to offer sound advice, and the other was to make a threat of sorts. Now, it is my intention, I may need the help of both of you gentlemen as we progress, but it is my intention to answer the questions put to me as truthfully and as fully as I can without violating the law . . . . It may not always be easy, but . . . I intend to do that.

Flierl and Tenney wrangled some more in the deceptively ritualistic language we lawyers use, as the time for me to back out passed quietly by. The hostages' lawyers questioned me for what turned out to be about a hundred pages while Flierl sat largely silent. I told, under oath and on the record, much of the Attica story I had never told before. This unburdening was a strange release, finally sharing some more of my pent-up knowledge about where the literal and figurative bodies lay.

I declined to name grand jury witnesses or suspects the few times I was asked to do that, and I avoided direct references to the jury. I hoped Flierl did not think I was going too far, but I thought the State might have trouble calling my testimony a crime after an assistant attorney general sat by and let it proceed. As a silent counterpoint while I testified, I planned how I, as a prosecutor, would build a criminal case against me. During lunch Bill Cunningham said cheerfully that he would defend me free of charge if I was indicted. He and I laughed. Tenney looked serious.

The General did not seek the release of Volumes 2 and 3 during the seven weeks after the *Jones* and *Hardie* decision that he had claimed to be waiting for. By letter of July 20, I renewed my request to the General for prompt action and shared some other thoughts:

> Your opposition to the release of the full Meyer Report [in *Jones* and *Hardie*] is 180° contrary to Governor Carey's requests to you . . . .
>
> * * *
>
> Instead of paying compensation for the gunshot hostages, you resist their claims in Court; you use that litigation as a vehicle to oppose the release of the full Meyer Report, in conflict with the request of the Governor; and you, through Mr. Flierl, threaten me with criminal prosecution when I testify in aid of those gunshot hostages.
>
> Your actions do not appear consistent with Judge Meyer's conclusion that the prosecution's failure to expose and prosecute crimes by law officers at Attica was unintentional. Your actions, however, are fully consistent with my conclusions that this coverup was intentional and that it continues today. I would appreciate being advised of any reasons why my conclusions are unsound, as I am writing a book about all this and want to be fair.

The General never sent me any such advice and later declined my request to interview him. I wondered whether Governor Carey approved of his disobedience, wasn't paying attention, or did not want to tangle with him over Attica. A letter, dated July 25, 1977, from the General's executive assistant, replied to mine of the twentieth:

> Now that the various motions made by the claimants, Hardie and Jones, in the Court of Claims actions have been decided by the courts, papers are being prepared (subject to any unforeseen proceedings in such civil actions) by this office in connection with an application before Judge Ball respecting Volumes 2 and 3 of the Meyer report. Governor Carey has been kept informed of the progress of the claimants' motions. Copies of the application will be served upon you and others referred to in the Meyer Report.

My gadflying was far from the only reason the General was moving. Tom Goldstein of the *Times* had been calling him, too. Tom had been fascinated when I showed him the Lefkowitz response to my letter in May. He thought there was a story in the Attorney General's overt defiance of the Governor's orders. Apparently his editors disagreed. Casting about for an alternative, he said he might try a human interest story about me, on where the whistleblower was two years later.

"I greet that idea with mixed emotions," I said. My net feeling was pleasure.

"You may have to submit to it," Tom said somberly. Somber was one of his ways of being funny, though I was not always sure when. He interviewed me for two hours in the house I had moved into in 1976. Weeks passed. "You're a hard person to write about," Tom told me.

He also said he had called Lefkowitz. The General allowed that it was in the public interest to release Volumes 2 and 3 but said he feared that they would help the people who were suing his clients. "That puts you on the horns of a dilemma, doesn't it?" Tom ventured helpfully. Lefkowitz agreed. Tom's story appeared in the *Times* on August 3, 1977. It said in part:

> Unlike most silent dissenters in public office who discreetly resign, Malcolm H. Bell deserted the Attica prosecution and went public.
>
> He is writing a book on his Attica experiences that no one seems interested in publishing and is pressing for the release of a confidential report that he has been told will damage his reputation . . . .

"The only thing it has cost me is money," said Mr. Bell, who had to divide his Connecticut house in half to bring in rental income. "I feel great, I feel terrific. It was the right thing to do. It has given me a very solid feeling."

* * *

Mr. Bell has been calling the Attorney General and has written rather stiff letters in which he has told Mr. Lefkowitz that his failure to release the volumes "smacks of suppression."

More like a teacher scolding a distracted pupil than a former state employee addressing the state's highest law enforcement officer, Mr. Bell recently wrote: "Frankly, General, you have not evidenced the interest in the publication of the rest of the Meyer Report or of the facts which underlie it."

"I have a divided responsibility," Mr. Lefkowitz said. "It is in the public interest to release the report. But I am also defending the State of New York and former officials in lawsuits, and evidence brought out in the report may be damaging to my clients."

Conflict of interest was more like it. As Attorney General, he was particularly bound to obey the law and ethics of pretrial discovery in the hostages' suits. If he had overseen the Attica prosecution properly in the first place, the facts in Volumes 2 and 3 would have been public knowledge years earlier. If the General found himself on the horns of a dilemma, his wounds were self-inflicted.

Over seven months after Governor Carey directed the Attorney General to act promptly, but only two days after the *Times* publicized his disobedience, the General served an "Application" by himself and the Governor asking Judge Ball "for a judicial determination as to the publication of volumes 2 and 3 . . . ." This was a minirerun of April 1975. As Judge Robert E. Fischer himself wrote to the court, "Now, once again, a belated application is made to this court, apparently precipitated by a news story addressed to unrevealed events."

Lefkowitz's affidavit in support of his application discharged his public trust in a single sentence: "It is felt that it is in the public interest for the public to know what transpired to the end that confidence in our system of justice be restored." But he felt "obliged as an officer of the Court to bring the following facts to the Court's attention for its consideration." He spent the next eight pages arguing why Volumes 2 and 3 should remain suppressed and attached letters from the State Police and prison guards predicting tragedy or worse if the volumes were released. My own submission to the Court said:

24. We still live in a democracy. The governors are still the servants of the governed. It is long past time that the State finished answering to the people for Attica. That is also the best way to prevent another Attica.
25. Will the Court peel back some of the secrecy that still shrouds Attica, or will it seal the lid with its imprimatur? When all the interests have had their say, that is the question. That question allows only one answer.

Déjà vu rose with the sun on September 8 as I took the American Airlines early flight to Buffalo for the hearing on the General's application. Instead of traveling with Investigators Ed Burbage or Lenny Brown, I ran into inmate leader Big Black (he of the football balanced between chest and chin) and his "radical" lawyer, Liz Fink, who represented the inmates who had been shot and assaulted and the next of kin of the dead in a class action for four billion dollars (including punitive damages) in federal court.

The General did not show up. The State Police lawyers I used to see around the jury were there, as well as Mark Benenson for the guards, several lawyers for the hostages, and, helping the State, Dave Flierl and two more of my old teammates. Nelson Cosgrove for the hostages berated an assistant for "stonewalling." Generally, though, the atmosphere in the courtroom was that of a happy reunion. Former antagonists shook hands, shared legal papers, and chatted amiably. Surprised, but also part of it, I reflected on the powers of time and human nature to heal (when they do not kill).

Judge Carman Ball strode into the courtroom looking more tense than I had ever seen him. He asked several times if the assistant who was there for the Attorney General wanted an injunction against the release of Volumes 2 and 3. No, the assistant simply wanted a determination on whether the grand jury references they contained required them to be suppressed. State Police lawyer Bud Malone argued that the Attorney General's conflict of interest required him to be replaced in the proceeding. Judge Meyer was not there but submitted papers—far better reasoned and written than Volume 1—attacking the General's affidavit and urging the release of the rest of the Report. A lawyer for

Russell Oswald made the strongest plea for total suppression, urging that "the public does not have a right to know." Though Mark Benenson requested suppression, he made his strongest pitch merely to delete the names of his clients, the correction officer suspects. (I agreed and have, of course, done so in this book.) Liz Fink, the hostages' lawyers, and I argued for release. Before I started to speak, Judge Ball warned me not to violate grand jury secrecy.

At the end, the assistant attorney general handed the judge the thick, green-bound Volumes 2 and 3. Except for the assistant, neither the judge nor any lawyer present had read them. I hoped that the fact that they criticized Judge Ball (as Volume 1 said they did) would not sway his judgment. He reserved decision and strode out of the courtroom clutching the bulky volumes against his black robe in the manner of the Statue of Liberty.

* * *

New York law on releasing grand jury secrets was not entirely simple; in essence, it gave Judge Ball discretion in this unique situation. By memorandum of November 29, 1977, he found that:

> the public interest lies not in the disclosure of selected excerpts of grand jury testimony for the purpose of supporting conclusions of the Meyer Report, but rather in guarding the secrecy of grand jury minutes.

He directed the General "to redact and exclude any and all reference to grand jury testimony," and he provided for those of us discussed in Volumes 2 and 3 to receive the redacted copies thirty days before public release so that our rebuttals could come out at the same time. The heart of his reasoning on Meyer was that to allow one person to determine the facts and the law, to condemn and absolve can only precipitate debate in the public minds as to what happened in Attica. Rather than closing the book, it is opening Pandora's box.[8]

So much for the strength of democracy residing in an informed public opinion. At least Judge Ball did not opt for total suppression; he said he had no control over the portions of the volumes that did not contain jury information.

No one pushed very hard on the appeal. More than a year later, it was argued in the Fourth Department. The State Police joined the correction officers in urging full suppression. I was somewhat bemused to stand before the court on the same side as Judge Meyer, arguing for full release, so that what came out would not be as full of holes as an indigestible Swiss cheese. On May 22, 1979, the Fourth Department affirmed Judge Ball's decision to protect the sanctity of "jealously guarded" grand jury secrets. A stinging dissent by Justice John H. Doerr said:

> When prosecutorial conduct is placed under a cloud, where charges of coverup clearly places it, the need for invasion of Grand Jury secrecy is compelling . . . .
>
> The faithful administration of the laws of the state in a just and even-handed manner is clearly within the public interest. This interest cannot be served by conducting an investigation (by Judge Meyer) in a vacuum and then suppressing findings by a rigid allegiance to secrecy.
>
> * * *
>
> Redaction of these [grand jury] matters as ordered by the court below and approved by the majority would in many instances reduce the report to an inane compilation of words and phrases and consign the entire Meyer investigation to a futile gesture.[9]

Though Democrat Robert Abrams had replaced Louis Lefkowitz as Attorney General at the start of 1979, I was opposed to his office's redacting the grand jury materials from Volumes 2 and 3, since it was so obviously in its interest to construe "any and all reference" to jury testimony as broadly as possible and to redact with a meat ax. To no avail. The redacted volumes were finally submitted to Justice Frederick M. Marshall since Judge Ball, too, had retired. Whether or not the surgery was overzealous, Judge Marshall held, on November 20, 1980:

> I am not convinced under the circumstances presented here that release of these two emasculated and incomprehensible Volumes is in a public interest which "transcends the policy of maintaining the utmost secrecy in grand jury proceedings." . . .
>
> Accordingly, the Court directs that Volumes II and Ill of the Meyer Report be permanently sealed.[10]

It was Governor Carey who had directed the release of those volumes. It was as a lawyer for the Governor that Judge Meyer had argued in the Fourth

Department for full release. I wrote immediately to the Governor's Counsel (no longer Judah Gribetz) saying that I was not in a position to take an appeal from Judge Marshall's decision, but urging him to. No appeal was taken. The body of the Meyer Report remained buried.

Chapter Forty

The Grand Jury Got It!

As the years began to pass after my work at the Investigation broke off in the middle, a big mystery hung in my mind: Where was it leading? Would I have gotten indictments if given the chance? Was the cover-up worth the State's effort, or was it simply a needless precaution? What of the Supplemental Grand Jury, the silent eye at the center of the turmoil? Between the destruction of evidence by the police, my lack of grand jury experience, and the alleged bias of the jury, would these citizens of Wyoming County have failed to indict the criminals even if I had been permitted to keep working with them?

To find out, I spoke with six jurors.[1] Since the prison is a major industry in their area, many of their friends and relatives work there, and many of their neighbors still believe that inmates killed the hostages, I do not name them. With one exception, they said pretty much the same thing about their experience on the jury though with varying degrees of specificity and fervor.

It may help at this point to recall the numbers that govern a grand jury: The full complement is twenty-three people. It takes sixteen to make a quorum; if only fifteen show up, they cannot function. It takes twelve votes to indict someone, twelve being barely more than half of twenty-three but three-quarters of sixteen.[2] The fewer jurors present, therefore, the harder it is to get an indictment.

I believe that what follows is substantially accurate, though, perceptions varying as they do, some jurors may disagree on some points:

After Simonetti and Perry told the jury in the fall of 1974 that they had received a very thorough presentation and had only two more weeks to sit, Simonetti and eventually Alfred Scotti continued them for another year and a half, though they met only a few times in the winter of 1975–1976. The prosecutors never explained this radical reversal of plans. They simply smiled and said, "Things have changed." Another juror's reaction on hearing Perry tell them "only two more weeks, tops" in November 1974: "Hey, what's going on? You're not going to find nothing out in two weeks. We couldn't believe that."[3]

Simonetti "ran the jury with an iron hand. There were enough sheep for him to lead," rendering the others unable to take control. After he left, "things freed up a bit, but by then it was too late." Ned Perry and Dave Flierl made most of the day-to-day presentation after I was gone. "They were pleasant and easy to work with," but they failed to probe with their questioning, so that "the witnesses simply told the same story over and over again. At first we grew hot under the collar . . . indignant at wasting time . . . but eventually just bored to death. You can bore someone just so long."

Division grew among the jurors as the months went by. The quieter ones were generally more conservative than the ones given to asking questions. The majority saw that the officers had "done terrible things, committed crimes," though a couple of jurors "felt the officers could do no wrong, and even if they had, [those jurors] weren't going to do anything about it," and a couple more seemed reluctant "to rock the boat" by saying that officers were criminals. The longer the jurors sat, the more they inclined to the view that "our neighbors in Wyoming County meant more than the prosecution."

During 1975, physical attrition set in. Several times the jury failed to make a quorum. One woman met a man on her vacation in Alaska, married him, and moved away. A death in the family took another to another state for several months. Jury service placed a financial burden on all the jurors who had jobs. A young man who had a night job and dozed a lot in the jury apparently fell asleep at the wheel of his truck one morning and died in a head-on collision.

One juror started to speak out strongly for the State Police, reportedly after they started to frequent his place of business. (Their good-buddy tactics again? A crime of tampering?) Some jurors finally told a witness, "He doesn't speak for us." That juror stopped coming to the jury after that.

While I remained at the jury, a witness would tell them something, and "you would look at us as if to say, 'Remember that.' You were making points and we were hearing the points . . . . We were fully aware that you were in it heart and soul and cared and were the only one who did."

"You were the only one who asked questions that got anywhere. Everyone else was tippy-toeing, never trying to [cross-examine the troopers or] get them to say what they didn't want to." Another juror: "You were a bulldog pulling bones out of the fire." A third juror: "I wish they'd let you continue. Those next guys didn't ask much." A fourth juror said that she herself did not ask nearly so many questions after I left because my successors "made me feel uncomfortable, so I backed away."

When I left, the jurors were disturbed that "the only prosecutor who was really into it and rooting for us was gone . . . . After you left, no one guided us, and we floated."

The jurors "reacted strongly" against my sudden departure. They got together and wrote a letter of protest. "The prosecutors replied that the subject was closed . . . . They gave us no alternative." Jurors speculated that my removal was "a backstabbing operation because Simonetti wanted the whole show for himself." When my cover-up charges went public the next April, they realized that my superiors feared that "You would indict troopers." A second juror: "I hoped you weren't kicked into the backwoods." A third juror: "You were getting too close. They didn't like it."

The jurors generally agreed that the Attica prosecution was covering up. Even the propolice juror thought that they were not being shown "slides and rolling pictures" and that the jury was closed down before they were done. According to one count when I went public, "seventeen or eighteen of us wanted to raise hell, but were told to lay off." Notwithstanding the fact that the jurors had an excellent and unique perspective on my charges, the Meyer Commission never questioned them.[4]

"There was no way to call the prosecution an honest effort . . . . It was a miscarriage of justice." Another juror: "It was terrible . . . . I don't believe too much in justice now." A third juror: "I would definitely do it again. I think justice should be for everybody, no matter who."

The jurors were painfully aware of the prosecution's failure to present the necessary National Guard witnesses and other evidence of the postretaking brutality. "When we asked about that, the prosecutors said, 'Later.' Later never came."

Another juror noted all the inmates who had been present at the shootings and said she had wanted more inmate witnesses. "That big black man with the football on his chest—how could anybody not notice that?" she said when I asked what she thought of the troopers who had been in A Yard but denied seeing him.

The jurors were told that a report on the retaking was being prepared for them to make, but they never saw it.[5]

Some jurors took the hodgepodge presentation of evidence as "a calculated effort to confuse us." The August Switch "confused us greatly."

Many jurors were appalled that the State Police kept no lists, no records, and "talked so much about the terrible acts of the inmates." Second juror: "I couldn't see [the police] shooting when the inmates didn't even have guns. . . . They should have dropped the tear gas and not shot nobody." Third juror: "There shouldn't have been any shooting at all after the tear gas." First juror: "If some inmate raised a stick, that was cause to shoot everybody in D Yard . . . . The State Police were so busy protecting brother officers they didn't care who they shot . . . . The guys at the top did not do their duty when they let the hysterical State Police retake Attica, after days of trading insults and so forth." Second juror: "I thought they cut the shooting out of the film . . . . I do believe the guards and the State Police did wrong. I would have indicted a lot; I really do [think so]. I really think [Trooper A] was guilty."

Though witnesses lied to the jury obviously and often, the Investigation never let the jury vote on these perjuries (with, I believe, one late exception). That frustrated and discouraged the jurors. "The troopers all gave the same answers. We knew they were lying, but how do you prove it?" (The Investigation could and should have proved it.)

Simonetti angered them when he immunized Major V and Captain T, snatching away the decision whether to indict them. Apparently frustrations reached the point after I left where one juror remarked, "Everyone who was really guilty got immunity."

Another juror: "Most troopers were evasive. [Captain T] was very evasive. I wouldn't be surprised if he was in the cover-up." A third juror: "I was really disappointed in [Captain T]. I think he committed perjury, lied through his teeth. You could tell he was lying; he'd say something and contradict himself two or three times."

Jurors felt that many cases that should have been presented to them for indictment never were. "I don't care if it's a trooper or what, if someone is wrong, he's wrong. A lot of them were wrong. Troopers should know better. If troopers don't know anything, what have we got?" Another juror: "If they're guards or police or inmates, if they're innocent, they're innocent; if they're guilty, they're guilty. I don't care who they are. I know you were working for someone who didn't feel that way."

At the times of the votes they did get, the prosecutors did not really marshal the evidence or put each case together in a separate specific episode. It was necessary to do that after so sprawling a presentation, yet instead of reading back the testimony, "they would simply tell us, 'You remember so-and-so said such-and-such.'" The jury had no way to put the fragments together to form cases.

A juror also complained that the prosecutors failed to impress on them that voting on an indictment was not a vote upon the actual guilt or innocence of a suspect; it was only on whether the State had sufficient evidence to require him to stand trial. Some jurors cast their votes against indictments, that juror told me, on the premise that they were voting on guilt or innocence. The propolice juror I spoke with kept talking about their votes on whether or not to "convict." The distinction did not seem to faze a third juror: "There would have been more convictions if you'd stayed and we could have asked more questions. You'd add your questions to the questions we'd ask. The other guys wouldn't ask enough questions." But a fourth juror, "It's hard to say whether there would have been more indictments."

The propolice juror was a hearty, engaging man. The jurors who disagreed with him liked him, and so did I. His views on inmates: The police at the retaking "was mowing them right down. I thought they was doing a good job." When I asked him if it was right for the trooper to shoot through the ankle the inmate who was lying on the ground screaming, he said, "No, I suppose he should have hit him over the head."

What surprised the jurors most about Nelson Rockefeller's appearance in the summer of 1975 was the reappearance of Tony Simonetti. He had not come before them in months. "We nearly fell on the floor" at seeing him again. He walked back and forth, asking his questions. The jurors remained too much in awe of the Vice President to question him much themselves. A prosecutor who wanted to, a juror said, could probably have put them enough at ease to have questioned him. Another juror: "Rockefeller did nothing [on the stand]. We were not allowed to ask enough questions." A third juror: "You could tell you couldn't ask Rockefeller what I wanted to."

One juror suggested rather astutely that it had been a mistake to start them as the Investigation did on murder indictments, "where the feeling was, 'Gee, this trooper could be in for life.'" It would have been better, the juror felt, to start them on smaller crimes like perjury or reckless endangerment, so they could get their courage up before turning to murder. Would that have been unfair to the troopers? I thought not. The jury would merely have been rising to do the job they'd sworn to. Did Simonetti plan it to work as it did, I wondered, or was he simply lucky? So much for his decision not to let me present the perjury, Trooper Wildridge, and the other reckless endangerment I had prepared to present before the August Switch. Several jurors told me that if I had presented those cases on August 1, 1974 (as I'd planned to), the jury would have indicted those officers.[6]

When the jury finally indicted Wildridge in October 1975, the vote was close. "Many more troopers would probably have been indicted if the prosecution had handled us more professionally. There were times [when I was there] the evidence outraged us so much we would readily have voted indictments. Things were quiet, though, by the time the votes finally came." Several no bills apparently resulted from that, as well as from the slapdash manner of the prosecutors' presentations. Another juror was not surprised at all by the indictment of Wildridge; she thought it would "start the ball rolling" even at that late date.

"What are you calling your book?" a juror asked me.

"The Turkey Shoot."

"It certainly was that," she said.

After saying "later" on evidence that never came, the prosecutors finally said, "Time to call it a day." When that happened, "we felt cheated." Another juror: "I couldn't believe it when they closed us down." A third juror: "I thought several times something was being pulled away from us . . . . The jury fizzled out. We couldn't get answers." A fourth juror: "They were getting close to something they didn't want us to know. I don't think they'd finished their business." It was Ned Perry who came before them and told them they were finished.

"If this is what you call justice, I don't want any part of it," June Bardeen, the foreman of the jury, told him. "I don't know what's behind this, but I know it's something."

"You shouldn't feel that way," Ned replied.

"How do you expect me to feel after all this time getting nowhere?!"

* * *

Judge Ball strove to select the Supplemental Grand Jury for their freedom from bias. Tony predicted they'd do a good job because they didn't want to serve. They heard more evidence than any other citizens about events inside Attica during and after the turkey shoot. I had hoped I felt their readiness to indict the officers who deserved it; now I heard members of the majority say they had been ready. The jurors' testimony gives the lie once again to the Official Version that too little evidence remained on which to prosecute, and that a Wyoming County grand jury would never indict troopers.[7]

Besides aborting many indictments, the superficiality, disorganization, and the iron hand took their toll on the jurors' morale. "We did what we were told, good little jurors." Another juror: "We were fighting City Hall. We lost before we started . . . . [The jury] was a big farce, a waste of taxpayers' money. Nothing came of it."

"We never took things into our own hands. When we were ready to, we didn't know what to do." "You hear about runaway grand juries. We weren't." Yes, I had heard about runaway grand juries, most recently from Tony Simonetti. The specter had haunted him. He told me he was glad the law had been changed to make it harder for a grand jury to take matters into their own hands.

Another juror: "I think Simonetti was on the State Police and correction officers' side . . . . He didn't come out and ask the questions that made sense. [His questions] didn't hit the nail on the head. He'd leave you hanging. He asked questions that made it look good, but it meant nothing . . . . I think he was a very intelligent man, but he used his intelligence backwards. He was there to help cover up . . . . He was part of government politics."

On learning what it had been like for these jurors, I felt a vindication but also the pain and poignancy of their frustration. We had been in it together, and we had been put out of it together when it looked as though we were going to do the job that the System required but that those who ran the System feared. I felt for the jurors as I had not for myself; their hands were tied much tighter than mine.

"We were a shameful grand jury."

"No. You were conscientious, honest, interested. Your attendance was marvelous. You asked good questions. You were my first grand jury. I was very well impressed." Not very adequate, I thought, after blurting that into the telephone.

Add more casualties to Attica, these citizens of Wyoming County who tried for two years to do their job, those who saw the evidence as I did, the quiet minority who disagreed. The State did its interests proud when it put these jurors away.

Forty-one

New York Justice

The State's reluctant admission that the Attica prosecution had been grossly one-sided, coupled with its determination not to prosecute officers, led it to dismiss the kidnapping and other serious charges against inmates. The same logic of equal justice required that John Hill (Dacajeweiah), convicted of murdering William Quinn, be released from prison. But constitutional logic, it seemed, was not enough to spring the convicted killer of a prison guard. As noted before, Governor Carey made Hill eligible for parole when he closed the book on Attica at the end of 1976; two weeks later the Parole Board determined to keep Hill in, reasoning that his release "could cause a widespread negative community reaction and would probably promote disrespect for the law."[1]

Justice moved at a familiar pace while Hill did time in Green Haven prison. In spring 1978, Michael Kennedy, one of Hill's lawyers, asked me to make an affidavit in support of an application to get Hill out. Principle was one thing, but me help directly to spring a convicted killer? When Kennedy made his request, I had already determined that I would tell whatever I knew to whoever asked me, since the Sixth Amendment and the just principle behind it give everyone the right in a criminal case to call witnesses in his favor. I dictated and swore to a forty-two-page affidavit, which, incidentally, outlines the cases described in Chapter 14.

The court in Buffalo denied Hill's application. In January 1979, while another appeal was pending, the Parole Board tentatively granted parole to Hill, provided that he offer a program for himself that the parole authorities found suitable. That March they released him.

With Hill's freedom, roughly equal justice came at last in full measure to the Attica prosecution—not, as I have said, the equal justice that I sought, but a far cry from the charade the State was peddling before I went public. The roughness of the equal justice should not be glossed over: whereas sixty-two inmates spent several years under indictment for 1,289 criminal acts, one trooper spent less than five months charged with one crime, and the rest of the officer-perpetrators suffered perhaps no more than a few bad moments when they thought they might not get away with it. More broadly if unmentioned, however, the inequality of justice was only shifted. If State employees who committed crimes at Attica were not seriously prosecuted and the proceedings against indicted inmates were dropped, why ever prosecute anyone for anything?

If we glance at equal justice beyond Attica, the vista is disturbing for more reasons than this. For example: Corporate price-fixers who lift millions from the public's pockets historically serve fewer months (if any) than many small-time pickpockets. While thousands do time for peddling dangerous and not-so-dangerous drugs, the nation's leading addictive killers, cigarettes, are advertised and subsidized, and none of their dealers go to prison. In March 1974, the very month that Tony and I were obtaining a fresh grand jury to consider a mere thirty-nine homicides, the failure of McDonnell-Douglas to fix their DC-10 baggage doors, which they knew could blow off, resulted, in fact, in their blowing off and causing a crash that left the bodies of 346 people—nine times the number the police killed at Attica—strewn in some 18,000 pieces across the soil of France;[2] no one was ever prosecuted for that carnage. But my witness, Daltry, got four years in Attica for stealing a box of tools.

* * *

In making his Report, Judge Meyer had divided up the topics among his staff. Though they met and talked about one another's work, Meyer had the final say and "accept[ed] full responsibility for the conclusions."[3] Some Meyer people I talked with (Meyer himself declined to be interviewed) told me that his staff generally considered him honest, conscientious, fair, and hard-working. One of his staff told me that Meyer was comparatively slow to draw conclusions from facts. Does that, rather than ambition, explain his refusal to see the cover-up in the facts that showed it to him? As already described, it took me longer than some to see the prosecutorial cover-up myself, even when I became an object of the effort; but my reasons for not wanting to see it had to be different from Meyer's reasons. Nor do I doubt that Meyer's staff is as loyal to him as I was for so long to Simonetti.

Though Meyer's findings made bold to slap the wrist of a sitting Vice President, they ventured not a whisper about the Attorney General, who had overseen the "skewed" Investigation from the beginning and who, with Carey, had appointed Meyer. Lefkowitz had admitted having been in frequent communication with Fischer and Simonetti about their progress; the frequency of his communications with Simonetti increased sharply immediately after the August Switch, i.e., the Rockefeller nomination. He had admitted how serious my charges were against his subordinates, but he had maintained that he had done all he could to deal with them simply by telling Judge Ball and Governor-elect Carey about them in December 1974. He did not explain how Ball or Carey was supposed to investigate Simonetti's conduct inside his own Department of Law, or why he himself was not supposed to, except that he claimed the Quinn homicide trial, which ended just before I went public, somehow prevented him.

I find Lefkowitz's refusal to look into my charges against Simonetti inexplicable, except as part of a deliberate cover-up. For Lefkowitz to recognize the seriousness of my charges but refuse to look into them or obtain Simonetti's full explanation or ask me a single additional question was *in and of itself* covering up. Why look into serious charges only to see your face in the mirror?

I cannot fathom, and (according to my information) the Meyer people did not press Lefkowitz to explain, how Louis Aidala's trial of one case against two inmates in Buffalo rendered the General impotent to inquire whether Simonetti was aborting the prosecution of law officers. The wonder was not that the General said these things—again, I admired his creativity and the nerve it must take to purvey such figments—but that Meyer bought them without the slightest hint in his findings that the General was guilty of malfeasance or nonfeasance or anything else.

* * *

A dream came true for Bernard S. Meyer in May 1979 when Governor Carey appointed him from a field of five candidates to fill a vacancy in the New York Court of Appeals. Meyer had continued to head his law firm on Long Island. He told reporters when his name was placed in nomination that his only ambition had been to be a judge and that to sit on the Court of Appeals was "the highest honor bestowed upon a practicing lawyer."[4]

In July 1981, with Judge Meyer writing the opinion, a unanimous Court of Appeals held that all but one of the hostages' widows and related claimants, twenty-four in all, were barred from recovering damages from the State for these deaths and injuries because they had accepted relatively small Workmen's Compensation payments, which automatically became their exclusive remedy. A widow received about $5,000 a year unless she remarried. The highest compensation to a wounded hostage was $1,200, for having part of his head shot away. These claimants were not thrown out of court until they had been on trial off and on for four years.[5]

That left only the claim of Lynda Jones, widow of Herbert Jones, Jr., the young prison accounts clerk whose skull was shattered by an unidentified trooper's .270 bullet. Acting on "gut instinct," her lawyer, Bill Cunningham, had advised her not to cash a $21 Workmen's Compensation check she had received. He took her case to trial in October 1977 as planned, winning it five years and 7,000 pages of testimony later and after State officials had unsuccessfully sought to disbar him for accusing the State Police of murder. In 1978, Judge Robert M. Quigley held nineteen troopers and guards in contempt after they took the Fifth Amendment and refused to answer questions about the retaking. Throughout the litigation and the change in Attorneys General, the State made no effort whatsoever to settle the case.[6] The Fourth Department, affirming Judge Quigley's eighty-page decision, held in November 1983 that:

> The proof is overwhelming that much of the firing was haphazard and directed indiscriminately at the group of prisoners and hostages in D yard and that most, if not all, of it was unwarranted as a reasonable means of protecting the hostages from harm. Under any conception of the proof, this massive use of fire power directed at a group of inmates and hostages (with the obvious risk to the hostages, some of whom were held as shields for the inmates) cannot have been necessary and cannot be considered to have been the employment of a degree of force that was appropriate or one that was justified by any or all of the existing circumstances.
>
> * * *
>
> Having armed the men and directed them to fire into the crowd whenever in their judgement it was required, *the state may not now claim that it was not its intention to wound or kill, for this was the inevitable consequence, and indeed, the very purpose of the firing instructions.*
>
> * * *
>
> Here the risk of death or injury by gunfire was . . . deliberately created by the state in devising and implementing the plan for retaking the prison by armed assault. Injuries to those subjected to that risk must be held to have been intentionally inflicted.[7] [Emphasis added.]

The Court of Appeals in June 1984 declined to hear the State's appeal from this decision. Finally in March 1985, the State's check arrived for Mrs. Jones—$550,000 in compensation, plus interest, a total of $1,062,000.

The federal claims of the inmates who were shot and otherwise assaulted, and their next of kin, have not reached trial as of this writing.

It seems plain that, motive aside, Attorney General Lefkowitz's obstruction of civil justice was of a piece with his adoption and ratification, if not instigation, of the prosecutorial cover-up. His stonewalling of the civil suits took place in the open, though apparently few noticed; it further exposed his thrust in the prosecution. Apart from crimes by inmates, the purpose and effect of his civil defense and his criminal Investigation were precisely the same: to hide the facts and evade the responsibilities. No reason exists to accuse him of inconsistency. His efforts to bury the body of the Meyer Report were more of the same. The enormity of Attica has hung stinking in New York's official closet like a great dead albatross. The key rested snug and safe in the General's pocket.

* * *

In August 1977, a woman cook was found dead of stab wounds inside a cooler in the kitchen at Attica. The State Police promptly sent thirty troopers to investigate that one homicide, which was the first at the prison since troopers stopped shooting in September 1971. Bob Fischer, defending himself against a suggestion that the Attica Investigation had been too understaffed, was quoted in 1976 as saying, "The size of a staff doesn't mean a thing."[8]

On September 19, 1971, Simonetti, Max Spoont, and three other OCTF people had given Fischer their joint opinion that the Investigation required eight lawyers and fifty investigators. Yet Fischer swore to the Meyer Commission that in the fall of 1971 it was impossible to make any definite statement about staffing needs and that he never made any assessment of those needs.[9] Since Rockefeller had to and did take the overt position that Fischer could hire as many people as he needed,[10] the only way to keep the Investigation too small to do its job was for Fischer not to hire them.

Fischer, too, is the visible source of the decision to investigate the shootings and brutality last, though we can be sure that (at a minimum) he discussed the decision with Lefkowitz and Lefkowitz did not insist that the thirty-nine homicides, etc., required serious prompt attention. Fischer wrote to Lefkowitz in June 1972 that his staff was getting ready to present the retaking to the grand jury. He reportedly hoped to end that job about October 1, 1972; and from all that appears in Meyer Volume 1, he expected the inquiry into all the shootings to result merely in a grand jury report.[11] The Rochester *Democrat & Chronicle* reported on December 24, 1972, "A source close to the [Attica] grand jury investigation said there's a strong possibility that no guards or state troopers will be indicted."[12]

Fischer had shown his allegiance from the start. He put an inordinate number of his tiny staff onto Rockefeller's theory of a conspiracy to riot. On September 15, 1971, he imposed his blackout on all officials' statements, which he and Rockefeller immediately breached. On the sixteenth, Fischer held his joint news conference with Major Monahan at which they gave an Official Version of the retaking and released photographs showing hundreds of inmate weapons; the public's right to know was thus satisfied in a way calculated to take the heat for all the shootings off Rockefeller and the State Police. Also on the sixteenth, Rockefeller assured the press that the hostages had been caught in a "crossfire" and that the massacre he had unleashed was all "justifiable homicide."[13] Rockefeller assured the Meyer Commission, "I know Judge Fischer very well. He is totally independent, totally his own man . . . . [H]e would be influenced in no way by anything I said."[14]

* * *

Nelson Rockefeller's seventieth birthday, a year and a half after his term as Vice President had expired, prompted James Reston to write in the *New York Times*:

> [H]e now joins the long list of political also-rans who might have been very good Presidents but didn't quite make it . . . . [H]e was never able to persuade or capture the conservative forces in any Republican Presidential nominating convention.[15]

Nelson Rockefeller's moral responsibility for the intentional cover-up by the Attica prosecution is absolutely clear. He had the power, ability, and interest to have had a full and fair prosecution if he had wanted one. As Governor, he had the duty to have one whether he wanted it or not. He failed on both counts. He may or may not have been legally culpable for the cover-up, but any such guilt (or its absence) cannot now be proved. Simonetti, Schechter, the jury, and I all had serious questions worth pursuing on that score, but that investigation, too, was aborted.

"Attica reflected Nelson Rockefeller's emotional and political approach to the world." So wrote Lance Morrow, not among his greatest fans.[16] I must agree that Attica was Rockefeller at his worst, though there was plainly more to the man than that. His decision not to involve himself and his able Executive Chamber creatively in the negotiations with convicted felons may have been smart politics, but it was not statesmanship. Rockefeller did not go, he did not give, he ordered the assault with scant effort to avoid the massacre he knew it meant. Then he had the effrontery to call it "extraordinary" and "a miracle" that more hostages were not sacrificed.[17]

We shall apparently never know how active or passive Rockefeller's role was in the prosecutorial cover-up, thanks to that cover-up. I think, though, that Scott Fitzgerald was close to the mark in *The Great Gatsby* sixty years ago, when he wrote of wealthy people whose selfish irresponsibility resulted in Gatsby's death:

> They were careless people . . . they smashed up things and creatures and then retreated back into their money or their vast carelessness, or whatever it was that kept them together, and let other people clean up the mess they had made. . . .

After Attica, Rockefeller retreated back into his money, carelessness, and power. How much responsibility does he bear for what he did and failed to do? The cover-up comes down to a wry irony, in that the underlying crime of Nelson Rockefeller both during and after Attica was his irresponsibility.

* * *

At the end of 1978, Louis Lefkowitz retired from public service after twenty-two years as Attorney General and became counsel to a prestigious Manhattan law firm. The General's parting advice for office seekers was to concentrate on presenting a good TV image.[18]

Rockefeller devoted the final months of his life to making reproductions of his vast art collection available to the public at relatively moderate prices. On the evening of January 26, 1979, he suffered a fatal heart attack while staying late at the office with—it was first denied and then uncovered—a young woman with whom he had a close relationship. The night Rockefeller died, Louis Lefkowitz, then seventy-five, appeared at the hospital at 2:00 A.M. to console the widow.

As of the mid-1980s, Robert E. Fischer was still dispensing justice from the Supreme Court, Sixth Judicial District. Bernard S. Meyer was still sitting two levels above him on the New York Court of Appeals. The members of the Meyer Commission were holding annual reunions; in 1985 they celebrated their tenth. Judge Ball, though retired, was still hearing cases. Of these three judges of Attica, I think he comes off the best.

Robert B. McKay of the McKay Report wrote, on the Op-Ed page of the September 15, 1976, *New York Times*: "Those of us who experienced Attica even secondhand were radicalized by what we learned."

Myron Farber passed the hard test of his profession superbly in 1978 when he submitted to imprisonment for forty days in order to protect his sources in the Dr. X murder case.[19] Ed Hammock became chairman of the Parole Board. Governor Carey appointed Eric Seiff to head the State Investigation Commission at the end of 1976 but dismissed him in 1979, in part at least because Seiff had angered certain Republican leaders by investigating insurance commissions that had been paid to Republicans for little or no work during the Rockefeller administration.[20]

Dr. John Edland made a new life for himself teaching in another state. Dr. Michael Baden became Chief Medical Examiner of New York City in 1978, only to be dismissed by Mayor Edward I. Koch one day before he was to receive tenure. Years of controversy and litigation followed. I considered it a shame for Baden and a loss for the City that a person of his competence and character had to go through all that.[21]

Lenny Brown and Alfred Scotti died. In March 1984, Capt. Henry Williams was promoted to colonel and made head of the 700-member BCI. Robert Douglass became an Executive Vice President of The Chase Manhattan Bank. Big Black became legal investigator and process server for Liz Fink's law office in Brooklyn a few blocks from where I grew up.

Many perpetrators of the turkey shoot continued to ride around New York in their fast, blue-and-yellow cars, carry their big pistols, give out speeding tickets, pursue other criminals, and come to the aid of people in distress.

In January 1980 the bloodiest riot after Attica broke out at the overcrowded New Mexico State Penitentiary near Santa Fe, when one thousand inmates seized the prison, took twelve hostages, and killed thirty-three inmates, some by holding blowtorches to their faces. Perhaps, though, something had been learned. The authorities retook the prison without killing anyone.

* * *

Tony Simonetti and I did not stay in touch after my resignation. I understand that after leaving the Investigation, he headed an organization to aid in enforcing the laws against obscenity and that he then became a prosecutor in another state. In time, I came to wish him well and hope that his current performance outweighed any considerations about his conduct of ten and more years earlier.

Nelson Rockefeller and the New York State Police were the main beneficiaries of his conduct, and it served the purposes of Louis Lefkowitz; but Simonetti took the heat for it alone. What would have been the future of a State prosecutor who repudiated Rockefeller's pronouncements that the troopers did a "superb job" and all thirty-nine homicides were "justifiable"?

Simonetti was out front in the prosecution and prosecutorial cover-up after Fischer left for the bench. I went out front in opposition to the cover-up and in support of the prosecution. I was alone, and the State partly isolated "what's-his-name," though it did not drive him to point the finger higher up. The Official Version magnified our conflict, falsely saying its origins were personal not professional, calling him an incompetent or worse and me a maker of unfounded charges.

The game plan that the State followed by instinct or design: Let Simonetti and Bell struggle against each other like two drowning people, give them both a little downward shove, the waters shall close serenely over, and the ship of State shall not be rocked. That it did not quite work out that way was not the fault of Lefkowitz's burial of my serious cover-up charges, the Lefkowitz-Gribetz pfumpf, or the Meyer findings. Anyone inclined to judge between Simonetti and me might consider that he was the loyal team player, and I was the maverick who refused to play the orderly and customary game.

* * *

Attica changed my life. It brought me freedom, fulfillment, and fun. It cost me several years of regular income and opportunities for traditional advancement. It opened my perspective, cleared my outlook; some say it radicalized me. Life was good before, but the years since have been the best years. Like most people, I am several selves; Attica brought out the one I try to favor. Jimmy Webb said, "I will take my life into my hands and I will use it."[22] I did that. Bob Dylan said, "He not busy being born is busy dying."[23] So, more or less, did St. Paul. Fighting the Attica cover-up gave me a new sense of myself independent of any organization or job, and a new sense of peace. While it did not alter my flaws, the changes it wrought amounted in their way to a rebirth.

Knowing that I could have turned to my family for help freed me to continue spending time on Attica and to start my own law practice. I remained pleasantly surprised at how small an effect my decimated income had on the things I did and the people I saw from day to day. I probably ate hot dogs more often than was good for me, but I worried only that the car would die. Fortunately in 1978, I finally gained a well-paying client just before it did.

My law practice proved to be fascinating though not lucrative. In early 1979, I was offered a job as an antitrust counsel with a major corporation for which I had a high regard, but I turned it down without even reaching the question of salary. My routine became: work hard, take short naps after lunch, and enjoy a delightful amount of freedom. I left Darien, registered as a Democrat, remarried, and joined the Religious Society of Friends.

Attica, of course, does not end on personal notes. I have some recommendations to offer and a perspective to share.

Forty-two

Whistleblowing

My brothers and I found the .45 automatic and .45 revolver that our father had carried in France during the First World War after he died in 1981. Since none of us wanted them, one of my brothers asked around and received an offer of $150 for the pair. But I wanted to make sure that these guns, at least, never took a life. My brothers said all right.

One sunny spring afternoon, I laid the pistols down on my driveway and swung the blunt end of a splitting maul onto them again and again, banging their fatal symmetry into dusty twisted junk. It felt oddly like killing a snake. I drove to Long Island Sound, climbed out on some rocks, and threw the pieces, one by one, as far as I could across the brine. It occurred to me later that but for Attica, we would probably have collected that $150.

Refusing as I do to own a gun, I depend for my family's safety and my own upon the ability and sense, and ultimately the honor, of the police. In view of all the opportunities to serve that so many police seize so willingly and well, it is a shame when they work against themselves and their brother and sister officers, as many did at Attica. If, as Joseph Conrad says in *Lord Jim*, a "real significance of crime is in its being a breach of faith with the community of mankind," then crime by an officer entrusted to uphold the law is one of the worst; the breach of faith is one of the greatest.

Recall the State Police lawyer who complained that his clients thought they were above the law. Police routinely break the law each time they break the speed limit when they're not chasing a speeder or meeting an emergency. This habit may kill few people a year, but their bosses should end it, to curb the attitude it betrays and fosters.

Recall, too, the outcry of the Police Benevolent Association at the Investigation's convening of the Supplemental Grand Jury and again at the indictment of one trooper. Police unions often cry out, demonstrate, or otherwise carry on when a cop is charged with violence. They appeal to the 77 percent of Americans who reportedly believe that the cop who kills on duty is automatically justified.[1] They go on to claim the officer is being persecuted "for doing his duty." But it is never a duty to commit murder, manslaughter, reckless endangerment, or assault. The charge is that the officer did *not* do his duty. The police are not above the law. They, too, are American citizens.

Terrible as the inmates' riot was, it was lawless police who made Attica a massacre. Then, with very few noble exceptions, the brother officers of the guilty police were determined that not even one trooper would answer for their horrible crimes. To hell with cooperating with the prosecutors or telling the truth under oath to the jury. To hell with principle, law, right, justice, and the chosen purpose of their lives. The brotherhood came first. Call that loyalty if you choose.

It is not fair to single out the police at Attica for covering up. Nor were the New York officials who did it afterward unique among politicians trying to avoid scandal and protect ambition. In Washington, they do it in the name of national security. Doctors and hospitals do it to avoid malpractice claims. Executives do it to put a product onto the market and to avoid product liability. Merchants do it to make sales, and used car dealers even lobby for the right to do it. They all do it to preserve their honor, which then, of course, becomes an illusion. We congratulated ourselves that "the System worked at Watergate," but Watergate may have been an exception. We never know how often the System does not work, but we know the tendencies.

During the spring of 1985, police in New York City committed a number of crimes that police who witnessed them refused to talk about. Some officials decried "the code of silence" and "the blue wall of silence." Mayor Edward I. Koch remarked, "You know who is quiet? The Mafia is quiet."[2] At the Investigation, of course, we ran into the gray wall of silence.

Rat, fink, squealer, snitch, tattletale. We learn early not to admire the child whose object and delight is to get another child into trouble. But blowing a whistle is a far cry from telling a tale. For responsible citizens, especially for those who choose the job of enforcing the law, there comes a time to put away childish things, among them the criminal's code of silence. Loyalty to coworkers who do wrong does not justify disloyalty to the law, truth, and public.

Under West Point's venerable honor code, each cadet is bound by honor and the threat of expulsion not to lie, steal, or cheat, or tolerate those who do. If he sees another cadet cribbing on an exam, he must turn him in. Such a code seems particularly appropriate for people whose job it is to catch law-breakers. Former New York City Police Commissioner Patrick V. Murphy tells me that he considers such a code to be "an appropriate ideal." Police departments everywhere that have not already done so should adopt and enforce a code whereby officers must report misconduct by brother and sister officers. That is their duty anyway; attitude and enforcement are the problem. Such a code wouldn't work perfectly, but it can only work better than much common experience today. Surely it is not too much to ask of police that they substitute a code of honor that upholds the law for a code of silence that breaks it down.

* * *

Though the massacre by the State Police at Attica was unique in this century, those police were not isolated miscreants when it comes to killing people. The Philadelphia police were notoriously quick to shoot while Frank Rizzo was mayor. An agency of the Philadelphia Bar Association charged that 299 out of the 469 killings by the Philadelphia police during the previous nine years were illegal.[3] During the decade 1967–1976, police shot to death over six thousand people varying in age from ten to eighty-one, many of whom were unarmed. Former Commissioner Murphy (who stepped down in 1985 as President of the Police Foundation) assured me that the trend was toward substantially greater restraint, though problems still exist. While it is impossible to generalize accurately as to the lawfulness and necessity of all those six thousand-plus killings, Lawrence O'Donnell, Jr., has commented:

> ... An obvious symbiotic relationship exists between prosecutors and police. In most of their work prosecutors rely heavily on police officers. They are both part of the same law-enforcement team and they usually behave accordingly. The secrecy of a grand jury is the ideal cover for local or Federal prosecutors who want to avoid bringing homicide cases against police officers. Because grand jury proceedings are secret, prosecutors who control them can exclude incriminating evidence and insure that no indictment will be returned.[4]

Police are often merely transferred, disciplined, or dismissed for acts that would put other citizens in prison. We hear that sure, swift justice deters crime, and that must be true for lawless shootings and other crime by cops. But how do we approach sure, swift justice for them?

Three years after four American churchwomen were raped and murdered in El Salvador in 1980, a Lawyers Committee for International Human Rights found that the prosecutors were "alarmingly uninterested and wholly unprepared" for a trial of the five low-ranking National Guardsmen who were finally charged with those crimes, and that no meaningful inquiry was made to determine whether the accused were acting on higher orders.[5] That sounded familiar. That was Attica. That was also how the Justice Department's inquiry into the break-in at The Watergate was going before public outcry forced the appointment of an independent prosecutor.

Independence measures the candor and accuracy of the several inquiries into Attica. The McKay Commission was most independent and most trustworthy. Rockefeller, Lefkowitz, Fischer, Simonetti were least, with Meyer (ambitious within the System) next, and Scotti (a bureaucrat with character, the independence of old age, and the help of Meyer's start) closer to McKay.

The New York City Police Department consisted of some twenty-seven thousand cops, one of the largest standing armies in the world. Who would have thought that Frank Serpico and David Durk and precious few others could have triggered a revolutionary reduction in brutality and corruption in such an organization?[6] At the end of Serpico's long, lonely, and nearly fatal fight against the corruption he encountered among his brother officers, he made one simple recommendation:

> Basic changes in attitude and approach are vital. In order to insure this, an independent, permanent investigative body dealing with police corruption . . . is essential.[7]

Our System puts noble and comparatively effective restraints on the over-zealous prosecutor, but the sometimes underzealous prosecutor is inherently well positioned to get away with it, as this book illustrates. Perhaps ways can be found to keep better track of what prosecutors don't do, without inhibiting their necessarily broad discretion. A sure safeguard, however, is to free prosecutors from the conflict of interest that inheres when circumstances call on them to investigate cops and fellow bureaucrats, including their own bosses. Every government that can afford one should have a permanent, independent prosecutor, with independent investigators, to look into charges against law officers and all other government employees. If we want fair and equal prosecutions, we shall hire such people. If we don't, we won't.

* * *

Whistle blowing is not a popular sport. "Here I stand; I can do no other," said Martin Luther, perhaps the most notable whistle blower, triggering as he did the Protestant Reformation and the Catholic Counter Reformation. The great example of my youth was Anthony Eden, who quit the British Cabinet and spoke out against Neville Chamberlain's appeasement of Mussolini and Hitler. Part of my object in writing is to show that the grimness generally attributed to it is often exaggerated and to encourage others to blow the whistle when events, as they must, go awry. But the risks and price—lost income, lost opportunities, the unpleasant surprises of ostracism, and maybe even psychological damage— are real and not to be ignored.

Sometime after I went to the *New York Times*, I found two books very useful to learn the experience of others and see myself in perspective: *Resignation in Protest, Political and Ethical Choices between Loyalty to Team and Loyalty to Conscience in American Public Life* by Edward Weisband and Thomas M. Franck,[8] and *Whistle Blowing! Loyalty and Dissent in the Corporation* by Alan F. Westin.[9] I recommend the full text of *Resignation in Protest* and particularly the first-person narratives in *Whistle Blowing!* to anyone who is considering either of those acts and still has time to read.

Blowing the whistle can and at times does protect the public from dangerous practices and products, stop waste, mismanagement, discrimination, or corruption, maybe even avoid a war. As Weisband and Franck discuss, there are inordinately high

> costs of a system based above all on the value of "team play." Men and women in places of power and responsibility who choose not to pay the price of personal integrity merely succeed in shifting those costs to society as a whole.
>
> * * *
>
> . . . the policies that led to the morass [of Vietnam and Watergate] might have been arrested earlier by courageous public defection of key disaffected members of the Johnson and Nixon administrations. In each instance there was some halfhearted private questioning of policy, but when that

failed, the overriding rule, devoutly adhered to, was: loyalty and team play above personal conscience.[10]

As whistle blowers go, I was doubly fortunate: First, I had a comparatively large and positive impact on events. Second, the negative impact on me was comparatively small and far outweighed by the pluses. My personal values helped me greatly to do what I did and accept—even thrive on—the consequences. It may not hurt for anyone who considers blowing a whistle to ask himself or herself: What do I want from life? What matters?

Forty-three

America Can Do Better

Enter the busy Criminal Courts Building in lower Manhattan. If you look from certain windows, you will see the New York County Courthouse, only six stories high but massive through its girth. Let it stand for the enormity of Attica. Behind it you will notice the United States Courthouse rising thirty stories to its gold pyramid peak, even as the prison system looms behind Attica. If you shift your gaze slightly, you will see behind both courthouses the great bulk and spires of the financial district, as society rises behind its prisons.

My narrative has been of a riot, massacre, and cover-up that State officials and a man who would be President found inconvenient. Yet it would be an evasion to dwell on Attica without considering the prison system that spawned it and the society that our prisons serve.

Some people, it seems, must be put away until they change or die if the rest of us are to be reasonably safe. But in this efficiency-oriented age and nation, prisons are exquisitely counterproductive, inordinately more copious than necessary, and still largely organized to promote the uselessness, dependency, and hostility of their graduates—meaning 95 percent of everyone now in prison. To the extent that prisons harden criminals, they create crime victims. A century or so hence, I trust, Americans will look back upon our present prison system and ask, How could they? The big answer to prisons, of course, is to reduce crime radically.

Injustice is an iceberg, of which crime is only the glaring tip. Why, in this land of relative plenty and of the longest prison terms in the western world, do so many people kill and wound other people and steal their property? Why is overcrowding such a problem at our Atticas, and the building of new Atticas such an issue? Why the devastating rate of crime?

"The only way to stop crime is to uphold the law," wrote conservative columnist William Safire in the April 8, 1985, *New York Times*. That view, which I take to be widely held, misses the dynamic and more than half the point.

Upholding the law stops crime when it physically blocks the perpetrators or catches them in the act or the fear of it deters them beforehand. Law enforcement holds the lid on the pressure cooker some of the time, but it does not address the causes of the pressure.

Decency and inhibitions also stop crime. To the extent that parents, teachers, and clergy do their job—not to mention the fine example of truthful, law-abiding police, politicians, and particularly Presidents—there will obviously be fewer people growing up to commit crimes.

But the combination of deterrent and inhibition still misses the dynamic and half the point. As they say in detective stories, consider the motive. The greater the motivation or temptation or pressure that leads to crime, the greater must be the inhibition or deterrent if crime is not to occur. The less the drive, the less brakes are needed. Since the capacity of a free society to apply brakes is inherently limited, it is sensible and humane to reduce the power of the drive.

I love my country but find it hard to imagine a free society that does more to motivate its people to commit crimes, to inflame their greed, envy, frustration, and hostility, and to reduce their compassion for their victims. If things and money mattered less, fewer people would take them. Making people covet is the object of advertising and the linchpin of the economy. Racism, macho posturing,[1] and the wildly popular entertainment called shoot-the-bad-guys all induce crime; all, I suspect, pulled some triggers at the turkey shoot. Even people's inherent hostility, cussedness, and other forms of distress will produce less crime if society turns more gentle and compassionate, less hard-driving, and less driven.

Sufficient food, goods, and health care for everyone, full employment, and shortened hours of work are, technologically, more achievable now than ever before. The present System is not achieving them. It is not seriously trying. Unemployment and poverty flourish. However many people do not commit crimes, it seems certain that the greater the pressures, the more people will yield to them.

We seek the good life but often seem hell-bent to distance ourselves from any sort of peaceable kingdom. As I see it, the high crime rate is part of the price we pay for the way we choose to live, for our values and the broad injustices we tolerate and perpetuate. The people who commit crimes are, of course, to blame. So are the rest of us.

Attica reflects disturbing attitudes toward peace as well as justice. When Nelson Rockefeller ordered the armed assault before he had exhausted peaceful alternatives, he showed his fitness to be President of the United States. Though we executed top Nazis for, among other things, the crime of making aggressive war, we often use force against weaker nations that do not follow our wishes, doing unto others what we'd be damned if we'd let them do unto us. This country, according to the Pentagon, has used military force—meaning death, risk of death, threat of death, mainly to foreigners (there are no foreigners)— over two hundred times since World War II.[2] No one has yet blundered into the big war, but the posturing and honing of the hair trigger on both sides proceeds apace, and it's business as usual with the little wars, armed interventions, etc., that can escalate. The same impatience, aggressiveness, posturing, and rigidity that informed Rockefeller's approach to Attica pose a great and needless threat to peace.

Vexing national attitudes cannot be changed overnight. But recognizing that reality does not require one to surrender to it. The more one can do in a lifetime about such attitudes, the better.

* * *

At the end of World War II after the horrors of Nazi Germany became widely known, it was, as I recall, a commonplace for people to chide the Good Germans who minded their own business, did what they were told, and looked the other way when the smoke rose from the death camp ovens. How, we asked, could they have failed to rock the boat or make waves, and allowed the horror to continue by ignoring it? But how many of us would have done otherwise?

Hitler's Germany reflected a triumph of order over what we consider law. So do many dictatorships, where the streets may be safer than the churches. The Attica prosecution was a drama of order versus law. To the extent that the cover-up succeeded, order won. The cover-up's failures were victories for law and democracy. I hope that people who read this book will know in their hearts never to hyphenate the phrase "law and order."

Cover-ups are a genus of comfortable pretense that nothing is wrong. They often amount to a concert of smiles, silence about what matters, and unruffled intercourse between the deceivers and the deceived. Behind the red-domed cover over Attica stands the gray-domed cover over the prison system, and behind that, the white-domed cover over the injustices that riddle society and threaten war. The Good Germans covered over while Hitler set out to make the world safe for Germany and murdered millions who did not meet his petty standards for humanity. Need it take a Holocaust to show Americans how wrong it is to be Good Germans?

* * *

The story of Attica has no ending. That may not satisfy, as reality often doesn't. But satisfaction ends the challenge; it creates illusions that invite disaster. We do not live happily ever after, and it is risky ever to assume that we do. Watergate did not end when Nixon resigned as President, and Attica did not end when Carey closed the book (or when this book is closed). The Watergates continue, the Atticas continue, but so does the decency of most people to respond once they are able and willing to face what is. My friends who attend Alcoholics Anonymous say that the hardest hurdle for the drunk is to admit the problem. Too many of us are drunk on complacency. Why should we choose to face evil? Is it really so dangerous to turn one's back upon the beast? No one said that not being a Good German is easy.

A rabbi visiting my church one day talked about the Old Testament tradition of Hebrew prophets who worked outside the System for the sake of the System. The alternative to leaving the System is not necessarily to be a Good German, close both eyes to injustice, and say, "My country, company, etc., right or wrong." Our society has layers; one may work outside some of them while inside others.

Even in May 1985, a former prosecutor was reassuring me that the troopers at Attica were merely following orders. So was Adolph Eichmann. Hitler's favored Field Marshal Wilhelm Keitel admitted to the court in Nuremberg before he was hanged, "What I never realized was that simply being a good soldier and following orders was not enough. *Das ist mein schuld* [That is my guilt]."[3] But this is America. Following is a matter of choice. When things are wrong, we are free within the System to do something about them. Each person knows best, if he or she wishes, what to do. Shift your gaze slightly and you will see it.

Our society stresses results, the bottom line. That stress, when it isn't goading us, often tends to immobilize us. Why make an effort if you can't see that good will follow? You can't fight City Hall, so why try? But if we are true to the best within us, we will do our best regardless of results. And that, happily, is the best way to get results. I tested the System and accomplished far more than I had any reason to expect. If my story stands for anything, it is that in this great and complicated nation, one person can still make a difference.

The commuters I still sometimes ride with to the City bury themselves in their newspapers before they go equably about their business. One evening at supper a Maryknoll nun named Sister Susan Rech told my wife and me that every morning she has a choice: she can go equably about her business, or she can pick up the newspaper and grow angry at what she reads. The anger leads to action. She and her sisters refuse to follow the wishes of many people that they stay in their cloisters and pray. Rather, they and many like them serve across the nation and the world, risking their lives and sometimes losing them, for peace and justice.

There are many ways to serve. Being a good cop or a just politician is among them. Each of us does make a choice, and it is easy to choose none of them.

A few Sundays after I went public back in April 1975, I was invited to give the sermon at the still-dear Establishment church that I belonged to in those days. Something I said to my friends there is how I want to close:

> I used to wonder during Watergate whether I'd resign if I were in the position of those people. I still don't know for sure, because their position was different from mine. We each live out our lives the best we can, and now and then an Attica or a Watergate happens to one or another of us. I don't think it matters that much to our lives whether it happens or not, because we are who we are, regardless. Some of you would have done what I did if you were in my place, and some of you would have done it better.

Epilogue

White thunderheads rolled through the sky behind the walls and towers of Attica on the bright breezy afternoon of September 13, 2011. The dwindling band of onetime hostages, their wives, the widows of dead hostages, and the middle-aged children and frisky grandchildren of all of them had gathered in their usual space outside the prison wall to observe the fortieth anniversary of their common tragedy; they chatted in an open-sided tent across a green lawn from a line of framed photos of the eleven guards and civilian employees who were taken from them so long ago. A candle flickered in a red glass jar beside each photo; and behind the photos stood a gray granite tablet bearing the names of the eleven dead, along with two flags at half-staff, and, to one side, a lectern and chairs for half a dozen speakers.[1] Teams of color guards, comprised of correction officers who had come from across the nation, ranged themselves on the grass with their own flags fluttering and dull black weapons in repose.

Behind these men and women stood a large and imposing formation of correction officers; C.O. Sergeant Mark Cunningham, whose father Sergeant Edward Cunningham was one of the men being remembered at the ceremony, told the audience that following the 1971 riot these officers had trained to suppress any future riot, so that the State Police need never again be the ones to restore order inside a prison. A bagpiper wearing a plaid cap and kilt and a white shirt looked down on the array from the parapet of the central gun tower. Below him the door of the main gate, which is nestled in a Gothic arch embedded in the wall, stood open, allowing some of those sitting in the tent to glimpse another green lawn inside the prison.

During the memorial service, the challenge for some of us who spoke was simply to keep the breeze from snatching our papers off the lectern. Others had to pause during their talks, sometimes often, to fight back tears. It had been the same the previous morning at a symposium called "Attica 40" at the University at Buffalo Law School. Grown men wept or struggled not to. Time had not healed all wounds; they still ran deep and opened easily. A second sign of the fragility of all the years' healing was the extent to which some people still clung to fictions, sincerely believing facts that do not exist, most notably that inmates had killed the hostages who died during the retaking.

Recall Dr. John Edland, the medical examiner who autopsied the dead hostages and refused to go along with the Official Version of their deaths, which the responsible media had duly repeated, that inmates had slashed their throats. In fact, he told the world, it was police gunfire that had killed them. This was a shocker, as was the official lie that had claimed otherwise—twin prongs of the turkey shoot first bared by his devastating truth. For his honesty, Dr. Edland suffered years of vilification, harassment, and ostracism that gnawed at his health and spirit, finally driving him and his family to move far from New York. He died of congestive heart failure in 1991 when he was only fifty-seven, many years before his time. Jack Edland was another victim of the Attica massacre, a martyr to truth, cut down by people who would rather lash out than face it. *Requiescat in pace.*

Bob Patterson, my sometime lawyer discussed in chapter 34, became a federal judge in 1988 and died in 2015, at the age of 91. Trying to be fair about the vagaries of our attorney-client relationship was the hardest part of writing this book.

As you have seen, my story had its lonely moments. The writing of it that made me the happiest was chapter 40, reassuring me as it did that in the grand jury room I was not alone.[2] My conversations with those six jurors show that my pursuit of justice in Wyoming County was not quixotic; that the majority of jurors—which is all it takes in a grand jury—were with me and would most probably have done their duty; that I was right to hope, and the officials above me and probably Nelson Rockefeller were right to fear, that if given a fair chance, the jury would have indicted the troopers who committed violent crime against their fellow men—leaving it to trial juries to decide whether to convict them. The men and women of this grand jury deserve an honored place on any list of people who sought truth and justice over Attica.

Around the time I went public about the cover-up in 1975, the book called *Resignation in Protest*, which I discussed in chapter 42, warned me that, however well-founded such a resignation is, the people who do it tend to grow increasingly extreme in their later lives.[3] I have tried to avoid doing that, how well others may judge. On the other hand, a sound reason for appearing radical (if I now do) dawned on me several years ago as I listened to a tape of Professor Arnold Weinstein of Brown University giving a lecture on Nathaniel Hawthorne's classic *The Scarlet Letter*.[4]

The story's heroine, Hester Prynne, is partially ostracized from her seventeenth-century Puritan community in Massachusetts for the sin of committing adultery. While this psychic exile makes her daily life hard, it gives her a new ability to see her society from the outside, free from the fears, taboos, and no-nos that bind and blind its members. I, too, was partially ostracized from a goodly part of our society for the sin of kicking its anthill and rocking its boat—as I was keenly aware at the time. This experience left me, I believe, with more of the outsider's perspective that Hawthorne portrayed than I had in 1975 or even while I wrote this book. I mention this because some conclusions that I draw in this epilogue may strike some readers as extreme rather than, as I hope, sensible and overdue.

It has been said that Tom Wicker's Attica experience "radicalized" him, though he remained a moderate man. I believe it radicalized me in a mild sort of way, as I just intimated. For Tom, me, Robert McKay of the McKay Report by his own admission, and probably others, I believe that Attica opened our eyes to a darker side of reality than we had previously seen; yet we must see the darker side if we are to come close to seeing a full picture.

My main regret about the original edition of this book is that while I was happy to accept Tom Wicker's kind words in his foreword, I neglected to make clear that it was his decision to take seriously the summary of the Attica cover-up that I gave him during our fateful conversation of March 25, 1975, that led to the exposure by the *New York Times* of the cover-up and to so much that followed.[5] He was among the Observers (mediators) who risked their lives in D Yard trying to peacefully resolve what Governor Rockefeller claimed was an impasse between the State and the inmates (but it wasn't) over whether to grant the inmates immunity for such crimes as they had committed during the riot. Wicker did his eloquent best to persuade Rockefeller to come to the prison rather than order the bloodbath that he assured him an armed assault by angry troopers would be, and it was, because Rockefeller failed to take the simple steps—come to the prison and talk, or at least refrain from ordering the assault—to forestall the tragedy, which by then he alone could have forestalled. Most tragedies pass with their participants into oblivion with their lessons unlearned, but Wicker gave us *A Time to Die*, a truly significant book that illuminates the steps on the march to avoidable violence.[6] And on that early spring day when he and I met in his office, he launched the process that led to such equal justice as finally followed in the wake of the violence at Attica. In an age plagued by passivity and indifference, he acted upon his reason, courage, and decency for the good of all concerned, and much good came from what he did.

It was only when I observed the fortieth anniversary by rereading *A Time to Die* that I noticed the man who was not there, the curious absence of Louis Lefkowitz from the march to tragedy during the rebellion. Neither Wicker's book nor the McKay Report nor this book mentions Lefkowitz as playing any role at all in that story. Yet when one considers that the key issue that dominated the settlement talks and triggered the turkey shoot was legal amnesty for the inmates' crimes, and that the inmates' key fear was that all 1,300 of them would be charged with killing William Quinn,[7] it is clear that the State's Attorney General, as its chief law enforcement officer who most likely would and in fact did head the Attica prosecution, should have advised Rockefeller that he could assure the inmates that only Quinn's actual killers would be prosecuted, and then only if they could be identified. Rocky was the Man, the ultimate authority in the eyes of the inmates. Such an assurance coming from him might well have enabled the riot to end peacefully. Did Lefkowitz dodge his duty to tell Rockefeller what Rockefeller needed to know? Whether or not he told him in private, Rockefeller did not give this assurance to the inmates. Rather, the man whose place was at the prison chose to remain in his luxury, look tough, and order the bloodbath. In the end, of course, Governor Carey more or less amnestied all the culpable inmates, law officers, and officials.

And it is now clear that Rockefeller had believed beforehand that the assault could well be a massacre. As the fortieth anniversary of the uprising approached, Professor Heather Ann Thompson, who wrote the foreword to this edition, and Teresa Lynch, then an adjunct professor at the University of New Hampshire, shed further light on Rockefeller's decision to storm the prison when each of them uncovered a tape recording of him talking on the phone with Richard Nixon on the afternoon of the fatal September thirteenth. We hear him casually tell the President, "*And when we went in, we couldn't tell whether all 39 hostages would be killed and maybe two or three hundred prisoners.*"[8] (My italics.) So Rockefeller had believed what Tom Wicker and the others had warned him. His newly discovered words shed a garish light on his prompt praise of the State Police for their "restraint [that] held down casualties among the prisoners as well."[9] And they remove any doubt about his willingness to sacrifice hundreds of human lives rather than go to the prison and find out whether direct negotiations with him, the Man, could save those lives.[10]

Tom Wicker died in 2011 at the age of eighty-five. Among other participants in the Attica tragedy who have died since this book was written are Henry Williams in 1986, Robert B. McKay in 1990, William Kunstler in 1995, Louis Lefkowitz in 1996, Bernard S. Meyer in 2005, Robert E. Fischer in 2006,

Carman Ball in 2012, Liz Fink in 2015, and Don Jelinek in 2016. As far as I have ascertained, Tony Simonetti, Mike Baden, Myron Farber, Eric Seiff, and Ed Hammock are still old men like me.

Though I am about to relate the three happy endings that I promised in the Author's Note, Attica remains a grim story. Please consider why it is that many people believe even now that inmates killed the dead hostages; why some of them hounded Dr. Edland into his early grave; why talk of prison reform is usually a nonstarter; why, as we shall see, some people disliked a former guard for maintaining that another guard shot him intentionally during the assault; and more broadly and recently, why most Americans ducked the debate over the alleged efficacy of torture during the 2004 Abu Ghraib scandal; why so many smart and knowledgeable people failed to see the 2008 financial train wreck coming; and why nearly all Americans decline to know about U.S. support for the murders during the latter part of the twentieth century of upwards of 300,000 civilians in Central America, that is, the murders of 100 times more people than were killed in the 9/11 attack. While answers to these questions vary, the element they have in common is that each threatens to prick us with a sharp thrust of reality. Yet the harder it is to face an unsettling reality, the more important it may be to face it—perhaps about Attica and surely about much else.

I

One person who had no trouble in facing the reality of the turkey shoot was attorney Elizabeth M. Fink, the inmates' champion in their huge civil suit to hold Governor Rockefeller, Corrections Commissioner Oswald, and other ranking people liable for causing or allowing lesser officers to savage them. Liz says she began life as a red diaper baby (i.e., a child of communists); she was not a socialist but cared deeply about securing justice for disadvantaged people. She would tell the occasional prosecutor, "Don't call me a liberal! I'm a radical!"[11] But she is also a pragmatist.

After starting out in Brooklyn (as I did), she attended Reed College in Portland, Oregon, where she belonged to the Students for a Democratic Society (SDS), and graduated from Brooklyn Law School in 1974 at the age of twenty-six. A few weeks later, she drove up to Buffalo with her pet dog and joined the Attica Brothers' criminal defense team. Though the civil suit was filed that September, as the three-year statute of limitations was about to bar it forever, she was not recruited to work on it until 1981. She was back in Manhattan by then, and the civil case was about to be dismissed for other lawyers' failure to move it forward, when Frank "Big Black" Smith, the inmate leader who had been forced to lie naked with a football on his chest,[12] and another inmate leader, Akil Al-Jundi, both of whom she had befriended while defending them in the criminal cases, came to her and said, "You can't let it happen." "They laid on me," she recalled, "and I said O.K., though I'm not a civil lawyer." But she became one, and in 1982 she became the chief counsel on the case.

Liz spent the best part of the next eighteen years pressing the civil lawsuit forward, a Sisyphus rolling a boulder up a hill with the steadfast help of Smith and, until his death in 1997, Al-Jundi. In addition to Liz, the heart of the legal team consisted of Dennis Cunningham from San Francisco, Michael Deutsch from Chicago, and Joseph Heath from Syracuse. Of them she says, "These are my boys. The Attica lawyers are me, Michael, Dennis, and Joe. Danny [Meyers, who had signed the complaint that launched the suit] helped, but he's not an Attica lawyer. Ellen Yacknin [an old friend] was enormously helpful all these years, but she was not us. We're talking about the people who gave up their lives and went to Buffalo in the criminal cases, and then [did the same] in the civil case. There were only four of us who sacrificed our lives and just totally did what we had to do." In all, the civil case ran for more than a quarter of a century without a payday for any of these lawyers. Liz managed by taking on sundry criminal defenses and, in her words, "my mother helped me a lot; she was our firm supporter." Liz also kept her overhead down by maintaining a tiny walkup office on Atlantic Avenue in Brooklyn, where I would occasionally stop in to see her while I was writing this book.

The rituals of this litigation moved sinfully slowly. In 1988, the federal District Court in Buffalo dismissed the case against Nelson A. Rockefeller—actually against his estate, since he had died in 1979—fourteen years after it began. A year later the federal Court of Appeals affirmed the dismissal, concluding that we have yet to find a case in which the Governor of a state has been held liable for deprivation of constitutional rights or unlawful conduct arising from a decision to retake a prison and rescue hostages held by rioting inmates . . .

With that blandly deceptive version of Rocky's role, the court refused to let a jury decide whether the Governor, after being reliably informed that an armed assault would be a bloodbath, was liable for ordering unleashing of the bloodbath anyway, with its predictable orgy of brutality against the survivors. The court's decision did not catch Liz off guard because, she said, "I never expected Rockefeller to stay in the case, just by the nature of the fix." While I have no knowledge of an actual fix, I think the court bent its judgment to favor Rocky, much as Judge

Meyer had bent his judgment of the Attica prosecution.[13] In later riots, Governors of other states have generally gone to the prisons and waited out the rioters.

Justice crept forward. The District Court decided to split the enormous case into a trial by one jury to determine whether the remaining defendants were liable to the inmates, and, if so, then many additional trials by other juries to determine the money damages due to each. Liz, on the initial trial, which occurred in 1991–1992: "We just won liability against [Assistant Deputy Superintendent of Attica, Karl] Pfeil and hung juries against everybody else. But one liability, they tell me, is good. I thought we couldn't win with those jurors, but we were even able to convince them." While Karl Pfeil was not a man of wealth, any damages assessed against him would be paid by New York State, so the inmates still had a reasonable chance for a measure of justice.

"In 1992 when we had won liability," Liz said, "we immediately went into a settlement process." (Most large "class action" cases like this one were settled.) Not liking the way it was going, they consulted an outside authority, she says, "and he came up with the twelve million dollar figure. I didn't love it, it was before the damages [trials, and] I said O.K." But soon, she says, she learned that then-Governor Mario Cuomo would not consider paying any money at all to Attica inmates.[14] The settlement process fizzled, and onward plodded the litigation toward the many separate jury trials to determine the damages due to each injured inmate.

The high point came at the first such trial in mid-1997 when another Buffalo jury awarded Big Black $4 million, a huge sum for a felon claiming that he was abused in prison. In the next trial, a man named David Brosig, who had endured far less abuse than Black, was awarded $75,000. Thus Liz and her team won verdicts on behalf of convicted criminals from all three Buffalo juries. She said that notwithstanding many daunting obstacles, "We won, we couldn't lose, because the evidence was so overwhelming." It was much the same evidence, I suppose, that had horrified most of the members of my Supplemental Grand Jury in 1974.

Recall that a flaw in a Times Square gate that had slumbered for forty years enabled the Attica riot to explode in 1971.[15] Now a flaw in the first trial judge's jury instructions that had slumbered for seven years exploded the hard work and huge victories on behalf of Big Black, David Brosig, and all the other inmate claimants. Liz: "It went to the appellate court and, you know, fuck us."

And what was the fatal flaw that resulted in overturning all three hard-won jury verdicts? The Court of Appeals explained in its opinion in August 1999:

The lynch-pin of the [1992] liability award was a verdict sheet that on its face did not require findings [by the jury] sufficient to support class-wide liability or even liability to particular, identifiable plaintiffs. Absent a valid finding of liability, the damage awards [of 1997] to Smith and Brosig must be reversed.[16]

The flaw in the verdict sheet, according to the court, was that it asked the jury to decide whether Pfeil should "be held liable to the plaintiffs or any of them . . . ." The jury answered, "Yes." But did that yes mean that Pfeil was liable to Black or to Brosig or to some other plaintiff(s) or to all of them? There was no way to tell. And since the verdict did not establish that Pfeil was liable to any particular person, there was no support for an award of money damages to any person. The decision was more complicated than this, but this was the nub of it. (Liz remained convinced, she said, that the flaw in the verdict sheet was "harmless error" that did not warrant overturning the jury verdicts.)

Aware at last of the slug-like pace of the case, the court went on to say:

Given the long history of this matter, we direct the district court to give it expedited treatment . . . . We respectfully suggest that [its] Chief Judge . . . consider assigning this matter to the judge best able to expedite its resolution. We note that the defendants in this case, who are functionally the State of New York, have done all they could—frequently not without the court's acquiescence—to delay resolution. That strategy can no longer be tolerated . . . .

Thus prodded, the District Court moved. Senior Judge Michael Telesca replaced the previous judge and reportedly told the parties, "Don't tell me you can't afford to settle. You can't afford *not* to settle." Four months later they settled for $12 million, eight for the inmates, four for the lawyers.

Liz: "The twenty-five years made us settle. They had us over a barrel. We were going to continue to fight and get nothing, or we were going to take chump change, and that's what we did." I replied that it wasn't chump change but enough money to make the public take notice. "Oh, yes, it's the largest settlement in the history of prison litigation," she said. "Black's verdict was the largest verdict in the history of prison litigation." But Liz was right; compared to prevailing damages for such intentionally inflicted injuries, eight million dollars divided among what would now be 502 claimants was chump change. On the other hand, she believed that "the only reason why we got that money was because they knew we were nuts and we weren't going to go away."

The $4 million lawyers' fee may seem hefty—until we consider that they had worked up to twenty-five years without a payday and needed to divide the fee among themselves after subtracting their expenses itemized at $575,000, though, Liz said, they were close to twice that sum. Referring to her struggle to keep the case going, she said, "I lost most of the $500,000 family money I invested in the case. Big Black and I gave most of [our awards] up to properly pay off the prisoners."

And so Liz and her team had won three jury verdicts and the largest settlement ever on behalf of convicted felons. Not bad. In fact, a splendid achievement!

I asked Liz if she thought Attica had benefited any inmates. "Oh, yeah," she replied. "Frank is the perfect example. Attica itself, no. The fight for justice, yes. The fight for justice changed the lives of a lot of people for the better. Black was just a street person, older than most, without any politics. As a result of what happened to him at Attica and the fact that he was taken into a leadership role changed his whole life, and he became this incredibly powerful paralegal investigator. Akil was a Muslim, and came out of prison and devoted himself to the Attica Brothers. [He] got this job at Legal Aid, and died in '97 after twenty some odd years with the Legal Aid Society winning every award, being famous.[17] And that was all from that."

After Attica, she continued, "The entire nature of the American prison system changed for the better for ten years, and it produced statistics which are ignored today but which are absolutely powerful on the efficacy of educational and vocational trainings in prisons, that the higher degree of education a prisoner has, the less likely they are to go back to prison. Duh! Surprise, surprise! [Today] the nature of prisons in this country is containment for the underclass, because they've killed educational and vocational programs in prison."

Knowing that Liz had used this book in preparing for her trials, I asked her if she would comment on it. "Without you we couldn't have won," she replied. "Without you the real story of what happened at Attica would never have gotten told." This was nice to hear, and I had indeed opened the door to the information that she and her team developed; but the main reasons that they won were the terrible wrongs inflicted on their clients and their own abilities and perseverance.

Now the problem was to divide up the $8 million settlement money fairly among all those inmates, some of whom had suffered as gravely as Black and many of whom had suffered as comparatively little savagery as Brosig. Judge Telesca's solution was to have each of them tell his own story under oath in open court or by sworn statement or by someone who could speak for one who had died, or by telephone or video conference from whatever prison he was still in: whatever it took to get their stories on the record as reliably as possible.

The judge, to his credit, wanted to do more than simply divide up the money fairly. He seized the opportunity to let the world finally see what the State had worked so hard to cover up, namely, what law officers had done to their fellow human beings. He did this by having the inmates and former inmates speak for themselves and submit their medical records, as we shall soon see. Aware that some State officials would not like this, he first put the inmates' $8 million beyond the reach of any such official by having the State pay it "into the Registry of the Court subject to the Court's control."[18]

The hearings to take the testimony of about 200 inmates began in Judge Telesca's courtroom in Rochester in May of 2000. By August, he had divided all the inmates into five categories according to the severity of the injuries inflicted upon them. Big Black and fourteen others in the highest category received $125,000 each; Brosig and the other 261 men (or their survivors) in the lowest category received $6,500 each. Of the twenty death claims, nineteen were awarded $25,000 each, and one got $27,000 because it took the man two days to die. (Claims were not submitted on behalf of nine of the men whom the police shot dead, including Edward Menefee, who took nearly two weeks to die from the buckshot a trooper had fired into his torso.[19]) Judge Telesca noted that the majority of the awards were "of a modest sum," adding that for many of the men, "the privilege of recounting their odyssey was of greater value than achieving compensation." Comparing the $4 million the jury awarded Black to this $125,000, and Brosig's $75,000 to this $6,500, suggests what it may theoretically have cost the inmates to settle. But Black would die of kidney cancer in August 2004 at the age of seventy.[20] Even if he had gone through another trial, won another large verdict, and prevailed after the inevitable appeals, the chances were slim that he would have received any payment at all before he died. Other claimants, too, were soon to die. David W. Chen concluded in the August 29 *New York Times* that "the landmark settlement caps one of the longest and most ignominious chapters in American criminal justice history . . . an episode that has become a symbol of prison life and state-sanctioned brutality."

In sum, the State had delayed unconscionably, awarded the inmates only paltry compensation for their pain and suffering, and refused to admit its wrongdoing. In historian Heather Ann Thompson's words: "And so what the men had gotten wasn't justice. It wasn't even close to justice. But it was the closest thing to justice that these men would ever get."[21]

In a larger sense, though, the settlement was a tribute to our often-dishonored principle of equal justice. It showed that while people who commit crimes may be imprisoned as the law prescribes, they may not be tortured any more than anyone else may be tortured; and if they are tortured, they deserve to be paid for their pain and the PTSD that often haunts their lives. The State had done its best to block such justice—a justice that upset many people. "They started the riot, but they got paid" was a common protest. In fact, some inmates started the riot, nearly all were tortured, and torture is not an acceptable penalty for rioting or anything else. Those whom the inmates' settlement offended, on the other hand, did not seem to mind that each law officer who had committed the tortures that gave rise to the inmates' claims enjoyed absolute impunity for his brutal crimes.

I see the inmates' settlement as a bright spot in the sorry Attica saga. As Judge Telesca put it in his Decision and Order that ended the lawsuit:

> The events of the morning of September 13, 1971 left indelible impressions upon each of the plaintiffs . . . . Although they have left Attica, Attica has not left them. After having been assured that nothing would happen to them if they [surrendered], they were nonetheless shot at and beaten . . . . Many cannot shed the bitterness of that betrayal . . . . Attica is the ghost that has never stopped haunting its survivors—including both the inmates and families of the deceased guards and prison personnel. But at least the settlement of this case provides the basis for the former inmates to close the book on the past and to focus on the future.

In the fall of 2015, Liz Fink's legal teammate Joe Heath wrote to me the following about Judge Telesca's settlement hearings during the summer of 2000, "What I remember the most was the respect he showed each of the Brothers who testified and that each of them broke down and cried while on the stand."[22]

II

In 1992, I experienced a small personal irony, when some police nearly killed me—not New York State troopers but New Canaan, Connecticut, town police engaging in what has aptly been called "macho mayhem." It seems that two shoplifters had boosted about $50 worth of merchandise from a CVS drugstore. The police roared after them in a high-speed chase that ended when the fugitives' car slammed into my car and then into a tree, the first chase car slamming into theirs. The impacts injured five people, including two cops, and bashed in my car's body a few feet behind me. Later a former NYC police commissioner told me that he was appalled that these police had engaged in a high-speed chase over a minor property crime.

What appalled me was that even after the fugitives had been handcuffed, an officer had been carried from his shattered cruiser in a neck brace and on a stretcher, and several cops were standing around, none of them noticed my obvious wreck until I finally told one of them that I wanted to report an accident. Did they ignore me, I wondered later, for the same reason that New York refused to admit the dire needs of the Attica hostages and their families that resulted from the macho mayhem of its State Police? Does acknowledging a victim threaten to undo a perpetrator's retreat into denial? Whatever the reason, the callousness with which Rockefeller & Co. treated these loyal State employees who were innocent victims of the Attica massacre was Part Two of the callousness with which the troopers shot their way into the prison in the first place. To summarize:

- The State maintained the prison as such a perilous workplace that it could and did explode.
- During the ensuing negotiations, Governor Rockefeller refused to come to the prison upon his untrue claims that his coming would do no good and there was nothing left to talk about.
- Rockefeller & Co. decided, instead, to sacrifice the hostages in order to get the prison back, though it wasn't inmates but police who then did the killing.
- Having thus sacrificed its employees, the State was clearly obligated to take care of the widows and survivors. Commissioner of Corrections Russell Oswald assured them that this would happen. But, instead, the State swindled them. It issued them innocuous-looking checks for, say, $30, ostensibly to cover little expenses. Then it claimed that by cashing these checks, as all except widow Lynda Jones did, they had thereby waived their rights to fair recompense. Though New York's highest court upheld the State's claim in 1981, the State was in fact cruel, sneaky, and wrong. As Francis X. Clines put it in the *Times*, "They were gulled by

state officials in the early days of grief into accepting token workers' compensation and thus signing away their right to sue."[23]

For example, two widows with six children each were left living below the poverty line. Many families subsisted without adequate housing; for years, a family with several children did not have a furnace. A widow with five children received $230—less than $40 for each person to live on—per month. Another widow received $16 a month for her baby daughter, which did not pay for the diapers and formula.[24]

Comes the year 2000, and these surviving hostages, widows, and their families see that the inmates are receiving $8 million. The inmates had been serving time, they started the riot, and they got all that money. The hostages had been serving the State, and all they got was grief. The enormity of the injustice they perceived infuriated them; their righteous indignation aroused them to act. They organized themselves as the "Forgotten Victims of Attica" and began pressing New York to give them: (1) An apology for the wrongful deaths and physical injuries, the emotional injuries to all of them, and the State's "duplicity regarding compensation." (2) Release of the State's records of the riot to provide (they hoped) closure for themselves and to "expose the cover-up that the state perpetrated" (which they readily saw though Judge Bernard Meyer had claimed not to). (3) Counseling for those still suffering the emotional effects of the initial injuries and subsequent injustice. (4) The right to conduct a memorial service on the prison grounds every September thirteenth. (5) "Compensation that is deemed fair by the victims."[25] At heart, they wanted the State to recognize that they existed and had been sacrificed for it.

Everybody I know about except attorney Donald Jelinek (about whom more soon) believed that after New York's highest court had ruled against their claims, the Forgotten Victims of Attica (FVOA) had no remedy that they could pursue in court. Their quest, then, depended upon the decency of New York State officials—as we have seen, not a rosy prospect. But they clearly had enormous moral authority, and they sought to bring it to bear on then-Governor George Pataki, a Republican, and other officials in every way they could think of. The main mover of their campaign was a cheerful dynamo named Deanne Quinn Miller, the eldest of the three daughters of murdered Correction Officer William Quinn. Former C.O. Michael Smith was their main speaker. Gary Horton became their pro bono counsel, deeply committed to their cause yet standing fairly clear of the emotions, as a good lawyer must. Other members of the FVOA pitched into their common effort as needed.

All I had known about the travails of the surviving hostages and their families is pretty well summed up in the little I said about them on pages 364–365 of this book, and I, too, had forgotten them—until four of them and Gary Horton sat with my wife, Nancy, and me in our home in Vermont on a sunny midsummer morning in 2000. They had asked if they could come over and talk. Knowing it must be important to them to drive so far, I had said yes.

The four were Mike Smith and his wife, Sharon, and John Stockholm and his wife, Mary. By the grace of God and fine surgery, Mike had survived four bullets that had shattered through his abdomen as he sat blindfolded on A Catwalk with inmates poised to kill him.[26] Early in the riot, inmates had struck John on the head and neck hard enough to knock him out. Friendly inmates dragged him, bleeding, into a cell along with another guard, where they hid until the other inmates realized they were missing and it became prudent to surrender. He, like Mike, was one of the eight hostages whom inmates took to the catwalks in their vain effort to prevent the attack. When the shooting started, "I fell directly down to the ground. I could feel cement chips hitting me. And you could hear the sounds and the smell of pain and death . . . they have haunted me for over thirty years. It keeps replaying in my nightmares."[27] A powerfully built man, John was so traumatized that he, like several other ex-hostages, spent his remaining years at Attica assigned to gun tower duty and other jobs that did not require him to mingle with inmates.

As Nancy and I got to know these people on this pleasant morning, the violence that two of them had survived seemed far away. We saw immediately that the State had treated them shamefully and they deserved justice and recompense at last. I wasn't sure what I could do to help but resolved to do what I could.

The first thing they suggested was for Nancy and me to visit the entire group of Forgotten Victims, as we did in September in their usual meeting hall close to the prison walls. I found myself deeply moved to stand before this group of aging men and women and their adult children whose pain I had only read about. They had given up so much to serve the State; in return the State had treated them like jetsam. I don't remember what I said. Afterward some of them greeted me warmly; I particularly appreciated a great emotional hug from Mary Ann Valone, daughter of slain C.O. Carl Valone. Some of them seemed shy. Some were hard to read. I felt that it was only natural if some of them resented my past efforts to prosecute their fellow law officers, yet they were as deserving of recompense as all the others. (Later I realized that some of them must have felt the same hostility toward me that, as we shall soon see, they felt toward Mike Smith and Don Jelinek.) It did please me that then and at later gatherings, some of them brought up copies of this book for me to sign; several said that they had not read it before and now learned for the first time what had really happened to their loved ones. During the next few years, I spoke for the FVOA, wrote letters on their behalf, and testified before a commission set up by Governor Pataki to consider their claims.

The FVOA were diligent to recruit outsiders like me to their cause. Tom Wicker wrote an op-ed column on their behalf in the *New York Times* and later a review of the fine Court TV documentary, "Ghosts of Attica." Elliott Spitzer spoke up for them while he was New York's Attorney General. Jonathan Gradess, the Executive Director of the New York State Defenders Association, worked for the FVOA as their Albany insider and pro bono cocounsel. Bill Cunningham, the lawyer who had won the $1+ million judgment for hostage widow Lynda Jones, spoke for them and gave them useful information that he had discovered during that lawsuit.[28]

Seeing Bill Cunningham again led to a haunting moment the following September. Since he was donating his cartons of Attica papers to Bethune-Cookman College in Daytona Beach, Florida, college officials invited him, Big Black, and me to speak on Sunday, the 10th, at a ceremony to receive the donation. Afterward Nancy and I took a late evening flight back to Boston and found ourselves walking through the warm, nearly deserted halls of Logan Airport just a few hours before a handful of young men with box cutters walked those halls on their way to change America forever.

The 9/11 attack confronted the Forgotten Victims with a hard choice. They had planned a major memorial service for 9/13, the 30th anniversary of their tragedy. Should they go ahead with it? Correction officers and other guests had gathered from as far away as California. There would never be another 30th. But the nation was in shock. As all commercial flights were grounded, some people who had planned to attend couldn't; and others who were already there couldn't fly out. They decided to go ahead. Bill Cunningham and I were among the scheduled speakers. No problem for Nancy and me to drive over from Vermont, but Bill was still in Florida. Never easily defeated, he rented a car and drove the 900+ miles to the prison, earning applause from the Forgotten Victims.

The 9/11 attack also created a larger problem for the FVOA: responding to the attack absorbed State officials' attention and much of the funds at their disposal. One result was that the State would insist on spacing out over six years the money it eventually agreed to pay, during which some of the Forgotten Victims would inevitably die. On the other hand, the settlement would be simplified by Gary Horton's steady refusal to accept any compensation for his massive legal services, which he rendered in addition to serving as the Genesee County Public Defender, going to court for indigent people, and running the Public Defender's Office in Batavia.

Liz Fink offered to help the FVOA, as she was well equipped to do, but they turned her down. She was anathema to some of them for having championed inmates, though others agreed with Gary when he said: "I don't know anybody who would have had the perseverance that she had in representing the inmates; I have nothing but respect for what she did." Likewise, Dee Quinn Miller had "great respect for her; she did an amazing job for all the inmates." The decision to reject Liz's help was not based on the FVOA's personal feelings about her, but on a tactical concern that associating with the inmates' chief counsel would be off-putting to some of the officials—perhaps including the Governor—whose goodwill they were courting.

In May 2001, Big Black took it on himself to write the Governor a long, powerful letter on the Forgotten Victim's behalf and to tell everyone who would listen that they deserved the justice they were seeking.

In 2002, the quest of the Forgotten Victims came to the attention of my old courtroom legal adversary and longtime friend Don Jelinek in Berkeley. "I wanted to return to Attica and lend a hand," he said. "This was an authentic civil rights battle and I certainly knew the players."[29] That June he and his wife, Jane, flew east at their own expense to meet with the FVOA in their hall outside the prison—a difficult meeting for him and surely for at least some of them since he, like Liz, had represented inmates. The result: the FVOA put on hold a plan he advanced to sue the State because they felt that at that point such a move could be counterproductive, but they accepted the rest of his generous offer to help them. After that meeting, Dee wrote to me, "I am still a bit apprehensive about [Don]. I get the feeling he likes to really take charge of things and he's a bit intense. Other than that, he's OK." Understanding that I'd been asked for a reference, I replied:

> I know he comes on strong, but that can be an advantage for you or anyone else he represents or advises. At the same time, he is practical, not bullheaded. I believe he knows how to yield and adapt . . . . Don has a very strong component of idealism and wanting to help people he thinks have had a raw deal. That probably explains much or all of why he represented the inmates—though not everyone will understand that. Earlier in his career, he risked his life for long periods in the South to help blacks during the civil rights movement.

(In hindsight, I would change none of the above except to add a fact I find significant: each Fourth of July Don reads the full Declaration of Independence; he told me that he always found something new in it.) Dee replied, "I have faith that Don is a good man and good hearted (overzealous and intense), but I'll deal with that."

Besides relating his efforts on behalf of the Forgotten Victims, Don's book, *Attica Justice*, gives a fascinating account of his work for the inmates whom my office had charged with crimes.[30] Time and again as I read it, I found myself admiring the creativity, boldness, and dash with which he did his best for this unruly, violence-prone crew and their other volunteer defenders—"herding cats" vastly understates it. Recall, for instance, that Tony Simonetti, Max Spoont, and I had been concerned that "cause lawyers" may sacrifice the best interests of their clients in order to trumpet some noble cause. Unbeknownst to us, we had a substantial ally within the opposing camp; Don worried about the same thing, with good reason, and suppressed it whenever he could among the rest of the defense team. His most trying moments came after he was back in Berkeley, during the 1975 trial of John Hill for murdering Bill Quinn, when Don's friend and role model, Bill Kunstler, who was defending Hill, said more for the causes and less for his client than Don (or I) thought a defense lawyer should have. "Helplessly reading accounts in the *Times*," Don wrote, "I felt I was watching an epic disaster unfold in slow motion." Hill of course was convicted. Kunstler was a founder of the Center for Constitutional Rights and probably the nation's leading leftist champion of the rights of underdogs; he, too, had risked his life in D Yard trying to prevent the bloodbath; but in defending Hill, his passion, which included a seven-hour summation to the jury, may have backfired into more justice than he had sought.[31]

Of particular interest to me in Don's book was his account of a visit that he paid to my barn apartment in November of 1975, where we discussed Attica and his civil rights work on tape for three straight days. During lunch in Oakland a few years ago, he showed me a draft that said I'd been covering my windows with blankets at night lest someone take a shot at me. I did not recall that and denied that I'd done it—until I phoned my son Brian, who was at work across the Bay in San Francisco, and heard him describe the pale blue and tan blanket I'd been hanging over the windows that faced my desk. What, me in denial? I guess the lonely winter after I resigned in protest had a deeper impact on me than I realized at the time or these many years later.[32]

The Forgotten Victims found it hard to absorb the sharp thrusts of their own reality. As Dee recalls it, "People knew how their loved ones were killed but wanted to believe that it was more of an accident in the retaking of a building. Many of us were climbing up the hill of this evolution [to seeing that] there was intentionality, there was recklessness." The group's steepest challenge came when Mike Smith told them that another correction officer had intentionally shot him—one of their own had tried to murder another one of their own. "When I first heard it," Dee told me, "I thought it was preposterous. [It] made the group horrendously uncomfortable. I got phone calls after that from people saying, 'Do you really think that someone tried to murder him, specifically?' I still remember when I came to fully agree that Mike was a target. I didn't want to believe, but sadly the facts said otherwise." Some of the group, though, disliked Mike for his conclusion. At another meeting, Don Jelinek (with Mike's permission) brought up the attempt on Mike's life. Even though Mike had been saying it, and those who had read this book saw me reach the same conclusion, Don perceived that "as an outsider talking about their dirty linen, I had really enraged everyone in the room."[33] In the end, some of the group accepted the realities of the retaking; others clung to their assumption that the shootings of hostages were purely accidental—sincerely believing facts that do not exist. At least, Mike Smith's and Don Jelinek's disturbing honesty did not arouse the degree of wrath that had beset Dr. John Edland.

At times I cannot separate fact from fiction. For instance, I reported (and now have deleted) the story that inmate Elliot Barkley had been killed while running in D Yard during the assault and added that so far as I knew, the story that he had been executed later was not true, because the oblong entrance wound in his back strongly suggested that he was hit by a tumbling bullet that had ricocheted off something else and thus could not have been aimed at him. My conclusion rested on a convincing presentation by Dr. Michael Baden during the 1973–1974 shooter conferences plus a similar analysis on page 396 of the McKay Report. In 2011, however, an enterprising filmmaker named Christine Christopher learned from Dr. George Richard Abbott, who had been Dr. John Edland's assistant and performed the original autopsy on Barkley, that the hole in Barkley's back was not oblong, but round. Christopher and I later examined the shirts that the State Police had tagged as having been removed from Barkley's corpse. The white undershirt, whose fabric had deteriorated, bore a hole that might or might not be considered oblong, but the hole in the dark green outer shirt was small and squarishly round, indicating a direct shot fired either during or after the assault. There were eyewitnesses for both versions of Barkley's death. Some of them believe a fiction, but which ones?

A widespread fiction that persists to this day has it that National Guardsmen joined the law officers in shooting people during the assault.[34] But as the McKay

Commission put it in 1972, the National Guard's role "was carelessly and inaccurately reported. Guardsmen carried stretchers and administered first aid . . . and left their rifles outside."[35]

By mid-December 2004, the Governor's office had raised its offer to the Forgotten Victims to $8.5 million, and they had lowered their request to $15 million. Dee told me that she was alone when a call came raising the State's offer to $10 million. Without consulting anyone, she said no. Then the magnitude of what she had done began to hit her. Had she cost these fifty families, her own family, and friends who trusted her, all that money, which most of them badly needed? Within a day or so, her anxiety was so acute that she checked herself into a hospital emergency room and told an astonished therapist that she had just turned down $10 million. There followed several long days without much Christmas spirit. On the 22nd came the call she feared would never come, bringing the offer up to $12 million. She took the offer to the group, and they accepted it. Merry Christmas!

Dee, Gary, and Mike remained the driving force of the FVOA's quest; and when the talk grew heated between her and Mike, she says, Gary served as a liaison and a buffer between them. "When our mission is to shame the State," she added, "because it's our only opportunity for recourse, the three of us worked very well together." Her conclusion: it was *shame* and (echoing Liz Fink's insight) the fact that State officials "knew we weren't going to go away" and the people who kept telling the Governor to "do the right thing" that combined to carry the day for them.

The FVOA's strategy had been to tell their stories as clearly and widely as possible because, Gary Horton explained, "the public didn't know what happened to them [after] the riot. Telling those stories and the impact of how they were treated eventually was what helped us win the day. The stories are so powerful [that] if you keep telling them, you gain ground. We gained support from corrections unions, from the public, from people like Frank Smith, and it kept growing and growing upon itself."

In the crucial telling of the FVOA's story, Mike Smith spoke time and again with a simple eloquence that deeply moved his audiences. Gary saw Mike as "the picture of Attica that the public sees because he's a very good speaker and his story has a great deal of power because of the severity of his injuries and the person he is. He's a good man who was hurt, and that made him an almost perfect spokesman."

When I asked Gary why he volunteered very large amounts of his own time to the FVOA during five years, he replied too modestly, "I did it because once in, I couldn't walk away from it. There were times when I felt like it, and I just couldn't bring myself to do it." Dee put it more simply: "He did it for *justice*." The Forgotten Victims, she added, "are *very* thankful and they know that we could not have done this without him."

Nor without her. As noted before, Dee was the main mover of the Forgotten Victims' quest. I asked Gary about her role. His analysis: "In any cause like this, it's essential that there be one person that has the time and the willingness to be a central clearing house. It was a huge job. She did it willingly and did a great job."

When inmates bludgeoned Dee's father to death, she had been a girl of five. Had he survived, he would surely have been proud of her for what she accomplished for his family, fellow guards, and their families. I believe that in whatever Hereafter awaits us, he *is* very proud of her.

And so, nearly five years after the FVOA began their campaign, Governor Pataki finally recognized, in his words, the State's "moral obligation" to pay the agreed sum. This made him, in my view, the first New York Governor to come out on the positive side of the Attica ledger.

Though the Forgotten Victims' settlement was not in federal court or any other court, both sides chose federal Judge Telesca to administer it. Indeed, Gary told me, the office of the Governor had trouble understanding why the Forgotten Victims would want the same man who had managed the inmates' settlement. "But," Gary said, "we thought he [had] a good process and [was] very fair for the inmates, and we were happy to have him do it."

As he had with the inmates, the judge divided the claimants into categories according to the circumstances of a hostage's death or the seriousness of his injuries. Of course he included Bill Quinn, who technically had not been a hostage but whose family the State had treated as shabbily as though he were one. To the surprise of some, State Police Lieutenant Joe Christian, who endured permanent damage to his leg from friendly gunfire, was also on the list.[36] The families of Bill Quinn and of Harrison Whalen, who had been shot in the head, spinal cord, and pelvis and took until October 9th to die, received $550,000 each. The families of the other nine hostages killed by gunfire received $500,000 each. Payments in the other categories ranged from $380,000 to $100,000. In his order of July 13, 2005, which concluded the settlement, Judge Telesca wrote:

> Hopefully, the survivors and their families of the Attica riots of 1971 will no longer feel "forgotten" and those who suffered and continue to suffer will feel some measure of comfort at least from the fact that the matter is concluded and some measure of justice was served.[37]

I asked the judge whether his saying the Attica riots, plural, of 1971 was a typo. No, he said, he meant to include *all* of those riots. I took that to include the race riot by the State Police.

There is, I suspect, another group of forgotten victims of Attica, namely, the troopers and guards who have had to live with the horrible things that they did or saw their fellow officers do during and after the turkey shoot. I don't suppose there has been any relief for these men except to maintain a veneer of indifference or a fiction that they did a tough job well, or else to open themselves to the care of their loved ones or private therapists. And there are these officers' families. A young man at a 1991 symposium on Attica, held in Buffalo, NY, announced that he was the son of a trooper who had participated in the retaking. With anguish in his voice, he said that he often wondered whether his dad was a murderer. Later I checked my list and, no, his dad was not on it; but I still couldn't disclose who was or wasn't (I hope he reads this). In any case, being on my list would not have meant that a man was a murderer, just that maybe he was.

Welcome as the settlement may have been to the Forgotten Victims, it lacked the few key words that would have been enormously important to them— more important for some than the settlement money they received—and to the honor of the State: Pataki refused to issue a simple apology to these people for the ways the State had abused them during a major portion of their lives.

For the fortieth anniversary of the rebellion and massacre, the current Governor of New York, Andrew Cuomo, a Democrat, was asked to issue the apology that would have meant so much. He ignored the request. And so, as the father had refused to consider compensating the convicts whom State employees had tortured, the son refused to say the necessary words to employees whom State officials had abused. For want of these few words, the Attica albatross still taints the State of New York.

Readers may wonder, as I did, what became of Ann D'Archangelo, the young woman with the long dark hair in the first sentence of this book, so I asked her. She was twenty-two years old and had been married for three years, she said, when her husband John was taken hostage. Four months earlier, she had nearly died giving birth to their daughter. As she was about to undergo a C-section, John said to her: "I've just talked to the priest and I've been to the chapel, and I told God that if He saved you and Julie, He could take me." Of course, it was not God but a wanton trooper who took John's life, ironically, as he was about to become a trooper himself.

Governor Rockefeller phoned Ann around 2:45 on the fatal day and read her a speech—she could tell he was reading—which said that inmates had killed her husband.[38] Ann received many other phone calls in the midst of her grief, anonymous voices that told her in words or substance, "We're glad the pig got killed, we're going to get your daughter."

Commissioner Oswald visited Ann with a Workmen's Compensation official who told her that she had to sign a paper that was, as she put it, "the State's way of taking care of my baby for the rest of her life." So she signed it, and they received a paltry $16 apiece a week until Julie was sixteen—by which time Ann had remarried and all payments stopped. With her new husband, Ann bore a son, Mark; and in 1980 she returned to school because, she said, "I had this burning desire to become an RN—I had to be in a helping profession because I couldn't help John." She went on to care for inmates in the Auburn prison for twenty-eight years. While she knew at the time that John had been shot to death, it was not until she read this book that she learned how he actually died—a rude shock, to say the least. Now Julie has three children of her own. Ann is retired, delights in her grandchildren, and says that her life is peaceful. She calls the State's refusal to apologize to the Forgotten Victims "beyond belief."[39]

Judge Telesca told me he feels that while the judicial system was late in responding to the Attica situation, it was vindicated when it oversaw both settlements and let the inmates and hostage survivors tell their stories. I agree on all counts. The adage "justice delayed is justice denied" fits Attica with a vengeance; it took twenty-five years (during which hundreds of the inmates died) before the federal Court of Appeals stopped tolerating that denial of justice. But once the first trial judge left the case and Judge Telesca took over, *then* the system worked.

And unbeknownst to all the judges and everyone else, it would take this tardy working of the system in the inmates' case to galvanize the Forgotten Victims to join together and press their claim. To this extent, the Forgotten Victims owe the success they achieved to the much-maligned success of the inmates. It would have been doubly just if the inmates' case had settled years earlier.

A word about a name: they may have been Forgotten Victims when they started out, but they became Well-Regarded Survivors. By uniting and working together, they benefited not only themselves but also the State of New York, by giving it an opportunity to do something decent about Attica that it had no legal obligation to do. We ask people to take on three dangerous jobs for our own safety. We know what firefighters and the police do and the price they sometimes pay, but prison guards are, in a sense, our forgotten risk-takers—out of sight, out of mind. By telling their own stories and persuading the State to give them the respect and a bit of the compensation they deserved, the Well-Regarded Survivors benefited their whole profession.

In the end, it was the persistence of the inmates' legal team and of the Well-Regarded Survivors and their friends that finally made the settlements possible. Way back, my own decisions to resign in protest and to talk with Tom Wicker, and his decision to take my concerns seriously, led to an equal justice in the criminal prosecutions that was, as I said on page 337, "different from what I had sought, but radically better than what had existed before I went public." I hope I do not presume too much if I think that those decisions and this book also had a role in leading to both settlements. Then it was indeed the judicial system that finished the main elements of Attica business. Governor Carey had tried to close the book on Attica in 1976, but no one could have done that then. Three decades later, while history books may yet be written about Attica and further facts may yet be revealed, Judge Telesca has closed the book on the big jobs that needed doing, and he closed it with integrity, compassion, and about as much justice as was still possible.

III

Fine as Judge Telesca's work was in administering the inmates' settlement and the Forgotten Victims' settlement, his finest achievement, I believe, was not simply to close the book on Attica, but literally to write a key concluding chapter during the course of the inmate settlement—so fine an achievement that it deserves this separate telling.

To understand the significance of what he did, it may help to consider what no one had done before—indeed, what the officials in charge of the prosecution had diligently avoided doing (and kept me from doing). Their early decisions to investigate crimes "chronologically," underfund the prosecution, and send many inmates to other prisons enabled the architects of the cover-up to create a vast gap in the evidence. BCI detectives generally asked inmates what they saw and heard only up until the assault began; for the most part, they asked only law officers for their versions of the events that followed; and my office lacked the staff and the will to complete most inmates' interviews. So we ended up with full accounts by the perpetrators of the carnage and their brother officers, but only spotty accounts by the victims. Until Judge Telesca got the inmates' case.

During the settlement hearings in mid-2000, he encouraged each inmate to tell his story as fully as he wanted to and so reveal at long last the full horror (insofar as words can convey the sounds and smells and agony of horror) of the officially condoned savagery that the police and guards inflicted upon them. As the hearings of the live testimony began, he told everyone assembled in his courtroom:

> Let me set the record clear. We're going to dispense with normal court-room procedures . . . . I want to hear what each plaintiff has to say. There may be objections to relevance in a very pure sense, but I consider it all relevant. Whatever they want to say, I want to hear it.[40]

Time and again he would ask an inmate who was finishing up whether there was anything he wanted to add and tell him to return to court if he thought of more later. The testimonies moved the judge deeply. Significantly, he found these convicts "for the most part to be credible. And some understated the extent of their injuries and how those injuries affected their lives." (On reading their testimonies, I, too, found them mostly credible, sadly more credible than those of many of the police I had questioned.) He also found that their accounts of their injuries and lack of medical attention were generally consistent with the examples included in the McKay Report.[41]

Finally, Judge Telesca took the extraordinary step of writing out his own synopsis of each of these 502 inmates' accounts (omitting such parts as he did not find credible) and their medical records; and he had them all conveniently included as appendices to his published settlement decision. While the transcript of the inmates' testimonies is a public record and often fascinating to read, I regard the synopses, vetted as they were by a veteran trial judge who observed the witnesses' demeanors and correlated their words with their medical records, as being the most accurate record we have and are ever likely to have of the law officers' torture of inmates who had surrendered.

The testimonies disclosed significant new facts about the shootings. More significant, while much had been reported about the torture of inmates by the media at the time, and later in the McKay Report, Tom Wicker's book, this book, and other places, the inmates' testimonies as summarized by the judge raised the revelations about the law officers' barbarity to a new level of specificity and power. And of course, the judge's synopses included, as those early reports could not, the physical and emotional anguish, the crippling, and the medical procedures that these men endured over the next three decades of their lives. There is more than enough detail in the 502 synopses to turn a strong person's stomach.

Back in 1974, I had been very curious to know what the inmates would have told the State Police interviewers if the latter had not been instructed to write down nothing the inmates said they saw, heard, smelled, or felt after the tear gas came down and guns opened up at 9:45 a.m. on that fatal September thirteenth, 1971.[42] Now, thanks to Judge Telesca, I could finally find out. Yet weary perhaps of the sharp thrusts of Attica's reality, I possessed a copy of the judge's synopses for about ten years before I finally dug into it, and it was like reading the newspaper accounts of the tortures at Abu Ghraib and of what terrorism suspects said they had endured when the CIA sent them off to be interrogated (tortured) in other countries. It was all so horrible and sad and unnecessary. Here are my abridgments of a few of the judge's synopses:

- Alfred D. Plummer fell to the ground after being shot in the abdomen and leg. A trooper ordered him to get up and walk into A Yard, but he couldn't, so the trooper aimed his pistol at his head and fired. Plummer passed out twice, the second time coming to in the morgue where National Guardsmen found him and two other inmates still alive. He underwent surgery to repair his abdomen and spine, a colostomy for damage to his intestines, and a separate surgery to remove the bullet from his brain. Later surgeries removed the colostomy and put a metal plate in his skull. He lost peripheral vision in his right eye, developed epilepsy from the brain damage, and continues to have recurring nightmares "of being shot in the head at point-blank range."
- Willie James Sullivan took a .270 bullet in his spine that left him lying in the mud of D Yard. A trooper ordered him to remove the football helmet he was wearing, then kicked it off his head, leaving a permanent scar on his forehead. As an ambulance drove him to the hospital, a correction officer told him, "Nigger, we're going to open the door on this ambulance and dump you into the road when we get over the top of the hill so that a truck can run over you." The ambulance stopped, the back door was flung open, and Sullivan prayed they would not dump him. "I thought I was going to die," he testified, "but God saved me." A particularly sadistic mock execution. He is unable to raise his right arm and is permanently disabled from being shot.
- Anthony Scales was on A Catwalk where he saw several inmates shot, some fatally, one as he was pushing Scales to safety. "Everything that moved they hit—they didn't care." Officers threw him off the catwalk into A Yard nearly fifteen feet below, where they kicked him in his head

and testicles and beat him with pick-axe handles, knocking teeth loose, chipping bones in his elbows and knees, and breaking an ankle and some ribs. Back in his cell he was threatened with a shotgun. He continues to suffer from flashbacks and nightmares. Of the retaking, he said, "That's not law enforcement, that's murder."

- <u>Chris Reed</u> was shot four times in the lower left leg and once in the right foot. A bullet to his left thigh "exploded and took out a big chunk." As he lay on the ground, troopers debated whether to kill him or let him bleed to death. Some of them jammed their weapons into his wounds and threw powdered lime on them and on his face. He finally passed out, awakening "stacked up with dead bodies." The lime was burning his face and eyes so badly that he tried to rub it off in the bloody mud beneath him. Meanwhile the authorities told his mother he was dead and asked her to come in and identify the body; seeing him move, she suffered a heart attack and had to be hospitalized. Eventually he was placed on a stretcher where officers jerked on his wounds until the pain caused him to pass out again. A prison doctor put a cast on his leg without properly cleaning his wounds; later the cast was cut off so ineptly that the knife went into his thigh leaving scars that are still visible. Screaming in agony, he was told to "Shut up." His lower leg became gangrenous and had to be amputated at the knee; it took two more surgeries to close the stump. Severe physical and emotional distress continues to plague him. Yet Reed graduated from college, married, had two sons, and became a tax auditor for New York State.

If Chris Reed's life testified to one inmate's resiliency and pluck, then the shooting of helpless Alfred Plummer marked another success of the State Police cover-up.[43] Until I read the judge's synopsis in 2011, I had never heard of this incident, which sounded like a case of attempted murder. So far as I know, my office did not know about it, just as it had not known, until I asked Mike Smith to let down his pants in 1974, that Mike had been nearly killed by a C.O.'s automatic weapon. Nor did the McKay Report mention the shootings of Plummer and Smith. What, I wondered, became of the bullet that the surgeons plucked from Plummer's brain? Did it have sufficient markings on it to trace it to the pistol and trooper who fired it? Was it turned over to the State Police, who somehow neglected to inform my office about it? Did my office lose track of it? These questions should have been answered in 1972, and not only the shooter but anyone who hindered his prosecution should have been considered for indictment by the Grand Jury. Once again, it's too late now.

Sometimes a synopsis filled out a story that I'd heard part of long ago. Recall the inmate who sat up and chanted on his stretcher until guards dumped him off it and beat the hell out of him.[44] That inmate was Akil Al-Jundi, who went on to have that fine career. The judge's synopsis of his claim says that he was shot through the hand by one bullet and struck below the right eye by fragments of another:

> While he was lying on the ground, he saw corrections officers torturing another Muslim leader, James Richey, by using their rifles and sticks and jabbing them in Richey's abdominal gunshot wounds. To divert their attention, Al-Jundi sat up on his stretcher and began to chant. The officers turned on him, dumped him on the ground and beat him with clubs . . . . Still bleeding badly several hours later, he was finally transferred to the hospital . . . . Surgeons performed sixteen major and sixteen minor operations to reconstruct the hand, including bone grafts, skin grafts and insertion of a plastic implant over the [bullet] hole . . . . Mr. Al-Jundi's face and left hand were permanently scarred by gunshot injuries. Use of his left hand was permanently impaired. He suffered flashbacks, nightmares, and severe avoidance problems.

Recall, too, that after the retaking, two naked inmates were forced to lie with shotgun shells balanced on their bent knees in A Yard next to Big Black with his precarious football.[45] The judge's synopsis of one of these men, Gary Haynes, says that Haynes:

> remained in that position from morning until dusk, being subjected to officers spitting on him, throwing lit cigarettes on him, swearing at him, and threatening to kill him. After the other inmates were gone from A Yard, a correction sergeant sodomized him with the barrel of a shotgun. After enduring the A Tunnel gauntlet, he was forced to climb a stairway lined with guards who struck him on the chest, back, legs, arms, feet, and head with their rifles, night sticks and some planks. At the top of the stairs, he was kicked so hard in the stomach that he fell back down the stairs and again had to run the gauntlet to the top. Later when he tried to urinate, he discharged pure blood with extreme pain. He told a guard he needed

medical attention but received none for seven days. Permanent damage to his kidneys has since required him to be hospitalized more than 60 times.

Besides being serially beaten and kept naked and hungry in their cells, a great many of the inmates were subjected to terrifying games of Russian roulette and other forms of mock execution, which, of course, they did not know were mock until they realized they were still alive. Many did not receive medical care for their bullet wounds, broken bones, and other serious injuries for days or even weeks. Imagine being put in a dentist's chair, as at least two inmates were, and having a bullet pulled out of you without anesthetic. Most of the inmates testified that they still suffered nightmares, flashbacks, and other plagues of post-traumatic stress disorder.

What the police did at Attica was compared at the time (with some exaggeration) to the My Lai massacre in Vietnam. But couldn't it be seen today as a domestic Abu Ghraib? Descriptions of sadistic tortures like those quoted above impart too sharp a thrust of reality for many people to face, as they seem to have been too much for my own comfort zone during the years I let the judge's synopses languish unread.

Often as I had contemplated (or avoided) looking through Attica's window into hell, its awfulness came home to me as it never had before on the cold November morning in 2011 that I stood in an unheated warehouse of the New York State Museum a few miles west of Albany and examined the shirts in which Elliot Barkley had died and especially the outer shirt of C. O. Sergeant Edward Cunningham, who had foretold his own death on TV if Rockefeller did not grant amnesty.[46] Cunningham left a wife and six children. The shirt that I held between my hands was black and stiff and wrinkled from the red flow that had gushed out of his head. On it was written, not in words but in blood, the history of needless human violence.

Judge Telesca did not have to expose the barbarity that the State had worked so long and hard to suppress. In assigning inmates to categories, he could have relied on a much simpler record, as he would do with the Forgotten Victims. Nothing compelled him to write out any of these synopses, and he was criticized for writing them; for example, the well-known broadcaster Paul Harvey called him "a felon-friendly federal court" on a national hookup.

But justice required the great Attica cover-up to be defeated to the extent still possible, Judge Telesca saw a chance to defeat it, and he took it. He told me that he wanted to be open, to let the sunshine in, to let the inmates tell their stories, and let the world know what happened and what the inmates went through. A great irony of the Attica saga is that this fullest, most reliable record of the turkey shoot and the following orgy of sadism is the version that New York State tried the hardest to cover up, that is, the *inmates'* version. In the world of Attica, the people whom society considers least trustworthy turned out to be the most trustworthy, and those we count on to be most trustworthy were the least.

In 2004 Judge Telesca told historian Heather Ann Thompson that holding the inmates' hearings and creating his record of what law officers had actually done to them "was the most fulfilling thing I ever did."[47] The sunshine that Judge Telesca let into the Attica cover-up illuminates both the humanity that exists within these convicted felons and the savagery that likely lurks at some level within many if not all of us—and that our early ancestors may have needed ages ago for us to survive and evolve to our present level of civilization. I suppose that most of the troopers and guards who inflicted these horrors do not usually deport themselves like the Nazi SS; but the lifelong pain and suffering of their victims make it irrefutably clear that during several days of that long-ago September, the veil of civilization parted and the beast within many of those law officers did indeed spring forth. As it often has before and since, as at Abu Ghraib. It is also true, of course, that many officers managed to restrain themselves. Honest prosecutions, of course, encourage such restraint.

These truths about Attica can do no good if we avoid them. As the moon has a dark side, so does human nature; and it may be natural for most of us to seek the peace of pretending it isn't so. Yet as Anton Chekhov observed long ago, "Man will only become better when you make him see what he is like."[48] And in words attributed to Jesus and emblazoned on a wall inside the CIA's headquarters in Langley, Virginia, "Know the truth, and the truth shall make you free." And, one hopes, deter other Atticas and wars and worse.

IV

So far this epilogue has related the three happy endings within the Attica saga that I promised in the Author's Note. Now come the four recent sequels that I promised. The first involved the quest to open the State's hidden files on Attica. While I doubt that any such quest could still yield major revelations, it was surely worth pursuing. The Attica saga is too significant not to be fully knowable by historians and the rest of us—especially the FVOA, inmates, correction officers, and State Police.

On April 25, 2014, author, journalist, and human rights activist Scott Christianson summarized the still-suppressed material as follows: "more than 100 boxes of Attica-related files . . . the bulk of records that were compiled by the . . . McKay Commission . . . artifacts which the State Police removed from bloody D Yard . . . [and] Rockefeller's Attica records, tape-recorded or otherwise, are nowhere to be found."[49] Christianson compiled this list in response to a New York State court decision handed down the previous day that drove another nail into the lid of secrecy that still partly hides the enormity of Attica. Here are some highlights of the long, seesaw struggle between truth and denial:

- September 13, 1971: Officials falsely claimed that inmates had killed the dead hostages.
- September 14, 1971: Dr. Edland reported the fact that law officers had killed them.
- September 15–16, 1971: Governor Rockefeller falsely claimed that the troopers had done "a superb job" and their killing of hostages had been "justifiable homicide."
- September 1972: The McKay Report found, to the contrary, that the police had done "much unnecessary shooting" and then tortured the 1,200 or so inmates who had surrendered.
- 1971–1973: The Attica prosecution falsely represented that it was doing its job as fairly and rapidly as feasible.
- August 1974: Upon Rockefeller's nomination to become Vice President, the first systematic presentation to a Grand Jury of criminal cases against law officers was halted long before it was finished; it was never seriously resumed.
- April 1975: I disclosed the prosecution's intentional cover-up of police crimes.
- December 1975: Judge Meyer said I was wrong, but most of his basis for saying so was suppressed.
- December 1976: Governor Carey tried prematurely to close the book on Attica.
- June 1997: A jury awarded $4 million to Big Black (reversed due to an error in an antecedent case), thus rendering a citizen's damning verdict on the law officers' conduct.
- August 2000: Judge Telesca published as full an account as there will ever be of the brutality that law officers inflicted on inmates.

- December 2004: The State's agreement to pay the FVOA $12 million amounted to an admission that it has swindled them.

Since 2001 the FVOA had been pressing for the release of all the Attica records, including the suppressed portion of the Meyer Report. As you may recall, Judge Meyer, in Vol. 1 of his report, declared that, however wrongheaded, all of the officials' choices that resulted in aborting the prosecution of police crimes were innocent; but the courts sealed Vols. 2 and 3, which contain his main basis for saying so. Finally, in 2013, with the approval of Governor Andrew Cuomo, Attorney General Eric Schneiderman filed a motion asking the court that had first sealed these volumes to release them to the public.

The overt problem, which had originally moved the courts to suppress the volumes, was that they contain extensive Grand Jury material that the law soundly requires to be kept secret, mainly to protect the confidentiality of prosecutors' work and the identity of witnesses and suspects, unless a court in its discretion finds a "compelling and particularized need" to release it. (The unspoken problem was that many people still resisted further revelations about official crimes.) But at this late date, most of the basis for keeping these secrets had vanished, and the Attorney General had undertaken to redact the names of suspects and witnesses who might be hurt by being identified. (The FVOA opposed these redactions; I supported them.)

The Attorney General's motion papers made an excellent argument that the unique historical significance of the Attica tragedy demonstrated the required "compelling and particularized need" to make public all the information that the volumes contained, while the redaction of names as well as the passage of forty-plus years protected the pertinent identities. The accompanying affirmation of Executive Deputy Attorney General Martin J. Mack aptly summed it up:

> The passage of time has made it clear that—like the shootings at Kent State, the violent police attacks on civil rights demonstrators in the 1960s, the My Lai massacre and the Watergate scandal—Attica is more than just a profoundly tragic event; it is an historic event of significance to generations of Americans.[50]

In addition, the A.G.'s motion papers argued that since the Meyer investigation and report had been prompted by my cover-up charges, "The citizens of this State are entitled at long last to know . . . why, contrary to the charges leveled by Malcolm Bell so long ago, Meyer determined that New York's investigation and prosecution . . . were not corrupt and did not 'lack integrity.'"[51] Wanting to support the A.G.'s motion, I filed an affidavit that picked up on this point and argued that if Meyer's basis in Vols. 2 and 3 for his finding of official innocence had merit, the public deserved to see it. Or if, as seems likely, it was more of the same sycophantic sophistry that marred Vol. 1—that is, if the State had no case against my cover-up charges—then we surely deserved to see it. I was fine with asking the court to publicize the State's strongest case against me while, at the age of 81, I was still around to respond. To show why the public still needed to see these volumes, and to illustrate Meyer's flaws that probably pervade them, my affidavit made the following points about Meyer's Findings in his Vol. 1— which, I believe, also help in appraising his conclusion of no cover-up:

Meyer's Finding No. 5 claimed that my cover-up charges were "not sustained by the record" in part because: "The deficiencies in evidence gathering immediately following the retaking left so little available to the investigation that determination of possible criminal liability in shooter cases became inordinately difficult in all but a few extraordinary cases." This was not true. By saying it, Meyer resurrected the Official Version that had prevailed—and had been the main excuse for the prosecution's failure to indict any police—until January 1974 when I reached the rather obvious conclusion (see Chapter 10) that the felony of reckless endangerment in the first degree gave the prosecution the "handle" it needed for convicting perhaps six dozen (72) or more troopers and guards upon the evidence that we had. Tony Simonetti and Max Spoont had agreed with me. Putting these cases together was the main job of the shooter conferences that Tony conducted that winter; the Supplemental Grand Jury was impaneled largely to consider indicting these dozens of officers for committing this particular crime; with Tony's guidance and, I believe, Lefkowitz's knowledge, I gave the jury voluminous evidence of these crimes for three months; and even after Tony clamped down on me and the jury, they managed to indict one trooper for it. But it was much easier for Meyer to deny a cover-up if the prosecution had botched only a few cases rather than dozens of reckless endangerments that deserved to be competently put to a Grand Jury vote. So Meyer had to "disappear" all those cases before he could claim that it would have been too hard to prosecute "all but a few extraordinary cases." And it wasn't just Max Spoont's judgment, and Tony Simonetti's and mine, that Meyer, the newcomer to criminal law, rejected. Shortly after Meyer's report was released, veteran prosecutor Alfred J. Scotti, who had been New York City's Chief Assistant District Attorney for nearly twenty years, looked at the same evidence that Meyer had and reached the opposite conclusion, saying that this evidence "strongly suggests that the crime of reckless endangerment was committed by many law enforcement officers during the Attica retaking."[52] So how did Meyer explain away all those cases that the rest of us saw, and thus shrink the scope of the cover-up until it became so small he could claim he didn't see it? We needed Vols. 2 and 3 to know whether his reasoning was or was not as absurd as his conclusion appeared to be.

Meyer Vol. 1 on pages 42–44 said that he was listing the charges of covering up that I had made in my 160-page report to Governor Carey. Among them, I had written these two:

> [1] The Investigation was grossly understaffed from the start . . . . The meager forces of the Investigation were deployed in inverse proportion to the magnitude of the problems they faced . . . . [2] The decision to investigate the riot before the retaking, and inmate crimes before law officer crimes, was crucial to the failures of the Investigation to date.

But Meyer's list of my charges omitted these two big ones, thus bolstering the false Official Version that my charges merely amounted to petty squabbles between my boss and me. But these two official decisions, which had struck a one-two punch to the heart of the prosecution, were too blatant for Meyer to ignore, so in order to find no cover-up, he needed to claim that, wrong as they were, they were made in good faith. As to the first one, he said in his Finding No. 3: "The Attica Investigation was from the outset woefully understaffed. The responsibility for the inadequacy of the staff rests largely with [Robert E.] Fischer, and not with the Executive Chamber or Simonetti." So Rockefeller and Lefkowitz had no responsibility? According to Meyer, the buck stopped with their subordinate—who supposedly did not intend to conduct a sham prosecution but was merely exercising bad judgment. But Rockefeller and Lefkowitz were powerful and effective men, whose ambitions the slaughter at Attica had threatened. They commanded the Investigation and Fischer, and the Investigation was a part of the Department of Law, which Lefkowitz headed. The fact that they did not get a proper prosecution must mean that they had not wanted one. But Meyer refused to see or say this. He did not admit that Rockefeller and Lefkowitz were ultimately responsible for *their* failure to assure that the Investigation always had enough people to do the job. Was Meyer as blind to the culpability of these big guys in Vols. 2 and 3 as he was in Vol. 1?

Meyer Finding No. 4 faulted the idiocy (cleverness) of the decision to finish dealing with inmate crimes before seriously starting on police crimes: "The decision to conduct the investigation sequentially or chronologically rather than topically," he wrote, "was a serious error of judgment . . . which skewed the investigation's inadequate manpower away from possible . . . crimes by law enforcement personnel . . . ." Thus did Meyer dismiss this keystone decision in the arch of the prosecutorial cover-up as being merely Fischer's "serious error of judgment." Again Meyer failed to mention that Rockefeller or Lefkowitz or both should have corrected the error. Nor did he mention the likelihood that one or both of them had approved the decision—if they had not made it.

Meyer Finding No. 10 concluded that my

charge that the investigation switched in August 1974 from shooter cases to possible hindering of the investigation crimes . . . in order to frustrate presentation of possible cases against enforcement personnel is not sustained by the evidence. Those decisions were made in good faith, and except as to the brutality area, in the proper exercise of prosecutorial discretion.

Once again, Meyers's assertion of official innocence hangs unsupported in mid-air. He simply said it. Only access to Vols. 2 and 3 can permit historians and the rest of us to evaluate his basis, if any, for concluding that these decisions were not made in order to accomplish what they in fact did accomplish, namely, they protected Rockefeller's ambition to become President of the United States by seizing the sudden opportunity that President Ford gave him to become the Vice President.

In short, the only way to test the cover-up (since no one confessed to it) was by examining the totality of all the decisions and deeds that had aborted the prosecution of law officers' crimes. So far as appears, Meyer did not do this. How could he possibly manage not to connect the dots that showed the obstruction of justice by the highest State officials? Glaring as the cover-up was, how could he not see it? Again, we cannot fully know unless we see Vols. 2 and 3. Whether Meyer lacked the capacity to see the prosecutorial cover-up, or else understood that he was not supposed to see it and that seeing it could thwart his own ambition to sit on New York's highest court,[53] or whatever the reason was, his denial of the cover-up had the effect of furthering the cover-up. Many people still believe there wasn't one because he authoritatively said there wasn't.

On April 24, 2014, having declined to hear oral argument (in which I had hoped to participate) on the A.G.'s motion, Justice Patrick H. NeMoyer rendered his Decision and Order that released so much of Vols. 2 and 3 as did not contain Grand Jury material but refused to release the portions that did.[54] The decision disappointed. Not that I expected much news from the bits of Grand Jury evidence that Meyer must have cherry-picked to support his conclusion of no cover-up—I suppose that I had put many of those bits into the Grand Jury record—but the decision clashed with the new official openness that the current governor and attorney general had shown by making the motion to release these volumes. Most significant, releasing *this* Grand Jury material would have set a strong precedent for releasing all the rest of it that remained suppressed.

Though I disagreed with NeMoyer's refusal to release the Grand Jury material, I think he was sound in saying that when he weighed the public's interest in evaluating it against the residual interest in Grand Jury secrecy, the former would have weighed more heavily if he had been asked to release *all* the material rather than merely the fragments that Meyer had selected. Would a new motion to release all the Grand Jury material succeed? Perhaps we'll see.

A small point in the grand scheme but galling to me was Judge NeMoyer's statement on page 12 of his decision that "Bell advocates for the full release the Meyer Report." This is not true. In fact, the affidavit I submitted to him in support of the Attorney General's motion asked in two separate places for the *redaction* from Vols. 2 and 3 of the names of all suspects and witnesses. Over the decades I have made it a point *never* to reveal any of these names, so now the judge goes on record with the untrue assertion to the effect that I wanted them revealed. He did not respond to my letter asking for a correction.[55]

Attorney General Schneiderman decided not to appeal NeMoyer's decision; and I do not quarrel with his choice. It is very hard on an appeal to overturn a judge's exercise of discretion; and if the appellate courts affirmed this decision, that would probably make it harder for a later motion to release the entire Grand Jury material to succeed.

A year went swiftly past, and on May 15, 2015, the Attorney General's office, having redacted what the court required, released Meyer Vols. 2 and 3. The original report was 570 pages, of which Vol. 1, made public in 1975, was 130 pages. Of the remaining 440 pages in Vols. 2 and 3, the redacted version that was released came to a bare 46 pages—actually fewer than 40 pages, since many of the 46 had large white gaps. So more than 90 percent of Vols. 2 and 3 remained suppressed.[56] The portions I saw teased and tantalized. They made me wish for more. As I read them, I kept wondering what came next, but nothing came next. It was like watching a preview of a movie that would never be shown. Even so, I am glad that, thanks to the first Attorney General to actively favor disclosure, these fragments became public.

Of all the questions I discussed above that needed answers about Meyer, the released portions answered none of them. Most frustrating to me was their failure to shed any light on legerdemain by which Meyer had caused the host of reckless endangerment cases to vanish. Overall, though, the released portions showed, even further than Vol. 1 had shown, that by finding no cover-up, Meyer had given a big boost to perpetuating the cover-up.

Some of what was released was actually useful, for instance, the part that related incidents of police and guards' brutality to inmates that my office had failed to pursue. But shocking as these criminal assaults were, they were also cumulative to the extent that the media had reported many such horrors shortly after the riot ended; and the McKay Report related many similar acts in 1972, long before Meyer did his work. (This book reported several such incidents in 1985, and Judge Telesca published his vast compilation of them in the federal reports in 2000.)

The redacted volumes failed to give any basis for Meyer's exculpation in Vol. 1 of Rockefeller and Lefkowitz for the overall failure to prosecute law officers' crimes or for the sudden switch of the Supplemental Grand Jury away from the shooter cases upon Rockefeller's nomination for Vice President. On the other hand, they contained two more instances of the distortions that Meyer indulged in that enabled him to call conduct innocent or innocuous that was neither.

First, Meyer found no problem with the bizarre State Police Night Riders effort to obtain statements from local undertakers repudiating Dr. Edland's finding that gunfire had killed all the dead hostages, because, he wrote:

> the State Police had turned the bodies over to the medical examiner who had already publically announced that the deaths were caused by gunfire and knew that independent pathologists had been retained. It was, therefore, unrealistic to believe that obtaining the statements was a coverup effort by the State Police.[57]

To the contrary, it was totally realistic to conclude that the Night Riders were part of the State Police cover-up. Though they were fully aware that Edland was correct, the State Police, desperate to discredit his findings, tried to get undertakers to swear that "in [their] opinion there was no evidence of a gunshot wound to the body . . . ." Even more bizarrely, the police tried to convince the independent pathologists, Drs. Baden and Siegel, that the dead hostages had not been shot to death—and they partially though temporarily succeeded with Siegel.[58]

Second, Meyer claimed to see no point to my efforts to obtain any transcript or tape that a *New York Times* reporter had made of the State Police radio transmissions during the retaking, writing on page 479 that

> it was not of major importance because it would simply fill in the chinks in a picture of what happened on the 13th of which the investigation already had the broad outline and exact times of events would not be too important.

Here, too, Meyer's bland speculation was not true. In the first half of 1974, both Tony Simonetti and I had wanted to know whether any such transcript or tape existed since it might well contain spontaneous utterances such as the one on a Corrections Department tape that "the officer next to me was firing into the bodies on the [cat]walk and I pushed the rifle away."[59]

Particularly galling was Meyer's assertion that "exact times of events [during the retaking] would not be too important." In fact, those exact times could be crucial. I had been working hard to establish whether, as part of their cover-up, the State Police had cut their videotape of the retaking to eliminate the curiously absent scenes of troopers shooting people, as I and apparently the grand jurors suspected they had. If, say, the videotape showed that the surge of gunfire when an inmate felled Lieutenant Christian came four minutes into the assault but the immediate call on the radio of "officer down" came seven minutes in, that would strongly suggest that the tape had been cut.[60]

In addition to these two elements of the cover-up, the redacted volumes made cryptic references, on pages 189 and 195, to the death of inmate Edward Menefee, but they failed to mention the possible murder case against Trooper J, described on pages 113–114, above, that I had not nearly finished exploring—in particular, whether or not Menefee was the inmate into whom Trooper J admitted firing his shotgun—when I was removed from the shooter cases.

So far as I can discern, redacted Vols. 2 and 3 did nothing to support Meyer's finding of no intentional cover-up. Indeed, his specious reasoning pointed the other way. But during the last forty years, his report's lack of visible support has not kept some people from trusting it as though it were established truth. A not-random example of such blind trust appeared in a short review of this book in the April 6, 1986, *New York Times Book Review*, which concluded that though the book "makes a good case that the state police covered up the crimes of their own," Meyer's finding of no cover-up reduced the book to being merely "Mr. Bell's vehicle for rehashing his allegations." This put-down was about as erroneous as calling a six-week jury trial a "rehash" of a one-page indictment. The book reviewer was free to be persuaded or not by my evidence—meaning my whole account of how the cover-up unfolded—but his implication that this evidence did not exist was not honest. Even worse, treating Meyer's specious finding as authoritative gave it a measure of credibility. While I would like to think that no one at the *Times* intended such a result, it was ironic that this great newspaper, which had done so much to lift the lid off the cover-up, ran a review that sought to put the lid back down.

Paradoxically perhaps, the passing years have strengthened, not weakened, the Meyer Report's effectiveness in denying, and thus furthering, the cover-up. When the report first appeared in 1975, many people had ample reason for disbelieving it. After the McKay Report euphemistically found in 1972 that the police had done "much unnecessary shooting," the prosecution's failure to indict any police for their carnage had led many people to conclude, or at least suspect, that a cover-up was in progress. Then several months before Volume 1 appeared, the media had given much coverage to my cover-up charges and all the evidence they unearthed that supported me. And after Meyer's report appeared, it was widely criticized as being the whitewash it was.

But the passing years simplified the story. It became simply that an assistant prosecutor charged a cover-up and an official investigation concluded that there wasn't one, period. While the Forgotten Victims had no trouble in seeing the cover-up in the early 2000s, what are all the people who know little, or have forgotten much, about Attica supposed to believe? Especially people who don't doubt the veracity of official reports. I hope that what I have written in Chapter 36 and in this epilogue counters any assumption that because Meyer was official he was right.

The less-than-satisfying result of the Attorney General's motion to release Vols. 2 and 3 in their entirety did not end the efforts to exhume the rest of the Attica secrets. The motion itself demonstrated a new openness in that office. And there are all those other State files for the FVOA, Joe Heath, Scott Christianson, and other concerned citizens to go after. The Rochester

Democrat and Chronicle's reporter Gary Craig has been unearthing Attica material for many years, as has reporter Paul Mrozek of the Batavia *Daily News*. Michael Virtanen, a wire service reporter, and veteran reporter Tom Robbins of the Marshall Project have recently joined the quest. Professor Heather Ann Thompson of the University of Michigan has unearthed an enormous amount of material for *Blood in the Water*, her sweeping history of the Attica saga.[61] Perhaps someday, State officials and judges will notice that the longer they resist full disclosure of the Attica records, the longer they keep the drama alive. The Watergate scandal taught the folly of such resistance; but since some officials seem to think the lesson does not apply in the Empire State, the Attica saga continues.

The morning after Judge NeMoyer's 2014 decision came down, Executive Deputy A. G. Martin Mack phoned to thank me for my interest and support for the Attorney General's motion. This was good to hear. It marked the first time since I resigned in protest in 1974 that any State official took an initiative to thank me for anything I had done about Attica.

V

In 1974 I had not yet reached the case of inmate Sam Melville, whom a State Police detective had admitted killing, before I was shut down. Finally in 2014, the case reached me via Sam's son Josh, who was nine years old when his father died and had devoted considerable effort ever since to learning the truth about his profound loss. Now Josh wanted to know what I could tell him about his father's death, but I knew little more than I had said in this book, which he had already read.[62]

But he had somehow obtained copies of Dr. George Richard Abbott's report of his father's autopsy; two statements purportedly written by the BCI (Bureau of Criminal Investigation) detective who fired the fatal shot; and a statement by a BCI witness. I told him that while I would neither affirm nor deny that the man named in the statements had killed his dad, I'd assume it for our discussion. I found it stimulating to dig into them—as though I were starting in on my first shooter case in forty years—and consider at last the big question they raised: was Sam Melville's death a provable murder?

Dr. Abbott's autopsy report was not exceptional, and I was able to discuss it with the doctor on the phone. It showed that a one-ounce lead shotgun slug made a one-inch entrance wound in the upper left of Sam's chest and split in two against his third rib. One jagged piece formed a lump against the inside of Sam's back; the other piece tore through his left lung. The rib that split the slug was broken by it, causing two jagged ends of bone to protrude inwards, perhaps further tearing the lung. "CAUSE OF DEATH: Gunshot wound of chest. FRAGMENTS OF LEAD MISSILE." Essentially, Sam bled to death from his torn-up left lung, though Dr. Abbott said that he may have been able to move around for a minute or so while he was dying.

The immediate question was: could the shooter justify his shot? One of the statements, written in longhand purportedly by the shooter and dated "9-13-71" but not signed, said that after he and some other BCI men had followed the assault troopers down the C Catwalk and he was standing on the B Catwalk on the far side of Times Square and well above D Yard:

> I saw some commotion over to my right and it was a male inmate and he kept running in and out of the bunker or barricade [down in the yard]. I lifted my gas mask and shouted to him to "Stop." I put my gas mask back on and then motioned with my hand for this inmate to stay down. He continued to run back and forth about four or five times. The last time he came from behind the bunker he had a Molotov Cocktail in his right hand and he had his right hand cocked to throw the Molotov Cocktail up on the Catwalk B—or other troopers who were already in D Yard. It was then I fired one round at him and he went down behind the bunker . . . . I was about 20 yards away from the Inmate when I fired at him . . . .

For the most part, the statement of the BCI witness backed up this version; and the testimony of both men to the McKay Commission gave much the same accounts.[63]

I didn't believe them. It sounded incredible that this late in the assault, with armed troopers commanding the B and D Catwalks above this part of D Yard and other troopers with shotguns already down in the yard, any inmate would be running in and out of a barricade, or would have tried to throw a bottle of gasoline in order to commit suicide-by-cop. As noted in my book, a number of troopers conjured up Molotov cocktails to justify their shootings.

McKay's account cast further doubt on the BCI men's testimony:

> Neither man was absolutely certain that the inmate was about to throw a Molotov cocktail and neither could say whether it was lit. The [BCI

witness] said that 15 minutes later he went down into D yard to examine the body and could not find a Molotov cocktail near it.

If I could have established that the unsigned handwritten statement, which admitted the homicide, was authored by the shooter—which should have been easy to do back then—and that the Molotov cocktail threat was a fabrication, a provable case would have been well along.

And there was more. As noted in the book, two inmate witnesses contradicted the law officers' version. One said that he saw a man walking toward the brick wall at the edge of the yard with his hands on top of his head trying to surrender when a trooper up on the catwalk shot him in the chest. The second inmate said that he was actually in the makeshift bunker with Sam when they saw troopers coming down the ladders and starting for the hostages, so they decided it was time to surrender; this inmate watched Sam go out and get shot as he tried to do so.

The second purported statement of the BCI shooter, which was typed and also unsigned, was even less credible than the first. It started out much like the first but then had the shooter saying that he noticed

in the lower corner of the prison yard, a male, who was behind a barricade. . . . I saw him take a knife from his pocket and run to a ditch which was located nearby, which contained hostages which were prison guards. As he attempted to stab all of the guards, I fired the shotgun striking him. He then ran back behind the barricade. Then . . . I descended into the prison yard where I observed a subject behind the barricade, apparently deceased.

So the Molotov cocktail became a knife, and the hostages moved from the Hostage Circle forty or fifty yards away into a nearby ditch, which, if I remember correctly, actually served as an inmate latrine. And the inmate was trying to stab thirty or so men? I doubted that the actual shooter authored this fantasy; rather, it looked as though some BCI person who knew little of the retaking but considered the Molotov cocktail defense insufficient had concocted it, much as senior SP officers had created several troopers' "supplemental statements" described in the book.[64]

If we put aside this bizarre typed statement, we have the dubious accounts of two law officers against the plausible accounts of two inmates. But Chris Christopher, the filmmaker who had revised my view of Elliot Barkley's death, discovered another witness to Sam's death, a man named Frank Hall who had been a sergeant in the Monroe County Sheriff's Office and led a squad of stretcher-bearers down the A Catwalk behind the assault force. After Hall passed Times Square, he saw a trooper or prison guard (he wasn't sure which) shoot an innocent inmate with a shotgun. "The guy wasn't doing anything from what I could see from the catwalk and he just shot him," Hall told Chris. She then asked him whether he knew "what the state felt it needed to cover up."

> Yup . . . . I can't say . . . whether the guy was coming towards him and he had a knife in his hand or something . . . it didn't look like it from where I was . . . it was a shock to me to see that guy shot right down in front of me. It didn't look to me like he was doing anything wrong but wanting to give himself up . . . .[65]

Hall, who served twenty-one years with the sheriff's office and attained the rank of major, told me on the phone the essential details that the shooter was on the catwalk and the man he shot was down in the yard. From what I knew of who died where and how, it was evident that the shooter could only have been the BCI detective and the victim Sam Melville.

If a diligent filmmaker could discover a key witness four decades after the event, how many more witnesses should our professional investigators have found at the time? The Supplemental Grand Jury should have heard all the witnesses, seen the other evidence, and voted whether or not to indict the BCI man for murder or maybe manslaughter. Would they—or a trial jury if it came to that—have concluded that the detective had honestly if mistakenly thought that he needed to shoot this inmate in order to save himself or brother officers from death or grievous bodily harm? Another instance of the Attica cover-up producing mystery instead of justice.

There is an even more disturbing question: was Sam Melville's murder planned in advance, perhaps with accomplices? As my book noted, some inmates claimed that correction officers on the catwalks had pointed out certain inmates for execution and troopers shot them. Again from who died where and how, the only person who I thought could have been executed in such a manner was Sam Melville—until 2011 when Chris's research added Elliot Barkley as a possible. Both men must have infuriated many law officers. Melville (a.k.a., the Mad Bomber) was perceived as a radical leftist who had bombed several office buildings in order to make political statements and, during the days of the standoff, served as the inmates' most notorious weapons-maker. Barkley's eloquent rhetoric, some of which had been broadcast on national TV, had inflamed both sides during the negotiations. The McKay Report concluded that neither Melville nor Barkley "was removed from the yard and executed after the assault"; but this conclusion, which I think was correct, left open a real possibility that they were executed in D Yard late in the assault.[66]

Now Josh asked me the fascinating question, What was a BCI detective doing with a shotgun? Following after the assault force and armed with his pistol, the man would not likely have been issued one. I do not recall that any other BCI man on the catwalks had one—a fact that would have been easy to check. Here is how the BCI man explained the shotgun in the handwritten statement:

> Capt. [Henry] Williams instructed me and others to follow the assault group out and if any of the Troopers dropped their weapon we were to secure them. When I got to T.S. [Times Square] area an unknown trooper standing to my left handed me a shotgun. He was holding two of them. He stated that another trooper had dropped it.

Two false notes struck me at once. First, I can't believe that Williams gave this instruction; it would have been as needless as telling the detectives to tie their shoelaces. In the video I saw of Williams briefing the police, he instructed them to keep control of their weapons but said nothing about securing any dropped weapons. But putting these improbable words into Williams's mouth set up the shooter's even more improbable claim of how he acquired the shotgun.

Second and more basic, I cannot conceive that any trooper, trained and instructed to control his weapons, would have been so irresponsible and incompetent as to leave a loaded shotgun lying on that crowded pavement. As far as I know and as you'd expect, none of the troopers in the assault forces and in the Rescue Detail who climbed down the ladders into D Yard dropped their shotguns and abandoned them.

So what was the real reason this detective had this shotgun? And how did it come to be loaded with slugs, which are the perfect ammunition for executing a person in a crowded area because a single slug will strike only the person aimed at, unlike the more commonly used pellets, whose spread can easily hit unintended people? Why would a detective shoot an inmate who was trying to surrender unless there was a plan to execute him? And if Sam Melville's murder was planned in advance, doesn't that add to the likelihood that Elliot Barkley's was, too? The cover-up foreclosed the answers, guilty or innocent, to these questions.

Like Josh's effort to come to terms with the events that left him without a father, Elliot Barkley's sister, Tracee Barkley, has borne the gnawing burden of her brother's death for most of her life. How many loved ones of the Attica dead have endured similar years of pain while the killers lived out their lives with impunity?

In some societies, Josh would have sought revenge against the man who shot his dad. Indeed, forestalling such acts is one reason that civilized societies have lawful prosecutions—except that the lawful prosecution of the worst felons at Attica was aborted. Or Josh might have dwelt on his father's death to the point of being unproductive. In fact, though, he has lived a life that is successful by most standards and is writing a book about the tragedy that overshadows it. I look forward to reading it.

VI

On March 1, 2015, another story of violence at Attica, accompanied by a large and surprisingly gorgeous photo of the prison in snowy nighttime blue, dominated the front page of the *New York Times*.[67] The article reported the following:

> One summer evening in 2011, three white prison guards (who weighed 240 pounds, 300 pounds, and 260 pounds) entered the cell of a black inmate named George Williams (170 pounds), ordered him to strip for a search, and when he had done so, walked him out to a darkened dayroom for what they said would be a urine test. They apparently believed that he had earlier shouted obscenities at them after the inmates had been locked in their cells for the night, though other inmates would later say that the guards took the wrong man.
>
> A punch to the ribs knocked Williams to the floor. Trying to protect himself, he doubled up as the three burly officers struck his head and body with their fists, boots, and stout wooden batons. One of them jumped on his ankle, causing him to scream in pain. He saw another draw back a leg to kick him in the head. He thought he was going to die. Inmates in nearby cells saw all this and heard him screaming and begging for his life as the guards continued to pound his flesh and bones. Other officers rushed in, not to stop the orgy, but to join it.[68]
>
> When they ceased, Williams, whose ankle was broken, could not walk. They handcuffed him and dragged him to the top of a staircase, where one of them ordered him to walk down or he'd be pushed. He said he couldn't walk. They pushed him and he landed on his shoulder at the

bottom. They picked him up and rammed his face into the wall, splattering his blood across it.

They tried to put the badly injured man into the Box, the prison's solitary confinement unit, but the guard in charge of it said, "We can't take him in here looking like that," and directed them to take him to the infirmary. There a nurse named Katherine Tara, who had been working at Attica for only ten months, saw his injuries and the blood on his mouth and clothing. He told her that his vision was blurry and he thought some ribs were broken. Having treated other "use of force" cases, Tara considered this one excessive and insisted that he be sent to an outside hospital. The prison doctor concurred. Doctors at the nearby Warsaw hospital saw that his injuries were more severe than they could treat and sent him on to a larger facility in Buffalo. The doctors there found that Williams had suffered a severely fractured left eye socket, a broken shoulder, several cracked ribs, two broken legs, one of which required a plate and six screws to realign it, and numerous cuts and bruises. There was a large amount of blood in one of his sinuses. The doctors were able to save his left eye.

Back at the prison, inmates said, the guards had them clean up a large amount of Williams' blood and take a bag of bloody shirts out to a courtyard to be burned in the officers' barbecue pit. The guards officially reported that Williams had had a weapon hidden in his underwear, a razor blade (which another inmate said he saw a guard break out of a plastic razor), but a subsequent investigation failed to find any of Williams' DNA on the blade. One of the C.O.'s reportedly took home several batons, an act that violated prison rules, sanded Williams' blood off them, and refinished them.

Williams said of Nurse Tara, "She was a blessing. If she hadn't of [sic] said I needed a surgeon, I would have been dead."

The Corrections Department's Inspector General and the State Police investigated, though of the fifteen guards whom the latter tried to interview, eleven refused. Several inmates, fearing retribution, also refused to talk to investigators (or to the *Times*' reporter) until they were transferred to other prisons. In December of 2011, a Grand Jury sitting in Warsaw—how well I remember that redbrick courthouse—indicted the three guards on charges of gang-assault in the first degree, a Class B felony that carries a sentence of five to twenty-five years in prison. Other felony charges against them included conspiracy, filing false reports, and tampering with evidence.

These indictments were unprecedented—the first time, according to officials, that criminal charges had been brought against prison guards for non-sexual assault. The inmates were reportedly astonished, not by what the guards had done to Williams, but by the official efforts to hold guards accountable. The guards and their union fought the prosecution with the sort of bluster and hyperbola that the State Police union had used in 1974 when my office seemed likely to indict troopers. Loyalty before law. But the Corrections Commissioner had referred the case to the prosecutors because, he said, the "beat-down" of Williams was the worst one he knew about during his time in office and, "It was clear to me that a number of officers had acted together."

The *Times'* reporter met with Williams in a restaurant in New Jersey in November 2014 and saw that Williams' left eye was more sunken than his right eye and he was continually dabbing his nose as a result of the damage the guards had inflicted on his sinuses. One leg bothered him continuously. He said he suffered headaches, nightmares, and had much difficulty sleeping. Like so many of the inmates whom law officers savaged in 1971, he had been diagnosed with PTSD.

"This is awful," I thought on reading the article. It could have been Judge Telesca's 503rd synopsis: same Attica, same barbarity, four decades later. But except for a whiff of affinity with the nurse who spoke up, I felt that this latest Attica horror story has nothing to do with me . . .

Until I read in the *Times* two days later that as the felony trial of the three guards was about to begin, they all copped pleas to a single misdemeanor under which they would (a) quit their jobs and never work as prison guards again, (b) serve no time in jail, and (c) keep their pensions.

Déjà vu! This was nearly the same impunity that the law officer criminals had enjoyed in the 1970s. Williams called the deal "crazy." Many called it worse. Former state senator and Attica riot Observer John Dunne said: "It's a terrible indictment of the system. If defenseless people can't find justice in New York's legal system, who can expect them to believe in it?" Once again privilege trumped justice at Attica.

The prosecutors allowed that they had had a powerful case; they rightly claimed that it was a victory to move even as far as they had against felonious guards; but they said it would be hard to win a jury verdict against correction officers in rural, white Wyoming County, in which prison employees abound.[69] One of them even acknowledged that the case had "never been about jail for these officers."[70] All the same, I was clear that the prosecutors should have put the case to a jury. What did they have to lose since, if the report of their conduct was close to accurate, these guards should never be allowed to work in a prison again even if they had not been prosecuted? These slaps on their wrists told the world that maiming and nearly killing an inmate was trivial. If the trial jury convicted them, justice would finally have triumphed. Even if the jury acquitted them, other guards would still know that such barbarity could put them in serious trouble, maybe even in prison. I have long hoped, perhaps in vain, that the failed prosecution that followed the turkey shoot had a deterrent effect on at least some of the State Police.

It was absurd but true that pressing criminal charges against three corrections officers as far as it went could honestly be called a victory. A follow-up editorial in the *Times* put it simply: "The guards should have gone to prison." After citing official claims that guards were currently "using less force against inmates"—less force than what, it did not say—the editorial noted that inmates reported that "some guards still commit unchecked violence and then justify savage beatings by concocting false charges of inmate misconduct." It concluded, "The attack on Mr. Williams shows that there are still deep problems at Attica." Problems, I would add, not only with violence against inmates, but also with the impunity that encourages such violence, and with the notion of enforcing the same justice for everybody. At least in this case, nobody died—probably thanks to two people who did the right thing, the guard at the Box and Nurse Tara.

After thinking about all this for a while, I phoned Sergeant Mark Cunningham, who was by now one of the most senior C.O.'s at the prison, and asked him for his take on the reports about the attack on Williams. He had not been aware of any such incident at the time, he said, and if he had come upon one, he would have broken it up. When an inmate assaults a guard, he explained, "We do what we have to do, but after the inmate is under control, we don't touch him." He said, too, that sick and injured inmates were often sent to hospitals outside the prison. I have no reason to doubt Mark Cunningham, who I believe has served the people of New York long and well; and after talking with Gary Horton about the Williams case, I have no reason to doubt the account of it in the *Times*. As to the Williams case, the near impunity of those guards shows that injustice may occur without prosecutorial misconduct. Sometimes bad judgment is merely bad judgment.

This horrifying glimpse behind the walls of today's Attica illustrates a point I reported regarding the Forgotten Victims, namely, that unlike the decent cops and firefighters whom everyone sees doing their dangerous jobs for the rest of us, decent prison guards like Mark Cunningham work out of sight, usually out of mind, and often for too little pay. Instead, we hear about guards who, by brutalizing inmates, degrade the public's opinion of their calling. I hope the account of the Forgotten Victims in this epilogue, as well as Don Jelinek's *Attica Justice* and Heather Thompson's *Blood in the Water*,[71] will help to improve people's perceptions of prison guards.

VII

While much of the unwarranted shooting on the fatal September thirteenth, being indiscriminate, claimed victims both black and white, it was evident that race hate and/or fear pulled many police triggers and that the retaking of Attica was a race riot by certain police. Indeed, it is a paradigm for the too-frequent instances in which law officers get away with unjustifiably gunning down black men and boys. Then the officers make up stories like the Attica shooters' BCI statements, which, however feeble, usually result in impunity. Rights groups have long sought to end these unpunished murders, manslaughters, and criminally negligent homicides; recently the Black Lives Matter movement has joined the effort. Black lives plainly did not matter to the troopers at Attica who bragged, "Got me a nigger," and too many police have still failed to free themselves from such homicidal racism.

While black males are the main victims of this racism, the police are also victims. There were decent troopers at Attica—you have met some in this book—but they ever after bore the opprobrium created by brother officers who perpetrated the wanton killing and racist crowing. People wondered about *any* trooper who participated at Attica—leading to questions like that of the young man who wondered, "Is my Dad a murderer?" Today many decent police experience the hatred, fear, distrust, or simply the dislike that racist officers provoke.

And police officers sometimes experience worse. In apparent revenge for the killings of unarmed black men, women, and children, certain black men have murdered randomly chosen police officers, giving rise to "Blue Lives Matter." Both kinds of homicide are obviously inexcusable, and the perpetrators belong in prison. And as Jelani Cobb has noted, "if the killing of an officer carries wider social implications, a killing at the hands of an officer does, too."[72]

When grand jurors decline to indict a cop for shooting someone, I often wonder whether the prosecutor presented the case to them properly. Given grand jury secrecy, we can't usually find out. But the mutual dependence of police and prosecutors in doing their work, and the propolice bias of many prosecutors, are evident in this book and other sources. Using independent prosecutors is probably the best way to assure that such cases will be properly presented. Which is the last thing that many people seem to want.

At Attica the authorities barred the Observers from observing the retaking, and the State Police operated (or not) the only cameras. Today police board and body cameras and the cell phone cameras of onlookers have occasionally made unwarranted homicides harder for cops to get away with; but there is apparently little or no lessening of the problem of prosecutors who won't seek justice dispassionately against their partners in law enforcement. Clearly we need more cameras as well as independent prosecutors, and an end to racism—or, realistically, far less of it. Then, perhaps, more black men will survive to love and be loved by their grandchildren, decent police will no longer be tarred with the brush of their barbaric fellow officers, and all of us will live in a more civilized society.

To sum up: When the State Police rampaged through Attica on that wet Monday morning, the racism that seethes beneath the surface of much American life burst out like pus from a boil. The racism seeped out more broadly though less violently as white supremacists and other hate groups burgeoned across the land during the years of our first black President.[73] And so America continues to pay the price for its vast sin of kidnapping and enslaving millions of Africans, paying unto the third and fourth generation and then some. It's easier said than done, apparently, to understand that we are all God's children—or for nonbelievers, that everyone is a human being—and that those black and white bodies bleeding on the catwalks were as human as you and I and the cops who shot them and the cops who held their fire.

VIII

For the Forgotten Victims' memorial service on the forty-fifth anniversary of their tragedy, the grass outside the prison was as green, the air as warm, and the sun as bright as they had been at the memorial service five years earlier, but there were no thunderheads in the sky, and fewer people were sitting in the open-sided tent across the lawn from the candles that flickered in red glass jars, the photos of the eleven men being remembered, and the granite monument that bore their names. Of the thirty-two hostages who had survived the retaking, twenty-three had now died, and many of their children were in their fifties and sixties.

I was the first person to speak that afternoon and I was angry. After the State sacrificed those eleven men, I said, it swindled the surviving hostages and all their families "with a cruelty and deceitfulness that I find incomprehensible."[74] Then a challenge:

If New York State ever owed an apology to anyone, it is to you Forgotten Victims. For Governor Andrew Cuomo . . . I have one word: apologize! If a great-hearted person like Abraham Lincoln were governor today, we know that he would apologize in a heartbeat. If Governor Cuomo is half the man that Lincoln was, he *will* apologize. Not only for your sake but for the honor of New York and for his own honor, he will say the simple yet profound words, "I apologize!"

Jonathan Gradess, the Forgotten Victims' cocounsel, speaking next, reminded us that he and I had asked for the apology five years ago to no effect; he, too, renewed the call for it now. Mike Smith read a touching poem that he had written about the death of his friend, hostage John D'Archangelo, and the State's refusal to admit that it had wronged anybody. Most moving for my wife, Nancy, me, and, I'm sure, many others were the words of Kent Monteleone, the fifty-two-year-old son of hostage John Monteleone, whom another correction officer had shot dead. It was Kent's first talk in public, though he sounded wholly at ease.

He and his mother and her other children, he said, had rarely spoken about the riot or his dad's death. Those events, which broke over him when he was seven, had aroused an anger that he carried within him for years. "I had thought I was the only one who had the feelings I had," he said, but when the Forgotten Victims came together in 2000, he met other people who had locked in the same emotions. Only then did he and a close friend from high school discover that both of their fathers had been hostages. Talking about the loss of his dad, Kent said, has brought him great peace.[75]

We have seen how deeply the murder of her father marked Dee Quinn Miller, who led the Forgotten Victims and organized today's memorial service. And how deeply what I will call the murder of Sam Melville marked his son Josh, who has written a book about his father's life and death called *American Timebomb*. And how deeply the death of Elliot Barkley marked his sister Tracee. Many if not most of the loved ones of the men who died by the law officers' guns were, I suppose, deeply marked.

Mixed with the solemn service at the prison that day came the good news that the Attorney General's office had created a website called "The Attica Uprising and Aftermath: Selected Documents from the Office of the Attorney General."[76] At last that office had begun the disgorgement of its Attica files; it said that more files would be posted. Papers such as grand jury transcripts, most of the Meyer Report, and my confidential report to Governor Carey would of course remain suppressed. The suppression, though, had become a bit less galling since Heather Thompson's *Blood in the Water*, which appeared the previous month, quoted liberally from many of these papers, which she had managed to access in spite of their being suppressed.

For that day's *Democrat and Chronicle*, longtime Attica reporter Gary Craig had written an aptly titled article, "Dr. John Edland: An Attica riot hero and victim," about his ordeal and that of his family in Rochester and the life they made for themselves after they left in 1977.[77] Jack and his wife Gwen, for instance, had allowed their three little girls to walk to school unaccompanied because that was America back then, but not to answer the home telephone because anonymous voices would utter obscenities or death threats at any hour of the day or night. Anonymous letters arrived at the house too, saying, for instance, "May your throat be slashed and violence come upon you and your family."

"I specifically remember the phone ringing and my mother hanging up abruptly, saying someone is calling to harass us," the Edlands' eldest daughter, Gretchen Edland Perry, told Gary Craig. All the girls had been younger than ten years old when the verbal assaults began.

When my son Brian and I visited the Edlands in 1976 (as described in chapter 37), I had known that the abuse had driven Jack into depression and sometimes to drink, but I did not sense what he had been through emotionally or know that he had recently spent six months in the Institute of Living, a psychiatric hospital in Hartford, Connecticut, where Gwen and the girls would make the long drive across New York to visit him.

After the Edlands left Rochester, Jack's life became more settled. He joined the faculty of Vanderbilt University in Nashville, Tennessee; in 1981 he became a dean at Creighton University in Omaha, Nebraska. He refused to be an expert witness for prosecutors, but he would offer his help without charge to criminal defendants who might need his medical expertise. "I'm no longer interested in the state's case," he explained in 1981, "because it seems they have so much power and the poor little guy on the other end who, though he may be guilty, ultimately has not much going for him."

Gwen, who is now eighty-two, said that after Jack died in 1991, she never wanted to remarry, and she didn't. Instead, she became a nurse who traveled to some seventy-seven countries doing Christian missionary work. Of Jack she said, "In spite of difficulties, he always looked after his family well and made sure they received a good education." She called him "one of my heroes who could not be bought off."

The Edlands' three daughters are all married and have children. Gretchen teaches the violin and plays it professionally in and near Huntsville, Alabama. Gretel Rowland is a nurse practitioner in the Tennessee community where her mother has now settled down. Gaele Craig teaches in Elkhorn, Nebraska.

Gary Craig put me in touch with Gretchen, and we had two long, pleasant conversations on the phone. She remembered the "Evel Knievel" bikes they had in Rochester but not riding around on them with Brian during our 1976 visit. I told her that her dad was one of my heroes, and she said I had been one of his. That was nice to hear, and interesting because what he and I both did was to do our jobs and say what we had to, though we knew that the men who ran the State required a different version of the facts. I guess his message was more displeasing than mine for people who make anonymous verbal assaults. It is a tribute to American freedoms that neither he nor I went to prison for what we did.

There is a detail that I found very moving yet hesitated to include here until Gretchen said she hoped I would. On Labor Day of 1987, Jack wrote in her copy of this book, "This is family history. It explains me. I hope it helps you understand why it all happened. Love, Dad."

Though Gretchen was always interested in the Attica tragedy, she began to delve into it seriously in her early twenties and came to appreciate her father's rare and quiet nobility. She wished to talk with him about those events but sensed that, while the pain never left him, he was reluctant to discuss the trauma that had shattered his life—the vengeance of those who wished to delude the public and those who wished to remain deluded. "I think he was at peace knowing he did the right thing. But . . . the consequences and ramifications of what he did, I think that was always with him."

And so innocent people and their children and grandchildren continue to pay a price—some more, some less—for Nelson Rockefeller's premature, self-serving, and craven decision to abandon words and turn to guns at Attica. But at least he did not become President and then launch needless wars that killed thousands in Panama or hundreds of thousands in Iraq or millions in Southeast Asia. There have been worse sinners than Nelson Rockefeller, though this fact does not absolve him of his sins at Attica.

IX

Were the often racist violence that ended the Attica uprising, and the corruption of justice that followed, merely aberrations that we may perhaps lament and then forget? Or are they paradigms that shed light on a dark side of the American way? A major reason for the enduring interest in the Attica rebellion and its aftermath, I believe, is the degree to which they exemplify broad issues that existed in the 1970s and remain current today. Attica, for all its complexity, presents a microcosm of much that besets America. Tom Wicker's book *A Time to Die* (1975) and Heather Ann Thompson's *Blood in the Water* (2016) address our nation's cruel and counterproductive prison system. Don Jelinek's *Attica Justice* (2011) addresses both the prison system and the justice system that sends people there. As you have seen, this book touches on inequalities in U.S. justice on page 362, and Chapter 43 addresses several other issues.

Since the book was first published, I have come increasingly to believe that the issue it illuminates most glaringly is the gulf between the justice accorded the privileged and the rest. The story of the Attica cover-up is, above all, a demonstration of who gets impunity and who does not. Recall the BCI detective who said he never expected the State Police to be prosecuted over the turkey shoot because of the "brotherhood of the police."[78] Their guns and expectations of impunity gave those officers liberty to exercise the power of life and death over men they hated, despised, or merely looked down on; we have seen that while many officers restrained themselves, many did not, and no one paid the price that the law and equal justice demand, as the State officials who arranged impunity for the guilty law officers also arranged it for themselves.

In a recent example that is far larger than Attica, prosecutorial discretion not to proceed against well-placed transgressors has given de facto impunity to nearly all the financial manipulators whose crimes played a major part in devastating the U.S. economy in 2008 and forcing thousands of families out of their homes. Pulitzer Prize-winning reporter and columnist Jesse Eisinger has reported that whereas the savings-and-loan scandals of the 1980s led to the prosecution of 1,100 people "including top executives of many of the largest failed banks" and the conviction of 839 of them, the recent financial meltdown has led to the conviction of only one Wall Street executive.[79]

Nobel Prize-winning economist Paul Krugman similarly observed that the financial schemes that led to the 2008 crash "in many cases amounted to outright fraud—and it is an outrage that basically nobody ended up being punished for those sins aside from innocent bystanders, namely the millions of workers who lost their jobs and the millions of families that lost their homes."[80] In short, the impunity of the privileged that followed the crash was Attica writ large.

There are at least three ways to enjoy impunity for one's crimes: not get caught: not be prosecuted; and secure the decriminalization of one's heinous conduct, often by deploying money and influence. Refusals to prosecute apparently account for only part of the impunity of many perpetrators of the 2008 financial crisis. In addition, the pertinent laws and regulations had become curiously forgiving of much of their predatory conduct. Writing in the *New Yorker*, Nicholas Lehman went so far as to say that "little-noticed changes in laws and regulations were far more important in causing the 2008 crash than was law-breaking by the heads of the financial industry . . . . As [former Congressman] Barney Frank . . . said when I spoke to him, 'A lot of that shit was legal!'"[81]

In chapter 41, I alluded to what I believe to be a particularly breathtaking failure to prosecute—or even to talk about prosecuting—certain privileged people for committing mass murder for profit. I mean the cigarette executives who have marketed their wares, knowing that cigarettes kill while insisting that they don't, thereby luring vast numbers of Americans to addiction and death. Such people clearly belong in prison if anyone does, and I believe they could be sent there under the various state murder statutes that are akin to the New York reckless endangerment statute (discussed in Chapter 10) under which, in 1974 and 1975, the Attica Investigation began to prosecute several dozen perpetrators of the turkey shoot.[82]

The New York statute is Penal Law Section 125.25, which says, "A person is guilty of murder in the second degree when . . . [u]nder circumstances evincing a depraved indifference to human life, he recklessly engages in conduct which creates a grave risk of death to another person, and thereby causes the death of another person."

"Cigarette smoking causes about one of every five deaths in the United States each year," according to the Centers for Disease Control and Prevention (the CDC), which means more than 480,000 Americans each year or close to five million Americans a decade.[83] It is not the fully informed free choice of smokers that produces this horror. Rather, the people who run the tobacco companies have for decades hidden and denied the facts, deceived and lied to the public about this fatal addiction, and even doctored their products to *increase* their power to addict—all for profit. What could be more "reckless" and "depraved" than pushing a deadly poison into the hands and lungs of millions of people while intentionally deceiving them about the risk?

Federal Judge Gladys Kessler aptly wrote, in a suit for civil damages, that cigarette makers "have marketed and sold their lethal products with zeal, with deception, with a single-minded focus on their financial success, and without regard for the human tragedy or social costs that success exacted."[84]

Sending these respectable merchants of death to prison for life would, one hopes, cause their companies to collapse—who would want to step into their shoes and thence into their cells?—and discourage people from importing of these lethal drugs. Since cigarettes currently kill nearly half a million Americans a year, consider the number of lives that such law enforcement could save.

Would these prosecutions succeed? I believe they should, though I'm not certain they would. It seems, though, that given the amount of suffering and death at stake and the obvious justice of such law enforcement, they are surely worth attempting. But given the ease with which Big Money influences government actions and the extent to which states and stockholders currently benefit from the blood money of Big Tobacco's profits, the likelihood remains that these prosecutions will not be brought. At least Judge Kessler, like Judge Telesca, let the sun shine in upon the filthy conduct of privileged killers who lied and connived to cover up their crimes.

Addressing our unequal justice generally, Senator Elizabeth Warren wrote in 2016 that

> Corporate criminals routinely escape meaningful prosecution for their misconduct . . . . Justice cannot mean a prison sentence for a teenager who steals a car, but nothing more than a sideways glance at a C.E.O. who quietly engineers the theft of billions of dollars.[85]

Senator Warren might as well have been writing about the man I called Daltry who got four years in Attica for stealing a box of tools.[86] Jeffrey Reiman and Paul Leighton summed it all up in the title of their book *The Rich Get Richer and The Poor Get Prison.*[87]

And what happens when the poor get to prison? Underlying the story of the turkey shoot, we may still glimpse the vast failure of the American penal system. Since the Attica rebellion, the number of people serving time in state prisons has risen more than 700 percent, at an average cost now of more than $31,000 per inmate per year; this huge jump is due far less to any increase in crime than to harsher penalties.[88] The tough-on-crime approach, which enthralls so many sincere Americans and demagogues alike, does keep many people who have committed crimes (along with quite a few who have not) off the streets; but nearly all prisoners get out under a system that makes it very hard for them to then earn an honest living. We Americans spend more and more of our tax dollars on the luxury of keeping our counterproductive prisons the most expensive and populous in the world in both total numbers and as a proportion of our population. Instead of preparing prisoners to succeed, nearly all U.S. prisons prepare them to fail.

Tom Wicker epitomized the uphill quest for prison reform when he wrote in 1994:

> For years, I seized every opportunity to speak and write about the need for changes in the squalid and inhumane U.S. prison system, for a measure of rationality in the treatment of offenders in America . . . . I long ago concluded . . . that my small personal crusade was in vain—that prison reform, in fact, was the most hopeless social cause this side of gun control. The fear of crime was and remains so great in this country that people are not only willing but anxious to 'lock 'em up and throw away the key.' That the dollar cost of this policy is insanely high, while its social purpose of reducing the incidence of crime has abjectly failed, seems to a fearful citizenry to be irrelevant.[89]

Now, more than twenty years after Tom Wicker wrote these words, there seems to be gathering recognition—though not yet enough—among some of America's leaders that he and other reformers have been right all along. According to most reports, this belated common sense is motivated mainly by a hope, not of reducing needless human misery, but of saving money.

The privilege that too often trumps justice throughout our society seems to arise from at least three factors: wealth, position, political clout, or some combination thereof. Regarding Attica, the State Police, the corrections officers, and Louis Lefkowitz had position and clout. Nelson Rockefeller, of course, had all three.

A necessity that permits improper impunity to occur (much impunity is not improper) is that prosecutors have, *and must have*, wide discretion about whom to go after and how far to proceed. The classic example is giving immunity to the little fish in a criminal enterprise in order to catch the big fish—as Tony Simonetti and I decided to do while the Hindering Prosecution case was still on track. While our laws and practices keep a reasonably tight rein on what prosecutors may do, they enjoy large and often unchallengeable discretion over what they choose *not* to do. Whatever else the Attica cover-up was, it was an egregious though far from unique exercise of prosecutorial discretion not to do a job that needed doing. When a prosecutor says, "I don't have enough evidence," who besides an insider like me has enough information to challenge this official claim? Who knew enough to show, as I hope I have shown, that the Attica prosecution was worse than inept? Or to challenge the solemn but untrue claim of the Meyer Report that all the officials who aborted the prosecution of police crimes had no intention to obstruct the pursuit of justice?

Here, incidentally, is another way that Attica changed me: As I wrote (or almost wrote) in chapter 2, I originally sought a job in a prosecutor's office in order to learn how to be a criminal defense lawyer. Paradoxically perhaps, that was a common way to receive the training one needs for this practice, which is more complex than people often suppose. But if I had it to do over, I might well become a career prosecutor. I learned in law school and still believe that a prosecutor wins as surely when an innocent person goes free as when a guilty person goes to prison. Too many prosecutors, though, seek simply to convict suspects.

One may reasonably suppose that the advent of actual equal justice would precipitate swift, sure penal reform. If privileged people who commit crimes were convicted as surely, sentenced as harshly, and sent to an Attica (instead of a minimum security camp) as regularly as other people, then isn't it likely that the levers of power would be pulled, sentences would shrink, prison conditions would improve, recidivism would decline, and a large blemish would vanish from America's image in the world? We can't know the answer of course unless really equal justice arrives, and what is the likelihood of that?

Inscribed over the front entrance to the Supreme Court of the United States are the words "Equal Justice Under Law." We Americans are said to strive for this ideal. Though I strove for it and I hope some of you will, too, a lesson of this book—or of reading a daily newspaper—is that privileged people too often avoid equal justice. No one is above the law? Only if we insist.

It is said that we are called not to be successful, but to be faithful. It was not their success or failure in achieving justice, but their quests for justice that enno-bled people as different from one another as Elizabeth Fink, Frank Big Black Smith, Akil Al-Jundi, Lenny Brown, Deanne Quinn Miller, Gary Horton, Michael Smith, Donald Jelinek, Jonathan Gradess, and Judge Michael Telesca.

The pursuit of justice helped me and it can help you, if it hasn't already. If there were more justice in our society, there would be less need for justice in our courts and less need for our Atticas to exist. It is true today, as it was back when I wrote it in Chapter 1, that preventable tragedies such as those that occurred at Attica will cease, it seems, only as America understands them and in its decency cries out, Enough!

Notes

Author's Note

1. Memorandum of Law in Support of Attorney General's Motion to Renew, dated October 13, 2013, *In the Matter of Carey*, New York Supreme Court, Wyoming County, Index No. 15062. This motion is discussed in epilogue, part IV.
2. In contrast, Professor Heather Ann Thompson considered it her duty as a historian to publish the names of quite a few Attica suspects in her book *Blood in the Water* even though she knew this would "reopen many old wounds and cause much new suffering." Each viewpoint had its adherent, and *USA Today*, the *New York Times*, and other media duly reported the controversy during the summer of 2016.

1. The Challenges

1. Quoted from historian Robert Perkinson, *Texas Tough: The Rise of America's Prison Empire* (New York: Metropolitan Books, 2010), p. 302.
2. *New York Times*, September 14, 1971, p. 30; September 17, 1971, p. 31. Deputy Director of Corrections Walter Dunbar called the retaking an "efficient, affirmative police action." *Times*, September 14, 1971, p. 1.
3. *Attica: The Official Report of the New York State Special Commission on Attica* (Westport, CT: Praeger Publishers, 1972; paper, New York: Bantam Books, 1972) (hereafter cited as the McKay Report, for its chairman, former Dean Robert B. McKay of New York University Law School), photo no. 29 after p. 248.

2. "An Honest Prosecution"

1. The quotations in this book are either verbatim or else very close paraphrases taken from notes or my clear recollections. That is why there are comparatively few of them. It is possible that some statements, particularly by State Police, that were made to me in conversation also turn up in their secret grand jury testimony. If so, the latter do not bar me from reporting the former.

4. Lawmen Restore Order

1. Calling the riot a "riot" is for many people a political act. It connotes the System, the Establishment, neutrality, or indifference. Better for them is "uprising," "insurrection," "revolt," or "rebellion." Using those terms is equally a political act for people who think in terms of political acts—such thinking itself being a political act, and so on. I stay with "riot" because, since the event did not start according to a plan,

it seems the most neutral descriptive word ("event" being nondescriptive and "incident" being nondescriptive and perhaps belittling), and it is the easiest to type.

2. Captain Anthony Malovich, in conversation with the author outside the grand jury room in 1974.
3. McKay Report, p. 140.
4. Ibid.
5. Charles "Flip" Crowley, quoted in Tom Wicker, *A Time to Die* (New York: Quadrangle/The New York Times Book Co., 1975), p. 97
6. McKay Report, p. 293.
7. McKay Report, p. 367.
8. New York Penal Law, Section 35.30.
9. McKay Report, p. 357.
10. Wicker, p. 272.
11. Investigator Lenny Brown and I tried for a long time one night to count the shots on the soundtrack of the A Roof videotape, replaying it, slowing it down, etc. Each time through the tape we came out with numbers that differed noticeably from each other's and from our own previous counts. Many shots came in clusters, and the echoes off the cellblock walls multiplied the problems. And a clear echo could be louder than a muffled shot.

5. "You Will Not Be Harmed"

1. All of the direct quotations in this chapter, except the one by Russell Oswald, appear in chapter 18 of the McKay Report.
2. Russell G. Oswald, *Attica—My Own Story* (New York: Doubleday & Company, Inc., 1972), p. 289.
3. The McKay Report states, p. 454, that hundreds of inmates filed claims for their personal belongings lost in A Block, but since their claims were notarized only once rather than in quadruplicate (the notary at Attica being a guard), Attorney General Lefkowitz's office elected to treat them "as a nullity" and relented only months later after protests from Legal Aid and others.
4. Members of the Ohio National Guard shot four students dead at Kent State University in May 1970. People sometimes confuse the shooters at Kent State and Attica. At Attica, they fired ten times as many shots, killed ten times as many people, and were *not* National Guardsmen.
5. McKay Report, photo no. 29 after p. 248.

6. *Programmed to Fail?*

1. Inmate attorney Donald Jelinek told me that he calculated this figure of 1,289 crimes; and since no one else mustered the energy to challenge it, the figure acquired a life of its own.
2. Robert B. McKay, "Attica: The Anatomy of an Investigation," 49 Chicago-Kent L. Rev. 139, 147 (1972).
3. I had two other inmate cases besides Indictment No. 10, but since the defendant in each remained at large, I never got into them. One of the Indictment No. 10

defendants was Thomas Hagen, who had been convicted along with two other men of killing Malcolm X. That made him somewhat anathema to the Attica Brothers Legal Defense, many of whom considered Malcolm X a hero. All three of the men convicted maintained that Hagen was the only one of them who was guilty. Hagen also said that his name was Hayer and "Hagen" resulted from careless record keeping that officials refused to correct.

4. I have changed the names of a few people who do not need this book in their lives. Daltry is one of them.

7."Much Unnecessary Shooting"

1. McKay Report, p. xxxix.
2. On p. 402.
3. Heinz Guderian, *Panzer Leader* (New York: Ballantine Books, 1972), p. 53.
4. McKay Report, pp. 385–386.
5. It has never been established where all of the dead were located when they received their fatal bullets.
6. McKay Report, p. 393.
7. See chapter 18; see also McKay Report, p. 324

8. What Evidence?

1. McKay Report, p. 374. Judge Robert M. Quigley put the number of accounted-for shotgun pellets at between 2,349 and 3,132, in *Jones v. State*, N.Y. Ct. of Claims, Claim No. 54555, decision dated August 31, 1982, p. 52.
2. E.g., *New York Times*, September 14, 1971, p. 1.
3. McKay Report, p. 459.
4. New York Penal Law, Secs. 205.50–205.65.

9. Report But Not Prosecute?

1. *Report of the 1970 Grand Jury*, U.S.D.C., ND. IL, E.D., 1970.
2. In fact, this fear proved to have some substance, as described in chapter 39.
3. We assumed that we would not be hampered by the rules against disclosing grand jury secrets, since we had the same information before it reached the jury.

10. Behold a Handle of Justice

1. See Lee B. Kennett and James LaVerne Anderson, *The Gun in America, The Origins of a National Dilemma* (Westport, CT: Greenwood Press, 1975), pp. 137–138.
2. *Jones v. State*, 352 N.Y.S. 2d 169 (N.Y. 12/27/73).
3. New York Penal Law, Sec. 120.25.
4. New York Penal Law, Sec. 120.20 makes reckless endangerment in the second degree a class A misdemeanor. The differences are that the defendant need only have acted "recklessly," not with "a depraved indifference to human life"; and the risk he creates need only be "a substantial risk of serious physical injury," not "a grave risk of death." At the Investigation we considered that the use of firearms and other factors at Attica made reckless endangerment in the first degree the likely crime (the

opposing memo writer dissenting), so I have not discussed reckless endangerment in the second degree beyond this note.

5. I was never convinced that throwing a spear up at a catwalk justified a fatal shotgun blast. After all, if the inmate had thrown it, he had thereby disarmed himself. So far as I know, no officer at Attica ever claimed to have received the slightest injury from any of these crude devices.

6. *People v. Graham*, 342 N.Y.S. 2d 361 (2d Dept. 1973).

7. *People v. Nixon*, 309 N.Y.S. 2d 236 (3rd Dept. 1970).

8. 238 N.Y. 188, 192 (1924).

9. New York Penal Law, Sec. 125.25 (2); McKinney's Consolidated Laws of New York, Practice Commentaries (by Arnold Hechtman), at page 399.

10. New York Penal Law, Sec. 35.30.

11. Several troopers admitted firing blindly into holes, then changed their stories to say they fired into the ground in front of the hole. As prosecutors we were free to use either or both versions against those troopers. The opposing memo writer was apparently willing to consider only the "corrected" version.

12. McKinney's, p.117.

13. Delineators are the metal stakes that go along the edge of the highway to show the snowplow driver where to go; inmates made them in the metal shop at Attica.

14. New York Penal Law, Sec. 265.35 (4). (Subd. (4) was changed to (3) in 1974.) This is the "prohibited use of weapon, a class A misdemeanor," referred to in the first quoted paragraph of my memo.

12. Trouble Ahead?

1. Memorandum, dated September 4, 1973, from Investigators Al Gonzales and Bill Blackford to Tony Simonetti.

13. A Proper Grand Jury

1. This information has been disclosed by others.

2. The Appellate Division, Fourth Department, which is the intermediate court of general jurisdiction in New York, the Court of Appeals in Albany being the highest, and the Supreme Courts of the various counties being the lowest. In New York, at least, the term "Supreme Court" is a bit misleading.

3. The judge also discussed with us a New York statute, CPL § 190.20(6), which permits grand jurors "impaneled at the same court term" to be transferred back and forth from one jury to another "for a good cause." Could we ask someone from the second jury to complete a quorum on the first? That puzzled us. We never tried it.

4. Rochester Democrat & Chronicle, April 17, 1974, pp. Al, A3.

14. Cases against Shooters

1. Given on June 28, 1978, at the request of Michael Kennedy, Esq., as part of his legal effort to get Dacajeweiah (John Hill) out of prison after all other Attica defendants had been dismissed or pardoned. See chapter 41.

2. The case against Trooper B is the one described at the start of chapter 9. The first jury's votes on Trooper B have previously been disclosed. Since no officers except Gregory Wildridge have ever been formally charged, I do not think it right for me to identify them by name, no matter how guilty I consider them.
3. I have long since forgotten which was the first.
4. See chapter 21.
5. See chapter 15.
6. See chapter 16.

15. The Grand Jury Hits Its Stride

1. What the shooters personally told our investigators was admissible in evidence as admissions, such "admissions against interest" being a common exception to the hearsay rule, which generally excludes secondhand communications from evidence. Our investigators also showed the troopers copies of their BCI statements and asked them whether they had signed them. Of course the troopers had to say yes. That further admission entitled our investigators to put those BCI statements into evidence, even though they had not been present when the BCI detectives took them.
2. The McKay Report (p. 505) does not show Michael Smith as having received any injuries at all on the thirteenth.

16. The Cases Build

1. Tony did not want them asking the questions directly, since they might not ask them in admissible form. I made it a practice to check after I'd asked the jurors questions to be sure I'd covered what they wanted me to.
2. Some of the troopers declined to follow the State Police's obstructive practice of not talking with us outside the jury, a help to us and credit to them.
3. That photo somehow always looked strange. It showed Lieutenant Joseph Christian lying on the ground with tents and parts of the Hostage Circle behind, as I now recall it, but something about it may not have been right. I would not put it past the State Police to have put together a composite in order to locate Christian in line with the Official Version, given the other things they did about Attica; but I do conclude on the basis of other evidence that Christian lay where the photo shows him.
4. McKay Report (pp. 391–393) notes but does not resolve some Christian mysteries. McKay's perception differs somewhat from mine. For example, it cites Lieutenant Christian as saying that he crossed D Yard far out front; but so far as I am aware, Christian did not look back so could not know this. Perhaps he had been told and was reporting the Official Version of where the other troopers were. And add this to the Christian mystery: the *New York Times* of September 16, 1971 (p. 48), reports that "a state trooper said that a fellow trooper had been shot . . . in Cellblock D. 'But he didn't mind because there was a nigger on top of him,' the trooper said casually." Christian was the only trooper shot, so "Cellblock D" had to mean D Yard. Hicks was a black. Were Christian, Hicks, and hostages in the Circle shotgunned *after* Hicks was down?

5. McKay Report (p. 403) notes that the trooper said that "fellow officers [encouraged them] to embellish their accounts of inmate activity."
6. See pp. 187–188, below, concerning "waivers of immunity."
7. McKay Report, pp. 397–398.
8. Quoted in *Life*, October 1, 1971, p. 28.
9. Quoted in Annette T. Rubinstein, *Attica, 1971–1975* (The New York Charter Group for a Pledge of Conscience, 1975), p. 4.

17. The August Switch

1. Joseph E. Persico, *The Imperial Rockefeller: A Biography of Nelson A. Rockefeller* (New York: Simon and Schuster, 1982), p. 294.
2. *New York Times*, November 28, 1979, p. 26.
3. *New York Times*, August 6, 1974, p. 1.
4. *New York Times*, August 8, 1974, p. 23.
5. Francis X. Clines, *New York Times*, August 21, 1974, p. 27.
6. Vice Presidents Truman, Nixon, Johnson, and Ford became President. Alben Barkley, Hubert Humphrey, and Spiro Agnew did not.

18. "Who's Going to Tell Gerry Ford?"

1. Wicker, pp. 214–222.
2. McKay Report, p. 322.
3. McKay Report, p. 324.
4. In *A Time to Die*, Tom Wicker wrote a compassionate analysis of Rockefeller's decision, pp. 217–222, 264–265.
5. They had to, and those I have asked told me they did. To the same effect, see the McKay Report, p. 265.
6. The full text of James's letter appears in the McKay Report, pp. 248–249.
7. In March 1978, I wrote to Nelson Rockefeller requesting an interview about Attica. His assistant, Hugh Morrow, replied that "Mr. Rockefeller has testified and commented at length on the whole Attica matter. Everything of significance that he knows about this subject is a matter of record and he has nothing to add." I wrote to Mr. Rockefeller again and asked if this possibility for ending the deadlock in the negotiations had been considered at the time. There was no reply.
8. See McKay Report, p. 327. The McKay Commission "would not . . . have ruled out some concessions on amnesty," such as not prosecuting for kidnapping (i.e., taking hostages) and larceny committed during the riot.
9. *New York Times*, September 16, 1971, pp. 1, 31.
10. *New York Times*, September 14, 1971, p. 30. Dr. Fox also ventured the opinion that "The primary reason for the use of force is always to create an image for the public." The motive for the armed assault, he said, was to give Rockefeller's administration "an image of strength with the public."
11. Superintendent Kirwan being one of the very few State Police officers to sign a waiver of immunity for the Supplemental Grand Jury, it is a matter of public record that he testified there. His lecture had nothing to do with any grand jury matter. Wilson lost anyway.

12. Simonetti is the witness for this; under all the circumstances, I do not believe he would have said it if it had not happened that way.

19. The Rockefeller Runaround

1. All the questions to this point were included in the chapter on the Rockefeller Runaround in my January 1975 report on the cover-up to Governor Carey. The Investigation eventually questioned Rockefeller in the Supplemental Grand Jury, in the summer of 1975, after he had become Vice President, as did the Meyer Investigation in his Manhattan office. Each of them had a copy of these questions, and they would be logical questions to explore in any event. I would be interested to know to what extent, if any, they did so.
2. When the Observers went into D Yard during the most tense negotiations, thus incurring far greater risk than they would have by watching the retaking from A or C Block with the riflemen, they had simply been required to release the State from liability. Locking up the Observers during the assault may be an admission by the officials who did it that they, too, expected the bloodbath.
3. Oswald, p. 293.
4. McKay Report, p. 321.
5. House Select Committee on Crime, *American Prisons in Turmoil* (Part 2), 92nd Cong., 2d sess. (Washington, D.C.: Government Printing Office, 1972), p. 698.
6. This is generally an excellent rule. I understand that, until fairly recently at least, federal prosecutors in the City did discuss cases with their grand juries off the record, giving them free rein to prejudice the jury in the guise of telling them what was going on. "This witness is going to say so and so, but you'll know he's lying because . . . " is an example that a federal prosecutor gave me of what they would tell their juries.

20. Evidence of Obstruction

1. Fischer told Tony, who shared the confidence on a "need to know" basis with enough people at the Investigation so that it likely passed through our sieve back to the State Police. Still feeling the constraints of the confidence when I wrote my report on the cover-up to Governor Hugh Carey in January 1975, I consciously omitted it. Given the balance of obligations, I think now that this was a mistake. Not that it would have made a particle of difference.
2. Though the rifles and shotguns had been turned in two days earlier by then, the troopers, being professionals, may well have made notes of their serial numbers, as at least some of the riflemen interviewed on the thirteenth apparently did.
3. McKay Report, pp. 402–403.
4. Under New York Penal Law, Sec. 210.20, perjury maybe proved by showing that two sworn statements are irreconcilably inconsistent, without the need to show which one is false.
5. N.Y. County Law, Sec. 674 (1) is, I believe, what Simonetti referred to.
6. There may have been more. I recall seeing only two for certain.
7. Dr. Edland relayed these two quotes to me in Rochester in August 1976. See chapter 37.

8. Dr. Edland told me he heard it on CBS News.
9. This, too, is from Dr. Edland, who was not there. Dr. Baden confirms what he did.

21. Obstruction of Evidence

1. McKay Report, p. 380; House Select Committee on Crime, *American Prisons in Turmoil* (Part 2), 92nd Cong., 2d sess. (Washington, D.C.: Government Printing Office 1972), 1498–1499.
2. See *Richardson on Evidence*, Sections 469–472. *Richardson* was a basic text on what was admissible in New York.
3. Memorandum to Simonetti, dated October 18, 1974, from Investigators Nicholas Mattarazzo and James LoCurto regarding interview with Warren Cairo on September 30, 1974.
4. *New York Times*, September 17, 1971, p. 1.
5. By Edward M. Shaw, Esq., a former federal prosecutor, while he was questioning me for the Meyer Investigation, described in chapter 36.
6. I understand that Shapiro later denied that "We've got to get something on" Edland is how anybody in Rockefeller's Executive Chamber thought. Moran, however, was clear in his recollection that Shapiro had said it either to Moran or to another OCTF person named Ed Crosswell, and that Moran and Crosswell had discussed Shapiro's remark between themselves both at the time he made it and later.
7. Persico, *The Imperial Rockefeller*, pp. 138–139.
8. The 7-2-7 figures stuck in my mind. It is my best recollection that this sheet showed assignments in 1971, or possibly in early 1972, when BCI detectives still worked at the Investigation. I have some recollection, though not a firm one, that the sheet showed a few other investigators with miscellaneous other assignments.
9. *New York Times*, September 14, 1971, p. 30.
10. One of the strangest things that happened to me was not being able to remember specifically which investigators and assistants said this to me, even though I remembered so much else and this became so important later. While I could make what I considered highly reliable guesses, I always refused to do that. My recollection that several *did say it to me* is clear. I have no explanation for not retaining a specific recollection of any of their identities.

22. Bathing a Big Fish

1. Criminal Procedure Law, Sec. 190.40. See also, Sec. 190.45.
2. A startling exception occurred as I was questioning a sergeant who had gone out on A Walk. Our staff had not listed him as a shooter. I unsuspectingly asked him what he did next as he went down A Walk. He answered that the next thing he did was to fire his shotgun at an inmate down in A Yard. I suspended his examination and discussed with Tony in New York what we could possibly do; we decided there wasn't anything: he had his immunity. We were planning cases against three other troopers whom we knew to have fired at that inmate, who was likely the deceased William "Taxicab" Allen.

3. Seventy-four was the number used thereafter, though it was actually seventy-three because I had written one man's name twice.

4. We could not be sure how many of the 128 had been shot by correction officers, though it must have been comparatively few.

23. Immunizing the "Chief Perpetrator"

1. "How come Paul [O'Brien] never got indicted?" Chuck [Colson] asked [in prison]. "Because Silbert and Glanzer [the original Watergate prosecutors] gave him immunity early on. Neal told me it was just another example of how they blew it. He says as soon as Paul got immunized his memory went bad. They've never even used him as a witness." Quoted in John Dean, *Blind Ambition* (New York: Simon and Schuster, 1976), p. 392.

24. Playing Catch-22 with the Commissioner

1. See Oswald, p. 122. A *New York Times* editorial of September 18, 1971, concluded that, "The 28 concessions . . . were all reforms that the State should have undertaken on its own initiative long ago." Oswald (p. 336) quotes a blunt question by State Controller Arthur Levitt: "If the twenty-eight demands . . . were acceptable by the state immediately, then why the hell could this not have been done before?"

2. McKay Report, p. 323. The Official Version put it that Oswald ordered the retaking and that Rockefeller merely authorized and approved the order.

3. *Brady v. Maryland*, 373 U.S. 83 (1963).

28. Rocky's Men Speak No Evil

1. Some statements in the memo indicate that Tony may have written parts of it substantially earlier.

2. Since Tony used [ ], as well as ( ), my words are enclosed in { }. I have continued to substitute "Trooper A" for that man's name.

3. A. G. Simonetti, fifty-three-page memo of August 1974 (hereafter cited as Memo), p. 19.

4. Memo, p. 20.

5. Memo, pp. 21–23. The Meyer Report (p. 64) says of Simonetti's confrontation with Infante, "Simonetti was quite impassioned and stood while he spoke."

6. Memo, pp. 25–26.

7. Memo, pp. 29–30.

8. Memo, p. 35.

9. Memo, p. 33.

10. See pp. 156–157.

11. Memo, p. 27.

12. Memo, p. 29.

13. See pp. 169–171.

14. Memo, p. 30.

15. Memo, p. 10.

16. Memo, pp. 31–32.

29. Leads Going Nowhere

1. We had some grounds to suspect that the State Police, besides cutting the A Roof videotape, had also suppressed or radically altered another tape. A State Police lieutenant told us he had seen two videotapes of the retaking, of about equal quality. We knew of only one tape that was any good, the A Roof tape. Another tape existed, but its depiction of the retaking was technically so awful as to be worthless; the police, we were told, had tried unsuccessfully to run that TV camera off a car battery. I recommended to Tony that we show the lieutenant both our tapes to see if that clarified his recollection, one way or the other. Tony refused, saying by memo of November 13, 1974, which is discussed in the text, "there is no need to accomplish [this] work . . . as the investigation re same answers the [question] . . . ." Tony's answer was not responsive. Nothing that the Investigation had done answered the question of whether a second useful videotape of the assault had ever existed. It would have been simple to invite the lieutenant down, show him the tapes we had, and consider his response.

2. See pp. 171–172.

3. The time printed in the *New York Times* is "9:45." It seems clear, however, that the 4 and 5 were transposed in printing this number, since it comes between messages at 9:52 and at 9:55.

4. Tony said as much in a memo dated September 23, 1974.

5. The news story standing alone was hearsay, but Ferretti's testimony that it was accurate and was what he wrote in the ordinary course of his business as a reporter should have made it admissible. The way he told it to me sounded convincing.

6. Of the 9,000 pages of transcript, about 500 pages were comprised of Judge Ball's voir dire (i.e., selection) of the jury and of assistants addressing the jury.

7. See pp. 91–92.

8. The "11/22/74" memo, which I also received on the afternoon of 11/21, enumerated my memos that the 11/21 memo referred to.

9. The rest of paragraph three of my memo says: "The first memo, dated 11/7/74, on Mr. Perry's list was written to suggest a solution to a problem raised several times to me by Messrs. Bradley and Nitterauer. The second and third memos concern questions which logically should have been asked Supt. Kirwan and Major V in the Grand Jury but were not; Mr. Simonetti said he concurred in the latter on seeing it in writing. The fourth is a memo of law which is integral to the shooter cases, particularly in view of doubts expressed by several attorneys that a shooter's admission that he shot somebody has any evidentiary value if his statement also contains false exculpatory language [i.e., the "Divisible Lie"]. The fifth is my response to a project proposed by Mr. Perry in his memo of 11/8/74. The sixth is a file r ecord of a phone conversation with an attorney [Mark Benenson] which may well prove important if his client is indicted. The seventh was specifically requested by Mr. Simonetti. The eighth and ninth concern information of great potential importance to the cases I am assigned to prepare. The tenth was written in furtherance of a written assignment by Mr. Simonetti (his 11/13/74 memo, p. 2)."

32. The General Tips His Hand

1. Jack Anderson was a widely read investigative journalist who had exposed a number of scandals and I expected would expose this one if it came his way.
2. The October 17 memo about immunizing Major V that Tony threw at me.
3. Perry sounded as though he was repeating Tony's dictation when he offered the confidence of "the office." Telling the office meant telling the State Police. The informant was right to refuse.
4. Following a suggestion by Judge Ball on the 10th, I wrote a second letter to the General in which "I affirmatively request to see you, at your convenience."
5. When I had asked Tony about that, he had denied saying it.

33. My Report to the Governor

1. Here are the contents:
   1. Introduction
   2. Early Aspect
   3. February–November
   4. Jury Presentation
   5. The Shooter Cases
   6. The August Switch
   7. The Hindering Prosecution Case
   8. The Uninvestigated Rehousing Cases
   9. Chaperoned and Shut Out [of the jury]
   10. Immunizing Major V
   11. Immunizing the "Chief Perpetrator"
   12. Playing Catch-22 with Commissioner Oswald
   13. The Rockefeller Runaround
   14. Thursday in the Sky
   15. The Cairo Close-Out
   16. Fall Witnesses
   17. Only Two Weeks
   18. Appraisal of Small Value
   19. The Bell Gag
   20. The 74 Witnesses
   21. Leads Not Followed
   22. Resignation
   23. The Divisible Lie
   24. Judgment [matters of]
   25. The "Cumulative Witness" Fallacy
   26. Hearing [before Lefkowitz]
   27. Conclusion

34. Waltzing with the Perps

1. See *United States v. Projansky*, 44 F.R.D. 550 (S.D.N.Y. 1968).

2. The client can waive the privilege, but the lawyer cannot without being released by the client. I have since released Bob from the privilege.

3. "Pfumpf" may derive from the Yiddish "*fonfer*," meaning inter alia a mumbler, double-talker, a specialist in hot air, baloney. See Leo Rosten, *The Joys of Yiddish* (New York: Pocketbooks, 1970), p. 119.

4. See p. 223 above.

5. See, e.g., *New York Daily News*, November 13, 1980, pp. 1, 3, 40.

6. Any prospective whistleblower may wish to note how this worked.

7. "Me and Bobby McGee," words and music by Kris Kristofferson and Fred Foster. Copyright © 1969 by Combine Music Corporation. International copyright secured. All rights reserved. Used by permission.

35. The Cover-up Hits the Fan

1. As noted, I looked forward with guarded relish to any disbarment, libel, or even criminal proceedings that Lefkowitz or Simonetti might instigate or initiate for what I was doing to expose the cover-up. I felt I was serving the public interest and acting within the law. Plainly to violate the grand jury secrecy laws, on the other hand, especially when it did not seem necessary to the public interest, is what I saw no reason to do and every reason not to.

2. *Time*, April 21, 1975, p. 58.

3. Don Jelinek in conversation with the author in November 1975.

4. *Boston Phoenix*, May 13, 1975, p. 5.

5. Ibid., p. 30.

6. Ibid., pp. 30–31.

7. A notable exception came when I said in a speech in Connecticut that I wanted to give the grand jury the evidence and then they would indict or not indict. The local paper dropped "or not indict." As the worst example, that is not so bad, considering all I said and how technical some of it was.

8. *New York Times*, April 15, 1975, p. 26

9. Ibid.

10. *New York Times*, April 16, 1975, p. 27.

11. *New York Times*, April 15, 1975, p. 40.

12. *New York Times*, April 17, 1975, p. 78

36. A Judge Misjudges

1. *New York Times*, December 22, 1975, p. 37.

2. *New York Post*, May 31, 1975, p. 20; magazine p. 2.

3. Ibid.

4. Peter C. Dorsey was not the U.S. Attorney referred to at p. 7, above.

5. *New York Times*, August 8, 1975, p. 18.

6. *New York Times*, August 30, 1975, p. 16.

7. I am among the people who believe that Lee Harvey Oswald did shoot President John F. Kennedy, but not alone.

8. *New York Times*, October 11, 1975, p. 38.

9. *Rochester Times-Union*, October 11, 1975, p. A15.

10. In 1983 I was able to repay them $5,000 (i.e., with some interest). They wrote that they were surprised and touched and kindly suggested that I send the check instead to the National Conference of Black Lawyers, so that I could take the tax deduction. That was by far the largest contribution to anyone or anything I've ever made in my life and must have mystified them on arrival. A friend who knew about the episode gave my name to David Rockefeller, who thereupon sent me two personal, big-giver type letters of solicitation for another cause.

11. Four were old no bills by the first jury, one of them following the presentation I attended in November 1973; see pp. 60–61 above. I could have found out how the other three of those cases had been presented while I was at the Investigation by simply reading the transcripts of the presentations, but I had not taken the time to do so since I was not yet close to considering resubmissions. Three of the four cases had been presented without the benefit of much of the evidence that had been developed at the Shooter Conferences and in the second jury, and all four might well have benefited if I had been allowed to continue with the Shooter Cases in that jury. As to the three cases voted by that jury after I left, I was totally skeptical about the quality of the presentations.

12. It never crossed my mind that it might have been released to delude the public into believing that all the officers except Wildridge were innocent. Having now thought of this as a possibility, I still do not think it was the reason.

13. My Report to Governor Carey, p. 4.

14. Carey Press Release, December 22, 1975, p. 5.

15. Meyer Report, p. 8.

16. Meyer Report, pp. 7–8.

17. Meyer Report, p. 11.

18. Meyer Report, pp. 12–13.

19. Carey Press Release, December 22, 1975, p. 1.

20. Meyer Report, p. 41.

21. *New York Times*, December 22, 1975, p. 34.

22. *New York Post*, December 22, 1975, p. 2; *New York Times*, December 22, 1975, p. 34.

23. *New York Times*, December 22, 1975, p. 34.

24. Ibid.

25. *Time*, December 29, 1975, p. 3.

26. Here are some examples of Meyer's analysis that bothered me:

" . . . it was hardly foreseeable that so much bloodshed in the retaking would be caused by State Police personnel . . . ." (p. 47)

" . . . the Governor testified that he had complete confidence in Fischer's independence and impartiality (NAR 8660), and Fischer had been openly critical of the State Police role as OCTF's investigative arm before September 1971 . . . . Thus, Fischer had amply demonstrated that his conduct would not be colored by any favoritism towards the State Police occasioned by their role as his investigative arm at OCTF." (pp. 48–49)

"Immediately following the retaking and in several later instances during the early weeks after September 13, 1971, the Governor made statements in praise of the actions of the State Police in the retaking. He testified that he was speaking of the State Police as a group and their action in saving hostages, and not about individual troopers (NAR 8691, 8695-8696, 8769), and that inhibiting the investigation was the furthest thing from his mind (NAR 8750-8571, 8773). Since he was prepared to fund the investigation to whatever extent needed, see Subd. E(2) below, the statements clearly were not improperly motivated . . . ." (pp. 54–55)

27. The Goldman Panel, headed by Justice Harry Goldman, the Presiding Justice of the Appellate Division, Fourth Department. On September 14, 1971, Governor Rockefeller asked him to form a panel of impartial observers to monitor the prison. Bob Patterson served on it. See McKay Report, pp. 463–464. The Report of the Goldman Panel is printed in full in Russell Oswald's *Attica—My Story*, pp. 401–418.

37. Dr. John F. Edland

1. Dr. John F. Edland told me this in conversation in April 1976.
2. The descriptions in this chapter of what happened to Dr. Edland are close paraphrases of what he told me; many of the words are his even when quotation marks are not used.
3. Dr. Edland's mention of Captain Giangualano tantalized me. He was the one Troop A captain about whom I had heard virtually nothing at the Investigation, though he had to know a lot. I had had it in mind to bring him to the jury, though I had not thought to put him on the hastily prepared list of 74 witnesses.
4. In an interview, *New York Post*, August 21, 1979, p. 23.
5. McKay Report, pp. 461–462. Fischer first imposed the official silence on the fifteenth.

38. The Prosecution Peters Out

1. *New York Times*, December 7, 1975, Sec. 4, p. 5.
2. *New York Times*, January 27, 1976, p. 28.
3. *New York Times*, February 27, 1976, pp. 1, 62; February 28, 1976, p. E5.
4. Carey Press Release, December 22, 1975, p. 1.
5. Statement of Alfred J. Scotti, Special Deputy Attorney General, To Be Made In Court On February 26, 1976 Before The Honorable Frank P. Bayger, p. 5.
6. *Buffalo Courier Express*, March 21, 1976, p. 12.
7. *New York Times*, February 27, 1976, p. 62.
8. *Buffalo Courier Express*, March 31, 1976, p. 12.
9. *Buffalo Courier Express*, April 8, 1976.
10. Carey News Release, April 22, 1976; *New York Times*, April 23, 1976, p. 71.
11. *Ithaca Journal*, April 23, 1976, p 6.
12. *New York Times*, July 21, 1976, p. 1.
13. *New York Times*, September 9, 1976, p. 37.

39. The Book Won't Close

1. *New York Times*, December 31, 1976, pp. Al, A10.
2. *Jones v. State*, 352 N.Y.S. 2d 169 (N.Y. 12/27/73).
3. *Jones v. State*, Deposition of Nelson A. Rockefeller, April 22, 1977, pp. 34, 40.
4. See *Jones v. State*, 403 N.Y.S. 2d 935, 939, 937 (4th Dept. 1978); also Judge Quigley's decision therein, dated August 31, 1982, p. 9.
5. Carey Press Release "Attica Background," December 31, 1976, p. 6.
6. "In his representation of his client, a lawyer shall not . . . (3) Conceal or knowingly fail to disclose what he is required by law to reveal." Disciplinary Rule DR 7-102, American Bar Association, *Code of Professional Responsibility*.
7. I also suggested that they subpoena the Report I had sent to Governor Carey. We recognized that the grand jury material it contained prevented me from giving it to them without the court's permission, but issuing the subpoena, and receiving my response saying (a) how valuable it would be to them and (b) that I could not just give it to them, would provide a basis on which they could ask the court to rule. Judge Quigley did rule, however, that he could not authorize the release of my Report since it contained secrets of Judge Ball's grand jury.
8. *In the Matter of the Application of Carey*, 402 N.Y.S. 2d 100, 109 (Sup. Ct. Wyoming Co. 1977).
9. *In the Matter of the Application of Carey*, 416 N.Y.S. 2d 904, 913 (4th Dept. 1979).
10. *In the Matter of the Application of Carey* (not reported) (Sup. Ct. Wyoming Co. 1980).

40. The Grand Jury Got It!

1. Before discussing the jury with any juror, I set a rule for both of us that I did not want to hear, and the juror was not to disclose any evidence or the name of any witness or suspect that I did not already know, or the result of any vote, so that neither of us would break the grand jury secrecy laws. The quotations from colloquy in the jury are the recollections of jurors, which I take to be accurate in substance though not always *in haec verba;* they have not been compared with the jury transcript.
2. Criminal Procedure Law §§ 190.05, 190.25(1).
3. References to "another juror," "a third juror," etc., are to show speakers additional to the one first quoted on a given topic. The same individual, for example, may be the third juror on one topic, the first on another, etc.
4. It may be asked whether the jury could be questioned about the presentation by the prosecutors, without tainting any indictments they voted later. Without laboring the point, I am sure that a way could have been found if there had been the will. Perhaps at a minimum, Judge Ball could simply have asked them if *they* had any questions about the presentation they were receiving.
5. See pp. 61–63, above, on Simonetti's plans for a grand jury report on the riot, regardless of who was or was not indicted. After the Supplemental Grand Jury was empaneled, he determined that this jury would issue the report on the retaking and

other areas involving misconduct by officers, and preparations went forward in the office for that report.

6. It should be noted, however, that under my ground rules, we did not discuss whether the evidence against Wildridge that they actually voted on in October 1975 was the same as what I had prepared to give them fourteen months earlier.

7. If, as I expect may happen, someone talks to some jurors to check my report in this chapter, I hope he or she will protect the anonymity of their views.

41. New York Justice

1. *New York Times*, January 19, 1977, p. B18, February 22, 1979, p. B8.

2. Paul Eddy, Elaine Potter, and Bruce Page, *Destination Disaster, From the Tri-Motor to the DC-10: The Risk of Flying* (New York: Quadrangle/The New York Times Book Co., 1976), pp. 242–249.

3. Meyer Report, p. 34.

4. *New York Times*, April 20, 1979, p. Al.

5. *Werner v. State*, 441 N.Y.S. 2d 654 (N.Y. 1981); Gene Tenney in conversation with the author, July 1985.

6. Tom Wicker, "Justice for One," *New York Times*, March 22, 1985; Bill Cunningham in conversation with the author, June 1985; Gene Tenney conversation with the author, July 1985. A judge, unlike most juries, need not hear a trial all at once. At 150 to 200 pages a day, 7,000 pages of transcript is 35 to 47 trial days.

7. *Jones v. State*, 468 N.Y.S. 2d 223, 226–227 (4th Dept. 1983); Judge Quigley had found "overpowering" evidence of excessive force.

8. *Juris Doctor*, May 1976, p. 36. Fischer put the same notion more elaborately in his December 20, 1975, letter to Carey and Lefkowitz: "It has been my experience, gained in the process of gathering staffs in other investigations, that the quality of an investigative product cannot be measured by the number of investigators (or lawyers) retained for the long term investigation but that careful selection with attention to the particular investigative needs was the key factor." Simonetti told me some time after the August Switch that "Fischer was too nice a guy" to ask for an adequate staff. But being a nice guy does not excuse an abject failure to employ enough people to do the job.

9. Meyer Report, pp. 77, 85–86.

10. Meyer Report, pp. 54–55, 77, 87–88, 118.

11. Meyer Report, pp. 97–110.

12. P. 2B.

13. McKay Report, pp. 461–462; *New York Times*, September 17, 1971, pp. 1, 31.

14. Meyer Report, p. 72.

15. May 28, 1978.

16. Lance Morrow, *The Chief* (New York: Random House, 1985), p. 232.

17. *New York Times*, September 17, 1971, p. 31; Oswald, p. 321.

18. *New York Times*, December 6, 1978, p. 26; announcement, dated January 1, 1979, of Phillips, Nizer, Benjamin, Krim & Ballon.

19. See Myron Farber's excellent book *"Somebody Is Lying": The Story of Dr. X* (Garden City: Doubleday & Co., Inc., 1982).

20. *New York Times*, May 12, 1979, p. 25; May 25, 1979, p. 82.
21. Baden was called into the Dr. X case in New Jersey. Myron Farber wrote, "Dr. Baden . . . was one of the most talented and versatile pathologists working at the confluence of medical science and law." (*"Somebody Is Lying,"* p. 129.)
22. "MacArthur Park" by Jimmy Webb. © 1968 Canopy Music, Inc. International Copyright secured. All rights reserved. Used by permission.
23. "It's All Right, Ma (I'm Only Bleedin')" by Bob Dylan. © 1965 Warner Bros. Inc. All rights reserved. Used by permission.

42. Whistleblowing

1. *New York Times*, November 26, 1979, p. A21.
2. *New York Times*, March 29, 1985, p. B1.
3. *New York Times*, April 22, 1979, p. 44.
4. *New York Times*, November 26, 1979, p. A21.
5. *New York Times*, March 24, 1983, p. A30.
6. *New York Times*, November 29, 1982, pp. B1, B5. ("Decade After Knapp Inquiry, a Sense of 'Revolution' Pervades Police Force," by M.A. Farber.)
7. Peter Maas, *Serpico* (New York: Bantam Books, 1974), p. 304. (In 1972, the NYPD had over 30,000 officers.)
8. New York: Grossman Publishers, 1975.
9. New York: McGraw-Hill Book Company, 1981.
10. Weisband and Franck, p. 1, and Preface, p. ii.

43. America Can Do Better

1. See David Rothenberg, "Out on a Limb," *Fortune News* (The Fortune Society, New York, Spring 1983), p. 3.
2. Studs Terkel, *"The Good War,"* An Oral History of World War Two (New York: Pantheon Books, 1984), p. 192.
3. Ibid., p. 461.

Epilogue

1. People who think it unfair that there is a memorial for slain hostages but not slain inmates may not realize that correction officers raised the money to buy this monument to remember their own. Theoretically, inmates might do the same.
2. Though Grove Press under Barney Rosset stood for courage among publishers, one of his editors (unbeknownst to Barney, I'm sure) wanted me to delete the jury's chapter, chapter 40, convincing me that he didn't comprehend the book.
3. Edward Weisband and Thomas M. Franck, *Resignation in Protest: Political and Ethical Choices between Loyalty to Team and Loyalty to Conscience in American Public Life* (New York: Grossman Publishers, 1975).
4. Arnold Weinstein, *Classics of American Literature* (The Teaching Company, 1997), Part II, Lecture 16.
5. This conversation is described on p. 283 of the book.
6. Published by Quadrangle/New York Times Book Co., 1975; paper, University of Nebraska Press, 1994, and Haymarket Books, 2011.

7. See pp. 163–164.

8. Amy Goodman broadcast the recording on her radio program "Democracy Now" on September 16, 2011, <http://www.democracynow.org/2011/9/16/40_years_after_attica_rebellion_new>. Historian Heather Ann Thompson relates that shortly before Wicker and other Observers urged Rockefeller to come to the prison in order to prevent a bloodbath, his top advisor, Robert Douglass, had advised him not to come or engage in any further conversation. Rockefeller agreed, and that same day President Nixon told him on the phone that he supported his position. *Blood in the Water*, at pp. 146–147, 154–155. But whatever the conflicting advice that Rockefeller received, the decision to let police guns continue the conversation was his alone.

9. See p. 2 hereof.

10. Some apologists have said that if Rockefeller had gone to the prison, the inmates would have taken him captive. But no sane person was suggesting that he go among the inmates in D Yard.

11. My quotes of Ms. Fink are from interviews of April 16, 2001, and November 17, 2011, and several phone conversations in 2011 and 2012. At the time of the latter interview, she was part of the legal team representing the Occupy Wall Street protesters in New York City. See also pp. 350–351.

12. See p. 28.

13. *Al-Jundi v. Estate of Rockefeller*, 885 F.2d 1060 (2d Cir. 1989), quoted at p. 1067. Re Judge Meyer, see pp. 316–319 of this book. In Fink's opinion, Rockefeller's drive to become President "wasn't his serious motivation. His serious motivation was he was Nelson fuckin' Aldrich Rockefeller, and nobody was going to do that to him, right? What he said was, 'Fuck them, those bunch of niggers. We're going to show you what happens when you do this.'" While Rockefeller's culpability may have resulted, as Fink theorizes, from motives in addition to coveting the Presidency, the fact that the August Switch related in Chapter 17 coincided with his nomination to be Vice President affirms the strength of this motive. It is beyond my scope to weigh his motives further.

14. By an e-mail of Feb. 7, 2012, to his New York City law office, I asked former Governor Cuomo to confirm or deny that he took this position. He did not reply.

15. See p. 20.

16. *Blyden v. Mancusi*, 186 F.3d 252 (2 cir. 1999). Quotes: "the lynch-pin . . . " at p. 257. "Should be held . . . " at p. 260. "Given the long . . . " at p. 272.

17. Akil was fifty-six years old, had served fifteen years for murder, and reportedly died of complications from diabetes. According to his obituary in the Aug. 21, 1997, *New York Times*, "Mr. Al-Jundi, who credited a conversion to Islam to saving his life, became a demon for education. He obtained a high school equivalency diploma and began a lifelong habit of reading every book he could get his hands on . . . . To Legal Aid Society lawyers, judges, prosecutors, and others . . . [he] was a consummate professional who prepared presentencing reports with such meticulous care and argued for leniency with such persuasive passion that more than a few of the convicted criminals he represented had their sentences reduced or were routed to drug rehabilitation programs, mental health clinics, or other alternatives to prison."

18. *Al-Jundi v. Mancusi*, 113 F. Supp. 2d 441 (W.D.N.Y. 2000). Quotes: "paid into the . . . " on p. 444. "of a modest sum" on p. 446. "the privilege of . . . " on p. 447. "The events of . . . " on pp. 448–449.

19. See pp. 113–114.

20. Black described his early life as that of a street hustler. He was sent to Attica for robbing a dice game in New York City; but by the time of his death, Judge Telesca said of him, in an obituary in the Aug. 3, 2004, *Buffalo News*, "In my view, he was a giant of a man because he had a passion for justice." Black's *New York Times* obituary of the same date cited Liz as saying that Black had volunteered as a substance abuse counselor and in suicide prevention efforts, and he took mentally ill people into his own home.

21. *Blood in the Water*, at p. 504

22. Email of November 26, 2015.

23. See pp. 363–364. Mr. Clines's quoted article was published on September 19, 2006.

24. These examples are from the FVOA report, "A Time for Truth," February 13, 2003 (unpaginated); my conversations with Deanne Quinn Miller; and an undated letter of Frank Randazzo, a supporter of the FVOA.

25. The five requests are amplified in a booklet, dated January 11, 2004, that the FVOA addressed to each New York State legislator.

26. See pp. 119–129.

27. As quoted in "A Time for Truth," op. cit.

28. See pp. 364–365 and 345–347.

29. *Attica Justice, infra*, p. 379. See also p. 41 of this book.

30. Donald A. Jelinek, *Attica Justice: The cruel 30-year legacy of the nation's bloodiest prison rebellion, which transformed the American Prison System* (Jelinek Publishers, 2011).

31. *Attica Justice*, pp. 309–310 and generally pp. 305–313; see also p. 289 of this book.

32. During one of these lunches, Don pointed out an error in this book. On page 145, I wrote that not until the morning of the assault had the inmates been soaked with rain; in fact, they had been rained on before.

33. Don Jelinek and I had several conversations in 2011 about this epilogue; that December 15 he told me that at this point in his dealings with the FVOA, he was fed up with the Manichean view that he found among many of them that guards were all good and his former client inmates were all evil. Besides pointing out that a good guy had tried to murder a good guy, he reminded the group that inmates had risked their own lives to protect the hostage from other inmates during the rebellion's four-day stand-off. Not surprisingly, this meeting ended Jelinek's efforts to help the FVOA. See *Attica Justice*, pp. 390–391. Re: Michael Smith, see pp. 119–120 of this book.

34. See, for instance, Richard Norton Smith, *On His Own Terms: A Life of Nelson Rockefeller* (New York: Random House, 2014), p. 604.

35. McKay, p. 425. Richard Norton Smith, *On His Own Terms: A Life of Nelson Rockefeller* (New York: Random House, 2014), p. 610. The confusion may arise from the fact that it was Ohio National Guardsmen who shot and killed four unarmed students at Kent State University in 1970. I understand that during the

1970s, the shooting deaths of those four college students received more media attention than the shooting deaths of 39 inmates, correction officers, and prison employees at Attica.

36. Christian did not order the assault; he did not plan it; as far as I know, he did not shoot anyone; and it appears that he made a brave attempt to protect the hostages. See p. 51

37. *In Re Attica State Employees Victims' Compensation Fund*, Amended Order, 05-Misc Cv. 6017T (U.S.D.C., W.D.N.Y., July 13, 2005), p. 9.

38. Who wrote that speech and on what basis? Note that Rocky phoned Ann while some of his aides were at the prison with State Police who were trying to whisk the hostages' bodies into the ground without being autopsied by a competent medical examiner and State officials were announcing that inmates had killed them. See pp. 168–169 and 335–336.

39. Telephone interview of Ann D'Archangelo Driscoll, on May 18, 2011. Regarding John D'Archangelo's death, see pp. 1 and 74.

40. Transcript, *Al-Jundi v. Pfeil*, U.S.D.C.,W.D.N.Y., 75 Civ. 132, May 24, 2000, pp. 51–53.

41. The judge's opinion and appendices are reported as *Al-Jundi v. Mancuso*, 113 F. Supp. 2d 441 (W.D.N.Y. 2000), p. 445. While the McKay Commission took the testimony of many more inmates all within a year of the event when their recollections were fresher (though we do tend to remember our traumas vividly, when we do not blot them out) and the McKay testimony may someday be released, it presumably was not, and never can be, vetted for veracity by an experienced trial judge observing the witnesses' demeanors, nor can it be simultaneously corroborated by up to 29 years of medical records. The synopsis of Plummer is on p. 558, of Sales on p. 538, of Reed on pp. 559–560, of Al-Jundi on pp. 556–557, and of Haynes on pp. 553–554.

42. See p. 166.

43. Plummer's testimony begins on Transcript, op. cit., p. 1619, and Reed's on p. 1404.

44. See p. 32.

45. See pp. 28, 126.

46. See pp. 20, 74, 135–136.

47. *Blood in the Water*, p. 500.

48. As quoted in Anton Chekhov, *About Love and other Stories* (Oxford: Oxford University Press, 2004, Rosamund Bartlett tr.), p. xix.

49. In an editorial in the online *Nation* magazine, at <hppt://www.thenation.com/print/article/179546/forty-years-after-bloodiest-prison-uprising-us-history-attica-cover-continues>.

50. Mack affirmation of October 25, 2013, para. 39.

51. The Attorney General's memorandum of law, pp. 45–46.

52. See p. 339.

53. See pp. 307–308.

54. *Matter of Carey*, Supreme Court, Wyoming County, Index No. 15062.

55. I wrote to the judge on May 8, 2014, asking him to correct this error. He did not reply. As of this writing, he has not corrected it.

56. In this regard, I should note that Professor Heather Ann Thompson lists me as the source of a number of suspects' names in her book *Blood in the Water*. While this is true, I did *not* provide her with any of these names. Rather, I understand that she unearthed them from still-suppressed internal documents of the Attica Investigation that I wrote while I worked there in 1973–1974 and from my 1975 confidential report to Governor Carey.

57. The fact that Dr. Thompson was able to access these documents does nothing to reduce the need for the State and the courts to make them public. Rather, I believe, it increases this need. If I had had my way, all of these documents would have been made public, with all of these names redacted, forty or so years ago.

58. The pagination of the released volumes further suggests the magnitude of the redactions; the only pages and parts of pages released were numbers 131–142 (i.e., the first pages of Vol. 2), 189, 195, 246–248, 264–286, 324–326, and 477–479.

59. See Meyer's pp. 324–325.

60. See my p. 239.

61. See my p. 176.

62. See my pp. 20, 56, 135–136.

63. Her book tells much more than this one does about the run-up to the rebellion and the aftermath. Mine tells more about the turkey shoot itself, the prosecution, and the cover-up. I believe that the two books complement each other.

64. Except as otherwise noted, all the references in this epilogue, part V, to my text are to pp. 135–136. Sam Melville's death was not among the cases summarized in Chapter 14.

65. All my citations of the McKay Report in this part V are from pp. 396–398 thereof.

66. See p. 166, also p. 84.

67. Transcription: Major Frank Hall, Interview conducted September 17, 2011, by Christine Christopher, p. 29.

68. McKay reached the same conclusion about inmate Tommy Hicks. It seems clear from Hicks's few and randomly spaced, shotgun-pellet entrance wounds that this is correct and that he was not executed anywhere but, rather, was shot at a considerable distance most probably in D Yard during the assault. See also p. 133 of the book.

69. Veteran reporter Tom Robbins of The Marshall Project wrote this and two follow-up articles for the *Times*. The Marshall Project, according to its website, is "a non-profit news organization that focuses on criminal justice issues." According to its founder, Neil Barsky, it "represents our attempt to elevate the criminal justice issue to one of national urgency, and to help spark a national conversation about reform."

70. The facts and quotations in this and the following paragraphs about George Williams's torture and its aftermath are taken from Tom Robbins's news articles of March 1, 3, and 5 and a *Times* editorial of March 4, 2015.

71. These same circumstances had not kept most of my Supplemental Grand Jurors, all of them from Wyoming County, from being eager to do their civic duty and serve

justice, nor had they kept the present Grand Jurors from indicting these guards, though it is easier to get an indictment than a conviction.

72. As quoted in a *New York Times* editorial, December 18, 2015.

73. Epiloge Part II; *Attica Justice*, op. cit.; *Blood in the Water*, op. cit.

74. In the July 25, 2016, *New Yorker*.

75. See the following articles published by the Southern Poverty Law Center: Mark Potok, "For the Radical Right, Obama Victory Brings Fury and Fear," November 7, 2012; Morris Dees, "Attorney General Holder Is Right: Racial Animus Plays Role in Obama Opposition," July 15,2014.

76. The eleven men were the ten hostages whom police killed plus C.O. William Quinn, whom the inmates killed.

77. I did not take notes of Kent's talk and have depended for this account on the article that Gary Craig wrote about it in the September 14, 2016, Rochester *Democrat & Chronicle*.

78. The collection may be found at <http://www.archives.nysed.gov/research/oag/attica-documents>.

79. What follows about the Edlands is based partly on the Gary Craig article, partly on my Sept. 19 and Oct. 9, 2016 phone conversations with Gretchen Edland Perry.

80. See p. 127.

81. In his article "The Fall Guy" in the May 4, 2014, *New York Times Magazine*. Eisinger reports for *Pro Publica* and writes columns for the *New York Times*. Pulitzer Prize-winning business reporter Gretchen Morgenson flagged the same contrast between the over eight hundred prosecutions for the savings-and-loan crimes and the fact that "not one high-ranking executive at a major... firm was held to account for the crisis of 2008," in her article in the November 11, 2016, *New York Times* (November 13 in the print edition) titled "How Letting Bankers Off the Hook May Have Tipped the Election."

82. *New York Times*, Dec. 18. 2015. In the same vein, another Nobel Prize-winning economist, Joseph E. Stiglitz, has written that "America has become a country not 'with justice for all,' but rather with favoritism for the rich and justice for those who can afford it—so evident in the [mortgage] foreclosure crisis, in which big banks believed that they were too big not only to fail, but also to be held accountable." As quoted by Thomas B. Edsall in his review of Stiglitz's book *The Price of Inequality*, in the August 3, 2012, *New York Times*.

83. In the Nov. 11, 2013 issue.

84. New York Penal Law Section 125.25, for example, provides, "A person is guilty of murder in the second degree when . . . [u]nder circumstances evincing a depraved indifference to human life, he recklessly engages in conduct which creates a grave risk of death to another person, and thereby causes the death of another person." What is more reckless and depraved than pushing a deadly poison into the hands and lungs of millions of people while intentionally deceiving them about the risk?

85. Smoking & Tobacco Use" at <cdc.gov> for the years 2005-2009, as of January 25, 2016.

86. *United States v. Philip Morris USA*, 449 F. Supp. 2d 1 (D. D.C. 2006), a civil racketeering case, quoted on p. 28. The appeals court affirmed, and the Supreme Court declined review.

87. New York Times, Jan. 29, 2016.

88. See pp. 43 and 362.

89. *The Rich Get Richer and The Poor Get Prison: Ideology, Class, and Criminal Justice* (New York: Pearson, 9th ed., 2009).

90. The PEW Center on the States, "Time Served: The High Cost, Low Return of Longer Prison Terms," June 2, 2012, pp. 1, 2 (www.pewstates.org). See also, Robert Perkinson, *Texas Tough: The Rise of America's Prison Empire* (New York: Metropolitan Books, 2010), pp. 1–2, 6–9.

91. In his preface to the University of Nebraska 1994 paperback edition of *A Time to Die*, p. xiii.

Index

Acknowledgments
For the 1985 edition

I am deeply grateful to Nancy Greene Bell, Jennifer Atkinson, Knox Burger, Howard Cady, Angus Cameron, Don Conover, Ann Crawford, Dorothy Davis, Liz Fink, Sam Fogal, Deloris Gausch, Larry Hansen, Evelyn and Mike Harris, Agnes Haviland, Alex Hoffman, Charlotte Hoffman and her writers' workshop, Brown Meggs, Barney and Lisa Rosset, Roger Whitbeck, and Tom Wicker for their help, support, patience, and judgment.

From the vantage of 2016, I want to express particular gratitude to:

Barney Rosset for his decision to publish this book after many publishers had turned it down. He was a courageous pioneer among book publishers; and I believe that, given whom I had publicly accused and would be continuing to accuse through this book, it took courage to publish it—much as it took courage for Connecticut's U.S. Attorney Peter Dorsey to offer me a job in 1975 when other employers would not consider me (see pp. 312, 302).

Knox Burger, my then-agent, a gruff man who loved books, spoke his mind, and did well for me. Knox died in 2010 and Barney in 2012.

Jennifer Atkinson, my Grove Press editor who went over every page of the book with me with great care and patience.

And Nancy, my main inspiration, supporter, and first editor in writing and in so much else.

For the 2016 edition

For the surprising amount of effort that it took to produce this revised edition, I am deeply grateful to:

Mike and Sharon Smith and Dee Quinn Miller for keeping me in the loop for the past sixteen years with pertinent documents, Western New York newspaper clippings, and good conversation.

Don Jelinek, my onetime adversary and longtime friend, for helping me with my writing as I helped him with his, through our many phone calls and emails and our annual three- or four-hour lunches at an Oakland diner when Nancy and I visited our sons Brian and Chris in the Bay Area.

My agent Amaryah Orenstein for selling the book, of course, and for her astute and sensible editing, her knowledge and judgment that I called on time after time, and her unfailing good nature in the face of the trial I can sometimes be.

The team at Skyhorse Publishing: Tony Lyons for making the still-bold decision to republish the book; Joseph Craig for his keen and patient editing; Jordan Koluch for production; Leslie Davis for publicity; and Rain Saukas for the strong and apt new cover.

Again and always, my wife Nancy for inspiring, editing, and sustaining me.

Insofar as this edition improves on the first one, much credit goes to Joe, Amaryah, and Nancy. Insofar as it doesn't, I plead guilty.

MALCOLM BELL

About the Author

A former corporate litigator, Malcolm Bell decided midcareer to seek greater fulfillment by pursuing criminal law. While serving as a New York State prosecutor, he bravely blew the whistle on the State's refusal to hold law officers accountable for the extensive torture and murder that they committed during the 1971 Attica prison riot. Though he paid a stiff price for this stand, it brought him much satisfaction. Later, as an activist in the Sanctuary Movement of the 1980s, he stood in solidarity with—and offered safe haven to—illegal refugees fleeing the state-led, US-backed terror in Guatemala. He has written about this experience and is completing a series of spiritual reflections aimed at encouraging readers to explore their own beliefs. He lives in Weston, Vermont, with his wife, Nancy, who is a retired school teacher.